D1120969

THE GATES OF POWER

WITHDRAWN

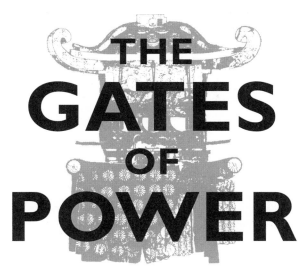

THE
GATES
OF
POWER

*Monks, Courtiers, and
Warriors in Premodern Japan*

MIKAEL S. ADOLPHSON

University of Hawai'i Press
Honolulu

© 2000 University of Hawai'i Press
All rights reserved

Printed in the United States of America

05 04 03 02 01 00   5 4 3 2 1

Library of Congress Cataloging-in-Publication Data

Adolphson, Mikael S., 1961–
The gates of power : monks, courtiers, and warriors in premodern Japan /
Mikael S. Adolphson.
p.   cm.
Includes bibliographical references and index.
ISBN 0–8248–2263–3 (cloth : alk. paper) — ISBN 0–8248–2334–6 (pbk. : alk. paper)
1. Japan—Politics and government—794–1600. I. Title.

DS850. A36   2000
952—dc21   00–023448

Publication of this book has been assisted by grants from
the Reischauer Institute of Japanese Studies
at Harvard University and the School of Hawaiian, Asian,
and Pacific Studies, University of Hawai'i.

University of Hawai'i Press books are printed on
acid-free paper and meet the guidelines for permanence
and durability of the Council on Library Resources.

Book design by Kenneth Miyamoto
Printed by The Maple-Vail Book Manufacturing Group

For my parents
Sven and Gunvor Adolphson

CARLETON COLLEGE LIBRARY

CONTENTS

DS
850
.A36
2000

121101-257624

MAPS AND FIGURES

ACKNOWLEDGMENTS

This manuscript evolved from a long-standing interest in the secular aspects of religion in premodern Japan. I have traveled a long and crooked road, spanning three continents, to complete this study, and I owe much to those who have encouraged me to pursue a career in a field that I was told did not exist in my native Sweden. First and foremost, I would like to thank my parents for having the courage to support their only child's efforts in a culture so distant from their own. Their faith in me, even during several odd excursions and seemingly hopeless situations, provided me with the extra energy and determination to succeed in my endeavors. It is unfortunate that my father passed away just months before this manuscript was completed, but I find comfort in the belief that he knows its completion was as much a result of his and my mother's resilience as of my own.

As a graduate student, I was extremely fortunate to have Professor Jeffrey Mass as my adviser. I cannot help but wonder if even the acolytes within the monasteries of premodern Japan could have expected such brilliant guidance and genuine concern from their masters. Jeff guided me most patiently through the many stages of becoming a scholar, while greatly facilitating my transition into academic life in the United States. Most of all, I am eternally grateful for his time-consuming efforts to refine my skills as a writer and for his allowing me to grow in the direction of my choice.

I would also like to express my gratitude to James Ketelaar, whose guidance into the realm of ideas has been groundbreaking for me. If I ever manage to integrate the spheres of politics and religion, my success would owe much to the theoretical and ideo-

logical training that I received from him as a graduate student at
Stanford. I have greatly benefited from the advice and encouragement of Joan Piggott and Peter Duus on several occasions. I am
also fortunate to count among my teachers Hal Kahn and Albert
Dien in the field of Chinese history, Philippe Buc as a fellow
medievalist, and Thomas Hare and Susan Matisoff in the area of
classical Japanese. I owe many thanks to my colleagues Karl Friday,
Carl Bielefeldt, Thomas Conlan, and Robert Eskildsen for sharing their experiences and knowledge so unselfishly, and I will
remain greatly indebted to Sidney Brown for his limitless kind-
ness, support, and advice during the various stages of this manuscript. I would additionally like to express my gratitude to two
colleagues in American history, Wayne Morgan and Robert Gris-
wold, for understanding the special needs of a premodern Japanese historian at the University of Oklahoma. Margaret Ann
Smith and Earl R. Chain at the university's Instructional Services
Center helped me understand and, to some extent, master the
computer technologies that lie behind the charts and maps in
this manuscript. Finally, I would like to thank those scholars in
Europe—in particular Carl Steenstrup, Olof Lidin, Eva Österberg,
and Bo Stråth—who gave me support and encouragement to
pursue my interest in the early stages of my education.

In Japan, I am forever indebted to many friends and colleagues.
Professor Ōyama Kyōhei has always been supportive and under-
standing of my views, and he has made my two sojourns at Kyoto
University most enjoyable. My skills in reading ancient and medi-
eval sources, in particular courtier diaries, government documents,
and handwritten documents, owe everything to my two tutors, Itō
Toshikazu and Satō Yasuhiro. Special thanks are owed also to
Yoshioka Masayuki of the Kunaichō shorikubu at the Imperial
Palace in Tokyo and Hodate Michihisa and Tajima Tadashi at
Tokyo University for giving me access to the excellent source col-
lections at those renowned institutions. For helping me obtain
illustrations, I am grateful to Professor Kondō Shigekazu of Tokyo
University's Shiryō hensanjo, Hashimoto Michinori of Biwako
Hakubutsukan, Ueno Ryōshin of Shiga kenritsu biwako bunkakan,
and Okano Toshiaki of Chūō kōron shinsha.

My many research trips and stays in the Kansai area were especially pleasurable because of a number of friends who helped me
in several ways. I was very fortunate to be able to stay with the
Takemoto family in Osaka, allowing me to focus full time on my

studies. I am afraid that I will never be able to repay them for their hospitality, generosity, and patience with my foreign manners except to say that I am eternally grateful and hope that the gods in some way will reward them. Mr. Murase Mitsuhiro of the Japan Volleyball Association, who sadly left this world much too soon, provided me with several opportunities to improve my skills in translation and interpretation, and I will always be grateful for his confidence in me. Jerker Bergström has helped me in various ways as a friend and as my most important link in Osaka, and I wish him the best in his career as he has always supported me.

The financial support of a number of organizations made this manuscript possible. First, I would like to thank Monbushō for giving me my first scholarship to visit Japan in 1986. Second, the generous support of the Japan Foundation provided the necessary means for two of the most important stages in my life as a scholar, first in 1992–1993, when the research for the basis of this manuscript was completed, and then in the summer of 1997, when I was able to locate and obtain additional sources at various Japanese archives. Grants from the Weter Fund, the Stanford History Department, and the Japan Fund of the Institute for International Studies at Stanford University supplied financial support to refine my argument and writing. While at the University of Oklahoma, I received crucial support from the College of Arts and Sciences on several occasions, allowing me to continue my research without any major interruptions. Finally, I would like to express my gratitude to the Reischauer Institute for a generous grant at the final stages of this project, which I hope will shed light on the importance of religion and its institutions and practitioners in premodern Japan.

A NOTE ON TRANSLATION AND JAPANESE NAMES

Historians dealing with foreign cultures and languages face the challenge of making their works accessible through adequate translations while not distorting the meaning of the original terms. Though some scholars prefer to use a large number of Japanese terms to avoid the problem, I find this custom self-defeating, since it not only makes the work complicated to nonspecialists, but it also excuses the author from making sufficient effort to grasp the meaning of words. Therefore, I have attempted to find English equivalents that convey the proper meaning to all historical concepts in this study, and only the most important and unique terms are occasionally noted in Japanese. One of the central terms in this study, for example, is *"gōso,"* which literally means "forceful appeal." Although an acceptable translation, it can also be misleading since it omits two important connotations; *gōso* were demonstrations in the capital staged by a few monasteries with the help of divine symbols. Thus, I prefer the term "divine demonstrations," frequently also using the Japanese word *"gōso,"* since it is central not only for this study but also for the understanding of religious institutions in premodern Japan in general. To further assist the reader, Japanese terms and names that appear frequently in the text are explained and listed with their Chinese characters in a separate glossary.

With the exception of cloisters within the main monasteries, names of temples, which are always Buddhist in this study, are consistently given as proper nouns. Thus, I speak of Enryakuji, not "the Enryaku temple," "the Enryaku-ji," or "the Enryakuji temple." In the case of Kūkai's monastic complex on Mt. Kōya, properly known as Kongōbuji, I frequently refer to it as Kōyasan, since it is more commonly known under that name. Religious centers primarily dedicated to the native gods are called shrines, whose names present more of a problem since they varied more than temples not only over time but also depending on their rank. The terms *"yashiro," "jingū," "taisha,"* and the suffixes *"-sha"* and *"-gū"* all refer to shrines whose differences are hard to discern even by specialists. I prefer to retain the pronunciation of shrines as they are presented in the sources of the Heian and Kamakura eras. Therefore, although Enryakuji's shrine affiliate is known today as Hiyoshi taisha, it was known as Hiesha in the pre-Muromachi period. Since Western scholars have accepted the habit of referring to shrines in their translated version (e.g., the Kasuga shrine) I will occasionally use such terminology, although most shrines, technically speaking, consisted of a number of smaller shrines.

The divine entities of Buddhism and the native cults (Shintō) present another problem. In Buddhism, I talk about deities or buddhas and bodhisattvas, and give their names exclusively in Japanese. Shintō deities are referred to either as the native gods or under the Japanese term *"kami."* The term "deities" is applied across the board, becoming in this case the terminological link between the two systems of belief. In distinguishing between the members of temples and shrines, I prefer the term "monk" for Buddhist clerics, since it implies membership in a particular order and the taking of specific vows. The term "priest" is reserved for performers of Shintō rituals, as its meaning is broader, reflecting adequately the different duties of the servants of the *kami.* There were also a wide variety of lay followers of temples and shrines who are simply called "supporters," "service people," or "attendants" in this study.

Japanese names are given with the surname first, and, as with the names of religious institutions, I have tried to retain the practices of the premodern era. Thus, the genitive *"no"* is retained in names of large and high-ranking families (e.g., Fujiwara no Michinaga), since that was the practice during the Heian and Kamakura eras. For years and dates, I have ignored the differences between the lunar calendar, which was employed in Japan at the time, and our Gregorian calendar for two reasons. First, it is accepted praxis among virtually all Western historians to use the hybrid form—giving the Western year followed by the month and day of the lunar calendar—in academic works. Second, it is simply not worth the trouble to translate every single date into our calendar, as it would create severe inconveniences for other scholars attempting to refer to Japanese works. Only when the original era name is of outstanding importance have I included it in the main text. The Japanese era names are, however, consistently listed in the footnotes in order to facilitate locating entries in diaries that are cited in this study.

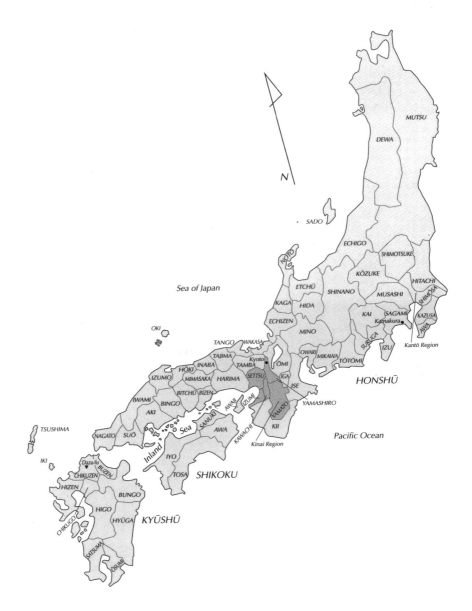

Map 1. The provinces of premodern Japan. Reprinted from *The Origins of Medieval Japan,* edited by Jeffrey P. Mass, with the permission of the publishers, Stanford University Press. © 1997 by the Board of Trustees of the Leland Stanford Junior University.

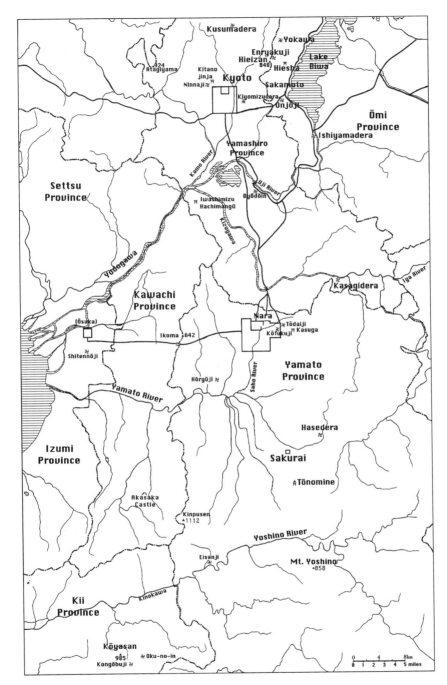

Map 2. The Kinai region. Adapted from *Nihon no rekishi*, volume 4: *Ritsuryō kokka* (Tokyo: Shōgakkan, 1974).

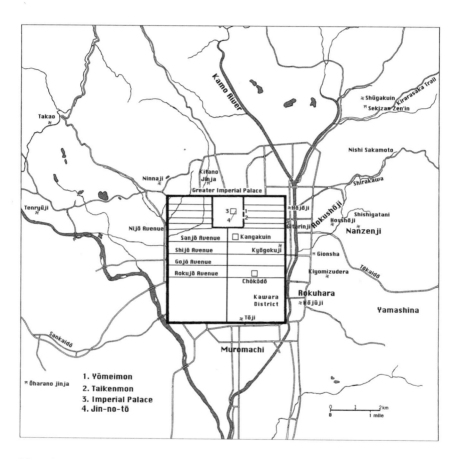

Map 3. The Kyoto area. Adapted from *Nihon no rekishi*, volume 8: *Ōchō kizoku* (Tokyo: Shōgakkan, 1974).

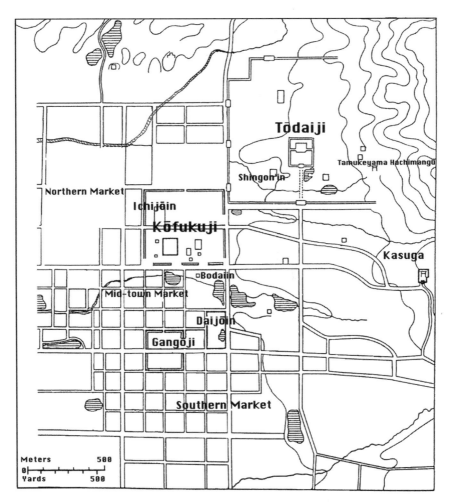

Map 4. Eastern Nara. Adapted from Nagashima Fukutarō, *Nara-ken no rekishi* (Tokyo: Yamakawa shuppansha, 1980), 77.

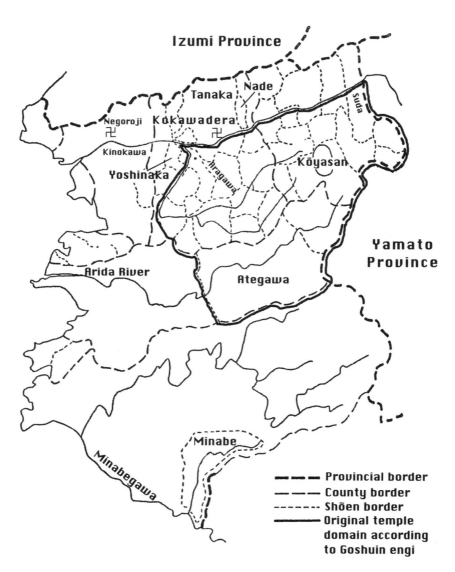

Map 5. Estates in Kii Province and Kōyasan's Goshuin engi domain.
Adapted from *Kōyasan ryō shōen no shihai to kōzō*, edited by Toyoda
Takeshi (Tokyo: Gannandō shoten, 1977), 500.

1
Introduction

The warrior class dominated the political landscape of Japan perhaps longer than in any other culture, and it is only natural that it has been, and still is, the most popular theme among historians. From its rise in the late Heian age (794–1185) to its complete dominance in the peaceful Tokugawa age (1600–1868), eventually also spearheading the fall of this last shogunate, the samurai is not only a historical figure heavily researched by scholars but also a legendary hero and an ideal that can be found in today's popular culture in Japan and many Western countries. Though the popular samurai image continues to compete with scholarly interpretations, serious students of Japanese history now have access to many works in English that dispel the common myths and offer a more balanced view of the warrior's social and political roles in different eras. Indeed, considerable progress has been made in the last few decades among Western historians, who are now able to offer a more refined understanding of the warrior class, not only challenging earlier views but perhaps even contributing actively to scholarly discussion in Japan.[1] For example, though Japan's first warrior government (the Kamakura Bakufu) was established as a national power in 1185, scholars have realized that it was not as dominating as previously thought and that the traditional elites in Kyoto still wielded considerable power.[2] As a result, the age of the warrior has been pushed forward to the fourteenth century, when the second warrior government (the Muromachi or Ashikaga Bakufu) assumed all the responsibilities and qualities of a national government and warrior culture truly began to dominate Japanese society.[3]

These revelations have put the momentous social and political

changes of the fourteenth century into a sharper focus, greatly
advancing our comprehension of how the warrior class adapted
and became the rulers of Japan. But this interpretation also has
important consequences for the era preceding the Ashikaga age
(1336–1571). It now appears that the period from the emergence
of the warrior class in the late Heian period to the establishment
of the Muromachi Bakufu has no identity of its own. If it was not
the beginning of the warrior age, then what was it? Though some
scholars might be satisfied to call it a transitory phase into true
warrior rulership, such an identification would not explain why it
took more than two hundred years to complete. Nor do attempts
to characterize this era as a simple prolongation of the Heian
style of rulership offer any valuable insight, since they overlook
substantial differences between the mid-Heian and Kamakura
(1185–1333) systems. In short, to account for these changes exclusively within the framework of the Heian system would be to do
injustice to the realities of contemporary historical documents.
Researchers must instead consider rulership from a more encom-
passing perspective, taking into account both adjustments and continuities in the transition from an imperial bureaucratic system of
the early and mid-Heian eras to a warrior-dominated polity of
the fourteenth century. One of the main goals of this book is to
address this problem and to provide a coherent synthesis of rulership from the late eleventh to the late fourteenth centuries.

Warriors and courtiers were not the only elites wielding authority in the late Heian and Kamakura eras. Most scholars are at
least vaguely aware that there were also a number of temples and
shrines, Buddhist monks, Shintō priests, and secular followers of
various religious centers with enough political, economic, and
military power to pressure, or even challenge, the secular authorities. Perhaps it is this worldly aspect of religion that has induced
previous scholars to ignore this age, concluding that the religious
disturbances in the late Heian and Kamakura eras were simply a
sign of the imperial court's decline and the inevitable rise of the
warrior class. The following quote, attributed to the otherwise
dominating Retired Emperor Shirakawa (1053–1129), has been
used frequently to support such views: "The flow of the Kamo
river, the roll of the dice, and the mountain monks [of Enryakuji]
are things I cannot control."[4] The sources in which this quote
appears were written some two centuries after Shirakawa, and its
reliability must therefore be questioned, but it leaves no doubt as

to the perception of the secular influence of Buddhist temples in the late Kamakura era. More important, there are also contemporary records indicating that Buddhist monks and their followers could cause trouble in the capital during Shirakawa's era. In 1108 the monks from Enryakuji and Onjōji, normally rivals over the leadership of the Tendai sect, joined forces to protest Shirakawa's appointment of a monk from another sect (Shingon) to perform an important ritual even though it was, according to precedents, Onjōji's turn. The retired emperor refused to oblige the monks, although several courtiers noted that there was reason in the Tendai protest. In response, the monks approached the capital, and Fujiwara no Munetada, a courtier in Shirakawa's service, fearfully noted in his diary: "Previously, the clergy were clad in protective armor when they came to the imperial palace, [but][5] this time, they are already armed, carrying bows and arrows. It is possible that the mob now reaches several thousand. Truly, it is a frightening situation when the court has lost its authority, and [the palace] must be defended with all available might."[6]

The armed protesters never reached the capital in 1108, but such quotes led the pioneering British historian George Sansom to conclude that Buddhist temples during this age "failed miserably to provide the moral force that the times demanded, since the influence of the sects with the greatest power and greatest responsibility in medieval Japan was on the whole an evil influence breeding disorder, corruption and bloodshed."[7] This view may appear archaic today, but its basic tenets are still predominant among scholars in the field. In fact, despite a growing awareness of temples and shrines as social and political institutions in the West in the last two decades or so, religious institutions are sadly missing from most surveys on premodern (ca. pre-1600) Japan, and when incidents or skirmishes involving religious followers are described, they are rarely explained in their political context.[8]

In a ground-breaking article, Neil McMullin has argued that the reasons for this negligence are to be found above all in the historians' own milieu. Most historians have depoliticized religion by taking it "out of its socio-political-economic-cultural setting" and have thereby tended to treat religion as a subject strictly distinct from other social sciences and in particular, one might add, from history. Such a division, McMullin argues, is based on the modern idea that religion and politics are and ought to be separate entities, which has led to a critical attitude toward "the clergy and religious institutions seemingly in direct proportion to the degree of economic, political and military power that the clergy and the monastery-shrine complexes possessed." Stated differently, scholars have assumed that religious institutions with secular power and influence are signs of corruption and degeneration, whereas noble hegemons who acquired unprecedented wealth and influence have been heralded as heroes.[9] Most historians today would probably agree with McMullin, as do I, that such simplistic dichotomies need to be discarded.

McMullin's article is important not only because of its lucid analysis of the problems of dealing with religious institutions, but also because it represents a new spirit among current scholars. A few pioneering studies have demonstrated the importance of incorporating temples and shrines as vital components of the political order and the *mentalité* of the premodern age.[10] The merit of such works notwithstanding, however, they cover widely different periods and give little more than a glance at the general interaction between religious and secular power. In particular, religious institutions have not yet been treated over an extensive period, making it difficult to grasp the framework within which they worked or the range of characteristics among various temples and shrines. Studies on temples as secular powers in the long term are thus, to put it simply, long overdue.

Three Religious Gates of Power

The current study focuses on the secular power of three of Japan's most powerful temples—Enryakuji, Kōfukuji, and Kōyasan—from the late eleventh to the late fourteenth centuries, in an attempt to explain the role of these temples in the larger context of the ruling structures of the Heian, Kamakura, and early Muromachi eras. Enryakuji was arguably the most influential temple in premodern Japan. Located on Mt. Hiei just northeast of Kyoto, the complex housed some three thousand monks, well known for their various ways of putting pressure on the imperial court in issues that concerned the temple. Fighting even occurred occasionally between Enryakuji and other religious centers, in particular Onjōji, a sibling within the same Buddhist sect (Tendai). However, perhaps the most striking evidence of Enryakuji's political influence are the many divine demonstrations, known as *gōso* (literally "forceful protests"), that the temple staged to pressure the government in Kyoto to act in the temple's favor. It can be estimated that some three hundred protests were staged by religious institutions in the capital from the late eleventh to the sixteenth centuries, and more than one-fourth of them were staged by Enryakuji.

In spite of its prominent political position, Enryakuji has received surprisingly little attention by historians. While there are a number of studies on Tōdaiji and other temples as proprietors of private estates, no such studies are available for Enryakuji. In fact, few scholars, even in Japan, have attempted to place protests and conflicts involving the monks on Mt. Hiei in their historical context.[11] One reason for this oversight is the prejudice against temples with political power and the consequent unwillingness to deal seriously with such issues. Another, much more poignant, is that the temple and its entire archive were destroyed when Oda Nobunaga put the torch to the complex on Mt. Hiei in 1571.[12] As a consequence, scholars have tended to avoid Enryakuji as a topic for historical study, assuming a lack of adequate sources. However, a number of useful sources survive that shed considerable light on the history of Enryakuji and its role in the premodern Japanese state.

First, there are several contemporary diaries that are extremely valuable in describing the temple's involvement in capital politics. Though many of these sources have been used to explain events in Kyoto, they also contain much of interest on Enryakuji. Since the diarists, who were high-ranking courtiers, often participated in the litigation process, there are entries that not only describe the outcomes of appeals and lawsuits from temples and shrines but also offer detailed explanations of the origins of the conflicts themselves. Second, a variety of chronicles provide additional information about the temple, although they were written at a later date. The most useful source in this category is the *Tendai zasuki* (Records of the Tendai Head Abbots), a collective scripture telling the story of the head abbots of Enryakuji from the temple's founding in the late eighth century to the early Shōwa era (1926–1989).[13] Though essentially an appointment record, the *Tendai zasuki* provides crucial information about the most important events under each head abbot, often citing related documents in full in the process. Other records in this category include legends and war tales such as the *Heike monogatari* and the *Genpei seisuiki*. Such sources are less reliable because of their tendency to glorify certain events, lineages, or clans, and they tend to be biased against religious institutions, condemning their secular power. Nevertheless, they do offer some insight into aspects of events that are not readily available in contemporary sources. The last category of sources consists of a small group of government documents pertaining to Enryakuji that can be found at other locations. For example, since governments issued their verdicts to opposing parties during a dispute, some of these documents survived at temples that had been in conflict with Enryakuji.

The Kōfukuji complex was founded in the old capital of Nara (710–784) early in the eighth century, giving it a head start and a slight advantage over Enryakuji in terms of ties with the imperial court. As is well known, Kōfukuji became the clan temple of the powerful Fujiwara family, allowing the temple's monks and the Hossō sect to dominate the religious establishment in the early Heian period. The Hossō center's fortunes were thus tied to those of the Fujiwara clan, as both prospered immensely for the several successful centuries of the Fujiwara regency (ca. 858–1068). Records regarding the temple's landholdings are not conclusive at this point, but there are indications that Kōfukuji controlled over three hundred estates (most of them in Yamato Province, where it dominated; see Map 1) as late as the sixteenth century.[14] Though Kōfukuji also rivaled the size of Enryakuji in terms of monks and secular supporters, the temple complex itself did not encompass as large an area, since it was confined to the city of Nara. The distance from the capital of Kyoto did not, however, discourage Kōfukuji's monks from staging some seventy divine demonstrations to pressure the imperial court to act in its favor. In fact, monks from Kōfukuji and Enryakuji combined for a vast majority of disturbances both in and around the capital, and most scholars still begin with the "armed monks of the southern capital [Nara] and the northern ridge [Mt. Hiei]" *(nanto hokurei no sōhei)* when addressing the phenomenon of armed conflicts involving religious institutions.[15]

Unfortunately, the two temples are also similar in their paucity of contemporary records and original documents. Kōfukuji suffered a devastating destruction at the hands of warriors late in 1180, when forces of the Taira clan attacked the temple for opposing its hegemony in central Japan during the Genpei War (1180–1185). Kōfukuji's oldest buildings date to the reconstruction during the next several decades, but a large part of the complex was

destroyed again in the fourteenth century during the conflict between the two imperial courts (the Nanbokuchō era, 1336–1392),
which involved cloisters of Kōfukuji on opposing sides. There are
fortunately frequent references to Kōfukuji and its supporters in
several diaries, which appear to be especially informative regarding the Hossō center, since many of them were written by Fujiwara
nobles. Other useful sources are also similar to those regarding
Enryakuji, including a small number of documents contained in
other collections as well as monk appointment records such as
the *Kōfukuji bettō shidai* (Precedents of the Kōfukuji Head Abbot)
and the *Sōgō bunin* (Appointments to the Office of Monastic
Affairs) from the Hossō center.[16] Another interesting and useful
temple chronicle is the *Kōfukuji ryaku nendaiki* (An Abridged
Chronicle of Kōfukuji), which lists appointments of ranking Hossō
offices in relation to developments in the Fujiwara clan.[17] Scholars
can thus reconstruct much of Kōfukuji's history and involvement
in politics from the same type of sources as for Enryakuji, though
there are also the same limitations concerning the extent of landholdings and branches under the control of these monastic complexes.

Kōyasan provides a contrast to Enryakuji and Kōfukuji in several
ways. First, it was located on Mt. Kōya on the Kii peninsula at a
considerable distance from the capital, as indicated by imperial
pilgrimages, which took about six to eight days. Thus, regardless
of its importance as a retreat for esoteric studies founded by the
legendary monk Kūkai (who also chose the mountain as his grave
site) and its ranking as one of the two major Shingon centers, the
temple's direct involvement in political matters in Kyoto and Nara
was more restricted. Second, since the Kōyasan clergy skillfully
avoided direct involvement in any wars from the late Heian to the
early Muromachi eras, a considerable number of original documents still exist, most of which have been published in eight
volumes of the *Dai nihon komonjo: iewake* 1 as *Kōyasan monjo*. As a
result, numerous studies of Kōyasan and its estates in Kii Province
have been published as both articles and book-length studies in
Japan. In fact, many classic studies of Japan's private estates *(shōen)*
grew out of the rich Kōyasan document collection.[18]

On the surface, it may thus appear that Kōyasan does not fit
the traditional mold of elite temples because of its location and
rare involvement in factionalism in the capital. However, since the
Shingon sect was one of the main providers of ceremonies for the

imperial state, represented primarily by Tōji in Kyoto, an avenue
for promotions was readily available also for monks from Mt.
Kōya. More important, Kōyasan was a significant, though more passive, player in the religious and political systems, and it received
much attention from noble and warrior patrons in the form of
donations of land and other income-generating titles. Similar to
Enryakuji and Kōfukuji, it operated as a *ryōke* (proprietor) of
most of those estates, with members of the Fujiwara or imperial
families as patrons *(honke)*. Furthermore, though the monks on
Mt. Kōya may have focused less on making headway in and around
the capital than did their colleagues on Mt. Hiei and in Nara,
they were representatives of a religious elite institution who were
valuable allies during times of disturbances and war. Indeed, it is
not until the late thirteenth and early fourteenth centuries, as
Japan was experiencing momentous social and political changes,
that Kōyasan developed characteristics that clearly set it apart
from other monastic complexes located closer to the capital. Japanese scholars see this transition as one from *shōen ryōshū* (*shōen*
overlord) to *zaichi ryōshū* (local resident lord), according to which
the temple alienated itself from a reliance on status from the
capital and took direct control of estates and inhabitants close to
the temple.[19] Stated differently, Kōyasan abandoned the old style
of rulership based on elite status in favor of a local territorial lordship. Kōyasan will therefore—although it is not as central to this
study as Enryakuji and Kōfukuji—serve as an important point of
reference, indicating some of the variations among the most
powerful religious institutions in premodern Japan.

It is through the many appeals, demonstrations in the capital,
and conflicts with other elites that the political power of Enryakuji,
Kōfukuji, and Kōyasan is most visible in the sources.[20] Though
some of these incidents have been noted by earlier scholars, they
have not been analyzed in conjunction with other political developments. This study is therefore devoted to explaining these
conflicts during the period when they were most frequent, from
the late Heian to the early Muromachi eras, from a perspective
that illuminates the polity as a whole. The central themes involve
various land and appointment conflicts and what in contemporary terms were known as *hōki* (mobilizations), *gōso* (forceful
appeals), and *kasen* (battles). Such conflicts became, interestingly
enough, most frequent and most violent during the tenures of
three retired emperors: Shirakawa (1086–1129), Go-Shirakawa

(1159–1192), and Go-Saga (1246–1272). Their eras are consequently the topics of chapters 3 to 5, where I explore and analyze the origins of conflicts involving Enryakuji, Kōfukuji, and Kōyasan, in a larger historical context. It is during Shirakawa's era that the imperial family reasserted its power vis-à-vis the Fujiwara regents, establishing in the process new factions and competition involving other gates of power as well. The sudden emergence of conflicts involving religious institutions was, in fact, a result of Shirakawa's efforts to control the elites of the late Heian governmental structures, thereby threatening the established balance of power. During Go-Shirakawa's violent times, the importance of these temples becomes even more apparent as their influence and activities in capital politics increased while they were courted by all sides during the factional conflicts of the 1160s and 1170s and the ensuing Genpei War. Go-Saga's era in the mid– and late thirteenth century was characterized by an imperial resurrection with the assistance of the Kamakura Bakufu, which resulted in further involvement by the still influential centers in the capital region. Yet the social and economic changes of the late Kamakura age also affected the elite temples in various ways, forcing them to adjust or to risk losing their position within the imperial state.

Chapter 2 provides an in-depth survey of the early history and development of Enryakuji, Kōfukuji, and Kōyasan as organizations and temple communities from their establishment to the end of the Heian age. Although I aim here to familiarize the Western reader with important terminology and background information related to these monasteries, I also emphasize the significance of secular factors in religious developments and vice versa. Chapter 6 focuses on the different forms of protest that the monks of the most influential temples, most notably Enryakuji and Kōfukuji, used to pressure the imperial court to respond to their pleas. Though these protests are vital indicators of issues that concerned the elite temples and of the methods used in communicating their concerns, they have not been the topic of any English-language scholarship. The forceful appeals supported by spiritual symbols will receive special attention, as they were the most common form of actual protest, but they also raise important questions regarding religious beliefs among members of the secular leadership, the role of the elite temples within the state, as well as general political structures. Finally, in Chapter 7, I show how the establishment of the Ashikaga Bakufu and the increasing influence of the warrior class in the fourteenth century gradually eliminated a governmental system within which the elite temples had actively participated. These temples were not rendered powerless; rather they were excluded from matters of national rulership, resulting in their disassociation from government and complete independence, as the bakufu declined from the second half of the fifteenth century. By thus treating four different eras of intense conflicts involving religious institutions and paying particular attention to the means of communication and conflict solution, this study will present a theory of rulership spanning several centuries.

The *Kenmon* Theory

Few scholars have been able to offer a synthetic interpretation of ruling structures taking into account the power of religious institutions in premodern Japan, since most have failed to disengage themselves from the conventional periodization, that sees the Heian, Kamakura, and Muromachi eras as all but mutually exclusive. However, Kuroda Toshio (1926–1993) opposed such restrictive views, arguing for a different approach that recognized the leading Buddhist temples as legitimate co-rulers of the premodern Japanese realm. He was a pioneer in constructing the first, and perhaps only, theory that took into account the different expressions of political and religious power in more than one era. His influential theory is commonly known as the *kenmon taisei* (the gates of power system).[21]

Though Western scholars in the field of Japanese history owe much to Kuroda Toshio's theory positing religious institutions as important co-rulers of what he called the medieval state, his contributions have been little acknowledged until recently.[22] Few indeed are those, in both Japan and the West, who have responded to Kuroda's own exhortation to analyze religious riots and monk disturbances "in conjunction with other political and military incidents."[23] Although most Japanese scholars acknowledge the importance of religious elites in the Heian and Kamakura eras, attempts to follow up on or adjust Kuroda's synthesis of shared rulership have been all but nonexistent.[24] In contrast, his more doctrinal interpretation of "Japan's medieval ideology," which Kuroda termed the *"kenmitsu taisei"*—the exoteric-esoteric system, named after the exoteric *(ken)* scriptures and the esoteric *(mitsu)*, orally transmitted, rituals that dominated the religious world in the Heian and Kamakura eras—has left more tangible traces among today's scholars.[25] Kuroda developed this doctrinal theory in opposition to the traditional view that the new popular sects of Buddhism, in particular Hōnen's Pure Land and Shinran's True Pure Land sects, dominated religiously as early as the Kamakura age. Instead, he claimed that the eight traditional sects, which combined the six teachings of Nara, headed by the Hossō sect of Kōfukuji, and the somewhat later Tendai (Enryakuji) and Shingon (Tōji and Kōyasan) sects continued to provide the general ideological framework until the fifteenth century. Unfortunately, the frequent discussions of the ideological aspects of Kuroda's theories have resulted in a tendency to neglect the larger theory (the *kenmon taisei*) that concerns itself also with the political environment and the ruling structures.

Kuroda introduced his theory of shared rulership, the *kenmon* theory, in the mid 1960s in an attempt to describe the sociopolitical system in Japan from the eleventh to the fifteenth centuries.[26] According to this theory, the highest authority in the state was shared by a number of private elite groups known as *kenmon* ("gates of power" or "influential families"). These elites were the leaders of three power blocs—the court nobles *(kōke* or *kuge)*, the warrior aristocracy *(buke)*, and temples and shrines *(jisha)*—which ruled the realm together by sharing responsibilities of government and supporting each other's privileges and status. Cooperation was a fundamental principle in the *kenmon* system of rule despite occasional conflicts between the blocs. In fact, Kuroda stated that the *kenmon* were mutually dependent on each other to maintain their status and wealth: one *kenmon* was never powerful enough to rule without the support of other elites. During the twelfth century, for example, the retired emperor dominated the political scene but relied on warrior aristocrats to supply military force. A similar dependence existed between the court and the warrior government in the thirteenth century.[27]

But how did the *kenmon* evolve? It is well known that Emperor Kammu (ruled 781–806), an astute and forceful sovereign, was responsible for moving the capital from Nara (Heijō-kyō) to present-day Kyoto (Heian-kyō) in 794.[28] But Kammu could not have foreseen that strong and direct imperial rulership would not last long after his death. From the mid–ninth century, the Fujiwara clan, though the most ardent supporter of the imperial-bureaucratic system and the emperor, had been the dominating faction at the imperial court. The Fujiwara chieftains virtually monopolized the right to provide consorts for imperial princes and emperors and came to exercise their power as maternal relatives of reigning emperors, assuming the post of regent *(sesshō)* or chancellor *(kanpaku)*. As the most important courtiers in the realm, the Fujiwara obtained substantial private privileges, including a large portfolio of tax-exempt estates, known as *shōen*. The clan's assets were managed by the chieftain with the help of other subordinate Fujiwara members and a private family headquarters *(mandokoro)*. In addition, the head of the clan used this wealth as well as his personal retainers to promote his own career at the imperial court and to perform his duties as the leading government official. The distinction between public and private thus became increasingly blurred, and, by the eleventh century, considerable private wealth as well as powerful allies and retainers were needed to attain important posts in the government. Yet, since the Fujiwara were still primarily dependent on government titles to rule and to maintain their position (even within their clan), Kuroda claimed that these events did not signify the beginning of *kenmon* rule per se.[29]

The first signs of a *kenmon* system appear, according to Kuroda, late in the eleventh century when members of the imperial family reasserted their dominance as retired emperors. Beginning with Shirakawa, who retired from the throne in 1086, the imperial house transformed itself into a private elite, amassing estates and attracting retainers of its own. The period from 1086 to 1185 is therefore known as the era of "rule by retired emperors" *(insei),* though Kuroda also pointed out that other elites, such as the Fujiwara, were never completely eclipsed. The crucial point at this juncture was that rulership now took place without high government offices, indicating that government was becoming increasingly privatized. Rulers typically retired to be able to exert their power.[30] Bureaucratic titles thus mattered little to the imperial family or the Fujiwara leaders in the twelfth century. In short, direct control of estates, provinces, and manpower was more important than government titles in order to influence or dominate the government. The *kenmon* style of rule was then further expanded in the twelfth century as the privatization of power and property continued and other elites came to share the responsibilities and privileges of government. These "new" members—religious institutions and members of the warrior aristocracy—had performed functions within the state for centuries, but they now acquired enough independence and power to assume the characteristics of *kenmon*.

According to Kuroda, the *kenmon* all shared five characteristics that defined their elite status. First, they had their own private headquarters, which handled administrative and economic matters within the *kenmon*. The Fujiwara clan and many religious institutions developed such organizations early in the Heian period, while other elites followed later in the eleventh and twelfth centuries. The retired emperor had his equivalent in the *in-no-chō* (the retired emperor's private headquarters), and the warrior elites followed with their own versions during their rise to national prominence in the second half of the twelfth century. Second, these headquarters issued edicts to convey orders from the head of the group, controlling matters pertaining to land and internal disputes. Such orders, though not entirely supplanting government edicts, took on a public character as they became virtually indistinguishable from those issued by official organs. Third, each *kenmon* had a number of retainers or followers who were loyal only to its leader. These retainers included both armed and civil personnel, and they were frequently employed in tasks for the state, as the elites increasingly used their private resources to perform government functions. For example, military retainers were used to maintain peace and to protect the palace area against demonstrations by the monks from Nara and Mt. Hiei. Fourth, the head of each elite had complete judicial rights—that is, rights to self-rule—over his own family or lineage. Promotion within the Fujiwara family or a temple was, in other words, an internal issue, even if the imperial court held a nominal right to confirm or (on a rare occasion) deny it. Indeed, the appointment of a head abbot at Kōfukuji was normally made by the Fujiwara chieftain on the recommendation and approval of the clergy. Fifth, the *kenmon* also had immune control and jurisdiction (another aspect of self-rule) over its assets, which came to include a large number of private estates. This privilege bordered on extraterritoriality, since the authority of government officials did not extend into private estates and the temple compounds, which could serve as a refuge for criminals, although the proprietors were expected to extradite them. It should also be noted that the *shōen* contained a vertical division of rights *(shiki)* that was an integral part of the *kenmon* system.[31] In fact, these terms were inseparable, since the *kenmon* constituted the political elite of a socioeconomic system based on *shiki* and *shōen*. Kuroda's argument is quite convincing, since the term *"kenmon"* itself first appears in *shōen* documents of the mid-Heian period.[32]

These several elites, Kuroda argued, joined to make up three larger power blocs, which performed specific duties (administrative, military, and religious), thus sharing the responsibilities of rulership while receiving judicial and economic privileges in exchange. The court nobility, consisting of the imperial family and the capital aristocracy, held the administrative and ceremonial responsibilities of the state. Supported by their private organizations and assets, the nobles maintained their privileged access to government offices and remained the formal leaders of the state. The emperorship, however, was above the system as the outstanding symbol of the state itself, ensuring its exceptional survival through ages of both peace and turmoil. It was the emperor who made all important appointments, including the shōgun and monks for important Buddhist ceremonies at the imperial court, even though such appointments at times existed in name only and the imperial power per se may have been limited. In other words, the three power blocs all needed this figurehead in whose name they ruled and prospered.[33]

The warrior aristocracy was responsible for keeping the peace and physically protecting the state. Beginning in the mid–twelfth century, these duties were entrusted to prominent warrior leaders from the Minamoto and Taira clans. This unofficial division of responsibilities was formalized with Minamoto no Yoritomo's (1147–1199) establishment of the warrior government in the east (the Kamakura Bakufu) in the 1180s, which Kuroda saw as a second phase of the *kenmon* system. Although the bakufu could easily outpower the court and its supporters in the capital area (which actually happened in the Jōkyū War of 1221), it could not eliminate the court and rule on its own, since it lacked the administrative and bureaucratic apparatus to extend its rule over all classes in thirteenth-century Japan.[34] Its main responsibility was rather confined to maintaining peace and controlling the warrior class. The court and the bakufu consequently complemented each other in an overlapping rulership that has been termed a dual polity by some historians.[35]

The third member of the ruling triumvirate—the religious establishment—supplied the state and its members with spiritual protection. It also supported a vertical differentiation among the rulers and the ruled through magical and expensive rituals that only the most prestigious courtiers could afford. Since the power of religious institutions is the subject of this study and since the religious bloc is the most controversial part of Kuroda's theory, it will be useful to explore his analysis of temples and shrines in some depth.

During the ninth century, the most popular Buddhist sects (the *kenmitsu* schools) developed close relations with the most powerful families in the capital. However, after two centuries of patron-client relations, the larger temples became less dependent on direct and voluntary support from the capital nobility. By the eleventh century, these temples had private estates of their own, a vast number of monks, lay followers, and branch institutions over which they held exclusive judicial rights. Administrative duties and the management of these assets were handled by the temple's own headquarters. A head abbot, often of noble birth, represented the temple and served as the channel of communication with the other elites. Even though the head abbot was principally a chosen leader, his leadership within the sect was not unlike that of the Fujiwara chieftain or the retired emperor. In effect, these religious centers had been "*kenmon*-ified."[36] By approximately the same time, a doctrine that supported the interdependent relationship between the imperial court and Buddhism developed. It is known as *ōbō-buppō sōi* (the interdependence of the Imperial Law and the Buddhist Law), representing the idea that the state and Buddhism were dependent on each other as the wings of a bird or the two wheels of a cart. Tangible evidence for this ideological concept, which also includes the idea that the Shintō gods *(kami)* are vital in protecting the Buddhist deities and institutions, exists from the mid–eleventh century both in religious sources and in documents of more secular character. The *ōbō-buppō sōi* concept provided the ideological foundation for the participation of Buddhist institutions in government, while linking together the realms of the *kami*, the buddhas, and the living.[37]

Kuroda's *kenmon* concept is especially appealing because it treats religious institutions as political powers both in their own right and as providers of doctrines and spiritual support. Moreover, the idea of shared rulership in medieval Japan can help explain a number of complex relationships involving the elites from three different groups. However, it can also be misleading, since it labels religious institutions as a coherent power bloc on the same level as the court and the bakufu. Three points illustrate the problems that occur with this idea.

First, it is difficult to imagine that the religious establishment had the same kind of power as the court or the bakufu. Taira Masa-yuki, Kuroda's student and successor, adjusted his mentor's theory in this respect. Taira states that religious institutions never had enough power to form an independent government as the war-rior aristocracy did. He further claims that temples never held ultimate authority in any way. That power only belonged to the secular powers.[38] Second, if religious institutions did not have the same kind of power as the other two power blocs, then how inde-pendent were they? Kuroda himself seems to have recognized a certain difference here. Temples, he concluded, were "half-dependent" on the court.[39] As this study will suggest, ties with the court were quite strong and much different from those with the bakufu and the warrior class in general. For example, the cere-monial and religious duties of the *kenmitsu* temples—their raison d'être—were almost exclusively directed at serving the members of the imperial court, and it was in an attempt to defend the right to perform such ceremonies that the monks of Enryakuji, Kōfu-kuji, and Tōdaiji staged many of their protests in Kyoto. Third, by claiming that the religious establishment constituted a separate bloc, Kuroda assumed that there was a sense of unity among the most powerful temples and shrines. As will be apparent in this study, this point is arguably the weakest in the whole *kenmon* theory. While the court and the bakufu were coherent in that they had clear apexes in their blocs, the religious establishment cannot be seen as a single hierarchy during the late Heian and Kamakura periods. Different doctrines and sects coexisted and competed for favors from the court in a system that can most aptly be de-scribed as one of doctrinal multitude. It is therefore misleading to treat the religious establishment as a collectively active body. Individual temples and shrines had *kenmon* status, but they were too diversified in power and structure to be compared with the court and the bakufu as a single bloc.[40] Though a handful of tem-ples had elite status and were actively involved in maintaining the centrality of the state, the religious establishment as a whole was clearly inferior to the power of the imperial court and the bakufu. In the end, I have found it more helpful to use the term "shared rulership," emphasizing the different elites involved as well as their functions, than to assume the existence of three distinctive blocs. The interaction between the elites, which is characterized by interbloc alliances and intrabloc conflicts, also indicates that a division into blocs can create serious misconceptions.

Based on these objections, how relevant is it to use the term *"kenmon"* to refer to religious elite institutions? Are they, for example, referred to as *kenmon* in contemporary sources? Surprisingly, these questions have not been posed by scholars in the West or in Japan. Kuroda used *"kenmon"*—a historical term—mainly as an analytical term in his works. The warrior government (bakufu) and religious institutions are not referred to as *kenmon* in historical sources. Rather, there are numerous examples where the terms *"kenmon"* and *"kenmon seika"* (powerful houses and influential families) are used expressly to distinguish the noble powers in the capital from religious institutions. Moreover, there is no exact contemporary religious equivalent to the compelling terms *"kōke"* (or *kuge;* the nobility) and *"buke"* (the warrior aristocracy), further belying Kuroda's idea that the religious establishment could be considered one coherent hierarchy.[41] Yet there is some evidence to support Kuroda's analytical usage. There are frequent references to the prerogatives of the *kenmon* and temples and shrines *(kenmon narabi ni jisha)* in documents and other contemporary sources, putting them on a level of parity. This impression is further strengthened by the term *"sōke,"* or *"shūke"* (sect lineage), which appears in several Kōyasan documents in the Kamakura era, indicating the kind of independence and authority associated with the *kenmon.*

"Sōke" most commonly refers to the head abbot *(chōja)* of Tōji, denoting his leadership of the sect, as in an edict issued from that temple in 1283.[42] However, it is the broader usage of this term that deserves full attention, as seen in examples for Kōyasan such as a document of 1239 that lists eight articles of the *sōke,* indicating the kind of power and authority that was both comparable to and independent of that of the secular and religious elites in Kyoto and the warrior aristocracy.[43] Such juxtapositions are also openly made between the *sōke* and the *buke* by a monk-manager of a local estate in pledges to Kōyasan in the late thirteenth and early fourteenth centuries.[44] Moreover, and most important, a document from the Kōyasan clergy of the seventh month of 1271 explicitly juxtaposes the *kuge,* the *buke,* and the *sōke.* It is evident from the contents of this *okibumi* (directive of regulations) and

from the honorific empty space that precedes all three terms that a concept of elite noble, military, and religious spheres of authority existed at this time. Undoubtedly, this document represents the best support for Kuroda's *kenmon taisei,* while it also reaffirms the close relationship between the elites and the *shōen* hierarchy.[45] Although these terms are thus far restricted to Shingon documents and evidence of a widespread usage is lacking, the claims nevertheless indicate that notions of freestanding religious powers were part of the intellectual environment in the capital region of the Kamakura age.

It is no exaggeration that the *kenmon* theory has made important contributions to the field. The notion of privately based elites that shared governmental duties is an important insight that facilitates comprehension of the ruling structures of Heian and Kamakura Japan. To be more specific, the *kenmon* theory brought attention to three important issues. First, the concept of shared rulership opposed the traditional view that the Heian and Kamakura polities were characterized by a sequence of elites in total control of government. Kuroda pointed out that the Fujiwara family, the retired emperors, and the Kamakura Bakufu, even during the heydays of their respective power, were never completely dominating. They were merely the *primus inter pares*—the dominating elite among other elites—who could not rule alone without the support of their peers. Conversely, the other elites were not completely eclipsed even when the balance shifted to their disadvantage. The Fujiwara family, for example, continued to play an important role in the capital throughout the reign of retired emperors and in the Kamakura period. Second, Kuroda questioned the view that the establishment of the Kamakura Bakufu in 1185 marked the transition from court rule to warrior rule or from the ancient to the medieval era. Indeed, historians have recently realized that there were more continuities between the Heian and Kamakura periods than were previously acknowledged, and as a result, studies that move away from the warrior-centered view of these eras have appeared in the last decade or so. The continued authority of the imperial court and the central proprietors is one important aspect of this revision. As part of this realization we should also consider Kuroda's claim that it was *kenmitsu* ideology, which maintained its multidoctrinal emphasis, and not the new populist sects that dominated thought and ideology at the national level in Kamakura Japan.[46] Third, Kuroda showed that religious institutions were not merely parasites who usurped authority from the imperial court. On the contrary, they were important participants in the government as providers of religious rituals for the well-being of the state and its officials. Such rituals were instrumental in creating and maintaining the social stratification that supported the court hierarchy, since the ability to finance and perform lavish and often magical ceremonies augmented the status of those involved. Moreover, religious institutions served as extensions of the state when they collected income in the provinces as the representatives and religious protectors of the state.[47] In sum, the *kenmon* theory made scholars realize that religious institutions in premodern Japan were sociopolitical institutions integral to the government and its rule.

In substance, the *kenmon* system was a ruling system in which a number of elites—"gates of power"—ruled through their private, or extralegal, assets, and it was the head of the most powerful *kenmon* who typically dominated the government. The headquarters of that elite thus assumed a more official character and issued documents to different government organs. The retainers of the *kenmon* leader also came to serve the government and received official titles. At the same time, not even the dominating *kenmon* chief had enough power to become an absolute ruler. He was dependent on the support of the other elites, who assumed specific public responsibilities (religious, military, or administrative) in exchange for confirmation and support of their private control of land and their own lineage. *Kenmon* rulership was, in other words, a ruling system in which private and official powers were combined to achieve efficient government over land and people.

Benefiting from the positive contributions of the *kenmon* theory, this study acknowledges that religious institutions in premodern Japan were not merely locations of worship and religious rituals, but also important members of the ruling elite. By politicizing religion and accepting the interdependence of religion and politics, poorly understood religious protests and conflicts can be explained in a coherent manner without resorting to simplistic theories of secularization and doctrinal semantics. My approach is thus to some extent like that of an *Annales* historian, as I address the least understood aspect of premodern Japanese rulership over the long term in order to construct a new synthesis of the framework within which rulers and subjects, monks and shrine

servants, warriors and courtiers acted. The object of this mono-
graph, therefore, is not only to provide new information or a
reinterpretation of known events, but above all to offer a comprehensive theory that can advance general understanding as well as
generate new questions regarding the era that has been known as
the late ancient and the early medieval in Japan.

2

Monastic Developments in the Heian Age

The *kenmitsu* temples were from their founding never separated from their sociopolitical environments. For example, the history of the Enryakuji complex, located on Mt. Hiei just northeast of Kyoto (see Map 2), is closely intertwined with the history of the old capital itself. Founded almost simultaneously around the turn of the ninth century, Enryakuji prospered while the capital became the center of the magnificent Heian court lifestyles that for many have come to signify the peak of ancient culture in Japan. The temple initially lived off the patronage of the capital nobility, and court nobles continued to play an important role within the complex when it became more independent late in the Heian period. Similarly, Kōfukuji, though not as close to the political nexus of the Heian period, so dominated Nara that the contemporary term for the temple's clergy, *"nanto shuto"* (the clergy of the southern capital), was synonymous with the entire religious establishment of the city itself, indicating a firm symbiosis between monastic complex and city.[1] Kōfukuji's ties with the Fujiwara, reinforced by the temple's control of Kasuga (the Fujiwara clan shrine), assured it consistent aristocratic patronage, prestige, and a steady flow of income. As an important center for the Shingon sect, Kōyasan also reached similar heights of power and independence, but because of its location on a distant mountain some thirty miles south of Nara, the temple was less directly involved in capital politics. However, since it was also represented by Tōji in Kyoto, and the secular elites there tended to support Kōyasan in conjunction with their general patronage of Shingon, the temple remained an important part of the *kenmitsu* establishment. The aristocratic links of these temples remained central throughout the premodern era, but the privatization of government that became evident in the mid–Heian period gradually forced the temples to rely on their own resources for economic support and physical protection. To comprehend such expressions of secular power and the role these temples played in the larger sociopolitical context, it is useful to place them in the general framework of Heian history by surveying their respective establishments and their development into powerful religious elites.

The Politics of Religious Patronage in Nara and Early Heian Japan

The handful of temples that can be characterized as elite institutions in premodern Japan have several common characteristics, such as prominent secular patrons and allies, large portfolios of private estates and branch institutions, fiscal and judicial immunities, as well as armed followers. But there were also important differences among them, unique features that depended to a large extent on the circumstances during their founding and subsequent years of growth and consolidation.

Kōfukuji was the oldest of the elite temples in premodern Japan, outdating even the grand imperial temple of Tōdaiji, which was founded in 741. Though Kōfukuji's exact origins are uncertain, the temple's history appears to begin with the patriarch of the Fujiwara family, Nakatomi no Kamatari. After having aided Prince Naka in the Taika coup against the Soga family in 645, Kamatari was awarded the Fujiwara surname and remained a close supporter of the assertive prince. In 668 Naka ascended the throne as Emperor Tenji and moved the imperial palace from Naniwa to Ōtsu on the shores of Lake Biwa, where he built a temple named Sufukudera.[2] At the same time, Kamatari's wife sponsored the construction of Yamashinadera, supposedly for the spirit of their first son, Mahito (642–665), who had studied Buddhism in T'ang China at a young age. Mahito had died in 665, apparently poisoned by an immigrant from the Korean kingdom of Paekche who feared that he might persuade the court to support T'ang-favored enemy kingdoms in the civil war on the peninsula.[3] Tenji himself died in 671, leaving the throne to his young son, but the new ruler was immediately challenged by Tenji's younger brother, Prince Ōama, who usurped the throne after a six-month-long conflict known as the Jinshin War. Ōama became Emperor Temmu and proceeded to move the imperial palace back to the Asuka region, where he had his own base of power. Interestingly, the Fujiwara-sponsored Yamashinadera followed the new ruler as well, a practice that continued during subsequent moves of the imperial palace. During the brief era of the Fujiwara capital (694–710), Yamashinadera appears to have merged with another Fujiwara-sponsored temple (Umayazakadera), until it ended up in Nara in 710, where the temple assumed the name Kōfukuji (Temple to Promote Posthumous Felicity), indicating that it had now taken over the responsibilities of services for the deceased members of the Fujiwara clan. In addition to such spiritual services, the temple served more immediate and worldly purposes for the Fujiwara, as the elaborate temple structures and the expensive rituals that took place there accrued prestige to the sponsors. Such displays of wealth and knowledge of the more developed civilization of T'ang China were important functions of temple sponsorship in the Nara period, as demonstrated also by the role played by Tōdaiji in consolidating the imperial family's position in the early Japanese state.[4] At any rate, Kōfukuji became an important and permanent structure in Nara, even though its connections to the Ōtsu region must have remained strong in memory, since both Heian and Kamakura sources often refer to the temple as Yamashinadera, from the name of its original location in the seventh century.

Extensive construction commenced at Kōfukuji under the supervision and patronage of Kamatari's second son, Fuhito (659–720) in 714, beginning with the completion of the main temple building, the Golden Hall (Kondō). Other structures were soon added, including the Northern Round Hall in 721, the Eastern Golden Hall (Tōkondō) in 726, a five-storied pagoda (730), the Western Golden Hall (Saikondō) in 734, and a lecture hall in 746, through the initiative of both Fujiwara and imperial members, in recognition of the temple's early popularity. Fujiwara no Nakamaro (706–764) provided Kōfukuji with some of its first landholdings, though small in size, in 749, 757, and again in 761, but the temple also began to take on a more official role, as evidenced by the appointment of a government official in 720 to supervise the ongoing construction.[5] By the end of the eighth century, the Fujiwara clan temple was one of the most important temples in Japan, overshadowed only by the imperially sponsored Tōdaiji.

Kōfukuji's doctrinal inclination was toward Hossō, which, because of its focus on reading and intellectual activities, became especially popular among the noble elites, as it served to distinguish the well educated and cultured from other aristocrats. The Yuima'e, a ceremony that celebrated the contributions of nonclerics to Buddhism, was the single most important aspect of the Hossō package. It became an annual lecture series performed for the court and the imperial state early on, and, more important, it was decided that it be held exclusively at Kōfukuji in 801. The mid–Nara period also saw, probably as a result of the efforts of Fujiwara no Nagate (714–771), the Kasuga shrine, located on the hillside just east of Kōfukuji (see Map 4), become adopted as the Fujiwara clan shrine, which prepared the way for the eventual merging of Kōfukuji and Kasuga into one large and powerful temple-shrine complex.[6]

Kōfukuji's early success is best evidenced by the influence of its school of thought (Hossō) on the *sōgō* (Office of Monastic Affairs) and the number of its monks on the *sōgō* staff. The *sōgō* was a government organ established in 624 for the purpose of supervising all Buddhist sects, monks, and nuns. Its responsibilities included ordinations, registration of monks, and reviewing the rules for each sect. The court staffed the *sōgō* with high-ranking monks of its own choice, though nominations were made by a monk's teacher or his temple based on his service within the temple and merits accumulated through the performance of prestigious Buddhist rituals for the imperial court. The number of members and their ranks changed over time, but there were three basic levels with subranks throughout the Heian period. The *sōjō* (grand master) was the highest-ranking monk in the realm, followed by the *sōzu* (monk supervisor or director) and the *risshi* (preceptor).[7] The composition of the *sōgō* tended to reflect the political balance among the different sects. Since both the Fujiwara family and the imperial court in general appreciated the Hossō sect's elitist philosophy and its popularity with the Chinese emperor at the time, Kōfukuji's monks came to dominate the *sōgō* in the Nara period. While extending its influence over other temples in Nara, the Hossō clergy used the *sōgō* to control the religious establishment and to suppress their opponents. In fact, although the Kōfukuji clergy unsurprisingly objected to Emperor Kammu's move of the imperial palace away from Nara in 784, causing some tension between the imperial family and the Fujiwara clan temple, it managed to retain a dominating position through its influence within the *sōgō*.[8] It was this power that put Kōfukuji in a position to oppose a young and ambitious monk named Saichō in the early ninth century.

Because of the legends surrounding Saichō (766/7–822), he has become the central figure in most accounts of the establishment of Enryakuji and Tendai Buddhism on Mt. Hiei. This hagiography may give undue credit to the founder of the Japanese Tendai sect because later scholars who recorded it had the advantage of knowing the temple's subsequent prominence. In fact, many of the accomplishments attributed to Saichō seem to have been coincidental, depending on factors beyond his control, and were it not for Enryakuji's able leadership in the ninth and tenth centuries, Saichō would probably not be the legend he is today. In particular the political implications of Saichō's religious preferences are important in understanding Enryakuji's subsequent developments in the Heian age.

After learning about Tendai Buddhism—a Mahāyāna school that preached that all human beings had the potential for enlightenment and held a fairly syncretic view of Buddhist practices —in Nara and becoming a full-fledged monk at Tōdaiji in 785, Saichō decided to return to his native Ōmi to live in a small hut on Mt. Hiei to continue his studies.[9] The reasons for Saichō's move away from the Buddhist centers in Nara have been discussed elsewhere, but his fortuitous choice of Mt. Hiei deserves to be explained. Two factors are especially vital here. First, there were Buddhist hermitages on the mountain in the years before Saichō. According to a poem in the *Kaifūsō* (a collection of poems from 751), a hut for Buddhist studies and meditation was built there by Fujiwara no Muchimaro (680–737), who was the grandson of the Fujiwara family patriarch, Kamatari. Interestingly, the Fujiwara leaders maintained a strong tie with Ōmi (both Muchimaro and his son Nakamaro served as governors there), which may have helped Saichō secure much of his funding for the construction of a temple on Mt. Hiei.[10] Second, and perhaps more important, there were strong traditions related to the native cults. The *kami* (native deities) associated with the mountain by the eighth century belonged to two distinctive but equally important traditions. The oldest shrines are believed to be dedicated to Yamasue-no-mikoto, an important agricultural deity of local origin. The other deity on Mt. Hiei was Ōnamuchi-no-mikoto, who was a protector of imperial residences and thus also indirectly a guardian of the imperial family. Originally established in Ōtsu

in 667, supposedly by Prince Naka (Emperor Tenji), the shrine
was probably moved to Mt. Hiei in 715 by the aforementioned Fujiwara no Muchimaro.[11] The deities on Mt. Hiei thus combined
strong local traditions with one of the most prominent imperial
gods, and their presence may have attracted Buddhist monks,
including Saichō, to Mt. Hiei during the eighth century. In fact,
monks commonly sought the support of the native cults from the
introduction of Buddhism in Japan, as evidenced also by the construction of Kōfukuji adjacent to the Kasuga shrine, which later
became the main Shintō affiliate of the temple.[12] In light of these
traditions, Saichō's choice of Mt. Hiei for his retreat becomes
considerably easier to understand.

Three years after settling on Mt. Hiei, Saichō named his small
temple Hieizanji. Many scholars consider 788 the founding year
of Enryakuji even though the name itself was not given until after
Saichō's death.[13] In 793, Saichō named the central building of the
complex the Ichijō shikan'in (One-Vehicle Meditation Hall),
indicating that he was leaning more and more toward Tendai.
The teachings of the one vehicle *(ichijō)*, which stated that all
human beings contain the potential for Buddhahood, constitute
a view that is most emphatically expressed in the Lotus Sūtra.[14]
Though this text was known at the time, Saichō's complete faith
in this concept was different from the view of the Nara sects, especially Hossō, which promoted a more difficult path, maintaining
that only a selected few holy men would achieve Buddhahood
after this life. Yet regardless of these innovations, there was nothing particular about Saichō's status, and his appointment as imperial court monk *(naigubu)* in 797 therefore seems unexpected.
The *naigubu* were a group of ten favored monks who performed
Buddhist rituals and gave lectures on certain sūtras at the imperial palace, in return for which they were granted financial support and two boy servants. Most important, the appointment
meant official recognition and opportunities for further support
from the nobility. Some scholars credit another court monk,
Jukō, for recommending Saichō to the imperial court. According
to this view, Jukō was impressed with Saichō's vows to stay away
from worldly matters until he had obtained wisdom.[15] Although
this explanation is appealing, because it lends support to Saichō's
reputation as a faithful and fervent Buddhist, it neglects other
important aspects of his promotion. Specifically, it is doubtful
that such merits alone could have propelled a young monk into

the spotlight at the imperial court, and again it is necessary also to consider the sociopolitical context of the 790s.

Construction of a new capital commenced at Nagaoka (south of present-day Kyoto) immediately after Emperor Kammu and the court left Nara in 784. Following several unfortunate events, this enterprise was abandoned ten years later, when the Kyoto plain, next to Ōmi Province, was selected as a more appropriate location for the imperial court. As Ronald Toby has shown, Emperor Kammu's line of the imperial family (the Tenji line) had its traditional power base in the vicinity of the Kyoto plain, while the opposing line (the Temmu line) was based in the Nara basin. But it should also be noted that the Fujiwara family benefited greatly from the transfer of the imperial court. In the second half of the Nara period, the influence of the Fujiwara family at the imperial court had declined, owing to a combination of powerful opponents and the untimely deaths of leading family members, which may also help explain why the ongoing construction of Kōfukuji stopped suddenly in 772.[16] However, after the move to Kyoto, the Fujiwara fortunes improved, and the family came to control more government posts than ever. In particular, it was the Northern Branch (the *hokke* branch) of the Fujiwara clan that emerged as the leader. It was also this branch that had strong connections with Ōmi Province.[17]

Both Emperor Kammu and the leaders of the Fujiwara family were thus socially (intrafamilial competition) and politically (control of government) motivated to move the court to the Kyoto plain. But, there were also religious reasons for relocating the capital in that area. In fact, most traditional historians have argued that the growing influence of the Buddhist establishment over government affairs was the principal reason that forced Kammu to leave Nara. Although that view is oversimplified, there is little doubt of an attempt by the Kammu court to broaden its religious base so that it would not become dependent on a single hierarchy of temples. It is as part of this restructuring that Saichō, a proponent of a different doctrine that was based away from Nara, was promoted to court monk in 797. Unfortunately, neither Saichō's role nor his situation during the transfer of the imperial court in 794 is known. Did his presence on Mt. Hiei influence the court in its decision to locate the capital close to the mountain? Although he may have been known to the Fujiwara, there is no evidence that Saichō was acknowledged by the court as a whole. His status as a monk was not exalted enough to support the notion that his presence influenced the court's decision. Rather, it was the rich spiritual presence around the Kyoto plain that made the area attractive religiously, especially considering that the abandoned Nagaoka had been perceived to be troubled by malevolent spirits. The guardian deity Ōnamuchi-no-mikoto on Mt. Hiei may have been considered important for the protection of the new capital, since evil spirits came from the northeast, according to well-known Chinese geomantic views.[18] In other words, Saichō probably became better known *after* 794, as a consequence, rather than a cause, of the move to the Kyoto plain. Location plus a willingness to promote new doctrines and new temples were thus the immediate backdrop to Saichō's promotion and rapid advancement after 797.

Following his appointment as a court monk, Saichō concentrated on collecting texts and lecturing on the Lotus Sūtra. After a successful appearance at a debate on the Tendai teachings at Takaosanji in 802, Saichō began to separate himself from the Nara sects more openly, criticizing them for their reliance on commentaries rather than the Buddha's original words. Saichō accordingly petitioned the emperor that original texts should be obtained directly from Buddhist masters in China. In the twelfth month of 802, Emperor Kammu granted Saichō permission to go to China and the money in gold to cover his expenses.[19] Again, the support Saichō received is evidence of the court's policy to promote monks who focused on Buddhist teachings other than those of the Nara sects. Another aspiring and ambitious monk from Nara was also chosen to study in China, traveling as part of the same mission as Saichō. He was Kūkai (774–835), the founder of the esoteric Shingon sect in Japan.

Kūkai was born of the Saeki family, a local branch of the more prestigious Ōtomo clan, on the island of Shikoku, but was fortunate enough to have an uncle on his mother's side who served at the imperial court. In 788, at the age of fourteen, Kūkai went to the capital, which at the time was being constructed in Nagaoka, to study Chinese. Though it was intended that he focus on Confucianism, Kūkai soon became dissatisfied with this school of thought and turned instead to Buddhism. He became a private monk, and when it was decided that the capital be moved again, he left Nagaoka to spread the word of Buddha on his own.[20] Kūkai's subsequent activities until he was suddenly chosen to join the mission to China in 804 are obscure, though it is unlikely that he was well known among the Kyoto nobles, and his selection for the mission to China in 804 thus seems surprising. The most sensible explanation must take into account the same factors that surrounded the choice of Saichō. Just like his contemporary, Kūkai preached Mahāyāna Buddhism and may have provided an attractive alternative for Emperor Kammu and his supporters to the Nara sects, which became disappointed when the court left the old capital. In addition, Kūkai had some supporters in the capital, most notably his uncle, who may have promoted the monk successfully in his capacity as an imperial tutor.[21]

The circumstances behind the selection of Saichō and Kūkai may thus have been similar, but the trip to China illustrates fundamental differences in their approaches. Kūkai, whose ship arrived first, ended up in the southern Chinese province of Fukien. A letter to the local governor ended a long wait, and Kūkai was allowed to travel to the capital of Ch'ang-an, where he arrived in the twelfth month of 804. After a three-month stay at a residence supplied by the T'ang court, Kūkai moved to the famous temple of Hsi-ming, built in 658. He eventually met the great master Hui-kuo (746–805), who was the transmitter of popular esoteric teachings based on the Mahāvairochana Sūtra (Dainichi-kyō in Japanese) that had been introduced in China almost a century earlier.[22] Although Kūkai intended to spend as many as twenty years in China, he decided to return to Japan after Hui-kuo's death in 805. Carrying with him a large number of Buddhist texts, mandalas (cosmic paintings used in meditation in esoteric Buddhism), and books of poetry, he left Ch'ang-an, where he spent his entire stay in China, early in 806 and arrived back on the coast of Kyushu later that same year.[23]

Contrary to Kūkai, Saichō and his interpreter, Gishin (781–833), never visited the grand capital of the T'ang dynasty. Instead, they went straight to Mt. T'ien-t'ai, where they immediately began the copying of various texts. Both Saichō and Gishin subsequently took the Mahāyāna bodhisattva vows, after which they returned to the Chinese coast only to discover that they had to wait for one and a half months for a Japanese ship. The time was well spent, however, as the two monks studied esoteric texts, and they eventually received corresponding initiations on the eighteenth day of the fourth month of 805.[24] On their return to Japan, Gishin went back to his native province of Sagami, while Saichō proceeded to

Kyoto, where he arrived in the seventh month of 805. At that time, Saichō found his main patron, Emperor Kammu, ill. Esoteric rites, which were believed to have healing effects, were known in Japan before Saichō, but with his return they reached a new level of popularity. Saichō brought back the most current esoteric routines from China, which became a bigger success in Kyoto than his own preferred Tendai doctrines. On the first day of the ninth month of 805, a *kanjō* ritual, the first esoteric ceremony of its kind on Japanese soil, was performed on behalf of the ailing emperor.[25] Kammu's health did not improve, however, and Saichō, realizing the danger of losing his principal patron, took steps to establish his teachings as a recognized school of its own. Accordingly, on the third day of the first month of 806, he proposed that the ordination system be revised and that two of the twelve yearly ordinands appointed by the court be from the Tendai sect.[26] Kammu had tried to obtain an even balance among the different sects and was concerned in particular with the Hossō sect's dominance in Nara. He was therefore in favor of Saichō's petition, since it would reduce Kōfukuji's ordinands from five to three. To some scholars, the acceptance of Saichō's proposal marks the official establishment of Tendai Buddhism in Japan.[27]

Emperor Kammu died on the seventeenth of the third month of 806. Saichō subsequently became a less central figure in the capital, mainly because the succeeding emperor, Heizei, cut back on government spending, forcing many temple projects to be halted. In fact, despite the edict of 806, the first Tendai monks were not ordained until four years later, just after Emperor Saga had ascended the throne.[28] Although activities on Mt. Hiei were increasing, Saichō had to struggle to obtain independence for the Tendai sect. He faced two powerful opponents in his endeavors. First, Kūkai, who returned to Kyoto in the seventh month of 809, immediately became a challenge to Saichō's position as a master of esoteric Buddhism. After returning to Kyushu in the tenth month of 806, Kūkai had sent a memorial to the imperial court in Kyoto, accounting for his achievements while asking for support to start a new esoteric school. He had to wait almost three years for a response, but the imperial court eventually allowed him to return and reside at Takaosanji, just northwest of Kyoto, although Emperor Heizei was known for not showing strong religious fervor. Kūkai's fortunes soon changed for the better as Heizei became ill and resigned in favor of Emperor Saga, who quickly became an avid supporter of Kūkai. Saga appreciated artworks, which were an integral part of Kūkai's teachings, and the two men also engaged in poetry writing and exchanges. This relationship gave Kūkai an important advantage over his competitors, and he had reached new heights within the political and religious hierarchies by 810. For example, he established a group of students and disciples studying esoteric Buddhism at Takao-sanji and planned to perform esoteric ceremonies. More important, he was honored by appointment as head abbot *(bettō)* of Tōdaiji, which eventually made it possible for him to incorporate esoteric rites in Nara by establishing a branch called the Shingon'in (822) within the imperial temple.[29] Between Kūkai and Saichō, there was now little doubt that the former held the upper hand, since he had studied esoteric practices, whose popularity dominated among the Kyoto aristocrats, extensively in the Chinese capital. Saichō's knowledge was not as comprehensive, and the esoteric course given on Mt. Hiei was at best a limited success, since most monks who had taken it defected to the Hossō sect in Nara within a couple of years.[30] This lack of a full esoteric program made it difficult for Saichō to retain his students, and he was forced repeatedly to ask Kūkai to lend him esoteric texts. In 812 Saichō and one of his disciples (Kōjō) even participated in an esoteric ceremony performed for them by Kūkai. Yet Saichō's attempts to master the esoteric teachings were effectively curtailed by Kūkai, who may have resented Tendai's syncretic emphasis on concepts such as monastic rules and meditation in addition to esotericism, and he became increasingly unwilling to share the texts he had brought back from China. The ensuing deterioration in the relationship between the two men is sufficiently known that it need not be recounted here.[31]

The Nara schools were Saichō's other opponent. The confrontation, as it has survived in the sources, focused on doctrinal differences. As noted earlier, Saichō believed that all sentient beings had the potential to attain enlightenment, an idea central to the Mahāyāna (the greater vehicle) doctrine. The Nara schools, and in particular the Hossō school, were in practical terms closer to the Hīnayāna (the lesser vehicle) doctrine, according to which Buddhahood could be achieved only by a privileged few who had attained a certain level of wisdom. This difference of opinion forced Saichō into discussions with other monks that often centered on the issue of ordinations of monks, which were based on

Hīnayāna principles during Saichō's time. Since Saichō was unable to gain acceptance in Nara for the Mahāyāna precepts, he began to petition the court to allow a separate platform at Hieizanji and to designate it a Mahāyāna temple. Though Saichō continued to debate these issues with the Nara monks, at the time of his death in 822, they still had not been resolved.[32]

Although the religious antagonisms of the day have received much attention, most scholars have failed to see that the conflict between Saichō and the Nara monks was only one element in a larger picture dominated by factionalism and political regrouping. The move to Kyoto in 794 is the single most important event in this process, but the restructuring continued into the ninth century. In fact, imperial power was firmly consolidated in Kyoto through a series of events that took place in 809–810. In the fourth month of that year, Emperor Heizei fell ill and retired in favor of his younger brother, who became Emperor Saga. In the twelfth month, however, Heizei recovered and moved to Nara with his entourage and various court officials. Among those who accompanied Heizei were his favorite consort Fujiwara no Kusuko and her brother Nakanari. Heizei now elected to honor both of them with government titles, creating, in the process, a challenge to Saga's court in Kyoto. The initial response from Kyoto was weak, but when Heizei ordered the capital back to Nara on the sixth day of the ninth month of 810, Saga and his court reacted with force. The troops that were sent out from Kyoto quickly surrounded Heizei and his followers, who surrendered after only three days. Heizei was forced to become a monk, and Kusuko committed suicide.[33] The result of this conflict, known as the Kusuko Incident, was twofold. First, there was a distinctive shift of power within the imperial family and the Fujiwara clan. Saga eliminated Heizei's descendants as eligible candidates to the imperial throne by "granting" a surname to the deposed line, and all subsequent emperors were accordingly descendants of Saga. This secularization of surplus royals became a common technique during the Heian age, designed to restrict competition for the throne and to avoid factionalism at court.[34] A similar consolidation took place within the Fujiwara family. Fujiwara no Fuyutsugu of the Northern Branch emerged as the undisputed leader following the elimination of Kusuko and Nakanari of the Ceremonial Branch. The second implication of this incident was a distinct shift in favor of the imperial court in the Kyoto plain at the expense of Nara. However,

since the country's most prestigious and powerful religious institutions—in particular Tōdaiji and Kōfukuji—were still located in
the old capital, the court needed to establish new religious centers
that could legitimize and support its rulership. The court's patronage of Kūkai and Saichō, both outside the old capital, following
the move to Kyoto, was integral to this policy.

Though Saichō's efforts to establish Tendai as an independent
sect coincided with the court's ambitions, resistance from the
temples in Nara remained considerable. Tendai was a threat to
the established Nara schools by virtue of both its proximity to the
capital and the favoritism shown to Saichō under Kammu and the
hokke Fujiwara. But the Nara schools were more a problem to
Saichō than the other way around. Saichō's difficulties in retaining his monks on Mt. Hiei have already been mentioned. Although twenty-four Tendai monks were ordained between 807
and 818, only ten remained on Mt. Hiei (half newly arrived
novices). Even worse, at least six of the defectors joined Tendai's
main opponent, the Hossō school, which also dominated the
Office of Monastic Affairs. In fact, a Hossō monk named Gomyō
(749/50–834), who was appointed to the *sōgō* a month after the
death of Emperor Kammu, became one of Saichō's chief antago-
nists. With the office thus staffed with his opponents, it became
necessary for Saichō to obtain independence from the *sōgō*.[35] In
the many petitions that he sent to the court beginning in 818, he
concentrated on three objectives. First, Saichō requested that the
monks studying at Hieizanji should not be removed from the lay
registers, thereby exempting them from the *sōgō*'s jurisdiction.
Second, he sought acknowledgment that Tendai monks should
remain on Mt. Hiei for the entire twelve-year training period.
Although Saichō's sincerity regarding religious training cannot
be denied, this policy was also a way of retaining monks.[36] The
third and most controversial part of his program was the request
for an ordination platform on Mt. Hiei. During Saichō's time,
there were three platforms in Japan, all controlled by the *sōgō*.[37]
Moreover, the final ordination for Tendai monks always took
place in Nara. Under these circumstances, it is hardly surprising
that the *sōgō*, headed by Gomyō, fiercely objected to Saichō's petition, opposing a separate Tendai platform. In effect, Saichō was
asking that Tendai be placed beyond the control of the government's duly constituted agency.[38] While Saichō continued to
argue with the monks in Nara, he in no way desired a complete

separation from the state. On the contrary, he stressed that the monks and temples of the Tendai sect would serve "to pacify and to protect the state" *(kokka wo chingōsu)*.[39] It was of utmost importance for Saichō to stress such service for the state, since his quest for independence simultaneously required support from outside the established channels.

Saichō died on the fourth day of the sixth month of 822 without having achieved full recognition for Tendai's independence. Yet only seven days after his death, Saichō's petitions were approved, perhaps as a memorial tribute, though the first ordinations on Mt. Hiei did not take place until 848. It appears that the doctrinal polemics and other issues of personal pride subsided among the monks with Saichō's death, enabling the court to recognize Tendai's independence, which is also indicated by the granting of the name Enryakuji on the twenty-sixth day of the second month of 823 to what had been known as Hieizanji. The importance of this development should not be underestimated, as other temples followed suit, obtaining independence from the *sōgō*.[40] As a result, it was now possible for temples to manage their own affairs more efficiently and to establish more direct ties with their patrons, marking the first important step toward the privatization of the religious hierarchy and the development of religious institutions as co-ruling elites.

In contrast to Saichō's desperate efforts to gain recognition for his Tendai sect, Kūkai encountered very little resistance. He performed several esoteric rituals not only for noble members at the imperial court, but also with monks from other sects attending. For example, Kūkai led two esoteric ceremonies late in 812 with Saichō among the eager attendants on both occasions. In another ritual at Takaosanji in the fourth month of 813, some ninety-four participants, including Saichō and one of his disciples (Kōjō), received esoteric initiations. The success and popularity of esoteric rites in Japan are further reflected in Kūkai's decision to dispatch monks to several provinces in Japan in order to spread knowledge of the teachings he had brought from China.[41] Thus boosted by an increasing number of disciples and rising popularity at the imperial court, Kūkai asked Emperor Saga for Mt. Kōya, where he intended to build a temple that would serve as a center for meditation and esoteric rites.[42] Located several days' walk from the capital on the Kii peninsula and boasting an altitude of 3,230 feet, the mountain had a strong presence of prominent local *kami,* not unlike Mt. Hiei. According to the legends, Kūkai often paid tribute to the native deities of various locations, establishing protective *kami* for both Takaosanji and Tōji. In the latter case, he selected the powerful Hachiman, who was later promoted on Mt. Kōya as well. The sacred ground of the mountain was, however, originally affiliated with two other local deities; Kōya myōjin and Nibu myōjin. Kōya myōjin, eventually settled at Amano jinja (Amanosha), became the most exalted protective deity of the mountain, and Nibu myōjin, a deity associated with sources of water and productivity, became the second-ranking *kami* of Kōyasan. Another reason for Kūkai's choice may have been the difficulties of isolating a monastic center from other doctrines and ideas in the capital, where monks often became multisectarian. Such practices may have induced Kūkai to look for a more distant location where his monks could focus exclusively on esoteric studies and meditation.[43]

Kūkai did not climb Mt. Kōya until late in the twelfth month of 818, since Emperor Saga, who was troubled by an illness, needed the monk's services in the capital. Ground was broken for the central area of the temple in the fifth month of 819, and the borders were marked in a consecration ceremony in Kūkai's presence. He named the central temple Kongōbuji (Diamond Peak Temple)—the official name for the complex on Mt. Kōya—representing the center of the Buddhist world, using the surrounding peaks to complete this worldly map of the Buddhist cosmos. In true esoteric fashion, he also commenced construction of a Grand Pagoda to symbolize the supreme Buddhist being of Dainichi nyōrai (Mahāvairochana) and the Ultimate Realm within the monastery itself. However, he was unable to supervise the construction personally most of the time, returning, in the seventh month of 819, to the capital, where his services both as a religious leader (he was appointed to the Office of Monastic Affairs in 812 and served there for twenty-four years) and as an educated man known for his organizational skills were in high demand.[44]

On the nineteenth day of the fourth month of 823, Kūkai was appointed to head Tōji (the Eastern Temple), one of two temples established by Emperor Kammu in the southern part of Kyoto to serve as protectors and monuments of the state. Emperor Saga, who was now nearing his own retirement, had granted an independent ordination platform to Tendai the previous year, after Saichō's death, and he may thus have felt inclined to grant a sim-

ilar favor to Kūkai by giving him the opportunity to transform this
temple into an esoteric center in the capital itself. A more compelling reason, however, may have been Kūkai's reputation as an
effective administrator with technical skills. The monk not only
had completed improvements on the temples he already headed
(Tōdaiji and Takaosanji) but had also been asked to reconstruct a
reservoir in his home province of Sanuki, which he did successfully in 821 after the governor had failed. Since Tōji was as yet
unfinished in 823, Kūkai may have been appointed specifically to
erase the poor impression the construction site made on visitors.[45]
Kūkai, for his part, accepted the honor, fully understanding the
importance of staying on good terms with the secular leaders.
When Emperor Junna ascended the throne in the fourth month
of 823, Kūkai, counting on continued imperial support, sent a letter to congratulate the new sovereign. On the tenth day of the
tenth month of that year, undoubtedly an important moment for
Kūkai, an imperial decree stated, in response to a request by
Kūkai, that only monks from the Shingon (True Word) sect could
reside at Tōji. Not only does this decree mark the official recognition of the Shingon sect, but it also allowed the sect the unusual
distinction of being exclusive of other sects, contrary to the practice among the Nara sects and Tendai to study several different
doctrines.[46]

From 823 to his final retirement at Kōyasan in 832, Kūkai was
the undisputed master of Buddhism as well as one of the most
popular figures at court in general. Though he may have wished
to spend more time supervising the construction on Mt. Kōya
personally, it was difficult for him to leave the capital region. For
one, there were now two Shingon centers in Kyoto (Takaosanji
and Tōji), and he had established a firm foothold in Nara through
the Shingon temple hall (the Shingon'in) at Tōdaiji. Moreover,
his official status continued to improve as he was promoted to the
office of *dai sōzu* (Grand Supervisor) of the *sōgō* in 827. He also
established a private School of Arts and Sciences in 828 close to
Tōji, which holds the distinction of being the first educational
institute in Japan open to anyone.[47]

Suffering from deteriorating health in 831, Kūkai announced
his wish to resign from the Office of Monastic Affairs. His request
was initially denied, but he was soon allowed to retire to Kōyasan,
where he stayed until his death in the third month of 835. But
Kūkai was anything but inactive even during his retirement, and

he continued to secure important privileges for his sect from a compassionate imperial court. The two most important accomplishments came within a few months late in 834 and early in 835. First, Kūkai was allowed to establish a Buddhist hall within the imperial palace, where annual Shingon rituals would be performed for one week in the first month of every year. This series of rituals was known as the Mishiho and became one of the prestigious services performed annually for the welfare of the imperial court and the state throughout the Heian era.[48] Second, Kūkai was granted the ordination of three new state-supported Shingon monks every year. As in the case of Saichō and the ordination of Tendai monks, this stipulation signified the recognition of the sect as one of the state-sponsored Buddhist sects. Further confirmation of this recognition came the next month, when Kongō-buji was designated a *jōgakuji* (specially designated temple), providing special protection for the imperial state.[49] By Kūkai's death on the twenty-first day of the third month of 835, Shingon Buddhism was, like Tendai and Hossō, a recognized part of the Buddhist establishment, marking the early form of a multidoctrinal system with competing and coexisting sects within the framework of the imperial state.

The Coming of Age of the Monastic Complexes

The establishment of Kōfukuji, Enryakuji, and Kōyasan reflects the activities and ambitions not only of their founders but also of their patrons in an integrated display of politics and religion. But the subsequent leadership in the early Heian age must not be overlooked in relating the development of each of the monastic centers. One of the most important issues of state and religion was the relationship between the secular rulers and the monasteries. By controlling ordinations, the public monk hierarchy as well as head abbot appointments for important temples, the imperial court kept a watchful eye on the clergy and was on occasion even able to use them in factional struggles in the capital, as evidenced in the infamous Dōkyō Incident of 769.[50] The *sōgō* was staffed with the most prominent monks of the realm and was still the main organ for controlling monk promotions and head abbot appointments, but the early ninth century saw the number of exceptions grow, as in the case of Enryakuji. Ironically, these developments actually gave individual members of the imperial court more direct influence over important religious appointments. In particular, the court quickly focused on the Enryakuji head abbot *(zazu),* who functioned as the official link between the clergy and the imperial court. He represented the monks in the capital when needed, but the flow of communication more commonly went the other way, as he was also expected to respond to the demands of the court. Imperial orders were issued to the head abbot, who conveyed them to his head administrators in "letters of instruction" *(zasu mikyōjo)* before an order *(Enryakuji mandokoro kudashibumi)* was issued to the clergy. Importantly, the first three head abbots were appointed by the Council of State (the *daijōkan*), but beginning with the fourth *zasu,* Anne, in 864, the appointments were made directly by the emperor.[51]

The creation of such direct ties between Enryakuji and members of the imperial court thus compensated for a lack of representatives within the *sōgō.* Indeed, only a day after Emperor Saga granted the name Enryakuji to Saichō's temple in the second month of 823, it was decided by the Council of State that the yearly candidates for ordination would be questioned by two lay administrators *(zoku bettō),* who were to be in charge of Tendai matters at court.[52] Thus, while it was now possible for Enryakuji monks to perform their ordination ceremonies independently from the *sōgō,* the court still controlled what the new monks were to study as well as appointments to various ceremonies.[53] Serving as representatives for Enryakuji at court, forwarding requests for funding, these lay administrators would likewise ensure that the government could maintain some control over the temple. For example, they signed documents confirming monk ordinations in the fourth month of 823. This new office became popular with other sects as well, and *zoku bettō* were subsequently appointed to Kongōbuji on Mt. Kōya in 836 and to Tōji and Tōdaiji in 838. Moreover, though the first recorded instance of a *zoku bettō* at Kōfukuji dates to 884, there is compelling evidence that one was appointed some fifty years earlier, simultaneous with other prominent temples. These appointments were typically made through a consensus vote within the imperial court, though the Fujiwara chieftain reserved the right to control appointments for Kōfukuji, indicating their importance as offices of control for the capital nobles. Regular appointments were made well into the eleventh century and sporadically even during the Kamakura period. For example, *zoku bettō* were assigned to Tōdaiji during times of major repairs when a mechanism for contact with the court was required.[54]

There were two reasons for the success of the *zoku bettō* office. First and foremost, it succeeded in bypassing the *sōgō*, which meant that opposition and resistance from monks of other sects could be avoided. Second, since the lay administrators were ranking courtiers usually in a position close to the emperor, they became an attractive and important link to the highest level of authority in the state. In short, the establishment of the *zoku bettō* laid the foundations for private and direct contacts between powerful court nobles and the temples, a pattern that was to become dominant during the Heian period. This court-temple symbiosis put a distinctive mark on the development of the early Heian temple communities, although the particular circumstances of each monastic complex differed.

Enryakuji after Saichō: Succession Disputes within Tendai

Owing to the creation of the *zoku bettō* office and a lack of involvement in the *sōgō*, Enryakuji was less rigorously controlled externally than were the Nara sects, but its internal organization remained loosely structured even into the tenth century. Though Saichō was concerned with establishing doctrinal rules for Tendai, he failed to provide any guidelines for the temple organization itself, a task that was left to the subsequent leaders on Mt. Hiei.[55] Saichō also left a heritage of rivalry for the abbotship of Tendai that became a recurrent problem for several centuries. In 812, when Saichō was ill, he named his disciple Enchō (771–836) to succeed him. However, just before his death in 822, Saichō changed his mind, designating Gishin as his successor (see Figure 1).[56] Gishin's training in China and his seniority as a Tendai monk combined to play an important role in this decision, and he was consequently appointed the Tendai head by the Council of State on the twenty-second day of the sixth month of 824.[57] Just before he died in 833, Gishin named a disciple of his own, Enshū (735–843), to succeed him, leading Saichō's original disciples to protest against this "private" appointment. The latter supported Enchō, Saichō's original selection from 812. The dispute remained unresolved while petitions, over an eight-month period, were forwarded to the emperor as well as to one of the temple's lay administrators. Eventually, the court issued a decree removing Enshū, who left the mountain together with his followers, while Enchō was ap-

pointed head abbot *(zasu)* of Enryakuji on the sixteenth day of
the fifth month of 834.[58] Although the appointment of Enchō temporarily stopped the animosities on Mt. Hiei, this incident marked
the beginning of a long-lasting rivalry that was initiated by Saichō
himself. His change of heart in 822 and his failure to determine
how a leader should be selected created an uncertainty over the
leadership and its duties that had to be worked out in the next
several decades, if not centuries.

When Enchō died in 836, no new head abbot was appointed.
In fact, the next *zasu* was not appointed until 854, which indicates
that the head abbot post had not yet been institutionalized. The
de facto leader of Enryakuji for these eighteen years was Kōjō
(778–858), also a direct disciple of Saichō.[59] Even though Kōjō was
close to the capital nobility, managing to receive funding for a
bell tower and sūtra repositories, he struggled to keep Tendai
apace with the Shingon sect. Shingon monks had superior knowl-

Figure 1. Early head abbots of Enryakuji
Italics indicate tenure as head abbot.

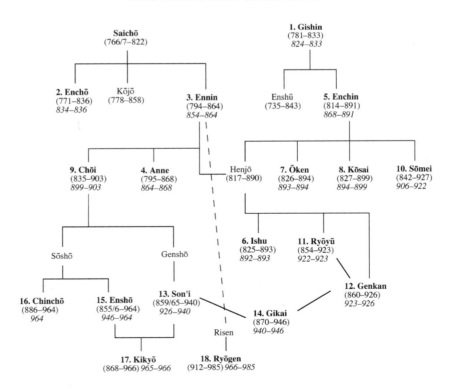

edge of the secret rituals of esoteric Buddhism, which were highly popular at court because of the benefits they were perceived to provide in this life. In addition, these ceremonies, which included the burning of rare fragrance and the display of expensive art objects, became powerful symbols of status and rank. Kōjō therefore attempted to improve Enryakuji's position by synthesizing Tendai with the esoteric teachings, but he had little success.[60] However, Enryakuji's fortunes improved drastically with Ennin's return from China in 847. Ennin (794–864) had been sent to China in 838 to study the esoteric teachings on what was the first official mission there since Saichō. Although he never actually made it to Mt. T'ien-t'ai, he obtained knowledge and scriptures from the monks in the T'ang capital and from the monastic complex at Wu-t'ai-shan. When he returned to Japan, Ennin received a hero's welcome from an excited court. In the following years, he performed several court-sponsored Buddhist ceremonies in the capital, including, for example, rituals at the initiation ceremony for the new emperor (Montoku) in 850. Eight years later he led a ceremony in which the succeeding emperor, Seiwa, together with 140 high-ranking nobles, took Buddhist vows.[61]

On the third day of the fourth month of 854, Ennin was appointed *zasu*, making him the second in a row of Saichō's disciples to lead the Tendai sect. However, the authority of the *zasu* was still limited at that time. In fact, on the day of Ennin's appointment, the aforementioned Kōjō was appointed head administrator, which suggests that the highest authority within Tendai was divided between a doctrinal leader *(zasu)* and an administrative director *(bettō)*. The two duties seem to have come together with the appointment of the next *zasu*, Anne (795–868), in 864. There is no evidence of a *bettō* appointment at that time, and, more important, the signature of the *zasu* now started to appear on documents of administration. At the same time, the importance of the lay administrators *(zoku bettō)* began to decline as the *zasu* took over such responsibilities as the approval of ordinations, demonstrating that the head abbot now served as the link between the court and Enryakuji. This link was even more direct than before, since *zasu* appointments, which had hitherto been made by the Council of State, now were made by the emperor. The relationship between the leaders in Kyoto and Enryakuji was thus finally institutionalized in the mid-860s. A further proof of Tendai's higher level of recognition is that Anne became the first Tendai monk to obtain a position in the *sōgō*, showing that Tendai monks had joined the Nara monks in the competition for influence and, indeed, for control over the whole religious establishment.[62]

When Enchin (814–891) was appointed head abbot on the third day of the sixth month of 868, the competition for the leadership took what in hindsight seems to be an irreversible turn toward a split within the Tendai sect. Enchin was the first disciple of Gishin to head Tendai, and though he tried to prevent disputes between the emerging Saichō and Gishin factions, the competition between them eventually led to a geographic split a century later. Yet Enchin himself, just like his predecessors, continued to expand Enryakuji's religious and physical realm in what can only be described as a very successful leadership. Enchin's monastic career resembles that of Ennin in many ways. Indeed, it has been suggested that he was sent to China by Gishin's followers in response to Ennin's trip there. Enchin went to China in the eighth month of 853 and came back to Kyoto five years later, when he was greeted by the court with lavish gifts and much excitement. He soon performed several esoteric rituals in the capital, including an ordination ceremony in 864 for Emperor Seiwa and several leading nobles. Enchin's services earned him an appointment to the Office of Monastic Affairs in 883. Five years later, he was even invited to be head lecturer for the Yuima ceremony at Kōfukuji, but he declined the honor, probably because he anticipated protests from the Hossō monks.[63] Nevertheless, the invitation itself shows how much Tendai's status had improved in only four decades.

To continue the comparison between Ennin and Enchin, both established new temple areas as their personal strongholds with their own groups of followers. When Ennin was appointed *zasu*, he was living at Enryakuji's Yokawa section, a secluded area about three miles north of the main temple on Mt. Hiei (see Map 2), where he had withdrawn in 831, when there was scarcely more than a hut there. As his popularity rose, however, new temple buildings and halls were constructed, and a group of disciples gathered around him. Ennin left Yokawa only reluctantly, but he finally moved to the main area to assume his duties as head abbot in 854. He entrusted Yokawa to his disciple Anne, who also succeeded him as head abbot in 864, roughly a month after Ennin's death.[64]

Whereas Ennin had sought out a desolate area, Enchin took up residence at Onjōji (also known as Miidera), a temple established southeast of Mt. Hiei facing Lake Biwa. Onjōji has its origins in Emperor Tenji's Sufukudera in the early 670s but came under the sponsorship of the powerful Ōtomo family, as it was built on their land. After siding with the losing side in the Jinshin War of 671–672, the Ōtomo rebuilt the temple between 680 and 686, renaming it Onjōji soon afterwards.[65] Enchin received this temple as a donation in 862, and it was probably made into a Tendai detached cloister (betsuin) some four years later.[66] There were thus two religious sections, Yokawa and Onjōji, that were not only distinct from the main area but possibly also centers of opposing cliques by the late ninth century. Perhaps this situation is what Enchin was referring to when he wrote in his "will" of 888 that there should be no animosities between the disciples, respectively, of Saichō-Ennin and Gishin-Enchin.[67] All was to no avail, however, since the conflicts between these two branches became increasingly manifest. After Enchin, six of the seven succeeding head abbots were of his branch (see Figure 1), but monks from the Saichō-Ennin lineage came back to monopolize the zasu post from the early 940s.[68] Little is known of Enryakuji and its activities during the early tenth century except that it suffered a decline. Several temple buildings were destroyed by fire, and funding was too scarce to finance reconstruction, which hurt the Yokawa section the most, as Enryakuji was dominated by monks from the Enchin line. Consequently, the growth that Tendai had experienced during the Ennin-Enchin era was arrested for a period of some decades until the situation improved considerably during the tenure of the eighteenth zasu, Ryōgen (912–985), who has been credited with reviving Enryakuji and bringing it into its "golden age." Ryōgen was a resourceful monk, who chose to settle at Yokawa in 939, after sixteen years of training, in order to revive this desolated area of Enryakuji.[69] Benefiting from close ties with Fujiwara no Morosuke (908–960), who served as regent, and other powerful nobles in Kyoto, Ryōgen secured funding to reconstruct the area while climbing the monk hierarchy rapidly. With such support and a strong record at religious debates, he became zasu in 966 at the mere age of fifty-four, making him the youngest head abbot in twelve appointments, bypassing several senior monks at Enryakuji.[70] Several buildings that had deteriorated or been destroyed by fire on Mt. Hiei were reconstructed during Ryōgen's tenure, and new landholdings were granted to the temple. As such tax-exempt holdings increased, Enryakuji obtained a firm financial base, allowing it to support a growing number of monks on the mountain, which appears to have increased substantially from a couple of hundred to some 2,700 late in the tenth century. Indeed, the clergy on Mt. Hiei were referred to as "the three thousand monks" from that juncture.[71] Ryōgen's tenure as head abbot was thus a dramatic turning point in Enryakuji's history. A century later the monastic complex on Mt. Hiei had enough of an economic foundation to sustain a powerful and active clergy that became much feared in the capital, sometimes exercising a will of its own.

Early Shingon: One Sect, Two Centers

The challenges facing the Shingon sect in the ninth century were similar to those of Tendai. Both sects struggled with the succession to leadership posts, while the patronage from their secular allies played an integral role in the ensuing disputes. Shingon's rift may have been deeper from the outset, though, since there were already two esoteric centers (Tōji in Kyoto and Kongōbuji on Mt. Kōya) during Kūkai's times, with an additional disadvantage for Kongōbuji, located at quite a distance from Kyoto. The Shingon monks also had to compete more and more with monks from other sects, which had adopted several of the popular esoteric rites. In part, this development can be attributed to the very success and popularity of Kūkai himself, who introduced esoteric rites at other temples in the capital region. Most temples, especially in Nara and Kyoto, were favorable to such changes, since the magical rituals were the most popular at the imperial court. Thus, other sects also learned esoteric practices, enabling them to offer such magical ceremonies in competition with Shingon.

The popularity of esoteric rituals is also what allowed the establishment of two Shingon centers and several detached cloisters. While some of these, such as the Shingon cloister within Tōdaiji, were founded by Kūkai himself, others were founded by his disciples.[72] And, as in the case of Saichō, Kūkai did not designate a successor, nor did he give any firm guidance of where the Shingon headquarters should be. With many eminent disciples and numerous cloisters associated with Shingon at different locations, it is hardly surprising that a conflict over the leadership of the sect broke out almost immediately after Kūkai's death in 835. He designated a young monk named Shinnen (804–891) as the abbot of Kongōbuji, but it was Jichi'e (Jitsu'e) who came to shoulder the mantle of the sect, since he had served under Kūkai the longest (see Figure 2). Jichi'e was appointed to the rank of *gon risshi* (assistant preceptor) within the *sōgō* as well as abbot *(chōja)* of Tōji on the tenth day of the intercalary fifth month of 836, assuming the effective leadership of Shingon, which also included administrative authority over Kōyasan. It was also this Jichi'e who,

Figure 2. Abbots of Kongōbuji and Tōji

Boldface indicates tenure as *chōja* (head of the Shingon sect), italics tenure as *zasu* (abbot) of Kongōbuji.

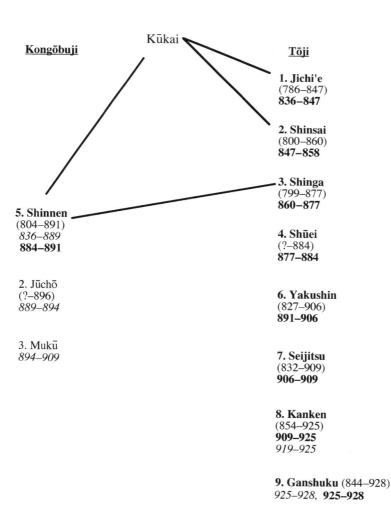

Kongōbuji Kūkai **Tōji**

1. Jichi'e
(786–847)
836–847

2. Shinsai
(800–860)
847–858

3. Shinga
(799–877)
860–877

5. Shinnen
(804–891)
836–889
884–891

4. Shūei
(?–884)
877–884

2. Jūchō
(?–896)
889–894

6. Yakushin
(827–906)
891–906

3. Mukū
894–909

7. Seijitsu
(832–909)
906–909

8. Kanken
(854–925)
909–925
919–925

9. Ganshuku (844–928)
925–928, **925–928**

learning from the developments at Enryakuji, managed to create a direct tie with the imperial court by establishing a *zoku bettō* (lay administrator) for Kōyasan in the seventh month of 836 and for Tōji two years later.[73]

Jichi'e died in 847 and was succeeded by Shinsai (800–860, also a direct disciple of Kūkai), who was equally successful in the capital as he climbed the traditional ladder within the Office of Monastic Affairs, reaching the highest post of *dai sōjō* (Great Grand Master) in 856. The most important development during his tenure as Tōji head abbot was, however, an expansion in 853 of the yearly Shingon ordinands from three to six. But this success also created new problems as Shinnen, the abbot of Kongōbuji, complained that the construction on Mt. Kōya had not been progressing while existing buildings were deteriorating and argued that Kongōbuji should be the location for these ordinations, since the founder was buried there. Shinsai agreed to allow three of the new monks to be ordained at Kōyasan, but he never kept his promise, busying himself with both religious and political matters in the capital. Eventually, his political engagement and neglect of Kōyasan's welfare caused Shinsai's demise, as a growing opposition within the sect forced him to resign in 858 and live his last two years in seclusion. This development paved the way for improved relations between Tōji and Kongōbuji under the next *chōja*, Shinga (appointed in 860), who was also one of Shinnen's teachers. Benefiting from his ties with the new head abbot, Shinnen was granted funding to repair Kongōbuji's Great Pagoda in 861, and he was additionally promoted to Assistant Preceptor *(gon risshi)* in 874, at the age of seventy-one.[74] Spiting the opposition of several Tōji monks, Shinnen even managed to borrow from Tōji the thirty scrolls of esoteric sūtras that Kūkai had copied in China, which were already at that time considered one of the most valued possessions of the Shingon sect. Following unsuccessful attempts by the next *chōja*, Shūei (appointed in 877), to have the scrolls returned to Tōji, the opposition subsided in the early 880s, when Shinnen, who apparently was a tenacious monk, successfully climbed the religious hierarchy in Kyoto, while improving conditions at Kōyasan.[75] In the fifth month of 882, he finally managed to realize what Shinsai had promised almost twenty-five years earlier, as it was determined that three of the yearly ordinations should indeed take place at Kōyasan. He was promoted to assistant head abbot of Tōji the next year and finally became *chōja* in the third month of 884 at the advanced age of eighty-one. Shinnen was now one of the most prominent monks in Japan, as evidenced by the increased number of Shingon temple halls built and his attendance at the initiation ceremony for the new temple hall of Nishiyama goganji (later renamed Ninnaji) in the northern part of Kyoto in the presence of Emperor Kōkyō in 886. As might be expected, Shinnen also took the opportunity to attempt a consolidation of the Shingon hierarchy, which he did by changing the title for the Kongōbuji abbot from *bettō* to *zasu*. This change signified that Shinnen intended to establish Kongōbuji as the leading Shingon temple by imitating the Tendai hierarchy. Shinnen now had an official title to match the possession of the thirty scrolls, which also implied leadership of the sect.[76]

In spite of his efforts, Shinnen's strategies proved untenable in the long run. Though he was succeeded by one of his disciples, Jūchō, at Kongōbuji in the third month of 889, and two more monks of his lineage followed, the *zasu* office did not add any prestige to Kōyasan in the competition for the sect leadership against Tōji. Moreover, Shinnen's successors faced an unusually resourceful and influential monk in Yakushin (827–906), who succeeded Shinnen as Tōji *chōja* in 891. As a former abbot of Tōdaiji, Yakushin was already well connected, taking Emperor Uda with him on a pilgrimage to Kongōbuji in 900 and initiating the sovereign into the esoteric teachings the next year. Yakushin performed several ceremonies on behalf of the imperial family, but, more important, he constructed a new Shingon cloister at Shinnen's Nishiyama goganji for the retirement of Uda. He renamed that temple complex, which was located in the northwestern outskirts of Kyoto, Ninnaji, and it became an important retreat for many young princes throughout the Heian period. Supported by the most powerful members of the imperial court, Yakushin also began to reassert Tōji's leading position within Shingon, while attempting to gain the thirty scrolls back from Mt. Kōya.[77]

Yakushin's successor only lasted three years, but Kanken (853–925), appointed in 909, was yet another forceful head abbot, who continued to promote Tōji's leadership of Shingon. Riding on the recent success and popularity of Shingon rituals with the imperial family, Kanken managed to unify the sect while augmenting its general status. His first step was to demand the return of the thirty scrolls to Tōji in 911. When his orders were ignored by the Kongōbuji *zasu* Mukū, he sought the help of Uda, who was now retired. Uda supported his Buddhist teacher by replacing Mukū with Kanken as *zasu* of Kongōbuji on the nineteenth day of the ninth month of 914, giving the Tōji monk control of Kōyasan as well. Moreover, the retired emperor dispatched an order to Kōyasan in the twelfth month of 915, stating that the scrolls should be kept at Tōji, in effect acknowledging its leadership of the Shingon sect. There was now little the monks on Mt. Kōya could do to stop Kanken, and the scrolls were returned to Tōji in 919, signifying the surrender of Kongōbuji's claim to the head abbot-ship of Shingon. For the next several centuries, the Tōji *chōja* was the leader of the sect and commonly the abbot of Kongōbuji. Kanken's successful strengthening of Tōji's position brought im-portant consequences for many Shingon temples. Not only was Kōyasan transformed into a *matsuji* (branch temple) of Tōji, but other temples with Shingon inclination, such as Ninnaji, Tōdaiji, and Daigoji, now had their abbots appointed by the Tōji *chōja*.[78]

Even though he managed to raise Tōji's status within Shingon, Kanken nevertheless had no intention of ignoring other branches, indicating that his primary concern was unification and general prosperity for the sect. For example, in response to problems in maintaining buildings on Mt. Kōya, Kanken established a new office *(shitsugyō)* charged with local administration. In addition, he secured an imperial decree that granted Kūkai the posthumous name Kōbō Daishi (The Great Teacher Kōbō) on the twenty-fifth day of the tenth month of 921, some fifty-five years after Saichō had been honored with the honorific name Dengyō Daishi. Kanken himself is said to have carried this decree to Mt. Kōya, inspiring the Daishi cult, according to which Kūkai is in a sleep-ing stage and expected to return to this world at some point. It is in this context that the Oku-no-in, a temple hall close to Kūkai's tomb, was restored by Kanken in 933.[79] Ironically, Kanken's suc-cess in raising Tōji to the top led to near disastrous results for Kōyasan in the politically distant mountains of Kii Province, as the temple was increasingly overlooked. Matters took a sharp turn for the worse in 952, when lightning hit one of the buildings, causing severe damage to the complex, and no funding was made available for reconstruction. Kongōbuji subsequently became less attractive to aspiring monks, and the last ordination of new annual Shingon monks took place on Mt. Kōya in 983. By the end of the tenth century, Kongōbuji was all but forgotten in the capital, and only the most ardent and devoted Shingon monks would dare the bitter conditions on the mountain at that time. Disaster struck again in 994, when more central structures were destroyed in a fire caused by another thunderstorm. Although funding was granted for reconstruction this time, the provincial officials who were entrusted with the project assessed taxes of their own, thus diminishing funding that was earmarked for the temple. At this point, the monks left Mt. Kōya in protest, leaving it desolated and with little hope, it would seem, of Kongōbuji ever becoming the cosmoslike temple complex that Kūkai had envisioned.[80]

Early Kōfukuji Prosperity

Of the three temples examined in this study, Kōfukuji was the most successful during the ninth and tenth centuries. Hossō monks continued to dominate the Office of Monastic Affairs, though that organ's ability to control the Buddhist clergy had declined as temples such as Enryakuji, Tōji, Tōdaiji, and Kongō-buji created special ties directly with the capital elites. However, Kōfukuji also caught on to these changes, as evidenced by the establishment of a lay administrator as an important link between the temple and the Fujiwara chieftain in the 830s.[81] Perhaps even more important to Kōfukuji's early stability was its uncomplicated procedures for selecting head abbots under the firm guidance of the imperial court, making internal politics much less of a problem in Nara than on Mt. Hiei or between the Shingon centers in Kyoto and on Mt. Kōya. Unfortunately, the records are unclear regarding the early leadership of Kōfukuji, though it appears that the monk Jikun (?–777) was the first to be appointed head of the temple in 757 (see Figure 3). The appointment was mostly a reward, however, following Jikun's services at court, in particular prayers for Emperor Shōmu, who was ill in 756. The actual administration of Kōfukuji was handled by Ninshū, one of Jikun's disciples. That the abbot, called *bettō* at Kōfukuji, was not yet an institutionalized or firmly defined office is further supported by the next head, Eigon, who was nominally appointed in 779, two years after Jikun's death, but held little real power. It was only with the appointment of Gyōga (728–803?) that the *bettō* accomplished anything of significance for Kōfukuji. A native of Yamato, Gyōga took the Buddhist vows at the age of fifteen and went to China in 753, to remain for more than thirty years. He excelled in the teachings of Hossō when he returned to Nara, becoming head abbot of Kōfukuji in 791 and serving in the *sōgō,* where he reached the level of *sho sōzu* (Minor Supervisor). Most important, during his tenure the court determined that the Yuima'e, which became one of the most prominent and popular Buddhist ceremonies for the imperial court through its emphasis on the contributions of the secular elites, should be held at Kōfukuji every year, giving the Hossō center a substantial advantage over other temples within the imperial court.[82]

Subsequent head abbots were unproblematically selected from disciples of previous abbots, earning ranks within the Office of Monastic Affairs along the way. This stable leadership, combined with consistent support from the Fujiwara, allowed Kōfukuji to obtain important privileges in terms of grants for performing prestigious ceremonies for the clan as well as for the state and reaping the economic rewards from having such a powerful patron. Needless to say, Kōfukuji's ties with the Fujiwara leadership were key in the temple's prosperity when the clan chieftain started to dominate the imperial court as regent for reigning emperors from the late ninth century. The basis for this relationship was laid during the chieftainship of Fujiwara no Fuyutsugu (775–826), who was responsible for the construction of a new temple hall named the Nan'endō within Kōfukuji. In cooperation with Gyōga and his successor, Shūen (771–835), Fuyutsugu made Kōfukuji the ceremonial center of the *hokke* Fujiwara. Subsequently, under the chieftainship of Fuyutsugu's second son, Yoshifusa (804–872), who also became the first Fujiwara regent *(sesshō)* for the young Emperor Seiwa in 858, Kōfukuji experienced a dramatic increase in both ritual responsibilities and funding. This trend further continued during the regency of Yoshifusa's adopted son and successor, Mototsune, who gave more than six hundred *chō* of land in Echizen to Kōfukuji in the seventh month of 881.[83] By the ninth century Kōfukuji was the most influential religious complex in Japan, though it never dominated completely, since the duties of protecting the state, as well as the benefits, were shared with other privileged temples such as Enryakuji, Tōdaiji, and Tōji.

Doctrinal dogmatism was clearly not an issue for the nobles at the imperial court, as they saw the various doctrines and the different ceremonies as complementary. Nor was religious exclusivity an issue to many monks. Shūen, who served as Kōfukuji head abbot from 803 to 822, was a student of Saichō as well as of Gishin, although he had entered Kōfukuji at a young age. Esoteric teach-

Figure 3. Early Kōfukuji head abbots
Boldface indicates approximate years as head abbot *(bettō)* of Kōfukuji.

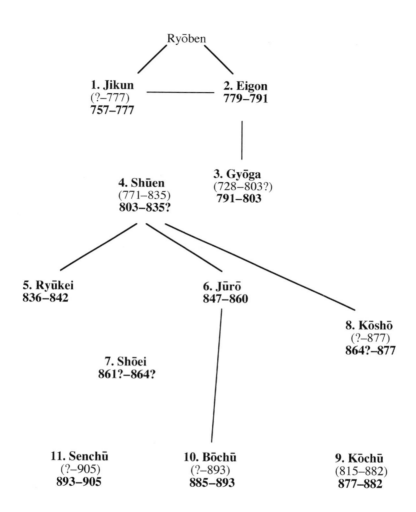

Ryōben

1. Jikun
(?–777)
757–777

2. Eigon
779–791

3. Gyōga
(728–803?)
791–803

4. Shūen
(771–835)
803–835?

5. Ryūkei
836–842

6. Jūrō
847–860

8. Kōshō
(?–877)
864?–877

7. Shōei
861?–864?

11. Senchū
(?–905)
893–905

10. Bōchū
(?–893)
885–893

9. Kōchū
(815–882)
877–882

19. Jōshō
(911–983) **971–983**
Son of Fujiwara no Morotada
Fourth-ranking Tōji *chōja* in 969

ings, in particular, were highly popular, and it is telling that even Kōfukuji monks made an effort to incorporate such ceremonies in their practices. In fact, the monk Jōshō (911–983), who became Kōfukuji *bettō* in 971, learned the esoteric teachings of Shingon so well that he was appointed fourth-ranking head abbot of Tōji two years earlier and abbot of Kongōbuji in 979. The son of a high-ranking courtier, Fujiwara no Morotada (920–969), Jōshō entered the clan temple at an early age, embracing two of the dominating doctrines of the era: a typical representation of the prevailing syncretism of both the aristocracy and the religious leadership.[84] Interestingly, Jōshō's tenure coincides with the beginning of another important expansion of Kōfukuji's influence. In particular, pilgrimages increase to both Kasuga and Kōfukuji, accompanied, as was the custom, by various favors and donations. One milestone was achieved in 989, when Ichijō became the first emperor to go on an official pilgrimage to Kasuga, and the great Fujiwara no Michinaga visited the shrine ten years later. Kōfukuji's land possessions subsequently increased, especially in the Nara region, at the same rate that regents and members of the imperial court visited Kasuga. For example, Eisanji, a temple south of Nara (see Map 2), affiliated with the southern branch of the Fujiwara *(nanke)*, was absorbed by Kōfukuji in the middle of the eleventh century.[85]

The most important acquisition was the gradual absorption of Kasuga, resulting in a greatly expanded influence for the Hossō center. Kōfukuji first extended into Kasuga in the mid–ninth century, when a reading of Buddhist scriptures within the shrine area took place. Moreover, an appeal asking that Kasuga receive tax exemptions for its annual festival, forwarded on the shrine's behalf by Kōfukuji in 883, provides firm evidence that the two complexes had developed common interests. The implications of this important appeal are twofold. First, it demonstrates that an institutional relationship had been established between Kōfukuji and Kasuga as well as between the *kami* and the buddhas, though it is clear that the shrine still maintained its independence. Second, the appeal for tax exemptions indicates that the festival fulfilled some function for the imperial state through its tie with the Fujiwara chieftain. Indeed, in the well-known Jōgan Code of 869–871, the Grand Rite of Kasuga assumes the importance of a state ceremony, and by the Engi Codes of 927, the ritual was fully sponsored by the state. Furthermore, readings of the Lotus Sūtra were held at

Kasuga once a year from 947, with monks from Kōfukuji partici-
pating. By the early eleventh century, these lectures were performed regularly twice a year, marking another important step in
Kōfukuji's takeover of Kasuga, as the funds earmarked for these
rituals were controlled by the Hossō clergy.[86] By the time of the
first known Kōfukuji protest in the capital in 1093, the Kōfukuji-
Kasuga association was unquestioned, and the divine symbol of
the shrine—a sacred branch of the *sakaki* tree—was carried to
Kyoto in support of the temple's appeal. Also from this time there
occurs a dramatic increase of Kōfukuji followers, a result of the
addition of the many secular supporters (usually men of local
power, *kokumin*), known as *jinnin,* that were associated with Kasuga
and employed in various estates in Yamato.[87]

By the late tenth and eleventh centuries, Kōfukuji and Enryakuji had matured into wealthy monastic complexes leading the
religious establishment in a system that allowed for the participation of several sects and temples. In both cases, the ability of the
leadership was crucial in this development, and their close ties to
the most influential elites within the imperial court were equally
vital. Though Kōyasan became an elite institution in its own right
somewhat later, its basic organization and economic foundation
developed along the same lines, and it is therefore appropriate to
survey these more mundane and secular aspects of the temples
here.

The Economic and Social Foundations of Heian Monasteries

The ties between the secular elites and the temple leadership remained crucial for the survival of the early monastic centers, while
mutually benefiting the nobles and clerics involved throughout
the Heian and Kamakura eras. But internal temple matters were
essentially beyond the reach of the imperial court. Most important, whereas a career in the noble hierarchy was unthinkable for
anyone outside the immediate circle of the capital elites, a provincial monk could advance in the temple rankings, as evidenced by
the early abbots of Enryakuji and Kōfukuji. Not only were all levels
of the temple hierarchy at least theoretically open to anyone in
the Heian period, but the organizational structure itself allowed
each member of the clergy a voice within the community, and
promotions were regularly based on the number of years served

as a monk. It is thus no exaggeration to claim that the monastic communities exhibited a degree of democracy not seen in any other central organizations in Heian Japan.

At the top of each monastery, there was usually a cabinet of head administrators, known as *sangō* at both Enryakuji and Kōfu-kuji. It originally consisted of three members, a presiding officer *(jiza)* who supervised Buddhist ceremonies, a director *(jishu)* responsible for the management of construction within the temple complex, and a provost *(tsuina)* overseeing daily financial matters, but eventually assistantships were added to each office.[88] As at most other temples, the administrative cabinet handled judicial, eco-nomic, and administrative matters, in particular those related to rents from estates. The practical matters of administration such as the collection of dues, summons for meetings and ceremo-nies, and preparation of rituals were handled by a body of lower officials referred to as *"shoshi"* (custodians). At Kōfukuji they were collectively organized in an administrative organ called *"kumonjo."*[89] Each monk also participated in matters regarding the temple in general, since all clerics, regardless of pedigree or rank, had a right to vote in matters concerning the temple. The most basic level was a meeting of the whole monk assembly, which included the lowest-ranking clerics, often referred to as "worker-monks" *(dōshū).* These more democratic meetings were called to nominate monks for promotions and candidates for the head abbotship, and in particular when the clergy wished to protest something in the capital. But even in such cases, there were rules guiding the temple's petitions to the government, since the con-sent of the entire clergy was needed for a formal appeal to the capital. If a section acted independently, it was on its own in the event of repercussions.[90]

At Enryakuji, this meeting was known as the *santō sengi* (the meeting of the three pagodas), after the three sections on Mt. Hiei. The first and oldest section was Tōtō, or the Eastern Pagoda, including the ordination platform and Enryakuji's main building (the Konpon chūdō), which served as the location of meetings of the monk assembly. Saitō, or the Western Pagoda, which is located about a mile from Tōtō, was developed in particular by Enchin, and it became the most thriving area on Mt. Hiei by the mid–tenth century. Although surpassed by its eastern counterpart at the end of that century, Saitō was equal in size to Tōtō, and it con-tinued to prosper and to play an important role in both administration and internal politics. The third section, Yokawa, is located at some distance from the other two and was not considered a section in its own right until 973, when its monks appealed for the same status as the other two sections. The acceptance of this petition marked the beginning of a three-section organization that lasted through the entire premodern era. Each section was further subdivided into five or six smaller temple halls or cloisters, which functioned as the most basic units of cohesion and decision making.[91]

Despite some variations, there were similar meetings of the general clergies at Kōfukuji and Kōyasan, usually referred to as "*daishu-e*" (meetings of the large clergy), which, in the case of the Hossō center, met at the grounds in front of the Kondō—the temple's main building. Whereas the Enryakuji clergy was named after the three pagodas, the Kōfukuji monks were known as "the six directions" *(roppō)*, after the main residence areas within the monastery, where they lived. These "directions" were actually only four, including northwest *(inu-i)*, northeast *(ushi-tora)*, southeast *(tatsu-mi)*, and southwest *(hitsuji-saru)* from the Chinese zodiac, to which were added the two nearby cloisters of Ryōkain and Bodaiin. Though the social status of the *roppō* changed somewhat in the Kamakura period, the majority of this group usually corresponded to the lowest class of monks, known as "*gerō*" (lowest seniority) or "*dōshū*" (worker-monks), whereas the upper echelons were the educated *gakuryō*, ranked immediately below the temple leaders *(sangō)*.[92] There are no exact and reliable figures regarding the size of the Kōfukuji clergy, especially since other monks and supporters residing in Nara, though only loosely connected to the Hossō sect, could easily join the main clergy at times. Nevertheless, the main clergy may have been close to Enryakuji's in size, numbering some two thousand monks in the early eleventh century. By contrast, the monastic complex of Kōfukuji was necessarily more confined, and therefore more unified, than Enryakuji and Kōyasan, since the Hossō center was located in the more populous city of Nara.[93]

Kōyasan's clergy was also organized in three tiers, but in a slightly different manner from the Tendai and Hossō centers, as it matured somewhat later, toward the end of the Heian and Kamakura eras. The ranking clergy was known as "*gakuryō*" and was further divided into "the learned" *(gakushū)* and the "pupils" (*higakushū*, literally "the uneducated"). The second level were

the "*gyōnin*" (corresponding to the worker-monks), who performed various menial tasks within the temple community, such
as accounting, maintenance of residences and temple halls, and
provision of meals. The "*hijiri,*" or wandering monks, though also
present in smaller numbers at Enryakuji, were in several aspects
unique to Kōyasan, as they were recognized as a separate entity
within the temple. Because of Kōyasan's location and greater
need to establish and maintain a tie with local powers, these *hijiri*
were of special importance in recruiting local support and labor
for the temple on the Kii peninsula.[94]

The central unit on Mt. Kōya was Kongōbuji, whose abbot
served as the leader of the temple community though ranked
considerably lower than the heads of Tōji. Together with five
neighboring cloisters, Kongōbuji constituted the central section
that was controlled by the *gakuryō*. Other sections of the monastic
complex, including the influential Oku-no-in where Kūkai's tomb
was located, were dominated by other groups, such as the *hijiri*.
Since most monks, as in the case of Enryakuji, identified themselves with their masters and cloisters, competition and conflicts
between the various sections were not unusual. In addition, many
capital patrons, including retired emperors and imperial consorts, eventually sponsored their own cloisters on Mt. Kōya, resulting in economic differences between the sections. Indeed, a
serious breech developed in the late Heian age, as Kongōbuji's
leadership of the monastic complex was questioned by other
cloisters on several occasions.[95] But even such conflicts could not
have broken out were there nothing to dispute.

It is well known that monastic complexes such as Kōfukuji, Kōyasan, and Enryakuji possessed enormous wealth by the late Heian
period, but the resources available in the preceding centuries were
much more limited. Funding for specific ceremonies, the maintenance of buildings, and the livelihood of the monks was originally
provided by the imperial court through specific grants. The private landholdings of the early monastic communities were, in
other words, quite limited, affirming their initial financial dependence on the imperial court. Kōyasan's problems in maintaining
and rebuilding ruined structures, followed by monks leaving the
complex, have already been mentioned, but Enryakuji also experienced funding difficulties in the early Heian period. The Tendai
center's main support originally came from public grants that consisted of rice taxes, other temporary taxes, and interest from agri-

cultural loans, but they proved to be insufficient, and the original temple estate was too small to support the monks living on the mountain.[96] Even Kōfukuji had only minor landholdings in the early Heian age, though it received a steady flow of revenue for its services to the imperial court. However, additional funding was occasionally granted to monks who performed important rituals at court. These personal grants tended to be quite generous, often providing the receiver with rights to land that later became a private possession of the temple. Such donations were attractive to all temples, but they became even more popular as public grants declined in the tenth century. Temples such as Enryakuji, Kōfukuji, and Kōyasan were now forced to seek a more reliable and independent financial base, which they found in two kinds of tax-exempt holdings: branches—shrines (massha) or temples (matsuji) —and private estates (shōen).[97]

Private estates became the main source of income for most temples during the late Heian and Kamakura eras. The extent and the development of Enryakuji's possessions are little known because of a lack of original documents, but there is little doubt that the number of private estates under its control increased substantially in the late twelfth century and throughout the Kamakura era. Incomplete as they are, the records do indicate that close to three hundred estates were registered in Enryakuji's name in the premodern era. Many of these shōen were donated by aristocrats to secure spiritual and political support from influential monks and temples, but noble chieftains also donated estates to support a son who had retreated to a monastery. Eventually, these estates were taken over by the temple community, thus adding to its general portfolio. A notable exception were those estates that were donated to the noble cloisters (monzeki) of the twelfth century and the Kamakura period. These estates, although theoretically part of the Enryakuji portfolio, remained under the private control of the cloister while retaining the bond to the donor. In shōen terminology, the donor remained patron (honke) and the cloister became the proprietor (ryōke).[98]

Kōyasan was far removed from capital politics, and even though it received some estates from local strongmen close to Mt. Kōya in the mid–tenth century, the fire of 994 was devastating to the complex. Pleas to restore the temple were in large ignored by the Kyoto elites, and it remained in the backwaters compared to Enryakuji and Kōfukuji. For example, the Kongōbuji abbot (zasu)

Ninkai (955–1046) wrote a letter to Emperor Ichijō (ruled 986–1011) to ask for funding, but the appeal was never forwarded by the governor of Kii Province, who was also the lay administrator *(zoku bettō)* for Kōyasan. However, the preceding abbot, Kanchō, had established ties with Fujiwara no Michinaga's older sister, Higashi Sanjō, who donated six villages to an affiliated shrine (Amanosha). Insignificant as this donation might appear, it provided a link to Michinaga, eventually resulting in the first pilgrimage to Kōyasan by a Fujiwara chieftain on the twenty-third day of the tenth month of 1023. This visit yielded not only a new bridge, cloisters, and monk residences but, more important, also created a tie between the capital elites and Kōyasan that would continue to grow during the next century. In the tenth month of 1048, Yorimichi followed his father's example with his own pilgrimage to Kōyasan, accompanied by a donation of several estates. Fujiwara no Morozane (1042–1101) did the same in 1081, funding the construction of a pagoda.[99]

But it was the pilgrimages of the resurgent imperial family in the late eleventh and twelfth centuries that truly propelled Kōyasan into a wealthy and vibrant religious institution. Shirakawa began a virtual parade of imperial visits with his pilgrimage to Kōyasan in 1088, two years after he resigned as emperor. He provided the temple with two private estates in support of the livelihoods of thirty *hijiri*. Additional estates were donated on several subsequent pilgrimages, culminating with the 1127 visit of two retired emperors, Shirakawa and Toba, who were particularly generous during a celebration ceremony for the reconstructed Grand Pagoda. One of the more popular ceremonies took place at the Oku-no-in, which became increasingly important as the place of worship focusing on Kūkai himself.[100] These pilgrimages gave more fuel to this Shintō-inspired Kōbō Daishi cult, while several imperial sons who had taken Buddhist vows were placed at the temple to further augment its status. In the end, the combined pilgrimages of the four great retired emperors (Shirakawa, Toba, Go-Shirakawa, Go-Toba) in the late Heian and early Kamakura eras have been calculated to total nine, illustrating well the extent of the benefits enjoyed by the temple. Further, the Fujiwara leaders also continued to support and visit Kōyasan in the twelfth century, adding more prospects for donations. The processions could be quite large, including several hundred retainers and servants, making the costs of the stay at Mt. Kōya quite expensive, often requiring additional taxes from nearby *shōen* and public land.[101] The Kongōbuji complex on Mt. Kōya was not only on its way to recovery, it now joined the other elite temples as an important political and religious institution in its own right, controlling over one hundred estates at its peak.

The Kōfukuji-Kasuga complex was probably wealthier than both Kōyasan and Enryakuji in late Heian Japan, and some scholars maintain that it was the third largest landholder after the imperial family and the Regent's Line of the Fujiwara (the *sekkanke*). Many of these holdings were a result of the recognition given the Kōfukuji-Kasuga complex by the Fujiwara chieftains for the valuable assistance provided by the buddhas and the *kami*.[102] Indeed, after receiving extensive support from Michinaga and his son Yorimichi in the eleventh century, Kōfukuji began to dominate Yamato. To a large extent, its dominance was due to the increasing popularity of Kasuga, whose main shrine (Ichinomiya) became the protector of Yamato Province, resulting in more estates under Fujiwara and Kasuga control. Kōfukuji benefited heavily, since it came to control Kasuga's administration, but it also attempted to expand in Yamato on its own, despite resistance from the governors. By using personal ties with warrior leaders, Kōfukuji added to its own holdings, as evidenced by the ranking monk Hanshun, who obtained a Tōdaiji estate through support from the Taira in 1100.[103]

In spite of the declining fortunes of the Fujiwara during the *insei* era (1086–1185), the developments in the twelfth century merely consolidated Kōfukuji's position. In 1116 Fujiwara no Tadazane built the Western Pagoda at Kasuga, which now recognized Kōfukuji as its master temple *(honji)* outright. Through the construction of the Wakanomiya shrine within Kasuga in 1135, Kōfukuji, Kasuga, and the tutelary deities of the Fujiwara clan were effectively combined into one body, further increasing the temple's status. Though the construction was not controlled by Kōfukuji, the Wakanomiya's festival was completely funded and administered by the temple. Not only did this new shrine mean that the temple could extend its influence over Kasuga's many service people *(jinnin)*, it ensured Kōfukuji's dominance in Yamato Province. Frequent imperial visits to Kasuga thereafter resulted in additional prestige for Kōfukuji as well, and the many land donations that followed became part of the temple-shrine complex.[104]

Following this consolidation, Kōfukuji continued to expand in

Yamato as well as in some neighboring provinces. Using a combination of the divine threat from Kasuga, whose claim to Yamato had already been established, and warriors, who were recruited strongmen in the region, Kōfukuji kept increasing its influence at the expense of existing temples. Many temples in this region, no matter how old and religiously removed from Kōfukuji, were unable to escape the Hossō center's ambitious growth. For example, Kinpusen, located southwest of Nara, was eventually absorbed despite early resistance. Tōdaiji was able to protect most of its estates but lost one of its branches, Hasedera in southern Yamato (see Map 2), to the Hossō center. In addition, many other landholdings not claimed by the imperial temple were taken over by the Hossō center. Only the shrine-temple complex of Tōnomine appears to have been able to resist the Kōfukuji onslaught successfully, aided by its connections with Enryakuji and by enlisting the help of local *dogō* (upper-class farmers). Yet by the mid–twelfth century, Kōfukuji was firmly entrenched and the dominating power in Yamato, and it would not tolerate challenges to its authority, not even by the Fujiwara regents. For example, when Regent Tadamichi received Yamato as a hereditary province *(chigyō koku)* in 1144, he ordered one of his warrior retainers, Minamoto no Kiyotada, to perform a land survey. Kōfukuji resisted by claiming its and Kasuga's rights to Yamato, detaining some of Kiyotada's followers and demanding the exile of Kiyotada. Tadazane was forced to oblige and retracted his men, resulting in further consolidation of Kōfukuji's position in Yamato. The temple's expansion continued into the thirteenth century, when Hōryūji was made into a Hossō branch, and Kōfukuji was subsequently acknowledged as the *shugo* (military governor) of Yamato by both the Kamakura and early Ashikaga shogunates.[105]

The incorporation of shrines into the temple organization was an important step toward more influence and independence of government funding for the elite temples in the capital region.[106] As demonstrated above, Kōfukuji's control of Kasuga augmented its spiritual status and power with the imperial court, enabling the temple to expand in Yamato. By the late tenth century, Enryakuji had also begun the transformation into a temple-shrine complex. Seven shrines on the eastern slopes of Mt. Hiei housed *kami*, who were believed to be local representations of the buddhas and the bodhisattvas, and different legends and doctrines developed in support of these institutional conglomerations. The highest-ranking deity was Sannō myōjin (the Mountain King deity), who emerged as the local manifestation of the Buddha and the all-encompassing protective deity of Enryakuji by the mid–Heian era. The integration of these temples and deities was in fact a gradual process that began in the ninth century. In Enryakuji's case, the first clear evidence of an assimilation dates back to 887, when funds were granted for two priests to perform services and read sūtras for the two deities of the Hie shrines, then known as Ōhie and Kobie (Obie).[107] The Enryakuji complex continued to grow during the late Heian and Kamakura eras, as shrines in regions distant from the capital became affiliates of Enryakuji, which used its status to provide protection and immunity from taxes and government officials. By the Muromachi period, the Hie shrine complex consisted of a network of more than two hundred shrines.[108]

Shrines were vital components of the *kenmon* temple organizations, since they provided important spiritual and human resources. On the spiritual side, the native deities were used to support the appeals of Enryakuji and Kōfukuji. Shintō symbols, not Buddhist images, were carried to the capital to support forceful appeals. Shrines also added manpower, since their organizations often encompassed a large number of service people who could lend military power in case of conflicts. In fact, the *jinnin* often played a prominent role in protecting temple possessions and occasionally participated in Enryakuji and Kōfukuji demonstrations in the capital. Affiliated branches were consequently not primarily religious outposts with independent economic bases, as one might expect. Rather, they were financial and human assets of the main temple *(honji)*, which had the right to appoint chief administrators and to collect a fixed amount of rice tax and labor services from the branch every year. Typically, these branches were listed in the main temple's estate records together with private estates. Enryakuji's first branches were actually detached cloisters *(betsuin)*, which, strictly speaking, were different from *matsuji*. While detached cloisters had their abbots or head priests appointed by the government, branch temples were under the total jurisdiction of the main temple.[109] From 840 to 882 eleven *betsuin* were attached to Enryakuji, some of which were as far away as the provinces of Mutsu and Shinano. Although these relations were not permanent, many detached cloisters were eventually converted into *matsuji* (branch temples) or *massha* (branch shrines).[110] This development was an important step toward the privatization and expansion of Enryakuji's possessions.

Like the *shōen,* mutual interests lay behind the creation of ties between a provincial temple or shrine and elite temples like Enrya-kuji and Kōfukuji. First, since estates that belonged to prominent central temples were much easier to convert into tax-immune hold-ings, regional temples could relieve their tax burdens by becoming a branch. Second, the temple patron, just like the *shōen* patron, would protect the rights of its client by bringing complaints to the imperial court. I have already noted Kōfukuji's appeal on behalf of Kasuga in 883. To mention one Tendai example, Enryakuji monks protested in the capital in 1177 about illegal intrusions of a provincial governor on behalf of the branch of one of its branch temples.[111] In return for such protection, the main temple not only received income from its branches, but also manpower, since the branch could offer monks or warriors to support the claims of the main temple. For example, the *Taiheiki* describes an incident from the mid–fourteenth century when monks from some 370 branches were called in to support the Enryakuji cause.[112]

Among the numerous supporters of the elite temples and shrines were an increasing number of armed followers, who, from the eleventh century, were used to defend or emphasize the inter-ests of their temple. Historians call these figures *"sōhei"* (monk-warriors), but this usage is anachronistic and inappropriate, since the term was first used in Japan by a Confucian scholar in 1715.[113] The contemporary terms relating to conflicting parties that can be found in various kinds of documents— *"akusō"* (evil monks), *"shuto"* (clergy), and *"daishu"* (clergy)—do not imply a distinction between specific monk-warriors and other clerics.[114] In fact, there is little evidence that these bands were coherent groups of monks also serving as professional warriors during the Heian and Kama-kura eras. Instead, there are references to other groups, such as worker-monks *(dōshū)* or lay shrine servants *(jinnin),* that appear to have been more loosely connected with the monasteries, and skirmishes between government warriors and protesters appear unplanned. Yet it cannot be denied that conflicts involving reli-gious forces became common from the eleventh century, when the elite temples became substantial landholders and elites in their own right. In general, such armed forces were most frequently involved in internal conflicts, intertemple rivalries, or disputes be-tween temples and the provincial governor class.[115] Little more is known about the religious forces, although Japanese scholars have much debated the causes of their emergence. Some have claimed that the increase of private monks outside the control of the Office of Monastic Affairs led to more aggressive and secular behavior among the clergy. Others have stressed that the decline in the *sōgō* itself caused a secularization of monk behavior. Yet another theory maintains that a general decline of the state of Buddhism caused the emergence of armed monks.[116] The most insightful explanation, however, relates the trend to the general process of privatization of rulership and land that took place from the mid–Heian period. Religious forces satisfied the need for protection of private possessions, much like the emerging warrior class *(bushi)* did for the capital nobility. In fact, Kuroda Toshio called the *akusō* and the *bushi* a pair of twins that emerged from the sociopolitical development of the Heian period.[117] Since the armed monks and the *bushi* emerged at the same time and also functioned and behaved similarly, this characterization stands out as the most helpful and accurate of those presented so far, although further research is needed before the character and role of these religious forces can be properly understood. In any case, with such human, social, and economic foundations in addition to their spiritual influence on society and rulership, it is easy to understand the significance of temples in Heian and Kamakura Japan.

Internal Divisions within Tendai and Shingon

The prosperity and growth that the elite temples began to experience in the middle of the Heian period also brought new conflicts. On the one hand, disputes began to occur between temples for land and income as the arable land in central Japan was carved up into private domains by nobles and temples from the mid–Heian age. On the other hand, as the temple-shrine complexes became wealthier, more resources and power fell under the control of the head abbots, which exacerbated existing tensions and seemed to threaten the temple communities' basic unity. Within the Tendai sect, monks from the Saichō-Ennin and the Gishin-Enchin branches found it increasingly difficult to coexist on Mt. Hiei. Head abbot Ryōgen (912–985) seems to have been determined to solve this problem in favor of his own lineage, as he attempted to unify the Saichō-Ennin branch and restore its supremacy on Mt. Hiei by suppressing the Gishin-Enchin monks.

In 980, for example, he excluded a number of monks, most of them from Onjōji, from the monk registers. Furthermore, the Gishin-Enchin monks were almost completely neglected in important rituals that same year.[118] The Gishin-Enchin line was, however, ably defended by Yokei (918–991), who competed with Ryōgen for the patronage of the Fujiwara leader. When Yokei was honored in 981 with the abbotship of Hosshōji, which had been built in Kyoto in 925 by the former regent and chancellor Fujiwara no Tadahira (880–949), Ryōgen protested, claiming that the post was a monopoly of the Saichō-Ennin branch. Some 160 Ryōgen supporters subsequently went to Grand Minister Fujiwara no Yoritada's (924–989) mansion in the capital to convince the Fujiwara leader to confirm their right to the abbotship. This first Enryakuji demonstration forced Yoritada to cancel the appointment, setting an important precedent for successful protests.[119]

Ryōgen resigned as head abbot in 985 and was succeeded by Jinzen, who was not only his disciple and the master at Yokawa, but also the son of Ryōgen's patron, Fujiwara no Morosuke.[120] However, Jinzen resigned four years later because of difficulties cooperating with the head administrators, and Yokei was appointed *zasu* on the twenty-ninth day of the ninth month of 989. The Saichō-Ennin monks disapproved of the selection, and hundreds of monks descended to the foot of the mountain trying to stop the appointment. Even though Yokei assumed his post a month later, he was forced to resign within three months, lacking the approval of a large majority of the monks.[121] In 993, two years after Yokei's death, monks of the Gishin-Enchin faction raided the Sekizan zen'in, an Enryakuji temple-shrine on the western slope of Mt. Hiei (see Map 3) associated with Ennin. In retaliation, Saichō-Ennin monks burned some forty residences within the main temple area belonging to their foes. At that point, the whole Gishin-Enchin clergy (possibly up to a thousand monks) simply left Mt. Hiei and settled at Onjōji, marking a physical separation of the two branches.[122] From that time on, the Saichō-Ennin lineage was known as the "mountain gate branch" *(sanmon monto)* and the Gishin-Enchin line as the "temple gate branch" *(jimon monto)*.

The organizational separation did not finalize the split, nor did it stop the competition between the two branches.[123] When the twenty-seventh *zasu,* Kyōmei of the *sanmon* branch, died in 1038, the abbot of Onjōji, Myōson (967–1060), saw an opportunity to become head abbot of the Tendai sect. However, when his ambitions became known to the *sanmon* monks, they descended to the capital to protest at Chancellor Fujiwara no Yorimichi's (990–1074) mansion. Since Yorimichi was close to Myōson, he was reluctant to appoint another monk, maintaining that the *zasu* office had not been the monopoly of either branch. The *sanmon* monks responded that a monk of a branch temple *(matsuji)* could not, according to precedent, be appointed head abbot.[124] Rhetoric aside, the monks' argument and their presence at his mansion were imposing enough to prevent Yorimichi from appointing Myōson as *zasu* at that point. But the abbotship remained vacant for several months, and at one point, during a skirmish between Yorimichi's warriors and *sanmon* followers, one monk took his own *zasu* candidate (Kyōen) hostage and escaped after having injured one of the warriors. Repeated protests finally forced Yorimichi to comply with the demands, and Kyōen was appointed the twenty-eighth Tendai head abbot on the twelfth day of the third month of 1039. Myōson was eventually appointed head abbot in 1048, but again the monks protested and tried to stop the appointment. Myōson's tenure lasted only three days.[125]

In response to the *sanmon* monks' unwillingness to accept a *jimon* monk as head abbot, the Onjōji monks attempted to complete their separation from Enryakuji. Starting in 1040, they appealed for an ordination platform of their own, much in the same manner that Saichō had done in his struggle for religious and political independence from the Nara sects more than two centuries earlier. However, at no point did the monks on Mt. Hiei allow any concessions, not even when the retired emperor gave permission for ordinations to take place at Onjōji. On some occasions, the Enryakuji monks simply attacked their foes and burned down their buildings.[126] Despite such disasters, the Onjōji monks kept demanding their own ordination platform. Kageyama Haruki, a well-known scholar of Enryakuji, has aptly likened Onjōji's dilemma to that of a university without rights to confer degrees to its graduates.[127] In other words, the Onjōji monks were in a no-win situation. On the one hand, they were denied influence in the Tendai sect, since they were barred from the top post. On the other hand, they were not allowed complete independence through an ordination platform of their own. These issues became a source of constant conflict between Enryakuji and Onjōji, erupting into violent confrontations on several occasions in the late Heian and Kamakura eras.

After having endured hard times in the mid–Heian period, the Shingon center on Mt. Kōya benefited greatly from Shirakawa's promotion of Shingon during his *insei* (1086–1129) as well as the patronage of his successor Toba, as each of these sovereigns visited the temple three times. One monk was especially instrumental in this process. Kakuban (1095–1143), the son of a provincial officer in Echizen, took Buddhist vows at the imperially sponsored Ninnaji in 1100 but also studied at Kōfukuji and Tōdaiji. In 1114 Kakuban entered Kōyasan, and he soon became popular because of his extensive knowledge of the esoteric rites of both Shingon and Tendai. He gained additional fame as a close spiritual adviser of Toba, who gave the monk both important support in his religious career and extensive funding, including seven *shōen*. In 1129 Kakuban started construction of his own cloister on Mt. Kōya, the Denpōin, which was expanded and renamed the Daidenpōin in 1132. It was for the maintenance of this cloister, which soon emerged as one of the two most important centers (the other being the Mitsugon'in) within Kōyasan, that Retired Emperor Toba donated the seven estates. In 1134 the two cloisters were designated imperially vowed temples *(goganji)*, but this led to resistance among other monks on Mt. Kōya, who forwarded a protest to the sect leader *(chōja)* at Tōji, claiming that two of the estates given to Kakuban already belonged to Kongōbuji. Toba protected his monk-confidant by making him abbot *(zasu)* not only of the Daidenpōin but also of Kongōbuji, breaking the more than two-hundred-year-old tradition that the Tōji *chōja* also be Kongōbuji abbot.[128]

Kakuban consequently gained control of Kōyasan despite resistance from some of its monks, but he had also earned the animosity of Shingon monks in the capital, who saw Tōji's grip on Kōyasan threatened. The dispute was too much for Kakuban to handle, and he resigned in the second month of 1135 by transferring both abbot offices to his disciple Shin'ei. The Tōji clergy managed to retain control of Kongōbuji's abbotship the following year, and Kakuban, deeply disappointed with the bickering within the sect, secluded himself at the Mitsugon'in. However, his many enemies at Kongōbuji continued to harass him, and he sought help from a renowned warrior (Minamoto no Tameyoshi) in Toba's service, leading to skirmishes on Mt. Kōya itself. Kakuban eventually left Mt. Kōya in 1140 with seven hundred followers after several serious confrontations in which the Kongōbuji monks destroyed a large number of the Daidenpōin's structures. He subsequently attempted to return to Mt. Kōya but was not able to do so in spite of several edicts from the retired emperor. Kakuban instead established a new Shingon complex, later known as Negoroji, on a plain not far from Mt. Kōya. Toba demonstrated his continued support of the monk when he visited Negoroji in the second month of 1143, granting it the status of *goganji* as well. Kakuban died at the end of 1143, and it took his disciples another four years and more edicts from the retired emperor before they could return to Mt. Kōya. But the seeds for a long-standing conflict had been sown, creating in effect a rift between Negoroji and Daidenpōin followers, on the one hand, and the Kongōbuji clergy, on the other, which would split them for good in 1288.[129]

From Aristocratic Patronage to Aristocratization

From Saichō and Kūkai to the late tenth century, the character of noble patronage did not change fundamentally for Enryakuji, Kōyasan, or Kōfukuji. While specific public taxes were set aside for certain rituals and in support of a limited number of monks in the early Heian age, the most important support came through direct and personal relations with nobles in the capital. Emperors Kammu, Junna, and Saga as well as other prominent courtiers were instrumental in helping Saichōto establish the temple on Mt. Hiei while also supporting Kōfukuji. Remarkably, the Fujiwara leaders saw little contradiction in supporting Saichō while some of his most ferocious opponents came from their own clan temple. I believe that this dual sponsorship was in fact necessary. While the Fujiwara maintained Kōfukuji as the clan temple, Saichō's temple, which was more favored in Kyoto, helped the leaders of the Northern Branch to dominate the clan. Generous court patronage also made it possible for Ennin and Enchin to study in China and learn more about the increasingly popular esoteric teachings. This support coincided with the *hokke* Fujiwara's drive for control of the imperial government. Fujiwara no Yoshifusa (804–872) and his adopted son, Mototsune (836–891), were extremely successful in eliminating their opponents at court while establishing the Northern Branch of the Fujiwara clan as the most powerful aristocratic family in the capital. The Fujiwara reached, and maintained, this position by becoming the main supplier of imperial consorts, making the chieftain the maternal

grandfather of the emperor. This dominance was institutionalized through the establishment of the regent *(sesshō)* and chancellor *(kanpaku)* offices. Yoshifusa served as the first *sesshō* between
858 and 872, and Mototsune was the first *kanpaku* from 884 to
887. During this aggrandizement, Yoshifusa and Mototsune supported Enryakuji, where esoteric rituals had gained considerable
popularity, to boost their own status. Since the *kenmitsu* (exoteric-
esoteric) ceremonies were extremely costly, only the most prestigious elite could afford them. Thus, by sponsoring the copying of
sūtras, the production of artistic objects, and the rituals, the clan's
supreme status was effectively displayed and reinforced. Moreover, since participation was limited to the most prestigious
courtiers, the rituals also served to reinforce the ties between the
participants, the emperor and the Fujiwara chieftain.

The Northern Fujiwara family remained close to both Enryakuji and Kōfukuji throughout the Heian period as its leaders continued to promote specific cloisters and monks to boost their own
political status. A particularly interesting example is the previously mentioned relationship between Ryōgen and Fujiwara no
Morosuke, which has been analyzed by Neil McMullin. He has
convincingly argued that Morosuke's patronage of Ryōgen and
sponsorship of several temple construction projects, especially at
the Yokawa section, were part of Morosuke's strategy of establishing a new temple-shrine network loyal to his subbranch of the
Northern Fujiwara. In fact, several Fujiwara leaders established
family temples in addition to the clan temple with hopes of creating new spiritual centers in support of their own power during
the tenth century. By donating Fujiwara-associated shrines and
temples to Enryakuji, Morosuke was trying to augment his own
status beyond the power already associated with the clan's reli-
gious-cultic center of the Kōfukuji-Kasuga complex based in
Nara.[130] Indeed, without awareness of these conditions, it is difficult to understand Enryakuji's expansion at that time. For
example, according to the *Konjaku monogatari,* a collection of
stories from the eleventh century, the Enryakuji takeover of the
Gion shrine-temple complex in Kyoto in the 970s was caused by a
dispute over the blossoms of a tree and resolved by Ryōgen's
ghost.[131] This collection of stories also describes how yet another
shrine complex, Tōnomine, south of Nara in Yamato Province,
became a *betsuin* of Enryakuji. Both of these complexes were
central to the Fujiwara clan and had been under the control of

Kōfukuji. The Gion shrine had been an important outpost in Kyoto for Kōfukuji since the ninth century, while Tōnomine, which became affiliated with Enryakuji in 947, is said to house the tomb of the clan patriarch, Fujiwara no Kamatari (614–669).[132] Kōfukuji lost both these religious centers to Enryakuji through Morosuke's efforts to secure his family's grip on the family headship.

By the late tenth century, the relationship between the capital nobility, on the one hand, and Enryakuji and Kōfukuji, on the other, began to change. First, public grants were replaced by donations of tax-exempt estates, which served as a tie between the temple and the donor, as the latter often remained patron of the donation. Second, instead of being outside supporters, many nobles now had their sons enter the temple as privileged monks, often assuming important leadership roles. The first case in point in this "aristocratization" was Jinzen (the eleventh son of Fujiwara no Morosuke), who became the nineteenth Enryakuji head abbot in 985. After that, two more Fujiwara head abbots appear before the twenty-fifth *zasu*, Myōku (945–1020), the grandson of Emperor Daigo, became the first son of an imperial prince to reach that position in 1019. Then, in 1156, Saiun (1103–1162), the son of Emperor Horikawa, became the first imperial prince to head the Tendai sect.[133] At Kōfukuji, an identical development took place when sons of the Fujiwara Regent's Line (the *sekkanke*) were appointed *bettō*, beginning in 1110. Though the appointment of an abbot stemming from the high nobility occurred later in Nara than on Mt. Hiei, social status quickly became a determining factor, as all head abbots of Kōfukuji from 1125 came from the *sekkanke*.[134] Subsequently, head abbots of prestigious temples were overwhelmingly sons of the Kyoto nobility throughout the Kamakura period. The nobility in fact monopolized high-ranking offices and religious ranks from the twelfth century, and sources show cases of commoners who were prevented from well-deserved promotions because of their lack of birth rank. Noble heritage was thus no longer an additional merit, but a necessity for a successful monastic career.[135]

This influx of nobles has been seen as one important reason for the decline in monastic discipline that, according to many scholars, characterizes Buddhism in the late Heian period.[136] Such analyses have led some scholars to conclude that "the Tendai establishment became *increasingly* involved in worldly affairs, catering to secular demands with esoteric rituals and ceremonies, and accumulating power and wealth" (emphasis added).[137] Although such statements are essentially true, they are nonetheless deprecatory for what they imply. They assume that religious institutions with secular influence are evidence of degeneration and that sects such as Tendai and Hossō in some way were "more religious" in their early stages than later on. In fact, it must be questioned whether the degree of secular involvement of temples and shrines is a relevant issue at all. Religious institutions in premodern Japan were at no point isolated from political events and trends; their religious and political developments were interdependent from the very outset. Thus, the question is not to what degree Enryakuji or Kōfukuji became secularized, but rather how the interaction between the central authorities and the temples changed.

According to one common view, an increasing impoverishment of the capital nobility caused more and more aristocrats to seek alternative careers as abbots of temples.[138] Others have related the trend to the Fujiwara family's dominance of court politics, making it difficult for other aristocrats to advance at court.[139] Both of these views are, however, mistaken, since the aristocrats who were appointed to leading posts at temples during the Fujiwara dominance were more often than not Fujiwaras. Similarly, monk-princes *(hōshinnō)* appear during the twelfth century when the retired emperor was the dominating figure in the capital. Accordingly, as Adachi Naoya has argued, the appearance of these noble abbots was not a sign of weakness and impoverishment, but rather of strength and desire to exert more control within the established monastic orders. Princely monks were placed by the retired emperor at Enryakuji, Onjōji, and Ninnaji as a means to control these powerful temples and, by extension, their followers.[140]

In 1099 Retired Emperor Shirakawa gave his son Kakugyō the title *hōshinnō* (Imperial Prince of the Law). He was assigned to Ninnaji with a considerable amount of funding that remained under the control of the imperial family.[141] Kakugyō subsequently came to control several important temples and cloisters in Kyoto, while gaining prestige within Shingon. Few sons of capital nobles settled at Kōyasan, since the purpose behind these princely monks was to remain close to the political and religious center of the capital, but Tōji and the Shingon sect in general undoubtedly benefited from these new religious elites. It was Kakugyō who sponsored and accompanied Shirakawa's and Toba's pilgrimages to Mt. Kōya, performing ceremonies there for the imperial family while securing funding for the temple in the late 1120s, when the Grand Pagoda was finally repaired.[142] The first princely abbot at Enryakuji was, as mentioned earlier, Saiun, who was appointed in 1156, and aristocratic and princely monks subsequently held most leading offices at Enryakuji and many other central temples throughout the Kamakura period.[143] The outstanding feature of these noble monks was their dual position as nobles and religious leaders. For example, they lived in specially designed sections called *"monzeki"* (noble cloisters), often located in the outskirts of Kyoto, where they could enjoy the benefits of aristocratic lifestyles while being involved in capital politics. The *monzeki* were constructed in the popular *shinden* style of the Heian nobility with a U-shaped structure facing into a garden with a pond, instead of the more austere settings of the traditional Buddhist monasteries.[144] In addition, their training as monks was considerably shorter than that endured by normal monks, such as the twelve years Tendai acolytes had to spend on Mt. Hiei.

"Monzeki" was originally a term for sects or groups of disciples, but from the late Heian period it was used to refer to the special residential and temple areas of noble abbots. The term also came to denote the abbot himself.[145] Among Enryakuji's five *monzeki,* the Shōren'in was the most important. It was established as the residence of the forty-eighth head abbot, Gyōgen (1093–1152), in the Tōtō section in the 1130s but was moved to the Sanjō-Shirakawa intersection in the eastern part of Kyoto by the mid–twelfth century. The third abbot of the Shōren'in was Jien (1155–1225), the author of *Gukanshō,* a well-known interpretative history of Japan.[146] Two other *monzeki* deserve to be mentioned. The Myōhōin, with origins in the ninth century, was established as a *monzeki* in Saitō by Yōsei, the first son of Emperor Takakura (1161– 1181). It was moved to Kyoto soon afterwards, during Go-Shirakawa's tenure as retired emperor. The third important *monzeki,* the Sanzen'in (also known as the Kajii or the Nashimoto *monzeki*) was founded in the 1050s in the same eastern section (Tōtō) as the Shōren'in. Monks of the Sanzen'in were often involved in disputes over estates and the *zasu* post with the Shōren'in clergy in the thirteenth and fourteenth centuries. In fact, the appearance of noble cloisters became grounds for new divisions within the Enryakuji complex. The monks increasingly identified themselves with their *monzeki,* and many internal conflicts took place between these factions in the Kamakura period.[147]

The developments within Kōfukuji were remarkably similar,

dividing it into a tripartite organization. The Kondō remained
the center of the complex, with a majority of the general clergy
belonging to this hall. The noble cloister of Ichijōin was founded
between 978 and 983 by the monk Jōshū, the son of the Minister
of the Left Fujiwara no Moroyasu (not of the regent's line), and is
as far as one can tell the first *monzeki* to be established in Japan. In
1087 another *monzeki* named the Daijōin was founded by the monk
Ryūzen, who became the assistant abbot of Kōfukuji in 1096. As at
Enryakuji, these *monzeki* were beyond the immediate control of
the general clergy, relying on the secular status of their cloister
heads *(monshū)* to compete for offices and honors, but also bringing with them the factionalism that characterized politics at the
imperial court. This factionalism should come as no surprise,
since the establishment of the *monzeki* was mainly a political strategy to begin with, as the Fujiwara chieftains scrambled to maintain their control in the face of a resurgent imperial family in the
early twelfth century. For example, the three most important Buddhist rituals for the state were controlled by Kōfukuji, but new
ceremonies were established by Shirakawa when members of the
imperial family gained important religious posts. As the imperial
bloc thus made gains in the capital, the Fujiwara regents responded
in kind with their own *monzeki*. In addition, the Fujiwara chieftains attempted to tighten their grip on Kōfukuji by assuming the
right to appoint head abbots to both Kōfukuji and Kasuga late in
the eleventh century. Some decades later, Fujiwara no Morozane's
son, Kakushin, became the first son of a Fujiwara chieftain to
become head abbot of Kōfukuji in 1110. Subsequently, Fujiwara
members increasingly competed for the office of *bettō* with one of
the *monzeki* as their base, indicating how important Kōfukuji had
become to the regent's line during the resurgence of the imperial
family.[148]

As various lineages of the Fujiwara supported the two cloisters,
they became the centers for competition for the head abbotship
in the middle of the twelfth century. In the process they overwhelmed the general clergy, as the noble abbots made it a habit
to bypass the tradition of promoting monks based on seniority, in
effect monopolizing important leadership posts. In 1164 Morozane's son, Jinkaku, became the first abbot of the Daijōin to be
appointed Kōfukuji *bettō,* and the office alternated between the
two *monzeki* from 1181, even as the main clergy opposed the noble
cloisters, effectively dividing Kōfukuji into a tripartite organization.

The noble leaders of the *monzeki* usually held the advantage in the competition against the main clergy, since they had direct and personal access to substantial resources. Their worker-monks, for example, were outside the influence of the main temple, and they controlled private estates that could be persuasive resources in gaining support for their candidacies for the head abbot office. More important, they had direct ties with the decision-making nobles in Kyoto, which gave them the opportunity not only to recruit supporters in Nara but also to gain a favorable decision or appointment by their peers in Kyoto.[149]

The prominence of these aristocratic abbots can only properly be understood by their dual character as nobles and monks. They were entitled to all privileges and leading positions within the temple complexes, but they also acquired independence from that same organization through their noble status. While earlier, donations that accompanied noble sons came under the control of the head abbot and the monk cabinet (the *sangō*) after the death of the recipient, estates that belonged to the *monzeki* remained exclusively with the noble cloister. These estates were transferred in wills and bequests from abbot to abbot without intervention by the temple's administrative headquarters, though the secular patrons may still have retained a voice in determining the ownership. For example, the imperial family required permission from itself in order to transfer such estates or noble cloisters within Enryakuji.[150] Even estates that were acquired by a *monzeki* remained the private possession of the cloister. For instance, Jien, although "only" a Fujiwara, incorporated land that had previously been under Enryakuji rule as *monzeki* estates in an effort to strengthen the Shōren'in. In addition, he received several donations from the imperial family and even managed to get confiscated Taira land from Minamoto no Yoritomo.[151] Just as the estates of Kōfukuji's two *monzeki* were beyond the control of the main clergy, such *shōen* belonged to the Shōren'in, not Enryakuji proper, and remained under the control of the abbot.

The noble abbots personified the new developments that took place within the temple organizations late in the Heian period. Enryakuji had relied on extragovernmental relations with leading courtiers from its establishment, and Kōfukuji developed similar ties with the Fujiwara soon afterwards, but with the emergence of the *monzeki,* the temples' own leadership became entirely based on private power and status. Enryakuji and Kōfukuji had, just like government (through the use of private retainers and resources to perform public duties) and landholdings (through the spread of *shōen*) in general, gone through a privatization process. This process was evident not only in its internal structures, but also in its modes of protection and enforcement. With the help of their human, religious, and economic assets, the elite temples adjusted and survived challenges both from the emerging warrior aristocracy and from below by merchants, traders, local warriors, and rebellious monks into the thirteenth and fourteenth centuries. In fact, both Enryakuji and Kōfukuji survived as important political forces for almost 250 years after the fall of the Kamakura Bakufu. Kōfukuji was confirmed as the *shugo* (military governor) of Yamato by both the Kamakura and Muromachi shogunates and remained a considerable presence in the region until the sixteenth century, when it may still have held as many as 344 estates in the Kinai and other scattered provinces.[152] Enryakuji was arguably the most powerful of the three temples in the Kamakura and Muromachi eras, and its presence, both spiritual and military, was felt in the capital until the late sixteenth century. Kōyasan was not as involved in the political shifts in the capital, but its influence and control actually grew under warrior rulership, as it became a tremendous local power on the Kii peninsula. Kōyasan's political and military role during the years of the two courts (1336–1392) may even have outweighed that of Enryakuji and Kōfukuji, as evidenced by the courting it received from the fighting sides. Most important, all three temples were integral to the imperial state itself for some three hundred years, sharing benefits as well as responsibilities with the secular elites. It is the secular and religious roles of Kōyasan, Enryakuji, and Kōfukuji during this age, from the late eleventh to the late fourteenth centuries, that will be the central concern of the following chapters.

3

Capital Politics and Religious Disturbances in the Shirakawa Era (1072–1129)

Buddhist monks and their many followers from both temples and shrines were involved in over four hundred disturbances, ranging from demonstrations to battles in the capital region, from the late eleventh to the late sixteenth centuries. Though these conflicts have been mentioned and occasionally described by Japanese scholars, attempts to analyze them in conjunction with their political contexts are still conspicuously absent. This flaw is to some extent understandable, since it is practically impossible for one scholar to treat all disturbances without merely creating a repetitive narrative of events. In addition, many incidents, which are known through brief entries in both contemporary and later documents, will remain mere footnotes, since the sources give no further information. These obstacles notwithstanding, it is possible to explain a large number of the conflicts by searching for clues beyond the temples itself, taking into account also factional competition among leading families and clans in Kyoto. In fact, my analysis of protests and other disturbances involving the leading temples shows that the vast majority of the conflicts were reflections of the social and political developments at court rather than the cause of its unsettlement. Specifically, conflicts were considerably more frequent and more violent during the *insei* (the rule of a retired emperor) of Shirakawa (1086–1129), Go-Shirakawa (1158–1179, 1180–1192), and Go-Saga (1246–1272) than during any other era. It is the reigns and the *insei* of these three monarchs, characterized by great political changes in the capital, that will provide the temporal framework for this and the following two chapters.

Though many earlier historians have described Shirakawa as a

despotic ruler throughout his more than five decades as emperor
(1072–1086) and as retired emperor (1086–1129), most scholars
today agree that he became the dominating figure at court only
some years after 1100. According to this view, his surge to power
was a direct consequence of the deaths of two Fujiwara chieftains
within the short period of two years (in 1099 and 1101), leaving a
young and inexperienced chieftain to head the clan. Based on
the conflicts examined here, the change seems less dramatic, but
I find no reason to question the basic tenets of this interpretation.
Indeed, the sources show that Shirakawa's influence at court,
while limited during his early years, increased considerably after
the Fujiwara misfortunes. It should be added, though, that Shirakawa's efforts to control religious centers and ceremonies more
directly during his early years indicate a more planned and gradual
surge to power. Eventually, Shirakawa's increased power tilted the
balance at court and directly caused several religious conflicts of a
more violent and more thoroughgoing kind than before. Yet it is
not the degree of violence in these disputes that concerns me
here but their causes. What issues caused the monks and other
followers of the leading temples to protest in the capital? Were
there conflicts that did not lead to demonstrations in Kyoto? In
other words, what were the specific circumstances that triggered a
protest? To answer these questions it is appropriate to begin with
a survey of the conditions just before and during Shirakawa's era.

Resurrection and Privatization of the Imperial Family

For two centuries before the enthronement of Shirakawa's father,
Emperor Go-Sanjō, in 1068, the chieftains of the *sekkanke* (the
Regent's Line) of the Northern Fujiwara were the most powerful
figures at the imperial court.[1] The Fujiwara dominance was established through the offices of regent and chancellor in the second
half of the ninth century. Through successful marriage politics,
according to which Fujiwara women were provided as consorts to
emperors and crown princes, the clan chieftain could exert influence by way of the reigning emperor's mother. These women
were, in an ideal setting, the daughters of the chieftain, but other
female relatives such as sisters or even adopted daughters could
serve the same purpose. The chieftain's main task once a male
heir had been born was to ensure that he be designated the next
crown prince.[2] Since the imperial consorts usually continued to

live with their Fujiwara relatives, these future emperors were raised under the influence and supervision of the *sekkanke* chieftain.[3] As a consequence, many emperors, put on the throne at a young age, were dominated by their Fujiwara relatives. Yet while this strategy was successful enough to sustain the dominating and luxurious lifestyle of Fujiwara no Michinaga (966–1027), its inherent weakness greatly troubled Yorimichi (990–1074), his son and successor. In fact, though Yorimichi spent over fifty years as regent or chancellor, dominating court politics even longer than his more famous father, he felt that the family's grip on the imperial throne was loosening because his daughters were not fortunate enough to give birth to any princes. He managed to maintain his influence until 1068, thanks to two of his sisters, Shōshi and Kishi (see Figure 4), who produced a total of three emperors. Shōshi was the mother of Go-Ichijō (reigned 1016–1036) and Go-Suzaku (1036–1045), and Kishi bore Go-Reizei (1045–1068). Thus, as the uncle of three consecutive emperors, Yorimichi could control the court, but the misfortune of his own daughters worried him, hampering the prospects of a continued Fujiwara control of subsequent emperors.

Yorimichi's real problems began in 1045, when Go-Suzaku abdicated in favor of his oldest son, Go-Reizei. Since the new emperor lacked male heirs of his own, Go-Suzaku instructed that Go-Reizei's younger half-brother, Prince Takahito, be named crown prince.

Figure 4. Genealogy of the *sekkanke* Fujiwara (early *insei* period)

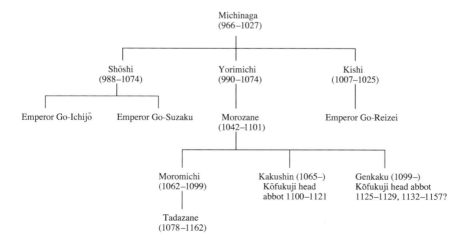

Yorimichi was reluctant to accept Takahito, since his mother was a princess without any ties to the Fujiwara family, but the pressure from his younger brother Fujiwara no Yoshinobu (who had adopted Takahito's mother) together with the realization that he had no candidate of his own forced Yorimichi to acknowledge the designation. Yorimichi continued to oppose Takahito, and he seems to have been intent on obstructing or even preventing the crown prince from becoming emperor. It took an unprecedented twenty-three years before Takahito ascended the throne. It is possible that Yorimichi stalled his enthronement hoping to find a means of replacing him with a prince more closely related to the Fujiwara. Such a reversal was surely not inconceivable, since there were previous examples of princes who had been denied accession. But Yorimichi's efforts were to no avail, as Takahito finally ascended the throne as Go-Sanjō in 1068 at the age of thirty-five, becoming the first emperor in a century without a Fujiwara mother.[4]

Go-Sanjō's short four-year reign is characterized by his efforts to reverse the trend of privatization of land. In 1069 he issued ordinances regulating the spread of *shōen*. All private estates created after the accession of Go-Reizei in 1045 were declared illegal and ordered to be returned to the public domain. In addition, older *shōen* would also be confiscated if the patrons or proprietors did not have the proper documents. To examine and judge these documents, Go-Sanjō established the *kirokujo* (Records Office).[5] But in contrast to these efforts, Go-Sanjō also added several new estates to the few imperial fields that already existed. These *chokushiden* (imperial edict fields) were mostly created from confiscated *shōen,* which ended up being transferred into the private hands of the imperial family under the assertion of restoring income to the state.[6] It is therefore difficult to know with certainty whether Go-Sanjō really intended to restore public land or whether he actually wanted to restrict the *shōen* of other elites so that more of the land could be brought under the direct control of the imperial house. In either case, his policies established a new strategy to combat the spread of private estates into the hands of the Fujiwara and religious institutions, increasing also the competition for land among both elites and the local managerial class.

Another important concern for Go-Sanjō was the imperial succession, in particular, keeping it outside the control of the Fujiwara. He abdicated in favor of his son, Emperor Shirakawa, in 1072, but since Shirakawa's mother was the daughter of a younger brother of Yorimichi (the aforementioned Yoshinobu), Go-Sanjō feared that the emperor once again would be subject to Fujiwara dominance. He therefore made the young Prince Sanehito, his son by a Minamoto consort, crown prince. In addition, he instructed Shirakawa to make another son (Prince Suke-hito) by the same consort the crown prince after Sanehito (see Figure 5). Go-Sanjō's efforts marked a momentous beginning in turning the tide for the imperial family, but most scholars believe that he had no far-reaching plans to restore imperial power in his retirement, though there are indications that he might have attempted to favor Tendai and Shingon monks over the Fujiwara-supported Kōfukuji clergy. However, because of his early death at the age of thirty-nine in 1073, possibly from complications of diabetes, Go-Sanjō was never able to enjoy his retirement, leaving it instead to his son and successor to restore the power of the imperial family.[7]

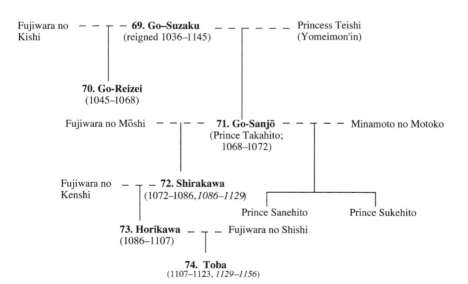

Figure 5. Imperial genealogy (early *insei* period)
Boldface indicates emperor; italics indicate tenure as retired emperor.
Numbers reflect sequence of emperors according to traditional accounts.

Politics and Religious Policies in the Shirakawa Era

Go-Sanjō's fears of a Fujiwara dominance of Shirakawa proved unwarranted, since Shirakawa was quite assertive, continuing his father's efforts to improve the imperial family's position. He too was deeply concerned with the matter of imperial succession. But whereas his father's efforts were primarily aimed at restricting the influence of the Fujiwara Regent's Line, Shirakawa was also determined to secure the succession for his own line. Since Go-Sanjō had stipulated that Shirakawa's two half-brothers, Sanehito and Sukehito, be designated as the next emperors, Shirakawa's own sons were all but excluded from the imperial line. Though it was not easy to ignore the wishes of his deceased father as well as the opposition of influential members at court, Shirakawa managed to put his line back in competition in 1085, when Prince Sanehito died in a smallpox epidemic. Shirakawa abdicated the next year, making his own son, Taruhito, Emperor Horikawa. Prince Sukehito, who would have been the rightful successor, was not even designated crown prince, even though there was no other candidate until a male heir was born to Horikawa eighteen years later (1104). Though Shirakawa was successful in securing the throne for his son, his first decade as abdicated sovereign showed no apparent indications of an imperial revival. Most court procedures continued as before. Ordinances were still issued by the imperial court, and no matters of national importance were decided without having been discussed during the meetings of the *kugyō* (the council of the highest-ranking nobles). In fact, Fujiwara no Yorimichi's successor, Morozane (1042–1101), though lacking the traditional connections with the emperor, was quite influential as regent and as the final judge in virtually all matters of importance at court.[8]

There is no evidence of hostilities between Shirakawa and Morozane, even though the latter seems to have been the more important figure immediately after Shirakawa's retirement. For example, on three occasions (in 1088, 1092, and 1093) Shirakawa's retainers were punished by the court without the retired emperor's intervention.[9] By contrast, Shirakawa's active involvement in major court issues reflects a dramatic increase in his power beginning in the Kōwa era (1099–1104). As many scholars have pointed out, two timely deaths within the Fujiwara family opened the door for this change. Morozane's son, Moromichi, became *sekkanke* chieftain and chancellor in 1094, showing signs of becoming yet another educated and forceful Fujiwara courtier, but he died in 1099 at the age of thirty-seven. Morozane himself died only two years later, leaving the young and inexperienced son of Moromichi, Tadazane (1078–1162), to sustain the political ambitions of the clan. The deaths of these two prominent Fujiwara leaders aided Shirakawa, who made Tadazane chief of staff of his own administrative headquarters *(in-no-chō)* in 1093, thus dominating the *sekkanke* by having its chieftain as one of his own retainers *(kinshin)*.[10] The retired emperor prevented Tadazane from becoming regent only to grant the Fujiwara chieftain the position in 1105, usually an internal Fujiwara decision, after a six-year vacancy. The ensuing relationship between Shirakawa and Tadazane is illustrative of a new political balance in Kyoto. Although previous retired emperors had been little involved in court matters, Tadazane was now forced to go to Shirakawa's palace to ask his opinion. The diminished influence of the Fujiwara is furthermore reflected in the clan's membership in the *kugyō*, which decreased from fourteen (out of twenty-four) in 1071 to eleven in 1103. By contrast, mid-ranking Minamoto courtiers, many in the service of the retired emperor, increased from nine to twelve. Shirakawa's power was reaching unprecedented heights for a retired emperor, and contemporary court diaries leave no doubt that he was now beginning to dominate capital politics.[11]

The central feature in the imperial revival was Shirakawa's success in expanding his control over a large number of estates. Initially, his land policies focused on curtailing the spread of *shōen* through the same means of regulation as his father. Supported by mid-ranking nobles—some were even members of the Fujiwara clan who hoped to benefit from a decline in the *sekkanke*'s dominance—Shirakawa issued his first *shōen* ordinances in 1075. He encouraged further regulations as retired emperor in 1087 and 1099, indicating that the initial ordinances were not as successful as he had hoped.[12] Indeed, it was not until Shirakawa implemented more aggressive land policies designed specifically to increase the imperial family's private estates that the retired emperor became a true contender for supreme power in the capital. This expansion, which continued throughout the twelfth century, occurred in three different patterns. First, estates were created in the name of imperial consorts after they had produced male heirs to the throne, thus bringing *shōen* under the control of the imperial house. By the mid–twelfth century, large blocs of land were created in the names of Taikenmon'in (Fujiwara no Shōshi, 1101–1145) and Bifukumon'in (Fujiwara no Tokushi, 1117–1160), for example.

A second means was Shirakawa's assignment of "proprietary provinces" *(chigyō koku)* to the retainers of his own administrative office *(in-no-chō)*. The practice of assigning the public land of a province, including all its taxes and revenues, to privileged nobles began late in the tenth century, but it was first used as a successful method of rewarding private retainers by Shirakawa after his grandson Toba became emperor in 1107.[13] For example, in 1108, following the appointment of Tadazane as chancellor, Shirakawa granted the Fujiwara chieftain, who was still his retainer, Sado Province. Shirakawa gave some thirty provinces to his confidants in the post-Kōwa era, which indicates that these proprietary provinces became a successful bond between the retired emperor and his supporters.[14] But the privatization of provincial domains also added more pressure on land as this second private hierarchy became a "public" alternative and a forceful challenge to the *shōen* pyramid. Confrontations between the provincial governor class, which benefited from the imperial revival by representing the provincial proprietor, and the *shōen* proprietors, most frequently religious institutions, became a recurrent theme during the twelfth century. The increase in conflicts between temples as well as between the elites in general can thus be attributed to this expansion of the retired emperor's power.[15]

A third method, which further attests to Shirakawa's ingenuity, was his use of religious institutions and head abbots to further the interests of the imperial family. Though his religious policies may seem traditional and mostly spiritually motivated, Shirakawa pursued an agenda that was designed to support his efforts to dominate capital politics. These policies are of particular interest because they show a continuity from his earlier years, suggesting that Shirakawa's surge to power was less coincidental than hitherto assumed. At first glance, Shirakawa's frequent visits to temples and pilgrimages to more distant religious centers seem to reflect a genuine concern with the spiritual world and the state of his own soul. For example, he traveled south to the Kii peninsula to visit the Kumano shrine and the Shingon center at Kōyasan nine times and three times respectively. Taking part in religious ceremonies at these sites, he then rewarded the ritualistic leaders with funding and promotions. Occasionally, he donated more extensive funding, estates, or taxes for the construction of pagodas, cloisters, or Buddhist images or the copying of sūtras. Shirakawa also visited the main temple hall at Enryakuji (1089/5/21) and the Hie shrines twice (1091/2/11 and 1093/10/3).[16] But while these pilgrimages and generous donations—both of which were levied on the proprietors of public land and local *shōen*—may be seen as proof of a genuinely religious personality, there were other advantages that could be reaped from a close relationship with large religious centers. Spiritual support mandating imperial rulership had been integral to the Japanese state since the Nara era, and assistance from temples and shrines was necessary for a successful reign. Such support may have been even more important during Shirakawa's era as temples such as Enryakuji, Kōfukuji, and Onjōji had become not only centers of learning and Buddhism, but also important allies with considerable wealth and numerous followers. Shirakawa's construction of a new cloister (the Kajii or Nashimoto *monzeki*) on Mt. Hiei was, for example, an attempt to combat the Fujiwara family's influence over Enryakuji through the Mudōji cloister. His financing of other temple halls and pagodas within the monastic complexes of Enryakuji and Kōyasan further attests to his efforts to win more support from these established temples.[17]

Shirakawa's donations and pilgrimages, although more frequent and more extravagant than those of his predecessors, were mainly a traditional way of creating and maintaining ties with religious institutions. What set him apart was his desire to attach a new set of loyal temples to the imperial family. Shirakawa seems to have realized that most powerful temples were less dependent on support from the imperial family than they had been earlier; as private sponsorship replaced the official endowments of the early Heian period, religious institutions had begun to receive funding from a variety of sources, making them less vulnerable to the desires of a single patron. Enryakuji, for example, claiming to be the protector of the state, could withstand some pressure from the imperial family, since it also received considerable support from the Fujiwara. Likewise, Kōfukuji, which had risen to prominence as the Fujiwara clan temple, assembled enough assets as one of the main providers of imperial ceremonies to challenge even the Fujiwara chieftain late in the Heian period. Consequently, though most temples still considered it the ultimate honor to perform rituals at the imperial palace, they were not unconditionally dependent on their main patrons. It seems that it was such loyalty, or control, that Shirakawa sought when he began to construct new temples under his own, exclusive control.

Yet innovative as these strategies were, Go-Sanjō, Shirakawa's father, had already taken important steps in the same direction. Enshūji, which was completed under Go-Sanjō's patronage in 1070, quickly obtained high status and recognition while serving as a challenge to the three most prestigious annual ceremonies, known as the Sandai'e. These annual lecture-rituals, which were held at Kōfukuji, at Yakushiji (both located in Nara), and at the imperial palace, were controlled by the Fujiwara chieftain and had been instrumental in the regent's ability to obtain funding, including private estates, for Kōfukuji. Participation in and performance of these ceremonies, especially the Yuima'e at Kōfukuji, were also crucial for determining promotion of monks to the Office of Monastic Affairs, which still constituted the main framework for the top-ranking offices in the religious hierarchy. However, Go-Sanjō as well as a large number of nobles in the capital favored the esoteric rites of Tendai and Shingon, whose monks were thereby offered an avenue of promotion without merit from the traditional exoteric rituals, from which they were excluded.[18] Encouraged by his closest spiritual adviser, the Tendai *zasu* Shōhan, Go-Sanjō ensured that only Tendai monks were used in Enshūji ceremonies, which focused mainly on the Lotus Sūtra, the central Tendai scripture. In addition, a Shingon monk was appointed abbot, a princely monk from Ninnaji (also Shingon) head administrator, and Shōhan became assistant abbot, in another effort to exclude the Kōfukuji clergy. While Go-Sanjō avoided outright favoritism of either Enryakuji or Onjōji, his support of Tendai and Shingon seems to reflect an attempt to promote these sects at the expense of the Nara sects and the Fujiwara, though one can only speculate about his true intentions, since he died in 1073, shortly after his retirement.[19]

Shirakawa initially continued Go-Sanjō's policies by sponsoring ceremonies at Enshūji, but he soon superseded his father's efforts by constructing several temples of his own in the same area of eastern Kyoto (see Map 3). Hosshōji was the first and most formidable of these temples.[20] Construction of the main temple building (the Kondō) began in 1075, and it was designated an imperial temple *(goganji)* the next year. Led by the Tendai head abbot

Kakujin (1012–1081, *zasu* 1077–1081), the opening ceremonies of the Kondō in the twelfth month of 1077 were attended by a substantial number of other high-ranking monks and nobles as well as Emperor Shirakawa and his closest retainers. Construction continued for several years, adding a grand octagonal, nine-story pagoda, which measured an impressive eighty-two meters in height, initiated in 1083, and a large number of Buddhist images. In addition, Hosshōji was soon followed by other imperially designated temples such as Sonshōji, Saishōji, Enshōji, Itokuji, Rengezōin, and Jimyōin, which also became proprietors of large portfolios of *shōen,* contributing to the increase of the private wealth of the imperial family. Hosshōji itself possessed at least thirty-three estates spread across fifteen provinces.[21]

These new temples were not merely a means to gain control of *shōen;* they also became the institutions through which Shirakawa attempted to establish new religious rituals. As noted, the Fujiwara chieftain controlled the three prestigious annual lecture meetings that were held at Kōfukuji, Yakushiji, and at the imperial palace. Shirakawa now sponsored a different set of lecture meetings, which eventually became known as the "Lecture Meetings of the Northern Capital" (Hokkyō no sandai'e), held at Enshūji and Hosshōji. The Northern Lecture Series focused on readings and commentaries of esoteric sūtras, which gave Shingon and Tendai monks many opportunities to lecture, perform rituals, and receive rewards. It was the Tendai head abbot Kakujin who led over 160 monks through the opening ceremonies at Hosshōji in 1077, and he was also the master of ceremony at the initiation of the Grand Pagoda six years later. Furthermore, several cloisters belonging to Enryakuji monks were located just south of the area where the new imperial temples were erected, and the first abbots at Shirakawa's temples were selected from among Tendai and Shingon monks.[22] Appointments of monks from the Kōfukuji complex were, however, conspicuously absent. Accordingly, Shirakawa's temples were established in part to counterbalance the central position that the Fujiwara-sponsored temples had obtained earlier. The new imperial temples even became known as "the clan temples of the imperial state" *(kokuō no ujidera)* in direct opposition to the temples dominated by the Fujiwara. Admittedly, this expression was coined by the later Tendai head abbot Jien (1155–1225), who was critical of the retired emperors and their control of capital politics, in his famous chronicle the *Gukanshō.* Some

scholars have therefore questioned whether this expression accu-
rately reflects the imperial family's control over these temples,
since contemporary sources do not indicate that they were considered "private," but rather include them among the state-sanc-
tioned institutions.[23] But such objections seem to miss the point.
What matters is not whether Shirakawa sponsored the new temples
as the "private" head of the imperial family or the head of the
imperial state, but rather that they became a challenge to the
Fujiwara-dominated state rituals. Thus, terminology aside, there
can be little doubt that the new temples, under the direct control
of the retired emperor, were part of a strategy to reassert the
power of the imperial family.

For the imperial temples to be a successful instrument of rulership, Shirakawa also needed to ensure that he could control their
internal affairs. Earlier imperially designated temples *(goganji)* such
as Enryakuji and Tōdaiji had escaped direct control, and they
were now too large and too powerful to be dominated single-
handedly by the imperial house. Therefore, after having appointed
several Tendai monks as abbots of his temples, Shirakawa assured
the imperial family's control over the new *goganji* by placing another temple, Ninnaji (in the northern part of Kyoto), at the pinnacle of the order. Ninnaji, which was founded by the Shingon
monk Yakushin in the late ninth century, became a prestigious
monastic center, to which Shirakawa could bring monks from
Onjōji, Enryakuji, and Kōfukuji to serve in lower offices under his
control.[24] This extended control was exercised by appointing imperial princes as head abbots of Ninnaji. Along with the increasing "aristocratization" of cloisters and head abbotships, the establishment of these "monk-princes" *(hōshinnō)* represents one of the
most important religious innovations of the late Heian period, as
evidenced by their presence at Enryakuji and Onjōji half a century later.[25]

It was Shirakawa's third son, Kakugyō, who first received the
title of *hōshinnō* in an imperial order *(senge),* dated the third of the
first month of 1099. Following the example of Fujiwara no Kaneie
a century earlier, Shirakawa provided Kakugyō with a considerable
amount of public funding in support of his "retirement," setting
him apart from earlier princes who had taken the Buddhist vows.
The grants included estates, temporary provincial taxes, and the
designation of an administrative chief *(hōshinnō bettō),* who issued
edicts in the retired prince's name. The Fujiwara leaders opposed

the appointment, claiming that Kaneie's retirement did not con-stitute a precedent for *imperial* members retiring with public funds in that way, but Shirakawa enforced the edict with relative ease anyway.[26] Considering the subsequent importance of the *hōshinnō* as landowners and religious leaders, it may be argued that the appointment of Kakugyō marks as important a turning point in the power of the retired emperor as did the weakening of the Fujiwara Regent's Line (the *sekkanke*) with the death of Morozane in 1101. Realizing the potential influence of these monk-princes, Shirakawa made two more sons *hōshinnō* following Kakugyō, and one of them also became head abbot of Ninnaji.[27] While some *hōshinnō* settled quietly in a cloister *(monzeki)*, others made quite a career of their retirement, becoming head abbots of large reli-gious centers. Most important, the imperial abbots of Ninnaji soon assumed de facto control of the imperial temples as well as their estates. The monk-princes were, in other words, without peers in the religious world, since they maintained their imperial status even after their "retirement." Indeed, the *hōshinnō* was a junior version of the retired emperorship itself, since many princes continued to exert private influence over political matters in the capital. Shūkaku *hōshinnō,* for example, was much involved in the politics of the early 1180s, and he is even known to have been a supporter of Minamoto no Yoshitsune in the struggle against his older brother Yoritomo, the founder of the Kamakura shogunate.[28]

Though Shirakawa's political power during the early years may have been limited, his religious policies indicate that he intended to improve the influence of the imperial house even before the sudden weakening of the Fujiwara. As shown here, the main components in Shirakawa's strategies were the construction of Hosshōji—a new religious center controlled by the retired em-peror—and the establishment of princes as powerful abbots who could control religious estates on behalf of the imperial house. In implementing these policies, Shirakawa initially stayed on good terms with most religious centers, but as he attempted to extend his control in the post-Kōwa era, his religious preferences also became more pronounced. Shirakawa was now prepared to go beyond the act of balancing the different sects, by favoring his own set of temples and their preferred rituals and thus distancing himself from the established institutions. It is in this context of imperial revival and increasing competition for private wealth and status that religious demonstrations became more frequent and more violent.[29] Not only were the leading Buddhist institutions such as Enryakuji and Kōfukuji at risk of losing their privileges through diminished participation in important ceremonies; the imperial family's revival also added more pressure on a limited amount of land. The two issues that caused most conflicts, whether they resulted in outright battles, protests in the capital, or just local brawls, were land and religious appointments.

Local Competition for Land and Branches

In general, conflicts over estates involving the elite Buddhist institutions manifested themselves in two ways. On the one hand, there were conflicts of local origin that posed few problems in the capital. These disputes were part of a growing trend in which resident powers sought to expand their control without explicit support from central proprietors. Such conflicts rarely resulted in templewide appeals and demonstrations in Kyoto. On the other hand, conflicts that led to forceful protests at the Fujiwara mansion or the imperial palace were caused by decisions or policies that originated in the capital. In short, whereas the central conflicts were expressions of increasing competition and factionalism in Kyoto, the local disputes were part of a general trend toward increasing lawlessness. One can note a parallel development, according to which the central elites competed for land and influence in the capital, while midlevel managers, local monks, and warriors attempted to improve their own position in the provinces. Although unable to separate themselves completely from the hierarchy of the Heian patronage system, these local strongmen could occasionally expand their control by playing off one central proprietor against another. Such opportunities emerged when the competition between the capital elites intensified in the late Heian period, though it was the local conditions that dictated the specific circumstances in each case, as is clearly demonstrated in conflicts involving Enryakuji in the city of Ōtsu, located on the western shores of Lake Biwa.

The inhabitants of Ōtsu had perhaps more control of their own fate than most commoners in the late Heian period. Ōtsu was not only an important trading post linking *shōen* in central and eastern Japan with the capital area; it was also the administrative and mercantile nexus for the neighboring temple complexes of Enryakuji and Onjōji. Merchants, traders, and artisans lived side by side with monks and administrators who found it more convenient to perform their duties from their residences in the city. In particular, the administration of the temples' estates, the collection of dues, and the supervision of production for religious services were more efficiently handled from Ōtsu. To recruit able people for these tasks, Enryakuji extended its judicial immunities to include a large number of service people (jinnin)—usually affiliated with Hiesha—who were also employed to perform menial tasks associated with festivals, handicraft, transportation, and other tasks that required manual labor. The mutual advantages of such an arrangement put the area in the forefront of that era's socioeconomic development. The service people, benefiting from their tax exemptions and the advantageous location of Ōtsu, were encouraged to engage in commerce and other profitable enterprises that allowed them more freedom to travel in addition to increasing their opportunities for social mobility. One might thus infer that the Ōtsu inhabitants were on the whole more industrious and less restricted economically than the average shōen resident. The temple, for its part, not only needed many of the goods produced in the area, but could also count on the service people to support them on various issues. Such was the ideal relationship, but there were also specific circumstances in Ōtsu that weakened the tie. Both Enryakuji and Onjōji, frequent competitors in religious issues, had groups of their own supporters in the city, which effectively became divided between the two Tendai complexes. The commoners in Ōtsu were aware of this rivalry and were, as two incidents during Shirakawa's era show, able to use it for their own purposes.

The ninth day of the sixth month of 1081 marks an important, though not auspicious, date in the history of Tendai, as it was the first of many occasions in which followers of Enryakuji broke into the Onjōji compound and burned down several of its buildings.[30] The confrontation can be traced to the fourth month, when monks from Onjōji obstructed the annual Hie festival in Ōtsu. However, it was actually a third party that provided the spark for this conflict. Before the festival, the organizers assigned it a new location, which required additional workers and more taxes. These dues were imposed on the service people in the same way that any shōen proprietor would have assigned irregular taxes for projects like the construction of temples or palaces.[31] But the service people objected to the new imposts, and, well aware of the competing interests over Ōtsu between the Tendai siblings, they invited monks from Onjōji to help them resist the festival organizers. Perhaps the monks saw an opportunity to expand Onjōji's influence, for they led some armed followers to the city and managed to prevent the festival from taking place.[32]

The court condemned the disruption and issued an edict to the governor of Ōmi Province declaring that the festival should be rescheduled to the fifth day of the sixth month.[33] But the edict seems to have mattered little to the Onjōji monks, who simply ignored it, stopping also this second attempt. It was at that point that Enryakuji decided to take action by launching its first physical attack on Onjōji with a combined force of armed monks and secular retainers, burning down parts of it early in the sixth month. There were rumors that the monks at Onjōji were planning to retaliate, but the festival finally took place in the eighth month after a *kebiishi* (an imperial police captain) was sent out to prevent further fighting.[34] The court also tried to end the dispute by seeking to punish the guilty parties, and on the twentieth day of the eighth month, it ordered the two temples to forward their respective instigators (those who enforced the new taxes on Ōtsu and those monks of Onjōji who obstructed the festival). However, both Enryakuji and Onjōji avoided reprimands by claiming that they did not know who the criminals were.[35] The court's authority was thus restricted, and it was in fact unable to prevent the two temples from exercising their own justice. In the ninth month of 1081, monks from Onjōji climbed Mt. Hiei to avenge the attack on their temple three months earlier. While this action resulted in only limited destruction and casualties within the Enryakuji compound, the enterprise proved disastrous for Onjōji. The Enryakuji monks countered a mere two days later by burning the buildings at Onjōji that had not been destroyed previously. The incident thus ended without any firm government action, except for a report on the fourth day of the tenth month that the *kebiishi* had arrested inhabitants of a village who were alleged to be Miidera's (Onjōji's) armed servants.[36]

Aside from marking the first burning of Onjōji at the hands of Enryakuji monks, this incident is also valuable in providing some insight into three aspects of governance at the time. First, the service people of Ōtsu were well aware of the tensions between Enryakuji and Onjōji, and, more important, they were able to use it to further their own interests. Though the organizers of the festival had a customary right to impose extra burdens according to the tax policies of private estates, the service people were no ordinary farmers. Rather, they were entrepreneurs skilled in the ways of commerce and production, some probably even educated in writing and reading, and they were apparently able to play off one proprietor against another. Second, although the court became involved and sent out warriors to quell the conflict, it could do little since the dispute was essentially local in nature. Neither of the temples lodged a formal complaint with the court, because it was a matter, in the end, of private control of assets. The conflict did not originate in the capital, and the two highest authorities in Ōtsu were, in effect, the temples themselves. The imperial court merely intervened to mediate between the two temples, not to assert its power over the city. Third, Shirakawa was not involved in this incident at all. In fact, the matter seems to have been handled entirely by the regent Fujiwara no Morozane (Yorimichi's son), lending further support to the notion that Shirakawa's influence at this point (1081) was far from that of a grand and dominating sovereign. However, in a similar conflict in 1120, Shirakawa's role was quite different.

On the twenty-eighth day of the fourth month of 1120, fighting broke out between Enryakuji and Onjōji followers over the division of Ōtsu. The conflict began when residents living in the Enryakuji part of the city built a new torii (a gate marking the entrance to a shrine compound) at a different location from the old one. The Onjōji monks disapproved of the location, and, claiming that there was Onjōji property behind the new torii, they tore it down. Even though neither Enryakuji nor Hiesha had endorsed or even been informed about the new gate, the monks on Mt. Hiei supported their service people and drove away the Onjōji monks. The incident was reported to the capital, and meetings were subsequently held at the retired emperor's palace. The heads of both temples were called in to see Shirakawa, who instructed them to end the disturbance and control their clergy. Following statements from both temples, the members of the court engaged in lengthy discussions on the proper way of handling the incident. Enryakuji wanted the torii reconstructed at the new location, but Onjōji, though willing to finance the construction, wished to build it at the old site. Finally, Shirakawa decided in Enryakuji's favor but also added that those who had raised the new gate without permission from the main temple or the main shrine should now, immediately, be arrested. The verdict was satisfactory to both sides, and the Onjōji abbot reported that construction had been completed on the fourth day of the fifth month.[37]

The two incidents in Ōtsu lucidly demonstrate important aspects of rulership at both the top and the middle levels during Shirakawa's era. First, the retired emperor's role changed considerably during the long interim between the disputes. His limited involvement in the early incident stands in sharp contrast to his almost total control of the court and its decision-making process in 1120. Second, the service people of Hiesha were more than mere bystanders or victims in the Enryakuji-Onjōji rivalry, and, as both incidents show, they had the ability to act on their own, using the protection of one side or the other. Indeed, this use of central authority for personal aggrandizement was not unusual in the late Heian period, as also evidenced in a dispute between Enryakuji and Tōji over the rights to the Tado shrine-temple complex in Ise Province, in which local warriors, with the help of local monks, used the authority of the Tendai center to further their own interests.[38]

The Kōfukuji-Kasuga complex claimed exclusive control of Yamato Province by the late eleventh century, but it faced resistance from Tōnomine, another temple-shrine complex with a long and rich history, located some twenty miles south of Nara (close to present-day Sakurai City). The Tōnomine peak probably became the location for the mausoleum of Fujiwara no Kamatari, the Fujiwara patriarch, by the Nara period. However, a monk named Son'ei, who was trained at Enryakuji's Mudōji cloister, retired to Tōnomine, where he began to attract many students with his Tendai teachings in the early years of the eleventh century. Son'ei was succeeded at Mudōji by a certain Kenmei, who appears to have been close to the most dominating courtier at the time, Fujiwara no Michinaga. Since the temple community at Tōnomine lacked affiliation with a central temple and might therefore be vulnerable to intrusions by other local powers, Son'ei asked Michinaga (through Kenmei) to make it a branch of Enryakuji. Despite protests from Kōfukuji, Michinaga allowed Son'ei's temple, now known as Myōrakuji, to become affiliated with Enryakuji, making, in effect, the entire shrine-temple complex of Tōnomine a Tendai foothold in Yamato.[39]

Tōnomine subsequently became a serious obstacle to Kōfukuji's complete control of Yamato, especially since it represented such a powerful religious and political competitor as Enryakuji. Yet the first serious confrontation did not occur until 1081, more than half a century after Tōnomine became an Enryakuji branch, indicating that other factors also played a part in intensifying the tensions. In particular, increased pressure on land, caused by local warriors and other strongmen who attempted to exercise more authority and by the early resurgence of the imperial family, augmented the competition for a limited quantity of private assets. The conflict of 1081 began early in the third month, when some monks from Tōnomine apparently entered a *shōen* belonging to Kōfukuji, shooting at and setting loose horses in that estate. A local official managed to drive the intruders away, but the Kōfukuji clergy demanded more retribution. Just two days later, Kōfukuji followers entered the Tōnomine area and burned several buildings, so unnerving some residents on the mountain that they moved the holy image of the Fujiwara patriarch away from its shrine to protect it.[40]

As the head abbot of Tōnomine explained to the Fujiwara chieftain (Morozane), the removal of the holy image was a violation of and an insult to the spirit of Kamatari, causing one Tōnomine monk in Kyoto to delay the performance of an important ceremony to the dismay of many courtiers. The following day, the chieftain ordered the attackers arrested, but Kōfukuji responded that the clergy had never approached the mausoleum of Kamatari and that the attack had come from a different group of monks, including one from Tōnomine. The abbot of Tōnomine later admitted that the attackers never got close to the holy image, but he maintained that they had caused enough fear and concern among the monks to warrant removing the image from its shrine, though Morozane seemed unconvinced. Unhappy with the lack of support for their appeal in Kyoto, the Tōnomine monks approached the capital, which they entered on the twenty-fifth day of the third month of 1081. The records do not indicate exactly how the imperial court responded, except that the Fujiwara chieftain sent messengers to Tōnomine to investigate the matter. The image was finally returned to its shrine on the twenty-eighth, and the head abbot of Kōfukuji, Kōhan, was deposed for the actions of his clergy. The Tōnomine clergy rejoiced over this resolution, though Morozane soon pardoned Kōhan, who was reappointed *bettō* during the chieftain's visit to the Kasuga shrine late in 1081.[41]

The peace between Kōfukuji and Tōnomine turned out to be almost as temporary as the punishment of Kōhan, as the temples continued to dispute during Shirakawa's era. News of another conflict reached the capital on the eleventh day of the ninth month of 1108, when it was reported that Kōfukuji monks had attacked and burned residences at Tōnomine. As in the previous case, the Tōnomine clergy had moved the holy image with the intention of protecting it, though it might also have been a pretext to upset the spirits and perhaps cause the attackers to commit the even more sacrilegious act of damaging the image. However, though several buildings were burned down, the image remained intact, in a spiritual defiance, it would seem, of the furious charge.[42] The Fujiwara chieftain (Tadazane) immediately gathered his closest advisers and retainers and subsequently sent a messenger to the Kōfukuji head abbot, Kakushin, asking for an explanation. A day or so later, Tadazane received reports from a Tōnomine messenger regarding the extent of the damages on the mountain. Though the destruction of several buildings was serious, it was the removal of the holy image, which could only be returned on a day of good omens, that caused most concern. Tadazane even refrained from performing his official duties in the capital for fear of further upsetting the *kami,* and he proceeded instead to ask the advice of the retired emperor. The formal appeal from Tōnomine arrived at Tadazane's mansion on the sixteenth day of the ninth month. The Fujiwara chieftain again assembled several of the most influential courtiers and retainers to a meeting to discuss appropriate actions. It was decided that a verdict, based on the procedures of the 1081 resolution, should be reached after a discussion at the imperial court and in consultation with the retired emperor, following an investigation of the damages.[43]

On the eighteenth day of the ninth month, one of Tadazane's retainers, a certain Naritada, returned from Tōnomine with a detailed report on the damages. The extent of the destruction was clearly worse than expected, and the messenger painted a dark picture of burned down temple halls and shrines. In addition, Naritada reported that virtually all monk residences had been destroyed, leaving few, if any, buildings standing on the holy grounds of Tōnomine. Once informed of the damages, Tadazane wasted little time in contacting the Kōfukuji head abbot, Kakushin (1065–1121, head abbot 1100–1121), who was ordered to forward the attackers. The Fujiwara leaders were greatly concerned with these recent events. Not only were two temples closely affiliated with the clan fighting each other, but angered ancestors were not something to take lightly, even if they were dead. At any rate, to oblige the spirits, Tadazane sent several pledges to Tōnomine and even visited Kasuga on his own, while sending two representatives to two other important shrines (Ōharano and Yoshida).[44] On the twenty-fourth, Tadazane decided that those from both temples who had violated the peace should be forwarded and punished. Two days later the holy image of Tōnomine was repaired and put in place in its shrine on top of the mountain. Though one might expect that the Tōnomine clergy, which had not caused extensive damage, would be the least satisfied with the absence of a more severe punishment of Kōfukuji, it was the Hossō monks who reacted most forcefully. On the twenty-eighth, a Kōfukuji monk appeared at Tadazane's mansion conveying a message from the clergy that matters yet remained to be settled. The monks demanded that Tōnomine become a branch temple of Kōfukuji, threatening to cancel the important Yuima ceremony the next month and to stage a protest in Kyoto if the court would not realize the importance and righteousness of their demands.[45] This can only be described as a very bold and daring move by the Kōfukuji clergy. Not only had some members of their monk community almost wiped out the shrine of the Fujiwara ancestor, but on being ordered to forward the criminals, they now renewed their claims to Tōnomine. Tadazane was, however, not intimidated, and he displayed his knowledge of Tōnomine's history in a response that illustrates the unusual determination shown by the Fujiwara chieftain.

> Tōnomine was founded a long time ago as a cloister of [Enryakuji's] Mudōji; how can we in our time make it into a branch of Kōfukuji for the first time? There cannot be such a verdict. With regard to the originators, the ones that caused these evil deeds were from both Kōfukuji and Tōnomine, and they shall all be arrested. How can only one temple be punished? If [the Kōfukuji monks] approaching to the capital are not stopped, I will proceed to Uji and meet them there myself.[46]

Despite Tadazane's forceful actions and prompt response, matters did not settle for quite some time. There were reports of unruliness in Nara and rumors of protesting monks coming to Kyoto on several occasions late in 1108. The problems in Nara in fact appear to have lingered on for almost two years, eventually inducing Tadazane to issue an edict from his headquarters (a *chōja sen*) on the fifteenth day of the sixth month of 1110, reinforcing the prohibition for Kōfukuji monks on carrying arms.[47] Tadazane was, however, not successful in quelling the clergy, and, when he became ill two months later, he suddenly gave up his tough stance and pardoned all punished monks at both Kōfukuji and Tōnomine, fearing that his disease was caused by the angry spirits of the temple and shrine complexes.[48] The Kōfukuji-Tōnomine conflict, though distinctively local in origin, reached larger proportions because of the complex ties both complexes had to the Fujiwara chieftain. Fears thus spread throughout the imperial court, but it was a dispute that concerned primarily the Fujiwara leader, who did indeed, as expected, come up with a solution in the end.

Kōyasan provides an interesting contrast to Enryakuji and Kōfukuji, since the revival of the imperial family affected it quite differently. First, as noted in the previous chapter, Kōyasan suffered a decline in the tenth century in terms of both conditions on the mountain and a lack of funding to finance reconstruction. The temple's possessions were not even comparable to the number of estates and branches controlled by the Tendai and Hossō centers. However, owing to links created with the Fujiwara during Michinaga's era, Kōyasan slowly regained its status and popularity, which were further augmented with Retired Emperor Shirakawa's visit in 1088. More important, as Shirakawa began to patronize Shingon to curtail the influence of the more powerful religious centers, Kongōbuji on Mt. Kōya became one of the new beneficiaries. Thus, whereas Shirakawa protected or even encouraged retainers who challenged the private possessions of Kōfukuji, and eventually also Enryakuji, he promoted an expansion of Kōyasan's estates and influence in Kii. Second, Kōyasan's location at some distance from Kyoto (an imperial pilgrimage to Mt. Kōya took between six and eight days) allowed the temple to focus on expanding its influence directly in the home area, instead of spending resources competing for favors from the various secular factions in the capital.[49] These priorities generally resulted in ambiguous relationships with local strongmen (*dōgo*), who had military power and retainers in the area. On the one hand, pacts frequently granted the warrior leader protection from the jurisdiction of government officials and confirmation as manager in an estate from

Kongōbuji, while the temple obtained a steady flow of income. For instance, the Sakamoto family in northern Kii organized other local warriors as retainers, assembled the work force, and collected taxes for the local Amano shrine, for which the Sakamoto even made themselves chieftains *(Amano uji chōja)*. This shrine was linked to Kōyasan, which started its journey to recovery with the help of such local support.[50] On the other hand, as Kōyasan's status improved, the clergy attempted to obtain a more direct control of estates in the region, resulting in resistance from and new conflicts with local strongmen beginning in the late eleventh century. For example, in the Kanji era (1087–1094), tensions escalated in the Kanshōfu estate to the point where the Sakamoto head, Tsunekiyo, killed the Kōyasan administrator. As a result, the Kongōbuji head abbot ordered over eighty *chō* (approximately 196 acres) of land confiscated from the Sakamoto family and redistributed it directly to the farmers in the estate, reflecting a successful elimination of the middleman. A similar incident some thirty years later resulted in the same punishment, but this time the Sakamoto were also driven out of the estate, establishing a precedent according to which murderers were forced to leave their homeland.[51] Kōyasan was not always so successful in such confrontations, but as its claims to more estates close to the temple received active support of retired emperors throughout the twelfth century, it became increasingly powerful in Kii, resembling the other religious *kenmon* closer to the capital in terms of landholdings and patronage.

As these examples have demonstrated, the local conflicts were not directly caused by the central elites, nor did they result in any forceful protests *(gōso)* in the capital. Rather, they were initiated by local powers who acted on their own and used the mandate of one central power to challenge the weakness of another. Control of land was thus never completely separated from capital politics. The usage of such a strategy has important implications for understanding the symbiosis of local and central in the late Heian period. While it was clear to central proprietors that military force was necessary to exert their authority locally, it was equally obvious to midlevel warriors, city dwellers, local monks, and shrine servants that they needed central support, if sometimes only in name, to assert themselves. Control of land without central connections was simply inconceivable at this juncture. Further, the vertical hierarchy covered both issues of land possession and jus-

tice, since matters of protection and complaints were brought
to the closest associated elite in the capital. Although particularly
severe incidents could cause concern among patrons in the capital,
they rarely caused any of the elite temples to go beyond the regular means of forwarding appeals to their secular allies or the
imperial court. Rather, it was the competition between the ultimate elites themselves that resulted in conflicts that would make
the imperial court, and occasionally the whole capital itself, trem-
ble with anxiety. The stakes in such conflicts were much higher
than in those at the local level; to the clergies, the very existence
of their temples now indeed seemed threatened.

Capital Factionalism and Religious Competition

The local incidents described above show that there were lawless
monks just as there were lawless warriors. However, such monks
were not representative of the entire clergy of Enryakuji and Kōfukuji; nor were they necessarily the main forces behind protests in
the capital. In fact, contrary to most scholarly assumptions, there
was a persuasive rationale for demonstrating in the capital. Regardless of whether the issue of conflict was land or monk appointments, protests were staged because the patrons of those who had
challenged the temple's rights resided in Kyoto.

Competition for Land

Land intrusions during Shirakawa's era frequently involved mid-
ranking courtiers and warrior aristocrats, whose job was to protect estates or to execute land policies on behalf of their betters at
court, confronting religious proprietors in their dual roles as
servants to their patrons and breadwinners for themselves. Significantly, these disputes appear before Shirakawa's rise to power in
the Kōwa era (1101–1104), reflecting the increased pressure on
land that resulted from the new policies against private estates
begun already under Go-Sanjō. For example, in 1069, forces of
the Yamato governor clashed with monks from Kōfukuji over
land rights. Go-Sanjō, who had ascended the throne the previous
year, was adamant toward the Fujiwara family and its great estates,
and he favored the governor, since he frequently attempted to
recruit members of the governor class to gain more support.
However, when the emperor was about to issue a verdict supporting the governor, the Fujiwara chieftain (Yorimichi) stated that it

would be a tremendous embarrassment to the clan if the emperor did not rule in favor of Kōfukuji. Although lacking the resources to challenge the Fujiwara chieftain outright, Go-Sanjō still ignored Yorimichi's plea and issued his verdict as planned. Yorimichi, who had opposed Go-Sanjō's accession from the start, became furious and left his position within the imperial court in protest. In the end, Go-Sanjō could not run things on his own in the capital, and he reluctantly had to comply with the demands of Yorimichi and Kōfukuji.[52]

Shirakawa was forced to deal with a similar plea in the middle of the ninth month of 1092, when some thirty members of Hiesha complained at the regent Morozane's mansion that several shrine officials had been harassed and killed as they sought to manage the affairs of a *shōen* that belonged to the shrine. The alleged offenders were retainers of Fujiwara no Tamefusa and Fujiwara no Tadazane (Morozane's grandson and the future Fujiwara chieftain), both serving as middle-ranking officials at court. To assure a favorable outcome, the protesters increased the pressure on the court by threatening to have the whole Enryakuji clergy join them if Tamefusa and Tadazane were not punished.[53] Two days later Tamefusa lost his official titles at court, Tadazane was apprehended while practicing at the archery field, and the retainers responsible for the harassment were arrested. But when the members of the Enryakuji and the Hiesha communities realized that the punishments would go no further, letting Tadazane go with no more than a reprimand, they threatened to initiate a protest in the capital. In response, the *kugyō* (noble council) met at the imperial palace, while a messenger was sent to ask the opinion of the retired emperor. However, Shirakawa did not reply, and the imperial court proceeded to handle the matter on its own. On the twenty-eighth day of the ninth month, it was ruled that both Tadazane and Tamefusa had indeed encouraged their retainers to intrude on the Hie estate. Accordingly, both were demoted and exiled to distant provinces as local officials; Tamefusa was "appointed" vice governor of Awa Province, while Tadazane became governor of Aki Province.[54] Though these appointments may not seem much of a punishment, even temporary exiles were setbacks for young nobles. It should also be noted that the punishments were administered even though both courtiers had connections with two of the most powerful figures at the imperial palace. Tadazane was, after all, the grandson of Morozane, who dominated

the court at that point, and Tamefusa was one of Shirakawa's retainers. These connections were, however, helpful in reducing
the terms of the exiles, and both courtiers were pardoned and
allowed to resume their careers at court within two years. Shirakawa influenced the court in its pardon of Tamefusa, who was
restored to his rank and position as one of the former emperor's
retainers in 1093. Tadazane and his primary accomplice were
called back to the capital on the fifth day of the third month of
1094.[55]

A similar conflict over land that also involved the inappropriate
treatment of Enryakuji monks took place in the tenth month of
1095, when a small group of monks complained at the imperial
palace that the governor of Mino Province, Minamoto no Yoshitsuna, had killed a certain Ennō, a longtime resident of the main
temple community at Enryakuji. Yoshitsuna explained that the
killing, which occurred during a dispute over the rights to a local
shōen, was an accident, caused by a stray arrow. The court's decision to acquit Yoshitsuna angered the monks, who assembled at
the Konpon chūdō with several portable shrines from Hiesha,
threatening to stage a divine demonstration in Kyoto. In the end,
only a few monks approached the imperial palace to protest, and
they were soon rejected by a force of defending government
warriors. The imperial court prevented further protests from the
clergy by sending the Tendai head abbot and other high-ranking
monks (who resided in the capital) to Enryakuji the following day
to calm the monks.[56]

Though the sources do not reveal the exact origins of this conflict, there is enough information to understand it in the larger
context of competition for land. According to the diary of Fujiwara no Munetada, Yoshitsuna confronted the monks when they
were about to administer *(satasu)* a *shōen,* thus indicating that the
estate was established in Enryakuji's name. However, *Heike monogatari,* a war tale from the thirteenth century, explicitly states that
the incident was a result of Yoshitsuna's efforts to prevent the
establishment of new *shōen* in the area.[57] The issue is complicated
by the fact that governors often used their mandate to stop *shōen*
as a technique for increasing their own revenues. Thus, it is
unclear whether a *shōen* had already been established when
Yoshitsuna and the monks faced each other or whether the estate
was a fairly new one. But there can be little doubt that the incident was a result of increased tensions between *shōen* proprietors

and the governor class (who were under the protection of other elites) that the more aggressive land policies of the imperial court had created.

The conflicts just described reflect another important dimension pertaining to the political balance in the capital. In particular, they further confirm the interpretation that the Fujiwara chieftain was still the main figure at court in the 1090s. In 1092 the protest took place at Morozane's mansion, and three years later it was his son, Moromichi, who ordered the warriors to stop the monks in the capital. In fact, while Shirakawa's name is not even mentioned, Moromichi was cursed by the Enryakuji monks for the outcome in the later incident.[58] The retired emperor was almost equally passive when his own retainer was exiled in 1092, acting only to reinstate him after over a year in exile. However, three decades later, Shirakawa's actions to protect another retainer speak of a profoundly different situation. On the eighteenth day of the seventh month of 1123, monks from Enryakuji carried seven portable shrines of Hiesha to the capital to protest against Taira no Tadamori's harassment and arrest of service people who were about to collect taxes for the temple in Echizen Province. Acting as one of Shirakawa's most entrusted retainers, Tadamori had attempted to expand his, and indirectly also the retired emperor's, control in the province. When the protesters entered the capital, they encountered defending government warriors, who engaged them in a battle. The seven shrines were left in the vicinity of the Kawara district in the eastern part of Kyoto (see Map 3), while the demonstrators scattered. Some of them sought protection at Gionsha, but they were driven out of the capital by Tadamori and Minamoto no Tameyoshi—another influential warrior leader. Throughout this ordeal, Shirakawa never budged and continued to support (if not condone) the acts of his retainers, even though some members of the Enryakuji clergy were killed in the confrontations. In the end, Tadamori was never punished, but Shirakawa ordered that the shrines that had been destroyed in the scuffle be rebuilt at the court's expense.[59]

The contrast in Shirakawa's power before and after the Kōwa period is also clearly reflected in Kōfukuji's records. An incident in the early era begins with a somewhat curious entry in the diary of Fujiwara no Moromichi, the Fujiwara regent. On the sixth day of the eighth month of 1093, he writes that the sumō bouts that had been scheduled to take place that day were canceled because of reports that the Kōfukuji clergy were mobilizing and rioting. Four days later some monks from the temple approached the regent to deliver a letter explaining why the monks were dissatisfied. After proclaiming the importance of Kōfukuji and Kasuga as the protectors of the imperial state (not unlike claims from Enryakuji in this period), the monks accused Takashina Tameie, the governor of Ōmi Province, of entering an estate of Kasuga and taking control of it with the support of forged documents. However, the monks could not supply any documents in support for their own claims to the estate, causing Moromichi to doubt the temple's appeal. In fact, he discussed the case with his closest advisers and retainers, wondering whether land could really have been commended to Kasuga even though an imperial edict had been issued prohibiting such donations at the time, and no specific edicts exempting the estate from taxes had been issued.[60]

Two weeks elapsed without any judgment from the court, resulting in an increasingly enraged Kōfukuji clergy and rumors that the monks were about to stage a protest in the capital. These rumors were confirmed on the twenty-sixth day of the eighth month, when a monk appeared at Moromichi's mansion, proclaiming that since no verdict had been issued, the Kōfukuji clergy would come to demonstrate at the Fujiwara mansion before staging a protest in the capital. According to several sources, thousands of monks, not only from Kōfukuji but also from other temples in Nara, entered the capital later that day to support the cause of Kasuga. The demonstrators first approached the Fujiwara clan's political headquarters in Kyoto—the Kangakuin—restating their complaint against Tameie and his harassment of Kasuga's service people. This protest finally induced the court to act in Kōfukuji's favor. That same night, Tameie was removed from his post as governor of Ōmi Province and exiled to Tosa, a province far removed from Kyoto, reflecting the punishment of a serious crime.[61] Tameie's son, who was also involved in the incident, lost his appointment as governor of Awa, though he was reappointed soon afterwards.[62]

The records do not provide any specific information regarding Tameie's political affiliations, but his oldest son was a retainer of Shirakawa, which explains why he was pardoned so quickly. The confrontation thus appears to be a mirror image of the 1092 conflict involving Enryakuji and two members of the Fujiwara family described earlier. Both incidents emphatically show increased tensions between the governor class and temples, reflecting an intensification of competition for land and revenues during the early years of Shirakawa's retirement. It was this situation that caused a ranking courtier and Shirakawa's former tutor, Ōe no Masafusa, to state that "everything in this world is according to the wishes of the retired emperor," indicating that Shirakawa had cautiously begun to increase his influence already before the weakening of the Fujiwara *sekkanke* between 1099 and 1101.[63]

The tensions were further augmented after Shirakawa's rise to power in the Kōwa era, as many governors and other military aristocrats associated with the retired emperor gained additional leverage and saw new opportunities to expand their influence. In the case of Kōfukuji, this shift is evident in a conflict that took place in the eighth month of 1120. It began with an appeal lodged by the Kōfukuji clergy against the governor of Izumi Province, who allegedly harassed service people of the Kasuga shrine. The Fujiwara chieftain (Tadazane) responded by sending out high-ranking Kōfukuji monks from the capital to calm their brothers in Nara, but this effort failed, and the clergy reinforced their complaints instead, appearing at the Fujiwara headquarters in the capital (the Kangakuin) less than a week later. The Fujiwara chieftain normally handled matters regarding Kōfukuji, but he now seemed incapable of dealing with this kind of pressure, deferring instead to Retired Emperor Shirakawa. The monks demanded the governor be exiled, but Shirakawa determined that such a punishment would be too harsh for the crime. Instead, he deposed the governor and ordered the harassing retainers arrested. After some discussion, the monks returned to Nara, apparently satisfied with the verdict.[64]

The Kōfukuji incidents just described are important for three reasons. First, they lend further support to the notion of representative jurisdiction for religious institutions. Even though a verdict could be issued by the retired emperor, whose retainers often were among the accused, the monks at Kōfukuji communicated first and foremost with the Fujiwara chieftain. Second, they are convincing evidence for Shirakawa's growing power from the Kōwa era. Not only did he issue verdicts for the Fujiwara clan temple, but his influence is also evident in the frequent references to the Fujiwara chieftain's reports to and discussions with the retired emperor. Third, and most important, the conflicts have demonstrated that it was the imperial family's attempts to challenge private estates belonging to elites outside its own influence late in the eleventh century that created new and intensified tensions between temples and provincial officers. When governors and their followers "defended the public realm" on behalf of the retired emperor by intruding into *shōen* and other areas where temples and shrines had long-standing interests, the religious establishment reacted by confronting the hired hands of the governor and by protesting in the capital.

Religious Appointments

Though the right to grant religious promotions and to award ceremonial functions always belonged to the imperial court, the growing independence of different elite temples combined with the self-regulating structure of a multidoctrinal system (through precedents and appeals) had made it all but impossible for the secular authorities to control these appointments willfully. Yet it was exactly this right that the retired emperor relied on when he attempted to become more competitive and gain an advantage over his competitors at court. Shirakawa's attempts to extend his control into Kōfukuji in the Kōwa era provide the earliest evidence of these strategies.

The Fujiwara *sekkanke* lost momentum when the regent Moromichi died in the sixth month of 1099, leaving the elderly Morozane and his young grandson Tadazane in charge of the clan. A year later Morozane's son, who had taken the name Kakushin as a Buddhist monk, was appointed head abbot of Kōfukuji. Perhaps sensing the weakening of the Fujiwara, Shirakawa took a bold step only two months later, on the seventh day of the tenth month of 1100, by appointing the monk Hanshun assistant head abbot *(gon bettō)* of the Hossō center. Hanshun, who had served as one of Shirakawa's main Buddhist teachers in the capital for several years, was not only close to the retired emperor but also a Shingon (Tōji) monk, thus lacking the experience to head ceremonies at Kōfukuji. Needless to say, there was considerable opposition among the clergy to Hanshun, who was seen as little more than Shirakawa's pawn in his attempts to prevent the Fujiwara from gaining more influence within Kōfukuji. It is therefore not surprising that the clergy objected early in 1101, when Shirakawa recommended his protégé as lecturer for the Yuima'e. The retired emperor was forced to acknowledge Hanshun's lack of merit, but the tensions between Shirakawa and the clergy kept escalating until they erupted on the tenth day of the seventh month of 1102, when a messenger from Kōfukuji arrived hurriedly at the mansion of Tadazane, reporting that some of Shirakawa's retainers had forcefully entered Kōfukuji's Kizu estate in Izumi Province. Monks and shrine servants on the estate confronted the warriors, even capturing some of them. The monks now wanted Shirakawa's retainers and their warriors punished for the intrusion and for using violence against the servants of Buddha and the *kami*. After hearing the complaint, Tadazane immediately informed Shirakawa, who had the new Fujiwara chieftain in his service at the time. The court subsequently deliberated for days without reaching a solution, but a verdict was issued against Kōfukuji on the first day of the eighth month. Shirakawa, attempting to protect the interests of his vassals, additionally turned the tables on the appealing monks by having the Fujiwara-supported Kōfukuji head abbot, Kakushin, temporarily relieved of his duties.[65]

This important verdict had double implications. First, Kakushin was the son of Morozane and Tadazane's uncle and, more important, the first of several Kōfukuji head abbots from the main Fujiwara line (see Figure 6). He was appointed head abbot of Kōfukuji at the young age of thirty-six on the twentieth day of the eighth month of 1100 through the Kangakuin, in an effort by Morozane to increase his control of the temple and its assets. Interestingly, this appointment took place only a year after Morozane had unsuccessfully opposed Shirakawa's appointment of one of his sons (Kakugyō) as *hōshinnō* to head the new imperial temples in Kyoto. The placing of sons as head abbots of important temple complexes thus emerged as a new strategy during the Kōwa years, implemented almost simultaneously by both the retired emperor and the Fujiwara chieftain. However, Shirakawa's suspension of Kakushin in 1102, which was unusually severe by all accounts, temporarily halted an increased Fujiwara control of the assets of the Kōfukuji complex, while reminding the young and comparatively inexperienced Tadazane that he was still the retainer of the retired emperor.[66] The dispute over land was thus used by Shirakawa as a pretext to increase his control over Kōfukuji at the expense of Kakushin and, by extension, the Fujiwara only a year after Morozane's death.

Second, the monks and the service people of the Kōfukuji-Kasuga complex reacted with great anger and determination shortly after the verdict. The clergy first directed its anger toward

Shirakawa's protégé, assistant abbot Hanshun, as well as his disciples and supporters by attacking their dwellings while blaming them for not representing the interests of the clergy and Kasuga sufficiently in the capital. It appears, then, that the clergy was aware of the various affiliations of the leading monks, and the attack may therefore also have been a vivid expression of capital factionalism spilling over into the monastic world. The suspended Kakushin, for his part, sent a letter to Regent Tadazane's mansion, perhaps containing an appeal. Tadazane summoned the ranking Kōfukuji monk Jōshin, who was charged with running the administration during Kakushin's absence, to discuss the issue and to find ways to calm the monks. Considering the role the retired emperor played in this incident and his increasing claims to power in the capital, it is not surprising to find that Tadazane also thought it wise to have a messenger report to Shirakawa what was taking place at Kōfukuji.[67] This messenger was incidentally Fujiwara no Munetada, a minor Fujiwara who served as the head of the imperial police *(kebiishi bettō)*, spending much of his free time recording the events in the capital in his diary, which today serves as the most comprehensive source of information for Shirakawa's era. Munetada received a letter about the riots within the temple complex from Jōshin on the eighth day of the eighth month, 1102, and he brought the report to Retired Emperor Shirakawa the

Figure 6. Court factionalism at Kōfukuji in the early twelfth century

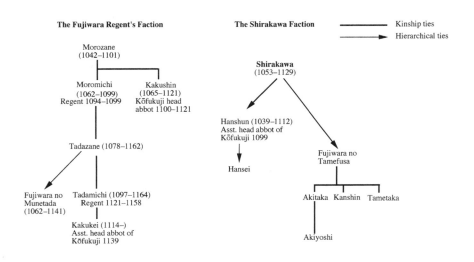

following day in an attempt to communicate the urgency of the matter. In his diary, Munetada, who apparently sympathized with Kōfukuji's situation, candidly blames Shirakawa for the disturbance, stating that "the reason [for the clergy's rioting] is the [previous] verdict by the retired emperor," though such a stance would be expected considering that the retired emperor's verdict was a setback for the Fujiwara as well. Nothing was accomplished in the meetings with Shirakawa, however, and the Kōfukuji monks became increasingly unruly. On the twelfth day there were rumors among the courtiers that the clergy was ready to enter the capital to stage a protest.[68]

These reports caused grave concern among courtiers in the capital, and even Shirakawa eventually became worried, calling on Munetada to restrain the monks. Accordingly, three of the highest-ranking Kōfukuji monks (who held *sōgō* titles) were sent to Nara to calm the clergy on the eighteenth. The monks returned the following day with a statement, which Munetada in common fashion immediately delivered to the retired emperor. A couple of days later, the three messengers, now accompanied by the aforementioned Jōshin, were called to Regent Tadazane's mansion to discuss the clergy's message in detail. Jōshin relayed the concerns of the clergy, claiming that they were unable to complete the construction of a new image of Buddha Kannon (the bodhisattva of great compassion and an attendant of Amida Buddha) because of the current crisis. A failure to pay proper tribute to one of the buddhas did not, Jōshin stated, reflect well on the retired emperor or the members of the imperial court. Still, Jōshin guaranteed that the Kōfukuji clergy had, despite the rumors, no intention of staging a demonstration in the capital. Within a few days, Jōshin sent Tadazane a letter from Nara, stating that he had managed to calm the clergy.[69]

However, Jōshin's control of the Kōfukuji clergy was not as extensive as he may have thought, or he may not have been entirely truthful in his letter to the Fujiwara chieftain, since the clergy was involved in new brawls soon afterwards. During a festival honoring the protective *kami* of Tōdaiji, some monks from Kōfukuji enjoyed their own festivities, performing a *dengaku* (a dance related to agricultural rites). This distraction apparently upset the monks from Tōdaiji, who shot some arrows at their adversaries. A physical confrontation followed, which eventually led to a partial destruction of some buildings on both sides. Jōshin hurried to the capital to report the incident, admitting that he was now unable to contain the Kōfukuji clergy. It became clear that the conflict with the monks of Tōdaiji, who incidentally staged a demonstration of their own in the capital with the holy cart of the Hachiman Shrine, was not the only source of discontent in Nara. The Kōfukuji clergy was still deeply dissatisfied with Shirakawa's opposition to Kakushin, who was unable to perform his administrative duties as head abbot during his involuntary convalescence. In the meantime, another monk named Ei'en headed Kōfukuji, but the clergy was unhappy that the Yuima ceremony had been performed in the absence of the head abbot and appealed to have Kakushin reinstated.[70]

The tensions were intensified late in the third month of 1103, when the Kōfukuji clergy threatened to come to the capital to demonstrate because of a court decision to appoint several junior monks, including a certain Shin'ei, over other more senior colleagues to function as the main lecturers at the Yuima ceremony. Though the monks admitted that Shin'ei was extraordinarily talented, they claimed that seniority should determine ranking and order of promotion among the monks. An imperial police captain was sent out from the capital to calm the clergy, but he failed, instead making the monks more aggravated, and some of them left Nara that night to protest at the Fujiwara headquarters in Kyoto. On the following day, the monks promptly appeared in Kyoto carrying sacred branches (*shinmoku* or *shinboku*) from the Kasuga shrine. The monks stayed in the capital for days, creating disorder and concern among the nobles, with added pressure on the Fujiwara chieftain, who received a message that the protesters would pay him a personal visit unless the matter was handled properly. The monks returned to Nara on the first day of the fourth month, after having been reassured that their demands would be heard, and the promotion of the young monks was subsequently canceled. To the delight of Tadazane and Kōfukuji's clergy, the retired emperor finally decided to pardon the previously suspended Kakushin, reinstating him as head abbot of Kōfukuji about a month after the protest. This proved to be a wise decision, since Kakushin managed to calm the monks after only a couple of days, resulting, at last, in a more peaceful atmosphere in both Nara and Kyoto, as evidenced by an offering at the monastic complex in Nara in the seventh month of 1103, with three hundred monks and high dignitaries from the Fujiwara family attending.[71] Though the reasons for the court's favoritism of Shin'ei and his young brothers are not known, it is clear that Shirakawa's suspension of Kakushin and promotion of Hanshun reflect an attempt to expand the retired emperor's control over Kōfukuji right after the Fujiwara had lost two of its most prominent leaders. More strikingly, it was the temple's own prolonged resistance, not the efforts of the Fujiwara chieftain, whose power had clearly declined, that prevented Shirakawa from making any substantial headway within Kōfukuji. Furthermore, it is significant that competition at court, rather than competition between temples and members of the imperial court, caused increased tensions in the religious sphere, and one might speculate that Shin'ei was yet another pawn in this competition.

The religious strategies of the imperial faction affected Enryakuji as well, as Shirakawa gained more confidence and implemented increasingly aggressive policies in the early twelfth century, causing incidents similar to those involving Kōfukuji. While land issues were important to Enryakuji, the most violent and intense conflicts were over religious appointments. Apparently, the monks' first concern was to maintain the temple's position as protector of the state, center of learning and Buddhist studies, and a preferred provider of religious rituals. Since these responsibilities also sustained the temple's status as a privileged elite, Enryakuji was extremely sensitive to changes that might diminish its role. Shirakawa's attempts to enforce such changes caused protests that came to be recorded as the most threatening incidents in over a century, and, in some cases, as the most disturbing religious protests ever.

One of the earliest Enryakuji demonstrations of this kind occurred on the last day of 1104, when service people of Enryakuji and its shrines protested against the appointment of Chōkan, an Onjōji monk, as master of the lecture meeting on the Lotus Sūtra at Enshūji.[72] The appointment of Chōkan came about as a result of unusual circumstances. Originally, Keizō of Enryakuji was appointed, but he became ill and was forced to decline the honor. At that point, Fujiwara no Tadazane, acting on Shirakawa's orders, appointed Chōkan as the new master without conferring with Enryakuji. The Enryakuji monks protested, arguing that all earlier selections among Tendai monks had been made on the recommendation of the Enryakuji head abbot. Although the claim was essentially true, the precedent was rather weak, since Enshūji was a relatively new temple, built by Go-Sanjō. Nevertheless, that claim, supported by the protest, was enough to make the court cancel the appointment.[73]

A similar appointment in 1108 resulted in more forceful protests, but this time Enryakuji appealed on behalf of Onjōji—its longtime adversary. On the twentieth day of the third month, Shirakawa appointed a Tōji monk to lead the *kanjō* ritual (an esoteric initiation ceremony) at Sonshōji, another of the newly established imperial temples in eastern Kyoto. The following day, Enryakuji claimed that it was Onjōji's turn to lead that ceremony. Enryakuji's support of its Tendai sibling is interesting, considering the fierce fighting that had taken place between the centers a mere two and a half decades earlier and the rivalry that characterized their relationship for centuries. It indicates that Shirakawa's patronage of Tōji and Shingon was considered serious enough to bring the competing Tendai branches together, even if only for a moment. Indeed, Fujiwara no Munetada also noted this rare instance of cooperation, commenting that "the monks from both temples forwarding an appeal together is truly [as unimaginable] as combining fire with water."[74] Munetada's fears came true on the twenty-third of the third month, the day before the ritual was to take place, when monks from both Enryakuji and Onjōji set out to demonstrate in the capital. Despite the court's fears, the protesters were not attempting to increase their privileges, but merely to underline what they considered their proper rights. In fact, the monks had precedent on their side, as courtiers in the capital also noted. Munetada wrote in his diary that it would be proper to bestow the honor on Onjōji, but the retired emperor was determined to do things his way. Shirakawa's explanation as quoted by Munetada speaks for itself:

> It is true that I have not followed the sequence of [appointments among] temples, but in other cases, there are numerous examples where promotions have been made rightfully. In the case of Tōji, there are no other particular routes of promotion besides this appointment. Therefore, with regard to the performer *(ajari)* for this *kanjō* ritual, many Tōji monks shall be employed, while Tendai monks will be used [only] occasionally. Thus, the *kanjō ajari* this year will be the Tōji monk Zen'yo.[75]

The ceremony subsequently took place according to Shirakawa's order, but the dissatisfied Tendai monks continued to mobilize and threatened to invade the capital in large numbers. Munetada described how the Enryakuji monks and government warriors prepared for a confrontation. He compared the different movements to a spectacular show of lights and reflections in the darkness of the Kyoto night: in the eyes of the Fujiwara courtier, the torches that the monks carried with them as they descended the mountains east of the capital seemed as plentiful as the stars in the sky. In addition, the naked blades of the warriors, who moved around to get in position to protect the capital, created reflections (of the moon?) that made it seem like daylight.[76] In the end, the monks did not enter the capital, but the pressure and the panic that spread as a result of the mere threat of a confrontation between Minamoto and Taira warriors, on the one side, and monks, on the other, were enough to make the court comply with the monks' demands. "In the future," the court stated, "the ceremony should be performed alternating between the lineages of Kūkai [Tōji], Ennin [Enryakuji], and Enchin [Onjōji]."[77] In other words, several members of the court candidly disagreed with Shirakawa's willful appointment, and Munetada, who seemed less concerned with the appointment itself, also noted that if precedent had been followed, life would have been much easier for the farmers, whose rice fields had been trampled by the government warriors in the eastern part of Kyoto.[78] While this incident did not result in actual confrontations, it might indeed have ended that way had not the court complied with the Tendai demands so quickly. Again, it was the retired emperor's appointment, contrary to customary procedures, that caused the conflict, whereas the Tendai monks were determined to uphold their own status and the accustomed balance of patronage among the different religious centers.

The Tendai demonstrations against Shirakawa's appointments in 1108 provide important evidence for yet another aspect of the retired emperor's manipulation of religious appointments to promote his own interests. Besides attempting to curtail and control Enryakuji and Kōfukuji directly, Shirakawa's policies of favoring Shingon monks in the post-Kōwa era reflect his efforts to weaken these traditional religious centers as well. If there was any sect among the established ones that was suitable for this purpose, it was Shingon. It contained the same esoteric rites and art as had been adopted in particular by Tendai, but neither of the two main Shingon centers (Kōyasan and Tōji) had the kind of political leverage that the Tendai and Hossō centers possessed. The first imperial pilgrimages to Kōyasan in 1088 and 1091 laid the foundation not only for a comprehensive revival of the temple but also for a new, reinforced partnership between the Shingon center and the retired emperor. In 1103 Kōyasan's popularity among the capital elites reached a milestone, as offerings were made in honor of the newly erected Grand Pagoda.[79] Soon after, Shirakawa's fourth son, Kakuhō *hōshinnō*, became head abbot at Kōyasan, and the retired emperor subsequently began to appoint an increasing number of monks from Tōji and Ninnaji for important court ceremonies, while attempting to change the balance among the highest-ranking monks by promoting more Shingon monks to the Office of Monastic Affairs.[80] Shirakawa's religious policies were thus designed to regain control over the religious order by, on the one hand, appointing loyal monks to offices within Tendai and Shingon and, on the other, strengthening the position of Kōyasan and Tōji monks and conversely weakening the influence of Kōfukuji and Enryakuji.

This context of a two-front assault explains another unusual appointment by Shirakawa in 1105, which caused a serious conflict between Enryakuji and Iwashimizu Hachimangū, a prominent and independent shrine complex located south of Kyoto.[81] In the first month of that year, a report arrived in Kyoto from the regional headquarters (Dazaifu) in Kyushu, accusing monks from Enryakuji of harassing the administration of Kamadoyama, a shrine located in Hōki Province (present-day Tottori).[82] This shrine was a local branch of Daisenji, which in turn was a powerful branch temple of Enryakuji since the late ninth or early tenth century. Though far removed from Kyoto, Daisenji was not isolated from capital politics. Munetada noted in his diary a decade earlier (1094) that some three hundred members of this temple entered Kyoto to file a grievance with Shirakawa. It appears that the Daisenji clergy were dissatisfied with the Tendai *zasu* at that time, but it is not clear what their grievance was about or how the issue was settled.[83] In response to the accusations in 1105, Enryakuji soon filed a countercomplaint in defense of its members, stating that Kōsei, the chief administrator of Kamadoyama, had allied with one Suenaka, a local Dazaifu official, and attacked other members of the shrine.[84] Though this conflict may seem like a trivial incident between Kōsei and Enryakuji, its origin and relation to circumstances at the imperial court have far-reaching implications for understanding Shirakawa's ambitions. It was Shirakawa who appointed Kōsei administrator of Kamadoyama although it was, in fact, part of a complex that was a branch temple of Enrya-kuji. The office was therefore expected to be a prerogative of the main temple, and the appointment of Kōsei, who also was the head of the rival shrine-temple complex of Iwashimizu Hachi-mangū, thus became a direct threat to Enryakuji's rights to Dai-senji. Furthermore, the appointment may also have implied that the retired emperor arbitrarily could redistribute branches to other sects. Enryakuji's response was, however, not immediate. At the time of Kōsei's appointment sometime in 1104, a certain Keichō was the head abbot of Tendai. Unfortunately, little is known about this elderly monk (he was seventy-five years old when he became *zasu* in 1102), except that he soon became the target of the Enryakuji clergy's anger and was chased off Mt. Hiei. In part, the discord seems to have been caused by Keichō's unwillingness to protest on Enryakuji's behalf over the appointment of Kōsei as head administrator of Kamadoyama.[85]

One of Keichō's most powerful opponents was a monk named Hōyaku Zenshi, who was, according to Munetada's diary, exceed-ingly skilled in the way of the warrior and loved warfare to the extent that he was involved in every dispute on Mt. Hiei, partici-pating in theft and killings in the Kyoto area and controlling most of Enryakuji.[86] This Hōyaku Zenshi was apparently quite influen-tial on Mt. Hiei, since he was among the leaders when the clergy forced the head abbot Keichō to leave Mt. Hiei on the fourteenth day of the tenth month of 1104. Later in that month he pro-ceeded to send lower-class temple servants and service people of Hiesha to Kamadoyama to obstruct Kōsei's administration. How-ever, shortly after the monks reached Hōki, Kōsei's followers were aided by Suenaka, who became involved in a confrontation with the Enryakuji followers. There were some casualties during an exchange of arrows, though the Enryakuji monks appeared mostly upset that one arrow hit one of Kamadoyama's sacred shrines.[87]

The court discussed the two petitions in 1105 on the fourth day of the fifth month and the second day of the sixth month, but before they could reach a decision, another incident caused fur-ther anger among the Enryakuji monks. On the fourteenth day of the sixth month, the police captain *(kebiishi)* Nakahara Norimasa stirred up a fight with members of Hiesha as they were perform-ing a ceremony in Kyoto. The shrine people managed to chase

Norimasa and his followers away from the area, but, enraged by the harassment, they also proceeded to the imperial palace and later continued to the retired emperor's palace demanding that Norisada be punished.[88] The protesters remained in the capital for months, hoping that their presence would induce the court to comply with their demands. At the same time, the Enryakuji clergy was waiting for Kōsei and Suenaka to be punished for the incident at Daisenji. But Shirakawa and the court seem to have been at a loss as to what to do, failing to reach a decision or to induce the protesters to return to their homes. On the twenty-fifth day of the tenth month, Suenaka was deposed from his post, but no decision was made regarding Kōsei. Fearing that the court would give in to Enryakuji's demands, supporters of the Iwashimizu shrine finally entered the capital in defense of their abbot on the twenty-ninth. The two camps subsequently confronted each other in Kyoto, resulting in a brief battle in which the Iwashimizu followers were driven out. The victorious Enryakuji supporters remained in the capital, continuing to harass the inhabitants and frighten the nobles. On the last day of the tenth month, the court felt obliged to accommodate Enryakuji, suspending Kōsei, police captain Norimasa, and Suenaka. Satisfied with these punishments, the protesters returned to Mt. Hiei that night.[89]

The incident was not settled until the end of 1105. Norimasa was eventually pardoned for his harassment of the Hie shrine members in Kyoto, and Kōsei was reinstated as chief administrator for Iwashimizu, though three of his retainers were arrested. Suenaka's fate was more unfortunate, as he lost his rank and his office in Kyushu in addition to being exiled to Suō Province.[90] Yet it was undoubtedly Kōsei who was the most important player in the whole incident. What then was his relationship with Shirakawa, and why was he appointed administrator of a Tendai branch temple? Unfortunately, the sources do not provide any direct answers, but it is known that Kōsei had important ties with the imperial family and most likely with Shirakawa himself. His daughter, known as Lady Mino, was a female attendant of Taiken-mon'in, the adopted daughter of Shirakawa as well as one of his favorite ladies at the imperial palace. Lady Mino became a consort of Emperor Toba, Shirakawa's grandson, and gave birth to two sons, both of whom became hōshinnō. To provide for the livelihood of Lady Mino, her mother, Fujiwara no Kaneko, supplied her with land (Kawada-no-shō in Echizen Province) that later became part of the imperial portfolio.[91]

Though the evidence regarding Shirakawa's intentions is scarce, one can deduce that he would have accomplished two things had not Enryakuji protested. First, Shirakawa was attempting to control religious estates directly by appointing a monk of his own liking to the Enryakuji branch. Had this measure been successful, it would have set an important precedent for the retired emperor's right to assign administrators to any temple's branches, violating an old right of the main temple and, in effect, disqualifying branches as immune estates. Second, Kōsei, who was close to the imperial house, would have provided Shirakawa with indirect control of estates that belonged to Daisenji. It is even conceivable that the retired emperor was using the appointment to create a tie between himself and Kōsei, hoping that the monk would share some of his estates with the imperial house through Lady Mino. At any rate, Shirakawa's measures were irregular. Indeed, although the courtiers were upset over Hōyaku Zenshi's military power and control within the Enryakuji complex, the temple's right to manage the affairs of Daisenji was never questioned.[92] Some objections were raised against the behavior of the messengers Hōyaku sent to Daisenji, but it was clearly within Enryakuji's prerogative, according to *honji-matsuji* (main temple–branch temple) relationships, to manage its affairs. In the end, the court recognized the temple's right to do so, since it was the local official, not the Enryakuji supporters, who was punished for the confrontation.

The dispute between Iwashimizu and Enryakuji was thus triggered by Shirakawa's appointment of a monk from the rival temple complex to head one of Enryakuji's branches. In 1113 Enryakuji was on the receiving side of another controversial appointment by Shirakawa. In the intercalary third month of that year, monks from Kōfukuji petitioned the court to cancel the appointment of the monk Ensei as the abbot for Kiyomizudera, a Kōfukuji branch temple located in the eastern part of Kyoto. Though training in different doctrines, even at other temples, was not unusual, this appointment tested the patience of the Kōfukuji monks, since Ensei had been trained at Enryakuji.[93] The appointment of Ensei was closely parallel to that of Kōsei, and the threat it posed to the monks at the main temple was similarly serious enough to cause protests and even fighting. The Nara monks were worried that Ensei's contacts with Enryakuji might estrange Kiyomizudera—the most important Hossō branch in Kyoto—from Kōfukuji. They thus had good reason to be concerned, and there were rumors that more than a thousand Kōfukuji protesters had left Nara on the twentieth day of the intercalary third month for the Fujiwara chieftain's mansion to pressure the imperial government to replace Ensei. The imperial court subsequently complied by appointing another monk the following day.[94] By the end of the month, the Enryakuji monks, who had not been actively involved in the dispute so far, suddenly came to the capital by the hundreds and attacked Kiyomizudera. The attackers claimed that Kōfukuji monks had despoiled and stolen property from Enryakuji's branch shrine Gion at the time of the protest a week earlier. The retaliation was devastating, leaving much of Kiyomizudera in ruins. Enryakuji also wanted the Kōfukuji abbot Jikkaku exiled, an issue that the imperial court discussed at the retired emperor's palace. Shirakawa and the nobles were clearly not pleased with the monks' behavior and saw no reason to punish Jikkaku for any crime. Fujiwara no Munetada despaired, lamenting that the end of the world seemed near, since the power of the clergy now superseded the authority of the court.[95]

The sources portray Shirakawa and the court as all but helpless, even though they called in the Tendai head abbot, ordering him to calm the monks. The abbot responded that there was very little he could do to control the anger of the monks, and since even the warriors hired by the government were considered insufficient, the court was eventually forced to punish Jikkaku. Perhaps anticipating protests from Kōfukuji, the court also added an unusual clause that Enryakuji's rights to protest against that temple's appeals in the future were now limited. The anticipated appeal came only a few days later together with reports that the Kōfukuji monks were about to enter the capital again. The Hossō monks, as expected, demanded that Jikkaku be acquitted of all crimes. But they also wanted the Tendai head abbot, Ningō, and another high-ranking Enryakuji monk exiled because of the destruction of Kiyomizudera. Finally, in an attempt to break Enryakuji's influence in the eastern part of the capital, the monks also demanded that Gion be returned to Kōfukuji as one of its branch temples.[96] Though the last demand seems far-fetched and unrealistic, Gion had indeed been a branch of Kōfukuji before it was attached to Enryakuji late in the tenth century.

While the court again deliberated over a verdict, Enryakuji and Kōfukuji continued to prepare for an armed confrontation. Fear spread among the nobles, who were at a loss as to what they should do to stop the monks from coming to the capital. In a desperate move, the court agreed to send messengers to the seven most important shrines to pray for a peaceful solution. On a more concrete note, Fujiwara no Tadazane, now regent for Shirakawa's grandson Emperor Toba, sent a messenger to Nara to calm the monks, and he also assembled warriors to protect the capital. The combined efforts of Tadazane and the native gods may have worked, since the monks never left their temples, and the crisis was avoided for the moment.[97] However, the anger of Buddha's servants did not subside for long. On the thirtieth day of the fourth month, monks from both sides finally set out for the capital to settle the dispute on their own. While the Enryakuji followers descended from Mt. Hiei and entered the capital from the east, the Kōfukuji monks, including supporters from other branches and estates in Yamato, came from Nara and approached the capital from the south, arriving at Uji, where Tadazane's palace was located. Government warriors were dispatched to Uji under the command of Taira no Masamori, and fighting broke out between the two forces.[98] The confrontation resulted in some thirty followers killed on Kōfukuji's side, compared to only two among the government troops. According to Munetada's diary, the fighting began when a deer, seen as a divine messenger by the monks, appeared before the two forces. One of the government warriors attempted to shoot the deer, upsetting the Kōfukuji followers to the point that they then attacked the opposing troops.[99] The confrontation and the possibility of divine retribution led to words of fear in many noble diaries, and Munetada even stated that the incident was more serious than the infamous rebellion by Taira no Masakado.[100]

Meanwhile, on the eastern side of the capital, the scene was not quite as violent, though the situation was equally serious. Warriors under the command of Minamoto no Mitsukuni and Fujiwara no Morishige were sent out to stop the Enryakuji monks, but they failed as the monks proceeded to the Gion shrine, where they prepared for a battle should the Kōfukuji monks reach the capital. Since the latter were turned back at Uji, the Tendai monks returned to Mt. Hiei without incident on the first day of the fifth month.[101] The whole conflict ended with a pardon of Jikkaku but perhaps also a partial victory for Enryakuji, since no punishments were enforced for the destruction of Kiyomizudera.

In general, one can conclude that Shirakawa put more emphasis on extending his power within Enryakuji and Kōfukuji in the early years, as evidenced by the monk appointments in the Kōwa era, whereas he devoted more attention to promoting Shingon later on. This shift toward weakening, instead of controlling, Hossō and Tendai may have been a result of the resistance he encountered from the clergies on Mt. Hiei and in Nara. However, one strategy did not necessarily exclude the other, and Shirakawa in fact continued his attempts to reach a level of control within these centers by using his right to monk appointments. For example, in the selection of monks to perform the Yuima ceremony at Kōfukuji (which had normally been handled exclusively by the Fujiwara chieftain) in 1114, Regent Tadazane felt compelled to consult with Shirakawa. Since this ceremony accrued important credit for promotions and abbot appointments for the monks heading it, the selection was an issue of interest to the retired emperor. Although Shirakawa did not oppose Tadazane's recommendation, he renewed the efforts he had begun in 1101, when he tried to promote his monk-ally Hanshun, by adding two youthful monks on his own to the list. Kanshin, who was the son of Fujiwara no Tamefusa—a retainer of Shirakawa—is of particular interest. Lacking experience in any of the annual lecture ceremonies, he was eventually denied the appointment in 1114, but the retired emperor managed to have his way by appointing him lecturer for the Yuima'e of the following year instead. Not only was the appointment of such an inexperienced monk unprecedented, but there were no previous cases where such honors had been bestowed in a directive from a retired emperor, earning both Kanshin and Shirakawa fierce opposition from the Kōfukuji clergy.[102] An overt conflict was avoided again when Kanshin postponed his participation because of his father's death in 1115, but he made it to Nara for the Yuima'e in the tenth month of 1116. Once in Nara, he and his brother Tametaka, who accompanied him as an imperial messenger, met an enraged clergy, and they were both driven back to Kyoto. Tadazane sided with the monks and suggested that Shirakawa change the appointment, but Shirakawa persisted. The dispute ended in a compromise, where Kanshin was allowed to serve as a discussant-commentator (ikō) for attending student-monks, who presented their interpretations of various Buddhist texts and problems, and a Tōdaiji monk was appointed lecturer instead.[103] The driving force behind this incident was not only Shirakawa but also his retainer Tamefusa, who had suggested making his own son Kanshin lecturer at the Yuima'e in the first place. Tamefusa, it turned out, had good reasons to infiltrate the Kōfukuji clergy, since two of his own descendants—the eldest son, Akitaka, and his son, Akiyoshi (see Figure 6)—became involved in a land dispute with the temple in Sanuki Province in the fifth month of 1116.[104] From a larger perspective, these tensions reflect not only a fundamental shift in power away from the Fujiwara in favor of the retired emperor in the early 1100s, but also how increased tensions on land induced Shirakawa to meddle in internal Kōfukuji matters that normally would have been handled exclusively by the temple and the Fujiwara chieftain.

It is abundantly clear that Shirakawa was not only involved in but also initiated the incidents over religious appointments described above. In fact, there was only one such dispute after 1100 that did not involve—for reasons that are easy to understand—the retired emperor directly. In the fifth month of 1102, monks from Enryakuji protested at the mansion of the Fujiwara chieftain, Tadazane, to have the abbot of Hosshōji, Ningen, also appointed abbot of Hōjōji.[105] Hōjōji was a prestigious temple that Fujiwara no Michinaga constructed in the eastern part of the capital in 1019, and the Fujiwara chieftain thus held the right to appoint abbots. Until 1098 all abbots had been Onjōji monks, but in that year, an Enryakuji monk, the former Tendai *zasu* Ninkaku, was appointed for the first time, inviting competing claims for the office.[106] Consequently, when Ninkaku died on the twenty-eighth day of the third month of 1102, both Enryakuji and Onjōji had legitimate claims to the abbotship of Hōjōji. Following the logic of all protests in Kyoto at the time, the Enryakuji monks proceeded to Tadazane's mansion in Uji, since the Fujiwara chieftain was the formal authority in this case. With the support of the emperor, who saw no immediate advantage in supporting Enryakuji's claims at this point, Tadazane opted for a compromise in which two Onjōji monks were made abbot and administrative chief, while Enryakuji's Ningen was appointed deputy administrator.[107]

Though Tadazane consulted Shirakawa, the dispute over the abbotship of Hōjōji was primarily an issue for the Fujiwara chieftain. This incident is a watershed in two ways. First, Shirakawa became increasingly involved in internal Kōfukuji matters from this junction, as evidenced by his deposition of the head abbot Kakushin four months later. Second, whereas the Hōjōji issue was carried out and resolved peacefully, post-Kōwa protests brought about unprecedented intensity and violence. For example, though the appointment of the abbot of Kiyomizudera in 1113 was quickly changed in favor of a monk trained in the Hossō sect, the monks of Kōfukuji and Enryakuji still attacked one another and prepared to engage in battle to settle their differences. Other earlier appointments that displeased the monks at Enryakuji—even regarding the head abbot—had not deteriorated into such battles. What then caused this change of behavior? I believe that the answer lies embedded in the political turns within the imperial court. The increase in violence coincides with the implementation of Shirakawa's more aggressive policies, originating from the establishment of the *hōshinnō*. Thus, the religious protests during the decade from around 1101 reflect more the changes among the elites at the imperial court than a change of attitude or an increase in "worldliness" among the monks on Mt. Hiei and in Nara. Though Shirakawa tried to control the Enryakuji clergy through the head abbot, even extracting a pledge to behave from the monks in 1111, his own policies had already created a more competitive atmosphere that accentuated the rivalries between different temples and sects.[108]

Shirakawa's religious policies even contributed to increased tensions within the leading monastic complexes. On the whole, Kōfukuji seems to have experienced more problems with internal divisions than Enryakuji during the early *insei* era. Both temples encountered increasingly ambitious noble abbots who attempted to control their landed wealth, vast human resources, and military potential, but Enryakuji was more successful in retaining its unity, avoiding sharp divisions and conflicts between noble abbots and the clergy, until the last decade or so of the Heian period. Kōfukuji was not as fortunate, as it was under more consistent attack from two directions. Sensing the weakening of his clan at the imperial court, the Fujiwara chieftain tried to obtain more direct control of Kōfukuji by appointing relatives to important positions within the temple. For the same reason, Shirakawa opportunistically began to place monks loyal to himself within the Hossō center, attempting to nominate and appoint them to the very same offices. As a result, there formed a highly complicated and intricate web of ties between the imperial family and its retainers, on the one hand, and the Fujiwara chieftain and the Kōfukuji clergy, on the other, as illustrated in Figure 6 above.

The increasingly dissatisfied Kōfukuji clergy, which wished to maintain a high degree of independence from both of these factions, came into conflict with noble abbots who primarily represented their patrons within the imperial court. This weakening of internal ties caused severe problems for the ranking monks, who found it more and more difficult to control both the clergy and many of the temple's own branches. For example, in 1106, a dispute occurred over the appointment of a head abbot for Kiyomizudera, the branch temple of Kōfukuji in Kyoto. On the twenty-third day of the second month, Fujiwara no Tadazane sent one of his messengers to Kōfukuji to announce that the monk Jōshin, who had attempted to help the Fujiwara chieftain calm the clergy in the conflict of 1102, would become the head abbot for Kiyomizudera. That this announcement was made at Kōfukuji instead of Kiyomizudera illustrates once again the prerogatives of the main temple in the hierarchy. Two days later several monks from Kiyomizudera approached Munetada, stating that it was customary that the abbot reside at the temple, implying that Jōshin was an outsider. Munetada responded that he needed to confer with the Fujiwara chieftain (Tadazane), who subsequently became the object of concealed threats from some rowdy monks. Tadazane was, however, not moved, causing the Kiyomizudera clergy to resort to a more violent solution, as they attacked Jōshin and his entourage on their approach to the temple from Nara. The Fujiwara chieftain immediately ordered the administrators *(shoshi)* of Kōfukuji, through head abbot Kakushin, to forward the perpetrators, who accordingly were brought to the capital on the sixteenth day of the third month of 1106, to end the conflict.[109] It was a significant dispute for its time, demonstrating how factional politics in Kyoto concretely affected one of the elite temples, forcing the clergy to express itself in a new manner. The subjugation of the Kiyomizudera clergy owed much to the leadership of head abbot Kakushin, confirming the importance of strong ties with the leadership of elite temples such as Kōfukuji. Indeed, Tadazane invited several high-ranking courtiers to his mansion to celebrate a ceremony held in the honor of Kakushin late in the third month of 1106, where he expressed his appreciation for the head abbot, who was not only his own uncle but also the most popular and successful Fujiwara *bettō* to head Kōfukuji.[110]

Conclusion

Protests and conflicts involving temples in the Shirakawa era cannot be understood as isolated events caused exclusively by the clergy but must be seen as part of a larger context. In particular, the progression of these incidents shows that the conditions of rulership and the contemporary balance of power in the capital area determined the setting, development, and outcome of each conflict. Since each elite was expected to control its own estates and retainers, it was only natural that protests against certain policies would be directed at those deemed responsible in the capital. The incident of 1113 between Enryakuji and Kōfukuji provides an unusually clear idea of how this system of "representative justice" worked. Whereas Enryakuji targeted the imperial palace, the Kōfukuji monks directed their protests to the mansion of the Fujiwara chieftain, Tadazane, not because he was the most influential aristocrat at court at the time, but because he was the leader of the clan to which Kōfukuji catered and dedicated their ceremonies. These rules of conduct within the imperial court reflect the most intricate workings in a system where various blocs had both rights and responsibilities in late Heian rulership.

The incidents also mirrored a shift of power within the imperial court, orchestrated by Shirakawa, from the Regent's Line of the Fujiwara to the imperial house. In the early years, before the Kōwa era, covering his reign as emperor and roughly his first fifteen years in retirement, Shirakawa was not particularly influential at court, though he maintained his position as head of the imperial family. Indeed, it was the Fujiwara chieftains who still controlled the noble council and influenced most matters of importance, and even Enryakuji directed some of its protests to the Fujiwara mansion. But Shirakawa was not politically isolated or passive even as he was preoccupied with religious pilgrimages and the construction of temples. These activities were in fact crucial in creating the means by which Shirakawa could build a base of land and increase his control of important religious ceremonies, launching his surge to power later on. In particular, Shirakawa managed to allocate large portfolios of land under the private control of the imperial family through the establishment of a new set of imperial temples headed by monk-princes, favoring Shingon and Tendai monks.

During the later years of his retirement, Shirakawa continued and intensified his efforts to control land, religious rituals, appointments of religious leaders, and promotions of monks with a more distinct favoritism of Shingon. But while thus enhancing the imperial family's direct control of these elements of rulership, he unavoidably faced the opposition of the established religious elites. As shown in this chapter, this opposition was powerful enough to force Shirakawa to reverse his decisions in several cases, even putting limitations on his successful recovery of imperial power. With this background in mind, Shirakawa's lament that "the flow of the Kamo River, the roll of the dice, and the Enryakuji monks are things I cannot control," even if it comes from a thirteenth-century author, holds important meaning.[111] But this quote must be understood in the context of shared rulership. It was not the temples that usurped power from the imperial government, but the retired emperor who encountered resistance when he attempted to shift the balance among the secular and religious elites in his favor. It is evident that temples and monks needed to preserve, not break, the established system, and they consequently did not demonstrate against or oppose the retired emperor himself. Rather, they protested in the capital to defend their religious and political status as well as the favored position of their temple against decisions and policies that threatened those privileges. Shirakawa, however, disrupted the accustomed balance between the different sects and temples through his religious policies, which were aimed at increasing his control of the religious establishment, its private assets, as well as important state-sponsored Buddhist ceremonies. Since Shirakawa needed to displace the Fujiwara to reassert his power, he first targeted Kōfukuji and its control of the Sandai'e—the three most important annual Buddhist ceremonies—favoring both Tendai and Shingon monks in a new set of rituals in Kyoto. However, once he superseded his secular adversaries at court and established the *hōshinnō*, Shirakawa attempted to control Enryakuji as well, heavily favoring Shingon temples and monks under his control.

Shirakawa's attempts to restore imperial power affected not only the Fujiwara family, but virtually all other elites in the capital region. Central proprietors found that their estates could be challenged both by imperial directives aimed at restricting *shōen* and by the retired emperor's retainers, who felt free to take control of whole provinces in the name of the imperial state. The pressure on land multiplied, not only resulting in an increase in disputes over estates and branches between temples but also presenting opportunities for local powers to play the competing elites against one another. In addition, Shirakawa's attempts to manipulate the religious establishment for his own purposes further magnified the competition between different temples, resulting in a dramatic increase in protests as well as in the first wave of battles between them. It became clear to the monks of Enryakuji and Kōfukuji that they had to rely increasingly on their own resources and military strength to protect the temples' status and estates. As the next chapter will show, this trend toward independence and increasing rivalry had progressed even further by the end of the twelfth century.

4

Temples as Allies or Divine Enemies during the Tumultuous Years of Go-Shirakawa (1155–1192)

Scarcely a generation after Shirakawa had dominated court politics, the balance on which that rule was based began to disintegrate. Many large blocs were split into smaller feuding factions, each acting increasingly on its own in the competition for land and offices, making it considerably more difficult for one bloc to govern efficiently. As a result, the three decades following the Hōgen Disturbance of 1156 were plagued by continual struggles within as well as among the most powerful families. This chapter will explore how the elite temples fared during the unruly times when Go-Shirakawa reigned as emperor (1156–1158) and then during the long period of his retirement (1158–1192), when he experienced both supreme success in controlling court politics and frustrating setbacks at the hands of the emerging warrior aristocracy. What role did Enryakuji, Kōfukuji, and Kōyasan play in the political fluctuations of the time? What caused the monks to demonstrate during this era? To what extent were temples active players in the Genpei War? How did the establishment of the warrior government in the Kantō in 1185 affect them?

Two major social and political trends in the late twelfth century caused a marked increase in disturbances and outlawry. On the one hand, there was a slow-moving process in which local warriors increasingly used their military power to expand their own influence at the expense of central proprietors. This trend continued for several centuries until the warrior class neutralized the political power of the old elites in Kyoto in the fifteenth and sixteenth centuries. On the other hand, intrafamilial competition for leadership and supremacy within the great blocs of power was a more fast-moving trend, which became the immediate cause for several violent incidents late in the twelfth century. The developments within the different blocs and dominating families are thus central to the analysis of the role and power of Enryakuji, Kōfukuji, and Kōyasan during this period.

Factionalism and Succession Disputes in Twelfth-Century Kyoto

The consistent efforts of Go-Sanjō and Shirakawa reestablished the head of the imperial family as the governing figure in Japan. But Shirakawa's success and his manipulations to control the future of the imperial line also created new tensions within the ruling family. In particular, a faction formed around Shirakawa's grandson Toba (1105–1156), who was determined not to relinquish his line's claims to the throne. Toba succeeded his father Horikawa as emperor in 1107 at the age of four, making it possible for his grandfather (Shirakawa) to continue his domination of court politics. In 1123 Toba was forced to abdicate in favor of Sutoku,

Figure 7. Imperial genealogy (late *insei* period)
Boldface indicates emperor; italics indicate tenure as retired emperor.
Numbers reflect sequence of emperors according to traditional accounts.

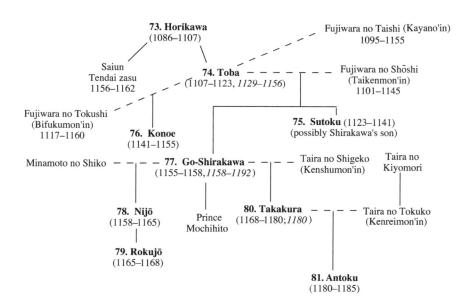

who, though officially recognized as Toba's son, was rumored to be the product of an affair between Shirakawa and Fujiwara no Shōshi (1101–1145), also known as Taikenmon'in (see Figure 7). When Shirakawa died in 1129, Toba returned to power as retired emperor, no less dominant than his predecessor.

As expected, Toba was adamant toward Sutoku, though the latter remained on the throne until Toba forced him to retire in 1141. The new emperor, Konoe, was the son of Toba's favorite consort, Fujiwara no Tokushi (Bifukumon'in). Unfortunately, Konoe was young and frail, and he died in 1155 at the age of sixteen without any descendants, leaving the imperial throne open to a number of candidates, including the son of the disenchanted Sutoku. However, Toba and Bifukumon'in settled on Go-Shirakawa (the legitimate son of Toba and Taikenmon'in) with the intention that he would eventually abdicate in favor of his son, Prince Morihito. Toba died the following year, giving Sutoku an opportunity to renew his line's claim to the throne. This challenge became one of the primary issues of the Hōgen Disturbance of 1156, which was further fueled by an intense and long-standing rivalry within the Fujiwara Regent's Line, following its decreased influence during Shirakawa's rise to power.[1] Fujiwara no Tadazane was only twenty-four years old in 1101 when he became the chieftain of the *sekkanke,* and he had little choice but to serve the older and more powerful Shirakawa at the time. However, the relentless Tadazane broke with Shirakawa and retired to his mansion in Uji in 1122 after a dispute over an arrangement between Toba and one of Tadazane's daughters.[2] After the separation, the retired emperor supported Tadamichi (1097–1164, regent 1121–1158), Tadazane's oldest son, who served as regent and chancellor at court. But Tadazane continued to be active, establishing close ties with Toba and extending his indirect influence within Kōfukuji through the influential monk and warrior leader Shinjitsu.[3] In that process, Tadazane also challenged his oldest son's leadership, thereby creating an important rift within Japan's second most powerful family.

Ironically, this intrafamilial competition seems to have brought the different blocs closer. For example, Toba did little to impede the establishment of new estates as he gathered a substantial number of *shōen* for the imperial family. Consequently, Toba's interests and ambitions coincided more with those of the capital nobles and religious institutions than with those of Shirakawa.

Indeed, during Toba's reign, the *sekkanke* cooperated with the imperial family, and there were considerably fewer and less violent religious protests than during the era of his predecessor. But, at the same time, the conflicting interests of different factions within these great blocs also began to surface, creating new ties of allegiance and new divisions within the court. In particular, Tadazane's return to court politics created an awkward situation, since his son, Tadamichi, was still the chieftain and held the most important offices. Tadazane subsequently supported the career of his second son, Yorinaga (1120–1156), in order to weaken Tadamichi and to reclaim his own position (see Figure 8). The two brothers engaged in a fierce competition to gain support among other courtiers and the imperial family by attempting to make their respective candidates, both adopted daughters, consort for the young Emperor Konoe. The scramble for allies and the maneuvering within the court were complex, but suffice it to say that both candidates became imperial consorts in 1150. More important, however, Tadazane now proceeded to divest Tadamichi of his position as the Fujiwara chieftain, which allowed Toba to elevate Yorinaga to the position of *nairan* (Inspector of Decrees) as a

Figure 8. Genealogy of the *sekkanke* Fujiwara (late *insei* period)

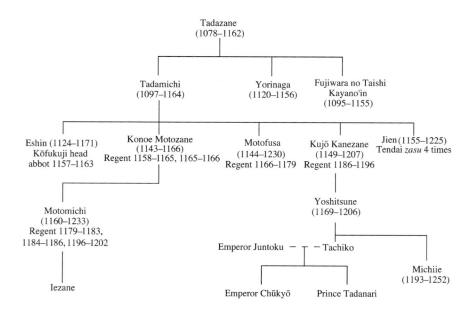

challenge to Tadamichi, who oddly enough managed to remain chancellor *(kanpaku)* until 1158.[4] But Yorinaga's position was precarious, since he relied on his adopted daughter to create a link with the imperial family by having a child with Konoe. The emperor's death in 1155 abruptly put an end to these hopes, and, to make matters worse, Tadazane's own tie with Toba, his daughter Taishi, also died that year. Yorinaga and Tadazane soon fell into disfavor with Toba, forcing them to retire to Uji with slim hopes of returning to power.[5]

Go-Shirakawa's accession in the tenth month of 1155 marked a serious setback to the Sutoku and Tadazane-Yorinaga factions at court, but they were provided with yet another opportunity to regain their power when Toba died on the second day of the seventh month in the first year of the Hōgen era (1156). Only eight days later, Sutoku assembled his personal retainers together with a number of dissatisfied warriors of the Taira and Minamoto clans, including Minamoto no Tameyoshi. That evening, Yorinaga brought his forces to one of Sutoku's villas, where they discussed how to proceed. However, before they were able to put words into action, warriors loyal to Go-Shirakawa attacked and quelled the attempted coup d'état before it had any momentum. In the end, the Hōgen Disturbance resulted in Yorinaga's death, Tadazane's complete and final retirement from capital politics, and the exile of Sutoku to Sanuki Province on the island of Shikoku, where he died in 1167.

Go-Shirakawa remained on the throne following the failed coup, strengthening his position as he became patron for most of the estates confiscated from the plotters. Two of his retainers, the Taira leader Kiyomori (1118–1181) and Fujiwara no Michinori (1106–1159)—the latter better known by his Buddhist name Shinzei—also benefited greatly from the disturbance. But the rewards that these two men obtained also bred envy and dissatisfaction among less appreciated warriors and courtiers who had sided with Go-Shirakawa. Shinzei, a non-*sekkanke* Fujiwara who had served as an adviser to Toba and also had close ties with Go-Shirakawa, augmented his status in particular after 1156.[6] His influence grew even more after Go-Shirakawa's retirement in 1158, causing additional resentment among his peers. Specifically, the opportunistic Shinzei blocked the career of another member of the Fujiwara clan, Nobuyori (1133–1159), who also was the head of the retired emperor's headquarters. In addition, Minamoto no

Yoshitomo, one of the most successful warrior leaders in the Hōgen Disturbance, became increasingly frustrated with Shinzei. Despite his meritorious services, Yoshitomo received few awards after the disturbance, while Taira no Kiyomori, the other prominent warrior leader, was generously rewarded with managerial rights to the confiscated estates. Furthermore, Yoshitomo tried to create a link between himself and Shinzei by offering his daughter to Shinzei's son, but she was rejected in favor of one of Kiyomori's daughters. Disgruntled and determined to improve their positions, Nobuyori and Yoshitomo joined forces and attacked Shinzei's mansion in the last month of 1159. Though Shinzei managed to escape, there was no one in Kyoto to protect him, since Kiyomori was on a pilgrimage to Kumano at the time, and the lay monk was subsequently arrested and executed. Nobuyori then proceeded to staff the court with loyal associates, mostly of the Minamoto clan, but his arrogant behavior seems to have turned some of his allies against him. Kiyomori, who was unable to attack Nobuyori without a mandate from the court, eventually got an opportunity to strike back when two of Nobuyori's disappointed allies convinced Go-Shirakawa to issue an edict condemning the new government. Subsequently, Kiyomori sent his younger brother Yorimori (1131–1186) and his son Shigemori (1137–1179) to attack the imperial palace, where they posted a quick victory (see Taira genealogy in Figure 9). Some of Nobuyori's forces, including the ill-fated Minamoto no Yoshitomo, attempted to retaliate by crushing the Taira headquarters in Rokuhara. They failed, and Yoshitomo escaped to Ōmi Province, where he suffered yet another defeat, and his uncle Yoshitaka was killed by some Enryakuji monks. The incident, known as the Heiji Disturbance (named after the era), eventually ended with the execution of both Nobuyori and Yoshitomo.[7]

By 1160 it was painstakingly clear to Go-Shirakawa that loyal military retainers were crucial to his own position at court. Although the Hōgen and Heiji disturbances eliminated important competing factions, new rivalries emerged to keep the imperial family and the court divided. When Go-Shirakawa retired in 1158 in favor of his son Nijō, he did so with the intention of controlling capital politics just like Shirakawa and his father Toba had done. However, Nijō, an adult at the time of his accession, had plans to rule as well as to reign, and father and son consequently came to head two new factions. Go-Shirakawa allied himself with the retired Fujiwara chieftain (Tadamichi), while Emperor Nijō joined forces with the regent, Chancellor Fujiwara no Motozane (Tadamichi's oldest son). It is in this context of factionalism and an increasing need for military power that Taira no Kiyomori was promoted to ranks unprecedented for any Taira or Minamoto. In return, Kiyomori supported Go-Shirakawa, who managed to sustain his power and a slight advantage over the rival factions. Matters continued to improve for the retired emperor when the reigning Emperor Nijō became ill in 1165, barely managing to put his infant son, Rokujō, on the throne before he died. Then Rokujō died only three years later, all but eliminating any substantial threat from Go-Shirakawa's opponents in the capital. Kiyomori also benefited from the retired emperor's good fortunes, and his position was further enhanced in 1168 when the son of Go-Shirakawa and Taira no Shigeko (Kiyomori's sister-in-law) became Emperor Takakura (see Figure 7 above).

For the next decade Go-Shirakawa and Kiyomori effectively controlled capital politics, but by the end of the 1170s, the Taira chief-

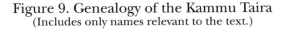

Figure 9. Genealogy of the Kammu Taira
(Includes only names relevant to the text.)

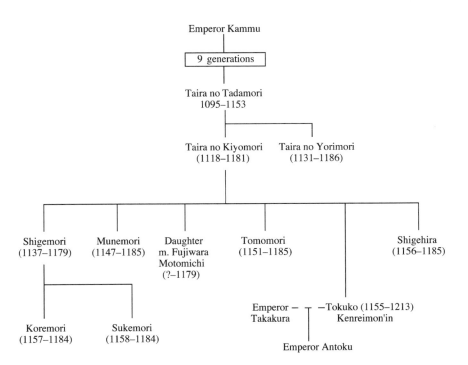

tain, while facing increasing opposition to his upstart career, began
to assert himself even against the retired emperor. In 1177 Kiyomori discovered and quelled a plot (known as the Shishigatani
Affair) against himself involving some of Go-Shirakawa's closest
retainers. Kiyomori did not punish the retired emperor, but the
relationship between the two former associates continued to decline until they became bitter enemies in 1179. In the sixth month
of that year Kiyomori's daughter died, and Go-Shirakawa quickly
proceeded to confiscate land that she had inherited from her
Fujiwara mother. Two months later Kiyomori's oldest son, Shigemori, also died, giving the retired emperor yet another opportunity to decrease land under Taira control as he recalled Shigemori's governorships. In the eleventh month Kiyomori finally
responded, dismissing his opponents at court and placing Go-
Shirakawa under house arrest.[8]

The military might of the Taira leader now overshadowed the
authority of the retired emperor, but Kiyomori failed to see the
benefits of shared rulership as he attempted to replace Go-Shirakawa at the pinnacle of the hierarchy, while excluding all other
elites except for his closest supporters. In other words, Kiyomori
sought to establish an autocracy within the Heian system, outdoing
his competitors primarily through traditional means. Thus, he
made himself the grandfather of an emperor on the twenty-first
day of the second month of 1180, when Antoku, only three years
old, ascended the throne. But three months later the resentment
against the Taira chieftain mounted, and a disenchanted prince,
Mochihito, urged the central elites to assist him in overthrowing
Kiyomori. The prince received only sporadic support in the capital region, and he was killed shortly thereafter. Whereas both
Kōfukuji and Onjōji opposed Kiyomori's usurpation, only Onjōji
took active part in the rebellion at this stage, and it was consequently heavily punished as the temple was completely burned
down by the Taira forces. Yet the resistance in the capital did not
subside, and Kiyomori found it increasingly difficult to govern
under those circumstances. In the sixth month of 1180, he
attempted to isolate his rivals in Kyoto by moving the imperial
court to his Fukuhara estate in neighboring Settsu Province on
the shores of the Inland Sea. Meanwhile, in the eighth month,
Minamoto no Yoritomo, an exiled son of the unfortunate Yoshitomo, declared war on the Taira from his base in the Kantō. But
though the war is named the Genpei War from the Chinese read-

ings of the Minamoto (Genji) and Taira (Heike) surnames, it involved more than the opposition of these two great warrior clans. As Jeffrey Mass has pointed out, it was above all an opportunity for Yoritomo to disengage the east from the rule of the central elites. In addition, the Minamoto-Taira opposition was used as a pretext by other local warriors to increase their local control as well as by disputing members within many provincial families.[9] In fact, Yoritomo did not engage the Taira himself and spent the first three years of the war consolidating his own base in the east, while loosely connected allies and relatives faced the Taira forces.

Changing his strategy from isolation to subjugation of his opponents in the capital region, Kiyomori for his part returned to Kyoto in the twelfth month of 1180, attacking and burning Kōfukuji and Tōdaiji to silence their unruly monks. Kiyomori fell sick shortly thereafter and died in the second month of 1181, never having succeeded at coming to terms with the religious establishment. The Taira kept their grip on the capital area until the middle of 1183, when the uncle (Yukiie) and the cousin (Kiso Yoshinaka) of Yoritomo entered Kyoto as the Taira forces retreated. Yoshinaka soon began to establish a despotic rule of his own in the capital, ignoring Yoritomo's government in the east. Go-Shirakawa, still alive and the foremost figure at the court after the Taira retreat, had not survived the Taira tyranny just to see one dictatorship replaced by another, and he proceeded to sanction Yoritomo's rulership in the Kantō in return for assistance to oust Yoshinaka. Yoritomo sent his younger brother Yoshitsune, who swiftly defeated Yoshinaka and restored peace in Kyoto.[10]

The Genpei War ended in 1185 with a resounding defeat of the Taira forces in a sea battle at Dannoura in the western part of the Inland Sea. But other problems that had surfaced during the war were still threatening the peace and could impede the reestablishment of governmental authority. One issue of concern was the ongoing intrafamilial rivalries that continued to plague many families where headship was worth fighting for. The antagonism that developed between Yoritomo and Yoshitsune at this time is the most famous sibling rivalry in all of Japanese history. Though the reasons for this rivalry are not wholly clear, most scholars agree that it was Yoritomo's envy of Yoshitsune's popularity in the capital that caused the rift. Indeed, Yoritomo probably had good cause to be suspicious, since both Go-Shirakawa and other courtiers supported Yoshitsune in the hopes of neutralizing the older Minamoto. Yoritomo managed to isolate his brother, forcing him to escape from the capital and to travel all the way to northern Honshu in order to find sanctuary with a Fujiwara branch that had refused to acknowledge Yoritomo's rule in the east. The situation proved to be a blessing in disguise for Yoritomo, who eliminated two of his most dangerous enemies in one blow during the Northern Fujiwara Campaign of 1189. A second issue that posed an even more serious problem to stability and order was the local lawlessness and challenge to central authority that had spread during the Genpei War. Though Yoritomo had established his own government in the Kantō in opposition to the central elites, his warrior rule was now recognized, but to maintain his authority, he needed to subdue the trend of which he was originally a part. Most important, the court needed him to control local warriors as well as to protect the interests of the elites in the capital. Yoritomo consequently found himself overwhelmed with petitions against warriors from central landowners shortly after the war's conclusion. But the new government lacked both the legislative and the judicial organs to deal with such a large volume of litigation, causing Yoritomo to support a strengthening of the court's judicial authority and to limit the bakufu's jurisdiction to its own vassals in 1188.[11] Thus was established a polity in which two governments coexisted and cooperated in order to control lawlessness, protect the rights of the elites, and contain local warriors through a system of rewards and obligations.

Go-Shirakawa's era was one of instability and great political change. Since the destiny of the *kenmon* temples depended on the imperial court as well as on general shifts in the balance of power, they could not avoid becoming involved in this movement, and their protests and conflicts thus reflected the political fluctuations. The following discussion traces the rule of Go-Shirakawa from 1155 to 1177 and Kiyomori's rise to power in the capital area and the Genpei War (1177–1185) and then explores the status of the elite temples in the immediate aftermath of the war.

Imperial Rulership and Religious Policies under Go-Shirakawa (1155–1177)

Go-Shirakawa was the main figure in the capital for more than two decades following the Hōgen Disturbance. Though described as cunning and conniving by some historians, he also earned a reputation as a devout Buddhist.[12] Indeed, though both Shirakawa and

Toba were frequent visitors to temples and shrines, their religious activities do not measure up to those of their successor. Go-Shira-kawa favored especially the imperially designated temples headed by Hosshōji, but he also visited the distant Kumano shrine thirty-four times and Hiesha more than thirty times. Enryakuji was honored on six occasions, the high point coming in the fourth month of 1176, when Go-Shirakawa received the Tendai precepts there.[13] Go-Shirakawa's devotion to Buddhism is further emphasized by his active role in the reconstruction of Tōdaiji, which was burned down by Taira troops late in the twelfth month of 1180. However, as Janet Goodwin has pointed out, the retired emperor was more than spiritually motivated when he supported this costly and time-consuming enterprise—it was also intended to augment his own status as a ruler. Go-Shirakawa attempted to portray himself as the ultimate protector of the most prestigious imperial temple, thereby reclaiming authority in a time when imperial rulership had been challenged by the rising warrior class.[14]

Though the retired emperor thus paid much attention to certain religious ceremonies, there is also evidence that he attempted to limit the economic and political power of the most powerful religious centers. Such measures did not reflect a desire to separate religious issues from other secular matters; Go-Shirakawa's primary purpose was to restrict the political power of temples and shrines, not to separate them from the state. Go-Shirakawa's efforts in these matters, in other words, were primarily designed to promote the interests of himself and his retainers. For example, in the intercalary ninth month of 1156, Go-Shirakawa and Shinzei issued an edict containing seven clauses ostensibly to restore order after the Hōgen Disturbance. The articles in this edict pertain in particular to religious institutions, and several of the most notable shrines and temples are specifically named. The edict had two objectives. First, it aimed to restrict the establishment of new *shōen*, in particular through the conversion of public land by religious institutions. As part of this strategy, the governors were ordered to forward records of estates belonging to temples and shrines in their provinces. Second, the edict reminded the main temples and shrines of their responsibility to control their monks and priests as well as their branches in the different regions. The illegal activities of service people *(jinnin)* and the atrocities of "evil monks" *(akusō)*, it was stated, should be reported to the imperial government so they could be punished accordingly.[15]

These clauses give the appearance of restoring order and cur-

tailing rampaging religious riots, but such an interpretation does
not take the historical context into account adequately. It assumes
that the edict was anticipated by an unusually high degree of land
intrusions and lawlessness on the part of temples and shrines, but
the records do not support such a notion. Not only were no religious centers actively involved in the Hōgen Disturbance itself,
the preceding five years were comparatively free of religious disturbances (see Appendix 1). Perhaps the edict is referring to several intertemple conflicts (involving Kōfukuji, Onjōji, Enryakuji,
and Kinpusen of Yamato Province) and three religious demonstrations in Kyoto (two by Kōfukuji and one by Enryakuji) that
took place between 1145 and 1150.[16] But then, why was the edict
issued in 1156, after several years of peace among the religious
institutions? Even if it is assumed that the edict was meant to
restore order and peace in the Kinai at the time, it is still unclear
why it targeted religious institutions. Once again it is necessary to
look at the larger context. A careful examination of Go-Shirakawa's
policies shows that the edict marks the beginning of more aggressive strategies pursued by the then emperor. By restricting the
establishment of new *shōen* as well as seizing recent ones, Go-
Shirakawa not only attempted to stop the carving up of public land
but also found a way of awarding his own retainers who served as
governors and deputies on these lands. The retainers received
revenues from the public fields as well as a mandate to resist the
private ownership of central proprietors. The edict thus indicates
that Go-Shirakawa considered religious institutions to be among
the most powerful and competitive members of that group. In
fact, he did not even mind that the provincial officials were often
prone to use their public offices as a pretext to expand their own
revenues at the expense of absentee proprietors, adding more
pressure to attractive farm land. It is hardly surprising that these
policies were supported by Shinzei, since he, a non-*sekkanke* Fujiwara with few holdings of his own, could only increase his influence at court if Go-Shirakawa's bloc acquired more power.

Go-Shirakawa's land policies were not new; they recall the strategies used by Go-Sanjō and Shirakawa. But his efforts to expand
his control over the established religious centers were different,
attesting to a stronger desire to rule the capital area directly without having to compromise his own position. Already before the
Hōgen Disturbance, in the third month of 1156, Go-Shirakawa
appointed Saiun (Go-Shirakawa's uncle and the son of Horikawa)

as the first imperial prince to head Tendai. This appointment provided Go-Shirakawa with an important link to Enryakuji that could help in bringing the temple under his control. Saiun was of the new type of head abbot, who resided and remained in the capital, shifting the loyalty and the location of the Tendai head closer to the imperial court.[17] The connection with Go-Shirakawa is further emphasized in the creation of Saiun's own administrative headquarters *(shinnō-chō)*, which was headed by Minamoto no Masamichi, an entrusted warrior from Go-Shirakawa's bloc. To extend his influence further, Go-Shirakawa also proclaimed that an imperial edict was required to complete the transfer of personal estates belonging to noble abbots within the Tendai center.[18] Go-Shirakawa was thus especially concerned with controlling Enryakuji in his early years, and Saiun apparently played an important role in accomplishing this goal, as evidenced by an incident that began in the third month of 1158, when reports reached the capital that the Enryakuji clergy had gathered at the Konpon chūdō (the central temple hall) to discuss whether to stage a protest in Kyoto. Though it was unusual for the court to act so quickly, Go-Shirakawa immediately sent Saiun and other leading Tendai figures to Mt. Hiei to calm the monks. Little more is known about this incident except that the Tendai leaders returned to the capital without extracting a promise of peace from the clergy.[19] Nevertheless, the strategy may have worked, since there is no record of a protest in the capital that year. Noteworthy are Go-Shirakawa's unusual attempt to quell a potential protest in the bud and also that the head abbot (the retired emperor's uncle) was used as an imperial messenger.

Go-Shirakawa continued to appoint Tendai head abbots that could be controlled, but it frequently became a lost cause. In 1167, for example, the new *zasu* (Kaishū) was forced to flee to the retired emperor's mansion after having been reappointed without the consent of the two main sections (Tōtō and Saitō) on Mt. Hiei. As a result, a much more popular monk named Myōun, who was to play an important role in Enryakuji's history until the Genpei War, became the new head abbot.[20] Go-Shirakawa's religious policies thus create the distinct impression that he, with the help of his supporters, was attempting to be forceful and determined toward Enryakuji. In particular, there is strong reason to believe, as Adachi Naoya has suggested, that the policy of promoting princely abbots was more than just the appointing of an imperially connected leader as the head of a major religious center; it was also a strategy to control the temple's estates, its important religious ceremonies, and its armed followers. In fact, Enryakuji was not the only temple that was targeted in this way, since an imperial prince was also appointed to head Onjōji at about the same time.[21] Interestingly enough, Go-Shirakawa was more successful in creating a link with Onjōji than with its Tendai sibling.

Whether it was because of his success in controlling the temple or for some other spiritual reason, Go-Shirakawa favored Onjōji over Enryakuji. The most direct expression of this favoritism can be found in later sources, which claim that Go-Shirakawa professed himself to be a disciple of the Onjōji line. But there is also evidence in contemporary sources to support that claim. In 1169, ten years after his retirement, Go-Shirakawa took the tonsure for the first time in a ceremony attended by eight monks—all from Onjōji.[22] It was only in 1176 that the retired emperor received the Tendai precepts at Enryakuji, the sect's main temple. These preferences sent a highly disturbing message to the Enryakuji clergy, indicating, in the worst scenario, that the retired emperor might promote Onjōji as the new Tendai center. Enryakuji therefore kept a watchful eye on promotions and ceremonies that seemed to question its authority within the sect. In particular, the matter of an independent ordination platform for Onjōji, which had been an issue of dispute for over a century, was a sensitive matter to the monks on Mt. Hiei. In other words, though there were differences in ceremonial procedures and rituals, the competition was predominantly political.[23] The Enryakuji monks perceived an independent Onjōji as a vital threat to the temple's privileged status vis-à-vis the imperial court and the Kyoto elites. Indeed, a second Tendai center would have become a challenge to the educational and ceremonial advantages that Enryakuji enjoyed. Undoubtedly, Go-Shirakawa and other leaders in the capital were aware of this situation and realized that an independent Onjōji would weaken the temple complex on Mt. Hiei.

Given the retired emperor's preference for Onjōji and a widespread suspicion against Go-Shirakawa on Mt. Hiei, it is not difficult to understand the protests that were lodged against Go-Shirakawa's plans to attend an initiation ceremony at an Onjōji branch temple in the third month of 1161. The ceremony was to take place at a cloister that was newly built at the Byōdōin in Uji, constructed by the abbot of Onjōji, Gyōkei, whom Go-Shirakawa seems to have considered his most important Buddhist master.[24] Monks from Enryakuji protested against the retired emperor's attending these opening ceremonies, wondering if the ritual was not, in fact, intended to initiate an Onjōji platform. Whatever his true intentions were, Go-Shirakawa felt it necessary to cancel the ceremony as it was originally planned. But he would not tolerate a total defeat, and defying an Enryakuji threat to attack Onjōji, he attended a less auspicious ritual, completing his visit on the seventh and eighth days of the fourth month. The ceremonies were thus completed without incident, and although Go-Shirakawa was upset with the Enryakuji monks' behavior, he did not punish them, since they had, in the end, refrained from carrying out their threat.[25]

Unfortunately, the sources do not reveal whether Go-Shirakawa truly intended to sponsor an Onjōji platform, but additional evidence does suggest that he was determined to promote Onjōji in order to weaken, or even to control, Enryakuji. On the fifth day of the second month of 1162, less than a year after the platform incident, the princely abbot Saiun became ill and wished to retire from his appointment as Tendai head abbot. While the court discussed rejecting his pledge, Saiun died on the sixteenth, at the age of fifty-eight. Saiun had been an important link between Go-Shirakawa and Enryakuji, and the retired emperor now had to find a new ranking monk who would suit his purposes. Go-Shirakawa chose a monk named Kakuchū, who subsequently became *zasu* on the first day of the intercalary second month. This Kakuchū could become yet another Tendai leader loyal to the retired emperor, since he was the son of Fujiwara no Tadamichi—one of Go-Shirakawa's closest supporters. But Kakuchū was also trained at Onjōji, which made the situation untenable with the Enryakuji monks, who had not seen a monk from their sibling monastery head Tendai in nearly a century. Kakuchū was consequently forced to resign after only two days, though Go-Shirakawa compensated for the monk's loss by elevating his monk rank and by making him abbot of the imperially favored Hosshōji three months later.[26]

Though the issue of Kakuchū's appointment did not last for long, the aftermath became considerably more serious. For the second time in a year Go-Shirakawa had attempted to strengthen Onjōji's position vis-à-vis Enryakuji, sending the message that the status and privileges of the clergy on Mt. Hiei were threatened. Accordingly, the monks acted forcefully against Onjōji in the wake of the appointment of Kakuchū. During the protest against him, the monks added to the dispute a doctrinal aspect that became the basis for further Enryakuji petitions. Specifically, the monks argued that since Kakuchū was ordained in Nara according to the rules of the lesser vehicle (Hināyāna), he could not head a temple of the greater vehicle (Mahāyāna). Using the ordination issue as a pretext, the Enryakuji clergy followed up that argument in the third month of 1163 by petitioning the court to prohibit Onjōji monks from being ordained in Nara. The court approved the request in a mere eight days, adding another clause some two weeks later stating that only a monk ordained at Enryakuji's platform could be appointed head abbot of Tendai.[27]

The implications of these edicts should not be overlooked. They gave Enryakuji control of its future leader, while effectively limiting the prospects of independence for its Tendai sibling. Needless to say, the Onjōji monks were dissatisfied, and they seem to have ignored the imperial court's stipulations. Enryakuji petitioned again, and new edicts were issued, requiring that all Onjōji monks now be ordained at Enryakuji's platform. The court even threatened to exclude Onjōji monks from state ceremonies if they did not comply with the ruling.[28] These orders were nothing short of a complete turnaround from Go-Shirakawa's intentions, since they would have shifted the balance immensely in Enryakuji's favor, making it possible for Enryakuji to extend its control over the Onjōji complex itself. Unfortunately, it is unclear why this change came about or what caused it. Perhaps Go-Shirakawa realized that he could not control Enryakuji to the degree that he wished and therefore decided to abandon his plans. In fact, the relationship between the temple and the retired emperor seems to have improved in the years following the incident, but now other powers were dissatisfied with the court's change of heart. The Kōfukuji clergy realized the danger in the advantage Tendai could gain if the court acknowledged Enryakuji's claims to superiority over itself and the other Nara sects. Kōfukuji thus demanded that the Onjōji monks be allowed to be ordained in Nara as well as on Mt. Hiei, but it received no support in Kyoto, as even the Fujiwara chieftain (Konoe Motozane) refused to act on their behalf. As a result, Kōfukuji—the clan temple of the Fujiwara—excommunicated a ranking member of the clan on the twenty-ninth day of the fifth month of 1163.[29]

Shortly thereafter, in the sixth month of 1163, monks from

Onjōji harassed and killed service people of Hiesha who resided in Ōtsu. Enryakuji responded by attacking Onjōji, burning down parts of the temple for the fourth time in less than a century. An imperial edict in the seventh month together with a stationing of government warriors at strategic places in Kyoto seem to have settled the issue, and there were no apparent problems when Go-Shirakawa visited Enryakuji in the fourth month of 1164.[30] However, the relationship between Enryakuji and Kōfukuji was seriously damaged. The doctrinal statements that the Tendai monks had inflicted upon the Nara sects were insulting, but, more important, the claims that Enryakuji's ordination was superior to that of Kōfukuji also had severe implications for the competition for sponsorship and privileges in ceremonies. An antagonistic mood between the two temples was thus developing, leading to a confrontation over religious status that broke out in 1165.

Emperor Nijō died at the age of twenty-three on the twenty-eighth day of the seventh month of that year, shortly after his retirement. During the funeral ceremonies that took place early the following month, high-ranking monks from both Enryakuji and Kōfukuji were among the participants. Inappropriate as it was, a quarrel broke out between them over the seating order during one of the rituals. The quarrel became a brawl, and some monks from Kōfukuji appear to have destroyed a number of Tendai buildings in the capital area.[31] Monks from Enryakuji retaliated within days, attacking and burning Kiyomizudera, Kōfukuji's branch temple in the eastern part of the capital. Not satisfied with that retribution, Enryakuji further demanded that the court punish several Kōfukuji monks as well as a number of government warriors. The sources are all but mute regarding how the court reached a decision, but a verdict was issued against Kōfukuji only a couple of days later. Kōfukuji's former head abbot was demoted, and eight of his followers were exiled together with a prominent warrior, Minamoto no Yoshimoto, who had sided with the monks. In response, the monks in Nara, clearly displeased with the verdict, began to plan an attack on Enryakuji. The Fujiwara chieftain sent a messenger in an attempt to prevent any further violence, but the latter was detained by the enraged clergy. The conflict was settled in the tenth month when Kōfukuji demanded, and eventually was granted, promotion of its leading monks in compensation for the burning of Kiyomizudera.[32]

So far, the readiness of the temples to defend their privileges when changes in the accustomed balance among the different Buddhist sects were imminent resembles that of the era of Shira-kawa. However, the conflicts of the later period were generally more intense, in part as a result of a weakening of the ties be-tween the elite temples and their patrons and in part as a result of increased pressure on land from local warriors. The overall trend is well known among scholars, but the developments that occurred between religious institutions and the other elites are still obscure. For example, Enryakuji's reliance on its bond with the imperial family could no longer be taken for granted, resulting in a more intense competition for patronage among temples and shrines (see Chapter 3). The Fujiwara chieftain's response to the request for assistance from Kōfukuji during the ordination dispute of Onjōji monks in 1163 further attests to this trend; Motozane rep-resented the interests of the court more than those of his own clan temple.

The ties between the religious and secular elites were thus be-coming increasingly temporary and contractual, as noble monks, who virtually monopolized the highest-ranking posts, became the main connections between the blocs. However, there were two inherent weaknesses in this arrangement, which made it difficult to sustain any control through these human linkages. First, it not only lacked a firm institutional basis, it also contradicted accepted customs of selecting leaders within the elite temples. Promotion and appointments to head abbotships were traditionally based on seniority and service within the monastic complex. The placing of noble abbots as leaders of important temples bypassed these cus-toms, while imposing on the comparatively equal monk commu-nity hierarchical rules based on pedigree. Second, most noble monks failed to obtain the necessary trust and support of the gen-eral clergy, since they protected the interests of their noble rela-tives instead of the monastery to which they belonged and that they attempted to lead. For example, in the seventh month of 1163, little more than a month after Kōfukuji opposed Enrya-kuji's increasing control of Tendai and excommunicated the Fuji-wara chieftain, the Hossō sect experienced its own internal breach. The Kōfukuji monks were dissatisfied with the head abbot, Eshin (1124–1171), and, taking matters into their own hands, they drove him out of the temple compound and burned down two buildings within his cloister.[33] As the son of Fujiwara no Tadamichi (see Figure 8), Eshin had benefited greatly from his noble ancestry and rose rapidly among the monks of the Fujiwara clan temple.

However, like so many of his fellow noble clerics, he spent most of his time in Kyoto and took up residence in Nara only in 1157, when he was appointed head abbot at the tender age of thirty-four, bypassing a number of higher-ranking and more experienced monks. Eshin's failure to support the clergy's appeals against Enryakuji and the subsequent refusal of his father, the Fujiwara chieftain, to act on behalf of the Kōfukuji monks must have contributed to their decision to attack Eshin's dwellings. Eshin was, however, far from a hapless young monk. Using his high status and connections in the capital, he commanded a sizable military force. Backed by these retainers, Eshin decided to retaliate against the monks, and, after assembling both warriors and other supporting monks in Kyoto, he confronted some of the Kōfukuji clergy in the capital itself in the eighth month of 1163. Headed by such renowned warriors as Daishōgun (Great General) Minamoto no Yoshimoto and Minamoto no Tadakuni, Eshin's forces attacked the Kōfukuji clergy, which, for its part, put up an impressive defense and managed to fend off the charging forces after three days of fighting.[34]

Eshin and his warriors lost face after this debacle, but he stubbornly refused to accept the defeat, and he sought revenge some four years later. In the middle of the night of the tenth day of the third month of 1167, the former head abbot brought his warriors to Nara and attacked a temple hall and several monk dwellings. This time, the clergy approached the emperor with an appeal to have Eshin severely punished for his acts. The court initially procrastinated, causing the clergy to threaten a protest in the capital with the assistance of the *kami* of Kasuga. The Kōfukuji monks never appeared in Kyoto, since a messenger from the imperial court eventually reassured the clergy that a prompt verdict would be issued against Eshin. But the court continued to delay, and after yet another appeal from the Kōfukuji clergy, an imperial edict sentencing Eshin to exile to a distant province was finally issued on the fifteenth day of the fifth month of 1167. However, Eshin adamantly remained in the capital, spiting both the imperial order and the Nara clergy, which again threatened to stage a protest in the capital if the sentence was not executed. The imperial court subsequently had a *tsuibushi*, an imperial police officer charged with apprehending criminals, send Eshin away to Izu Province, where the monk died in disgrace and shame some three years later.[35]

The weakening of the ties between secular patrons and the

elite temples were part of the general privatization and division of responsibilities of government that took place in the late Heian period. These trends also caused the laws and edicts of the imperial government to lose much of their efficacy, and direct control of land and the ability to defend it consequently became increasingly important for each bloc, leading to a scramble for assets and more intense conflicts. A dispute between Enryakuji and Kōfukuji that occurred in 1173 is indicative of this trend. Early in that year, Kōfukuji raised new toll gates in Yamato Province, where the Hossō center continually had attempted to increase its control. These gates naturally obstructed travel and transports along the established trade routes in Yamato, bothering especially monks from the temple-shrine complex of Tōnomine, who destroyed at least one of them in the fifth month. The destruction may even have been somewhat more extensive, since one source also indicates that the Tōnomine monks ravaged the general area, invading some estates of Kōfukuji in the process.[36] Tōnomine, an old Fujiwara religious site that had become affiliated with Enryakuji by permission of Fujiwara no Michinaga early in the eleventh century, was understandably a source of irritation in otherwise Kōfukuji-dominated Yamato Province. These tensions were intensified during Go-Shirakawa's era, and there were problems between the two centers in 1172, when the Kōfukuji clergy disrupted a Tōnomine festival by burning the residences of its organizers.[37] Kōfukuji and Tōnomine were thus already on bad terms when the latter destroyed one of the new toll gates in Yamato, which helps explain the furious retaliation by Kōfukuji supporters late in the sixth month of 1173, as they charged the complex on several occasions, destroying most of it by fire. The court tried to stop the attacks through the Fujiwara chieftain (Motofusa), who sent messengers to the clan temple, but all efforts were futile as the monks continued to charge Tōnomine even after the Kōfukuji head abbot and other ranking monks were stripped of their offices and ordered exiled, and explicit orders to cease were issued by the court.[38]

The charges eventually subsided, and Motofusa sent a messenger to assess the damages at Tōnomine in the seventh month, while the court discussed sanctions against Kōfukuji. Assurances were made to Enryakuji, which had appealed on behalf of its branch, that punishments were indeed forthcoming and that Kōfukuji monks would not be used in state ceremonies "for a long time." But, strengthened by the support of Tōdaiji, Kōfukuji continued to resist the capital nobles in various ways, refusing to forward the originators and demanding that Enryakuji be punished too. The court's repeated orders that Kōfukuji representatives come to Kyoto to answer for their lack of respect for the court's authority were disregarded as well. Finally, the Hossō monks sent a letter in which they agreed to appear at the court, but they did so in a way that must have seemed most threatening to the capital nobles. In response to the accusation that Kōfukuji had neglected to forward those who had instigated the attack and burned down Tōnomine, the clergy answered that "in regard to the burning of farming residences *(zaike)* and monk dwellings, the instigators are the entire clergy of three thousand monks, and they will, in accordance with the imperial order, *all* come to the capital" (emphasis added). Such threats would have forced the court to be cautious in its dealings with the Nara monks, and the temple thus managed to escape any severe punishment, indicating that the concept of a unique Kōfukuji justice *(Yamashina dōri)* indeed existed.[39]

The Enryakuji clergy had been relatively calm up to this point in the crisis, but in the ninth month there were discussions of an attack on Kōfukuji. In response to this new threat, leading Kōfukuji monks were sent both to the Fujiwara chieftain and to the court, in an effort finally to negotiate the exchange of a few guilty monks for a general pardon. But the talks failed, and the court threatened to exclude Kōfukuji from court rituals in the future, exacerbating the situation even more.[40] By the end of 1173, both Kōfukuji and Enryakuji seemed on the point of going to war. Kōfukuji was slightly more on the defensive, as it, for example, was compelled to order the influential shrine complex of Iwashimizu Hachimangū not to join forces with Enryakuji. However, it received support from Kumanodera a month later, spurring new plans to launch an attack on Mt. Hiei. Meanwhile, the court had exhausted all its powers of prevention, and even the Fujiwara chieftain had little success despite his assumed authority over Kōfukuji. In fact, Motofusa's mansion in Uji was under a spiritual siege, as the monks and servants of Kasuga stationed sacred branches of the *sakaki* tree outside the gates. Though the imperial court sent out government warriors, who managed to impede the protesters from entering the capital itself, the demonstration caused considerable concern among the nobility. At this point, Go-Shirakawa himself decided to step in, making threats that eventually forced the monks on both sides to desist from attacking one another. In particular, the former emperor declared that all *shōen* of both temples would be confiscated and reassigned as public land if any battles were fought. He also confirmed the earlier edict by the Fujiwara chieftain excluding not only Kōfukuji but also Enryakuji from state ceremonies. As a result, Kōfukuji gave up its harsh stance, and its leading monks pledged that those guilty for the initial attack on Tōnomine were not the entire clergy, but rather villainous bands among the clergy, who would indeed be forwarded for punishment. The imperial court subsequently punished only individual monk leaders by confiscating their personal estates, which were added to general holdings of the monastery.[41]

The threat of a major confrontation thus faded as 1173 ended, but the competition in Yamato continued as Kōfukuji targeted Tōnomine on several other occasions during conflicts with Enryakuji. Tōnomine's location in Yamato, not far from Nara, and its historical ties with Kōfukuji made that Enryakuji branch an obvious object of attack at the slightest sign of trouble with its old rival. Kiyomizudera was a similar target for Enryakuji in Kyoto. The burning of Tōnomine in 1173, then, was typical of the passion and the intensification of competition for land of that period. Moreover, the growing importance of military power was becoming evident at the same time that both Kōfukuji and Enryakuji acted more independently. Both the retired emperor and the Fujiwara chieftain were experiencing unheard of problems in containing what were still considered to be important temple allies. Other incidents involving temples and ranking warriors reinforce this impression.

The retired emperor stood at the apex of the "provincial" land system, which paralleled as well as competed with its *shōen* counterpart. He assigned provinces to his most trusted retainers as a way of rewarding them and assuring their loyalty. While defending public land against its transformation into *shōen,* these retainers were often involved in disputes with *shōen* proprietors and patrons. Such problems were, for example, evident in several estates close to Kōyasan, such as Aragawa-no-shō (just south of Mt. Kōya), which was established by Toba in 1129. Intrusions by a local warrior family, the Satō from the neighboring Tanaka estate, soon caused troubles, inducing Toba to have the patron of the Tanaka estate (Fujiwara no Tadamichi) issue an edict prohibiting such acts.[42] The Satō appear to have controlled their aggressions for a while, but new attempts were made to tamper with the borders and incorporate land from Aragawa, now under Toba's consort Bifukumon'in's patronage, not long after Toba's death and the Hōgen Disturbance. The Satō chieftain, Tadakiyo, was joined by the estate managers from another nearby estate, indicating perhaps that these local warriors saw a weakness in the imperial family's ability to defend its proprietorship, a clear expression of warrior challenges to central authority in the twelfth century. In the fifth month of 1159, Go-Shirakawa felt obliged to step in, issuing an edict that again prohibited the intrusions from the two neighboring estates. Apparently, this edict was ignored, and the donation of the estate to Kōyasan two months later, ostensibly to finance the copying of sūtras for Toba's salvation, was undoubtedly made with hopes that the temple would be better able to defend Aragawa and secure some of the rent to Bifukumon'in, who remained the estate's patron.[43] The problems were, however, exacerbated following the appointment of Minamoto no Tamenaga as governor of Kii in 1160, as this warrior leader, serving as a household retainer *(keishi)* of Taira no Kiyomori attached to Kenreimon'in (the Taira chieftain's daughter and the consort of Emperor Takakura), seemed fully intent on reaping immediate benefits from this post. Tamenaga broke the local prohibition against killing animals the next year (1161) by fishing in the river of the Aragawa estate. When Kōyasan monks tried to stop him, Tamenaga responded by leading several hundred warriors into the estate, arresting peasants, confiscating their possessions, and burning their homes. Not to be outdone, the aforementioned Tadakiyo opportunistically entered Aragawa, seizing property for himself in the mountainous border regions between Tanaka and Aragawa.[44] The border dispute subsequently continued between Tadakiyo and Kōyasan's followers in Aragawa, while Tamenaga for his part continued to extract irregular taxes and harass those who resisted, finally inducing Kōyasan to file a complaint through Tōji to the imperial court. As a result, an edict confirming Aragawa and part of the disputed border region to Kōyasan was issued by Regent Konoe Motozane in 1163, which temporarily halted the problems.[45]

Intrusions of the kind incurred by Tamenaga were not an unusual problem for the secular and religious elites in Kyoto, but conflicts involving the Tendai and Hossō centers were of much greater consequence to the capital elites and their factional struggles. Some of the best-known incidents of the entire period featured either Enryakuji or Kōfukuji on the one side and the retired emperor's retainers on the other. These conflicts demonstrate even more vividly how the private ties and personal powers of the elites had replaced most of the bureaucratic apparatus, even as the hierarchical system of the imperial court still provided the basic framework for competition. For example, in the ninth month of 1171, the Fujiwara chieftain (Motofusa) sent one of his retainers to calm the monks of Kōfukuji after hearing rumors that the clergy of the southern capital was planning to enter Kyoto. The reason for the clergy's discontent was the forceful entry of a certain Nobutaka, one of Go-Shirakawa's elite guardsmen, onto a Kōfukuji estate. Using a document of transfer (yuzurijō) from a monk, he attempted to take control of the Sakada estate, forcing his way by killing and harassing some Kōfukuji administrators. The Kōfukuji monks were enraged with the encroachment of Nobutaka, leading them to demand that he be exiled and the estate restored in the temple's name. Go-Shirakawa complied, but only selectively and halfheartedly. He immediately acknowledged that the estate belonged to Kōfukuji but procrastinated on the punishment of his retainer. In fact, the retired emperor seemed to have his doubts about the clergy's claims regarding Nobutaka's crimes on the estate, and he subsequently asked that Kōfukuji forward witnesses in support of the accusations. Apparently, the monks did not expect such a request, since they reacted quite adamantly. "Since ancient times," they stated, "there has not been one single case where witnesses have been forwarded during an appeal from the clergy." The monks further threatened to protest in the capital if the complaint was not addressed, though they also gave the retired emperor time to respond, as they indicated that they would not depart Nara until some two weeks later. Unfortunately, the sources give no indications of how this incident was resolved, but the absence of references to movements by the clergy or to any demotions or punishments of Nobutaka indicate at least that the intrusions stopped.[46]

Two Enryakuji incidents involving the retainers of Go-Shirakawa are also of particular interest, and they deserve to be treated in some detail. The earlier incident, which began in 1169, centered on Fujiwara no Narichika (1137–1177), one of Go-Shirakawa's most entrusted retainers, and the 1176–1177 Hakusanji Incident involved Saikō (Fujiwara no Moromitsu), another of the retired emperor's closest supporters.[47] As is frequently the case, the conflicts first appear in the sources at the point that protests were lodged in the capital. Thus, the Narichika Incident began on the seventeenth day of the twelfth month of 1169 with an appeal from Enryakuji on behalf of its service people in Hirano-no-shō in Owari Province. The monks complained that the deputy governor, Fujiwara no Masatomo, had harassed the people on that estate. But neither the court nor the retired emperor would hear their case, and the messengers were promptly sent back to the mountain.[48] Enryakuji did not take this rejection lightly, and on the twenty-third the monks carried eight portable shrines to Kyōgokuji, a branch temple in the eastern part of the capital. Once the group was assembled there, it proceeded as far as the inner grounds of the imperial palace to protest. The protesters demanded not only that Masatomo be exiled, but also that the governor, Fujiwara no Ienori, as well as Fujiwara no Narichika—the provincial proprietor of Owari—be punished.[49]

Given that Narichika was a retainer of Go-Shirakawa, it was only natural that the retired emperor would need to deal with the protesters. His first concern, however, was to remove the monks from the palace area, and he consequently ordered them to come to his mansion for a meeting. The monks refused, claiming that although Emperor Takakura was only a child (eight years old at the time), they would follow precedent and direct their protest to the imperial palace. But the former emperor was determined to remove the monks, using force if necessary. On the evening of the twenty-third, Go-Shirakawa therefore ordered Taira no Shigemori, Kiyomori's eldest son, to drive the monks away. However, though the order was sent to him three times, Shigemori refused, claiming that he feared the damage the monks might cause the palace in the dark. Shigemori promised to carry out the order the next morning, but the monks had already departed by the time the sun came up, leaving only their holy carts as a reminder to the courtiers of the anger of the gods.[50]

Shigemori's response may have reflected his fear of facing the protesting monks in the dark, but there were also other reasons behind his reluctance. Some scholars have interpreted Shigemori's disobedience as an early indication of a rift between the Taira and Go-Shirakawa. Indeed, Taira no Kiyomori continued to oppose the retired emperor's attempts to quell the Enryakuji monks when new appeals were forwarded against Narichika early in 1170.[51] It is therefore tempting to interpret this opposition, based on what is known about the split almost a decade later, as an attempt by Kiyomori to assert himself over his patron. But such an interpretation would be rash, since it is not supported by other evidence at that time. Rather than opposing his patron, Kiyomori was trying to avoid a confrontation with Enryakuji, since he was in the process, at that juncture, of seeking closer ties with the temple's leadership. Kiyomori's attempt to ally himself with Enryakuji, however, created a conflict of interest between his own ambitions and his status as a retainer of Go-Shirakawa.[52] Without the active support of his most powerful retainer, Go-Shirakawa was unable to calm the monks. Thus, on the day following the protest at the palace, the twenty-fourth day of the twelfth month of 1169, the retired emperor complied with the demands of Enryakuji by exiling Narichika, deposing the governor, and arresting Masatomo. Inasmuch as Go-Shirakawa had in a sense been coerced into making these punishments, he was probably never serious about letting the verdicts stand. Thus Narichika was pardoned four days later to regain his earlier rank two days after that. Instead, head abbot Myōun lost his post as *gojisō* (a monk who performs esoteric ceremonies and prayers for the emperor), and two lower-standing officials (Taira no Tokitada and Fujiwara no Nobunori) were made scapegoats and sent into exile for poor performance and for slandering Narichika during the incident.[53]

There can thus be little doubt that Narichika was a highly valued retainer of Go-Shirakawa, since the latter risked his relations with Enryakuji in order to protect him. As expected, the Enryakuji monks were not happy, and they renewed their demands in a matter of days to have Narichika punished. For a second time, Go-Shirakawa felt compelled to order Narichika into exile (1170/2/6), and on this occasion he was not able to recall him until late in the fourth month.[54] In the end, Go-Shirakawa failed to clear Narichika of responsibility for his actions, but the question of guilt really had very little meaning. What mattered was the status of one's bloc or, more precisely, of one's patron, and that the patron considered the retainer important enough to protect. For Go-Shirakawa, provincial proprietors such as Narichika were the basis of his wealth and power, and they were expected to respond to calls for extraordinary taxes and, in particular, military support. In return, they were offered the kind of protection that was needed in the competition they faced from powerful monastic complexes such as Enryakuji. Taira no Kiyomori was initially just another of those retainers, but as he gradually moved beyond the limitations of his subservient status, he began to seek his own independent ties with Enryakuji.[55]

In the Hakusanji Incident, Go-Shirakawa and Enryakuji were once again the central players, but the influence of Kiyomori had now improved to such a point that his ties with the temple played a crucial role in the conclusion of the incident. In fact, the matter had direct bearings on Kiyomori's own break with the retired emperor and on the Taira coup d'état of a couple of years later. The story begins in 1176, when the monks of Enryakuji lodged a complaint in the capital to have the governor of Kaga Province, Fujiwara no Morotaka, and the deputy—his younger brother Morotsune—exiled for burning residences and stealing from a *shōen* and a smaller branch (named Myōsenji) that belonged to Hakusanji, a branch temple of Enryakuji (see Figure 10).[56] Since no action was taken by the court at that point, the monks demonstrated again on the thirteenth day of the fourth month of the following year. In a wholly familiar pattern, they

Figure 10. The Hakusanji Incident of 1176–1177

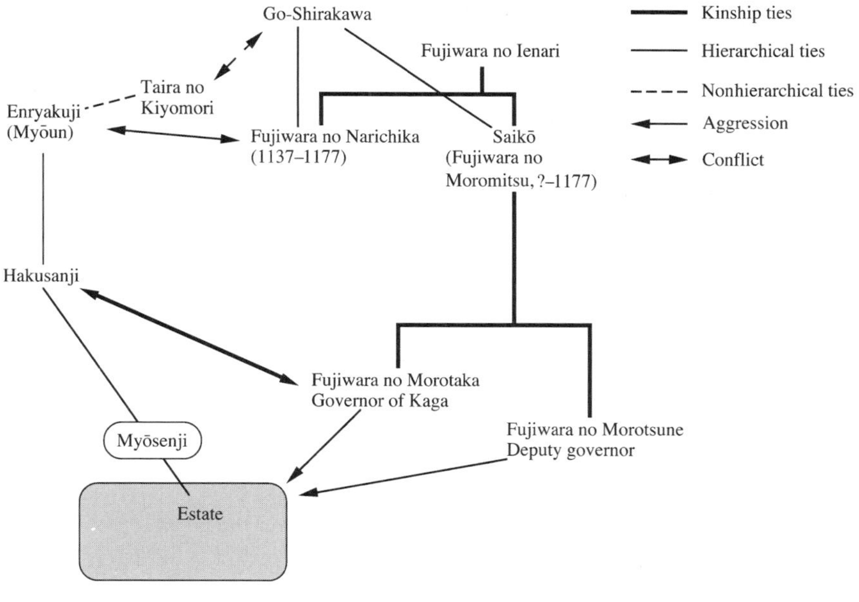

carried six of their portable shrines with them and assembled them at one of their branches in the capital before they proceeded to the imperial palace. This time the group was considerably larger; court diaries mention a total of eight shrines and up to two thousand protesters. Defending warriors confronted the demonstrators, and an exchange of arrows took place in which at least one monk and several service people were killed and two of the holy carts were hit. Both actions were considered highly sacrilegious, and the monks left their shrines in the palace area, escaping to branches of Enryakuji.[57]

Following this skirmish, the situation became exceedingly unruly in Kyoto. Not only did the spiritual threat of the abandoned palanquins trouble the inhabitants, there were also signs of renewed demonstrations by the clergy, as additional portable shrines were prepared on Mt. Hiei. As a result, the retired emperor fled to his mansion at Hōjūji in the southern part of the capital, and there were rumors of riots circulating everywhere in Kyoto. The courtiers' diaries leave little doubt of the panic that was now spreading, and one Fujiwara aristocrat (Sanjō Sanefusa) even noted that the many warriors at the imperial palace and at the retired emperor's mansion reminded him of the Heiji Disturbance. To calm the monks, Go-Shirakawa promised the Tendai head abbot, the increasingly influential Myōun, a verdict as well as punishments of the involved officials, but the monks continued to mobilize when it became clear that the retired emperor was merely trying to stall. Indeed, Go-Shirakawa was undoubtedly reluctant to accommodate Enryakuji's demands. On the seventeenth day of the fourth month, he issued an edict from his headquarters claiming that the area where the dispute had originated was not an estate of Hakusanji but rather public land. Here, in fact, was the essence of the conflict; it was a dispute over land between deputies of a central *shōen* proprietor (Enryakuji) and the retired emperor's retainers, in which the latter were defending the public domain as their private estate. Since the position of Go-Shirakawa lacks corroboration in other sources, one must conclude that the estate in question belonged to Hakusanji and that the former emperor was simply trying to protect his retainers and to avoid giving in to Enryakuji's demands. In short, his strategy was to reverse the tables on Enryakuji, making it the intruder and its monks rebels.[58]

Go-Shirakawa's efforts notwithstanding, Enryakuji's relentless pressure on the court forced the retired emperor to admit that the burning of residences on the Hakusanji estate as well as the shooting of arrows at the shrines were crimes that deserved punishment. Morotaka was consequently exiled on the twentieth day of the fourth month of 1177, and six of Taira no Shigemori's retainers were arrested for shooting at the protesters and the shrines.[59] Though forced to comply with Enryakuji's demands, Go-Shirakawa could not let the temple intimidate him or jeopardize his own status and power. On the fourth day of the fifth month, he struck back by arresting the head abbot, Myōun, for having sided with the monks instead of serving the needs of the court. Myōun was also indicted for the same crime during the preceding Narichika Incident in addition to being accused of having ousted the former *zasu*. This time, the retired emperor moved swiftly and forcefully, excluding Myōun from the monk register, deposing him as head abbot, and confiscating both his private and his public estates (attached to the head abbot office) within a couple of days.[60] A week later, the retired emperor ordered that Myōun be exiled, further angering the Enryakuji monks, who vowed to kill the head abbot rather than let him suffer the humiliation of being exiled. There were different opinions at court over the punishment; some disagreed vehemently with Go-Shirakawa's actions, but most nobles were, above all, amazed at this unprecedented verdict against a Tendai head abbot. Some courtiers washed their hands of the whole episode, stating that the verdict as well as the responsibility for possible repercussions were entirely on the retired emperor's shoulders.[61] But the unusual developments of this incident did not stop there. As Myōun was about to be exiled to Iyo Province on the island of Shikoku, the Enryakuji monks responded with an action that was just as unprecedented as Go-Shirakawa's verdict. On the twenty-third day of the fifth month, they intercepted the group that was escorting Myōun through Ōmi Province, freed their former leader, and carried him to Mt. Hiei. Go-Shirakawa demanded, without effect, that Myōun be handed over, but he also ordered provincial governors to survey the Enryakuji estates in anticipation of confiscating them. As a result, all thirty-nine of Myōun's estates, both those held privately and those he held as abbot at Enryakuji, were confiscated and distributed to Go-Shirakawa's retainers. In addition, the retired emperor met with Kiyomori, who agreed to bring his forces to the area around Mt. Hiei, though the Taira chieftain was clearly reluctant to comply with Go-Shirakawa's order.[62]

Kiyomori and Go-Shirakawa were thus still more allies than opponents at the time of the Hakusanji Incident, though their relationship was now more strained than in the earlier Narichika affair. Kiyomori had risen to unprecedented heights, but he was dissatisfied with the resistance he met from courtiers and other supporters of the retired emperor. Perhaps it was for this reason that he attempted to create his own network of support, aiming to make Enryakuji one of its most important elements. As revealed by the Hakusanji Incident and the riots of some eight years earlier, Kiyomori was unwilling to confront the temple. In particular, he was on close terms with Myōun, whom Kiyomori considered his main Buddhist master.[63] Given these conditions, it is understandable that Kiyomori's own priorities put him in a position opposite to that of Go-Shirakawa and his retainers during the Hakusanji affair. It was to a large extent this opposition that brought about a plot, known as the Shishigatani Incident, against Kiyomori. On the first day of the sixth month of 1177, only two days after he was told to lay siege to Mt. Hiei by Go-Shirakawa, Kiyomori discovered that some of the retired emperor's retainers were conspiring to oust him. The main figures in that plot were the familiar Fujiwara no Narichika and his younger brother, the novice Saikō (Fujiwara no Moromitsu, ?–1177); both were among the retired emperor's most trusted retainers, whose careers were impeded by Kiyomori's aggrandizement.[64] The plotters met at Shishigatani, the villa of the monk Jōken (the son of Shinzei), located in the eastern part of Kyoto, but one of the participants changed his mind and disclosed the conspiracy to Kiyomori. The Taira chieftain acted immediately, capturing and summarily punishing the plotters. Saikō was arrested, tortured, and killed, whereas others were exiled, and Narichika suffered the double punishment of being killed in exile. Kiyomori also executed the previously exiled Fujiwara no Morotaka (involved in the Hakusanji Incident) and some of his relatives, who apparently were involved in the plot too.[65]

Though the Shishigatani plot is best known for its anti-Kiyomori element, it was actually the Hakusanji Incident that led directly to the failed coup. Both incidents saw Kiyomori ranged against Go-Shirakawa's most powerful retainers, with Myōun serving as one of the central figures. Saikō's sons (Morotaka and Morotsune) were behind the intrusions of the Enryakuji estate, which was held by Myōun, and Saikō, who was the provincial proprietor of Kaga, confronted the Enryakuji branch in the area when he attempted to expand his control (see Figure 10). Following the punishment of his sons, Saikō was evidently upset with Myōun as well as with the latter's patron Kiyomori. There is thus reason to credit the account in the *Heike monogatari,* which blames the slander of Saikō for Go-Shirakawa's decision to punish Myōun.[66] Because of the Taira leader's relationship with the Tendai abbot, Saikō may have hoped that the punishment of Myōun would also weaken Kiyomori. Indeed, Kiyomori seems to have taken the attack on the monk very seriously; he listed the exile of Myōun as one of the primary reasons for the execution of Saikō.[67] Conversely, Saikō's motivation for participating in the Shishigatani plot should be seen in the light of his own and Myōun's competing interests in Kaga.

Saikō was joined in the plot by Narichika, who had his own reasons for resenting both Enryakuji and Kiyomori. His career had been blocked by Kiyomori and his son Shigemori, and he had been punished with exile at the hands of the Enryakuji clergy in 1170. There should be no doubt that both the Hakusanji Incident and the Shishigatani Affair were interrelated attempts by Go-Shirakawa's retainers to weaken and eventually to oust Kiyomori. Enryakuji had, through the popular head abbot Myōun, already been drawn, at this stage, into the factional positioning that led to Kiyomori's short dominance of Kyoto and then to the Genpei War. Go-Shirakawa's involvement in these affairs is difficult to assess, even though Saikō was considered the retired emperor's most important retainer at this time.[68] It is, however, clear that the trust between Go-Shirakawa and Kiyomori was now seriously damaged, and the two would never be able to revive their cooperation of more than two decades' standing.

Competing for the Friendship of the *Kenmon* Temples in Times of Instability and War (1177–1185)

Taira no Kiyomori took Buddhist vows in 1168 and is often referred to thereafter simply as the novice *(nyūdō)* Kiyomori. To today's historians, however, he is much better known for his opposition to the elite temples and for the later destruction of Onjōji, Kōfukuji, and Tōdaiji than for his Buddhist piety. By contrast, his adversary,

Minamoto no Yoritomo, is looked upon in a radically different light, owing to his considerable efforts to stay on good terms with individual religious centers in both the Kantō and the central region. In particular, Yoritomo's support of the reconstruction of Tōdaiji has come to stand as the symbol of his religious spirit. However, a closer examination of Kiyomori's career reveals that his confrontation with temples was not a question of spirituality (or a lack thereof). Nor was it really a designed strategy, but rather it was the product of his positioning vis-à-vis the established power structure. In contrast to Yoritomo, Kiyomori was obliged to build his influence within the existing system. He thus expanded his wealth and power by reducing the assets of noble and religious proprietors, thereby alienating himself in the process from the old elites in Kyoto.[69]

Kōfukuji first felt the expanding ambitions of the Taira in 1158, when Kiyomori ordered a land survey in Yamato, which he had received as a proprietary province from Go-Shirakawa following the Hōgen Disturbance. Though the clergy opposed these surveys, it seems that they were indeed performed, damaging the temple's exclusive claims to Yamato.[70] The sources indicate that the tensions between Kiyomori and Kōfukuji continued during the two decades before the outbreak of the Genpei War and the subsequent destruction of the temple at the hands of Taira forces. For example, in the twelfth month of 1172, service people of the Kasuga shrine confronted retainers of Taira no Shigemori (Kiyomori's oldest son) in Iga Province. It is not clear exactly what triggered this conflict, but it escalated into a physical confrontation, where some service people were killed. Kōfukuji subsequently filed an appeal to have the warriors punished, threatening to stage a protest in the capital if no actions were taken against the Taira retainer. The Fujiwara chieftain (Motofusa) managed to delay the monks briefly by sending his messenger to Nara to calm the clergy. However, many Fujiwara nobles were more inclined to support Kōfukuji's case, as indicated by Kujō Kanezane's opinion that there was "righteousness in the clergy's appeal." Since the imperial court and the retired emperor did not respond, the Hossō monks entered the capital a few days later with their divine symbol (the holy *sakaki* branch, or *shinmoku*) as promised, but they were turned back by defending government troops who were dispatched on the streets of Kyoto.[71] Unless the silence of the sources is misleading, this ended the conflict, which thus resulted in a rejection of

Kōfukuji's appeal and Go-Shirakawa's successful protection of his Taira retainers.

In spite of his antagonistic stance against Kōfukuji, it must not be assumed that the Taira chieftain categorically opposed all major religious institutions as some scholars seem to believe.[72] Though involved in a skirmish with Gionsha servants in 1147 early in his career, Kiyomori worked hard and consistently not to threaten Enryakuji, and he cultivated a close relationship with its most popular leader for over a decade. Kiyomori hoped to make Enryakuji a political ally, and his tie with Myōun was apparently crucial to him. The monk had been the master of ceremonies when Kiyomori took the Buddhist vows in 1168. But Myōun was also one of a few carefully selected aristocrats that Kiyomori supported within Kyoto, causing increasing resentment and envy against both himself and his associates. As seen above, his connections with Myōun ranged him against important elements close to Go-Shirakawa, leading, in 1177, to the Shishigatani Affair. Such resistance notwithstanding, Kiyomori never seems to have wavered in his support of the monk. Indeed, only four days after the plot against him was exposed, Kiyomori pardoned Myōun, and later that year he had the monk's confiscated estates returned to him.[73] In fact, even after Kiyomori's death (in 1181) and as the Taira warriors burned down important temples in the capital area, efforts were continually made to court and to stay on good terms with Enryakuji.

Following the Shishigatani Incident, Kiyomori continued his passive support of Enryakuji against Go-Shirakawa in another episode that took place early in 1178. On the twentieth day of the first month, Enryakuji monks acted on rumors that the retired emperor planned to visit Onjōji secretly to sponsor an initiation ritual. Such a ritual, the monks argued, would allow Onjōji an ordination platform, bringing to life again the old issue of Onjōji's independence. The retired emperor told Kiyomori to confront the monks, but he disregarded the order. As a consequence, under threat of Onjōji's being attacked, Go-Shirakawa had little choice but to cancel his visit. The retired emperor partially avenged his defeat in the fifth month by excluding Enryakuji monks from important state-protecting rituals at the imperial palace, but that may have been a small price for Enryakuji to maintain its dominance over the Tendai sect.[74]

At the midpoint of 1178, Kiyomori and Enryakuji were not

only successful in opposing Go-Shirakawa, but there were also possibilities that the nonaggression pact could develop into a more active cooperation. However, changes within the social structure of the temple put an unexpected stop to such a development. Enryakuji's strength during its appeals and protests was such that the whole united clergy, numbering some three thousand monks, plus innumerable service people could place considerable spiritual and physical pressure on the imperial court as well as on competing temples. But as princes and sons of other nobles settled in increasing numbers in designated cloisters, a breach was created that gradually widened between these Heian aristocrats and the rest of the clergy. In particular, two socially distinctive groups, scholar-monks *(gakushō)* and worker-monks *(dōshū)*, became identifiable on Mt. Hiei. The former were almost exclusively of noble birth and focused on reading texts and performing rituals. The latter were responsible for more menial tasks such as maintenance, administration, and military duties. In addition, it seems that many of the most skilled fighters were worker-monks. In theory, the two groups were not mutually exclusive, since it was possible for a commoner to become a scholar-monk after extensive studies. Nonetheless, the *gakushō* were in practice separated from the clergy, since all monks of noble birth, regardless of training, belonged to the more distinguished group and lived in their own quarters.

Such social differentiation appeared within several of the elite temples in the twelfth century and had caused internal conflicts within Kōfukuji already during the era of Shirakawa. Enryakuji retained its unity longer, but the distinction between scholar-monks and worker-monks accelerated during the second half of the twelfth century as the number of aristocratic monks increased. This influx also introduced another new aspect to the temple community. Many nobles provided their sons with financial support, usually estates that were designated as the private possessions of the monk. Contrary to earlier donations that followed aristocrats to the temple, these estates never became temple property, but continued to be controlled by the noble and his descendants. A good case in point is Myōun, whose private and office estates were confiscated by Go-Shirakawa. Such wealth was the basis for the scholar-monks' privileges and luxurious living conditions, which underscored the differences between them and the worker-monks. When Kiyomori attempted to develop closer ties with Enryakuji, he probably assumed that the unity demonstrated by the clergy in past protests would persist and that his liaison with Myōun would be the appropriate link to the entire group. Indeed, given his popularity among the monks on Mt. Hiei, Myōun was clearly the most suitable person to control the Tendai clergy. But, since a divided Enryakuji was not as effective an ally as Kiyomori thought he needed, his hopes were undermined by a dispute between the *gakushō* and the *dōshū* that broke out in 1178. It is not clear exactly what caused this conflict to erupt, and the progression is also hard to discern from the mostly sporadic entries during the more than one year that the dispute lasted.[75] Yet the sources provide sufficient information to outline the overall direction of the conflict.

The first clear indications of a dispute appear on the eighteenth day of the seventh month of 1178, when an edict was issued prohibiting "illegal activities" and fighting on Mt. Hiei. But the fighting apparently continued without interruption, and by the end of the ninth month the worker-monks' superior military power caused the scholar-monks to ask the court for help to stop their adversaries. On the fourth day of the tenth month, Go-Shirakawa ordered Kiyomori to attack the *dōshū*. It is not known if he responded, though it is conceivable, considering his support of Myōun, that he would have sided with the noble scholar-monks and carried out the order. In fact, it appears that the request for assistance was granted, since the *gakushō* were able to reverse the trend and then make more aggressive moves to subdue the worker-monks in the eleventh month.[76] Judging from an absence of further references in the sources, one might assume that the fighting stopped during the first part of 1179. However, the opposing camps confronted each other again on Mt. Hiei in the sixth month in an attempt to settle the dispute once and for all. Both the retired emperor and the courtiers were greatly disturbed, since the fighting was dangerously close to their homes and might involve some of their relatives. Finally, Go-Shirakawa ordered government warriors to attack the *dōshū* again late in the seventh month. To make the attack more efficient, the troops now also cut off all main passages to the mountain, carefully examining anyone traveling in the direction of Enryakuji. But nothing the court did could subjugate the furious monks. The attacks certainly weakened the *dōshū*, but they regained their strength every time the court hesitated to pursue the matter to its conclusion. At last, the

imperial court turned to more drastic measures when it attempted
to destroy the economic foundation of the worker-monks by burning three *shōen* under their control and several of their living
quarters early in the eleventh month of 1179. When this measure
failed as well, messengers were sent to the Enryakuji compound
in an attempt to negotiate or to enforce peace, but they could not
even reach the peak of the mountain. At that point, the scholar-
monks launched a desperate attack to drive out their enemies,
but it proved disastrous, as the battle turned into a devastating
defeat for the *gakushō*.[77]

By the eleventh month of 1179, the situation could hardly have
looked more discouraging for the capital nobles. On the one
hand, their aristocratic peers had just suffered a serious defeat,
and extensive government efforts to quell the worker-monks had
failed. On the other hand, Kiyomori must have shocked most
courtiers when he placed Go-Shirakawa under house arrest, put
his own grandson (Antoku) on the throne, and stripped the Fujiwara chieftain (Motofusa) of the clan headship and sent him and
forty of his retainers into exile, in order to assume the role of
head of state. Kōfukuji's clergy immediately protested against the
unprecedented exile of the Fujiwara chieftain, which was clearly a
retaliation for the latter's involvement in the confiscation of Kiyomori's daughter's estates following her death on the seventeenth
day of the sixth month of 1179. The monks were quite adamant
and would initially not listen to orders from their ranking monks
to stop mobilizing, though the commotion died out on its own
early in the twelfth month.[78] Yet whereas Kiyomori's coup caused
disarray in Nara and at the imperial palace, it also helped to solve
the two-year-long conflict between the *gakushō* and the *dōshū* on
Mt. Hiei. The head abbot Kakukai *shinnō*, who had replaced
Myōun two years earlier, was forced to resign on the tenth day of
the eleventh month because of his failure to control the clergy.
Six days later, Kiyomori had Myōun reappointed Tendai *zasu*, and
the fighting stopped miraculously within days.[79] It is possible that
Kiyomori wished to reestablish his ties with Enryakuji by appointing his monk ally at this point, but it is also likely that Myōun was
simply deemed to be the only one able to handle the monks.
Recall that Myōun had been freed by the monks when he was
about to be exiled earlier, and he was clearly a popular leader
who had a history of standing up for the interests of the temple in
spite of his noble birth. The monk now repaid his patron for his

long-standing support—Myōun's successful control of the clergy
facilitated Kiyomori's goal to govern the capital region. The head
abbot thus managed to achieve peace between the warring groups,
although the division and the differences persisted for some time,
weakening the temple's ability to act forcefully in political matters.

The Genpei War was the first conflict during Japan's ancient
era to reach the scale of a national civil war. Contrary to the incidents of the 1150s (the disturbances of Hōgen and Heiji), religious institutions could not avoid becoming involved in the jockeying leading up to and into the war, since their military strength
and divine power made them either forceful allies or fearful
enemies. Onjōji, which had been favored by Go-Shirakawa earlier,
felt obliged to act on behalf of the retired emperor when he was
put under house arrest by Kiyomori. On the seventeenth day of
the third month of 1180, monks from Onjōji contacted their
colleagues at Kōfukuji and Enryakuji about forming a united
front and retrieving Go-Shirakawa from his palace. Shortly thereafter, in the fourth month, the disenchanted Prince Mochihito
called the country to arms against Kiyomori, but a lack of immediate support in the capital region forced him to go to Onjōji to
escape the Taira troops. Onjōji, with its close ties with both the
retired emperor and the Minamoto in the east, reinvited Enryakuji and Kōfukuji to join the cause against the "tyranny of the
Novice Jōkai" (Kiyomori).[80] The Enryakuji monks did not respond
to the letter containing the overture, but it seems clear that they
were not prone to support Onjōji at that point. The *Heike monogatari* states that the monks were insulted that the letter posited
Enryakuji and Onjōji—the latter merely a branch in their opinion
—as equals. A second reason for their unwillingness to oppose
the Taira, according to the same source, was that Kiyomori made
a substantial bribe of silk.[81] Contemporary sources are vaguer, but
they do indicate that Myōun, perhaps in cooperation with Kiyomori and on the insistence of Regent Motomichi (1160–1233),
prevented the monks from joining Onjōji. Leading monks at
Kōfukuji also received a letter from the Fujiwara chieftain that
same day, telling them in no uncertain terms not to join Onjōji.[82]

Matters unraveled quickly from this point, however, as it became increasingly clear that the Fujiwara chieftain had little effective control of Kōfukuji, which could simply not be convinced to
stop opposing the Taira after more than two decades of conflicting interests in Yamato. In fact, when Motomichi sent his head

administrator (a certain Tadanari) to Nara on the twenty-fifth day
of the fifth month, in order to stop the clergy from rebelling, the
monks captured the messenger, ripped off his clothes, and sent
him in this embarrassing state back to Kyoto. The situation became
even worse in the Kinai the following day, as the Nara clergy
prepared to demonstrate in the capital, while Prince Mochihito
remained at Onjōji calling for a united uprising against the Taira.
In addition, some anti-Taira warriors fled the capital to seek support and protection at Kōfukuji, while other Kinai warriors, such
as Minamoto no Mochimitsu, began to rebel on their own.[83]
Among these menaces, it is clear that the Taira-controlled court
considered Kōfukuji and Onjōji the more serious threats, especially if they joined forces. Fujiwara no Kanezane commented in
his diary:

> Her Highness, the emperor's mother [Kenreimon'in],[84] said:
> "The clergies of both Onjōji and Kōfukuji are planning a rebel-
> lion. This is dangerous for the imperial state (kokka). Perhaps we
> should recall all [their] estates and branch temples?" I answered:
> "Now, this area has become rebellious, and [even though] there
> are imperial decrees [ordering a cease of the hostilities], the situa-
> tion has become very serious. It is too difficult for one person to
> handle, and we should call together the nobles of the imperial
> council quickly."[85]

Following Kanezane's advice, Kenreimon'in summoned the
court nobles, and Kiyomori himself left his mansion in Fukuhara
for the capital immediately. The next day, the twenty-seventh, the
most prominent nobles hurriedly assembled at the mansion of
Retired Emperor Takakura (who had replaced Go-Shirakawa with
the help of Kiyomori in the second month) to discuss what to do
with the insurgent temples as well as with Minamoto no Mochimitsu, who not only was gathering his own troops but also had
allied himself with Onjōji. A lively discussion ensued in which the
courtiers suggested various measures, ranging from attacking
both Kōfukuji and Onjōji and confiscating all their estates to initiating a more detailed investigation of who the rebels within
each complex actually were. In particular, there was considerable
disagreement over the treatment of Kōfukuji. Kanezane's opinion
seems to have reflected the view of most courtiers: "It would be
inappropriate to confiscate the estates and the branches of both
temples, [since] the people responsible for the acts [of treason]

are evil elements of the clergy. But the evil groups should be apprehended."[86]

Kanezane then suggested that a *tsuibushi* be dispatched to arrest the evil monks of Nara, reflecting more leniency toward Kōfukuji, which may have appeared to be less determined in its anti-Taira stance at this stage. In addition, the court seems to have valued the Hossō center more highly than the Miidera complex. An attack on Onjōji would only damage one of the two Tendai centers, whereas destruction of Kōfukuji would endanger the very existence of the entire Hossō sect. As Kanezane put it, "If government troops are sent [to Nara], all its temples and shrines are likely to be destroyed, which undoubtedly would result in the destruction of the entire sect."[87] Though some courtiers disagreed with Kanezane, his suggestions gained enough support to spare Kōfukuji, albeit temporarily, from encountering a punitive force. However, on that same day, the twenty-seventh, Onjōji, which had not received the support it had hoped for (Kōfukuji had initially responded positively, but it had not sent any troops even several weeks after the plea), was attacked and destroyed by Kiyomori's troops, headed by his fourth son, Shigehira.[88]

In contrast to Kōfukuji and Onjōji, which opposed the Taira outright, the leaders of Enryakuji still had much to thank Kiyomori for during the Tendai center's disputes with the retainers of Go-Shirakawa, and they were therefore inclined to support the Taira cause. However, Kiyomori's actions to strengthen his position and to withstand the opposition against him during 1180 also fueled resentment among many members of the clergy on Mt. Hiei. First, when Emperor Takakura abdicated in favor of Kiyomori's grandson (Emperor Antoku), Kiyomori had the new retired sovereign make his first shrine visit to the Heike-affiliated Itsukushima shrine in Aki Province in the third month of 1180. Previous retired emperors had more commonly made their first pilgrimages to Iwashimizu, Kamo, or Kasuga, though there were also some examples of visits to Kumano (Shirakawa) and Hiesha (Go-Shirakawa). The Enryakuji monks seem to have expected Takakura to visit Hiesha, but Kiyomori chose Itsukushima, evoking the resentment of many monks on Mt. Hiei.[89] Second, Kiyomori's move of the court away from Kyoto, in part caused by the resistance from Kōfukuji and Onjōji, to his mansion in Fukuhara early in the sixth month of 1180 was clearly not popular with the Enryakuji monks, who lost much of the direct influence on capital politics that the proximity of Mt. Hiei provided.[90] The location of their temple overlooking the capital from the northeast was a crucial aspect of its privileged status, also making it easy to apply direct pressure, whether spiritual or political. This very power together with Kiyomori's failure to obtain full support from Enryakuji may have contributed to the Taira chieftain's decision to distance the court from Kyoto. Only Myōun, who performed a ritual for Emperor Antoku, was still outright loyal to Kiyomori, while the rest of the clergy was becoming increasingly wary of the Taira leader.

In the end, the move of the capital angered the entire Enryakuji clergy to the extent that they threatened to take over the Kyoto area in the tenth month of 1180 if the court did not return to the Heian capital. Thus, as a consequence of Kiyomori's neglect of Enryakuji come the first indications that its entire clergy was prepared to side with Yoritomo. Retired Emperor Takakura met with ranking monks from Enryakuji and Onjōji to try to discern who the "traitors" were. However, in contrast to Onjōji, Enryakuji was not united in favor of one side; while the head abbot group supported Kiyomori, the worker-monks sided with Yoritomo. To further complicate the situation, and making it impossible for Enryakuji to be a reliable ally and for the Taira court to deal effectively with the entire temple, a third large group consisting mainly of lay members of the Hie shrines was divided between the two camps.[91] If anything, Enryakuji's indetermination favored Taira's opponents. When Taira no Tomomori (1151–1185), one of Kiyomori's sons, beat some Minamoto supporters in Ōmi on the sixth day of the twelfth month of 1180, he also earned the hatred of several monks on Mt. Hiei, since he set fire to peasant dwellings in the region. In fact, the incident prompted some three hundred to four hundred monks of Enryakuji's Mudōji section to join the remaining Onjōji monks in opposing the Taira. Soon thereafter, on the tenth day of the same month, there was a clash between Taira forces and some monks from Mt. Hiei (identified only as sansō, "mountain monks"). These forces were not of spectacular size, but rather consisted of twenty to thirty people on each side. Four Enryakuji supporters lost their lives and ten of the Taira warriors were injured before the monks retreated to seclude themselves either on Mt. Hiei or among their compatriots at Onjōji. The Taira troops thereafter attacked Onjōji in an attempt to get to the rebellious monks and their supporters. A small number of Enryakuji monks escaped into various areas of

Ōmi Province, and the Taira warriors, in an attempt to catch them and to discourage further opposition, again burned down temples, monk halls, and dwellings in the neighborhood of Miidera. This time more men were engaged in the confrontation, resulting in seventy injured Taira warriors. In the meantime, the Kōfukuji clergy, which had maintained its anti-Taira sentiments, was now busy assembling warriors from the temple's estates and branches *(matsuji shōen no bushi wo moyōsu)*, and plans were made to approach the capital together with supporters from the other temples of Nara. On the fourteenth it was reported to the court that the Kōfukuji monks would leave Nara on the sixteenth and enter Kyoto two days later. While accordingly making their intentions known, the Kōfukuji monks boldly asked the imperial court if it really wished for the decline of both the Hossō sect and Buddhism in general.[92]

The combined pressures from Kōfukuji, Tendai opponents, and groups of Minamoto supporters in the provinces of Mino and Ise finally forced the Taira to respond more assertively. After really allying himself with Go-Shirakawa, Kiyomori moved the imperial court back to Kyoto, and Taira forces, under the leadership of Kiyomori's sons, Tomomori and Shigehira (1156–1185), launched an offensive drive in the capital region, directing their attention first to Ōmi Province and Onjōji, which suffered defeat and destruction anew.[93] Then, after much planning and with rumors spreading in the capital of an attack on Nara, Shigehira left Uji to subdue Kōfukuji. Though some courtiers were still apprehensive about sending troops to Nara and were clearly hoping for, perhaps even expecting, a peaceful solution because of the apparent superiority of the Taira forces, Shigehira was now determined to deal the rebellious temples a crippling blow. On the twenty-seventh day of the twelfth month of 1180, he attacked Tōdaiji before turning his attention to Kōfukuji at the end of the day. Both temples were heavily damaged, as several buildings were burned to the ground, causing Kōfukuji monks and their supporters to escape in the direction of Mt. Kasuga, where they sought sanctuary. Even though the Kasuga shrine and the monks seeking refuge there were spared by the Taira troops, other monks were hunted down and killed, and some thirty heads were taken to be put on display in the capital. It is important to note in this context that the Taira attacked Onjōji as well as Kōfukuji and Tōdaiji well before they turned their attention to Minamoto supporters in Owari and Mino, leaving no doubt that these religious centers were considered the most formidable enemies in the area.[94]

The destruction in Nara had a profound impact on the nobles of the imperial court. They had clearly not expected this kind of destruction, and concerns for the future of the imperial state were now greater than ever. Kanezane wrote:

> All seven great temples [in Nara] are completely in ashes. This reflects the decline of both the Buddhist Law and the Imperial Law for the people in this world. I cannot find words, nor can I find the characters to write what I feel. When I hear these things, my heart and soul feel like they have been butchered. . . . I now see the destruction of our [Fujiwara] clan before my eyes. . . . Tōdaiji, Kōfukuji, Enryakuji, and Onjōji: these are our [state's] sects. Both Tendai centers have already been in ashes several times, but when it comes to the temples of Nara, it has never happened before. Because of these things it is evident that these are evil times, undoubtedly an era of decline.[95]

These concerns were, however, not shared by the Taira. In fact, following the destruction, Kiyomori further punished Tōdaiji and Kōfukuji by prohibiting their leading monks from performing court ceremonies, deposing them from public appointments, and ordering Kōfukuji's estates confiscated.[96] By thus adding insult to injury, it appears that the Taira leaders envisioned a rulership without compromising with the leading Buddhist institutions. Based on the strength of the entrenched system of shared rulership at the time and the wisdom of hindsight, one can only conclude that this unwillingness to cooperate with the religious establishment made it impossible to create a lasting Taira polity in central Japan.

The imperial court soon started to plan the reconstruction of both Kōfukuji and Tōdaiji. Reports listing the temples, halls, dwellings, other buildings, and Buddhist images that were destroyed within the compounds were soon forwarded to the court. Perhaps attempting to regain some of their confiscated estates, the Kōfukuji monks also complained that they could not manage such a reconstruction without their *shōen*. The pressures now mounted on the Taira. Kiyomori died after a brief illness early in the intercalary second month of 1181, and Taira no Munemori (1147–1185), the new Taira leader, felt compelled to return the estates to Kōfukuji. In addition, new estates and levies were assigned to the reconstruction by the imperial court in the middle of 1181, effectively reversing the earlier Taira confiscations. The reconstruction of Kōfukuji began on the twentieth day of the sixth month of 1181, and as the temple recovered its assets and began the reconstruction, the Taira family, which had lost its most magnificent leader, saw its star gradually falling.[97]

Because of the exclusion of the Kōfukuji clergy as well as other Nara monks from court ceremonies, Enryakuji monks were awarded the responsibility instead, also receiving the privileges and promotions that usually followed. Yet these rewards benefited mainly high-ranking Tendai monks of noble origin, while other sections of the Enryakuji clergy continued to oppose the Taira. In fact, the split within Enryakuji continued to impede it from taking sides, though there was no lack of effort from both the Taira and the Minamoto to entice the temple to join their respective causes. On the fourteenth day of the sixth month of 1181, a letter from the Kantō arrived at Enryakuji, asking the monks to support Yoritomo, in return for which he promised to confirm all the temple's landholdings in the east in addition to providing extra funding for Tendai services. However, Myōun, who was still the head abbot and loyal to the Taira, got hold of the letter and showed it to a courtier (Fujiwara no Sanesada, 1139–1191) on the Taira side. Myōun's act caused the clergy to stage a rare protest against him despite his widespread popularity, and there were even rumors of riots on Mt. Hiei.[98] The Taira, for their part, had not given up hopes of an amicable relationship with Enryakuji even after the death of Kiyomori early in 1181, and they continued to court Myōun, hoping that it would pay off somehow. On the twenty-ninth day of the twelfth month, he became head of the most important group of imperial temples—known collectively as Rokushōji—as well as of all of their estates.[99] Even Go-Shirakawa, who had been controlled by the Taira for several years, began to look for support from Enryakuji despite his hostile relations with the temple in the late 1170s. In the fourth month of 1182, he met with monks from Enryakuji during a visit to Hiesha, perhaps to work out the details of some new cooperation. The Taira leader, Munemori, heard of the meeting and sent warriors to Sakamoto to bring the retired emperor back to the capital.[100]

The competition for Enryakuji's support became especially fierce as the Minamoto approached the capital under the leadership of Kiso Yoshinaka (Yoritomo's cousin) in the sixth month of

1183. Yoshinaka came from the east by way of Lake Biwa, and he sent a letter to Enryakuji asking for either the monks' active assistance or at least a promise of nonintervention in the anticipated battle with the Taira forces. The monks were willing to support Yoshinaka but saw an opportunity to bargain and therefore asked for funding for Buddhist services and repairs of the holy shrines as well as for confirmation of *shōen* and branch temples.[101] In the meantime, Taira no Munemori, increasingly on the defensive, made a final desperate attempt to win over Enryakuji to his side. He sent a letter stating that Enryakuji would be made the clan temple *(ujidera)* and Hiesha the clan shrine of the Taira, if only the monks would choose to support him.[102] After much discussion, the monks rejected the Taira request, and Yoshinaka was able to climb Mt. Hiei, peacefully, on the thirtieth day of the seventh month of 1183. Though there is no indication that they met, Go-Shirakawa, who had fled the capital to escape the Taira, was also on Mt. Hiei, at the head abbot's residence in the Tōtō section, during Yoshinaka's meeting with the monks. In fact, a great part of the whole *kugyō* council had used Enryakuji as a refuge as the Taira hastily retreated with the infant emperor from the capital on the twenty-fourth day of the seventh month.[103]

As noted, capital politics affected Kōyasan to a much lesser degree than Enryakuji and Kōfukuji, enabling the Shingon monks to remain uncommitted and to focus on serving as a removed retreat while expanding the temple's interests locally. However, the emergence of a Taira polity and the positioning during the Genpei War were issues of much larger proportions that inevitably threatened to change conditions across Japan. Nevertheless, Kōyasan made strenuous efforts to maintain a middle stance, even though the Taira support of various provincial governors, who were prone to expand their own landholdings, was problematic to the temple. In addition, local warriors tended to ally themselves with the Taira to gain more influence against religious proprietors such as Kōyasan. For example, the Yuasa family in the Arida district became a prominent warrior clan during Shirakawa's era. Taira no Kiyomori was away from the capital on a pilgrimage to Kumano in southern Kii during the Heiji Disturbance of 1159–1160, when Kiyomori's associate Shinzei was killed in the capital. Kiyomori only had some fifteen retainers with him, and he was hard pressed to find forces to retake the capital. Fortunately, Yuasa Muneshige—a local warrior leader serving as *zaichō kanjin* (a resident official)—was in the area, and Kiyomori was able to return to Kyoto to beat the rebels Fujiwara no Yorinaga and Minamoto no Yoshitomo with the help of the Yuasa chieftain.[104]

Another interesting case involves Aragawa-no-shō, which had escaped intrusions from its neighbors in Tanaka-no-shō (see Map 5) for fifteen years. However, new problems arose in 1179 when Satō Yoshikiyo (the son of the ambitious Tadakiyo) used his status as one of the retired emperor's personal guards to ignore orders and edicts from the Fujiwara chieftain and to carve out pieces for himself from the Kōyasan estate. Then, in the tenth month of 1179, Taira no Munemori visited Kōyasan, apparently to seek spiritual consolation and advice. His older brother Shigemori had died two months earlier and his wife had passed away the previous year, inducing scholars to conclude that he sought consolation on Mt. Kōya for his losses as he was now put in a position to head the Taira clan at an important juncture. The Kongōbuji monks therefore took the opportunity to approach Munemori about the problems in Aragawa during this pilgrimage. Munemori had some of his administrators examine the situation and even called for both sides to appear at hearings in Kyoto in the fifth and tenth months of 1180. Kōyasan clearly had the stronger case, and the Satō attempted to avoid possible repercussions by not appearing for the second hearing, a common strategy for encroaching warriors. As a result, Munemori issued a verdict in Kōyasan's favor, which stopped Yoshikiyo's intrusions for a short time. However, on the eighteenth day of the fourth month of 1181, Yoshikiyo's younger brother and retainers attacked the southern part of Aragawa, burning residences and killing several inhabitants. Claiming to act on an order from Taira no Shigehira, Koremori, and Sukemori, the intruders continued to raid the estate and steal various objects that appealed to them. The Aragawa peasants fled to nearby mountains and forests but managed to send word to Kōyasan about the atrocities. The clergy contacted Munemori again, and it became clear that the Taira mandate Yoshikiyo's brother claimed to have was a forgery.[105]

Two years later, Yoshikiyo encountered opposition from another local warrior, Bitō Tomoyasu, who had lost his rights in the Tanaka estate after the Heiji Disturbance because of his alliance with Minamoto no Yoshitomo. However, the Bitō family continued to build a local network of retainers, and when Minamoto no Yoshinaka triumphantly entered the capital in 1183, Tomo-

yasu managed to become reinstated as manager of the estate.
Following a confiscation of Heike estates, Yoshinaka also stripped
the Satō family of its offices in Kii late in 1183, promoting Tomoyasu vis-à-vis his competition in Tanaka. The defeat of Yoshinaka
at the hands of Yoritomo's forces (led by his younger brother
Yoshitsune) somewhat surprisingly did not affect Tomoyasu, who
was even rewarded for his anti-Taira stance and confirmed as the
estate manager of the estates in the second month of 1184.[106] It is
interesting that the competition between the Bitō and the Satō,
both distant country cousins of the Fujiwara, took place within
the framework of the Genpei War's factions, proving the need for
central connections and legitimacy even during the chaos of this
nationwide civil war. Kōyasan largely maintained a dual stance
during the positioning and scrambling of the war, but its opposition to local warrior-retainers of the Taira, who appear to have
been the most aggressive ones in Kii, made the temple slightly
amenable toward local Minamoto supporters. In fact, small
numbers of Minamoto supporters escaped to the mountain in the
early stages of the war, remaining outside the control of—and becoming a source of irritation for—the Taira. Yet the temple somehow retained its ties with the Taira chieftain, Munemori, as well,
without actively supporting him during the war, making it possible to solicit edicts against local intrusions by aggressive warriors.

Back in Kyoto, Go-Shirakawa resumed his duties as senior
retired emperor once the Taira were ousted in 1183. However,
since Yoshinaka began to establish his own version of a warrior
government in the capital, the imperial court turned against him
and acknowledged Yoritomo's Kamakura Bakufu nationwide.
Yoshinaka attempted to rally support by asking the Kōfukuji clergy
to join him in attacking his cousin in the Kantō. Meanwhile, Retired Emperor Go-Shirakawa was on the run again, as he sought
protection on Mt. Hiei following a deterioration of relations between himself and Yoshinaka.[107] Then, in the eleventh month of
1183, Go-Shirakawa made a pact with Yoritomo against Yoshinaka,
who, for his part, responded by attacking and arresting the retired
emperor on his return to Kyoto. During the attack on Go-Shirakawa's Hōjūji mansion, several ranking monks from both Enryakuji and Onjōji who had responded to Go-Shirakawa's plea for
help were captured and executed. Among the victims was the
charismatic Myōun, whose leadership of Tendai displayed, perhaps more than in any other case, the political implications of

heading a powerful religious center at this time. It even seemed like Yoshinaka wanted to follow up these executions with an attack on Enryakuji itself, but he settled on appointing a new head abbot, Shungyō, who was born a Minamoto and was loyal to him.[108] The Enryakuji clergy was outraged over Yoshinaka's behavior, and the monks now had few problems in choosing between the feuding Minamoto. Early in the twelfth month of 1183, they mobilized their forces and descended to the capital, where they rioted and proclaimed to the remaining courtiers that the Buddhist Law was indeed in decline. As Yoshinaka reconsidered attacking Enryakuji, while several courtiers tried to convince him not to, the Tendai clergy finally sent a pledge of loyalty to Yoritomo on the twenty-first day of the twelfth month. Less than a month later, troops led by Minamoto no Yoshitsune (Yoritomo's younger brother) and Minamoto no Noriyori defeated Yoshinaka, ending his short rule of Kyoto. Head abbot Shungyō was forced to resign just a few days later, when the clergy drove him off the mountain.[109]

The Taira defeat at the battle of Ichinotani early in the second month of 1184 marked the beginning of the demise of the clan, and they were driven out from the Kinai later that year. Their departure must have caused great joy among most temples and monks in the capital region, considering the clashes that had occurred in the preceding years. The destruction of Kōfukuji and Tōdaiji had caused not only physical damage, but also great concern about the coming of the final age of Buddhism (mappō) among both courtiers and clerics. Reconstruction efforts were already under way in 1184, but the Nara monks were still hungry for retribution. Taira no Shigehira, who had led the forces during the attack on Nara in the twelfth month of 1180, was among those captured after the battle at Ichinotani. He was first sent to Kamakura, but Tōdaiji appealed that he should be punished for his deeds against the temples in Nara. Shigehira was extradited in the sixth month of 1185 and beheaded on the hill of Narazuka overlooking the streaming flow of Kizugawa.[110]

Yoritomo's Religious Policies in Central Japan (1185–1199)

Though the Genpei War itself ended with the defeat of the Taira forces at Dan-no-ura in the third month of 1185, peace was restored in Kyoto the previous year shortly after the battle of Ichinotani. Yoritomo's major concern was to suppress the lawlessness and the disputes that threatened the existence of both the court and his own newly established warrior government. By the tenth month of 1183, during the negotiations with the court against Yoshinaka, he had promised to restore all shrine and temple estates. After having issued edicts against the use of arms by monks (1184/5/2), Yoritomo kept his promise in the seventh month of 1184, when he confirmed all temple holdings in the Kinai area in an attempt to settle matters.[111] Such confirmations as well as Yoritomo's religious policies in general were far from revolutionary but rather were practical measures, designed to establish a working balance among the elites. His intentions notwithstanding, Yoritomo's unfamiliarity with local conditions in central Japan could also be used by ambitious powers to further upset established landholding patterns. For example, Kōyasan had ambitions to strengthen its financial foundations and control on the Kii peninsula, and it attempted to take advantage of the confusion during the war by extending its influence and claims into new areas. Indeed, the Kongōbuji clergy managed to have the Ategawa estate, located just southwest of Mt. Kōya, confirmed in its name under Yoritomo's general confirmations of temple holdings in central Japan on the second day of the seventh month of 1184, even though the estate belonged to Jakurakuji, a branch temple of Hosshōji in Kyoto. Yoritomo did, however, realize his mistake eventually, and he reversed his edict in the first month of 1186.[112]

Yoritomo and his new Kamakura headquarters must have appeared as a form of savior to many Buddhist temples. Contrary to Kiyomori, he was not interested in climbing the ladder of the court aristocracy or in assembling estates at the expense of the traditional landowners. More important, it appeared that Yoritomo was the only leader who could control, or at least slow down, intrusions by local warriors, and he was now willing to enforce and maintain peace and the status quo. As a result, Yoritomo soon became overwhelmed by a large number of complaints from the capital, and realizing that the bakufu did not have the law-making or the judicial apparatus to replace the court completely, he restricted the bakufu's jurisdiction to litigation involving Kamakura vassals, who were placed as managers in confiscated *shōen* and other unruly areas. Since Yoritomo had no ready-made formula to apply to all different areas and in all conditions, he was forced to experiment while making sure he proceeded cautiously. For example, to restore order in the capital area, Yoritomo enforced a wartime tax *(hyōrōmai)* and introduced a network of military stewards *(jitō)* to temple estates in the eleventh month of 1185, but the resistance of several religious centers forced him to exclude temple land from the tax (1186/3) as well as exempt them from some *jitō* appointments (1186/6/21).[113]

The *jitō* appointments thus seemed like a double-edged sword to most temples. On the one hand, local warriors received institutional support for their position, in effect reinforcing their power, while forcing the proprietor to split revenues with one more estate manager. On the other hand, the establishment of the bakufu also meant that proprietors now had an institution with which they could file grievances, whether factual or fabricated, against the troublesome members of the warrior class. Thus, it is hardly surprising that temples opposed *jitō* appointments while in fact appreciating the bakufu for its influence over the warrior class. Ategawa provides an unusually interesting case of such tensions. Yoritomo was now aware of the clergy's strategy of using the chaos to expand Kongōbuji's influence, as evidenced in the intercalary seventh month of 1185, when he commissioned one of his vassals (Ōuchi Masayoshi) to arrest the "evil monks" of Kōyasan. When Yoritomo subsequently reversed his earlier decision, acknowledging Jakurakuji as the proprietor and the Enman'in *monzeki* (of Onjōji) as the patron of Ategawa in 1186, Kōyasan had already sent out two local *shōen* administrators *(gesu)*. In response, Jakurakuji allied itself with the influential warrior-manager Yuasa Muneshige to drive away the Kōyasan intruders. Unfortunately for Jakurakuji, Muneshige remained in the estate after he accomplished his mission, leaving the control of Ategawa in contention. In the ninth month of 1197, the *gesu* office was awarded to Mongaku, a Shingon monk (heading Tōji at the time) who had gained the trust of Yoritomo through Go-Shirakawa, seemingly giving Kōyasan the upper hand in the estate. However, since he had no intention to oversee the estate by himself, Mongaku, who had a son of Muneshige among his disciples, transferred this office to Yuasa Munemitsu—another Muneshige offspring—within a month. Since Munemitsu was also a vassal of the bakufu, the stewardship was soon transferred from that of a *gesu* (under the direct control of the proprietor) to the more prestigious title of *jitō*, exclusively under Kamakura jurisdiction. Needless to say, local members of the warrior class preferred the *jitō* office, as it allowed more freedom vis-à-vis the proprietor, assuming perhaps also that the war-

rior government would support its vassals against the capital
elites.[114] At any rate, Ategawa remained the object of competing
claims by the Yuasa, Jakurakuji, and Kōyasan for most of the thirteenth century (see Figure 11). But it was Kōyasan that benefited
most from the bakufu's involvement, since it did not, contrary to
both Jakurakuji and the Yuasa, have any legitimate claims or any
history on the Ategawa estate.

The monastic complex on Mt. Kōya was also aided by the bakufu
in the highly problematic Aragawa estate. For example, on the
twentieth day of the fifth month of 1186, the temple managed to
obtain an edict from Yoritomo condemning the encroachment of
Aragawa-no-shō by the aforementioned Satō Yoshikiyo, who had
launched an assault anew by bringing tens of retainers together

Figure 11. The struggle for Ategawa

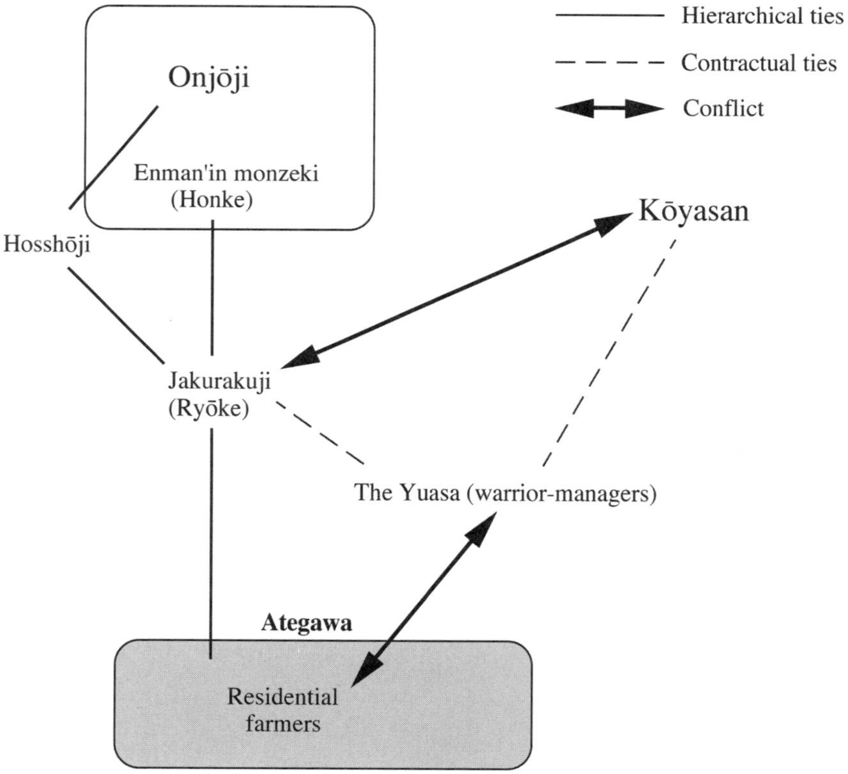

with a fraudulent Kamakura edict in order to override numerous imperial documents that confirmed Kōyasan's legitimate rights to the estate. When the bakufu ruled in Kōyasan's favor, the clergy joyfully promised to support Yoritomo (the bakufu) and pray for a healthy and long life.[115] Kōyasan further benefited indirectly from the bakufu's policies and ambitions, as seen in the case of Ōta-no-shō in Bingo Province. The estates in this province had been controlled by the Taira and were therefore confiscated by Yoritomo, who consequently appointed *jitō* there following the Genpei War. However, when an ambitious warrior (Doi Sanehira) was appointed to the Ōta estate, Go-Shirakawa, who was the patron *(honke),* responded by donating the proprietary rights *(ryōke)* in the fifth month of 1186 to the monk Hanna (?–1207) in support of ceremonies for the Grand Pagoda of Kongōbuji. The retired emperor's commendation of the proprietorship of this large estate was clearly more than just a pious act. Since Kōyasan had received a bakufu edict exempting its Kii estates from *jitō* appointments from the bakufu earlier that year, Go-Shirakawa was simply attempting to exclude the estate from land managers over whom he had no jurisdiction. The measure proved temporarily successful, even though Kōyasan soon encountered its own problems with the local land steward, prompting the bakufu to appoint a *jitō* a decade later.[116]

In short, Kōyasan relied primarily on the traditions of the *kenmon* hierarchy in asserting its privileged rights to estates and exemptions from taxes, but contrary to many of the temples close to the capital, it focused overwhelmingly on extending its local control, laying the foundation for what would eventually become a very powerful and independent complex in Kii by the Ashikaga era. There is thus some merit in the interpretation offered by many Japanese scholars that Kōyasan also had much in common with local landholding *bushi* in its local expansion, even as it benefited from its position as a member of one of the traditional Buddhist elite sects.

For Kōfukuji, the aftermath of the war was mostly a period of recovery and reconstruction. Whereas both the imperial court and the bakufu actively supported the reconstruction of Tōdaiji (Yoritomo visited Tōdaiji on 1195/3 to demonstrate his support), Kōfukuji had to rely almost exclusively on the contributions from the Fujiwara family and their supporters within the court. As a result, the reconstruction progressed slowly, and much of the financing and administration of this enterprise therefore engaged large numbers of Kōfukuji clerics. The complex was rebuilt considerably later than Tōdaiji, carrying over into the early thirteenth century.[117] In addition, Kōfukuji's ability to defend its assets appears to have declined, though the temple began to regain its momentum, as it managed, through several petitions, to have numerous confiscated and lost estates returned in the late 1180s, culminating, eventually, in the exemption of *shugo* (military governor) and *jitō* appointments on a large number of Kōfukuji *shōen*.[118]

Enryakuji's problems with local warriors were similar to those of Kōfukuji and Kōyasan, and it likewise managed to hold its own by appealing to the bakufu, as shown in the temple's confrontation with the powerful Sasaki family in Ōmi Province. On the twenty-ninth day of the third month of 1191, Enryakuji sent representatives to Sasaki-no-shō to collect dues that had not been delivered to the temple. This estate was especially important, since it was designated to support the daily living of many monks on Mt. Hiei, and a famine on top of the mountain had made the situation increasingly desperate, causing the temple to dispatch some ten shrine servants *(gūshi)* to collect rents. Sasaki-no-shō was also the home base of the Sasaki family, whose head, Sadatsuna, was the steward *(gesu)* of the estate, responsible for delivering the rents to the temple, but also a vassal of Yoritomo. It was thus to Sadatsuna's mansion in the estate that the shrine servants proceeded in order to collect the overdue taxes. Sadatsuna was in Kyoto at the time, but his son, Sadashige, received the Enryakuji messengers, who turned both aggressive and rowdy, demanding that the payments be made immediately. Sadashige apparently became enraged and mounted his horse together with a number of retainers, attacking the shrine servants. According to the Enryakuji complaint that was forwarded to the court early in the fourth month, the skirmish resulted in some fatalities and several injuries among the messengers. Enryakuji consequently wanted the court to punish both the father and the son for what is cited as three crimes: failing to deliver the dues, harassing the messengers, and destroying a holy mirror that was carried to the estate.[119]

The court was initially unable to respond to the appeal, since Go-Shirakawa was on a pilgrimage to Kumano. Enryakuji was asked to wait until his return, but the monks were eager to get a swift verdict, and a messenger was sent to the retired emperor's retreat. In addition, since Sadatsuna was a close retainer of Yoritomo, another messenger was sent to the Kantō asking for a verdict against the Sasaki. But as weeks passed without any response, the monks became increasingly impatient, and they proceeded to the capital with their holy shrines late in the fourth month, demanding the death penalty for Sadatsuna and Sadashige. The protesters confronted the palace guard before fleeing, leaving their carts behind. Sadatsuna, for his part, had escaped from the capital ten days before the protest, fearing that the monks would attack him. Following these events, Go-Shirakawa ordered that Sadatsuna and his retainers be arrested so that a punishment could be administered. Yoritomo, who had responded that he would not intervene in the matter since an appeal already had been made to the imperial court, supported the retired emperor's decision. The sentences were strict, ordering Sadatsuna and his three sons into exile as well as the detainment of five retainers. Sadatsuna was exiled to Harima Province (just west of Kyoto), while Sadashige's destination was Tsushima in the strait between Korea and Japan.[120]

Yoritomo's role in this incident is both interesting and surprising. First, the Kamakura chieftain did very little to protect Sadatsuna, even though the latter was one of his closest retainers in the capital area. Yoritomo's visit to the capital in 1190, which was aimed at making peace with Go-Shirakawa, was to a large extent financed by Sadatsuna. More important, it was in part this visit that had kept Sadatsuna from delivering the dues to Enryakuji since much of the funding had come from Sasaki-no-shō. Perhaps Sadatsuna was using these burdens as well as a recent flood as pretexts to withhold the rents, but, in any case, Yoritomo would have been expected to stand up for the vassal who had helped finance his Kyoto visit. Second, while Enryakuji had settled for banishments of the criminals despite its demands for death sentences, Yoritomo himself intervened to have Sadashige killed as he was about to be exiled.[121] Yoritomo's failure to stand up for such an important retainer reinforces the impression that his foremost concerns were peace and stability, and provides further evidence of the Kamakura chieftain's desire to revive the court's authority. Yoritomo also supported a new set of seventeen regulations that repeated earlier admonitions of "evil monks" and of local landholders allying themselves with shrine servants, issued by the court just weeks before the Sasaki conflict developed.[122] There was thus good reason for the Kamakura chieftain to avoid becoming involved, even at the expense of one of his vassals.

There are also indications in the *Azuma kagami* that Yoritomo considered it crucial to be on good terms with Enryakuji in the early 1190s. The chronicle states that Yoritomo provided the Enryakuji messengers with gifts when they arrived in Kamakura to protest early in the fourth month of 1191. In addition, though he refused to hand Sadatsuna over to the monks, he complied with all other demands, and when he sent Kajiwara Kagetoki—one of his most trusted generals—to Kyoto, he even gave Enryakuji half of Sadatsuna's land titles. But such favors were more the exception than the norm, perhaps necessitated by the circumstances, since he was at the time courting the nobles and the retired emperor in Kyoto (which he visited in 1190). Following Go-Shirakawa's death (1192), Yoritomo resorted to a more aggressive policy in the capital (culminating with his failed attempt to make his own daughter a ranking imperial consort), and he in fact pardoned Sadatsuna in a general amnesty in the third month of 1193. Sadatsuna was brought to Kamakura in the tenth month and appointed *shugo* of Ōmi Province, while his estates were simultaneously returned to him.[123] In other words, while the conflict had been resolved in Enryakuji's favor, the Sasaki family was quickly reinstated, even enhancing its position in Ōmi in the long run. These conditions paved the way for continued competition between the Sasaki and the temple for supremacy in the province throughout the thirteenth century.[124]

The issues that involved the Kamakura Bakufu and religious institutions in central Japan focused largely on possession of land, as the local warrior class, over which the Kantō held exclusive jurisdiction, was prone to expand its own territories at the expense of the legitimate proprietors. Since Yoritomo was firmly committed to maintaining peace and the status quo, most verdicts favored the capital elites against such intrusions. Needless to say, these policies gained the bakufu if not outright support, at least widespread acceptance among the elite temples, especially since the bakufu tended not to interject itself in religious disputes. Nevertheless, Enryakuji's extraordinary influence in the capital and its previous anti-Yoritomo stance made the relationship between the Tendai center and Yoritomo precarious, forcing Kamakura to act more aggressively on a few occasions. Moreover, the Minamoto clan had a long history of close ties with Onjōji, which in itself could be enough to make Enryakuji a dangerous enemy. Yoritomo himself counted an Onjōji monk named Hiin as one of his main Buddhist teachers, and another monk from Miidera visited him in Kamakura in 1181. Most important, Onjōji's good standing with the Minamoto leader was further confirmed when it received several estates that were confiscated from the Taira.[125] Many monks on Mt. Hiei, for their part, seem to have been suspicious of Yoritomo, perhaps because they did not know what to expect from him. The situation became especially strained in 1186 when Yoshitsune, now estranged from his brother, hid out at different temples, including Kōfukuji, Tōnomine, and Enryakuji. After having sent a stern warning to all temples in the capital region, Yoritomo dispatched several hundred mounted warriors to Kōfukuji in the ninth month of 1186 in an attempt to capture his younger brother. Some two to three hundred mounted warriors attacked Kōfukuji residences in an attempt to find and arrest Yoshitsune, who was supported by some of the Hossō monks. The clergy canceled both the Hokke (an annual lecture on the Lotus Sūtra) and the Yuima ceremonies in protest, causing great concern among the courtiers.[126] The grief that the Fujiwara chieftain Kanezane expressed in his diary is especially telling: "These matters [the entering of warriors inside the temple] are of the greatest consequences for our state. But I fear that the cancellation of the great lecture meetings is by far the hardest thing to endure for both the temple [Kōfukuji] and the chieftain. Should not the warriors also be made to feel this pain? Should we not raise our voice [in protest]?"[127] There was, however, little Kanezane could do to affect these rustic warriors, who had little or no respect for the old temples. Yet Yoritomo had learned the lesson from Kiyomori's burnings in Nara and wished to avoid an outright confrontation with the elite temples. In fact, a pledge from the imperial court seems to have dissuaded the Kamakura chieftain from attacking Enryakuji when he later heard rumors that Yoshitsune was hiding on Mt. Hiei. Although the temples thus escaped retribution, and there were no violent confrontations between the monastic complexes in the capital and bakufu representatives, Yoritomo's threat (indirectly strengthened by the earlier incident at Kōfukuji) to attack any temple that harbored his brother made it impossible for Yoshitsune to find allies among religious institutions, eventually forcing him to leave the capital region. Only a few monks dared to oppose the Kamakura chieftain, and when Yoshitsune was killed in the final showdown in 1189, two monks from Enryakuji were punished for their association with the younger Minamoto.[128]

In the wake of the elimination of his brother, Yoritomo's main concern was to prevent new disturbances, and, as the court had attempted before him, he wished to restrict the activities of Enryakuji and other temple communities. Though both Kiyomori and Yoshinaka had attempted to make an ally of Enryakuji, Yoritomo never sought to add religious forces to his own army. Thus removing himself from the intense scramble for allies among the capital factions, Yoritomo was the first warrior who was officially authorized by the imperial court to pacify the Tendai center. It was in this policing role that Yoritomo, relying on the combination of his private powers as a warrior leader and the authority of the state, was forced to deal with religious issues that hitherto had been the exclusive business of the court. For example, in the eighth month of 1188, Yoritomo ordered the arrest of a certain Enryakuji monk known as Zenkōbō, accusing him of being the ringleader of a band of thieves that roamed Kyoto.[129] But Yoritomo went even further, using traditional means of dealing with the Tendai center. For example, he hoped to gain some influence over Enryakuji by appointing a head abbot he could trust. Thus, in the third month of 1190, Kōken, who led several opening rituals at temples constructed by Yoritomo, was appointed *zasu,* but he was forced to resign after only a couple of days because of protests from the Enryakuji clergy. Whether it was an oversight on Yoritomo's part or not, it should have been clear that the appointment was destined to fail, since Kōken was an Onjōji monk who had been ordained in Nara.[130]

In a more determined effort, Yoritomo issued a set of regulations in 1188 that targeted the activities of the temple and the shrine communities. Similar regulations had already been issued by Go-Shirakawa and Shinzei, and Yoritomo simply followed this pattern when he prohibited monks from carrying arms and also arrested "evil monks." Supported by the Kamakura chieftain, the court issued several edicts in 1191, which were stricter and more specific in trying to regulate the monks' activities. In particular, to restrict the secular resources of monks and temples, it was stipulated that private land should not be donated to warriors, to shrine service people, or to "evil monks." In addition, a limit was set on the number of servants a monk could have, and there were new regulations regarding their garments, perhaps in order to prevent them from claiming undue authority or upsetting the monk hierarchy, and new prohibitions against monks leaving their temple in order to join forces with warriors.[131] In the end, these edicts had little impact on the lives of the monks in the capital area, and the establishment of a government that was capable of controlling warriors was, contrary to most scholarly assumptions, actually welcomed by the elite temples in the capital region.

Conclusion

This chapter has demonstrated the integral position of temples in the governmental structures of the late twelfth century. In particular, it seems that no ruler of Kyoto could dominate the region without having close ties with or controlling Mt. Hiei. Every time the political balance changed in the capital, Enryakuji became the target of new attempts to secure its support, or at least a promise of nonaggression, by the competing powers. For example, Go-Shirakawa attempted to control not only Enryakuji, but also its Tendai sibling more directly than any imperial head before him. To this end, he appointed princely monks head abbots while making another relative the abbot of Onjōji. Enryakuji's consistent resistance became an issue of great disappointment to the retired emperor, who subsequently attempted to weaken the power of the clergy on Mt. Hiei by favoring Onjōji within Tendai more exclusively. However, without the active support of Kiyomori, Go-Shirakawa could not muster enough political and military power to reduce Enryakuji's status to a position of subjugation.

The relationship between Kiyomori and Enryakuji is especially intriguing, as the Taira chieftain made consistent efforts to make an ally of the temple even as he competed fiercely with other powers in the area. However, he fell short of gaining the temple's support primarily because it lost the ability to act as a united force —caused by an internal division between aristocratic monks and labor monks—at a crucial point in Kiyomori's career. In the end, the social distinctions between scholar-monks and worker-monks may have worked to the temple's advantage, since the rift also divided the clergy over what side to support in the Genpei War, making it a potential ally for any faction. The Taira were severely hampered by the lack of commitment from Enryakuji, which otherwise might have made up for the clan's opposition from Onjōji and Kōfukuji. Most important, by not taking sides, Enryakuji was able to escape active involvement in the fighting as well as its repercussions, should it, by bad luck, have chosen the wrong camp.

Kōyasan maintained a middle stance during the uncertain times of the late twelfth century, much helped by its location away from the capital. Though the temple was not of the same political caliber as its Tendai and Hossō colleagues, it grew in importance during the late twelfth century as it received important land donations from capital nobles and extended its influence in the aftermath of the Genpei War. Remarkably, even when retainers of the Taira attacked Kōyasan estates, there were few indications that the complex would join the Minamoto. Instead, the clergy kept both doors open by simultaneously maintaining a tie with Taira no Munemori and harboring Minamoto supporters in other areas. As a result, Kōyasan managed to obtain land confirmations from both the Taira and the Minamoto chieftains, while maintaining its *kenmon* status through exemptions from war taxes and *jitō* appointments.

Kōfukuji, in contrast, had no choice but to take a strong anti-Taira stance. Kiyomori competed fiercely with several nobles at court, many of whom were members of the Fujiwara family. In addition, Kiyomori subdued two rebellions led by disgruntled Fujiwara leaders in the 1150s. Victory in these incidents also led to new titles for Kiyomori in Yamato, which put him on a collision course with the Fujiwara clan temple. Kōfukuji was thus unthinkable as an ally for Kiyomori, and it became instead an obstacle to his control of land in the capital region. Furthermore, Kiyomori's decision to move the imperial court to Fukuhara, caused in part by Nara's opposition of the Taira aggrandizement, was a poor one, as it failed to quiet Kōfukuji, earning him instead more opponents within the Enryakuji complex. Whereas Kōfukuji suffered physically for its anti-Taira stance, it was ultimately the Taira themselves who were most hampered by the destruction of the temples in Nara. Not only did this destruction fail to subdue the temples as intended, it also turned most courtiers who were uncommitted into opponents of the Taira. The combined opposition of courtiers and temples, on the one hand, and the gods and the buddhas, on the other, was clearly too much for a warrior family, even with noble ancestry, to handle.

The intensification of conflicts involving religious institutions was a consequence of the increased factionalism that took place during Toba's and Go-Shirakawa's eras. But another trend contributed to the way in which such conflicts manifested themselves: a growing distance between religious institutions and their secular allies. There can be little doubt that Enryakuji was perceived as a free agent, as it was solicited by any and all who aspired to control the capital. More important was the weakened tie between Kōfukuji and the Fujiwara. Not only was the Fujiwara chieftain unable to protect the clan temple as he had before, Kōfukuji also used new means of pressure against its ally. The excommunication of the chieftain when he refused to support Kōfukuji's attempt to hinder Enryakuji's domination of Tendai in 1163 marks the first recorded case of such a measure, providing a strong indication of the changed nature of the relationship between secular and religious allies. It was perhaps this growing distance that allowed several mid- and lower-level aristocrats, such as Fujiwara no Narichika, Morotaka, and Shinzei, to rise through the ranks. Heading their own group of retainers, they put pressure on powerful temples and their estates, appropriating some of the disputed assets for themselves in the process. In spite of these structural and social changes, however, the state was still guided by the principles of cooperation, though neither temples nor secular powers could take one another for granted, and ties and alliances thus needed to be confirmed continually through financial and political privileges. In other words, the framework for rulership remained the same even though the links between the main players were more contractual than before.

The methods by which the different elites—the retired emperor, courtiers, and warrior leaders—tried to control and contain the elite temples in the capital region were identical. The most common measure was to control the head abbot either by real kinship ties or by creating ties of allegiance with important monks within the complex. In the case of Enryakuji, such strategies were attempted, without much success, by Go-Shirakawa, Kiyomori, Yoshinaka, as well as Yoritomo. The failed career of Eshin at Kōfukuji provides another particularly telling example of how difficult it was to control the elite temples in the late twelfth century. Only Go-Shirakawa resorted to more extreme measures, as he reversed his policies and promoted other competing temples. In the end, warriors and courtiers alike were working according to the same rules, using similar means, and there were no indications that these procedures changed substantially after 1185. Thus, the establishment of the bakufu represented the institutionalization of the warrior elite within the *kenmon* state, where the warrior government's primary responsibility was to maintain peace and to support the existing system of shared rulership.[132] Since the new warrior regime developed within the existing system, it is not surprising to find that Yoritomo's methods in dealing with the elite temples, land disputes involving religious institutions, or problems with rowdy monks and shrine servants were rather traditional. But to evaluate the true impact of the new warrior government on the elite temples, it is necessary to move deeper into the Kamakura era. The next chapter will show what kinds of issues caused religious disputes and fights later in the thirteenth century, and how the court and the bakufu responded to these challenges.

5

Religious Conflicts and Shared Rulership in the Late Thirteenth Century

The previous two chapters have shown how the ambitions of two retired emperors, while affecting Kōyasan favorably, threatened the political position of Enryakuji and Kōfukuji, causing the clergies to lodge a large number of protests and to confront their respective rivals to maintain the privileges they were accustomed to. Though the establishment of the shogunate in Kamakura changed the composition of the Japanese polity, institutionalizing warrior participation in rulership and marking the beginning of a dual polity, it in fact served to stabilize the balance among the blocs even as the bakufu's influence grew. By the middle of the thirteenth century, the political balance had clearly shifted in favor of the east, as the Kamakura Bakufu, under the control of the Hōjō family, became the dominant power in Japan. Indeed, the warrior government began to assert its influence in areas that it had normally avoided, whereas the court, for its part, became more receptive to direction. For example, Go-Saga structured his private headquarters *(in-no-chō)* as retired emperor (1246–1272) according to the explicit wishes of the bakufu. But it was not the Hōjō's intention to replace the court, and the warrior government's main concern remained as before: to maintain the peace and to avoid new challenges to itself. As this chapter will argue, the capital elites retained much of their power, and though there was an increase in warrior encroachments in the thirteenth century, the *kenmon* temples continued to prosper, even enhancing their influence in some areas. Whereas Kōyasan continued to increase and secure its local control, Kōfukuji and Enryakuji expanded their economic power, owing to a large number of new land donations and increased control of merchant groups in the capital area. Moreover, though Go-Saga is often seen as a puppet of the bakufu, my analysis —based primarily on his relationship with three of the most powerful religious institutions in thirteenth-century Japan—will indicate that he had considerable influence in the capital and that he, not unlike Shirakawa and Go-Shirakawa, also had ambitions to restructure the political balance in Kyoto to his advantage. It was the policies of Go-Saga, not those of Kamakura, that precipitated the heaviest concentration of conflicts involving Enryakuji during these times.[1] A marked increase in forceful protests (gōso) by other temples as well in the capital region provide forceful evidence of Go-Saga's political endeavors and the expanded role of the imperial family compared to the preceding two decades.[2] What issues triggered protests and fighting during the period from the middle to the late thirteenth century, and what were the circumstances behind these conflicts? Given the power of the bakufu at this juncture, to what extent did it influence developments in the religious sphere in the capital region? Since the character of the bakufu and the changes in Kyoto have direct bearing on these issues, it is appropriate to begin with a brief general history.

The Development of Court–Bakufu Rulership

In 1184 Go-Toba—a four-year-old grandson of Go-Shirakawa— became emperor, replacing the young grandson of Kiyomori (Antoku) soon after the Taira had fled Kyoto. Go-Toba abdicated in 1198, only to continue the tradition of ruling as a retired emperor by reasserting his power a few years later. Taking advantage of his public status and his position as patron of what was now the largest bloc of private estates in the realm, he "wielded undisputed judicial power" in the capital region until he challenged and lost to the bakufu in the Jōkyū War of 1221.[3] The bakufu, for its part, gradually matured into a full-fledged government as the Hōjō (the family of Yoritomo's wife) established new political bodies to improve the bureaucratic work and the legal processing in Kamakura. These improvements not only benefited the bakufu itself, but were also designed to promote the interests and strengthen the position of the Hōjō, who consequently became the dominating clan in the east. At the same time, a set of fortunate circumstances, including the failure of the Minamoto line, facilitated their rise. Following Yoritomo's death in 1199, his oldest son, Yoriie (1181–1204), encountered severe problems in main-

taining the Minamoto leadership of the bakufu. In 1203 Yoriie
sided with his wife's family (the Hiki) against his mother (Masako)
and his grandfather (Hōjō Tokimasa) in an attempt to dislodge
the increasingly entrenched Hōjō. But the plot proved fatal to
Yoriie, who was defeated and then killed in a monastery the
following year, while the Hōjō tightened their grip in the Kantō.
Yoriie's younger brother Sanetomo became the next shōgun, but
he was little more than a puppet for the Hōjō leaders, who thus
created their own version of a regency. In fact, it is well known
that Sanetomo preferred the pleasures and the lifestyle of the
capital nobility, a change that his father would not have appreciated. As a result, the Minamoto line came to be all but excluded
from the operations of the bakufu little more than half a decade
after Yoritomo's death.[4]

In 1205 Masako and her younger brother Yoshitoki ousted their
own father, Tokimasa, and proceeded to assume effective control
in Kamakura. Later, in 1219, when Sanetomo was mysteriously
assassinated, Yoshitoki was able to consolidate his family's hegemony further. The Hōjō now could be accused of being usurpers,
which eventually provided Go-Toba with a suitable pretext to
challenge the bakufu, leading to the brief Jōkyū War of 1221. In
reality, the retired emperor was simply unwilling to share his authority with the bakufu, and he therefore tried to exploit what he
assumed was a widespread resentment against the Hōjō. As Jeffrey
Mass has shown, Go-Toba did indeed receive support from a wide
spectrum of the warrior class, but he miscalculated utterly on the
loyalties of the traditional elites. Indeed, the latter were probably
more content with a dual polity of two balanced governments than
with a single dominating nexus of power centered on the retired
emperor. In other words, while the bakufu did not threaten the
rights of proprietorship of the old elites, the retired emperor,
who was the most powerful patron in the *shōen* hierarchy, competed with other nobles, temples, and shrines for control of land.
Moreover, the central elites benefited from the bakufu, which,
soon after its establishment, had proved to be the only authority
that could protect their proprietary rights against the intrusions
of the rising warrior class. It comes as no surprise that most
religious centers in the capital area refused to support Go-Toba's
call for arms against the bakufu in the sixth month of the third
year of the Jōkyū era (1221). Enryakuji was, according to the later
chronicle *Azuma kagami,* one of the few temples that sent forces

to the retired emperor, but even that support was tenuous, as the
temple turned down a later request for additional troops. In fact,
the troops that Enryakuji sent seem to have been mostly a token
of the temple's close ties with the imperial family. As a result of
his failure to rally enough support among the traditional elites,
Go-Toba was quickly defeated only two weeks after the fighting
began.[5]

The bakufu was forced to extend its direct influence after the
Jōkyū War to contain a general outburst of local lawlessness, to
restore peace in Kyoto, and to assure that similar challenges would
not recur. The first step was to disarm the imperial family and to
punish the members that had participated on Go-Toba's side. Consequently, three retired emperors (Go-Toba, Tsuchimikado, and
Juntoku) as well as Emperor Chūkyō were exiled, and the bakufu,
in an unprecedented move, selected the next emperor (Go-Horikawa). The designation of the emperor's father, the monk-prince
Gyōjō, as retired emperor (Go-Takakura) seems even more peculiar, since he had never reigned. The bakufu also decreased the
imperial house's financial base, as many estates that were under
imperial patronage now became the sole possession of their noble
and religious proprietors. Consequently, many already powerful
religious institutions, in particular Kōyasan and Tōdaiji, received
numerous estates, further increasing their wealth and economic
independence. In the end, the imperial family lost its dominating
position, and, in the absence of any single ruling faction, a more
stable balance between the elites in the capital was established.[6]

It goes without saying that the bakufu itself had to grow as it
assumed more responsibility in central Japan. The shogunate's
flexibility and its ability to adjust easily made it possible for the
bakufu leaders to make important changes not only in the aftermath of the war, but continually and on a need basis for several
decades. First, though a bakufu representative had been appointed
in Kyoto earlier, two deputies (Rokuhara tandai) were placed in a
branch office in Rokuhara in the eastern part of the capital in
1221. These deputies were responsible for maintaining the peace
in the capital area, carrying out orders from Kamakura, and adjudicating in disputes in central Japan to relieve the bakufu from
an increasing burden.[7] The Kamakura Bakufu thus gradually expanded its political presence and authority in the Japanese polity,
and the issuance of its first set of laws in the seventh month of
1232 (known as the Jōei shikimoku, or the Goseibai shikimoku)

marks a milestone in that development. It was not a comprehensive law, and it was probably never intended to be more than a
complement to existing laws and practices, since numerous additional laws soon followed, but the bakufu was no longer merely a
military headquarters; it had acquired the characteristics of a
legitimate government.

Simultaneous with this shift of power in favor of the bakufu,
the Hōjō restructured their own clan hierarchy and made adjustments within the warrior government itself. Already the aforementioned Hōjō Yoshitoki had become the first *shikken,* or shogunal regent, in effect uniting the headships of both the Hōjō's
headquarters and the board of retainers *(samurai dokoro).* The
successful tenure of Hōjō Yasutoki (Yoshitoki's son) as *shikken,*
beginning in 1224, marked, in H. Paul Varley's words, "the
coming of age of the bakufu." Indeed, it was during Yasutoki's
leadership that the Hōjō found a working formula to dominate
the bakufu and to maintain their advantage. One important
means was the establishment in 1226 of the *hyōjōshū* (the board of
councilors), which provided the Hōjō leader with a body of judicial bureaucrats and warriors of the Hōjō lineage that could
broaden the base of support for the bakufu's policies. The power
of the imperial house, meanwhile, was severely restricted, but not
to the extent that the bakufu dominated all matters in the capital.
In fact, the issue of imperial succession was essentially handled by
the imperial court for two decades after the accession of Go-Horikawa in 1221. The bakufu only reluctantly responded to a court
request for its approval of the accession of Emperor Shijō when
Go-Horikawa decided to abdicate in 1232.[8] In the absence of
a powerful imperial house and with the bakufu reluctanct to
become too involved, it was two members of the Fujiwara clan—
Saionji Kintsune (1171–1244) and Kujō Michiie (1193–1252)—
who dominated capital politics for three decades.

Throughout much of their careers, Michiie and Kintsune
cooperated in their control of Kyoto. Michiie was born a member
of the Fujiwara Regent's Line, giving him a social and political
edge over Kintsune, who was of an inferior sublineage. The grandson of Kujō Kanezane (1149–1207), who lost favor with Yoritomo
and Go-Shirakawa in 1196, Michiie was raised to restore his lineage
in competition with the Konoe line (see Figure 12). However, the
heritage and expectations of the prestigious Fujiwara leadership
seemed to have weighed heavily on Michiie's shoulders, since he

was constantly preoccupied with restoring the clan's glory, causing him to engage in risky gambles. For example, his connections with the rebelling imperial faction during the Jōkyū War (he was the uncle of Emperor Chūkyō) cost Michiie his appointment as regent *(sesshō)*, and his post was subsequently awarded to Konoe Iezane of the rival lineage. However, Kintsune, whose daughter was married to Michiie, used his connections with the bakufu to help the Kujō chieftain recover. These connections were instrumental in 1226, when Michiie's son, Yoritsune, was formally appointed as shōgun after a seven-year vacancy. Moreover, on the recommendation of Kintsune, Michiie was reinstated as the head of the *sekkanke* two years later, and he subsequently became chancellor *(kanpaku)* for Go-Horikawa.[9]

In traditional fashion, both Michiie and Kintsune used their daughters to create ties with the imperial family. Michiie was particularly successful, as his daughter, Junko, became a consort of Go-Horikawa in 1229, giving birth to a son, the future Emperor Shijō, in the following year. The Fujiwara chieftain thus had good reasons to encourage Go-Horikawa to abdicate, as his grandson might then ascend the throne. With the support of Kintsune and the bakufu, Shijō became emperor in the twelfth month of 1232, and Michiie was once again on top of the aristocratic hierarchy in Kyoto. But the decade that followed proved disappointing for Michiie. In 1233 the mother of Shijō died, and only two years

Figure 12. Fujiwara genealogy for the early thirteenth century

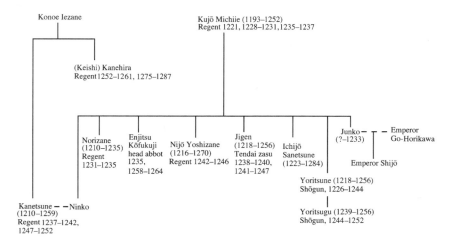

later a son (Norizane, 1210–1235), who had succeeded Michiie as Fujiwara chieftain in 1231, also died. To maintain his family's position, Michiie assumed the headship of the clan for the third time, while continuing to dominate the imperial family by providing relatives as consorts. Even though the reigning emperor was his grandson, Michiie made his eleven-year-old granddaughter the consort for Emperor Shijō in 1241. However, Michiie suffered another setback when the young emperor himself died on the ninth day of the first month of 1242, forcing him to arrange an earlier than anticipated succession. The task proved to be more difficult than most courtiers expected.[10]

The sudden death of Shijō might not have been so significant were he not the last male heir of the bakufu-preferred Go-Takakura line. Both Michiie and Kintsune tried to promote Prince Tadanari, who was the son of Michiie's sister and former emperor Juntoku. However, the bakufu was apprehensive, since Juntoku, who had been involved in the Jōkyū War, was still alive in exile. After more than two months of delay, the bakufu, under Hōjō Yasutoki, finally selected another candidate, Prince Kunito. Kunito's father was Tsuchimikado (reigned 1198–1210), who was also involved in the challenge against the bakufu, though his death in 1231 made his line the least threatening option at the time (see Figure 13). Despite much opposition in Kyoto, the bakufu prevailed, and Prince Kunito became Emperor Go-Saga on the eighteenth day of the third month of 1242.[11]

Michiie's and Kintsune's responses to the accession of Go-Saga were diametrically opposite, bringing their more than two-decade-long cooperation to an end. Kintsune, on the one hand, quickly shifted his support to Go-Saga when it became clear that Juntoku's son would not be approved. Michiie, on the other hand, turned away from court politics, placing his hopes on his son Yoritsune—still the shōgun—to expand the Kujō's influence in the Kantō. In turn, Kintsune moved to improve his and his family's position at the court. His granddaughter became consort to Emperor Go-Saga, and the Saionji thus replaced the Kujō as the main providers of consorts. The informal alliance between the families was completely broken when Kintsune made Michiie's estranged son Yoshizane (who was also the grandson of Kintsune) the regent for Go-Saga in the third month of 1242.[12]

As the ambitious Michiie turned to the east with hopes of gaining control of the bakufu, other developments intruded to create further uncertainty. Hōjō Yasutoki himself died only a few months after Go-Saga's accession, and Tsunetoki, Yasutoki's grandson, became *shikken*. However, the latter could not get along with the shōgun Yoritsune, who had built up considerable status as well as followers of his own after sixteen years in office. To redeem the situation, Tsunetoki forced Yoritsune to resign in 1244 in favor of Yoritsugu, the latter's six-year-old son. But the former shōgun remained in Kamakura and continued to work toward advancing the Kujō family's control over the bakufu.[13] Not long after these developments in Kamakura, Michiie's position in the capital suddenly improved when Kinstune died in the eighth month of 1244. Kintsune had been a loyal supporter of the bakufu throughout his career, and he had functioned as the warrior government's channel of communication with the court. Now, with Kintsune gone, this honor fell to Michiie, whose status received an unexpected boost, and he saw an opportunity to dominate politics in both Kyoto and Kamakura. As part of this plan, he supported Go-Saga's request to abdicate (1246) in favor of the oldest son, even

Figure 13. Imperial genealogy in the Kamakura Age
Boldface indicates emperor; italics indicate tenure as retired emperor.
Numbers reflect sequence of emperors according to traditional accounts.

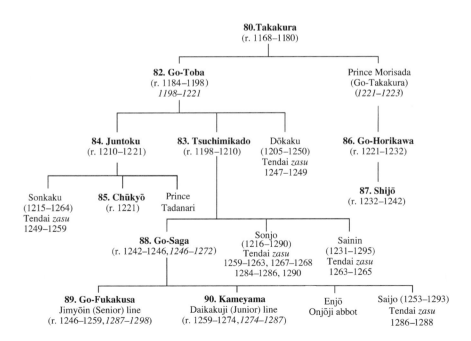

though the new Emperor Go-Fukakusa's mother was the grand-daughter of Kintsune.[14]

Michiie and Yoritsune were provided with another opportunity to improve their family's power when Tsunetoki became ill in the third month of 1246, causing him to pass on the shogunal regency to his nineteen-year-old younger brother Tokiyori. However, the two Kujō seem to have misjudged the latter's determination and level of support, as Tokiyori successfully withstood an uprising led by Yoritsune and dissident members of the Hōjō clan. As a result, Yoritsune was sent back to Kyoto in the seventh month, and the incident marked the end of Kujō power in the two capitals. The prestigious office of liaison officer *(Kantō mōshitsugi)* was transferred from Michiie to Saionji Kintsune's son, Saneuji, who was also the maternal grandfather of Emperor Go-Fukakusa. In addition, Michiie's other son, (Ichijō) Sanetsune, was replaced as the regent by Konoe Kanetsune in 1247 (see Figure 12), effectively ending the Kujō's attempts to monopolize that office.[15]

It is no exaggeration to claim that a new level of bakufu influence was achieved under the *shikken* rule of Hōjō Tokiyori. The Hōjō family council *(yoriai)* now came into its own, and the defeat of the Miura vassal house in 1247 underlined the new stature of the shogunal regent. According to most scholars, Tokiyori's influence was just as complete in Kyoto, making Go-Saga the puppet of the warrior government. Cameron Hurst, for example, writes that the "regent in Kamakura, Tokiyori, had thus reduced to the status of puppets all authority figures in the two capitals, including the ex-emperor, emperor, imperial regent, and shōgun."[16] In truth, Go-Saga had been enthroned by the Kamakura Bakufu, and his abdication in favor of his four-year-old son Go-Fukakusa in 1246 had required the consent of the warrior government. Moreover, Go-Saga agreed to establish a council on the model of the *hyōjōshū* in Kamakura to be staffed with members of the high nobility. Yet there is a second side to this debate, since Go-Saga operated without the intervention of the bakufu in many important areas. For example, it was he who commonly made religious appointments, and he also issued orders *(inzen)* pertaining to land from his private headquarters.[17] Above all, Go-Saga attempted to establish a closer relationship with important religious institutions by reviving the pre-Jōkyū custom of imperial pilgrimages to places such as Enryakuji, Iwashimizu Hachimangū, and Kōyasan. Thus, the era was one of successful partnership between the court and the bakufu, and of "a partial revival," to use Jeffrey Mass' words, of the imperial family.[18] Indeed, this relationship was con-firmed and strengthened in 1252, when the retired emperor's son, Prince Munetaka, became the first member of the imperial family to become shōgun. The dual polity had reached mature form. Seven years later, Go-Saga obtained the endorsement of the bakufu to force Go-Fukakusa to abdicate in favor of another son (Kameyama), though he never had a chance to arrange the succession for the next generation. Go-Saga himself died in 1272, and the bakufu, now under Tokiyori's son Tokimune, consulted with the empress dowager and initially supported the line of Kameyama, who abdicated two years later in favor of his own son Go-Uda. But when Go-Fukakusa brought his grievance to the bakufu in 1275, it shifted its preference to the other line. The well-known division of the imperial family ensued from this point, with consequences that would carry into the next century.[19]

Though the *insei* of Go-Saga was thus momentous in many ways, it has been neglected in deference to the bakufu and warrior power. When scholars have bothered to comment on Go-Saga, they have normally done little more than to characterize his rule as peaceful and stable, owing to his complacent attitude toward Kamakura. But there is more to this era than just that, because renewed demonstrations by Enryakuji and several attempts by leading figures in Kyoto to control the temple probably were that age's most prominent developments. Kōfukuji was also involved in severe confrontations and conflicts, characterized in particular by increasing problems between the main clergy and the high-ranking monks who represented the interests of the Kyoto nobility more than those of the temple. The Shingon complex on Mt. Kōya, less affected by capital politics, continued to focus its efforts on defending its interests against the increasingly ambitious local warrior class. A closer examination of the conflicts involving these temples and the context in which they occurred will provide important clues in understanding the religious policies of Go-Saga, the social trends, and the political structures of the era.

Religious Leadership and Court Rule in the Thirteenth Century

As the Buddhist clergy at the largest institutions gained more independence from their patrons in the thirteenth century, it became increasingly difficult for the imperial court and its noble members to control or to obtain the support of the *kenmon* temples. Yet the Buddhist establishment remained a vital part of rulership, and the secular elites still sought to extend their influence into the religious realm through traditional means, using in particular the office of head abbot, who they hoped could gain the respect of the clergy through his noble ancestry and status. However, two developments that had begun a century earlier made that strategy inefficient. On the one hand, the clergy was more diverse and the monks had developed loyalties among themselves that could not be controlled easily from above. Thus, the body of monks had, in a manner of speaking, come to live and prosper on its own without the guidance of the head. On the other hand, high-ranking monks, for their part, considered the head abbotship mainly a career opportunity outside the court hierarchy and a lucrative source of income. The aristocratic clergy lived close to their peers in the capital and enjoyed, in spite of their monastic status, a lifestyle that was no different from their secular siblings.

These trends notwithstanding, the members of the imperial court expected the head abbots to control their monks and to serve the interests of the court successfully. One might wonder why the secular capital elites did not notice how difficult it was to live up to these expectations, especially since there are examples of noble head abbots who had failed already in the twelfth century. The Kōfukuji head abbot Eshin in the late 1100s stands out for his failures to control and become accepted by his clergy, while Enryakuji's Myōun, who was deposed and sentenced to exile by Go-Shirakawa for his failure to perform for the court, provides an example at the other end of the spectrum. However, the problems associated with such expectations may be highlighted by the perspective of hindsight, and there were, in fact, noble abbots who managed to exert considerable influence within their monastic complexes, providing enough encouragement that a strategically placed relative or supporter could enhance the bloc's power. Thus, by Go-Saga's time, the expectations regarding the head abbots remained, though the estrangement of the sect leaders from the main body of monks had progressed even further, making such hopes more difficult to realize. This trend is evident on Mt. Hiei as early as 1238, four years before Go-Saga became emperor.

On the first day of the third month of that year, a mere twenty-

year-old monk named Jigen became Tendai head abbot *(zasu)*.
Not only was such a young head abbot unprecedented, but Jigen
also had surpassed several senior monks, including his own teacher
(the prince-monk Dōkaku) and the master of his ordination ceremony (Jiken). The selection of Jigen can only be explained by his
pedigree; he was the brother of shōgun Yoritsune and thus was
backed in the capital by his father Kujō Michiie and his grandfather Saionji Kintsune. Enryakuji held enough importance in
the mid–thirteenth century to induce Kyoto's two most powerful
courtiers actively to extend their control of the monastic complex
and its resources. However, although he was the leader of Enryakuji, Jigen spent most of his time in Kyoto performing important
ceremonies both in his role as the official head of Tendai and
more privately for his personal supporters. Whereas such duties
were performed in a grand manner, giving him prestige among
his noble peers, the young monk was less successful in controlling
the Enryakuji clergy. In fact, in the ninth month of 1239, he announced that he wanted to resign because he had failed to stop
the monks from carrying the seven sacred palanquins of Hiesha
to the main temple to prepare a forceful protest. Though Jigen's
initial request was declined, he was eventually allowed to resign in
the eighth month of 1240.[20]

Jigen was replaced by one of his masters, Jiken, but the new
head abbot became ill shortly after his appointment and resigned
within six months. Jigen was subsequently reappointed on the
seventeenth day of the first month of 1241, this time keeping his
position for six years. On the whole, it appears that he was on
better terms with the clergy during his second tenure, though Jigen
was also now kept exceedingly occupied with ceremonies in Kyoto.
For example, on Emperor Shijō's death early in 1242, Michiie
had Jigen perform a Tendai ritual that was believed to prevent
disaster for the imperial family.[21] The beneficiaries of Jigen's
prayers and services were primarily the imperial family, Michiie,
and Kintsune, further demonstrating that his position was indeed
well regarded in the capital. There is also evidence that Jigen himself saw the head abbotship as something more than an economic
privilege and a religious post. When his brother Sanetsune was
deposed as chieftain of the *sekkanke* by the bakufu early in 1247,
Jigen strategically announced, after an important ceremony at
the imperial palace, that he wished to resign. Even though both
the court and the Enryakuji clergy wanted the *zasu* to remain, they

could not convince the bakufu to accommodate Jigen, primarily because the issue had little direct bearing on the Kantō, and the resignation of the young monk was consequently accepted.[22] Using the head abbotship as a way of putting pressure on the secular authorities was not unique to Jigen, but the connection between the desire to resign and other political events was rarely as clear-cut as in this case. Unfortunately, the sources are not as informative about the reasons behind another request to resign that Jigen made some six years earlier, on the twenty-fifth day of the seventh month of 1241, although it may have been related to a bout of illness.[23]

Jigen's tenure reveals the continued political importance of the Tendai head abbotship in the mid–thirteenth century, and it is hardly surprising that there were extensive discussions at court regarding the selection of Jigen's successor. There seems to have been general agreement that the next head abbot should be an imperial prince, but the court had problems in choosing between two candidates, and it therefore sought the advice of the Kantō. Though the bakufu favored a third candidate, Dōkaku (1205–1250), it had some doubts about this monk, since he was a son of the rebellious Go-Toba (see Figure 13). Finally, after a two-month delay, the warrior government concluded that Dōkaku, who had never shown political tendencies, would be harmless, and he was consequently named the eightieth *zasu* of Tendai on the twenty-fifth day of the third month of 1247.[24]

Following the Kujō family's failure and Tokiyori's victories in 1246–1247, the resignation of Jigen can only be seen as the logical conclusion of the decline of the Kujō. Moreover, whereas Tokiyori tightened Hōjō's grip in Kamakura, Go-Saga saw an opportunity to reassert himself not only in Kyoto but also in Nara. Kōfukuji was undoubtedly the most powerful monastery in the southern capital, and the decline of *sekkanke* power in the mid-1240s made it possible for Go-Saga to expand his influence over the Fujiwara clan temple. It was the retired emperor, not the Fujiwara chieftain, who stepped in to protect the aristocratic abbots as conflicts between the lower echelons of the clergy and their masters within Kōfukuji suddenly increased in scope and intensity. For example, following a confrontation in 1246, Go-Saga issued an edict *(inzen)* to quell the lower clergy and to have the originators arrested and punished.[25] The retired emperor was forced to act again on behalf of Kōfukuji's ranking monks in

1248, this time by sending his own head administrator *(in-no-bettō)* to Nara to calm the monks.[26] Though Go-Saga appeared genuinely troubled by the disturbances in the southern capital, he also used them to widen his influence over Nara's most powerful monastic center at the expense of the Fujiwara.

Go-Saga's expansive ambitions are, however, most obvious in the case of Enryakuji, where the imperial family had been all but absent for more than two decades following the Jōkyū War. Indeed, the former emperor became the primary mover in issues that concerned the temple, using the princely head abbot who had replaced Jigen. In the fifth month of 1247, only two months after Dōkaku became *zasu,* Go-Saga called him to his palace several times to discuss an internal Enryakuji dispute between some monks and a shrine official. A police captain was sent out to arrest the monks, but one of them (a certain Shunpan) escaped, causing the retired emperor to order the head abbot to confiscate the monk's estates. Later, an appeal was sent to Go-Saga from the monks of the Mudōji in the Yokawa section, claiming that the shrine official in question had violated Hiesha by arbitrarily using the sacred treasures of the shrine. As a result, the retired emperor agreed to pardon Shunpan after other high-ranking monks had vouched for him.[27] Though conflicts between individuals from different religious centers were commonly handled by the court, it was, especially considering the inactivity of the imperial house in the preceding two decades, unusual for the retired emperor to act so forcefully and so directly in an internal Enryakuji issue that seems to have caused very little disturbance in the capital. But Go-Saga's political ambitions necessitated more direct control of the powerful complexes in central Japan, inducing him to proceed more aggressively in addressing both Kōfukuji's and Enryakuji's internal affairs. His actions the following year in the early stages of another dispute further support that impression.

Early in the eighth month of 1248, the retired emperor received a report from Mt. Hiei stating that the monks of the two noble cloisters *(monzeki)* Shōren'in and Nashimoto (or Kajii) were about to attack one another. The reason for the discord seems to have been the recruitment of novices and the right to perform a certain lecture series for the new members. On the sixteenth day of the eighth month, Go-Saga sent a directive to head abbot Dōkaku and the abbot of Nashimoto—an imperial monk-prince named Sonkaku (the fifth son of Juntoku)—ordering them to calm the monks. Since the edict did not have the anticipated effect, Go-Saga continued to explore different measures to control the monks, consulting with the nobles of his council. The dispute was completely resolved in the eleventh month, when the retired emperor decided that the two cloisters should have separate lectures for their respective monks and novices.[28]

Go-Saga's several directives to Enryakuji were designed to maintain order as well as to establish the retired emperor's authority over the Tendai center, but he relied heavily on the head abbot and other princely monks to execute his policies. Yet the loyalty of these aristocratic abbots was not guaranteed merely because the monks were imperial relatives. Though Dōkaku was the son of Go-Toba (and the uncle of Go-Saga) and Sonkaku was the son of Juntoku (thus Go-Saga's cousin), it was necessary, as with other allies, to confirm and maintain the relationship through gifts and services. In exchange for rituals on behalf of the imperial family, monk-princes *(hōshinnō)* were therefore rewarded with titles and promotions that also entailed financial privileges.[29] In addition, visits to cloisters or temples of these noble abbots served to confirm such crucial relationships. For instance, after a long absence of imperial pilgrimages to Mt. Hiei, Go-Saga visited the Enryakuji complex on the fourth day of the third month of 1248. The destination for this pilgrimage was actually Hiesha, but the retired emperor also went to the Nashimoto *monzeki*—the cloister under the management of Sonkaku *hōshinnō*. As usual, several monks, including the head abbot, received awards following the religious ceremonies.[30]

The importance of this pilgrimage should not be underestimated. According to the *Tendai zasuki,* which is meticulous in recording imperial visits to any parts of the complex, Go-Saga's was the first by an emperor or retired emperor since Go-Toba visited Hiesha on the twenty-sixth day of the ninth month of 1220, just before the Jōkyū War.[31] The mere absence of recorded pilgrimages in the *Tendai zasuki* does not necessarily mean that such trips did not take place. However, the stark contrast between the frequent pilgrimages just before the Jōkyū War and during Go-Saga's rule, on the one hand, and the complete absence of recorded visits in the period in between, on the other, reveals an important change in imperial policy and power. This notion is further strengthened by a number of pilgrimages to other important shrines, such as Iwashimizu Hachimangū (marking likewise the first pilgrimage to that shrine-temple complex since Go-Toba before the Jōkyū War) and Kasuga in 1246, Gion on several occasions, and Kumano early in 1250.[32] Eclipsed for more than two decades, the imperial family thus attempted to revive itself under the *insei* of Go-Saga, who displayed these intentions by establishing close ties with noble abbots, hoping to augment their, and in extension his own, control of shrines and their temple affiliates.

Shingon temples also received renewed attention from the imperial court under Go-Saga's leadership. Though Tōji, as the center of the sect and being located in Kyoto, benefited most in terms of religious status and funding, Kōyasan was also honored with pilgrimages and generous donations. For example, Go-Saga and Kujō Michiie's eldest son, Yoshizane, visited Mt. Kōya in 1257 and again the following year, resulting in new landed estates for the temple.[33] Unlike those to Enryakuji and Kōfukuji, however, such pilgrimages rarely yielded much in terms of religious status for Kōyasan's monks, who, for their part, appear to have been more concerned about the extent of the temple's—and their own —regional influence. This focus sets the temple on Mt. Kōya apart from its counterparts in the capital: it maintained ties with the secular elites and was granted privileges like any *kenmon* temple, but it also remained aloof of Kyoto politics and competition for participation in religious ceremonies at the imperial court. Conversely, Kōyasan was not as integral to court politics, except as a counterweight to other powerful institutions, despite its popularity, as suggested by the court's lukewarm response and inability to resolve severe internal disputes on Mt. Kōya. These conflicts were additionally of a different character from those at Enryakuji and Kōfukuji, where the most serious troubles stemmed primarily from social tensions between the aristocratic abbots and the main clergy. On Mt. Kōya, the division was instead between competing sections for the headship of Kōyasan, void of involvement by capital nobles.

Kakuban (1095–1143) founded the Daidenpōin on Mt. Kōya in 1132 with the strong support of Retired Emperor Toba and several important estates attached to it. Despite resistance from other cloisters, Toba made Kakuban head abbot (*zasu*) of Kongō-buji, leaving him in control of Mt. Kōya while taking away Tōji's control of it. However, the tensions overwhelmed Kakuban, who resigned in 1135 in favor of one of his disciples. The Tōji clergy retained control of Kongōbuji's abbotship the following year, while Kakuban secluded himself on Mt. Kōya. But his fellow monks continued to harass him, and he left the mountain with several hundred followers to settle at one of his estates, where the temple Negoroji had been established as a branch of the Daidenpōin. Kakuban's attempts to return to Kōyasan failed, but the animosity between the wealthy Daidenpōin and other leading cloisters continued even after the monk's death in 1143.[34]

The tensions remained for a century, as the clergies competed for the income from numerous estates and appointments for monk offices and ceremonies within Kongōbuji. For example, violence erupted in 1162 when followers from the two cloisters quarreled over the procedures for a Daidenpōin ceremony, bringing in armed supporters to intimidate one another and force a solution.[35] A particularly serious confrontation occurred some eight decades later, in 1241, when monks of the Daidenpōin employed inhabitants of villages belonging to the cloister of Jitsu-gon'in, which also belonged to the Kakuban lineage, to attack the Kongōbuji clergy. In retaliation, monks from the Oku-no-in, many of whom appear to have been heavily armed, charged and burned parts of the Daidenpōin during a ceremony there in the seventh month of 1242. The head abbot of Tōji, acting as the leader of Shingon, subsequently sent an order to Kōyasan's abbot Myōken to forward the evil investigators in an effort to quell the disturbance. But the fighting continued, for which Myōken and two other ranking monks on Mt. Kōya were deemed responsible and sentenced to exile early in 1243. The clergy of the Oku-no-in, using its clout as the largest and most powerful section on the mountain, now appealed to the Tōji head abbot, claiming that the Daidenpōin, which was a younger section of Kōyasan, did not obey the rules of main-branch *(honmatsu)* relations—an argument that is strikingly similar to the one used by Enryakuji against Onjōji in the late Heian age. The Shingon head abbot attempted to solve the situation by having the combating sections forward lists of names of the guilty instigators to be punished by Rokuhara warriors at the end of the seventh month of 1243. Some ten monks from the Daidenpōin and about twenty-six from the Oku-no-in were finally sent to the capital and detained some four months later. A trial-confrontation *(taimon)* followed, in which both sides appeared in Kyoto to explain their cases. It was, however, not easy to reach a verdict, since both sides, the sources say, "spread many lies, and no ground for crimes could be found."

Nevertheless, a decision to exile more than thirty of the instigators was issued in the first month of 1244, but it appears that all
convicted monks escaped before the verdict could be enforced.
Even high-ranking monks involved in the dispute escaped from
Kyoto to avoid repercussions, and the conflict was thus as unresolved as when it began some two years earlier.[36]

On the fifteenth day of the fourth month of 1246, the newly
retired emperor, Go-Saga, decided to step in, and he sent an
order directly to the Daidenpōin, stating that a thorough explanation of the conflict should be forwarded. Apparently, the Daidenpōin clergy was now the more aggressive and perhaps even
the more successful party, forcing Go-Saga to have Rokuhara investigate new riots. The problem of executing such orders was,
however, a familiar one; even though the main clergy wished the
shugo to enter and pursue the originators, he could not legally do
so because of the temple's exempt status. The internal tensions
on Mt. Kōya were indeed peculiar. Neither the retired emperor
nor the bakufu was successful in controlling the disputing factions. Their inability to offer a solution can be attributed to Kōyasan's own dual stance, as both a *kenmon* temple and a landholder
with direct control of its estates in league with local warriors,
putting it between the jurisdiction of the court and the bakufu.
In fact, although the imperial court had vested interests on Mt.
Kōya, the monastic complex also gained increasing support from
the warrior class, including the Hōjō themselves, in the form of
land confirmations, new tax exemptions, and donations.[37] With
its isolation from court politics in Kyoto and its heavy warrior
patronage, there seemed little Go-Saga could do to control Kōyasan and to subdue its internal disputes. As a result, the rivalry continued, and it only ended in 1288, when a large number of Daidenpōin monks left Mt. Kōya to found their own branch of
Shingon (known as Shingi Shingon) at Negoroji, which developed,
not unlike Onjōji, into a serious competitor to the main temple.

But the problems on Mt. Kōya hardly threatened Go-Saga's
ambitions in the capital directly, and it was instead to Enryakuji
that the retired emperor's religious policies were directed.
Following his first pilgrimage to Mt. Hiei in 1248, he maintained
close ties with the Tendai center's leading monks through several
other journeys to Hiesha as well as to branch shrines such as
Gionsha.[38] Though not as frequent a visitor to the Enryakuji complex as Go-Shirakawa, Go-Saga made more consistent efforts to

cultivate a good relationship with the princely monks, since they, as heads of the wealthiest and most powerful cloisters on Mt. Hiei, were his most efficient channels of communication with the temple. The vital importance of these monks to Go-Saga's policies helps to explain another unusual case of the former emperor's intervention in an internal dispute on Mt. Hiei.

At the end of the eleventh month of 1248, the retired emperor's council met to discuss among other things a dispute over the estates belonging to the Shōren'in *monzeki*. The issue was brought to the retired emperor's attention by the head abbot Dōkaku, who filed a complaint against his predecessor, Jigen, for continuing to hold the rights of administration over Enryakuji cloisters and their estates. Such internal conflicts over temple estates emerged occasionally, since the assets bequeathed from abbot to abbot were increasingly hard to distinguish from the temple's common estates—both of these categories were often administered by the same abbots. Yet most conflicts of this nature did not bother the imperial court or the bakufu unless they caused unrest in the capital area or otherwise threatened to deteriorate into violent outbursts. In fact, as seen throughout this book, the secular authorities rarely intervened at all before fighting and riots broke out or one of the parties filed an appeal. However, Go-Saga needed to be assertive in protecting the interests of his monastic relatives, whom he counted on to extend his control over Enryakuji and its wealth. He consulted with the bakufu, which was inclined to support the retired emperor's allies after the falling out with the Kujō. Backed by the Hōjō, the retired emperor then issued a verdict on the twenty-ninth day of the intercalary twelfth month of 1248, giving the rights to manage the estates and the cloisters to the incumbent head abbot.[39] Go-Saga thus managed to protect the interests of Dōkaku while restricting the influence of the Kujō-born Jigen. However, in spite of the former emperor's unconditional support, Dōkaku could not perform the functions Go-Saga had hoped for. In fact, the monk was forced to resign on the fifth day of the ninth month of 1249, because he was unable to quell the clergy's anger over an appointment to the abbotship of Shitennōji (see later in this chapter). Go-Saga replaced Dōkaku with another princely monk, the aforementioned Sonkaku, in a continuing effort to gain more efficient control of the clergy.[40]

Go-Saga subsequently continued to support Sonkaku, visiting Hiesha and the head abbot the following year. The retired emperor kept giving awards to Enryakuji's high-ranking monks during such visits, but the pilgrimages became less frequent in the early 1250s, coming to a complete stop in the middle of the decade.[41] This change reflects a turning point in the policies of Go-Saga, who, after several attempts to extend his influence through the head abbot, realized that his noble allies on Mt. Hiei simply did not have the power to control Enryakuji's entire clergy. As a consequence, the retired emperor now began to distance himself from the temple by turning his attention, and his patronage, to Onjōji, causing some of the most violent battles involving religious institutions in the thirteenth century.

The Enryakuji–Onjōji Rivalry Rekindled

There were sporadic eruptions of the rivalry between Enryakuji and Onjōji in the first half of the thirteenth century, but they were comparatively few and lacked the kind of violence that usually characterized such outbursts. Most important, the issue of an independent platform for Onjōji was dormant for almost a century after the conflict in 1163 (described in the previous chapter). The sources do not reveal exactly under what circumstances this matter recurred, but there is no doubt that Go-Saga's increased patronage of Onjōji was the main factor. The retired emperor shifted his support to Onjōji sometime in the mid-1250s, and this tie was explicitly confirmed in 1257, when his eldest son, Enjō *hōshinnō*, became abbot of that temple.[42]

It was this imperial support that inspired the Onjōji clergy to renew its demands for an independent ordination platform in 1257. Go-Saga apparently did not support Onjōji's wishes at this point, since he sent an order to Rokuhara to have the monks stopped, but the Enryakuji clergy, concerned about maintaining its control of Tendai, was not convinced, and it responded by sending a messenger to Go-Saga, asking him to reject the appeal. A week later, there were rumors in the capital that the monks on Mt. Hiei were preparing a forceful protest, but it was never realized, since the retired emperor proclaimed that a platform would not be permitted. Moreover, the bakufu supported the former emperor with another edict, ordering the Onjōji monks, who had left their temple in protest, to return to their compound. But once reopened, the issue of Onjōji's independence could not be resolved that easily. Tensions were felt in the capital even after the edicts, forcing the imperial court to postpone the Kitano festival in the seventh month of 1257.[43] The discord prevailed also later that year, causing the warrior government to send two ranking warriors—Nagai Tokihide and Ōsone Nagayasu—as envoys to Kyoto to examine the situation.[44] Although it is not known what these envoys actually did or how they dealt with the situation, it is clear that they were not successful in their attempts.

New demands were raised by Onjōji in 1258, but this time, perhaps as a result of the earlier problems, Go-Saga would not act without first consulting with the bakufu. Thus, on the sixth day of the third month, Saionji Saneuji was sent to the Kantō conveying the retired emperor's opinion that Onjōji's claims were, in fact, just. The retired emperor's change of heart may have been caused by the realization that only a strong Onjōji would make it possible to exert any real influence over the monks on Mt. Hiei. While soliciting the support of the warrior government, Go-Saga asked for the bakufu's opinion on the matter, but the latter could not make a decision either way. In the meantime, acting on rumors of Go-Saga's support for Onjōji's petition, the monks at Enryakuji carried seven sacred palanquins to Kyoto on the sixteenth day of the fourth month of 1258. In order to cause as much disruption and anxiety as possible, the palanquins were left at several strategic locations, including the imperial palace, the front of the building of the noble council (the *kugyō*), and a busy intersection. On the twentieth, Go-Saga issued an edict reassuring the Enryakuji monks that a platform would not be permitted. Yet the clergy were initially reluctant to end the protest, perhaps because they had little faith in the retired emperor's promise. However, since funding eventually was granted for the reconstruction of the damaged palanquins, the monks were satisfied enough to return to Mt. Hiei.[45]

Throughout this protest, Tendai was still headed by Sonkaku, but the records do not indicate what, if any, role he played. Nevertheless, he apparently did not perform satisfactorily, and he therefore resigned in 1259. Sonkaku was replaced by Sonjo *hōshinnō*, a son of Emperor Tsuchimikado, but the new *zasu* was equally unable to halt the animosity between Enryakuji and Onjōji, as monks from Mt. Hiei carried a total of nine sacred palanquins to the capital to lodge a protest on the sixth day of the first month of 1260. The situation was considerably more serious for Enryakuji this time, since an imperial edict had already been issued two days earlier, authorizing Onjōji to build an ordination platform. As during the protest in 1258, the palanquins were left at different locations in Kyoto, but the confrontations with warriors from the bakufu's branch in Rokuhara seem to have been a notch more violent this time, as the capital was overflowing with protesters and defending government warriors. On returning to their shrines and temples, the Enryakuji supporters proceeded to close all three sections on Mt. Hiei in addition to several branches in the capital area in order to declare a continuance of the conflict, even though the actual demonstration had been averted.[46] Moreover, several ceremonies—festivals and investitures of courtiers—at the imperial palace were postponed or abbreviated because of the presence of the Hie palanquins in the capital. While the court sent a messenger to the bakufu to ask for advice, Go-Saga admonished the monks to stop their rioting. However, the Enryakuji clergy merely responded by continuing to mobilize, and finally, on the nineteenth day of the first month, the permission for the Onjōji platform was recalled. But after several years of broken promises, both Enryakuji and Onjōji found it hard to trust the court, and the monks thus continued the dispute. Onjōji desperately appealed to the court again and then turned to the bakufu for help when that failed. In addition, many monks left their dwellings at Onjōji, and the bakufu, fearing that the Enryakuji clergy would seize this opportunity to attack its rival, ordered Rokuhara to protect the weakened temple. Though no attacks were launched against Onjōji, the monks on Mt. Hiei continued to riot, destroying and polluting their own shrines, while the court tried to placate them by granting funds for reconstruction.[47]

Though Go-Saga had thus managed to appoint consecutive Tendai head abbots of his own choosing, he had little success in controlling the clergy. His subsequent desire to promote Onjōji within Tendai was curtailed by the sometimes violent opposition of the Enryakuji clergy, resulting in the retired emperor's own wavering between prohibiting and allowing a separate platform for the "Temple Gate" (jimon) clergy. The key to understanding Go-Saga's failure to execute his religious policies lies in the limited authority of the head abbot over the Tendai clergy. Indeed, a discord between the monks of the Saitō and Yokawa sections over the rights to an estate eventually forced Sonjo also to resign on the sixteenth day of the eighth month of 1263. Following his previous pattern, the retired emperor appointed yet another monk-prince, Sainin (another son of Tsuchimikado), who was immediately charged with pacifying the clergy. It is not clear what role Sainin played in the next several months, but the dispute was settled, as Go-Saga issued an edict in favor of the Saitō section in the eleventh month of that year.[48] Yet Sainin proved to be just as unsuccessful as his predecessors in controlling the clergy over any longer period of time. Indeed, it was during his tenure that one of the most unyielding religious disputes of the century occurred.

There was no limit to the anger of the monks of Enryakuji in 1264. In the third month they burned several of their own temples on Mt. Hiei, which they followed up with a forceful protest at the retired emperor's palace, and in the fifth month they attacked and burned Onjōji. It was the combination of two separate issues, both ultimately related to Go-Saga's favoritism of Onjōji at the expense of Enryakuji, that upset the clergy: the appointment of an Onjōji monk as abbot of Shitennōji and the killing of service people belonging to an Enryakuji branch in Tanba Province. The issue of the abbotship of Shitennōji (often merely referred to as Tennōji) caused particular discontent among the clergy, and further explanation is required before it can be understood in the context of 1264.

The status of Shitennōji, located south of the capital close to the coast of the Inland Sea (in present-day Osaka), as one of the oldest Buddhist temples in Japan made its abbotship religiously and politically important. The temple was, according to popular wisdom, constructed by the Soga family and the legendary Prince Shōtoku in 587 after their victory over the anti-Buddhist Mononobe family. In spite of its age, however, Shitennōji could not match the size and the power of temples like Tōdaiji, Kōfukuji, or Enryakuji. As a result, Shitennōji was courted by several major centers that tried to make it into one of their branch temples. Many exalted monks visited Shitennōji, including Ennin, who is said to have given lectures there in 829. The first abbot *(bettō)* of Shitennōji was the Shingon monk Engyō of Tōji, who was appointed in 837. Though abbots were not always appointed, leaving the responsibilities of leadership and administration to the ranking monks at the temple, a variety of monks from different sects were subsequently given the honor. In 964 Jōe became the first Tendai monk to head Shitennōji, but from the mid–eleventh century the abbots were increasingly selected from the lineage of Enchin (Onjōji).[49] However, in the sixth month of 1180, the court punished Onjōji for having sided with Prince Mochihito and Yori-tomo in the early stages of the Genpei War by taking away that privilege. The post was subsequently assigned to the Taira-favored Myōun of Enryakuji, creating, in effect, a precedent for a long-lasting rivalry.[50]

Myōun resigned in the twelfth month of 1182, perhaps as a result of an appeal that the monks at Onjōji filed in order to retain their monopoly of the abbotship. However, Myōun was, ap-parently with the continued support of the Taira, reappointed in the first month of the following year, keeping the post until his death in the eleventh month of 1183. In the second month of 1184, Go-Shirakawa, who had regained control of the capital after the defeat of the Taira and of Kiso Yoshinaka, awarded the abbot-ship to an Onjōji monk. Then, in 1189, the former emperor issued an edict ordering that the abbotship of Shitennōji subse-quently be transmitted within the lineage of the Byōdōin cloister of Onjōji.[51] However, Onjōji's control of Shitennōji was challenged by Enryakuji in 1196. In a lengthy appeal, the Enryakuji clergy argued that Onjōji, which was not a separate lineage when the first Tendai monk became head of Shitennōji, had no exclusive rights to the abbotship. Therefore, the appeal concluded, the abbotship belonged to the Tendai sect (i.e., Enryakuji), not to an inferior branch (Onjōji). However, this gallant effort at rhetoric yielded no verdict in Enryakuji's favor, and the newly appointed Onjōji monk retained his office for over a decade. Nevertheless, on the death of that monk, the pendulum swung again, as the court appointed as his famed successor Jien, who held that office twice: in 1207 and between 1213 and 1223.[52]

The rivalry resurfaced on several occasions when a new appoint-ment was imminent. For example, when a princely monk of Enrya-kuji died during his tenure in the ninth month of 1239, the Onjōji clergy expressed its ambition to regain the post after six consecutive appointments of Enryakuji monks. Concerned that the court might accommodate Onjōji, the monks on Mt. Hiei mobilized their forces and prepared the portable shrines in front of the Konpon chūdō to stage a protest. The court, for its part, sought the advice of the bakufu, which sent warriors to protect the capital. In the end, no protest was staged, since the court acknowledged Enryakuji's right to the abbotship in the end of the eleventh month. Onjōji staged a more offensive drive in the third month of 1242, when the aforementioned Tendai *zasu* Jigen was appointed abbot of Shitennōji. Onjōji protested vehemently, emphasizing their demands by closing the gates to their temple. Though the sources are not clear as to what exactly happened subsequently, it appears that Jigen resigned in the fifth month as a result of the court's support of the Onjōji petition. However, no new abbot was appointed for seven years, undoubtedly because of the problems associated with the post.[53] On the fourteenth day of the eighth month of 1249, when rumors spread that the abbotship of Shitennōji was about to be awarded to the princely monk Ninjo of Onjōji, the monks of the Shōren'in *monzeki* brought some palanquins to the main temple building on Mt. Hiei to prepare a protest. The court, now led by former emperor Go-Saga, secured the support of the bakufu, and an edict was subsequently issued on the sixth day of the ninth month awarding the post to Ninjo. To placate the monks on Mt. Hiei, Go-Saga promised annual funding for ten new monks at Hiesha and promoted another monk. In addition, Go-Saga replaced the head abbot Dōkaku with Sonkaku *hōshinnō* following the incident because of the former's inability to control the clergy.[54]

After more than a decade without problems, the conflict emerged again late in 1263, when Go-Saga and junior retired emperor Go-Fukakusa determined that the abbotship of Shitennōji should belong to Onjōji. It was also promulgated that the costs of repairing a temple hall at Onjōji were to be levied on Tanba Province, where one of the Hie shrines had landed interests. It seems that Hiesha had previously received funding from the Kotada village in Tanba under the patronage of Fujiwara no Sanefuji, a prominent courtier in Kyoto. When Sanefuji's retainer, Fujiwara no Mitsunori, entered the area to collect taxes for Onjōji as ordered by the retired emperors, he confronted some priests from Hiesha, killing two of them. It was the combination of these killings and the discontent of losing Shitennōji's abbotship—both ultimately caused by Go-Saga's favoritism of Onjōji— that caused the monks from Enryakuji to mobilize and to forward an appeal on the fifteenth day of the first month of 1264. Go-Saga subsequently consulted with the bakufu, but more than two months passed without any concrete attempts to address the problem. Finally, the monks on Mt. Hiei ran out of patience, and, on the twenty-third day of the third month, protesting the delays of the verdicts, they set fire to several of their own buildings on the summit, including important structures such as the lecture hall and the Tendai ordination platform.[55]

This kind of self-destruction appears to be overly drastic, but within the mental framework of the thirteenth century, the actions made perfect sense, since the main purpose was to make a profound impact on the capital elites. Enryakuji played a pivotal role in both the spiritual and political well-being of the state, and, according to the prevailing doctrine of mutual dependence of the imperial law and Buddhism *(ōbō-buppō sōi)*, the destruction of Enryakuji would also result in the decline of the court itself.[56] In other words, it was understood that the Enryakuji complex was ultimately the financial responsibility of the court, not of the clergy. In 1264 the monks knowingly used this doctrine to their advantage when they damaged their own complex, and the burning had the desired effect on the capital nobility. Both Go-Saga and Go-Fukakusa interrupted their visit to the Kamo shrines, hurrying back to the safety of their palaces. Two days later the monks descended the mountain, carrying ten sacred palanquins to several important places in the capital, most notably to the imperial palace and the villas of both Go-Saga and Go-Fukakusa. Warriors were sent out to stop the demonstrators from reaching their destination, causing a skirmish in which some of the protesters were injured and one monk was killed, while the government guards escaped harm. On the twenty-seventh day of the third month, Go-Saga attempted to compromise with Enryakuji by arresting Mitsunori and sentencing Sanefuji to exile for the killings of the priests in Tanba. However, the retired emperor refused to change the appointment of the Shitennōji abbot. "The Tennōji abbot," he declared, "shall be appointed in the tradition of the imperial commands of the Kenkyū [1190–1199] and Kenchō [1249–1256] eras, according to the times and the circumstances."[57] Referring to the appointments of 1196 and 1249, when Enryakuji unsuccessfully had protested the appointments of Onjōji monks, Go-Saga was thus stating his right to appoint a head abbot of his choosing regardless of religious lineage.

The Enryakuji clergy was predictably not content with this proclamation, but instead of continuing to petition the court, the monks on Mt. Hiei turned their anger toward their fellow Tendai monks. This change of direction was, at least in part, caused by a ranking Onjōji monk (named Senchō), who, citing the recent loss of a platform on Mt. Hiei as a pretext, ordained some novices of his own. Therefore, although the palanquins were brought back to their shrines in the fourth month, large parts of the clergy were still upset and intent on continuing the dispute. In fact, some "evil monks" of the Saitō section intercepted those who carried the palanquins up Mt. Hiei, forcing them to abandon three of their carts midway to Hiesha.[58] Finally, the monks on Mt. Hiei took matters into their own hands and launched a forceful attack on their rival on the second day of the fifth month. The fighting lasted for hours that day and continued for another four days, as several important temple buildings and monk dwellings were destroyed by the superior Enryakuji forces. Few structures were left intact on the Onjōji compound by the aggressors, who also took some objects—most notably Onjōji's famous bronze bell—back to Mt. Hiei as symbols of their victory.[59] Following this attack, the sacred palanquins of Hiesha were once again brought to the capital, but all parties involved seem to have been more inclined to reach a peaceful solution at that point. Ranking monks from Enryakuji were called to Go-Saga's palace to answer for the attack, and a few days later the portable shrines were returned, while the court sent representatives to three of Enryakuji's most important shrines (Hiesha, Gionsha, and Kitano) to thank the gods for their cooperation. The issue was settled on the twenty-fourth day of the fifth month, when Go-Saga managed to award the abbotship of Shitennōji to Onjōji. Surprisingly enough, there was no reaction from the monks on Mt. Hiei this time. Perhaps they were tired of fighting, or perhaps it was more important to secure support for the reconstruction of the buildings and palanquins that had been burned or otherwise damaged during the protests. There may also have been some consolation in the court's earnest assessments of the self-inflicted damages on Mt. Hiei, since the survey was modeled on the one that took place at Tōdaiji after its destruction in the Genpei War. The repair work got under way quickly, and less than a month later, in the eleventh month of 1264, grand ceremonies, sponsored by the court, took place on Mt. Hiei as the newly reconstructed ordination platform was initiated.[60]

Bakufu and Court Involvement in Religious Disputes

Considering that Go-Saga is usually characterized as little more than an instrument of bakufu policy, one is struck by the near noninvolvement of the bakufu in the incidents of 1264. In fact, from its beginning to its settlement, the drama's main director was Go-Saga, who also must be blamed for initiating the conflict. It was thus only fitting that the grand finale in the tenth month of

1264 featured Go-Saga and the junior retired emperor (Go-Fukakusa) visiting Hiesha and the Nashimoto noble cloister to confirm the settlement and to reestablish amicable ties with the *kami* and the buddhas on Mt. Hiei. The bakufu was surprisingly passive, only being consulted occasionally by Go-Saga and providing limited military assistance through the Rokuhara branch in Kyoto. When the bakufu finally did act, it dispatched two prominent warrior leaders—Nagai Tokihide of the *hyōjōshū* (the bakufu's council) and Nikaido Yoshitsuna of the *hikitsukeshū* (the board of coadjutors)—together with several hundred mounted warriors to arrest those deemed responsible for the fighting. However, this act took place almost two months after the retired emperor had reached a settlement with Enryakuji.[61]

The bakufu was thus more active in the cleaning up. In the second month of 1265, for example, several "evil monks" from Enryakuji and one from Onjōji were extradited and then detained, though some of the criminals escaped and went into hiding to avoid punishment. More important, the conflict was deemed sufficiently serious to compel the two governments to attempt a more active role in controlling Enryakuji, leading to the adoption of two new measures. First, an imperial edict aimed at restricting the political power of the monks on Mt. Hiei was issued in the fourth month of 1265. It prohibited the use of arms on Mt. Hiei and in Sakamoto, and denied monks the right to gamble or to have "secular followers" *(sokutai no tomogara)*.[62] Retired Emperor Go-Saga endorsed this promulgation in an edict from his own headquarters in the eighth month, adding that all high-ranking monks of Enryakuji should now reside on Mt. Hiei. The latter was an important and innovative attempt to bridge the gap between the aristocratic abbots (who preferred their own cloisters in the capital area) and the clergy, demonstrating that the retired emperor realized that changes were necessary to make noble monks more instrumental to his religious policies.[63] Since there is no indication of similar edicts to other temples at that time, there can be little doubt that Enryakuji was a special concern in the capital area. Second, on the nineteenth day of the third month of 1266, the bakufu's envoys (the aforementioned Tokihide and Yukitsuna) consulted with Go-Saga before proceeding to enforce the appointment of a new Tendai head abbot (Chōkaku). In addition, the representatives designated estates for the *zasu* in order to secure his financial base and to foreclose internal disputes.[64]

The progression of the conflict over Shitennōji's abbotship in the 1260s aptly reveals the different responsibilities of the imperial court and the bakufu within the thirteenth-century polity. Go-Saga was undoubtedly the prime mover in religious issues, which was allocated to the sphere of court politics. Indeed, it was the visit of the two retired emperors to Hiesha in the tenth month of 1264 that officially ended the problems and also reconfirmed the tie between the imperial family and the Enryakuji complex. Go-Saga then made another pilgrimage to Hiesha in 1266, awarding ranking members of Enryakuji with promotions and funding. Between these pilgrimages, an additional tie was established when Go-Saga's son, Saijo, entered Enryakuji as a novice at the age of thirteen. Left to the bakufu and its branch in Kyoto were policing duties. The Rokuhara headquarters supplied military support when the court or Onjōji needed it, whereas Kamakura interrogated and punished those who had behaved improperly. Though the court reopened Shitennōji in the first month of 1267, it was the bakufu that actually obliged Enryakuji to return Onjōji's bronze bell three months later. This return marked the symbolic end to one of the most violent religious disputes of the entire thirteenth century.[65]

In spite of this denouement, the abbotship of Shitennōji remained an issue with both Tendai lineages in possession of legitimate claims. Go-Saga had made no future commitments, indicating that he expected there to be further competition; appointments, he stated, would be made according to the "circumstances at the time." Thus, unsurprisingly, Enryakuji renewed its claims to the abbotship by mobilizing its supporters and preparing a demonstration in the tenth month of 1282. Emperor Kameyama, who became the dominating power in Kyoto after Go-Saga's death in 1272, sought the support of the bakufu before addressing the monks' demands. In the interim, however, he issued edicts to the Shōren'in monks who had apparently instigated the movement, while affirming that the abbotship should belong to Onjōji.[66] The monks on Mt. Hiei continued to claim their right to Shitennōji's abbotship, and, in the first month of 1283, they entered the capital with six of their sacred palanquins. The protesters spread out within the palace area, placing their holy carts at strategic locations, but some of the demonstrators also seized the opportunity to loot and riot, causing a great deal of fear and despair among the nobles. Eventually, warriors from Rokuhara intervened and managed, without firing any arrows, to fend off the monks, who left their palanquins and returned to Mt. Hiei. The protest ended later that evening when service people from Gionsha brought the holy carts back to their shrines.[67] Greatly concerned, the bakufu this time decided on a more forceful response. In the seventh month of 1283, two of its messengers arrived with a multi-part edict that included the following: the monk Saigen, who was Tendai head abbot at the time of the protest, was to lose his rights to certain estates; the instigators of the protest were to be extra-dited and their estates confiscated; and warriors who had failed to protect the palace were to be punished.[68] The edict added further that since Shitennōji "was constructed by Prince Shōtoku as the first location of Buddhism, there is no reason for it to be a branch of any other temple." Consequently, it concluded, in the spirit of the deceased Go-Saga, that any meritorious monk at Enryakuji, Onjōji, Tōji, or the other old temples of Nara might, depending on the circumstances, be appointed Shitennōji abbot. On the tenth day of the seventh month, the Kantō envoys were given a pledge of cooperation by Enryakuji, which proceeded to forward a list of the instigators two weeks later.[69]

The bakufu's determined action in 1283 prevented a major inci-dent, but it did little to prevent future conflicts, as the abbotship was still open for competition. In fact, Enryakuji managed to reverse the trend again in 1286, when the Tendai head abbot Sonjo was appointed abbot of Shitennōji. As expected, this appoint-ment not only upset the Onjōji monks, but it also prolonged the conflict by reacknowledging Enryakuji's right to the post. As the competition thus continued, the clergy on Mt. Hiei renewed their demands early in the third month of 1291 that the court continue to grant Shitennōji's abbotship to an Enryakuji monk. The court, as was now typical, procrastinated, and a week later some monks from Enryakuji began to harass other monks and cloisters in the capital area in order to persuade them to join the protest. In the end, the court elected to comply with Enryakuji's demands, and it appointed yet another monk from Mt. Hiei on the seventeenth day of the third month.[70] The complicated history of Shitennōji along with a sequence of inconclusive verdicts by both govern-ments were clearly to blame for the prolonged dispute over Shi-tennōji's abbotship. In fact, the lack of firm action was but an integral part of shared rulership. The court preferred not to commit the abbotship to any particular lineage so that the ap-pointment might be used as a political tool to favor or to demote a temple of its choice. Such religious appointments had been used for centuries to balance the power of temples like Enryakuji Onjōji, Kōfukuji, Tōji, and Tōdaiji.

The rivalry over Shitennōji's abbotship reveals that the division of responsibilities between Kamakura and Kyoto defined the nature of the bakufu more than its military might. To put the matter directly, it was as a peacekeeper that the bakufu involved itself in Enryakuji issues, leading it to support, not supersede, the imperial court in Kyoto. Other cases of religious appointments reinforce this conclusion. For example, the head abbotship of Tendai was the traditional means by which the government attempted to control Enryakuji. Shirakawa, Go-Shirakawa, Taira no Kiyomori, Kiso Yoshinaka, and Go-Saga were some of the famous figures who attempted to use this office to extend their influence. However, the bakufu did not, as a rule, involve itself in monk promotions and appointments, leaving such matters to the powers in Kyoto. Yet in the second month of 1247, the court sought its advice on which of two monk-princes should be made the next Tendai *zasu*. The bakufu was willing to help with the selection at this point, since the leadership in Kamakura was itself in some turmoil, and the choice was a factional one that might affect its own future. Tokiyori had just overcome the opposition of the Kujō family, and he was therefore willing to support the imperial court—led by the newly retired Go-Saga—in its efforts to stabilize matters in Kyoto.[71]

Similar political circumstances caused the bakufu to involve itself in the selection process again in 1268, when the monastery on Mt. Hiei was plagued by internal disputes following several years of quarrels over the Shitennōji abbotship, and tensions in the capital over the appointment of the regent *(kanpaku)* caused further unrest. The bakufu accordingly intervened by replacing the incumbent chancellor, and the court appointed a new Tendai head "according to the wishes of the Kantō" in the same month. To prevent any further disturbances over estates held by Enryakuji, the bakufu also placed the two central *monzeki* of Nashimoto and Shōren'in under the management of the new *zasu*.[72] The contrast between a complete lack of bakufu involvement in Tendai head abbot appointments in the late 1270s and its more active participation in the selection process in the next decade must similarly be related to the issue of stability in the capital. For example, the selections of Dōgen and Kōgō were made by the court in 1276 and 1278, while Kamakura chose to give its advice in the appointments and resignations in the 1280s. As demonstrated, the bakufu's intervention in the 1280s was caused by the conflict over the leadership of Shitennōji.[73]

A number of other religious incidents during Go-Saga's era provide further evidence of the retired emperor's initiative, the cooperative spirit between courtiers and warriors, and the bakufu's peacekeeping priorities. For example, during an internal dispute on Mt. Hiei in 1246, it was the retired emperor who issued the edicts in an attempt to quell the disturbance. Failing to do so, he met with both Kujō Michiie and Rokuhara officials to find a solution, but the bakufu representatives appear to have been of little help.[74] It was partially the timing of the problems that made it difficult for the warrior government to respond in full force to such religious squabbles. The bakufu itself was in a flux as the Hōjō struggled to maintain their grip in the Kantō in the wake of Hōjō Yasutoki's death in 1242. Late in 1246 a young Hōjō Tokiyori was challenged by the former shōgun Kujō Yoritsune and then faced a rebellion by the Miura family in 1247, which the shogunal regent Tokiyori managed to subdue. Though the bakufu was interested in who the leader of the sect was, a minor incident within the Tendai center must have seemed inconsequential compared to the challenges the young Tokiyori and the Hōjō family faced from its own supporters. Indeed, neither did a more threatening conflict between Hossō and Tendai monks in the imperial palace area itself the same year lead to much of a response from the bakufu. This confrontation was a result of a disagreement between Enryakuji and Kōfukuji monks following the conclusion of the Saishōkō (the annual lecture held on the Sūtra of the Golden Light, which featured monks from Enryakuji, Tōdaiji, Onjōji, and Kōfukuji) ceremony on the twenty-second day of the fifth month. Ritual participation at the highest level still mattered to most ranking monks in the mid–thirteenth century, and conflicts over honorable and meritorious appointments among monks from the leading sects could cause arguments and squabbles among the Buddhist holy men. In this particular case, the assistant head abbot of Kōfukuji, *sōjō* (Grand Master) Kakuben, became involved in a brawl with an Enryakuji monk named Ken'un once the attending courtiers, which included among others the Fujiwara chieftain (Konoe Kanetsune), had departed. Both monks were of noble origin with Fujiwara ancestry, but Kakuben was ranked far above Ken'un, and though aged seventy-two at the time of the incident, he was apparently vivacious enough to confront a much younger cleric. The quarrel soon deteriorated as Enryakuji supporters brought their bows and arrows to fight their opponents within the palace area, where Kakuben was staying. Two or three supporters were killed on each side, but there is no record of any actions by the bakufu despite requests from the court, and Kakuben, in fact, became head abbot of Kōfukuji later in 1247.[75]

Although the era of turmoil in the Kantō that saw the transition from Yasutoki to Tokiyori and the former shōgun Kujō Yoritsune's uprising in late 1246 was not representative of the bakufu's overall role as a peacekeeper in the capital region, it is nevertheless indicative of the workings of dual government, where the initiative to act in religious matters rested mainly with the imperial court. For example, when the Onjōji monks left their temple during the dispute with Enryakuji in the third month of 1257, the former emperor asked the Kantō spokesman to dispatch warriors from Rokuhara to protect the deserted temple. However, since the court continued to encounter problems in resolving the conflict, the request was transmitted to the bakufu itself, which sent warriors to Kyoto to ensure a speedy resolution.[76] In a similar measure, representatives from Kamakura were dispatched to the capital in the first month of 1260 to protect Onjōji during the dispute over the ordination platform. The bakufu thus acted strictly in response to requests from the court, performing its policing duties within a polity of shared responsibilities.

Religious status and the proper etiquette during (and after) state ceremonies notwithstanding, the bakufu was considerably more active in land issues involving religious institutions in order to preserve the existing estate holding patterns, issuing edicts against unlawful intrusions by both warriors and clerics.[77] In this regard, Kōfukuji was particularly important and challenging to the bakufu throughout the Kamakura era despite its location in Nara, somewhat outside the immediate arena of capital politics. It was Kōfukuji's extensive landholdings in Yamato Province, giving the temple not only considerable income, but also access to a large number of followers at less than a day's march from the capital, that forced the bakufu to pay special attention to the Hossō monastic headquarters. As is well known, Kōfukuji's hold of Yamato Province was strong enough to deny appointments of *jitō* on its estates as well as *shugo* (constables) in the province for a good part of the Kamakura era. Though the bakufu could appoint a representative of its own in Yamato if it truly felt it necessary, it usually chose to allow Kōfukuji to control the province as long as peace prevailed. However, in 1236, when Kōfukuji challenged the bakufu's decision to ignore an appeal from the temple, the leaders in Kamakura made a rare statement by appointing both a temporary *shugo* and several new land stewards in Yamato. But such assertive bakufu behavior against Kōfukuji was the exception rather than the norm, as a more in-depth examination of this incident reveals.

The conflict that caused the bakufu to step in has its origin in a dispute between Kōfukuji and Iwashimizu Hachimangū, a powerful shrine-temple complex in its own right just south of Kyoto. In particular, Iwashimizu's extensive landholdings in the capital region, including Yamato Province, made it a serious competitor to Kōfukuji. A local dispute over water rights between the residents of two neighboring estates, Takigi-no-shō and Ōsumi-no-shō, put the two complexes on a collision course in the fifth month of 1235, causing the imperial court to ask Rokuhara to send out messengers to examine the situation. However, before a verdict was issued, some residents of Takigi, which belonged to Iwashimizu Hachimangō, attacked and killed peasants in Ōsumi. Since Ōsumi was a Kōfukuji estate, the clergy in Nara became agitated and set out to burn Iwashimizu. Rokuhara dispatched warriors to stop the Kōfukuji monks, who diverted their anger toward the Takigi estate instead, raging and burning more than sixty homesteads *(zaike)* in addition to killing some Iwashimizu supporters early in the sixth month.[78] The shrine servants of Iwashimizu were naturally appalled, and some members brought out the shrine's holy cart with the intention of taking it to the capital to stage a forceful protest. However, the imperial court made it clear to Iwashimizu's abbot, a certain Kōsei (1157–1235), who seemed reluctant to support the protest anyway, that no demonstration would be tolerated, especially since "the movement of the Iwashimizu holy cart is without precedent."[79] In addition, the court attempted to placate the potential protesters by donating an estate (Ōuchi-no-shō in Iga Province) to Iwashimizu, but the shrine members initially ignored the pleas of both their own abbot and the court. Only when the imperial court increased the donation to include all of Inaba Province (present-day Tottori) did the agitated Iwashimizu servants finally settle, bringing the holy cart back to its shrine.[80]

On receiving a report from the court, the bakufu found it pertinent to reach a swift conclusion and to discourage similar problems from occurring in the near future. A messenger was sent to the court, ordering an examination of the incident with the intention of punishing those deemed guilty. However, not much was achieved in this investigation, as both temples were reluctant to cooperate, and Iwashimizu was thus allowed to keep Inaba Province. The dispute appears to have been an issue beyond the bakufu's reach, as the complexes were protected by their immunity, but the matter of peace was clearly the responsibility of the warrior government. To contain the conflict, the bakufu proclaimed that the new Iwashimizu abbot, Shūsei (Kōsei died early in the seventh month), would be deposed and the demonstrators would be heavily punished if the holy cart was moved.[81] But these measures were evidently insufficient to put an end to the conflict. When Shūsei, in an attempt to calm his clergy, dispatched messengers to examine the borders between the two estates late in the twelfth month of 1235, they encountered some servants of Kasuga from Ōsumi, and a fight soon broke out in which some of the Kasuga people were killed. The Kōfukuji clergy was angered and demanded that both the abbot and his deputy be permanently exiled to distant provinces, that the official (a certain Katano Munenari) who led the attack be imprisoned, and that Takigi estate be awarded to Kōfukuji. Shūsei felt the pressure mounting at this point, and he pledged to arrest Munenari and to return Inaba Province. However, the Kōfukuji clergy, which had started to prepare a divine demonstration when the demands were lodged, still proceeded to march on Kyoto with the Kasuga *shinmoku* (the sacred *sakaki* branch). Once they reached the river of Kizugawa close to Uji, the Kōfukuji protesters encountered bakufu warriors, who had barricaded the bridge, temporarily halting their progression.[82]

The court subsequently tried to placate the Kōfukuji clergy by offering to finance a special temporary festival at Kasuga, to send a procession of court nobles to pay homage to the shrine, and to promote a past monk named Shin'en to the posthumous rank of *bosatsu yama sōjō* (Great Master Bodhisattva of the Mountain). All three of these privileges would have brought financial rewards as well as prestige, but the clergy would not listen. By this point, the

Kamakura Bakufu had received detailed reports about the incidents, and it sent an order that reached the imperial court on the twenty-ninth day of the twelfth month. The order stated that Munenari, who had been arrested once but freed by the Iwashimizu servants, should be imprisoned and that both sides should send statements explaining their behavior with pledges not to cause any further disturbances. In addition, the bakufu stated, if peace was not achieved even after the arrest of Munenari and the return of Inaba Province, it would send out its warriors to drive away the protesters with military might. Most of the Kōfukuji protesters then returned to Nara, leaving the Kasuga holy branch behind in Uji in an effort to maintain spiritual pressure on the capital elites.[83]

The threats of a *gōso* in Kyoto itself thus remained, as did the conflict, since the matter of guilt and punishment still remained to be solved in the minds of the Hossō monks. In the first month of 1236, the imperial court offered to depose Shūsei from his post as abbot of Iwashimizu in exchange for the removal of the Kasuga holy branch from Uji, but the Kōfukuji clergy would not accept anything less than the abbot's exile to a distant province. The monks threatened another protest and even managed to have Kasuga and Tōdaiji close their gates while they performed the same symbolic act of protest at Kōfukuji. The bakufu was consequently compelled to step in again, sending Gōtō Mototsuna with an ultimatum late in the second month. Unfortunately, it is not known exactly how the bakufu attempted to coerce or entice Kōfukuji to a state of peace, except for a promise to punish Shūsei, but the desired effect was achieved, as the clergy retired to Nara with the divine symbol on the twenty-first day of the second month. However, the bakufu never took any action against Shūsei, inducing the Kōfukuji clergy to close the gates to Kasuga and move the holy branch to the main temple building in anticipation of yet another demonstration in the seventh month of 1236. Mototsuna was dispatched from the Kantō anew the next month, and the roads to and from Nara were soon blocked by bakufu warriors, even preventing rice taxes from reaching Kasuga, in an effort to isolate the unruly protesters. The monks and their supporters responded by entrenching themselves and preparing for battle. After a standstill that lasted for two months, the bakufu decided to take more direct control over Yamato to subdue the temple, appointing a *shugo* for the province as well as several *jitō* to previously exempt Kōfukuji estates in the tenth month.[84]

These resolute acts demonstrate that the bakufu had the authority and the means to contain outbursts of violence between temples despite several failed measures vis-à-vis Kōfukuji and Iwashimizu in 1235 and 1236. Ironically, it was the warrior government's reluctance, even under Yasutoki's forceful leadership, to involve itself in conflicts between temples in the capital region that caused the Kōfukuji clergy's disturbance, forcing, in the end, Yasutoki to place a *shugo* and several *jitō* in Yamato. In response, the Hossō clergy attempted to reassert Kōfukuji's privileges by protesting through other means, canceling lectures on the Lotus Sūtra and the Yuima'e, which had been performed regularly since the early ninth century. The shutdown of such important Buddhist ceremonies combined with the bakufu's own desire to avoid involvement in religious issues were behind the warrior government's decision to recall all the appointed officers in Yamato in the eleventh month of 1236, as soon as the clergy had settled down and the holy branch had been returned to Kasuga.[85]

The Takigi-Ōsumi conflict was settled after almost two years, but the tensions that initially caused this bothersome conflict were not sufficiently solved. There was still disagreement about the water rights between the two estates, and the conflict reemerged in the ninth month of 1281, when Kasuga's holy branch was removed from its protected area in the main shrine and then carried to the capital early the next month. Bakufu-dispatched warriors succeeded in halting the protesters in the Uji area, but the holy branch was left at Hōjōji; a statement aimed at the Fujiwara chieftain (Kanehira), since that temple had been closely associated with the clan since its construction by Michinaga in 1019. Several lectures and ceremonies were, moreover, postponed or canceled altogether by the clergy, thus applying pressure from both the Buddhist and the Shintō deities. Kanehira accordingly succumbed by issuing an edict in the second month of 1282 in an attempt to solve the conflict. The first measure was to avoid confrontations between the representatives of the two religious complexes, which Kanehira effectively did by donating new estates to both parties while assigning new proprietors to Takigi and Ōsumi. In addition, he told the bakufu to punish the four warriors who had damaged a holy cart during a confrontation in Uji. Though the bakufu stated that it merely had sent out the warriors on the request of the imperial court and that such measures might be impeded in the future if the defending warriors were at risk of being punished, it did eventually comply—an important statement that religious issues had their own logic even to the leaders of the bakufu.[86] With these measures, the Takigi-Ōsumi conflict, which had begun as a dispute over water rights between the residents of two estates before developing into a display of spiritual and political pressures by two important religious complexes in the court-bakufu polity, finally ended.

Conflicts between temples over estates would normally fall outside the Kamakura Bakufu's jurisdiction unless the imperial court was unable to maintain peace, as in the Kōfukuji-Iwashimizu dispute. The more common scenario involved disputes over rights to estates between traditional temple proprietors and the local managerial warrior class. Such conflicts were highly problematic, since they forced the bakufu to reconcile two contradictory interests in thirteenth-century Japan. On the one hand, it wished to support the traditional elites of the *shōen* in order to ensure that local warriors would not attempt to aggrandize their power, causing chaos and war. On the other hand, the bakufu also needed to keep its warrior retainers satisfied, since its only raison d'être was to control and contain this growing class of armed men. The Kamakura Bakufu thus had to perform a precarious balancing act to which there was no simple resolution, as evidenced by the large number of disputes between local warrior managers, serving as *jitō* or *gesu,* and the estate proprietors that dominated the legal realm of the thirteenth century. For example, Kōfukuji appealed to the bakufu in the fourth month of 1257, asking that the *gesu* office of Suita estate in Settsu Province be confirmed to the temple and that incursions by a local warrior be stopped. Discussions over this matter had taken place at the retired emperor's palace, but the courtiers were unable to reach a decision despite a drawn-out debate. Finally, the matter was turned over to the bakufu, which issued an edict in Kōfukuji's favor in the twelfth month of 1258.[87]

Outright encroachments by warriors were not difficult to prove, and the bakufu certainly recognized the crimes committed in such cases, but there were other ways for a local warrior to expand his influence that might be more difficult to attack. For instance, he could decrease the amount of rent due to the proprietor by blaming poor harvests, have local peasants under threat support claims for a larger tax-exempt homestead for himself, or assess new taxes for various purposes. One interesting case, which first appears in an appeal early in the fifth month of 1264, pitted the Kōfukuji clergy against its own head abbot, Enjitsu. The sources do not provide any clear indications as to the origins of this dispute, but it appears that a large group of lower-ranking monks and shrine servants were upset with failures by local warrior-administrators to deliver rents to the temple, the assessment of irregular war taxes on Kōfukuji estates, and Enjitsu's failure to respond and support the appeals.[88] Enjitsu was another son of Kujō Michiie, who embarked on a promising career as a noble monk. In the third month of 1235, three years before his younger brother Jigen became Tendai *zasu*, Enjitsu was appointed head abbot of Kōfukuji at the young age of twenty-three, though he resigned at the end of that year. However, he continued to rise through the ranks as the head of the Daijōin, one of the two main cloisters within the Hossō center, reaching the highest level of *daisōjō* (Great Grand Master) within the Office of Monastic Affairs. In the tenth month of 1258, he was reappointed head abbot of Kōfukuji, and he managed to maintain that position until the 1264 dispute, when he failed to support the clergy's appeal.[89] The head abbot's lack of support created a stalemate in the capital, causing the Kōfukuji appealers to discuss a protest early in the sixth month. To initiate this process and to make the necessary preparations, the clergy sent messages to Kasuga, attempting to enlist the support of its shrine members while asking that the holy branch be prepared for a demonstration. Equipped with sacred mirrors, the *shinmoku* was moved from the main Kasuga shrine to the nearby Utsushiden, where the monks and shrine servants held meetings and performed ceremonies, marking the first stage of a forceful protest. The Fujiwara chieftain (Nijō Yoshizane, 1216–1270) called some Kōfukuji monks to his mansion to discuss a resolution, but no progress was made, in part because some of the chieftain's own retainers were among the accused (which might also explain why Enjitsu—Yoshizane's younger brother—did not support the clergy's appeal). After another month without any significant response from the imperial court, the *shinmoku* was moved to the Kondō of Kōfukuji, where the clergy discussed an appeal. By now the appeal had taken on larger proportions, as it included demands for punishment of Enjitsu, who, for his part, went to Kyoto to name the originators of the appeal. The clergy continued to prepare to march toward the capital, but it was consistently delayed as both bakufu representatives and supporters of the court were successful in their attempts to stall the protesters. For example, messengers from Rokuhara were sent to Nara to calm the agitated monks on the fifth day of the seventh month and again on the second day of the eighth month. Moreover, the abbot of Kōfukuji's other noble cloister (Ichijōin) attempted to delay the departure to the capital by inquiring about the precedents for the procedure, to which the clergy forwarded a detailed description of locations they might visit during the demonstration.[90]

The tensions gradually escalated in the middle of the eighth month until a physical confrontation broke out between Enjitsu's followers and the clergy in Nara. An enraged clergy attacked the dwellings of both Enjitsu and his closest supporter (named Bōjitsu), causing heavy destruction. Some high-ranking monks then appeared in the capital to report the events, while presenting demands that Enjitsu be exiled and Bōjitsu arrested. The pressure on the capital nobles as well as on Rokuhara was now considerable, and even though noble monks within the Hossō center attempted to calm the monks, a divine demonstration in the capital seemed only a matter of time. However, an unexpected death changed the course of events in favor of Kōfukuji. On the twenty-seventh day of the eighth month of 1264, news reached Nara that Hōjō Nagatoki (1229–1264), who held one of the most important posts as *shikken* (shogunal regent) in the Kantō, had died some five days earlier after a brief illness. The clergy was quick to point out that Nagatoki was a supporter of the *jitō* of Tanigawa-no-shō in Izumi Province, one of the Kōfukuji estates that had been assessed the additional war tax. Was this not, they wondered, the deed of Kasuga Daimyōjin, the great *kami* protecting Kōfukuji?[91] While Enjitsu was forced to hide out at a nearby mountain to avoid confronting the Kōfukuji clergy, the latter sent yet another petition to the court, with specific references to Tanigawa estate and head abbot Enjitsu, demanding a verdict, lest the entire clergy appear in the capital to voice their concerns. The bakufu was first to respond, inviting Kōfukuji representatives to the Kantō to settle the issue, which eventually resulted in an exemption from the extraordinary tax for Tanigawa. The court soon followed suit by deposing Enjitsu and ordering him exiled to Awa, to the joy of the Kōfukuji clergy, which brought the sacred branch and its mirrors back to Kasuga late in the ninth month.[92]

The tensions lingered, however, as long as Enjitsu was unwilling to give up his monastic career and remained in Nara with his supporters. In fact, the clergy attacked and destroyed the dwelling of an Enjitsu supporter within Kōfukuji in the eighth month of 1265. Then, two years after his deposition, Enjitsu returned to Kōfukuji, apparently with the support of some of his fellow ranking monks, in an attempt to regain the head abbotship. The clergy responded forcefully, demanding that Enjitsu be exiled forever. Again, the imperial court seemed unable to find a solution, and the bakufu was forced to intervene after some three months. Following an investigation, the bakufu forced Enjitsu to give up his prestigious monk rank as *daisōjō* and to resign from his post as a ranking monk administrator. Enjitsu subsequently kept his promise of not getting involved in matters regarding Kōfukuji's administration, but he remained in a cloister in Nara even though the bakufu had recommended that he leave the city. It is not known whether he was still perceived as a threat by the clergy or whether he actually attempted to control Kōfukuji indirectly through other means, but the monks of the main clergy eventually decided to take matters into their own hands to rid themselves of this unpopular monk. On the twenty-sixth day of the eighth month of 1268, several hundred monks assembled in front of the Kondō agreed on a strategy and proceeded to Enjitsu's dwelling to drive him out of Nara. Retired Emperor Go-Saga was deeply concerned, issuing an edict to Rokuhara telling the bakufu representatives to contain the clergy. The combined criticism and threats from the Rokuhara tandai, the retired emperor, and the bakufu were quite successful, most likely because the secular authorities declared that monks from the Hossō sect would be excluded from appointments to *daisōjō* for one generation if they did not calm down.[93] The clergy complied, thus ending a complicated and tenacious conflict, which reflects not one but several levels of tensions among monks, courtiers, and warriors.

On the most basic level, the appeal was lodged in response to local warriors' attempt to extract extraordinary taxes. Though the bakufu seems to have acknowledged the illegality of these acts, it was also reluctant to comply with Kōfukuji's demands univocally, and it disapproved of the clergy's demonstration, as revealed in the punishment issued against one of the originators of the protest in 1265. The incident also reflects the changing nature of the internal structures of Kōfukuji, where the gap between the clergy and their noble masters was widening. The term *"gekokujō,"* which is usually translated as "the lower overturning the higher," is aptly used to describe the changing social conditions of the fourteenth century, when local estate managers and warriors increasingly and successfully challenged the central elites. However, this process began even earlier within the religious centers, as seen in several internal conflicts pitching lower classes of religious servants against their masters in the twelfth and thirteenth centuries.[94] There had been tensions between the noble, more privileged monks, who monopolized leadership and other important posts, and monks of more humble origin within several temples in the late Heian period, but now there were occasions when the lower-ranking clergy was able to obtain more control in the long term within the major monastic compounds. In the case of Kōfukuji, the lower echelons of the Buddhist clergy as well as shrine members began to oppose the scholar-monks *(gakuryō)*, who held ranking positions such as head abbot and other leading offices within the temple administration in the mid–thirteenth century. In time, the worker-monks, who performed more menial and administrative tasks, even took control of the Kōfukuji's decision-making process by dominating the temple meetings *(sengi)*, a trend that is apparent during the Enjitsu dispute in the 1260s. In addition, a similar process took place in Kōfukuji's *shōen* and branch temples, where monk-administrators often allied themselves with *shōen* warriors *(shōhei)* to gain more control of the estate and its income at the local level.[95] Though the symptoms of these tensions, in the form of conflicts between the two groups, are unmistakable, the sources do not always provide enough information regarding what actually sparked the disputes. For example, in the eighth month of 1244, violent confrontations between senior and junior monks at Kōfukuji occurred, causing the opposing sides to barricade themselves and then battle it out within the compound. The origin of this conflict as well as its conclusion are unknown, though the older guard had to retire from the battle scene owing to the pressure from their younger brothers. Four years later, Go-Saga acted on behalf of Kōfukuji's ranking monks in 1248, when he had his own head administrator *(in-no-bettō)* calm the monks.[96] Thus, as shown most clearly in the Enjitsu conflict, a growing distance had arisen between the two noble cloisters of Daijōin and Ichijōin and the general clergy—an issue that will be treated further in Chapter 7.

A third realization gained from the Enjitsu conflict relates to the limited and declining influence of the Fujiwara chieftain, who was forced to defer to the cooperative efforts of the retired emperor and Rokuhara. In fact, the severing of the tie between the Fujiwara chieftain and the clergy of the clan temple that began cautiously in the twelfth century was now obvious even to contemporary observers in the capital. One of Go-Saga's closest retainers, Hamuro Sadatsugu, noted in his diary during an incident in 1246 that the Fujiwara chieftain completely lacked the power to control Kōfukuji, forcing, or perhaps creating the opportunity for, Go-Saga to intervene to preserve order.[97] The Kōfukuji monks had, in fact, turned the table on the Fujiwara chieftain, as the temple not only became more independent from the Fujiwara clan but also could exert unprecedented influence over its main secular patron in the late thirteenth century. For example, in a dispute over land, Kōfukuji supporters attacked and destroyed four Tōnomine locations with casualties on both sides in the eighth month of 1284. As a result, the imperial court issued an edict to various officials in the Kinai region, ordering that the originators be arrested. Instead of cooperating with the imperial court, as was expected, the Kōfukuji clergy responded by excommunicating Fujiwara no Kanenaka, whose signature appeared on the edict because of his assignment as a scribe-recorder *(kurōdo)*. The members of the imperial court were not only upset, but also fear-struck, as evidenced by another Fujiwara member's (Tsuneyori's) refusal to produce a document to report the situation to the Kamakura Bakufu. Despite his caution, Tsuneyori was also excommunicated in the middle of the ninth month, and the court appeared to be as much in disarray as in disbelief over the actions of the Kōfukuji clergy until both unfortunate Fujiwaras were reinstated the following month.[98]

The excommunications of members of the Fujiwara clan were part of a new trend. Thus, when monks and peasants in a Kōfukuji estate refused to forward portions of the annual rent *(nengu)* that belonged to the Kantō and Rokuhara wanted to examine the matter in the twelfth month of 1289, the monks responded by excommunicating the Fujiwara chieftain from the clan.[99] Moreover, in 1291, an Enryakuji monk was appointed for a court ritual even though that honor was usually reserved for Kōfukuji clerics. Again, the monks in Nara perceived that the Fujiwara chieftain did not represent their interests, and they excommunicated him in the first month of the following year. This strategy became the preferred modus operandi at this juncture, and other members

of the Fujiwara clan were similarly expelled in related incidents in
1292.[100] The excommunicated members were usually restored in
the clan by the temple later, but not until they had repented either
with donations or a declaration of cooperation in the future.
Times were indeed changing, not only for the Fujiwara, but also
for the *kenmon* temples, which simultaneously obtained a larger
degree of independence and were forced to rely more exclusively
on their own means for protection and to maintain their status as
they distanced themselves from their main secular patrons.

Kōyasan's Quest for Independence and Local Hegemony

Of the three temples in this study, Kōyasan may have engaged the
bakufu most frequently in various land disputes, perhaps because
it had more in common with the warrior class as a power attempting to assert local control. In addition, the temple was the most
popular of the established sects among the warrior class, obtaining donations from bakufu officials, especially the Hōjō and the
Adachi, and other ranking warriors, while serving as a retreat
for warriors who became lay practitioners *(nyūdō)*.[101] Therefore,
despite traditional patronage from the capital elites, the Kōyasan
clergy was prone to turn to the bakufu even when a conflict fell
within the responsibilities of the court. For example, supporters
of Kinpusen, a temple-shrine complex with Kōfukuji affiliations
located southwest of Nara, invaded Kōyasan property in 1223,
causing the latter to complain to the bakufu even though no warrior or retainer of the bakufu was involved. The bakufu handed
out a verdict in Kōyasan's favor, which, judging from the absence
of further records, resolved the dispute.[102]

The bakufu was also forced to step in frequently in a recurring
border dispute over water rights between Kōyasan's Nade-no-shō
and Kokawadera's Mionoya village.[103] The conflict has distinctly
local origins, dating to 1240, when Minamoto no Yoshiharu, an administrator of Nade-no-shō, attempted to divert water from Nade
to one of his own holdings in the neighboring Mionoya Estate
(see Figure 14). To accomplish this task, he conspired with the
deputy *jitō* of Mionoya, a certain Taira no Nagayasu, before proceeding to break an embankment to extract water for his own
fields. On the death of Yoshiharu soon thereafter, Nagayasu opportunistically claimed his former ally's entire landholding, some of
which was located in disputed areas on Mt. Shiio in the border

region between the estates, causing protests from the residents of Nade. The respective estate managers met on the thirteenth day of the fifth month of 1241 in an attempt to settle the issue, but Nagayasu broke the truce that night by cutting a good share of the harvest. The peasants of Nade would not quietly accept such behavior and proceeded to take possession of the remainder of the harvest the following night. At that point, monks from Kokawadera stepped in to support their estate manager, while forwarding a complaint to the imperial court as well as to Rokuhara, inducing Kōyasan to do the same on behalf of the Nade inhabitants.[104]

Matters were further complicated by the flow of Mizunagawa, a river that originated from two smaller streams flowing down the slopes of Mt. Shiio, marking the border between Nade and Mionoya. However, Mizunagawa had changed course from the time of the establishment of the two estates in the mid–Heian period, so that there was now also a dispute over the rights to the river as well as the land around it. Since the imperial court was in a transition, with factions positioning themselves and supporting various candidates for the imperial throne until Go-Saga was selected in the third month of 1242, it was not able to handle such a compli-

Figure 14. The Nade-Mionoya conflict
(graphic representation)

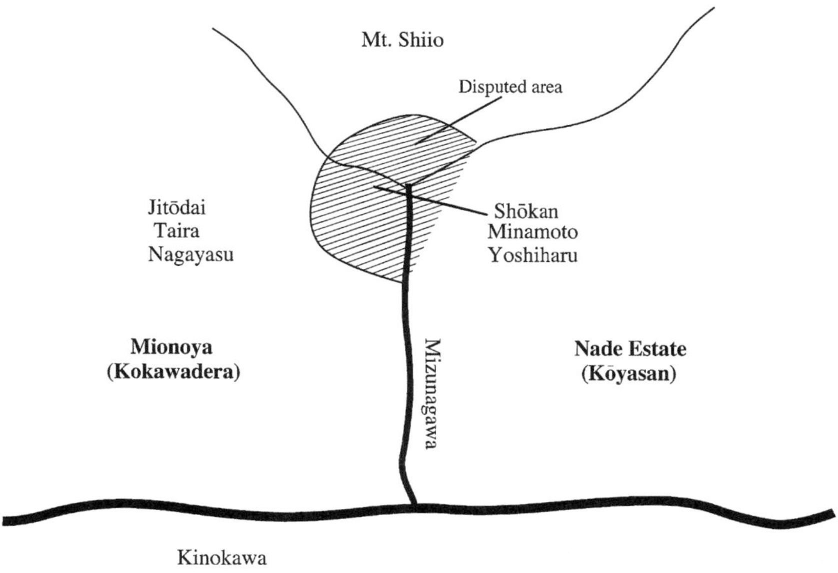

cated issue. Moreover, the dispute also involved a deputy *jitō* (Nagayasu), clearly putting it in the judicial sphere of the bakufu, which started the process of litigation in the seventh month of 1243 by ordering the Rokuhara deputies to find a solution. Yet it was not until the middle of 1244 that the Rokuhara representatives got around to a trial-confrontation *(taiketsu),* spending a full seven days during a period of one month listening to the pleas from representatives from Tōji (as the main temple of Kōyasan) and Kokawadera as well as the managers from each side. The dispute proved difficult to solve, however, because of the changing course of the river and the warrior government's unfamiliarity with local conditions. Thus, another year passed before Rokuhara finally sent representatives to the disputed area to examine the borders and create a new map of the area in question. But neither Rokuhara nor the bakufu was prepared or willing to issue a verdict even at this stage. Rather, the bakufu suddenly and surprisingly attempted to disengage itself from the conflict, claiming that, "border disputes in the west" *(saikoku sakai sōron)* were not issues for the warrior government to resolve unless they also involved criminal acts.[105] Left on its own, the imperial court finally made its judgment only several years later, in the twelfth month of 1250. Though the court stated that the Mizuna River did not belong to either estate, but was rather public property, the verdict was more favorable to Mionoya, despite poor documentation from both sides. The court rejected Nade's claim to Shiioyama and determined that the river's origin was located on the western side of the mountain, within the sphere of the Mionoya village.[106]

Instead of resolving the conflict, this verdict caused the disputing parties to enter a more violent stage, as disappointed inhabitants of Nade destroyed irrigation structures and raided Mionoya on three occasions during 1251 and 1252. One appeal claimed that residents of Nade estate, who appear to have been local rogues acting under the pretext of the water rights dispute, had invaded the neighboring village in full warrior attire, killing and injuring several people while ranging the area for objects worth stealing. Since these were clearly criminal acts, Kokawadera now appealed to the bakufu, which forwarded the issue to Rokuhara. In the seventh month of 1253, after Nade inhabitants had failed to appear at a trial in Kyoto, Kii's deputy *shugo* headed a force of bakufu retainers *(gokenin)* to calm the residents and to construct a particular kind of embankment that would allow both estates to receive equal amounts of water from the river.[107] But the inhabitants of Nade would not recognize the settlement or the arrangement and destroyed the dam the following year, resulting in new construction by the deputy *shugo,* who seemed unable or unwilling to deal with the deconstructive Nade people more harshly. Clearly, the Nade aggressors must have been quite organized, and perhaps they were even accomplished warriors, as indicated in an appeal forwarded by the Mionoya village deputy *jitō* Shinagawa Kiyohisa in the eighth month of 1257, asking for a punishment of the neighboring conspirators. The bakufu supported Kiyohisa, but the records do not indicate any punitive actions against the perpetrators. The story repeated itself some six years later, in 1263, when Nade inhabitants raided Mionoya, causing several fatalities. The deputy *shugo* now asked the help of Yuasa Munenari, one of the most powerful warriors and bakufu retainers in Kii, to enforce a punishment, but the Nade estate managers escaped, since the inhabitants claimed that they had been dismissed in favor of new officers. After new reports of Nade intrusions in 1268, the conflict finally seems to have died out on its own.[108]

The Nade-Mionoya conflict contained the traditional elements of competition for land and resources, but somewhat unusual is the lack of involvement of prominent warriors operating under the protection of the bakufu. Rather, the incidents were initiated by lower-class peasants and warriors, though the proprietors took an active role in defending the interests of their estate inhabitants. It was the Kongōbuji clergy that forwarded statements to the Rokuhara representatives during the trial, thus engaging itself in local management issues involving inhabitants not directly affiliated with the monastery to a degree rarely found for Enryakuji and Kōfukuji. Other land disputes involving Kōyasan reflect the more typical tensions between the emerging warrior class and the religious proprietor, as evidenced by two particular estates, where the temple struggled to maintain its control. First, Minabe-no-shō, located in the southern part of Kii, was an important *shōen* (established under Retired Emperor Toba), which provided not only rice but also other pertinent material such as lumber for the monastic complex on Mt. Kōya. It was desirable for the temple to maintain complete and direct control of this estate to assure a steady income, but the bakufu appointed a *jitō,* the first of whom was also the *shugo* of Kii. It is well known that the private ambitions of the *jitō* were often in conflict with his responsibility to collect and forward taxes for the proprietors, and there is, in fact, a record of orders from the bakufu to the *jitō* of Minabe in 1222, ordering him to forward taxes as promised.[109] When problems erupted again in 1247, Kōyasan appealed to the bakufu that the *jitō* kept three-quarters of the rice taxes, ignoring an order from Retired Emperor Go-Saga to forward the appropriate share. The Kōyasan clergy also took the opportunity to ask the bakufu to depose the *jitō* and to exempt the estate from future appointments. But it also seems that the *jitō* was not alone in trying to usurp income from the estate. The appeal additionally stated that local monks had attempted to extract taxes for their own sake by claiming they had permission to do so from the bakufu. The bakufu acknowledged the temple's rights and condemned the inappropriate acts of the *jitō*, who, though not deposed, was ordered to forward the temple's share.[110]

Another estate of tremendous wealth, Ōta-no-shō, located in Bingo Province, provides further evidence of Kōyasan's concerns with the local warrior class and the bakufu's high degree of involvement in the temple's land disputes. The estate was established by Go-Shirakawa in 1166, when the custodian title was awarded to Taira no Shigehira. Following the Genpei War, Go-Shirakawa managed to exempt Ōta from *jitō* appointments, and later he donated the entire estate to Kōyasan when the monk Kakua asked for funding for Buddhist services at the Grand Pagoda. In 1196, four years after the retired emperor's death, Yoritomo reversed his decision, appointing a *jitō* to Ōta, which already was staffed with managers from the temple, resulting in conflicts that would last into the fourteenth century.[111] An abundance of sources relating to Ōta remain, and the many other studies on the estate need not be accounted for here, but some disputes occurred during the thirteenth century that demonstrate important aspects of Kōyasan's status and character as a powerful monastic center and landholder. For example, the bakufu issued a verdict in 1235 ordering the *jitō* to stop appropriating rice fields in the estate. At the same time, it also ordered Rokuhara to examine local conditions to establish which fields actually belonged to the *jitō*, his deputy, and Kōyasan's manager.[112] The problems continued despite such verdicts, and there was yet another admonishment in 1263, when Retired Emperor Go-Saga issued an order from his headquarters (an *inzen*) to Kōyasan stating that intrusions of the Ōta estate should stop immediately. The conflict was a straightforward and familiar one: the *jitō* and the temple's administrator *(azukari dokoro)* quarreled over the division of taxes. The dispute reemerged in 1272, when the appeal was brought to the Kantō. Hōjō Tokimune, shogunal regent, ordered that the illegal activities by the *jitō* deputy cease and that taxes be forwarded according to a compromise *(wayojō)* that had been established between the temple's manager and the *jitō* in 1270.[113] Thus, regardless of the earlier verdicts of 1263 to secure income from Ōta, Kōyasan had been forced to sign a new agreement to divide the taxes with the *jitō*, but only two years after that compromise, the temple found itself scrambling to defend its rights. The authority of the bakufu was limited despite its attempts to support the rights of Kōyasan, as evidenced by repeated problems of nondelivery of taxes between 1274 and 1286, resulting in new compromises and divisions of revenues between the *jitō* and Kōyasan managers in 1301.[114]

While Kōyasan's struggles to maintain its right to and its income from Minabe and Ōta can be seen as typical expressions of the problems that most elite temples experienced during the late Kamakura era, there are also cases where the temple's activities set it apart from its religious colleagues in the vicinity of the capital. It cannot be denied that Kōyasan aimed at developing a kind of local rulership that came to stand apart from that of traditional *shōen* proprietors, showing the same kind of ambitions found among the leaders of the warrior class. The process is often referred to as *"ryōshu-ka"* (becoming a local proprietor), a vital step within the larger trend of local powers gaining control and independence at the expense of the capital elites. Japanese scholars have thus described the process in terms that are usually applied to local warriors, noting that Kōyasan controlled its estates directly without any middlemen by the fourteenth century, as most uniquely reflected in the land surveys that Kongōbuji performed on nearby estates.[115] Aragawa-no-shō offers a particularly interesting example. Despite the problems the Kongōbuji clergy had experienced on the estate in the twelfth century (described in Chapter 4) the temple managed to establish a firmer grip on Aragawa about a century later. Thus, in 1254, despite protests from the estate inhabitants, Aragawa was subjected to a survey in which the number of homesteads and expected taxes for Kōyasan were listed in an attempt to establish firmer control of the estate.[116] Two features of Aragawa allowed for these measures. First, the estate's proximity to Mt. Kōya made it geographically and militarily possible to control directly, a characteristic that Aragawa had in common with the several estates that Kongōbuji claimed as part of Kūkai's original temple domain (*goshuin engi;* see Map 5). Second, the absence of warrior managers allowed assertive peasants and lower warriors to mount their own collective resistance against various threats and pressures, becoming an important force for or against any proprietor or manager, as was the case in particular in the last third of the thirteenth century. In 1275 a resident of Aragawa, a certain Minamoto no Tametoki, was accused of killing the manager of a neighboring estate. The bakufu accordingly sent out local vassals, both of the formidable Yuasa family, and had Tametoki arrested. Several years later Tametoki somehow managed to return to the estate and attacked another village, killing more than ten people. Interestingly, the bakufu sent an order in 1285 to the Yuasa retainer, asking to have Kōyasan hand over Tametoki, indicating thus that the temple had taken measures to protect this rogue. Half a year later, Tametoki was active in Aragawa again confronting and killing some other local troublemakers. Kōyasan subsequently judged both the victims and Tametoki to be "serious criminals" and confiscated their possessions. In the second month of 1286, the *shugo* examined the incidents and demanded Tametoki be extradited, but Kōyasan, which seemed to be in control of the situation on its own, refused. In the tenth month Tametoki took Buddhist vows to become a lay practitioner and signed a twelve-clause pledge on Mt. Kōya, promising to abide by the rules of the Kongōbuji administrators.[117]

Yet problems erupted anew in 1290, when Tametoki, regardless of his Buddhist vows, spearheaded new criminal acts, such as the stealing of horses and oxen, and the burning of farming residences in Aragawa. Despite a new pledge to Kongōbuji to stop such activities, Tametoki's group continued to invade rice fields and residences into the next year. Not relying on bakufu warriors to preserve order, the Kōyasan clergy assembled its own forces of "evil monks," which joined a local warrior, Mike Shinjō (who was also a Kamakura retainer apparently acting on the temple's behalf), in launching an attack on Tametoki and his residence in 1291. Though the Kōyasan forces appeared to have the situation under control in the ninth month of that year, Tametoki countered with forces from Takanodera, a local branch temple of Enryakuji's Hiesha, enlisted with the help of a claim that timber belonging to the Hie branch was stolen during the attack on Tametoki's dwelling. Tametoki was attempting to add the power and authority of Enryakuji, hoping that its central *kenmon* status would help him reclaim his land from Kōyasan.[118] In fact, the Tendai head abbot, princely monk Jijō, immediately asked Tōji to examine the situation, thus approaching the highest level of the Shingon pyramid according to the practices of representative justice in the *kenmon* state. The workings of shared rulership were apparently still effective, since Kōyasan abandoned its attempts to solve the problem with its own military force, turning instead to the bakufu with an appeal. Tametoki immediately responded by getting the Tendai *zasu* to forward a similar complaint to Roku-hara, which sent out representatives to examine Aragawa late in 1291. Though the outcome of this case is not known, it appears that Mike Shinjō lost his posts as *kumon* of Aragawa and *jitō* of his own Mike-no-shō, whereas Tametoki finally disappeared from the scene, or at least from Aragawa, following the questioning in early 1292.[119]

Joint efforts by local peasants and warriors, organized in bands known as *"akutō"* in contemporary sources, are characteristic of the rise of the lower classes against the proprietors in the country-side that became common in the fourteenth century. Tametoki and his adherents were early proponents of this trend (as were the rebellious inhabitants of Nade), but their failure to oust the proprietor not only demonstrates that such self-government was as yet premature, but also reflects the increase of direct rulership by Kōyasan, which, by using the bakufu at opportune occasions, managed to assert its own local control of Aragawa in the late thirteenth century. Similar ambitions and results can be seen in Ategawa-no-shō, which the Kōyasan clergy had claimed as part of the original temple homestead since the eleventh century. Such claims were intensified in the thirteenth century, as evidenced by several appeals in the 1250s that challenged Jakurakuji's pro-prietorship (see Figure 11 above).[120] Since the appeals had not yielded any results, Kongōbuji attempted to extend its control in Ategawa by aligning itself with the local managers against the lawful proprietor. The aforementioned Yuasa family had its home base in Ategawa, serving as *jitō* on the estate and as bakufu repre-sentatives throughout the Kii peninsula, making for a powerful but also unreliable ally, skilled in both the legal procedures of the bakufu and the ways of the warrior. In 1259, for example, Yuasa

Mitsunobu countered an appeal from Kōyasan by stating that one of the temple's own monks, a certain Harima *hokkyō,* had caused the plundering and the riots on the estate.[121] Since the bakufu had no effective way of punishing the *jitō,* who was also the vassal of the warrior government, there was little it could do to halt the ambitions of the local warrior clan in the long run. Thus, less than ten years later, in 1266, Rokuhara was forced to order a stop to the intrusions by a Yuasa member of Ategawa again, and in the following year, it even summoned the *jitō* of Ategawa to Kyoto twice to ask about the forwarding (or lack thereof) of taxes and the complaints presented by Kōyasan, but none of these measures appears to have had any lasting impact.[122]

Kōyasan was, however, undeterred, and the clergy continued to ally itself with and play the Yuasa *jitō* against Jakurakuji's local estate manager (usually the *zasshō*), as demonstrated by the many complaints lodged by the proprietor's manager. But, the Yuasa strategies, which on occasion became quite violent and dramatic, could also result in fierce resistance from the local estate residents, making it difficult to accomplish the clergy's goals of establishing direct control of Ategawa. The most famous incident occurred in 1275, when farmers from a village submitted an appeal claiming that the *jitō,* Yuasa Munechika, forced them to work for him, cutting off their ears and noses and the hair of their women if they refused to obey. Since this letter represents one of the earliest known instances of an appeal from the farming population (although they were assisted by the steward sent out from Jakurakuji), written almost entirely in the simplified *kana* syllabary, it has gained much recognition and attention from scholars in Japan. It is also interesting to note that Munechika was accused of not forwarding rent to Jakurakuji, serving as an indication of Munechika's continued efforts against the legitimate proprietor.[123]

In 1278 the Kongōbuji clergy increased the pressure by threatening to close the entire monastic center on Mt. Kōya if Jakurakuji's "intrusions" of Ategawa were not stopped and the estate was not confirmed as a Kōyasan estate. Kongōbuji's claims were supported by the Yuasa, who needed the temple as an ally to offset the resistance of the farming population. The bakufu conveniently overlooked the role of its own vassal here and avoided issuing a verdict by maintaining that the incident was a conflict between two temples: Kōyasan and Jakurakuji. While the matter thus lingered at the imperial court, Kōyasan was able to put in place administrators, who collected taxes from Ategawa with the help of the Yuasa, and when the question of ownership of the estate came up again in 1304, Retired Emperor Go-Uda acknowledged Kongōbuji as the proprietor, though the Yuasa remained a local challenge to the temple's complete control.[124]

Kōyasan's primary concern was thus to maintain and expand its landed base close to the temple. In fact, no conflicts or appeals concerning religious privileges involving Kōyasan can be found during Go-Saga's era, which sets it apart from the other two elite temples. In addition, Kōyasan's success or failure to protect its estates depended more than anything on the location of the estates and its ability to assert its right through both legal and military means. Although not without difficulties, the temple managed to defend its position in Minabe and Aragawa and to establish control over Ategawa, paving the way for the temple's development into a strong local power in Kii. The situation was quite different on the more distant Ōta estate, where the temple had to compromise with the local warrior-managers to secure part of the rent it was entitled to. Land disputes most frequently became issues for the bakufu and its Rokuhara representatives, but such intervention did not stop the Kongōbuji clergy from using a wide array of strategies to extend and maintain its possessions, including enlisting local warriors to exert its own justice, forging alliances with more prominent local warriors, and appealing to the court in more traditional fashion with *kenmon*-like threats of closing the temple.

Conclusion

The similarities between the policies of Go-Saga and the retired emperors of a century earlier, as well as of the Fujiwara chieftains, indicate that the late Heian style of rulership continued throughout the thirteenth century. The initiative for making changes in the political balance among Buddhist sects and temples in the capital region was still held by the imperial family. The sharing of and competition for privileges among religious institutions were part of the workings of cooperative rulership; at no point are there protests in Kyoto that did not also involve leading factions in the capital. Indeed, the rivalry between Enryakuji and Onjōji, which had been practically dormant for decades, was revived not by the monks themselves, but by Go-Saga's attempts to augment his position in the capital area after a more than two-decade-long eclipse of imperial power. The well-documented rivalry for the abbotship of Shitennōji underlines this point. The matter became complicated for the first time in 1180, when Onjōji lost its monopoly over the post, giving both Tendai complexes legitimate claims to the office. Yet nothing in the sources gives reason to believe that the court, with the bakufu's help, was unable to resolve the issue once and for all. However, such a solution would have ensured an indefinite advantage to the favored temple, causing the court to lose control of the abbotship. In other words, the court wished to retain its privilege to appoint abbots from the two temples so that it might use the office as an ultimate form of leverage. Such impermanence was an integral part of the delicate balance that constituted a central element of shared rulership.

It is also evident that both the Kōfukuji and the Enryakuji clergies had gained further strength vis-à-vis their noble allies. Kōfukuji successfully resisted Enjitsu's attempts to take control in Nara, and Enryakuji withstood a challenge that combined the forces of Onjōji, the retired emperor, and the bakufu. The religious elites had distanced themselves from the secular elites with a higher degree of independence as compared to a century earlier. However, this distancing also brought about a weakening of the efficiency of the twelfth-century strategies of protest and communication. Divine demonstrations were not as successful, as Enryakuji monks began to instigate self-destruction, and their Kōfukuji colleagues made excommunications of Fujiwara chieftains a common strategy to make their demands better heard in Kyoto. To some extent, these new strategies may reflect less reliance on the established Buddhist centers in an era when the warrior government, which was clearly less dependent on the old sects, was expected to provide physical protection. A weakening of the bond between secular and religious elites in the capital region also meant a less effective Kyoto rulership, making the presence of the bakufu all the more important.

The Kamakura Bakufu, for its part, was at the peak of its power during the second half of the thirteenth century, but it did not dominate all aspects of capital politics. The Kantō leaders left (perhaps even shunned) several important matters to be determined by the capital elites, in particular the status and the privileges of the most powerful religious institutions, reflecting a continuation of the political context of the twelfth century in which

Enryakuji and Kōfukuji managed to maintain their positions. Although the bakufu occasionally intervened in spheres of traditional Kyoto authority, it did not do so with the intention of overthrowing the court or its associated elites, but rather to protect the style of rulership that it was, in fact, a central part of. The warrior government's willingness to allow Kōfukuji control of Yamato Province is one of the best expressions of this policy. There can be no doubt from the cases in which the bakufu failed to act, from its punishment of Kōfukuji (1235–1236), and from its endeavors to solve land disputes in Kii Province, allowing Kōyasan to extend its control vis-à-vis the bakufu's own vassals, that the warrior government in the Kantō was first and foremost committed to preserving the status quo and maintaining a system of shared rulership. Even the methods used by the bakufu to assert its policing authority—issuing edicts to restrict the monks and to prohibit the use of arms, and using the head abbot as the channel of communication and control—were traditional and undisruptive, imitating the policies of earlier retired emperors and courtiers.

While Kōyasan headed in a different direction from Enryakuji and Kōfukuji, focusing on establishing a local rulership with direct control of warrior bands, regional warrior leaders, and the peasantry, it also continued to use its more traditional elite status. Appeals were forwarded to both the court and the bakufu, claiming violations of the temple's traditional privileges granted it by past sovereigns for their salvation and for the protection of the state. These were the claims, whether valid or not, of a *kenmon* temple attempting to improve its local stakes. It did so using both "ancient" policies against the growing powers of local warriors and the more "medieval" strategies of an aggressive proprietor with a unique ability to spin a new web of control in a more limited yet concentrated area south of the center of politics.

In short, the second half of the thirteenth century was less dominated by the warrior government than many scholars have assumed. The Kamakura Bakufu relied on the court to exercise its bureaucratic power and on the religious elites to perform their duties, and it was thoroughly committed to maintaining this hallowed division of responsibilities and shared rulership. As providers of spiritual power, Enryakuji and Kōfukuji retained their traditional status, while Kōyasan used the bakufu to enhance its power within a polity that might still most aptly be termed the *kenmon* state.

6

Protesting and Fighting in the Name of the *Kami* and the Buddhas

Conflicts involving elite temples in the capital were closely connected to, frequently even directly caused by, decisions made—or in some cases, not made—by leading members of the imperial court. Ironically, Enryakuji, which was supposed to protect the capital from evil spirits from the northeast, was the temple that staged most protests in the capital, followed by Kōfukuji and Tōdaiji.[1] But why did the members of Enryakuji and Kōfukuji choose to express their discontent by protesting in Kyoto? Scholars in both Japan and the West have neglected to address this issue, thus failing to grasp the distinction between the different sorts of conflicts in the Heian and Kamakura eras. Though battles between religious centers, regional conflicts involving monks and warriors, and demonstrations *(gōso)* in Kyoto all emerged as a result of privatization of government and increasing factionalism, these conflicts were also expressions of distinctively different circumstances. The failure to recognize these differences has sustained the widespread misconception that religious protests in the capital were nothing short of violent attacks aiming to undercut the authority of the government. Thus, a thorough scrutiny of the *gōso* themselves as well as in comparison to other kinds of conflicts is long overdue. What was the rationale behind the *gōso?* What issues induced the monks to stage such demonstrations? What alternative means of applying pressure were used? How were the *gōso* perceived in the capital? How did the court and the bakufu respond to these divine demonstrations? And why were the protests so successful? In addition to providing a better understanding of the *gōso,* the answers to these questions reflect other important considerations, such as the temples' political rights and the religious beliefs of the elites.

The History of the *Gōso*

The term *"gōso,"* which literally means "forceful protest," does not appear in sources until late in the Kamakura period and first becomes common in the fourteenth century. Nevertheless, Japanese scholars consistently use it to refer to the protests that began to appear some two centuries earlier.[2] The contemporary terms for such appeals were *"uttaemōsu"* (to forward an appeal), *"soshō"* (a lawsuit), or occasionally *"ureimōsu"* (to state a grievance), and the demonstrations were commonly recorded as *"shinmoku"* or *"shin'yō juraku"* (the entering of the holy branch/holy cart into the capital). Yet despite the anachronism, *"gōso"* remains a helpful term, and it will be used in its analytical form here, since it most comprehensively connotes the phenomenon that is best described as divine demonstrations. The *gōso* were characterized by two important elements. First, they describe an appeal that was brought to the capital by monks from a temple, frequently also supported by service people from some of its branch shrines. Second, spiritual pressure was exercised by bringing symbols of the *kami* (the native gods) to Kyoto. In the case of Enryakuji, this symbol was a *mikoshi* (or *shin'yō* in contemporary sources): a sacred palanquin or a portable shrine that was believed to house a specific *kami,* represented by a holy object inside. The Kasuga and Kumano complexes employed a different symbolism throughout the late Heian and Kamakura eras, using a branch of the sacred tree (a *sakaki*), known as the *"shinmoku,"* carried on a small platform with holy mirrors attached to it.[3] These various components had diverse origins and did not come together until quite late in the eleventh century, during the *insei* of Shirakawa.

The practice of appealing in the capital against policies by the imperial court and its representatives began sometime late in the tenth century. One of the earliest protests may have been staged by Kasuga in the seventh month of 968, when a holy *sakaki* branch was carried to the capital for the first time. This case is difficult to verify in contemporary sources, though later Kasuga chronicles claim that the protest was caused by a land dispute between Kōfukuji and Tōdaiji. In the end, it cannot be known if the *shinmoku* was truly carried to the capital during this dispute, or to what extent Kōfukuji was involved. The timing is not unlikely, however, since the first confirmed appeal was lodged in 987 by a small number of service people of the Ise shrine, who, carrying a sacred tree, protested against the inappropriate behavior of the governor. Similar appeals were taken to the capital, though without any divine assistance, by commoners and farmers against the governors of Kaga (1012) and Ōmi (1036).[4] Moreover, the Kōfukuji clergy joined servants of Kasuga in an appeal regarding an estate belonging to the shrine in the capital in 1006, though there is no evidence that any sacred *sakaki* branches were used.[5] Imitating these early forms of appeals, Enryakuji brought its first appeal to Kyoto in the second month of 1039, when some monks proceeded to the regent Fujiwara no Yorimichi's mansion to prevent the Onjōji monk Myōson from becoming Tendai *zasu*.[6] Although this demonstration lacks the spiritual component of the *gōso*, it was an important precedent for later protests, as it bypassed established channels of appealing, targeting the powerful Fujiwara chieftain directly. Nonetheless, such protests were not the norm at the time, and the appeal of 1039 was an exception necessitated by the circumstances. Since the issue was the appointment of a new head abbot, who was normally the proper channel of communication, the monks were forced to approach the leading noble to voice their discontent.

The two main elements of the *gōso* were thus in place early in the eleventh century, but they were not combined and used by a Buddhist complex nor were they part of a regularized way of appealing until almost a century later. The exact date of the first divine demonstration is an issue of some disagreement among historians. For example, Nagashima Fukutarō, a scholar of the history of Nara, states that it was staged by Kōfukuji in 1093, when the monks went from Nara to Kyoto carrying the *shinmoku* from the Kasuga shrine for the first time. The issue was a familiar one: disputing over the income from a private estate, the protesters wanted the governor of Ōmi Province (a certain Takashina Tameie) exiled for not honoring an exemption of taxes, for appropriating income for himself, and for the harassment of service people of Kasuga.[7] However, Hioki Shōichi—who has done extensive research on armed monks in the premodern era—argues that the first *gōso* was staged in 1082, when members of Kumanodera carried sacred *sakaki* branches from their temple-shrine complex on the Kii peninsula to Kyoto.[8] Though Hioki does not specify his sources, there is reason to believe that Kōfukuji's protest in 1093 was indeed not the first divine demonstration by a temple. The custom of carrying a sacred symbol during an appeal was clearly known to the service people of Hiesha in the ninth month of 1092 when they protested at Fujiwara no Morozane's mansion against the harassment of Hie servants by other members of the Fujiwara clan. In fact, the protesters must have learned about the symbolism from earlier demonstrations by Kumanodera or Kōfukuji, since they carried a sacred *sakaki* branch instead of the holy carts that they came to use later. Moreover, a temple was involved in this protest, since the Enryakuji clergy supported the appeal in response to the court's light reprimand of the offenders, stating that a more severe punishment was needed to placate the anger of Sannō (the Mountain King deity) and to appease the buddhas and the bodhisattvas. The native gods and the buddhas had, in other words, found a way jointly to oppose decisions taken in the capital through the *gōso*, as suggested in a statement attributed to the Kōfukuji clergy during the 1093 protest against the Ōmi governor, claiming that "the shrine's grief is [also] the grief of the temple."[9]

Following the protests of the early 1090s, the *kami* gradually became more frequent participants in temple demonstrations and appeals. For example, when Minamoto no Yoshitsuna was acquitted by the imperial court after having killed an Enryakuji monk in a *shōen* of Mino Province in 1095, sacred palanquins from Hiesha were carried to the main temple building (the Konpon chūdō) on top of Mt. Hiei for the first time. The monks further threatened to bring the palanquins with them to the capital if their demands were not met, but Retired Emperor Shirakawa was not intimidated. Instead, he sent a message to the Department of Divine Affairs *(jingikan)* stating that the sacred palanquins should be stopped and that they were not to be feared.[10] In the end, the *mikoshi* never entered Kyoto, as only a handful of messengers were sent to the court to deliver the appeal.

It is not until 1105 that there is proof that sacred palanquins associated with the Enryakuji complex were actually carried to the capital to support an appeal. At that time, the issue was the appointment of an Onjōji monk as master of the lecture meeting on the Lotus Sūtra at Enshūji (see Chapter 3). Monks from Mt. Hiei descended to join members of Gionsha who carried their *mikoshi* to another branch (Kyōgokuji) in the capital. Thus supported by the *kami* from Gion, the protesters subsequently proceeded to the location of the noble council's meetings (the *jin-no-tō*), close to the imperial residence itself, where they stayed until the court nobles surrendered to their demands the follow-

ing day, thus making this first Enryakuji *gōso* a successful one.[11]
This success notwithstanding, divine demonstrations did not immediately become the preferred standard for appeals and protests.
For example, though a conflict over Daisenji in Hōki Province
between Iwashimizu Hachimangū and Enryakuji involved more
violence and even a direct confrontation of the opposing camps
later that year, the sacred palanquins were never deployed. Nor
did the attack of a police captain's retainers on some service
people of Hiesha cause any demonstrations supported by these
palanquins.[12] Furthermore, in 1108, when Enryakuji and Onjōji
joined forces to complain about Shirakawa's favoritism of Tōji,
members from both Tendai complexes entered the capital, though
apparently without palanquins.[13] The lack of divine symbols in
these important protests following the first *gōso* indicates that
such strategies were not immediately considered crucial for successful appeals. However, the palanquins became more and more
common in the protests of the second half of Shirakawa's *insei*.
In 1113, during the bitter conflict between Enryakuji and Kōfukuji, the sacred palanquins were carried around on Mt. Hiei, and
messengers were sent to the retired emperor's palace to appeal.[14]

It is no coincidence that Enryakuji began to demonstrate in
the capital during Shirakawa's era, when the retired emperor tried
to improve his own position by shifting the power among the *kenmitsu* sects. As Motoki Yasuo has pointed out, Shirakawa's religious policies also affected Kōfukuji in an identical manner, spurring simultaneous development of *gōso* from Nara.[15] In 1103, for
example, the imperial court decided to appoint several junior
monks, including a certain Shin'ei, over other more senior colleagues to function as the main lecturers at Kōfukuji's most important ceremony, the Yuima'e. Though the clergy admitted that
Shin'ei was extraordinarily talented, they claimed that seniority,
which was generally held as the determining factor for ranking
Buddhist monks, should determine the order of promotion. To
calm the increasingly agitated monks, the imperial court sent a
messenger to Nara, but it only made matters worse, causing the
clergy to leave their temples that night to stage a protest. On the
following day the monks promptly proceeded to the capital,
appearing at the Fujiwara clan's administrative headquarters in
Kyoto—the Kangakuin—with their sacred Kasuga branch. The
monks stayed in the capital for days, creating disorder and concern among the nobles, but they also attempted to apply additional pressure on the Fujiwara chieftain by stating that they

would pay a personal visit to him at his villa in Uji unless the matter was resolved in the clergy's favor. The monks returned to Nara only after having been reassured that their demands would be heard, and the promotion of the young monks was consequently canceled.[16]

The *gōso* were a new negotiating tool, based loosely on preceding protesting practices, that developed in direct response to the retired emperor's policies among temples most affected by such changes. Whereas the early protests in the 1090s were poorly organized and rather sporadic, the *gōso* in the later half of Shirakawa's era developed distinct patterns that were used for centuries to come. The standardized progression of Kōfukuji's *gōso* was essentially in place during the protest of 1103, but the monks also made regular the visit to the Fujiwara chieftain in Uji some ten years later in the fierce conflict with Enryakuji by adding it as a stopover before reaching Kyoto. The demonstrators' purpose was to make their presence known and to apply direct pressure on the clan chieftain, a strategy that the Kōfukuji monks used in most of their *gōso* in the late Heian and Kamakura eras. An additional stage was added in 1165, when the sacred branches were stationed at a temple hall known as the Utsushiden (The Moving Hall), located close to the Kasuga Shrine, in order to rally support among the clergy and send the first signals to Kyoto that a demonstration was being prepared.[17]

For Enryakuji, the standardized pattern emerged in a protest of 1123, when sacred palanquins of some of the seven main shrines of Hiesha were carried to Kyoto, marking the first time the *kami* were moved from Mt. Hiei to the capital. Demanding that one of Shirakawa's retainers be punished for the harassment of some Hie service people in Echizen Province, the demonstrators brought the *mikoshi* to the imperial palace to voice their concerns. However, after a confrontation with defending government warriors, the protesters left the palanquins in the palace area and were pursued to Gionsha, where they had secluded themselves. Apparently, the warriors did not respect the sanctuary of the Gion shrine and entered the premises to stir up another skirmish in front of the main shrine building, escaping punishment as retainers of the by now confident and influential retired emperor. Yet the *kami* remained a threat through the presence of the sacred carts in Kyoto, often overwhelming the military power of government warriors.[18]

Following Shirakawa's (and the imperial family's) rise to power, *gōso* became increasingly common in the capital, and there is little doubt that they caught the attention of the Kyoto nobles. An Enryakuji protest that was staged in the tenth month of 1160 was duly noted as marking the fifth time the *mikoshi* of Hiesha were brought to the capital.[19] In fact, by Go-Shirakawa's era, the *gōso* were not only a fairly familiar sight in Kyoto but a particular pattern of protesting had developed that was frequently used by the clergies of Kōfukuji and Enryakuji in a wide range of issues. For example, as seen in the Narichika Incident of 1169, palanquins from other branches were also used in Enryakuji protests; three *mikoshi* each from Hiesha and Gionsha were joined by two from the Kitano shrine. In addition to more spiritual pressure, the number of protesters also increased as other branches located in the capital were used in preparation for the appeal at the palace. Similarly, the protesters were now so numerous that they spread out to enter the palace area from two of its large eastern gates; the Yōmeimon and the Taikenmon (see Map 3), located close to the *jin-no-tō*, where the noble council held its meetings.[20] Additional shrines and divine symbols were also used to increase the spiritual pressure in Kōfukuji's protests, as the Hossō center sought support from various branches in the capital area. For example, Kiyomizudera became an important ally in Kyoto, as demonstrated in particular by Enryakuji's attacks on this center during Tendai-Hossō disputes. In addition, the *mikoshi* of the Yoshino branch and the sacred sword of Isonokami Nifuru Shrine (dedicated to the violent *kami* of thunder) were added in support of Kōfukuji during the 1173 dispute with Enryakuji, following an attack on Tōnomine.[21] Strength in numbers applied to the *kami* as well as the demonstrators, and so by using various shrines, the spiritual pressure could be gradually stepped up.

The development of divine demonstrations was thus much more gradual than many scholars have assumed. The individual aspects of what historians describe as *gōso* were essentially in place early in Shirakawa's era, and they emerged when leading powers within the imperial court sought to restrict privileges and tilt the accustomed balance among the elite Buddhist sects. Yet the standardized pattern that represents the *gōso* as a phenomenon did not develop until the last decades of Shirakawa's rulership, and they were not firmly in place until the very end of the Heian period. These ritualized protests are of great interest not only as evidence of the secular influence of the elite temples but also because they reflect elements of beliefs and represent a distinctive pattern of communication between the protesting temple and the ruling elites.

From Appeals to Divine Demonstrations

Despite the frequent occurrences of *gōso* in Kyoto, their symbolism, social meaning, and political relevance have not been systematically studied. Thus, Hioki Shōichi, for example, has been satisfied to argue that temples continued to protest with their sacred palanquins because it was the most successful means of pressuring the imperial court.[22] More important, Japanese scholars have yet to put these important phenomena into their proper historical context, and the *gōso* are still interpreted as predominantly aggressive attempts by monks and shrine servants to control capital politics, causing, in the long run, the demise of the Heian court. As a matter of fact, many historians still tend to view the divine demonstrations as attacks on the capital itself.[23] The *gōso* were not attacks on the capital or attempts to overthrow the government, nor were they necessarily meant to be violent. They were a last resort in the process of litigation by which temples showed their concern over certain policies or registered their displeasure with attempts to restrict their privileges. It is important to note that only elite temples, such as Enryakuji, Kōfukuji, and Tōdaiji, with a tradition of bringing appeals to the capital with the help of their *kami*, were entitled to stage a divine demonstration, reflecting the power of precedence and customs. Indeed, the ritualized behavior that came to characterize these *gōso* was accompanied by an increasingly standardized symbolism representing a means of communication that stood alongside the exhausted, more formal channels at this advanced stage of a dispute.

In the first place, one or more regular appeals rejected by the imperial court normally preceded a demonstration in the capital. For example, several months before followers of Iwashimizu Hachimangū and Enryakuji battled on the streets of Kyoto in 1105, both sides had filed appeals to gain control of Daisenji in Hōki Province. As described in Chapter 3, the court was unable or unwilling to make a decision either way in spite of extensive discussions, resulting in the opposing camps deciding to protect their interests in the capital proper.[24] Furthermore, in 1120, the Kōfukuji clergy lodged an appeal against the governor of Izumi

Province, accusing him of harassing service people of the Kasuga shrine. Instead of dealing with the appeal, the Fujiwara chieftain sent high-ranking Kōfukuji monks from the capital to calm the clergy in Nara. Unsurprisingly, the clergy responded by appearing at the Fujiwara headquarters in the capital (the Kangakuin) less than a week later.[25] To mention one more case, when Go-Shira-kawa refused to hear the plea from a small group of messengers from Enryakuji and Hiesha against Fujiwara no Narichika and his retainer Masatomo late in 1169, monks from Mt. Hiei entered the capital in great numbers with their palanquins, forcing the retired emperor to comply with their demands.[26]

By thus stalling or simply ignoring the appeals, the imperial court often tried to dismiss the claims of a temple, but such mea-sures served mostly to frustrate and anger the monks, inducing them to proceed to the capital to state their case more publicly. Delaying tactics were in fact consistently used by the secular au-thorities, as demonstrated by several intriguing cases. For example, when Go-Saga neglected for more than two months to act on En-ryakuji's appeal against his own favoritism toward Onjōji and against the killing of some priests in 1264, the clergy set fire to several of their own buildings on Mt. Hiei. Blaming the destruc-tion on the court's unfavorable policies toward Enryakuji, the monks subsequently entered the capital with a total of ten sacred palanquins, placing them strategically at the palaces of both the senior (Go-Saga) and the junior (Go-Fukakusa) retired emperors.[27] Go-Shirakawa employed yet a further technique of stalling. Facing the Enryakuji clergy for the second time in the Narichika Incident of 1169, the retired emperor promptly obliged the pro-testers, only to reverse his verdict and to reinstate the accused Fujiwara no Narichika as soon as the protesters left the capital. Unsurprisingly, this turnaround act resulted in new demon-strations the following year that forced Go-Shirakawa to exile his retainer again.[28] To mention one more example, it was the court's and the bakufu's inability to issue a verdict in a dispute over water rights between two estates that caused the Kōfukuji clergy to leave the sacred *sakaki* branches in the capital in 1235–1236.[29]

Divine demonstrations were thus not only a reaction against policies that ran counter to the interests of a temple, but also a direct response to the court's attempts to stall or to refuse to handle a case at all. Nevertheless, a rejected appeal rarely resulted in an immediate protest in the capital. Rather, the upset clergy went through a series of procedures and stages before ultimately marching to Kyoto. Though the *gōso* strictly speaking consisted of a protest with divine symbols in the capital, the larger process of preparing, rallying support, and marching toward Kyoto was as much part of the pressure applied on the imperial court. The progression of these protests serve as helpful reference points in understanding the *gōso* and their rationale.

A *gōso* could be initiated by any group of monks or lay followers with a grievance, and it was the shrine affiliate that provided the starting point. At Enryakuji, the first step was taken when the most persistent members of the community assembled at the compounds of the Hie shrines on the eastern foot of Mt. Hiei. The Hiesha complex consisted of seven main shrines, each corresponding to a native deity *(kami)* as a manifestation of a Buddhist counterpart, which were organized in order of their ranking.[30] To start a *gōso*, the discontented monks assembled in the compounds of several of these shrines, where their first objective was to receive the support of the gods that were believed to reside there. The *kami* were then transferred into their sacred palanquins *(shin'yō, or mikoshi)*, carried off to the top of Mt. Hiei, and placed in the vicinity of the Konpon chūdō (the central temple hall on Mt. Hiei). These portable carts were normally about six to ten feet high, twelve to fifteen feet long, and quite heavy because of their elaborate decoration, requiring a dozen or more servants to carry one on their shoulders. Besides the sacred mirror, symbolizing the supreme *kami,* contained in the cart, many *mikoshi* were also decorated with mirrors on the outside, probably in order to enhance the sacredness of the palanquin, especially in confrontations with warriors. Another important and frequent symbol was a golden phoenix *(hōō)*, which was placed on top of the cart. It is particularly interesting that Japan's oldest surviving *mikoshi* at Tamukeyama Hachimangū, dating back to the Kamakura period, is equipped with this symbol, as were many carts of the nobility.[31] Modern-day *mikoshi* frequently have a golden phoenix on their roofs as well, as depicted in Figure 15, which shows a cart from Hiesha before a festival. Although the symbolism of this sacred phoenix has not been explored, it is known to represent prosperity and wealth for the state and its dignitaries, indicating the symbiosis of the imperial state and the Buddhist/Shintō teachings. Still, further research on this topic will be needed before the use of the *hōō* and the ideology behind it can be properly understood.

Figure 15. Modern *mikoshi* (sacred palanquin) from Hiyoshi taisha in full decoration before a festival.

The earliest Enryakuji demonstrations were staged using the *mikoshi* of Gionsha, but it was the palanquins from Hiesha that became the principal symbols of the protests in the late twelfth century. The major difference was that, whereas the Hiesha carts had to be carried from the eastern side of Mt. Hiei via the main temple location on top of the mountain, the Gion carts were already in the capital area and thus excluded from the early stages of the protest and the march toward Kyoto. It is uncertain why or how palanquins from Hiesha's top shrines were chosen, but precedents played a big role, and there may have been a correlation between the rank of the shrine and the seriousness of a *gōso*. The records indicate that if the cart of the main shrine (Ōmiya) was brought out, support from other branch shrines, such as Gion, Kitano, and Hakusan, was almost inevitable.[32]

The monks at Kōfukuji in Nara employed an identical strategy during the initial stage of a forceful protest. After the first gathering of dissatisfied followers, the holy *sakaki* branch was equipped with mirrors (often referred to as *"shintai,"* the divine body) in representation of the supreme *kami* Kasuga myōjin, before it was moved from the Kasuga shrine to the nearby Utsushiden. Employing the same logic used at Enryakuji, the Kōfukuji clergy's purpose was twofold: to give Kyoto a first indication that the clergy was discontent and to gather Kōfukuji and Kasuga members for the protest by preparing the special *sakaki* branches with holy mirrors. If no response was forthcoming from the imperial court or the Fujiwara chieftain at this stage, the branches were taken to the main hall at Kōfukuji (the Kondō), where a meeting with the whole clergy *(roppō)*, was held, marking the beginning of the second stage of the *gōso*.[33]

The clergy meetings during the early stage of the *gōso* were vital to their success, since practices at both Enryakuji and Kōfukuji dictated that there be a general agreement within the complex to stage a protest.[34] At Enryakuji, meetings known as the *santō sengi* were staged in front of the Konpon chūdō once the palanquins and the agitated members reached the top of Mt. Hiei. Contemporary sources provide little information on what took place during these meetings, but later accounts provide some hints of the participants and the procedures. Two of these sources are picture scrolls describing, to some extent, life at the monastic complex on Mt. Hiei. The *Tengu sōshi*, composed in the late Kamakura period (probably in 1296), shows the many misdeeds caused by small demons *(tengu)* that were believed to inhabit the mountains, but it also depicts several interesting scenes from Enryakuji, Onjōji, Kōfukuji, Kōyasan, and Tōdaiji. One of the more famous paintings in the scroll, devoted to Enryakuji, shows monks sitting in a circle in front of the Konpon chūdō, discussing a *gōso* against Onjōji at an unspecified time (see Figure 16). These monks, who are distinguished from other participants through their strategic seats in the center of the circle, all wear white robes with hoods, but none of them seems to be armed. There are also a dozen or so supporters spread out around the assembly, appearing to apply some pressure on the monks with their heavy armor, bows, swords, and halberds (*naginata,* a popular weapon among armed religious forces). Furthermore, judging from their shaved heads, two of the armed supporters seem to have taken the Buddhist vows. However, they cannot be of prominent status considering their position outside the inner circle, and they probably represent the artist's idea of lower-ranking worker-monks, who were better known for their martial skills than for their devotion to the ascetic life of a Buddhist monk. It is further explained in the middle of the screen that monks from all three sections of the Enryakuji complex are deliberating on whether to take the seven palanquins to the capital in order to stage a protest in the area close to the *jin-no-tō*. The monks who agree with this strategy are energetically proclaiming "*mottomo, mottomo*"—that is appropriate, that is appropriate.[35]

Figure 16. Enryakuji *santō egō sengi* (Composite Meeting of the Three Pagodas) according to the *Tengu sōshi*. Courtesy of Chūō kōron shinsha.

Though a highly interesting source because of its focus on the behavior of the monks at five of Japan's most influential temples, there is good reason to use the *Tengu sōshi* with some skepticism. It was produced with the intention of discrediting the monks, and the artist ends each scroll with the *sens moral* that monks who were driven by greed and selfishness became those much-feared mountain demons *(tengu)* themselves. Interestingly, a picture depicting an identical meeting at Onjōji—known there as the *san'in egō sengi* (Composite Meeting of the Three Cloisters)—with hooded monks in white robes seated in a circle, shows no signs of armed participants (Figure 17).[36] The contrast is remarkable, considering that both Onjōji and Enryakuji had armed supporters. One can only surmise that the artists painted these meetings differently for a specific reason, perhaps intending to portray Enryakuji in a more negative light. In the end, the *Tengu sōshi* scrolls cannot be considered a reliable source in describing the appearance of the *santō sengi,* although they do give an indication of how these meetings of the Enryakuji clergy were perceived in late Kamakura art.

Another collection of picture scrolls, probably produced in the early part of the fourteenth century, focuses on the life of the Buddhist saint Hōnen.[37] One scene in this collection depicts the Enryakuji clergy in a meeting that took place in front of the main Lecture Hall in 1204, preparing a petition to have Hōnen's *nenbutsu* sect prohibited in the capital (see Figure 18). The picture strongly

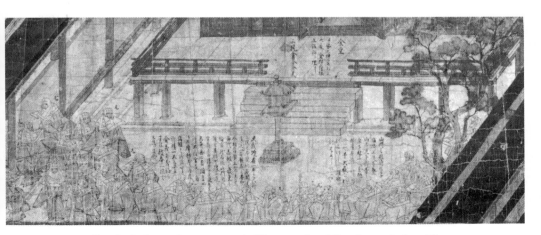

Figure 17. Onjōji *san'in egō sengi* (Composite Meeting of the Three Cloisters) from the *Tengu sōshi.* Reprinted with permission from Chūō kōron shinsha.

Figure 18. Enryakuji *santō sengi* (Meeting of the Three Pagodas) according to the *Hōnen shōnin eden*. Reprinted with permission from Chūō kōron shinsha.

resembles the one in the *Tengu sōshi,* with a number of monks in white robes (though some of the monks now also appear to wear brightly colored robes) and hoods seated in a circle. This time, however, a larger number of ranking monks are carrying arms, mostly swords. Surrounding them are, again, several followers in full armor with bows and arrows, and other secular supporters carrying only a *naginata.*[38]

The Hōnen scrolls are also one of the most important sources concerning the meetings at Kōfukuji, which otherwise are as scarcely depicted as the Enryakuji counterparts. Following Enryakuji's protest against the *nenbutsu* teachings in 1204, Hōnen and several of his followers submitted a pledge, promising to stop their verbal attacks on the established *kenmitsu* teachings.[39] Though this pledge was accepted by the Tendai clergy, the monks in Nara remained dissatisfied. Attempting to have Hōnen exiled, the Hossō monks staged a general meeting at Kōfukuji in the ninth month of 1205 to determine the appropriate course of action. The depiction of this meeting in the *Hōnen shōnin eden* shows hooded monks in white robes assembled in front of the main temple hall. In contrast to the Enryakuji meeting, the Kōfukuji monks are seated in rows on low benches facing the temple hall (Figure 19). More important, though several of the monks carry swords under their garments, there are no signs of lower-ranking members or secular followers trying to influence the monks.[40] It is not clear if these contrasts actually reflect differences in the way that the meetings

Figure 19. Kōfukuji clergy meeting in 1205 according to the *Hōnen shōnin eden*. Reprinted with permission from Chūō kōron shinsha.

were conducted at Enryakuji and Kōfukuji, but the viewer gets an impression of more chaotic and warlike conditions on Mt. Hiei. Nevertheless, since there appears to be no reason for the participating monks at Kōfukuji to carry swords, the viewer is also induced to interpret the high-ranking monks of Kōfukuji as aggressive warrior leaders.

Both the Hōnen picture scrolls and the *Tengu sōshi* are important sources in the context of late Kamakura history, but they may have been given too much credence in their descriptions of past events. The representations of the clergy meetings at Enryakuji, Onjōji, and Kōfukuji portray differences that appear exaggerated, reflecting a bias, in particular against Enryakuji and Kōfukuji, that calls into question their general credibility. In addition, their visual images cannot be corroborated by contemporary textual accounts, nor are they sufficiently supported by a well-known war tale. The *Genpei seisuiki*, which was compiled in the fourteenth century, pays considerable attention to matters pertaining to Enryakuji and its monks.[41] Though the epic was written more than two centuries after the events it describes, its detailed account of the meetings of the clergy on Mt. Hiei is commonly accepted as accurate:[42]

> The meeting of the three thousand monks of Enryakuji takes place with the whole clergy in the open space in front of the Lecture Hall. The monks all wear shredded robes and cover their heads. They carry a three-foot-long staff called "*nyūdōjō,*"[43] which they use to brush off the dew from the trails and the fields. Each monk carries a little stone, in which a small hole has been made. Disciples and novices dress themselves [in the same manner as the monks] sitting right next to them. They pinch their noses to

change their voices and proclaim, "Let us gather up the clergy of the whole mountain!" Then, they discuss the contents of the appeal. Those who agree with the complaint exclaim "that is appropriate, that is appropriate," and those who disagree proclaim "there is no reason in the appeal."[44]

According to this account, the *santō sengi* was controlled by the lower echelons of the clergy, whose shredded robes described here are fundamentally different from the artistic representations in the *Tengu* and Hōnen scrolls. The well-dressed monks in their white or colored robes depicted in the picture scrolls are now missing, but so are the arms. It is tempting to accept this description at face value, and it may, in fact, offer some indications of the meetings in the late Kamakura era, but it should be noted that the account also is strongly biased against Enryakuji, perhaps attempting to exaggerate the lack of order and hierarchy on Mt. Hiei. In fact, the milieu in which the *Genpei seisuiki* as well as the picture scrolls mentioned above were created was fundamentally different from that of the late Heian and Kamakura periods. In particular, the new Buddhist doctrines that proposed a simplified way to salvation began to spread only in the late Kamakura era among elites and commoners. The established temples, led by Enryakuji and Kōfukuji, resisted the privileges that were granted the emerging schools, and they were accordingly seen in a negative light by many proponents of the new sects and their patrons, which included both retired emperors and the bakufu. The Hōnen scrolls were actually commissioned by Emperor Go-Fushimi, a staunch supporter of Hōnen's ideas, to portray the hardships of the Japanese Pure Land patriarch as he tried to promote his Amidist beliefs in the face of resistance from the established sects early in the thirteenth century. Such patronage served two purposes. While the production of picture scrolls earned the patron merit, it also promoted the populist sects among commoners, merchants, and warriors, who were more impressed by and attracted to drawings and paintings than descriptions written in Chinese.[45] Another trend that contributed to the critical view of the clergy at Enryakuji and Kōfukuji was the social movement in which the lower classes began to challenge the authority of the central elites (*gekokujō*, "the lower overturning those above"). This trend was visible within the temple complexes on Mt. Hiei and in Nara as early as the late Heian period, but it became more pronounced in the late thirteenth and fourteenth centuries, earning the clergies a reputation for insubordination, as indicated in the *Genpei seisuiki*. In short, those who strove for order and a restriction of the political influence of religious centers in the late Kamakura era saw the old Buddhist schools as obstacles to these goals. The blame for disorder, present and past, was thus targeted at temples such as Enryakuji and Kōfukuji.

Such was the climate in which the *Genpei seisuiki* and the picture scrolls were compiled, giving good reason to use these sources with caution. Though detailed descriptions are admittedly scarce regarding the meetings on Mt. Hiei and in Nara, it is nevertheless remarkable that no contemporary accounts can be found to support the images in the picture scrolls of armed monks. Another problematic issue in these scrolls is the hooded garments, whose symbolism within the temple communities remains an intriguing topic. Hoods were originally used by younger and lower-ranking monks to conceal their identities in order to attend ceremonies they were excluded from. There is also evidence that hoods were later used by commoners who wished to become part of a temple community by concealing their nonreligious status.[46] The meaning and exact use of such hoods during protests and meetings remain unclear, as does the practice of wearing hoods within the monastic communities, calling for further exploration. The final and most troubling discrepancy in these later accounts is the lack of the sacred carts. Contemporary sources repeatedly state they were brought to the main temple for the meetings, yet they are nowhere to be found in the picture scrolls or in the *Genpei seisuiki*. In the end, it may be that the description in the *Genpei seisuiki* is the best source for the clergy meetings, keeping in mind that it also attempts to superimpose fourteenth-century images on its representations of the Genpei War. At this point, one can only conclude with certainty that a meeting of the clergy was a crucial part of the mobilization that took place on Mt. Hiei and in Nara in preparation for a *gōso*, which, in itself, is highly noteworthy. Since no protests were brought to the capital without the approval of the main clergies, there was a democratic aspect to this process. The main purpose of the meeting was indeed for the monks bearing a grievance and their servants to generate support for mounting a *gōso*. Protests could thus be initiated by regular monks and service people, but they needed the endorsement and the support of the temple's main sections as well as of the leading monks themselves. Occasionally, disagreement over an appeal or other actions could cause internal fighting or augment tensions between cloisters, but no protests were staged by individual cloisters in the pre-Muromachi era. Agreement over a protest carried a particular weight for the clergy, which was convinced that there had to be a sacred righteousness behind a complaint with so much support. This logic led to the development of *Yamashina dōri*—Kōfukuji justice—according to which the Hossō center claimed a divine justice that could override that of the imperial court.

The Kōfukuji and Enryakuji clergy meetings were never meant to be secret. On the contrary, they were designed to cause irritation and fear in the capital. Undoubtedly, the central feature of this stage of the preparation, known as *hōki* (mobilization), was the bringing of the sacred symbols to the main temple buildings. This act not only put pressure on the monastic leaders to listen to the monks and the service people, it was also immediately reported to the court to warn the Kyoto inhabitants of the impending protest. Contrary to Enryakuji, Kōfukuji often sent an additional messenger directly to the Fujiwara mansion to ensure that the chieftain understood the seriousness of the situation and would act in the interest of the temple. For example, when the court delayed in the Kōfukuji appeal against the governor of Ōmi Province in 1093, the clergy became enraged and began to riot in Nara. A monk then appeared at the Fujiwara chieftain's mansion, proclaiming that the clergy would bring the holy carts to the capital, since no verdict had been issued in response to Kōfukuji's protest.[47] It is clear from contemporary diaries that these early reports caused a great deal of concern among the nobles in Kyoto. Most important, the mobilizations of the clergy were at variance with contemporary combat strategies of warriors, which often included night attacks and surprise charges, in that they were intentionally manifest so as to give the court time to respond to the demands.[48]

Although some protests did not proceed beyond mobilization, the instances when the court yielded to the demands at that stage were few. *Hōki* that did not result in demonstrations in the capital usually died out on their own, perhaps because of a lack of support by the entire clergy. But issues that were deemed truly important tended to prompt a march toward Kyoto, executed according to established practices. For example, the descent from Mt. Hiei was made in the same demonstrative manner as the preparations, ensuring that no one in Kyoto could avoid knowing that the Enryakuji clergy was about to enter the capital. A popular method, as described illustratively by Munetada in his diary in 1108, was to descend at night with torches, creating long rows of lights along the western side of Mt. Hiei, which could be easily seen from anywhere in the capital.[49] It was extremely important for the protesters to make every stage of the *gōso* as visible as possible not only to send their message of concern to the imperial court, but also to impress on the decision makers the anger of the gods. Thus, contrary to the view of most scholars, the *gōso* were not attacks on the capital; they were the monks' final attempt to communicate their concerns to the authorities in Kyoto.

The descent from Mt. Hiei might take place along several trails leading from the summit. By coming down on the northwestern slopes, the monks had the opportunity to enter the capital from the north, close to the imperial palace. Another more commonly used trail, known as Kirarazaka, originated in front of the Konpon chūdō, passing the Saitō section, and then descending on the western side of the mountain. This trail also passed close to Sekizan zen'in, a branch dedicated to Ennin, where the protesters might pause or add the palanquins of that temple-shrine to their own. The procession then entered the capital from the northeast and proceeded to Gionsha or some other branch, such as Kyōgo-kuji or Gitarinji, in Kyoto (see Map 3).[50] Once the protesters reached the capital, they continued their strategy of giving the courtiers ample time to respond to their demands, which would have been well known in advance because of the earlier appeal. Another advantage in not proceeding too quickly was that it gave the courtiers time to consider the threat that the sacred palanquins and the *kami* presented to the court. The first stop in Kyoto was thus one of Enryakuji's branches, where the monks prepared themselves with rituals and various performances. This practice was already current during Shirakawa's *insei,* when the protesters began to assemble at Gionsha before the palanquins of that shrine were taken out to support the demonstration. Gion remained one of the prime destinations in those *gōso* during the whole of the premodern era, and as the first destination in Kyoto, the shrine often became the target of government warriors who wished to get an early start in their attempts to dissuade the protesters. For example, the imperial police captain Norimasa approached Gionsha in 1105 as a ceremony was being performed there. Intent on containing the protesters, some of his retainers became involved in a brawl with Gion service people. Some warriors were injured during a brief skirmish, and attempts to arrest the service people failed, as some forty to fifty shrine members drove the warriors away. That night, however, some two hundred service people went to the Yōmei Gate of the imperial palace, carrying their palanquins and demanding heavy punishments for Norimasa and his retainers. For his troubles, Norimasa was briefly suspended from his post.[51]

With the passage of time, other Enryakuji branches became increasingly involved, providing additional divine support as well as manpower. The third most frequent participant in such demonstrations after Hiesha and Gionsha was the Kitano shrine (Kitano Tenmangū). Located in the northern part of Kyoto, it was a convenient stopover for protesters who used the northernmost path to descend Mt. Hiei. Kitano was comparatively young, founded in the mid–tenth century, but it soon developed into one of the most influential shrines in the capital. As a popular shrine devoted to the deified courtier Sugawara no Michizane, Kitano controlled, at one time or another, at least 150 estates, varying from small lots in Kyoto to regular *shōen* in the provinces. Kitano also benefited greatly from the economic development of the thirteenth century as it became the patron for several of the more prosperous guilds, such as that of the malt producers.

Other locations that were used as stopovers and for final preparations were Kyōgokuji (a branch of Hiesha, located close to Sanjō in the eastern part of Kyoto; see Map 3), Gitarinji (east of the imperial palace close to the Kamo River), and Sekizan zen'in: all Buddhist temples. The first two were involved in the earliest protest in 1105, and they became regular destinations thereafter.[52] Though Zekizan zen'in was less centrally situated, its location close to the Kirarazaka trail made it a convenient destination, and its palanquins were often added to the protest. Apparently, the protesters hoped that the combination of pressures from different shrines and temples in the capital area would be enough to convince the court or the retired emperor to rule in their favor. In the event of failure, however, a procession to the heart of the capital—to the imperial palace or the retired emperor's mansion —might be necessary.

The vast majority of Enryakuji demonstrations approached the imperial palace from the east. The Yōmeimon, by far the most common target, was the eastern entrance in the wall of the Greater Palace area that led to the *jin-no-tō*. However, as the number of protesters increased in the late twelfth century, other gates, such as the Taikenmon, came to be frequented. In 1169, for example, during the protest against Fujiwara no Narichika, six palanquins were brought to the imperial palace. Four of them, Jūzenshi, Hachiōji, Marōdo (all from Hiesha), and Gion were taken to the Taikenmon, while two palanquins from Kitano were taken to the Yōmei Gate.[53] There were also cases when the demonstrations were directed to the mansions of powerful members of the court elite. In fact, Enryakuji's first appeal in 1092 was taken to the mansion of the Fujiwara chieftain (Morozane), who was the most influential figure of his day.[54] Moreover, the retired emperor's villa became a popular target especially during Go-Saga's tenure; for example, sacred palanquins were taken to his and to junior retired emperor Go-Fukakusa's mansions in 1264.[55] Most demonstrations were, however, directed to the imperial palace, and it was these protests that caused the most serious problems of all, since the presence of the *mikoshi* in the palace area forced the secular authorities to find a solution. Once the protesters had arrived at the gates of the outer wall, sometimes even entering the main palace area itself, the secular authorities had only two options: either to promise to comply with the demands or to dispatch warriors to fend off the protesters, which sometimes resulted in exchanges of arrows and blows that scattered the protesters. Unfortunately, scholars have focused almost exclusively on these confrontations, neglecting in the process the more important and manifest progression of the protests, which do not display any of the strategies associated with armed attacks.

Since Kōfukuji was located farther from Kyoto than Mt. Hiei, the protesters' route to the capital was different. The mountainous terrain between the two cities was not easily crossed, though there were a few roads that could be used. In particular, the protesters were aided by the river Kizugawa, which provided a narrow valley just across from the hill of Narazaka, leading into Yamashiro Province (see Map 2).[56] The Kōfukuji clergy's march to Kyoto was thus quite prolonged, but it gave the court ample time to respond while the protesters gathered more support at various branches. The Kōfukuji protesters approached Kyoto from the south, stopping first at the residence of the Fujiwara chieftain, their secular ally, in Uji after crossing the Kizu River. The purpose of this stopover was for the monks to state their grievances directly to the chieftain, with the divine symbols present just outside his courtyard. However, since the chieftain rarely would issue or overturn a verdict on his own, he would have to consult with other courtiers and the head of the imperial family. The effects of a protest were therefore much more far-reaching if the monks also reached the capital, spreading fear among other nobles and Kyoto citizens as well. Once in the capital, the Kōfukuji clergy continued to follow the principles of representative justice and approached the Fujiwara administrative headquarters, the Kangakuin. These procedures were established in 1093, when the clergy successfully convinced the Fujiwara chieftain and the court to remove and exile the governor of Ōmi for intrusions of a Kasuga estate.[57] Following a destruction of the Kangakuin in a great fire in Kyoto in 1177, the demonstrators directed their attention to Hōjōji, which served as the new Fujiwara headquarters until 1317, when the Chōkōdō —the administrative center of the senior imperial line—became the preferred target, reflecting the declining authority of the Fujiwara clan. Although the targets for the Kōfukuji protests in Kyoto thus changed, the basic strategies of the twelfth century still exercised considerable influence over the Kyoto nobility, as evidenced in a dispute over water rights involving Kasuga late in 1281, when the Kōfukuji demonstrators managed to secure a verdict in its favor by leaving the *sakaki* branch close to Hōjōji.[58]

Despite slightly different conditions and progressions, the methods used by Enryakuji and Kōfukuji were thus identical. Both approached their respective allies within the court, who were expected to protect the temples' interests. The monks were consequently not attacking an enemy in the capital, but rather "reminding" powerful courtiers of their political responsibilities toward their religious allies. In addition, both temples clearly relied on the same judicial and political privileges, and the basic concept of mutual dependence between Buddhism and the imperial state *(ōbō-buppō sōi)*. The religious protests can therefore be viewed as one of the most concrete expressions of the era's symbiosis of religion and politics as well as of the overlapping of public and private powers. The basic political structure that allowed for these conditions was the practice of shared rulership, according to which the privileges and responsibilities of rulership were shared by the imperial court, the warrior aristocracy, and the leading religious institutions. This concept even seems applicable beyond the elites, since the *gōso* show many similarities to peasant protests that were staged within the *shōen* in the same era. Like the clergies of Enryakuji and Kōfukuji, peasants borrowed the power of the *kami*, signing sacred oaths to support their petitions against wrongful treatment by estate officials. As a last resort, the peasants might abandon their fields and move to another estate, leaving the proprietor without any rent.[59] Neither of these ritualized acts was considered "illegal," and both have counterparts in Enryakuji's and Kōfukuji's *gōso,* in the clergy meetings and the closure of cloisters, respectively. Such strategies provide evidence not only of a system of shared rulership between different spheres among the elites, but also of a vertically integrated system in which even peasants had some rights and responsibilities.

Secular Responses to the *Gōso*

The most effective way for the court to squelch a *gōso* was to comply with the demands of the monks. But as demonstrated in the preceding chapters, the issues that caused the protests were integral to the competition for power at court and were thus too important to be compromised on that easily. The secular authorities may have wished to end these protests, but not at the expense of eroding their position. However, since the *kenmon* temples were quite independent judicially and economically, the means of controlling the monks and the *gōso* were often inefficient, leaving the court with few options. Despite their declining power over the clergy, the head abbots (the Tendai *zasu* and the Kōfukuji *bettō*) were still considered the most important link between the court and the elite temples throughout the late Heian and Kamakura eras. The Fujiwara chieftain's attempt to appoint his own descendant to head Kōfukuji in 1100 as a way to make up for the clan's diminishing influence at the imperial court represents one of the earliest and most telling examples of the hopes attached to the sect leadership.[60] Appointments of close supporters to such posts were subsequently made by a wide range of secular authorities, including retired emperors as well as warrior leaders, but they were only partially successful. The head abbot's dilemma was to live up to the expectations of his supporters without losing the trust of the clergy. As expected, most abbots could not satisfy both sides, especially since they continued to identify themselves primarily as nobles, typically spending more time in their aristocratic cloisters close to the capital than on Mt. Hiei or in Nara.

The expectations surrounding the head abbot were thus high,

and many were forced to resign or were deposed for their failures. For example, the young head abbot Jigen attempted to resign in 1239 after having failed to stop the Enryakuji monks from mobilizing. Later, Go-Saga attempted to use the office to increase his influence over Enryakuji and its valuable landed and human resources, but this strategy yielded little success. The princely monk Dōkaku therefore resigned in 1249, and another imperial monk, Sonkaku, was deposed ten years later, also failing to control the clergy.[61] There were also cases when the head abbot lost his office for failing to represent the clergy. For instance, when the Tendai head abbot refused to forward the clergy's complaint in 1122, he was driven from his cloister by the disappointed monks. Or again, when the clergy blamed the *zasu*'s lack of persistence for the light punishment of Taira no Tadamori in 1147, the head abbot was forced to resign in spite of his seventeen successful years as Tendai head.[62] At Kōfukuji, the situation was identical. For instance, Eshin, the son of the prominent Fujiwara no Tadazane, was appointed head abbot of Kōfukuji at the mere age of thirty-four even though he spent most of his time in Kyoto. When he failed to support the clergy's appeal in 1163 against Enryakuji, which had managed to obtain control over ordinations of Onjōji monks while indicating that the Tendai teachings were superior to those of the Nara schools (see Chapter 4), Eshin was attacked by his own clergy and driven out of Nara. He subsequently tried to retaliate against his opponents but failed despite enlisting some of the finest warrior retainers of the Fujiwara. A century later Jigen's older brother Enjitsu was similarly ousted by the Kōfukuji clergy for failing to support an appeal against taxes levied on several of the temple's estates.[63]

Since it accordingly became more and more difficult to control the clergies through the head abbots, the court's most common response to the *gōso* was to dispatch professional warriors, though the latter were not allowed to harm the protesters or to damage the sacred palanquins. In this vein, Retired Emperor Shirakawa ordered as follows in 1118: "No arrows are to be fired at the clergy. The warriors are only to protect [the imperial palace], but if any protesters try to enter the premises as they are being restrained, the warriors shall arrest them and bring them forward."[64] In other words, the guards were ordered to stop the protesters at all costs, even though they could expect to be punished if they used excessive force. It appears, then, that the members of the imperial court "sacrificed" their defending warriors, since they tied their hands knowing fully that only force could fend off the protesters. Shirakawa's orders in fact embody a general principle of the period—the punitive measures taken against warriors for violence against divine symbols or monks in order to appease the *kami*. The extent of such punishments were recurrent problems in the aftermath of a *gōso*, ranging from temporary demotions, to arrests, and ultimately to exile.[65] Yet since few other practical choices (apart from delay) were available, the warriors frequently ended up in a physical confrontation. Such encounters normally concluded with a scattering of the protesters, but since the palanquins were left behind, the *kami* were still battling, in a sense, for their cause. The *mikoshi* or the *shinmoku,* which were often damaged in the exchange, continued to pose a threat to those living in the palace area, since the native gods of these sacred objects would have been much angered, and only the shrine servants knew how to move the divine symbols without causing further disaster. For example, when the Kōfukuji clergy was unable to have a well-liked monk named Ryūkaku reappointed head abbot in the fifth month of 1150, a protest was brought to the capital. The protesters apparently roamed around in the capital, making noise and waving their *sakaki* branches, equipped with several mirrors, close to the palace of the newly retired emperor, Sutoku. On encountering government warriors charged with maintaining order, the monks left the sacred branches at the Kangakuin, which soon resulted in the imperial court's appointment of Ryūkaku as head abbot. Enryakuji demonstrators employed the same strategy in 1169, when they left the sacred carts in Kyoto on encountering government warriors who were sent out to drive them away from the palace area.[66]

This final stage of the *gōso* poses some interesting questions about the role of the *kami* and the power of religious beliefs. The issues that caused the monks to demonstrate with their holy objects were political, mostly involving patronage, religious status, or land. In turn, the monks' behavior has seemed to indicate a strong military threat.[67] However, contemporary sources reveal that the threat of the *kami* played the most decisive role in settling and concluding the disputes. In other words, though political decisions caused many of the protests, the pressures emanating from Enryakuji and Kōfukuji were not merely or even primarily secular; the power that the native gods exercised over courtiers remained compelling. Activities at the palace were interrupted or scaled back in the presence of the sacred palanquins or branches, forcing the court to settle with the demonstrators in one way or another. Though decisions were not always resolved in the grieving temple's favor, the importance of the *kami* and their symbols was readily acknowledged by having the portable shrines and *sakaki* platforms rebuilt at court expense, compensation paid to the shrine, and the warriors who caused the damages punished. A conflict was thus never settled until the sacred symbols were returned to their mother shrines *(honsha)* and the monks had been promised funding and compensation for their repair. There were even occasions when the court's stalling or negligence in fulfilling its promises caused new eruptions of protests and violence.

The court's contradictory behavior, as it on the one hand attempted to avoid complying with the demands of the monks and on the other prohibited government warriors from using their weapons against the demonstrators, was influenced by a genuine fear of the *kami*. But why did the warriors who attacked monks and palanquins seem so unaffected by these beliefs? Divine protests were only staged in Kyoto by the most prominent religious complexes, all of which were integral to the court system itself. By contrast, warriors were less attached to the court or the religious complexes, and they may thus have felt less threatened by the protesters and their gods. At the same time, by no means did all warriors engage in such activities, and some protests occurred without violent confrontations. Among the men of arms, whether they wore robes or armor, some were more willing than others to display their martial skills, hoping that this would yield prestige and status. However, as previous chapters have shown, the authority of the imperial court and central connections were still important, and any individual display of military power in the capital without the support of one of the traditional elites in the pre-Muromachi era was doomed to fail.

The Powers of the *Kami* and the Buddhas

The use of the *kami*, symbolized by either a *sakaki* branch or sacred palanquins, is one of the most intriguing aspects of the *gōso*. The native deities played an important role in protecting the interests of the temple-shrine complexes in Nara as well as on Mt. Hiei. But why should the *kami* have been preferred over the buddhas and the bodhisattvas? Though the success rate of the demonstrations undeniably reinforced the monks' confidence in their own ways, such a realization merely accentuates the need to analyze how the *gōso* were perceived and what body of beliefs supported them in the Heian and Kamakura eras.

The answer lies embedded in the cultural milieu of Heian and Kamakura Japan, and historians are thus faced with the difficult task of recreating the *mentalité* of that age.[68] I would like to offer two observations deriving from the Enryakuji and the Kōfukuji *gōso*. First, the *kami*, or at least their habitats, would appear to have been more mobile than their Buddhist counterparts. I know of no cases in which Buddhist images were moved in order to make a specific buddha or bodhisattva influence particular conditions. Second, the influence of the native deities was simply more widely felt throughout Japanese society. In other words, whereas Tendai and Hossō, like most of the *kenmitsu* schools, catered mainly to the Kyoto elites, the shrines that were associated with them received extensive support from other less privileged groups. Moreover, the *kami* can be viewed as more malevolent than the Buddhist deities, perhaps because they were considered local manifestations of the buddhas and bodhisattvas, protecting the Buddhist Law on the Japanese islands. Thus, whereas prayers to avoid disasters and to combat diseases and other misfortunes were made to both the buddhas and the *kami*, the latter were more capable of inflicting curses and creating misfortunes for the living. It was not uncommon to explain disasters, both personal tragedies and human suffering caused by nature, as the native gods' response to "political injustices," such as the neglect of one of the elite temples.[69]

The *Heike monogatari* offers an account that supports the impression that religious beliefs served as the basis for the divine threat in the *gōso*. The war tale describes how, in response to a protest over the killing of an Enryakuji monk in 1095, the Fujiwara regent Moromichi ordered a palace guard, Minamoto no Yoriharu, to hold off the demonstrators. Yoriharu confronted the protesters, killing or injuring some monks, before he eventually forced them to retreat. The monks became enraged and brought several *mikoshi* of Hiesha to the Konpon chūdō, where they read sūtras and called on the Hachiōji *kami* to bring down a curse on the regent. Moromichi fell ill, "which everyone attributed to the Sannō god's anger." The *Heike monogatari* then goes on to explain that Moromichi's mother made three vows, favoring the Lotus Sūtra and the *kami* on

Mt. Hiei, in an attempt to have her son spared, but the god remained implacable, responding through a medium as follows: "I
can never forget the misery I suffered when the authorities shot
and killed some of my priests and shrine attendants instead of
granting their modest request and when others of my people returned, wounded and weeping, to complain to me of their wrong-
doings." Yet because of the lady's compassionate vows, the *kami*
granted her son an additional three years.[70]

Though the account in some of its details is likely exaggerated,
there are some useful lessons here that further indicate the
dilemma for dispatched government warriors.[71] First, they were
expected to refrain from harming any of the protesters, since the
latter were under the protection of Enryakuji and its deities.
Second, it was a crime to damage any of the sacred palanquins
regardless of the *gōso*'s validity; an arrest for the firing of arrows at
a local palanquin in 1105 represents another early example.[72] In
fact, the court was consistent in punishing its own warriors for such
offenses. During the Hakusanji Incident of 1177, for instance,
arrows were fired at some of the *mikoshi*, leading to the arrest of
the six warriors deemed responsible.[73] Though the Kamakura
Bakufu may have been less intimidated by the spiritual pressures
from the *gōso*, it showed its commitment to maintaining the traditional system of rulership by supporting and continuing the verdicts of the court against warriors who harmed any demonstrators
or violated their divine symbols. A conflict between Enryakuji and
the Sasaki family of Ōmi in 1235 gives further support for this
notion, as the bakufu enforced severe punishments, including the
exile of the *jitō* himself, in response to the murder of shrine
servants.[74]

As the damaging of a *mikoshi* during an Enryakuji protest came
to represent the court's inappropriate treatment of an appeal,
any signs of damage or deterioration of the Kasuga *shinmoku* symbolized the decline of the Hossō sect and by extension of both
Buddhism and the state. For instance, during a dispute in 1281
over water rights between Takigi and Ōsumi estates, under the
patronage of Iwashimizu Hachimangū and Kōfukuji, respectively,
the Kasuga sacred *sakaki* branch was carried to the capital. The
protesters were met by bakufu warriors at Uji, where the *shinmoku*
was damaged in a skirmish, after which it was abandoned close to
Hōjōji (the Fujiwara administrative headquarters) by the fleeing
Kasuga supporters. The Fujiwara chieftain eventually managed to

avoid a more serious confrontation between the two religious complexes only by assigning replacement estates to both parties early in 1282. In addition, he asked the bakufu to punish the four warriors who had damaged the divine branch during the confrontation in Uji. The bakufu was initially reluctant to comply, since it had merely responded according to the request of the imperial court, and it warned that its vassals might be unwilling to shield Kyoto for the court in the future if they were punished for obeying orders. Nevertheless, the bakufu complied, indicating the consideration given by the bakufu leaders to the sanctity of servants of the Buddha and the *kami*.[75] Perhaps the warrior government felt compelled to act this way because of the court's respect for the religious establishment and because of its own desire to maintain the status quo.

The Muromachi Bakufu attempted to ignore the spiritual pressures of the established Buddhist centers, promoting instead its own set of Zen institutions. However, the powers of the *kami* and their worldly servants were not to be ignored even in the fourteenth century, as demonstrated when Kōfukuji complained about land intrusions and other illegal acts by the *shugo* of Echizen, Shiba Takatsune, late in 1364. The Ashikaga leaders initially chose not to punish Takatsune even though the imperial court had made a promise to that effect, causing the Hossō monks to bring the *shinmoku* to the capital in a protest. Since the bakufu and the court could not come up with a solution, the sacred branch remained in the capital for over a year. During that time several unusual events occurred that the court took as signs from the gods, an impression that was reinforced by the increasingly withering *sakaki* branch, which foreboded a demise of the temple-shrine complex and offered additional proof of the perceived spiritual power of the native gods. To make amends for its negligence, the bakufu finally decided to sponsor a *kagura* performance (a dance dedicated to the *kami*) at Kasuga in the sixth month of 1366, but various diseases raged in Kyoto the next month, indicating that the gods would not settle until the crisis with Kōfukuji had been solved. Finally, in the eighth month of 1366, nearly two years after the holy branch had been taken to the capital, the bakufu decided to punish Shiba Takatsune, inducing the monks finally to return the *shinmoku* to Kasuga.[76] That this incident appears anachronistic considering the control the warrior aristocracy had attained, indicates the strength of the old beliefs. One can thus concur with

Braudel and other *Annales* scholars that currents in the cultural sphere were considerably slower to change direction than in the political arena.

The strength of the *kami* is further evidenced by the court's willingness to finance the reconstruction of damaged palanquins regardless of the validity of the original protest. There were even cases of such funding when palanquins and buildings had been destroyed by the monks themselves. In fact, self-destruction marked a rationalization of the Enryakuji *gōso* indicating an even heavier reliance on the power of the *kami* than otherwise and based on the theory of mutual dependence between the Imperial Law and Buddhism. One of the earliest examples can be found in 1260, when the monks on Mt. Hiei destroyed and polluted their own shrines in protest against the court's reluctance to prohibit an ordination platform at Onjōji. The most blatant use of this strategy, however, occurred four years later, when the monks on Mt. Hiei felt threatened by Go-Saga's favoritism of their rival. In disapproval of these policies and in objection to Go-Saga's attempts to stall, the clergy burned several important buildings on Mt. Hiei before they proceeded to stage a *gōso* in the capital.[77] Several other examples of self-destruction soon followed this incident: in 1269 the monks damaged some of the sacred palanquins in front of the Konpon chūdō after an earlier *gōso* in the capital had failed to yield the desired result; six years later, several of the *mikoshi* were destroyed again by parts of the Enryakuji clergy.[78] The purpose of such self-destruction was twofold. First, it symbolized the damage that, in the eyes of the clergy, the court had inflicted on Enryakuji and, by extension, on the state itself. Second, by damaging their own shrines and palanquins, the clergy disturbed the *kami*, further adding to the distress of the court nobility.

Even when the court obliged the protesters, further measures were often deemed necessary to placate the gods. In particular, pilgrimages to the shrines of the *kami* were an important symbol for the reestablishment of peaceful relations. For example, Enryakuji's violent protests in 1264 finally ended late in that year as both retired emperors (Go-Saga and Go-Fukakusa) visited Hiesha, granting funding for a number of monks and priests.[79] To mention one example from Shirakawa's era, after having issued a verdict against Kōfukuji following the attack on Tōnomine in 1081, the Fujiwara chieftain apparently felt a strong need to reconcile with the clergy. Thus, he reinstated the head abbot of Kōfukuji only nine months after having deposed him and then celebrated and confirmed the bond with the temple-shrine complex during a visit to Kasuga.[80] Official representatives from the imperial court were also dispatched during the protests to offer prayers to the *kami*. These visits were shortened versions of official pilgrimages intended to ask the gods to stop the conflicts. For instance, when Enryakuji and Kōfukuji eagerly prepared to battle out their differences in 1113, the court, in a rather desperate move, sent messengers to several of the most prestigious shrines in the capital area, including Kasuga, Ōharano, and Yoshida on the Kōfukuji side, asking the gods to calm the rivaling camps.[81] Unfortunately, the records do not reveal in detail what was offered to the gods or if anything was offered to the shrines themselves to induce the service people to pray on the court's behalf. It is clear, however, that the *kami*, both as protectors of the Buddhist sects and as deities able to curse the living, were powerful enough to influence political decisions at the imperial court.

The responses to the *gōso* offer important indications of how they were perceived by the secular authorities from a legal standpoint. Though both the court and the bakufu attempted to regulate the behavior of monks, there is no indication that the demonstrations were ever prohibited or considered "illegal." On the contrary, it was understood that the elite temples were entitled to demonstrate their concerns in various ways. Indeed, when monks were actually punished for staging a *gōso,* it was not a question of legality, but rather they were punished for its lack of validity and unlawful content.[82] This attitude is even evident in the *Genpei seisuiki,* which, despite its notoriously critical stance against the monks of Mt. Hiei, states that the main problem with many protests was their use in unwarranted cases.[83] Perhaps the best known example of these special rights is Kōfukuji's reputation for enforcing its own kind of justice, known as *Yamashina dōri* (the justice of Kōfukuji), which was based on the idea that there had to be some kind of divine righteousness in an appeal supported by the entire clergy of the three thousand Hossō monks.[84] There was a certain "democratic" rationale in this reasoning, since both Kōfukuji and Enryakuji needed the endorsement of the entire clergy in order to exercise these special rights, which were used mainly by the complexes of Tōdaiji, Kōfukuji, and Enryakuji. It was in their capacity as legitimate co-rulers that the elite temples were entitled to protect their own position within the imperial state, even if it occasionally led to instances where the monks clearly made right out of wrong, like "making water from fire," as Fujiwara no Kanezane put it in response to an appeal forwarded in 1198. A similar idea is also visible in Kōfukuji's concealed threat that the entire clergy of three thousand monks were "guilty" in attacking Tōnomine in 1173 and that they would all appear in the capital in response to the court's demand that the originators be forwarded.[85] *Yamashina dōri* and the *gōso* were social and political expressions of underlying ideologies that sustained the temples' rights to protest unfavorable judgments. In particular, the notion of mutual dependence between the Imperial and the Buddhist Law provided a doctrinal basis for *kenmon* temples, as co-rulers, to communicate their discontent through demonstrations and other kinds of pressure. Indeed, it was this same interdependence that made the government ultimately responsible for the physical and financial well-being of these religious centers.[86]

The interdependence of *ōbō* and *buppō* had deep roots, referring in its simplest form to the claims of Tendai and Hossō as protectors of the state in the early Heian era. A document from the imperial court in the late tenth century contains one of the earliest known references to the mutual dependence, stating that a violation of the imperial law was also a crime against the divine law of Buddhism, which in turn served to protect the state.[87] An appeal from an estate manager of Tōdaiji in 1053 comparing the imperial law and Buddhism to the wings of a bird and the wheels of a cart demonstrates that such thoughts were also spread among the provincial elites before *gōso* became a common phenomenon in late Heian Japan. Further, Retired Emperor Shirakawa is said to have pledged in 1128 that while the *kami* help the Law of Buddha, it is Buddhism that protects the imperial lineage. Implied in these and other similar references of the period is also the notion that the state will deteriorate if Buddhism declines.[88] The very existence of the *gōso* and their relative success are, in fact, substantial indications of the importance of the *ōbō-buppō* concept in Heian and Kamakura Japan. Conversely, a deterioration of their effectiveness in the fourteenth century is indicative of a decline in the belief in the Buddhist Law. During the twelfth and thirteenth centuries, though, the symbols of the Buddhist Law were as untouchable as the state and the *kenmon* temples were inseparable.

Not only did the Buddhist monks rely on the *ōbō-buppō* concept, the court was also a willing supporter of this doctrine. Indeed, its ongoing commitment to fund the repairs of damaged buildings and palanquins as well as the genuine concerns that the *gōso* caused in the capital underline again the interdependence of religion and politics. The monks were aware of the power of this concept, since they frequently used it to enhance the pressure of their demonstrations. However, though the rationale behind the self-destruction employed by protesters in the late thirteenth century relied on the doctrine of *ōbō-buppō*, it did not originate from these ideas. Rather, it originated in the *gōso* themselves, allowing the clergy to rationalize the confrontation with defending warriors. The presence of the *mikoshi* in the palace area was a considerable threat to the courtiers, but the capital elites seem to have felt more pressure if the gods were believed to be further angered by the physical destruction of their portable shrines. Such damage was originally inflicted by defending government warriors, but the clergy, perhaps realizing the increased effectiveness of a *gōso* with damage done to the palanquins, soon began to "assist" in this process by handling the carts roughly as they left them behind in the palace area. In short, by destroying their own property, the monks used a forceful form of symbolism to show the damage the policies of the secular elites caused the temple, Buddhism, and the state itself. The impact of such acts was further enhanced by the idea of *mappō* (the final age of Buddhism) that became widespread late in the Heian period. The physical destruction of temples and shrines as well as monks demonstrating in the capital were frequently interpreted as signs (not as the cause) of the decline of the world and the end of righteous government, as demonstrated by numerous entries in courtier diaries.[89] It was clear to contemporary observers that the *gōso* did not cause these developments, but were simply expressions of the prevailing system of shared rulership and an informal means of communication in an age of increasing factionalism and reliance on private resources. In sum, the *gōso* were never illegal; the elite temples were entitled to voice their discontent in this manner. The complexes of Enryakuji and Kōfukuji constituted a privileged elite with responsibilities to the state, and their *gōso* were thus a further expression of the privatization that characterized rulership to the end of the Kamakura era.

The Power of the Sword

Granted the strength of the *kami* and the buddhas, what role did physical and military threats play during the divine demonstrations? Again, because of the scarcity of information in contempo-

Figure 20. *Gōso* by the Hōki Daisenji clergy in 1094. From the *Daisenji engi*. Courtesy of Tōkyō daigaku shiryō hensanjo.

rary sources, one must begin with the scroll paintings. One of the few descriptions available is a scene in a late-fourteenth-century picture scroll, which shows members of Enryakuji's branch temple Daisenji in Hōki Province staging a protest in the capital in 1094 (Figure 20). It depicts a group of protesters led by some monks, who are wearing white robes and hoods to cover their heads. Two of the monks are armed, one wearing his monk robe over an armored chest plate while carrying a *naginata*. Another monk, whose status is revealed by his shaved head ("decorated" with a headband—a *hachimaki*), is dressed entirely in regular warrior armor and carries a sword. The protesting monks are accompanied by armed and unarmed followers, who carry two holy carts. The entire carts are not visible, as they are half covered by a wall, leaving only the roofs of three carts visible.[90] This illustration is similar in style to the previously mentioned picture scrolls, thus indicating a later artistic representation. It is especially interesting that the artists chose to depict only six monks and three warriors, while there are at least eight unarmed carriers. Unfortunately, it is difficult to say whether those numbers were intended to reflect an accurate ratio, but it may suggest that the protesters were not as heavily armed as many scholars have assumed.

One more pictorial representation of a *gōso* in Kyoto is extant today. A pair of folding screens, made in the middle of the Tokugawa period in the influential style of the Kanō school, depict the progression of the *gōso* in two stages. In the first part, a *mikoshi* is carried by a dozen or so armed retainers, followed by hooded and armed monks, through the temple grounds of Enryakuji (Figure 21). The second screen shows this procession approaching the palace area, which is defended by some leisurely conversing warriors (Figure 22).[91] Though the names of the painters of these screens are known, scholars have been unable to identify who they actually were and for whom the screens were made. However, considering the era, it appears likely that they were made for either a warlord *(daimyō)* or possibly a rich merchant in Kyoto. The choice of scenery for a decorative object may appear strange, but war scenes were popular themes among the warrior elites in Tokugawa Japan, as were historical stories, Shintō festivals, nature scenes, and city life.[92] The images in these screens are somewhat different from the late Kamakura and Muromachi pieces discussed earlier. The holy cart, which is clearly shown with the phoenix on top, is now carried by fully armed men. Their heads are shaved and they wear *hachimaki*, indicating the stereotypical image of warrior-monks. There are no signs of any high-ranking monks without arms, but some monks in hoods and white robes, who carry bows and shields, are portrayed farther back in the progression. The images of monk protests in this Tokugawa work have proceeded to a new level compared to the picture scrolls of the thirteenth and fourteenth centuries. Taken together, these screens and the earlier picture scrolls thus demonstrate an interesting trend: the protesters appear more heavily armed as the distance from the thirteenth century increases.

Contemporary textual accounts are unfortunately of little direct help, as they rarely provide any details regarding the *gōso* except for the location, an occasional skirmish between warriors and demonstrators, and sometimes the injuries that occurred during such exchanges. Yet there are valuable conclusions to be deduced even from this lack of information. Though the authors of the diaries resided in the capital, there is almost a complete absence of records of armed protesters. In other words, contemporary records indicate that few monks seem to have been armed at all, and even those who were must have been ill prepared for confrontations with the government warriors. The demonstrators were consistently bested in the confrontations: one is stunned by the ease with which the warriors rejected the protesters, especially considering

Figure 21. Enryakuji *gōso* procession descending Mt. Hiei. Folding screen from the middle of the Tokugawa period, one of a pair with the screen in Figure 22. Reprinted with permission from Shiga kenritsu biwako bunkakan.

later accounts of furious and invincible warrior-monks. Most confrontations were over in a few hours—later accounts listing thousands of protesters who faced a few defending warriors are, as many scholars realize today, exaggerated. The *Heike monogatari,* for example, provides an unlikely account of how a palace guard with three hundred horsemen, facing a much superior force from Enryakuji, managed, in part because of his ability to compose poems, to convince the protesters to attempt to enter the palace area from a more heavily defended gate.[93]

There is, to my knowledge, only one account that indicates that the monks were armed during the course of the *gōso*. In

1108, when monks of Enryakuji and Onjōji joined forces to protest against Shirakawa's favoritism of Tōji, Fujiwara no Munetada
quoted what was said at the *kugyō* council's meeting of the twenty-
third day of the third month: "Previously, the clergy were clad in
protective armor when they came to the imperial palace, [but][94]
this time, they are already armed and carry bows and arrows. It is
possible that the mob now reaches several thousand. Truly, it is a
frightening situation when the court has lost its authority, and [the
palace] must be defended with all available might."[95] The forces
that frightened Munetada and the courtiers never came to the
capital, and no divine demonstration was staged. Yet there can be
no doubt of the court's fear, and it may indeed have been the
clergy's intention to frighten the nobles. Nevertheless, I have
found no contemporary sources that indicate that organized
groups of armed men actually participated in the *gōso*. In the end,
one might deduce that some of the protesters may have carried

Figure 22. Enryakuji *gōso* procession approaching the imperial palace. Warriors leisurely defend the gate while courtiers meet in the background. Folding screen from the middle of the Tokugawa period. Courtesy of Shiga kenritsu biwako bunkakan.

their personal arms, which caused later authors to exaggerate the actual military strength of the demonstrators, describing the *gōso* as attacks on the imperial palace. The sources leave no doubt that monks within the elite temples used more violent strategies in other circumstances. As Hirata has pointed out, arms were primarily used in internal conflicts, intertemple rivalries, or disputes between temples and the provincial governor class.[96] This study confirms his observation. In fact, noble diarists consistently note the extent of both preparations and battles between various temples, such as the attacks on Onjōji by Enryakuji monks. Similarly, Mune-

tada duly recorded the confrontations between Kōfukuji followers and defending warriors in Uji during the 1113 conflict with Enrya-kuji, even mentioning what appears to be a very precise head count of the fatalities.[97] The internal conflicts within both Tendai and Hossō were no less violent, as evidenced, for instance, by the monk Eshin, who led a group of warriors against Kōfukuji after being ousted by his former brothers in 1167.[98] The methods used during those conflicts, characterized by a high degree of military preparation, were quite different from the progression of the gōso.

In the end, though a conclusive statement is elusive, it appears unlikely that religious demonstrators were prepared to go to battle during a gōso. Even comparatively detailed accounts mention no more than the demonstrators yelling, shouting, and beating on bells, as noted by Fujiwara no Munetada during an Enryakuji pro-test in 1108.[99] The same observation is made in the *Hyakurenshō* (a

chronicle compiled at the end of the thirteenth century) regarding a Kōfukuji protest staged in 1150. In particular, it is noted that
some two hundred shrine servants carried around the *shinmoku,*
while making noise throughout the capital, before the protesters
retreated, leaving the divine symbols to continue the spiritual
protest.[100] Moreover, although there are references to warriors
injuring and killing protesters with arrows, I have found no specific references in contemporary sources to a monk or a shrine
attendant using the bow and arrow. Thus, while also taking into
account the success that the warriors had in fending off these demonstrators, one must conclude that the protesters were at best
poorly armed. Unlike conflicts that took place with other temples
and with members of the governor class, the *gōso* were not intended to become actual physical battles, since the demonstrators
were relying primarily on the power of the *kami* and their sacred
palanquins.

Other Means of Applying Pressure and Solving Conflicts

Though the *gōso* were unquestionably the most efficient means
of applying pressure on the capital elites, other methods were
also explored. For example, the clergy could close the temple or
selected cloisters, thereby ceasing to perform its spiritual duties
for the state and its leaders.[101] These methods were, like the *gōso,*
ideologically based on the *ōbō-buppō sōi* concept, since the closure
of an important temple would signify the decline of Buddhism as
well as of the state itself. The impact of such acts was further enhanced by the idea of *mappō.* The physical destruction and the
closure of temples thus became efficient means of protest, representing a decline in the understanding of the Buddhist Law and
the approaching end of righteous government.

The monks on Mt. Hiei were usually in favor of applying pressure on the court through *gōso,* although closures were also used
occasionally during the thirteenth century. For example, in the
eighth month of 1213, some members of the Enryakuji clergy set
out to attack Kiyomizudera in a conflict over land, but they were
caught by the personal guards of Retired Emperor Go-Toba. The
monks protested against the arrests and the treatment of their
colleagues by closing several buildings, putting out the eternal
flame in the Konpon chūdō, and secluding themselves on the
mountain. The protest proved successful, as the arrested members

of Enryakuji were pardoned and the guards conversely lost their posts. The same method was used again some two decades later when the Enryakuji clergy was displeased with the slow treatment of their appeal against warriors of the Sasaki family in Ōmi. On that occasion, the monks closed some of their buildings and threatened to seclude the entire mountain, eventually forcing the court and the bakufu to comply with their demands.[102] Overall, however, the Enryakuji clergy preferred the strategies of *gōso* to those of closure. By contrast, the strategy of closing the temple to apply pressure on the secular authorities appears to have been more common for Onjōji, which was rarely involved in divine demonstrations in the capital. For example, in the dispute over Onjōji's ordination platform in 1163, the clergy shut down the temple, because the court had declared that all Tendai novices be ordained at Enryakuji's platform.[103] Moreover, in 1242, Onjōji was closed in protest against the appointment of the *zasu* Jigen (of Enryakuji) as abbot of Shitennōji, and fifteen years later, the issue of independence caused the monks to resort to the same strategy. In 1260 the bakufu even felt compelled to send warriors to protect Onjōji during a closure, since it feared that the Enryakuji clergy might burn the unprotected compound.[104]

Kōyasan protesters were likewise uncommon in Kyoto, in part because Tōji was the head of Shingon and expected to represent the interests of its distant sibling in the capital. Yet *gōso* staged by any of the Shingon centers were extremely rare. Interestingly, Kongōbuji did use the strategy of closure quite effectively to influence verdicts in its favor from both the imperial court and the bakufu. The first instance dates to 1162, when the Kōyasan clergy left Kongōbuji in protest against the imperial court's unwillingness to issue a verdict against Kii governor Minamoto Tamenaga in a dispute over land.[105] The most successful application of this strategy, which was used as much as a threat as it was actually enforced, can be found in the temple's acquisition of the Ategawa estate (see Chapter 5). After more than a century of illegitimate claims from the Kōyasan clergy, Ategawa was incorporated in the temple's holdings in direct response to threats to close and leave Mt. Kōya desolated in 1278, and Retired Emperor Kameyama subsequently confirmed Kōyasan's complete proprietorship over the estate in the early fourteenth century.

The differences in the modus operandi of protesting between the Tendai siblings or between Kōyasan and Kōfukuji, for example, is a topic that deserves further attention. There is little doubt that the *gōso* were a privilege only for the most important temples such as Enryakuji, Kōfukuji, and Tōdaiji—the elites among the *kenmon* temples. But how was it determined which temples could or could not stage a divine demonstration in the capital? Distance from the capital played a part, though it was not enough of a deterrent for faraway institutions such as Daisenji and Kumanodera. Moreover, Onjōji clearly refrained from divine demonstrations in the capital despite its proximity, large number of followers, and high status within the religious establishment. Yet among the temples and shrines that did stage *gōso* in Kyoto, there was, in fact, a clear correlation between the frequency of protests and location. The correlation should not be taken simply as a matter of convenience, however, as proximity to Kyoto also meant more involvement in capital politics.

The most important and explicit criterion seems to have been that *gōso* could only be staged by certain privileged temples, as the Muromachi Bakufu stated in 1340: "Both Enryakuji and Nanzenji are imperially designated *(chokugan),* and there is no reason why only Enryakuji could stage a *gōso.*"[106] Yet there were more *chokuganji* than there were temples that staged protests in the capital, indicating that other factors also played a role. First, considering that neither Onjōji nor Kōyasan—which were both contenders for but not the formal center of two of the *kenmitsu* sects—staged any substantial protests in the capital, one can conclude that the *gōso* were primarily used by the main sect centers with ranking shrine affiliates. Second, precedent and tradition played an important role in legitimizing protests. The earliest *gōso* were staged by Enryakuji, Kōfukuji, and Tōdaiji in the tenth and eleventh centuries, and they were responsible for a large majority of all protests in the capital in premodern Japan. In addition, the supposed lack of precedent was used vehemently by the bakufu in 1235, as it tried to stop protesters from Iwashimizu Hachimangū from entering the capital with their holy carts in the incident between the Takigi and Ōsumi estates.[107] It is thus reasonable to conclude that the right to stage a *gōso* was most closely associated with tradition and *kenmon* status, while location was an important factor in terms of frequency. A more comprehensive study of *gōso* by other religious complexes in comparison to the procedures and circumstances of the temples examined here would undoubtedly shed more light on this issue.

The use of other strategies, such as self-destruction, to put pressure on the secular authorities became increasingly common among the monks of Mt. Hiei to rationalize the *gōso* from the second half of the thirteenth century. Their frequent use reflects a need for more desperate measures by the Enryakuji clergy to gain the attention of the imperial court as other established means of communication somehow became less effective. Whereas self-destruction appears to have been a unique strategy for Enryakuji, the excommunication of members of the Fujiwara family was equally original, and effective, for Kōfukuji, especially during the late Kamakura and Muromachi eras, which saw some twenty-two cases, affecting about forty-five courtiers, of this strategy.[108] As the secular ally of the Hossō center, the Fujiwara clan was expected to represent the political and financial interests of the temple in return for spiritual protection and services. The parties thus had mutual responsibilities toward one another, putting pressure on the Fujiwara chieftain in times of Kōfukuji dissatisfaction. The strategy of excommunicating Fujiwara members who had failed to live up to their responsibilities to the clan temple in general proved highly effective; most members felt obliged to make an effort to be reinstated within only a couple of days. The earliest example can be found in 1163, when Fujiwara no Kanesue was excluded from the clan by Kasuga for not supporting Kōfukuji's attempt to limit Enryakuji's control of Tendai and the issue of ordinations vis-à-vis Onjōji. The same strategy was used anew against Fujiwara no Nagakata and Shigekata, while other members of the clan were threatened with the same treatment only fourteen years later during the dispute between Kōfukuji and Tōnomine.[109]

Excommunications appear to be all but extinct in the sources for almost a century following these initial instances, but they re-emerge late in the thirteenth century to become a favored strategy for the Kōfukuji clergy, used several times in just a few years. First, the *kurodō* (scribe) Fujiwara no Kanenaka was banned for signing a document in 1284 that proclaimed that two Kōfukuji monks should be arrested for having burned Tōnomine property in Yamato. It took appeals from chieftain Kanehira and intervention by Retired Emperor Kameyama to have Kanenaka reinstated in the clan some two months later. Furthermore, in 1290 and again in 1291, the Fujiwara chieftain and other members of the clan were excommunicated for not supporting the temple's claim in the capital, and they were typically not reinstated until they had repented and offered additional donations to the Kōfukuji-Kasuga complex. This strategy subsequently became one of the most effective means for the Kōfukuji clergy in the fourteenth century of increasing pressure on the Fujiwara clan, as evidenced by a dispute between Kōfukuji and Tōnomine over an estate in Kawachi Province in 1307, when a member of the Fujiwara family was excommunicated for not acting to support the interests of the temple.[110] In 1344 two members of the Fujiwara clan were even excommunicated in unrelated instances. In the third month, Ichijō Sanetomi was banned because of problems that occurred in a Kōfukuji estate, and four months later, the clergy proclaimed the same punishment for the unfortunate Shijō Takakage, who happened to be the scribe for Retired Emperor Kōgon when he issued an edict prohibiting the temple's toll barriers.[111] While these measures were less dramatic than the self-destruction employed by Enryakuji, they proved equally effective. Fujiwara nobles were unable to continue their duties at the imperial court, demonstrating again the considerable power of the *kami* on politics. The increased use of such strategies in the late thirteenth and fourteenth centuries shows that the traditional means of protesting and communicating were becoming less effective—compelling evidence of a growing distance between the *kenmon* temples and the secular elites.

Going to battle against an opponent was usually the last resort for the clergy. Physical attacks on the leaders of the imperial court never occurred (contrary to the prevailing opinion), but the monks were not hesitant to attack their religious rivals. The Enryakuji clergy's readiness to attack their foes at Onjōji may be one of the best examples of this trend. Not only was Onjōji a Tendai competitor, it was also "conveniently" located close to the city of Ōtsu and Mt. Hiei. From the first attack in 1081, Enryakuji burned down its sibling on more than half a dozen occasions until the end of the Kamakura period.[112] Though these acts were condemned in the capital, and though individual monks were occasionally apprehended and punished, Enryakuji itself never suffered any retaliation from the court for these atrocities. Kōfukuji fought similar and recurring battles with Tōdaiji and the Tōnomine complex in Yamato Province, many of which were as devastating as the battles between the Tendai centers. Interestingly, Kōfukuji's first attack on Tōnomine occurred in 1081, the same year that Enryakuji attacked its Tendai sibling for the first time.

The proximity of the temples involved combined with the growing pressure on land and increased competition for religious status during the late eleventh century induced such direct attacks.

There were also several regional skirmishes between temple representatives and local warrior-officials, but it was the conflicts with religious competitors that most resembled outright attacks and battles. Unfortunately, contemporary sources do not contain enough information about the equipment of the aggressors or of the progress of even well-known skirmishes, to re-create these incidents in detail. Nonetheless, it appears that many of these confrontations, contrary to battles fought by the country's warriors, were disorganized and poorly planned. For example, during the conflict over the rights to a branch temple (Daisenji) between Enryakuji and Iwashimizu Hachimangū in 1105, the opposing camps had entered the capital with the intention of protesting, and a battle erupted as a result of the fact that both groups were there at the same time. Indeed, the sides clashed after both had attempted to state their cause to the court, entering the palace area from the neighboring gates of Yōmeimon and Taikenmon.[113] Other disputes that seemed destined to deteriorate into violent battles—most notably the conflicts between Kōfukuji and Enryakuji in 1113 and 1173—were effectively contained by the court and its warriors. The latter case, in particular, when monks from Kōfukuji and Enryakuji prepared large numbers of supporters in preparation for a confrontation to settle matters regarding Tōnomine, came to an unexpected halt when Go-Shirakawa stepped in to contain the conflict.[114] The monks were armed and prepared to battle on such occasions, but it seems that they were only somewhat better equipped during those incidents than during the gōso, despite the difference in attitude and aggressiveness. The professional warriors were clearly superior both in equipment and battle strategy. For example, when government warriors clashed with Kōfukuji followers in 1113, the sources list some thirty casualties among the Kōfukuji supporters against only two among the government warriors.[115]

The issue of the military prowess of temples and shrines during the Heian and Kamakura eras is thus more complex than hitherto assumed. Later war tales describe monks as fierce warriors equal to the most famous of the bushi, and scholars have tended to accept these accounts at face value. "Warrior-monks" such as the furious Jōmyō Meishū presented in the Heike monogatari; Hōyaku

Zenshi, who controlled Mt. Hiei for a while in the early 1100s (see Chapter 3); and the infamous Kōfukuji monk Shinjitsu in the 1150s, known in some sources as *Nippon ichi no akusō* (the number one evil monk in Japan), have given the entire ecclesiastical community a reputation of being more warriors than monks.[116] Though monks of this kind occasionally do appear in reliable sources, such figures were exceptional. The vast majority of monks and service people were poorly armed and had very little success against government warriors. In short, the images offered in the war tales and other fourteenth century sources were produced to convey a picture that exaggerated the military power of the clergy and had as its goal the discrediting of the established Buddhist schools in general.

Conclusion

The *gōso* have long been seen as the ultimate embodiment of the "evil influence" that religious institutions were believed to have exercised on the secular government during the late Heian and Kamakura eras. But such views lack historical foundation. The notion that all the main characteristics of the *gōso* fell into place at the same time is incorrect, as both Enryakuji and Kōfukuji only developed their strategies gradually, following the pattern of early shrine protest in the late eleventh century. The pieces came together only at the end of the Heian era, and the strategies reached full maturity in the late twelfth century. For Enryakuji, the standardized progression began with a meeting and a mobilization at the Konpon chūdō and was succeeded by a staged descent to the capital. Meetings and rituals then occurred at different branches in Kyoto, followed, finally, by a protest at the imperial palace or at the retired emperor's villa. The early stages of a protest were quite similar at Kōfukuji, where the procession to Kyoto was preceded by meetings and demonstrative moves in Nara. Though the pressure was mainly put on the shoulders of the Fujiwara family and directed to the clan headquarters in the capital after a visit to the chieftain's mansion in Uji, the pattern corresponds perfectly to Enryakuji's.

A second misunderstanding is the assumption that *gōso* were religious riots that were inherently violent and that aimed to harm residents of the capital if not actually to overthrow the government. A failure to accept the integrated roles of politics and religion is behind this misperception. In fact, the protesters relied more on the spiritual powers of their gods than on sheer force. They followed a schedule of ritualized behavior that gave the secular authorities opportunities to reach a solution at any time, indicating that the protests were an accepted means of communication (negotiation) though performed outside established structures. If the question of whether the monks and their supporters were armed cannot be answered conclusively as yet, the protesters were demonstrably no match for the defending warriors. At best the monks were poorly armed, again relying more on the power of the gods. Moreover, the ritualized destruction of shrines, *mikoshi*, and temples as well as the excommunication of Fujiwara members constituted a convenient replacement for actual confrontation, causing the same anger among the gods and exposing the court's failure to protect Buddhism.

Finally, the *gōso* were in no sense attacks on the capital, nor were they substantive protests against the system of rulership itself. Preceded by regular appeals, they constituted a last resort to solve important conflicts for the most prestigious temples of the imperial state. In general, the ability to influence decisions at court through a variety of strategies can be interpreted as one of the main criteria of *kenmon* temples, whereas the right to demonstrate in the capital with divine symbols was a prerogative of the elites within the religious establishment. In other words, the right to stage a *gōso*, though not written in any law codes and though open to contention, was a privilege held by the highest-ranking temples and shrines that had a precedent for demonstrating in the capital. In the end, the court's willingness to finance the reconstruction of sacred objects damaged during the protests and the harsh punishments of warriors who harmed monks or shrine servants provide the ultimate evidence of the legal rights of these temples to voice their concerns in a *gōso* or through other means. Stated differently, the *gōso* could not have had the currency they did were they not viewed as a function of the age's all-embracing shared rulership. They were a practical solution to the breakdown of the bureaucratic style of government and a further expression of the integrated role of temples in government and of the privatization that characterized rulership from the late Heian era to the end of the Kamakura age.

7

Religious Elites and
the Ashikaga Bakufu:
Collapsing the Gates of Power

The Kamakura Bakufu—Japan's first warrior government—actively sustained a cooperative polity with the imperial court, allowing the latter to continue exercising its judicial powers over non-warriors. Since the Kyoto-based system included governmental responsibilities as well as elite privileges for the most powerful temples and shrines, they also remained as they were in the late Heian period: active participants in capital politics and rulership. This point supports the recent view that the Kamakura period, while marking a shift in the power constellation, did not constitute the beginning of warrior dominance. Instead, it has been suggested, the beginning of a new rulership and an entirely new era one might call Japan's medieval age appears first in the fourteenth century.[1] It is from this time that discussions of national politics, religion, and culture increasingly must focus on the warrior class, as it became the dominating force in society. While the nobility could no longer contain the rising warrior class, the old Buddhist sects continued to exert considerable influence even after the establishment of the Ashikaga Bakufu in 1336. In 1368–1369, for example, monks from the Enryakuji complex entered the capital to protest the privileges that the bakufu had awarded to a Zen temple. Eventually, the bakufu complied with the monks' demands by exiling two prominent Zen monks and demolishing the gate of their temple. This conflict, known as the Nanzenji Gate incident, was not so much a dispute over economic privileges; rather, members of the Buddhist establishment were opposing the bakufu's attempts to promote Zen as its officially sanctioned sect.[2]

Based on these observations and, in particular, on the success Enryakuji had in resisting the Ashikaga Bakufu, Kuroda stated that although the *kenmon* system survived the establishment of the second warrior government, it simultaneously began to decline, as its economic base—the *shōen* system—started to disintegrate. This slow death, he noted, was caused by slow-moving socioeconomic changes on the local level. Villages as well as villagers began to question the authority of the absentee proprietors and formed horizontal alliances that resulted in more independent village units. The proprietor's control declined further as local warriors interjected themselves between the proprietor and the farming population. Subsequently, new kinds of conflicts appeared as whole regions rebelled against the old proprietors. In the end, it became increasingly difficult for the traditional elites in the central region—the imperial family, the high nobility, and religious institutions—to control and to collect dues from their estates.[3]

Other signs of the breakup of the old elite system were visible from the fourteenth century. Kuroda noted a decline in the prevalence of the *ōbō-buppō* concept, as it carried less weight with the new warrior rulers and was replaced by a renewed emphasis on Shintō. Moreover, he also observed that the spirit of cooperation between the various *kenmitsu* (exoteric-esoteric) sects declined, resulting in more tension and conflicts between different temples and scholars.[4] Though I find it difficult to substantiate any increase in conflicts between the established sects in the fourteenth century, the cooperative aspects of the old system of shared rulership did indeed disappear following Ashikaga Yoshimitsu's era (1368–1408). In particular, it was the emergence of new, populist sects, such as the Nichiren and Jōdo Shinshū (True Pure Land) sects, that changed the religious and political context. These sects offered new, simplified ways of achieving spiritual blessing, which challenged the complex and elitist rituals of the established schools. In characterizing Enryakuji's and Kōfukuji's aggressive responses and ensuing rivalries with the new sects, scholars have tended to stress doctrinal issues. But this opposition was not caused entirely by theological concerns. Indeed, even though disputes often centered on interpretations of Buddhism, the monks were less concerned with dogmatism than with maintaining their status and privileges. For example, when Enryakuji monks petitioned against Hōnen in 1204, followed by a more aggressive petition from Kōfukuji the following year, they simply tried to make him and his followers preach other fundamental Buddhist ideas in addition to Amidism. Both Tendai and the other *kenmitsu* schools were quite syncretic, allowing for different methods of salvation and, more important, a continuation of a multidoctrinal system of state-supported Buddhism. Only when this petition was denied and his followers maintained their exclusive stance was Hōnen banned. From that point on, the conflict escalated further, and Jien asked the court to prohibit the sect in 1211. Eventually, the leaders of Enryakuji even ordered its monks and estate officials to pursue the Amida believers and burn down their buildings.[5] This progression indicates that the *kenmon* temples' concern was not with the Amida doctrine itself (which was actually included in the Tendai teachings), but with increased competition for patronage from a sect that offered a simple and inexpensive way to salvation.

The Enryakuji monks similarly perceived Zen as a threat to Tendai's favored position with the imperial court. Consequently, Zen monks who would not compromise with Enryakuji's teachings found it difficult to preach their doctrine in the capital area. Dōgen (1200–1253), for example, rejected Tendai syncretism outright and stressed that only through *zazen* (seated meditation) could enlightenment be obtained. He was consequently driven away from Kenninji (an Enryakuji branch) in 1233, and he was forced to leave the capital because of opposition from the Enryakuji monks less than a decade later.[6] Eisai (1141–1215), in contrast, was less dogmatic and also quite successful in Kyoto even though the Enryakuji monks kept an eye on his activities. These tensions were even more acute in the early years of the Muromachi Bakufu, when the Ashikaga promoted Zen in an attempt to replace the *kenmitsu* sects as state doctrines. The emergence and promotion of Rinzai Zen would affect the nature of the cooperation between the religious and secular powers in the capital significantly.

While Kuroda duly noted such changes in the fourteenth century, he still argued that the *kenmon* system of cooperative rule somehow survived until the Ōnin War (1467–1477). Unfortunately, he did not explain how such an arrangement outlasted the Kamakura Bakufu by a full 150 years. He merely stated that the balance among the *kenmon* changed, as all the elites save the Ashikaga Bakufu lost power. It has even been suggested that, based on the continued economic and military power of the elite temples in central Japan, the *kenmon* system survived, at least in Kyoto, into the sixteenth century.[7] Kuroda has been much criticized for his inclusion of the Muromachi Bakufu within the *kenmon* system. In particular, Nagahara Keiji has objected to a single theory's appropriateness for the two shogunates, which were so fundamentally different from one another. He argues that Kuroda exaggerated the continuities between them, just as traditional historians had exaggerated the differences between the Heian and Kamakura polities.[8] This chapter will attempt to throw some light on this debate by examining the status and role of Enryakuji, Kōfukuji, and Kōyasan under early Ashikaga rulership. Did the fourteenth-century leaders regard religious institutions as a functional part of the state as had their predecessors? And, since many of the changes noted by Kuroda did not emerge suddenly with the establishment of the Ashikaga Bakufu, but rather gradually and more markedly from the beginning of the fourteenth century, how did the turmoil of the preceding decades affect the elite temples in central Japan?

Political and Religious Realignments under Go-Daigo

The importance of powerful temples as allies was all too obvious to Emperor Go-Daigo (1288–1339) when he began to search for support against the Kamakura Bakufu in the 1310s and 1320s. Indeed, it can be argued that the leading monasteries became hubs not only for their own factions and forces, but also for armies of more diverse origin in the fourteenth century, creating an overwhelming militaristic impression. The artistic (and usually exaggerated) representations of armed monks and secular followers in full battle gear in fourteenth-century picture scrolls of past events, beginning a long period of a critical attitude toward the influential monastic centers, reflect this trend. Go-Daigo's preoccupation with his own status vis-à-vis these powerful institutions provides further evidence of their leading role.

As described by Andrew Goble, Go-Daigo attempted to gain direct support from, and then control of, shrine servants (*jinnin*, or "purveyors," as Goble translates the term) of Hiesha early on. These officials held important posts as overseers of some 280 moneylenders and sake brewers under Enryakuji's jurisdiction, and the emperor managed to gain some ground against Mt. Hiei's temple-shrine complex by putting some of the *jinnin* under the jurisdiction of the Imperial Police.[9] Unusual as that strategy might have been in the Kamakura era, Go-Daigo in general resorted to more conventional methods to form ties with or extend his con-

trol over powerful temples. Specifically, two of his sons, Morinaga
—also read Moriyoshi—(1308–1335, Go-Daigo's third son) and
Muneyoshi (1311–1385, the eighth son), both became Tendai
head abbots at a comparatively young age (see Figure 23). Morinaga, who took the Buddhist name Son'un, was appointed head
abbot in 1328 at the mere age of twenty and again in 1330, though
he is better known for his activities as a commander after having
renounced his monkhood later that year. Muneyoshi adopted
the name Sonchō and became Tendai *zasu* several months after
Son'un's second resignation in 1330.[10] Go-Daigo also attempted
to extend his influence over Kōfukuji by bypassing the Fujiwara
chieftain and intervening in internal disputes between the two
leading cloisters of Daijōin and Ichijōin in the mid-1320s even
though no one within those factions asked him directly for help.[11]
Go-Daigo maintained an eclectic stance in attempting to build up
support from the religious powers, not unlike many of his prominent predecessors. While an avid supporter of Zen, as shown in
particular during the Shōchū debates between Tendai and Rinzai
Zen monks in 1325, he also continued to sponsor the esoteric
sects. Yet Go-Daigo never established himself as the undisputed

Figure 23. Imperial genealogy for the late thirteenth
and fourteenth centuries
Boldface indicates emperor; italics indicate tenure as retired emperor.
Numbers reflect sequence of emperors according to traditional accounts.

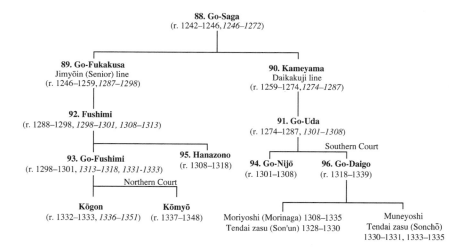

leader of the religious establishment, and he was forced to court virtually all major religious institutions, as evidenced by his activities in the third month of 1330, when he attempted to secure full support against the bakufu. Both he and his sons paid visits to the most powerful temples, such as Enryakuji, Tōdaiji, and Kōfukuji, as well as to several shrines, including Kasuga, Hie, Kitano, and Hirano. On Mt. Hiei, Son'un himself led ceremonies, with the assistance of his younger brother Sonchō, in which the warrior leaders in the east were cursed.[12]

At this point, still early in 1330, the outlook was fairly promising for the emperor and his sons. They appeared to have gathered some support from the most powerful temples in the Kinai region, and soon afterwards other mighty regional temples such as Daisenji in Hōki Province, its namesake in Harima, and Heisenji in Echizen joined the imperial cause. However, Go-Daigo never managed to gain the undivided support of any of the major temples. Although he was helped by uprisings staged by lower-level clergies and local warriors *(kokumin)* against the bakufu, these movements were less a result of local powers opposing the bakufu or supporting the emperor than part of the general trend of "the lower overturning the higher" *(gekokujō)* in a nationwide resistance against central elites and proprietors. In fact, though Go-Daigo's sons managed to gain control of some estates and to assemble several followers within the major temple complexes (in particular Enryakuji), the emperor's strategy was only partially successful. Scholar-monks and other prominent monks of the clergy, who still maintained control of estates and the organized armed forces of the elite temples, were rarely moved by Go-Daigo's call for rebellion. It was actually Enryakuji's ranking monks who forced Son'un to resign as head abbot in the fourth month of 1330, although the *Taiheiki,* a late-fourteenth-century war chronicle, claims that he did so voluntarily to head his own forces against the Hōjō.[13] Despite a lack of committed support from the religious elites, Go-Daigo relentlessly continued his spiritual attack on the Hōjō, having more curses performed at Sonshōji, Tōji, and Tōdaiji. Using the support he received from these temples, he then managed to depose the Tendai *zasu* Jigon, who had replaced Son'un, in favor of his other Tendai son, Sonchō, in the twelfth month of 1330. By this time, Kamakura had received increasingly detailed reports of Go-Daigo's rebellious activities, and in the fifth month of 1331, several monks who had been involved in ceremonies against the warrior government were called to the bakufu outpost in Kyoto, Rokuhara, to explain their actions. The emperor, now seeing that an armed conflict might be nearing, planned to make Mt. Hiei his central command post in Kinai, but those plans failed when Rokuhara responded by attacking both the imperial palace and Mt. Hiei in the eighth month of 1331.[14] Go-Daigo was clearly not as prepared as he would have liked to be at this stage, and he was forced to leave the capital, escaping to Mt. Kasagi in Yamashiro Province just east of Kyoto (see Map 2). This mountain, which housed armed forces under the control of the Kasagi temple, seems to have been a logical choice at the time, but Enryakuji's clergy was not pleased. Enduring a siege by up to three thousand bakufu warriors—an unprecedented attack, which incidentally seems to have shocked many nobles in the capital—because of their earlier affiliations with the emperor, the monks were gravely disappointed to see Go-Daigo and their own head abbot Sonchō, who accompanied his father, run off to another temple to seek protection. Enryakuji subsequently withdrew its support of Go-Daigo, and to make matters even worse, all the temples in Nara also declined the call from the emperor and his sons on Mt. Kasagi to join them against the bakufu forces.[15]

Though Go-Daigo did not receive the support he had expected from the Kinai religious institutions, he soon became, perhaps somewhat unexpectedly, the rallying point for disenchanted Kinai warriors with strong anti-Hōjō sentiments. The most important was Kusunoki Masashige (?–1336), who set up his own resistance in Kawachi Province (located south of Osaka and Nara) at his Akasaka fortress. The bakufu's forces responded by attacking Go-Daigo's stronghold at Mt. Kasagi while besieging also Akasaka throughout the ninth month of 1331. Go-Daigo was the first to succumb, as he was captured trying to escape from Kasagi together with a large number of noble and cleric supporters from Kyoto and Nara. Masashige endured another two months before being forced to abandon his fortress and escape. A new emperor (Kōgon) was installed by the Kamakura Bakufu in Kyoto, while Go-Daigo and his supporters were put under house arrest. Most nobles and temples appeared undismayed by these developments, and they simply adjusted by requesting confirmation of their estates and privileges from the new emperor (or by asking that earlier decisions be revoked if Go-Daigo's policies had gone against them).[16] Go-Daigo was banished to the isolated island of Oki off the northern coastline of Japan in the third month of 1332, and Soncho, deposed as Tendai head abbot earlier, was exiled to Sanuki, but many antibakufu forces were still at large. Prince Morinaga had escaped from Kasagi before it fell in order to join Kusunoki Masashige at Akasaka. When this fortress fell too, early in the twelfth month of 1331, Morinaga fled farther south to the Yoshino district, where he sought the support of Kinpusen, a shrine-temple complex with estates and local armed followers in Yamato Province. From this stronghold Morinaga attempted to gather more support from regional powers in Kii to attack the bakufu, though Kumanodera turned him down in the sixth month, and Koyasan maintained its middle stance, refusing several requests to send troops throughout 1332.[17]

The turning point in the rebellion against the Kamakura Bakufu, at least in hindsight, was instead provided by Kusunoki Masashige. He, too, escaped capture when his fortress fell late in 1331, and he continued to roam around in the Kinai area seeking to reassert his position. Carrying out a guerrilla-style warfare that proved difficult for the bakufu to eradicate—although the bakufu, for its part, did not commit all its forces to quelling the uprising —Masashige gradually gained enough strength to retaliate for the earlier loss. In the twelfth month of 1332, he managed to establish a new rebel fortress in the mountains of the Kawachi district, thus creating a visible symbol for the opposition to the bakufu. Together with Prince Morinaga, who gained a victory against a coalition of local bakufu warriors in the Suda estate close to Koyasan, Masashige subsequently secured the support of several temples, such as Kinpusen in Kawachi, Kokawadera in Kii, and Harima's Daisenji, which was also in alliance with a prominent local warrior named Akamatsu Enshin (1277–1350). Interestingly, most of the elite temples seemed reluctant to join the war actively at this point. Perhaps the risks involved in taking sides were simply too high at this stage, as suggested in the case of Toji, which, after having sided with Go-Daigo, was punished first by the Kamakura Bakufu and later by Ashikaga Takauji as well. In addition, even among provincial temples taking sides, many were driven by local strongmen *(kokumin)* seeking an opportunity to improve their position by joining one side or another. Since both sides were recruiting in the Kinai area, both the Masashige-Morinaga and the bakufu factions made a point of treating their lower-class supporters well, lest they lose their support.[18]

Go-Daigo's escape from Oki in the intercalary second month
of 1333 became another crucial step in the shaking up of the
bakufu, and it proved, in the end, to be the single most detri-
mental event in its demise. Even though he initially encountered
resistance from Hōjō supporters in Hōki Province, Go-Daigo received enough support from local warriors to emerge victorious
and begin a slow march back toward Kyoto. As the highest-ranking
and most symbolic challenger of the Hōjō thus escaped contain-
ment and remained at large, the former emperor quickly became
a concrete and dangerous rallying point for dissatisfied and oppor-
tunist warriors. Not even the most optimistic Hōjō supporter could
now avoid seeing the dangers posed by the combined dissatisfaction of many of its own warriors and the most charismatic
leader of the imperial family. Even the Yuasa family of Kii, traditionally one of the Kamakura Bakufu's most loyal retainers in
central Japan, fought Hōjō forces early in 1333. To make matters
worse, there were now fears in the capital that Enryakuji, with the
emperor back in contention, would send its armed supporters
against the capital to retaliate for the bakufu attack on Mt. Hiei in
1331. Threats soon turned into reality, and, as Enryakuji forces
began sporadic attacks against bakufu warriors, added pressure
was provided by Akamatsu Enshin's attacks on the capital itself in
the third month of 1333, forcing the bakufu to step up its own
involvement. The Rokuhara defense was initially successful, but it
could not defeat its opponents decisively, nor could it win the
Tendai monks over, as attempts to placate Enryakuji with donations
of new estates failed.[19] More important, the defensive success notwithstanding, the bakufu had yet to deal with the more dangerous
threats from Go-Daigo and the Masashige-Morinaga forces. The
Hōjō subsequently made the crucial decision to send Ashikaga
Takauji, one of the contenders for the headship of the Seiwa Minamoto lineage in the Kantō and hardly a reliable supporter of the
Hōjō, to lead an army from the east to deal a lethal blow to the
bakufu opposition in central Japan. In one of the historically most
significant switches of loyalty, Takauji declared himself a supporter of Go-Daigo and expressed his intentions to overthrow the
Hōjō on his arrival in Kyoto in the fourth month. Joined by the
forces from Enryakuji and other imperial supporters, Takauji
launched an attack on Kyoto, while Prince Morinaga and Kusunoki Masashige continued to battle Hōjō vassals in the Kinai
region. By the fifth month of 1333, the capital region was safe

enough for Go-Daigo's triumphant reentry into Kyoto. Later that same month, the remaining headquarters of the bakufu in Kamakura as well as in Kyushu were taken by anti-Hōjō forces, putting an end not only to Japan's first bakufu but also to an entire era of two coexisting and, for the most part, cooperating governments.[20]

When Go-Daigo returned to the capital to set up his government in the middle of 1333, he aimed at restoring the polity around himself. Since his policies have been treated comprehensively elsewhere, a summary of the strategies and developments relating directly to the religious sphere will suffice here. Sonchō returned from his exile in Sanuki and was reappointed head abbot of Tendai. Not unlike retired emperors Shirakawa and Go-Shirakawa two centuries earlier, Go-Daigo returned to the accustomed strategy of attempting to control important ceremonies and to contain the trends toward more independence among temples and shrines by having the head abbot in his corner. In a more innovative move, Go-Daigo also reestablished a provincial network of shrines under the direct patronage of the imperial family in an attempt to augment the cult around the divine emperor and the state *(shinkoku shisō)*, as noted by Kuroda.[21] More important, however, was his attempt to make Kyoto the center of Buddhism by promoting in particular Shingon and Tōji, a familiar policy that both Go-Uda and Go-Daigo had advanced in the first decades of the fourteenth century.[22] This strategy seemed especially aimed at Tōdaiji, which undoubtedly suffered most by Go-Daigo's policies. First, the emperor removed Tōdaiji from the nationwide network of temples, putting Saidaiji in charge of it instead.[23] Second, Go-Daigo attended to appeals from other religious complexes, such as Iwashimizu Hachimangū and even Kōyasan (despite its lack of support for the emperor earlier), before listening to the concerns of Tōdaiji. In fact, Kōyasan was even granted a confirmation of its original temple domain in the tenth month of 1333, according to its long-standing claims of land given to Kūkai close to Mt. Kōya *(goshuin engi)*, expanding and solidifying the Shingon temple's local control in Kii. With this confirmation, Go-Daigo was not only fulfilling a promise he had made two years earlier in exchange for prayers against the bakufu (though there is little proof that any prayers were actually performed), but also intended to win the loyalty of the Kōya clergy, while consolidating the support of Tōji, the centerpiece of his religious hierarchy. There can be no mistake regarding Kongōbuji's eagerness to take control of these estates:

administrators, accompanied by warriors, were dispatched as soon as Kōyasan received confirmations of its claims. In addition, new funding was granted for ceremonies and the construction of buildings and art objects in the fourth month of 1334, which finally induced the clergy on Mt. Kōya to support Go-Daigo against the resurgent Hōjō in the tenth month.[24] Kōfukuji received favors too, as it was allowed complete control of Yamato Province. Although such strategies were in part a counterweight to Tōdaiji, they also indicate a continuation of the imperial family's attempts to obtain some control over Kōfukuji now that the Fujiwara family was severely weakened. As Andrew Goble has pointed out, in order to make the established temples useful allies in his new state, it was necessary for Go-Daigo to reinforce their proprietary status, further strengthening the impression that his policies in the end were rather conventional. Go-Daigo's third measure against Tōdaiji was to abolish a number of existing toll rights that were a main source of income for many temples in a time of declining income from the *shōen*. Whereas this policy became a heavy blow to Tōdaiji, Kōfukuji was allowed to keep its toll barriers in Yamato, as was Onjōji for its support during the years of the rebellion.[25]

In addition to these restrictive policies, Go-Daigo actively promoted the sects he favored. Thus, Zen, which was politically insignificant compared to the established sects, became a favorite of the emperor, who invited Musō Soseki from Kamakura to Kyoto, where Zen temples such as Rinsenji, Kenninji, Tōfukuji, and, most notably, Nanzenji and Daitokuji, came to enjoy lavish support from Go-Daigo. However, this favoritism notwithstanding, Go-Daigo still relied mainly on the esoteric sects for religious ceremonies for the imperial family and the state. He simply could not act willfully in this area, but was forced to accept the arrangements that had been in place for centuries. Consequently, he used traditional strategies in confirming the bond between the imperial and the Buddhist realms through pilgrimages and donations. For example, Go-Daigo visited Iwashimizu Hachimangū, Tōji, Nanzenji, as well as the Hie and Kasuga shrines late in 1334. Most important, he dedicated a grand ceremony for the initiation of the pagoda at Tōji, although it had been rebuilt in the 1290s. Following these important ceremonies, Go-Daigo proclaimed that it was now Tōji that was the imperially designated protector of the state, taking over Tōdaiji's role as the center of the nationwide temple network.[26] Considering the efforts of previous sovereigns, Go-Daigo's religious strategies can hardly be called progressive or particularly innovative. Although he did intend a thorough reconstruction of the religious world by raising the emperor's authority over all temples, Go-Daigo was merely acting according to precedent, attempting to shift the balance within the established structures to accomplish his goals. Furthermore, he did not have the means simply to superimpose himself over the religious giants in order to transform the Buddhist establishment, while little of what he did satisfied or received the support of the military powers of the time. In the end, Go-Daigo's failure to accommodate the warrior class that had supported him brought about the conflict with Ashikaga Takauji that ultimately spelled the end of Go-Daigo's "Kenmu Revolution." The story is well known, but the movements of the religious complexes during the fallout deserve attention here.

It was in 1335 that Ashikaga Takauji turned against Go-Daigo, who had favored courtiers heavily with rewards and promotions during his regime, thus disappointing warrior leaders with expectations of land and offices. As one of the absolute prime warrior commanders in Japan and with the appropriate Minamoto heritage, the Ashikaga leader had expected to be appointed shōgun, but Go-Daigo bestowed that title on his own belligerent son Morinaga. Bothered more than the emperor by a resurgent Hōjō faction in the Kantō in the middle of 1335, Takauji then headed east on his own initiative without the shogunal command he had repeatedly asked for, although Go-Daigo actually commissioned the expedition eventually. Claiming a quick victory and retaking Kamakura, Takauji began to grant land to his own retainers without the specific approvals of the emperor. Go-Daigo subsequently exploited a breach within the Minamoto Seiwa lineage by having the leader of the competing Nitta branch, Yoshisada (1301–1338), attack Takauji. After losing the first couple of battles, Takauji turned the tide in the twelfth month of 1335 and eventually approached Kyoto, after which fighting between Go-Daigo supporters and Ashikaga followers spread nationally. Neither Enryakuji nor Onjōji was completely in favor of either side, but there were monks and secular followers who had made up their mind within each of the complexes. A monk from Enryakuji named Yūkan supported Go-Daigo's cause and fortified himself with over a thousand men at the Ikidai castle, but he was soon beaten by Kō no Moronao (?–1351), one of Takauji's premier generals. In the meantime, Nitta

Yoshisada suffered yet another loss, and Kusunoki Masashige, who remained with Go-Daigo, was besieged at Uji, all before the middle of the first month of 1336.[27]

The emperor escaped to Sakamoto, where he was joined by the young Kitabatake Akiie (1318–1338) in an effort to establish a stronghold on Mt. Hiei. At that point, the Tendai centers joined different sides, with Enryakuji making a commitment to Go-Daigo whereas Onjōji supported Takauji. Because of their proximity and the presence of Go-Daigo in Sakamoto, a confrontation between the two adjacent monasteries seemed unavoidable. On the sixteenth day of the first month, Go-Daigo's forces initiated the battle by launching a fierce attack against Onjōji, and even though Takauji sent one of his generals (Hosokawa Jōzen) to help the temple, the battle ended with a loss for the Ashikaga side and destruction of several temple halls at Onjōji. Takauji's forces suffered further defeats, and he found it best to withdraw to Kyushu to regroup in the second month of 1336. Takauji returned to the Kinai some three months later with fresh troops, including renewed support from Akamatsu Enshin, who was in turn supported by the armed forces of a local temple, Daisenji, in his home province of Harima. When Takauji's forces set out for Kyoto to battle Go-Daigo's armies, the outcome was anything but given. The emperor's forces may have had a slight advantage because of a greater familiarity in the capital area, but there was much lacking in terms of recruitment. Go-Daigo's failure to rally support among the powerful temples of Kinai hurt him badly during the war with the Ashikaga. None of the elite temples except Enryakuji made a firm commitment to his cause. Kōyasan insisted on its middle stance, despite Go-Daigo's renewed confirmation of the temple's original domain according to Kūkai's "hand-legend document," following the emperor's personal inspection and copying of the document. It is hardly surprising that Tōdaiji was reluctant to support Go-Daigo, considering the latter's policies against the temple only a year or so earlier. It may seem more surprising that Kōfukuji also remained uncommitted (though the Ichijōin cloister sided with Go-Daigo), but Takauji's strategy to bribe them with land donations (or promises thereof) to stay neutral certainly played a big role in the temple's early indecision, as it did for many other religious institutions with armed forces.[28] When the two forces approached a decisive battle in the capital area, there were consequently few religious forces involved. According to the

Taiheiki, Kusunoki Masashige at this point wanted to let Takauji into the capital, so that Go-Daigo's forces could recuperate, and then attack Takauji from the two strongholds on Mt. Hiei and in Kawachi. However, Go-Daigo would not allow a retreat from the capital and decided on a different strategy by sending Masashige to fight a much superior force, leading to the latter's famous and tragic death at Minatogawa in Hyōgo Province. Nitta Yoshisada, too, lost an important battle, finally forcing Go-Daigo to leave the capital for the safe haven of Enryakuji on Mt. Hiei. In the sixth month of 1336, Takauji entered the capital and immediately deposed Go-Daigo, setting up Kōmyō of the senior line as emperor.[29]

With the arrival of the forces of his brother Tadayoshi (1306–1352), Takauji ordered an all-out attack on the insurgent Enryakuji, approaching Mt. Hiei from three different directions. However, although Tadayoshi laid siege on Mt. Hiei for twenty consecutive days, he could not reach a conclusive victory. Some of the Ashikaga forces returned to Kyoto in the belief that Enryakuji was at least discouraged from continuing the fighting, but before long the western forces of Takauji were beaten by Enryakuji warriors, who had set out to strike at the unsuspecting enemy in the capital. This victory encouraged Enryakuji to the extent that plans were made for a heavy strike to retake control of the entire capital. Moreover, Nitta Yoshisada was prepared to join the temple's forces, sending a separate order to another temple (Kusumadera) to have its warriors join him in the attack on the Ashikaga. After some scrambling on both sides to prepare for the upcoming battle, it was the Enryakuji forces that moved first on the last day of the sixth month by descending the mountain and attacking Kō no Moronao's troops at Hosshōji in the Kawara area of the capital (see Map 3). The Enryakuji forces were victorious, giving them control of central Kyoto, which was consequently razed and set on fire. Nitta Yoshisada was not as successful, since he failed to beat Takauji, who was entrenched at Tōji, and was forced to return to Mt. Hiei. The battle consequently ended with mixed results, with the Enryakuji forces, which listed "mountain monks" *(yama hosshi)* among its leaders, more successful against Takauji's forces than such famous warriors as Nitta Yoshisada.[30] A tremendous change had occurred from the late Heian era, when warrior bands serving the imperial court consistently bested religious armed forces. In the fourteenth century temples commanded forces comparable to those of the most accomplished warrior leaders and were therefore not only essential allies or enemies in virtually all military and political battles, but also forces that by themselves could challenge most armies.

Tadayoshi, known as the more diplomatic of the Ashikaga brothers, attempted a different strategy following the defeat against Enryakuji. In a pledge to Hiesha, Tadayoshi promised to reconstruct the main temple hall on Mt. Hiei if his side was victorious. In addition, he stated that once those who supported Nitta Yoshisada had been apprehended and punished, he would guarantee the protection of the seven shrines of Hiesha as well as the "divine protection of the entire mountain." These measures were indeed bad news for Go-Daigo, whose armies not only suffered consecutive losses, but who would now have to worry about the loyalty of his most powerful religious ally. However, Go-Daigo managed to retain Enryakuji's loyalty by promising new and vast *shōen* donations in addition to Ōmi as a proprietary province for eternity. Furthermore, renewed efforts to gain Kōfukuji's support finally paid off, as a majority of the temple's monks and servants joined Go-Daigo's cause, though Nara's Tōdaiji and Saidaiji remained loyal to Takauji. Coordinated attacks from Kōfukuji and Enryakuji gave Go-Daigo renewed hope as the capital became entirely cut off, and as a result, starvation spread throughout Kyoto in the seventh month of 1336.[31]

But the forces on Mt. Hiei were short of supplies too. According to the *Taiheiki,* which has a tendency to exaggerate numbers greatly, some two hundred thousand men were entrenched on the mountain from the sixth to ninth months, and as Takauji's forces were beginning to cut off supplies from the outside, creating in effect an additional circle around the forces besieging Kyoto, the situation became increasingly difficult for Enryakuji. As a result, Go-Daigo agreed to make peace with Takauji on the tenth day of the tenth month, costing the lives of many monks and secular followers of Enryakuji, who were executed for their resistance. In a notable exception, the Tendai head abbot, princely monk Sonchō (Muneyoshi), managed to escape from Mt. Hiei to Ise. Go-Daigo himself discovered that he had been tricked when he was put under arrest, but he managed to escape in the twelfth month, heading off to the Yoshino mountains in Kii Province, where he joined Sonchō and Kitabatake Chikafusa (1293–1354), setting up his own Southern Court in a challenge to Takauji's Northern Court (headed by Kōmyō of the senior line).[32] As is well known, this marked the beginning of the era of the two courts, or the Nanbokuchō (Southern and Northern Court) period, lasting from 1336 to 1392, which was characterized by a great deal of uncertainty and political maneuvering.

Competition for Religious Allies during the Early Years of the Two Courts

One of the most important and complex issues for the two courts and the Ashikaga Bakufu (now established in Kyoto's Muromachi section) was the positioning of the many powerful religious centers in the Kinai. Convincing a temple to change loyalty was often outright impossible, and the strategy in many cases seems to have been focused more on preventing religious forces from actively joining one side or the other. As a result, several monasteries were courted by both sides, and the clergies knowingly attempted to benefit as much as possible without making sacrifices or commitments. For example, Kokawadera was asked to summon all its supporters to join the cause by both the Ashikaga and Prince Muneyoshi though it was only the third strongest religious force in Kii after Kōyasan and Negoroji.[33] Go-Daigo understood the importance of these monastic centers in the Nanbokuchō conflict well, and he remained highly active from his stronghold in Yoshino. In fact, he sent a letter to Kōyasan urging it to support him on the ninth day of the twelfth month of 1336, only seven days after arriving at Kinpusen of Yoshino. Although there had been some indications that Kongōbuji might support his cause, Go-Daigo received no immediate commitment. Takauji had actually pre-empted Go-Daigo by promising and granting confirmations of the old temple domain beginning in the sixth month. Unfortunately for the Southern Court, Kōyasan's "maybe" was one of the more positive responses it could muster from the influential temples in central Japan. As in the Kōyasan case, Takauji had acted earlier and he foresaw any moves the isolated emperor might make. For example, the Ashikaga leader confirmed landholdings for Kōfukuji in the ninth month of 1336, made donations to Tōdaiji's Hachimangū, and restored some estates for Saidaiji in several early attempts to secure support from Nara. Though these measures did not make the Nara temples complete Ashikaga supporters, they did ensure that the southern capital would not side with Go-Daigo.[34]

Nitta Yoshisada and Prince Muneyoshi, who resigned as Tendai

head abbot and gave up his monastic career (as Sonchō) to support his father, managed to flee Kyoto during the disastrous peace
agreement and began to assemble their forces to join Go-Daigo
early in 1337. At this point, the alignments started to fall into
place in the Kinai. Nara's temples sided with Takauji, as did Onjōji,
while Enryakuji now thought it best to remain neutral. Kongōbuji
displayed a slight inclination toward supporting Go-Daigo, even
though the Kōyasan clergy skillfully exploited its value by communicating with Kyoto as well in order to amass bribes from
both sides.[35] The strongest commitment came from Kumanodera's
clergy and *kokumin* (local strongmen associated with the shrine),
who gave Go-Daigo a good grip on the Kii peninsula by sending
warriors to the Southern Court. But these demarcation lines were
in no way absolute. The decision of the ranking monks of a temple to join one side or another did not necessarily mean that all
monks and secular supporters agreed or acted accordingly. For
example, the monk Seia (or Saia), a local strongman in Buddhist
robes under Kōfukuji jurisdiction, residing in the Yamato village
of Kaijū (in present-day Sakurai City), opposed his superiors in
Nara by siding with the Go-Daigo supporter Masaki Chōkon.[36]

Nara was actually an important checkpoint for the combating
forces of the Nanbokuchō era, not only because of its location
between Kyoto and Yoshino but also because of the many religious institutions in the area. Thus, in his charge against several
strongholds of the Southern Court beginning in the sixth month
of 1337, Takauji also attacked Kaijū, the village of the independently acting Seia. By the middle of the next year, the Southern
Court had suffered severe losses, as evidenced by Kitabatake
Akiie's death in the fifth month, followed by Nitta Yoshisada's
defeat and death in a battle two months later. Letters were sent
from Kyoto to attempt to entice Kōyasan to abandon its passive
support of Go-Daigo, but the clergy continued to waver between
the two camps, hoping to obtain more privileges. More important, both sides had little choice but to cater to the requests of the
clergy on Mt. Kōya, fearing that the temple's forces could tip the
scale in favor of the enemy. Takauji concomitantly issued edicts
protecting Kōyasan's rights against intrusions and exempting
temple land from war taxes on several occasions. For example,
in the eighth month of 1338, the Ashikaga Bakufu confirmed
the temple's possession of an estate in Izumi, prohibiting intrusions by various commoners. Several of these edicts concerned

the cloister of Kongō sanmai'in, whose abbot, Jitsuyū, was close to the Ashikaga brothers. Tadayoshi even appointed a new abbot to the cloister according to the clergy's wishes in the second month of 1339, demonstrating the Ashikaga's willingness to cooperate with the monks to gain their support. The Kōyasan clergy, for its part, used the attention it received from the Northern Court to bargain for more privileges. A successful attempt occurred late in 1338, when Retired Emperor Kōgon asked the bakufu to issue an edict exempting the transportation of the annual taxes from an estate in Echizen from toll dues late in 1338. In a measure of good-will and to ensure its success, Tadayoshi not only supported the appeal, which originated from the Kōyasan administrator *(zasshō)*, but also sent separate edicts to various toll gates ordering that the taxes be let through without any fees.[37] In the end, Kōyasan benefited immensely from the clergy's ability to solicit bribes from both sides. The biggest gain was Go-Daigo's confirmation of Kūkai's original temple domain, a late Heian period invention that was now established beyond any doubt. Even if the Southern Court saw through this forgery, it did not want to alienate the temple, which was free to establish absolute control of several nearby estates without any capital patrons involved. Though the first Kōyasan administrators, sent out to inspect and register paddy fields and cultivators, encountered some local resistance against the temple's attempts to establish a stricter proprietorship, Kōya-san came out of the Nanbokuchō era with a firm grip on almost all estates it had gained, owing to its unwillingness to commit itself in the war and to a new, more direct management strategy.[38]

The Southern Court experienced a revival when Kitabatake Chikafusa, based in Ise Province, managed to strengthen its de-fenses. Interestingly, it was Seia, because of the strategic location of his Kaijū village in Yamato, who acted as an intermediary be-tween Ise and Yoshino. Seia's resistance against the Northern Court was thus more than symbolic; it was quite problematic. In the tenth month of 1340, disagreeing with Kōfukuji's pro-Takauji stance and determined to reap some profits for himself, Seia invaded estates of the Kasuga shrine and withheld taxes that were earmarked for Kōfukuji's Yuima ceremony and offerings for Tōdaiji's Daibutsu. The Kōfukuji clergy, unable to control this local strongman, brought out the holy *sakaki* branch and, after pleading for sup-port among the temples in Nara, carried it to Uji and Kyoto in the twelfth month with an appeal to have Seia punished.[39] The pres-

ence of the Kasuga *shinmoku* in the capital greatly affected the
imperial court, which canceled several palace ceremonies, Buddhist rituals, and festivals, as it was forced to scale down its own
activities without the Fujiwara present.[40] It was left to the bakufu
to deal with Seia, which it did by sending out a force, led by
several renowned warriors, including Sasaki Dōyō (1306–1373),
in order to capture the renegade monk in the first month of
1341. The fighting between the Ashikaga and Seia lasted for six
months, until the latter suffered a severe loss, barely escaping certain execution. Though his fate after these events is largely unknown, there are later references to him and his son Ryōen (Yoshi-
maru) continuing the fighting for the Southern Court.[41]

Ashikaga's Yamato offensive in early 1341 appears to mark the
beginning of a more stable bakufu polity directed from its headquarters in the Muromachi area of the capital. As a result, most
religious institutions became convinced that it was most favorable
to accept the Ashikaga Bakufu as the legitimate government and
the Northern Court as the proper imperial court (at least for the
time being) of the realm. Enryakuji was still reluctant to partici-
pate actively in the fighting against the Southern Court, not because it felt morally committed to Go-Daigo, but rather because
its arch-rival, Onjōji, was unconditionally supportive of the Ashikaga Bakufu. The temples in Nara remained supportive of the
Ashikaga after Takauji's successful policy of courting them with
land confirmations and grants. Moreover, the Southern Court appeared to be in retreat when it came to Kōyasan, as Takauji and
Tadayoshi visited the complex in 1344, in an apparent attempt to
establish new ties and win it over. It must therefore be considered
at least a limited success for the Southern Court when it managed
to solicit promises in the third month of 1348 that forces from
Mt. Kōya would not enter the war on either side. Yet, at the same
time, edicts were issued stating that no one should be punished
for *not* joining the Southern Court, allowing individual monks or
cloisters to take sides and thus continue to invite bribes from the
two courts. In fact, Ashikaga Tadayoshi confirmed a division of
rents *(wayō)* from an estate only five months later.[42] There can be
no doubt regarding Kōyasan's intentional wavering, earning it
benefits and confirmations from both sides. But the courting was
far from equal, as more generous donations were forthcoming
from the Southern Court, whereas the Ashikaga Bakufu mostly
confirmed established estates and appointments, indicating its in-

creasing strength even in southern Kii. In fact, the Muromachi Shogunate established itself as the main governmental authority in central Japan from the early 1340s. It is under these improved conditions that one can begin to discern the bakufu's new ambitions regarding the role and status of religious institutions within the emerging warrior ruling structures.

The Ashikaga Bakufu's Religious Policies

Developments on the Kii peninsula were politically and militarily important to the Muromachi Bakufu, but the new national polity was created in Kyoto, where the most important trends within the realms of politics and religion were found. Though forced to court the powerful temples early on, the Ashikaga leaders also had their own religious agenda, which was not centered on the established sects. Rather, the leaders of the new regime promoted Zen throughout the fourteenth century in an attempt to create a new religious hierarchy that it could control. Zen was a relative newcomer with little economic and political power of its own, and with its earlier ties to the Kamakura Bakufu, it seemed a suitable doctrine to further the interests of the Ashikaga.[43] At the same time, the bakufu's religious policies, with its one-sided patronage of Rinzai Zen, threatened the old Buddhist schools as well as the entire system of doctrinal multitude. As a consequence, the age-old competition among the *kenmitsu* sects was now replaced by one between Zen and established temples.[44] Enryakuji in particular responded vehemently to the favors now granted Zen institutions. Two incidents demonstrate this point vividly. Though they are only two decades apart, they resulted in different conclusions, reflecting two different political complexions.

In 1339 Ashikaga Takauji, his brother Tadayoshi, Retired Emperor Kōgon, and the Zen monk Musō Soseki agreed to convert an imperial palace (Kameyama) in the western part of Kyoto into a Zen monastery. *Shōen* were provided by the bakufu to finance the reconstruction, but the temple was still not completed two years later. To increase the funding for the project, Takauji decided to send a trade mission to China and to give the profits to the temple. The enterprise was scaled down to a mere two ships because of protests from several of the *kenmitsu* temples, including Kōfukuji and Enryakuji.[45] The new temple, named Tenryūji, was finally completed in 1344. A memorial on the anniversary of Emperor Go-Daigo's death was planned for the next year, but once again Enryakuji protested. Since a Zen temple had never been the location of an imperial memorial service, the Enryakuji monks felt that Tendai's public role and religious status were now under threat. Such a perception is well demonstrated in the temple's appeals, issued between the twelfth month of 1344 and the eighth month of 1345, which emphasized the tradition of state protection by the *kenmitsu* schools.[46] As argued by Enryakuji, Tenryūji itself, which was described as little more than a private Zen hall, could scarcely, with justification, be made an imperially designated temple *(chokuganji)*. In particular, Enryakuji objected to the retired emperor's visiting such a place for the purpose of attending a memorial service. Clearly, the monks stated, it was Enryakuji that had served as the protector of the state since the capital had been moved to Kyoto originally (794).[47] In the monks' own words, "the safety of the state is through Enryakuji's protection," whereas Zen, in its neglect of the *kenmitsu* temples, represented the first step in the progression toward state destruction. In support of their claim, the monks did not fail to mention that the Kamakura Bakufu, which had favored Zen, no longer existed. Moreover, just as the Sung dynasty in China had succumbed to the Mongols because of its patronage of Zen, the monks argued, so would the imperial state decline, unless Tenryūji was demolished. Such demands were based on the precedents of Kagenji and Kenninji, two prospective Zen temples that had been stopped in the Kamakura era, under pressure from Enryakuji and Onjōji. Musō Soseki also received his share of criticism, as he was referred to as a beggar and an illegitimate monk, who threatened to destroy the state from its very core, and he therefore, according to his opponents, deserved to be exiled.[48] The mutual dependence of the Buddhist and imperial laws were thus, according to the Tendai monks, restricted to the established system of sects, the *kenmitsu* schools. They felt that the *kenmitsu* schools stood to lose immensely if Zen was favored, since its believers tended to reject other schools, making Zen incompatible with other Buddhist doctrines. It is not likely that the monks conceived the bakufu's policies as steps toward the creation of an entirely new hierarchy, but they were convinced that its patronage of Zen constituted an attack on the long entrenched multidoctrinal system.

Enryakuji stepped up its pressure early in the seventh month of 1345 by assembling some of the sacred palanquins on Mt. Hiei, threatening to bring them to the capital in a demonstration, and by calling its supporters together for a general uprising *(ikki)*. The court responded first by sending the abbots of the three main sections (Saitō, Tōtō, and Yokawa) from the capital, where they resided at a safe distance from the clergy, to attempt to pacify the enraged monks on Mt. Hiei. The abbots carried with them a promise that the retired emperor would not attend the ceremony and that Tenryūji would not be honored with an imperial designation. It appears that the ranking monks, probably influenced by the court-dispatched abbots, were willing to accept the compromise, but the clergy voted down the peace offer. Enryakuji forwarded a new, lengthy appeal, detailing Tendai's importance in the most sophisticated theoretical argument of the conflict. The court attempted to have the three *monzeki* abbots calm the clergy a second time, but these alienated noble monks now had little influence over the clergy on Mt. Hiei.[49] Instead, the Enryakuji clergy increased the spiritual pressure by bringing three of the Hie *mikoshi* (Seishinshi, Hachiōji, and Jūzenshi) to the Konpon chūdō on top of the mountain on the twenty-third day of the seventh month of 1345 and by forwarding another appeal early in the eighth month. In addition, Enryakuji invited Tōdaiji and Kōfukuji to join the protest with their divine carts and *sakaki* branches, showing not only that the Enryakuji monks saw the value of such support but also that it was indeed an issue with multidoctrinal implications. To entice the Hossō clergy and to emphasize common concerns, the Enryakuji invitation praised Kōfukuji for having destroyed the Zen temple Darumadera at Kataokayama in Yamato in 1305, spiting the subsequent exile of the responsible monk. In response to this increased pressure, the retired emperor finally decided to cancel his visit to Tenryūji in the middle of the eighth month.[50] However, the bakufu maintained a much tougher stance and was not ready to capitulate. Rather, it threatened to depose Enryakuji's three most prominent abbots as heads of the Saitō, Tōtō, and Yokawa sections and to confiscate the responsible monks' private and public possessions should they enter the capital. Prominent commanders were also dispatched to the palace to improve its defense in case the protesters came to the capital. These measures and threats apparently discouraged the clergy from staging a protest, enabling the bakufu leaders and a large number of prominent warriors to attend a grand ceremony at Tenryūji on the twenty-ninth day of the eighth month of 1345,

though without the presence of the retired emperor, who had to
wait with his visit until the following day. The ceremony itself was
an important statement for the bakufu: it displayed its own new
power and intentions while also rejecting Enryakuji's demands.[51]

The bakufu briefly controlled the capital following this incident,
but internal rivalries and the Southern Court's attacks on Kyoto
weakened its position considerably in the first half of the 1350s.
However, the Ashikaga regained control by 1355, and the second
shōgun, Yoshiakira, enjoyed a steady rule in the capital until his
death late in 1367. The next shōgun, Yoshimitsu, was only ten
years old, leaving bakufu matters in the hands of a council of warrior leaders. Such was the political situation when Enryakuji renewed its pressure against the bakufu's favoritism of Zen. The incident has its origins in 1367, when a novice from Onjōji was killed
as he tried to force his way through a toll barrier newly constructed
by Nanzenji. This Zen temple, located in the eastern part of Kyoto
(see Map 3) and heavily patronized by the bakufu, had been
allowed to build the toll station to finance reconstruction of the
temple's main gate. Onjōji and Enryakuji, both prohibited by the
bakufu to erect new tolls, also had interests in Ōmi Province,
where the toll gate was erected, and disapproved of what they
judged to be unfair competition. Armed servants from Onjōji proceeded to tear down the new barrier, with fatalities occurring on
both sides. The Zen leaders immediately appealed to the bakufu,
which decided to retaliate by dispatching warriors, who destroyed
three of Onjōji's own toll stations and then confiscated a number
of Onjōji estates. Since the larger issue was the bakufu's extensive
patronage of Zen, Onjōji managed to get the support of Enryakuji and Kōfukuji in its appeal to the imperial court. Facing the
combined powers of three such influential temples, the bakufu
and the court made peace with them in the eighth month.[52] The
opposition between the followers of Zen and Tendai did not disappear, however. Immediately after the peace agreement, in the
ninth month of 1367, the abbot of Nanzenji, Jōzan Sozen, wrote a
polemic (the *Zoku shōbōron*) in which he stated that Zen was the
only true Buddhist learning and that other sects were inferior per-
versions. He further mocked the Tendai monks, calling them
monkeys and toads.[53] In spite of such insults, the petitions from
Enryakuji throughout 1368 were more concerned with protecting
the traditional rights of the established *kenmitsu* schools, appealing in their name as it received the full support of both Onjōji

and the temples in Nara, while also discouraging the bakufu's patronage of Zen. Among other things, the Enryakuji monks claimed that the Shintō deities disliked Zen, that the state was protected by the eight *(kenmitsu)* sects, and that Enryakuji alone was the most favored temple of the sons of heaven.[54]

The bakufu responded with a three clause statement, attempting to defend Zen and Jōzan while discrediting the claims of Enryakuji. First, the bakufu claimed that Enryakuji was not the only imperial temple, displaying the bakufu's intentions to raise Zen to the level of the *kenmitsu* sects. Second, it avoided the issue of punishment of Jōzan by claiming that it did not know who the author of the polemic was. Finally, the edict stated that Enryakuji itself had been disloyal to the state four times since the bakufu had moved to Kyoto, attempting to discredit the Tendai center's right to appeal in the name of the state. It is not fully clear what these four incidents of disloyalty were, but Enryakuji's early support of Go-Daigo against Ashikaga Takauji is referred to.[55] A second incident may have been one of 1351, when some Enryakuji monks attacked Momoi Naotsune, a retainer of Takauji and the *shugo* of Etchū Province, on his way to the capital. The Tenryūji incident was most likely another sin on the bakufu's list. Enryakuji responded by reiterating the temple's protective role of the imperial state, claiming also that it was the Ashikaga forces that had initially attacked Mt. Hiei in 1336. The battles during this era were then defensive, according to the monks, who also rhetorically wondered if the entire temple really should be punished for the few "wild hearts" who engaged in military activities among the over three thousand monks on the mountain.[56] The bakufu avoided the issue of Zen as an exclusive state doctrine and the effects it would have on the old multidoctrinal system. For its part, Enryakuji, in its most comprehensive petition, revealed the depth of its concerns with the Ashikaga Bakufu and its religious policies in a new petition early in the eighth month of 1368: "The court and the bakufu have honored and favored Zen, but Tendai has not been bestowed such [honors]. However, this sect should not be neglected, and this mountain's Buddhism should not be forsaken."[57] In fact, the sources reveal that the monks had good cause to be worried. For while the bakufu was funding construction and repairs to Zen institutions, it was often reluctant to respond in the same way on Enryakuji's behalf. In 1350, for example, Enryakuji monks complained that taxes had not been forwarded from Sasaki-no-shō in Ōmi Province even though the Northern Court and the bakufu both had decreed that they be sent. Enryakuji even had a pledge from the Sasaki family acknowledging the temple's right to the taxes. In the end the bakufu not only denied Enryakuji's rights but even assessed the expenses of the Kamo festival on members of the Hie shrine.[58]

The Enryakuji monks were not alone in noting that the bakufu's policies disrupted the accustomed balance among the sects. For example, Konoe Michitsugu, a ranking courtier, was much concerned that these policies broke with the customs of old.[59] In addition, several of the bakufu's own warrior leaders wished to comply with some of the temple's demands and punish Jōzan, but the dominating figure at the time, Hosokawa Yoriyuki (1329–1392), who served as shogunal deputy (kanrei) from 1367 to 1379, continued to protect Nanzenji. When the bakufu heard that large numbers of Enryakuji supporters were ready to enter Kyoto in the eighth month of 1368, it responded with rigorous defensive preparations at several strategic locations in Kyoto, including the imperial palace, Nanzenji, Gion, and the mansion of the young shōgun, Yoshimitsu. Facing these forces, the demonstrators adhered to previous gōso practices, leaving several of the sacred carts, which included three from Hie (Marōdō, Hachiōji, and Jūzenshi) and at least one each from Sekizan zen'in, Gion, and Kitano, close to Ichijō Avenue in Kyoto to battle for their cause, before they were eventually relocated at Gion. The conflict now entered a stalemate as either side refused to budge for more than two months. Finally, in the eleventh month of 1368, Yoriyuki gave in and exiled Jōzan while also agreeing to delete his name from the register of monks.[60]

Encouraged by their partial victory, the Enryakuji clergy continued to demand that the Nanzenji gate be completely demolished. The bakufu applied delay tactics again, leading to a new protest in the capital in the fourth month of 1369, when the remaining mikoshi from Hie joined the original ones in the capital, while the clergy rejected pleas from the monzeki abbots to settle down. The bakufu dispatched warriors throughout the city anew, but the confrontation became several notches more violent this time, perhaps as a result of the challenge presented by the defending warriors. On the twentieth, the demonstrators broke through barricades on the western side of the palace area, leading to a skirmish with bakufu warriors. Although the protesters were successfully repelled, several holy carts were left close to the palace and in major intersections on Ichijō and Shijō, and some buildings were set ablaze by the retreating protesters, who continued to cause disturbances and uneasiness in Kyoto. Later sources state that the Enryakuji protesters were armed and ready to fight when they entered Kyoto, and even though contemporary sources do not indicate such a level of preparedness, the use of the term *"kasen"* (battle) to describe the confrontation seems to reflect a higher level of violence. In any case, the bakufu, still headed by Hosokawa Yoriyuki, finally complied on the nineteenth day of the seventh month of 1369, and the gate was torn down at the end of that month, marking a serious setback for the Ashikaga Zen hierarchy, while severing the ties between influential Zen monks, such as Shun'oku Myōha (1311–1388), and Yoriyuki.[61] The *mikoshi* were brought back to their shrines early in the eighth month, but the issue was not completely solved until much later. Since some of those palanquins had been damaged in the course of fighting with bakufu troops, the monks insisted, as was the custom, that they be rebuilt at bakufu expense. The warrior regime eventually agreed to build new shrines in 1372, but Yoriyuki never provided any resources to get the construction under way. It was only in 1380, following the ousting of Yoriyuki from the bakufu, that taxes were actually assessed and the reconstruction could begin. The Enryakuji clergy conveniently attributed Yoriyuki's fall to divine retribution from the Hie *kami* for his deceitful behavior against the Tendai center.[62]

Enryakuji was defeated, then, in the Tenryūji incident, but it was ultimately victorious in the Nanzenji Gate matter. The victory did not result from a change in the Ashikaga's religious policies. Rather it was a consequence of the bakufu's own power, which was now at low tide. The second shōgun, Yoshiakira, died in 1367, and the third shōgun, Yoshimitsu, was still too young to rule on his own. The leaders of the bakufu were far from united, and internal struggles prevented resolute decision making, though they remained committed to enforcing the policies introduced by the founders of the new warrior government. To the regime, Zen was a controllable sect and therefore to be favored over the older Buddhist schools. Consequently, Zen institutions were promoted and protected throughout the fourteenth century, and they continued to prosper as long as the bakufu remained vigorous. Yet at the same time, Enryakuji and the other *kenmitsu* schools continued to perform religious ceremonies on behalf of the imperial court, even as their overall influence was unmistakably declining.

The established sects were anything but passive facing these problems. The bakufu's promotion of Zen even resulted in an unusual spirit of cooperation among the otherwise competing sects of Nara and Kyoto, as evidenced by the decline in conflicts between the traditional sects in the first century of Ashikaga rulership. The few conflicts that can be discerned appear much less serious than the opposition to Zen or earlier conflicts between the established sects in the Kamakura era. For example, on the second day of the Saishōkō ceremonies at the imperial palace in the eighth month of 1367, a brawl broke out between Tōdaiji and Kōfukuji monks, on the one side, and Enryakuji monks, on the other. The conflict was actually the result of a protest from Onjōji, which opposed the composition of the performing monks, and since the Onjōji monks boycotted the ceremony, the proper offering could not take place. The monks from Enryakuji were apparently in a mood to support their Tendai brothers, resulting in a skirmish with some fatalities, but the fighting did not continue beyond the first day, as the Nara monks thought it best to retire rather than face the more numerous Enryakuji clergy. In spite of their differences, the disputing parties seemed to agree on how to resist the court's attempt to punish the responsible monks for causing such a violent conflict within the palace walls. Rumors in the capital that monks both in Nara and on Mt. Hiei were preparing to resist with the assistance of swords and *naginata* were apparently enough to let the monks off the hook.[63] Remarkably, despite this disturbance, Kōfukuji and Tōdaiji eagerly joined Enryakuji's protest against the bakufu's promotion of Zen less than a year later, indicating the relative insignificance of the palace brawl between the two leading monasteries in the capital region.

In short, the traditional *kenmon* temples, headed in particular by Enryakuji and Kōfukuji, and the Ashikaga Bakufu represented two fundamentally different approaches to the role of religious institutions in the Tenryūji and Nanzenji incidents. Whereas the temples represented a system of doctrinal multitude and interdependence, the bakufu sought to create a single system that it could control by itself. In so doing, it used both new and old methods. It was quite common for government leaders to support a particular sect to assure its total loyalty, although it would have been unimaginable for the bakufu to neglect completely the established

Buddhist schools in the thirteenth century. By promoting Zen, however, the Ashikaga Bakufu was not only favoring a particular Buddhist school, it was also attacking the underlying concept of doctrinal multitude. Monks and courtiers clearly noted this unprecedented change. The Tenryūji and Nanzenji Gate incidents, then, were less conflicts between the older schools and Zen than they were a defense by the former of their traditional rights vis-à-vis the bakufu.

Central Proprietorship and Territorial Lordship

The Ashikaga Bakufu's attempts to restructure the religious hierarchy in favor of Zen was a serious threat to the established *kenmitsu* schools, but it was not only the aristocratic members of the warrior class that threatened the temple elites. More long-ranging changes in the economic sphere were caused by the increasing power of the warrior class in general, as the flow of income from temple estates was disrupted, beginning in the Kamakura period. In particular, local warriors, often serving as land stewards *(jitō)*, sought to increase their share of revenues at the central proprietor's expense. The bakufu, whose principal role was to maintain peace, often judged against its own vassals, as demonstrated by numerous cases involving Enryakuji, Kōfukuji, as well as Kōyasan in the late twelfth and thirteenth centuries. But, if the Kamakura Bakufu was disposed to protect the legitimate rights of the *kenmon* temples, it became increasingly difficult to sustain such equilibrium in the fourteenth century. With local powers now questioning the authority of the central elites, divisions of estates *(hanzei)* with original proprietors began to occur. Like its predecessor, the Ashikaga Bakufu was concerned with the maintenance of stability, and it thereby confirmed *hanzei* in order to avoid friction. But at the same time, the bakufu was on occasion willing to recognize the proprietary rights of the *kenmon,* as can be seen from its confirmations of temple land on several occasions.[64] Some of its edicts condemned warrior intrusions on temple and shrine estates, whereas others prohibited the *hanzei* mentioned above. In any event, the frequency of such edicts suggests that the bakufu was less than successful in curtailing warrior encroachments. As a result, most central elites gradually experienced a decline in their income and control, with the notable exception of estates situated close to the main temple.

But what do the bakufu's confirmations of temple privileges indicate? Despite its religious policies, was the bakufu committed to supporting the system of shared rulership? And why did the Ashikaga Bakufu seek to slow its own warrior allies from taking control of the land? The answer is embedded in its desire to maintain the status quo on one level so as to be able to focus on the policies it wished to implement on another level. At the same time, the bakufu's control of even the capital region could be shaky, as, for instance, in the early 1350s during a momentary weakening of power because of internal disputes. Ashikaga Tadayoshi became engaged in a conflict over the bakufu's land policies with Kō no Moronao, the right hand of his older brother Takauji, in 1349. While Tadayoshi was inclined to maintain the privileges of the traditional elites, in a manner reminiscent of the Kamakura Bakufu, Moronao wanted less central control, siding with local warriors (*kokumin*) and confirming their land at the expense of central proprietors.[65] As a result of this difference of opinion, the two Ashikaga brothers became enemies, and Tadayoshi was forced to leave Kyoto the next year, seeking support with the Southern Court. After having launched an attack against Kyoto, Tadayoshi made peace with Takauji, but a new confrontation occurred in 1351. This time, Tadayoshi escaped to the north, fighting several battles along the way, including a big victory (and a sweet revenge) in Harima Province over Kō no Moronao, which eventually resulted in the latter's death. Tadayoshi later ended up in Kamakura, where Takauji finally killed his younger brother in 1352, ending the dispute that is known as the Kannō Disturbance after the era.

After ousting his brother, Takauji appointed his son Yoshiakira to handle bakufu affairs in Kyoto. But Yoshiakira, lacking his father's experience as a commander, soon found himself in a precarious position, and he was obliged to leave the capital in the intercalary second month of 1352, when forces of the Southern Court ousted both the rival court and the bakufu itself. A month later, Yoshiakira successfully recaptured Kyoto with the assistance of Sasaki Dōyo, thereby reestablishing the Ashikaga Bakufu in the country's capital.[66] With the bakufu's authority and position so seriously threatened, it was moved to compensate by adopting a favorable stance toward the powerful temples in the Kinai area. For example, both Takauji and Yoshiakira were unusually generous to Enryakuji as a way of assuring its neutrality during this conflict. Takauji granted it three *shōen* in 1351, and Yoshiakira responded in kind. In fact, not only did the second Ashikaga shōgun confirm Enryakuji's rights on several occasions, but he also granted it new estates as well as *jitō* perquisites.[67] Realizing the importance of having as many supporters (or as few enemies) as possible, the bakufu needed to maintain a precarious balance. The donations and confirmations to Enryakuji were both bribes and rewards for not allying itself on the side of the Southern Court.

It was also important for the Ashikaga to retain the loyalty, or at least the neutrality, of Kōfukuji during these lean years, and, conversely, the Hossō center was in need of support from the bakufu. Since the temple had numerous holdings in the area where the fighting between the two camps took place, and the southern armies were making headway at the time, opportunities opened up for illegal intrusions by various groups on the Kii peninsula. For example, in the eighth month of 1350, Kōfukuji and Kasuga sent no less than four appeals to the Northern Court and the bakufu, asking that various taxes be paid, estates be restored to the complex, and intrusions by *jitō* and others be stopped. Kōfukuji was additionally weakened by an increased number of internal conflicts, deriving from tensions between low- and high-ranking monks as well as shrine servants disputing over rights to titles and land. In addition, these disputes were often expressed in terms of support of or opposition to the Ashikaga, enhancing the hostility in these conflicts both within Kōfukuji and between many monks and the bakufu leaders. Just before his demise, Tadayoshi even sent a vassal to detain a bothersome Kōfukuji monk, who was eventually killed during the disturbance that followed the arrest.[68]

Another serious problem at Kōfukuji was the recurrence of competition for the office of head abbot between competing lines of the Fujiwara family. One of the leading branches at this time was the Konoe, which had obtained control of the Ichijōin—one of the two most powerful cloisters within Kōfukuji—in competition with the Tsukasa line. The Konoe line was headed by Tsunetada (1302–1352), but he was challenged by his cousins Mototsugu and Ietada for the regency in 1336. Tsunetada sided with Go-Daigo and left Kyoto to support the Southern Court even though Takauji agreed to appoint him regent for the Northern Court's Kōmyō. He returned to Kyoto in 1340 after a falling out with Kitabatake Chikafusa, but his basic loyalties appear to have remained with the Southern Court. It was Tsunetada's younger brother, Kakujitsu, who was the abbot of the Ichijōin during the Southern Court's offensive in 1350. To secure the Konoe's continued control of the cloister, Kakujitsu designated Jitsugen, the son of Tsunetada, his successor to this important office. Kakujitsu died in the fifth month of 1351, but monks from the Daijōin cloister, controlled by other Fujiwara branches such as the Kujō, Ichijō, and Nijō, who sided with the Northern Court, opposed Jitsugen's appointment, and a battle broke out between the competing cloisters. Interestingly, just after the Northern Court had sent Shijō Takakage to calm the monks, the Southern Court sent its own messenger attempting to accomplish the same thing.[69] Both courts claimed to hold the authority of and took credit for the truce at Kōfukuji, because of the different loyalties of the two cloisters.

The conflict erupted again in the eighth month of 1351, when the Ichijōin attacked its adversary with the help of forces from the Southern Court. Following the encouraging defection of Tada-yoshi and the ensuing defeat of Kō no Moronao (who had done much of the fighting for the Northern Court on the Kii penin-sula), the Southern Court sent a force under the command of the Ochi, a local warrior family (kokumin) of Yamato Province, to aid the Ichijōin. This force soon made the cloister its base and began attacking the opposing Daijōin. The conflict was more than a dis-pute between two cloisters by now; it was a battle for the leader-ship of Kōfukuji as well as a struggle between the Southern and Northern courts over control of one of the most influential temples and, by extension, also of Nara. Somehow, the remaining monks of the general clergy, who did not belong to any of the cloisters, assembled their own forces to strike back at the invading south-ern forces. To make the recruitment of other kokumin in the area successful, the Kōfukuji clergy offered Buddhist names as a sign of their special and new status. The ensuing battles, which con-tinued for nearly two months almost without interruption, were devastating, resulting in the burning of several of Kōfukuji's build-ings and the destruction of numerous Buddhist treasures.[70]

These drawn-out battles yielded no clear winner, but they affected Kōfukuji substantially in two ways. First, it became appar-ent that the Southern Court would not gain a foothold in Nara, since, apart from the Ichijōin, most temples and cloisters in Nara supported the Ashikaga. As the Muromachi leaders thus reestab-lished their hold of the capital region, the Kōfukuji complex came to favor the Northern Court more, as evidenced by the many appeals it sent to the bakufu. For example, five requests to stop intrusions of Kōfukuji *shōen* by named and unnamed warriors were forwarded to the bakufu and its prominent vassals (such as Hosokawa Akiuji) throughout 1352. The conflict between the cloisters lingered on, however, when the Ichijōin abbot Jitsugen attacked his foes in the third month of 1353 and again in the tenth month, but the bakufu, now firmly entrenched in Kyoto again, sent forces that easily quelled the disturbance, even though the antagonism between the cloisters would recur some twenty years later.[71] Second, Kōfukuji, severely weakened by the battles and extensive destruction, remained vulnerable to local intrusions after the Kannō battles, since the fighting continued in Yamato and Kii. Thus, it made a number of requests for assistance throughout the 1350s to the Northern Court, the bakufu, and even to individual *shugo* for protection of its estates. Though a lack of information in contemporary sources makes it difficult to estimate how often Kōfukuji's appeals were heard or its interests protected, a conflict in 1356, when the temple's pleas were not heard, indicates that more forceful measures were occasionally needed to involve the secular authorities in Kyoto. The Kasuga *shinmoku* was moved to the main temple building of Kōfukuji in preparation for a forceful appeal *(gōso)* on the thirteenth day of the seventh month of 1356 because of the lack of response from the Northern Court and the bakufu over a Kasuga appeal regarding the intrusions of two estates (named Hirai and Kawaguchi) in Echizen by its *shugo*. Not until three members of the Fujiwara clan were excommunicated for not supporting the appeal were actions taken to satisfy the monks, and the *sakaki* branch was finally taken back to Nara early in the third month of 1357.[72] It appears, then, that additional pressure was needed for Kōfukuji to make its voice heard, even in a case where there was no dispute over guilt, indicating the problems the Hossō center experienced in protecting its interests against the growing influence of the warrior class during the precarious 1350s.

Conflicts over land between Kōfukuji and different *shugo* were quite common, and they were particularly problematic because of the *shugo*'s importance as crucial allies of the bakufu and the most powerful figures in the provinces. One of the more interesting disputes broke out in the twelfth month of 1364, when monks from Kōfukuji and followers of Kasuga carried the holy branch to the capital in protest against the *shugo* of Echizen, Shiba Taka-

tsune (1305–1367). The protesters accused Takatsune of intruding into Kawaguchi-no-shō, which belonged to the Kasuga shrine.
Though essentially a straightforward and common dispute over
land in Echizen, the incident carries an important history. Shiba
Takatsune had sided with Ashikaga Tadayoshi in his war with Takauji during the Kannō Disturbance (1350–1352). Tadayoshi lost and
was eventually poisoned by his older brother in Kamakura. Takatsune, however, was not caught, and he sided against the bakufu,
opposing Takauji's son Yoshiakira, while playing an important
role when the Southern Court briefly took over Kyoto in 1352.
When the Ashikaga reconquered Kyoto, Shiba Takatsune quickly
changed sides again and managed to assume the post of *shugo* in
Echizen, which he kept from 1352 to 1364. The Shiba fortunes
rose during this long period, as Takatsune's son, Shiba Yoshimasa
(1350–1410) became an important member of the bakufu and
was appointed *kanrei* (shogunal deputy) in 1362. For his part, Takatsune apparently felt free to appropriate more income for himself,
enforcing a division of income *(hanzei)* from all estates belonging
to shrines and temples in Echizen. In the case of Kawaguchi, it
may have been even worse, since the Kōfukuji monks claimed
that Takatsune gave all the income from the estate to his own
retainers.[73]

To apply more pressure on the court, the Kōfukuji clergy argued
that the most important Hossō ceremony for the imperial state,
the Yuima'e, could not be performed, since the monks in Nara
were starving and would perish unless Takatsune's intrusions
were stopped. One must wonder if the rent from one estate could
cause such devastation for Kōfukuji, but the connection between
the temple's and the state's well-being was clear to everyone involved. The court subsequently promised to support Kōfukuji,
asking the bakufu to stop the intrusions, but the latter did not
send anyone to admonish Takatsune, most likely because his son
held the *kanrei* post. It was this neglect that caused the monks and
shrine members to carry the *sakaki* branches to the capital late in
1364. The protest caused considerable problems, since the emperor and the Fujiwara members found it difficult to perform
their functions with the holy branch left at the Chōkōdō—a temple
hall belonging to the junior (Jimyōin) line of the Northern Court
and the target for Kōfukuji demonstrations during the fourteenth
century—in the eastern part of Kyoto. The *sakaki* remained in the
capital for several months, and a number of strange events in

the fifth month of 1365 seemed to reinforce the protesters' resilience and put more fear into the minds of the Kyoto nobles. In particular, the records say that two deer, the most holy animal of the Kōfukuji temple-shrine complex, appeared in Kyoto and went to the southern gate of the Chōkōdō, where they stopped to cry four times. In addition, diseases became rampant, and a mysterious man with long hair but no nose or ears appeared in the capital just a few days before a ten-year-old acolyte apparently lost his senses at the Chōkōdō.[74]

As was customary when divine symbols were left in the capital during a protest, activities at the court were scaled down, but so were ceremonies that otherwise would have benefited the temple-shrine complex. The Kasuga festival, for example, was canceled early in the eleventh month of 1365. Then, in the sixth month of 1366, the bakufu sponsored a *kagura* performance (a Shintō dance) at Kasuga to placate the gods, since their *sakaki* branches were now withering (which, like the destruction of the *mikoshi,* symbolized the demise of the temple-shrine complex and the anger of the *kami*) in the capital. But the calamities appeared to accumulate as various diseases were raging in Kyoto in the seventh month, and many residents were wondering if these calamities were related to the unsolved crisis with Kōfukuji.[75] Finally, in the eighth month of 1366, nearly two years after the holy branches had been taken to the capital, Yoshiakira decided to punish Shiba Takatsune, who preempted the shōgun's actions by burning his own mansion in Kyoto and escaping to Echizen on horseback with about three hundred of his closest retainers. Yoshiakira sent several of his best generals, including Sasaki Ujiyori and Yamana Ujifuyu, to pursue the fleeing Takatsune and to beat him in battle if necessary. There are, however, no records of any decisive battles being fought, and Takatsune seems to have escaped his pursuers, as he died in his castle from illness the following year—which the Kōfukuji clergy attributed to the anger of the Kasuga deities. In the capital, the bakufu replaced Takatsune's son, Yoshimasa, with Hosokawa Yoriyuki as *kanrei* and issued a verdict in Kōfukuji's favor some four days later, on the twelfth day of the eighth month, after which the clergy quickly agreed to bring the holy branches back to Nara. Although the clergy was pleased with the outcome of the conflict itself, there was much discontent with the lack of support from the members of the Fujiwara clan. Thus, when Shijō Saneoto and Shijō Takatada failed to attend the offerings for the return of the branches to Kasuga after the bakufu verdict, they were excommunicated from the clan even though there were other members who also neglected to go to Nara.[76]

The bakufu was thus initially reluctant to respond to Kōfukuji's appeal, attempting to leave these matters to the capital nobles and waiting for word from the imperial court before it acted. Yet the Muromachi government could not accomplish its economic, religious, or political goals, nor could it function properly, unless it dealt with issues of unrest and proved itself as a legitimate police force and government, especially in the face of increasing disorder and weakening of the old central powers. Kōfukuji, in particular, continued to lose coherence and was gradually weakened by the devastating conflicts between the two main cloisters, the Daijōin and the Ichijōin, which caused multiple battles, burnings of buildings, and killings again in 1371 and 1372. Although twenty years had passed since his involvement in the fighting of 1351 to 1353, the ambitious and belligerent Jitsugen of the Ichijōin was still one of the most aggressive leaders in this destruction, opposing among others a certain Kyōshin of the Daijōin. This dispute, which centered on land and titles, was serious enough to cause the head abbot, who had lost control over these two powerful cloisters, and the main clergy to ask the Northern Court and the bakufu to contain the disputing parties. The clergy resorted to staging a forceful protest in the capital against both cloisters in the twelfth month of 1371, when they entered Kyoto with the *shinmoku*, excommunicating the Fujiwara chieftain in the process. The clergy specifically wanted the leaders of the conflicting cloisters, Jitsugen and Kyōshin, as well as other disputing monks exiled. But little was done to oblige the monks, and the entire year of 1372 was plagued by repeated confrontations and battles between the two sides, with the *sakaki* branch consequently still in the capital early in 1373. Even though the original dispute abated during this time, new issues provided more fuel for the clergy's discontent. In addition to demanding the fighting parties within the temple exiled, the Kōfukuji clergy lodged forceful complaints against various land intrusions. The deputy *shugo* of Settsu, Akamatsu Noriaki, was one of the targeted offenders, but the appeal was also directed against other *shugo* in general.[77]

The bakufu and the imperial court continued to procrastinate, inducing the Kōfukuji clergy to persuade the temples in Nara and Kasuga to close their gates, while the Northern Court was cursed at the Nan'endō. The imperial court belatedly responded to Kōfu-kuji's appeal in the eleventh month of 1373, exiling Noriaki to Echigo and a close relative, Akamatsu Seijun, to Shimosa, with the hopes that these moves would induce the clergy to bring their holy branches back to Nara. Yet it took a full six months, until the fifth month of 1374, before Noriaki and Seijun actually departed Kyoto on their way to their respective exiles, and the divine symbols remained in Kyoto, since the disputing abbots had not yet been punished.[78] Eager to achieve peace in the capital at last, the court acted as quickly as it could, issuing an edict for the exile of the fighting abbots in the sixth month and forcing them to depart five months later. Though the punishments were merely symbolic (the monks were "exiled" to neighboring provinces of the capital and allowed to return shortly thereafter), it was enough to convince the Kōfukuji clergy to end the *gōso* and bring the divine symbols back to Nara in the twelfth month of 1374. The *sakaki* branches were consequently stationed in Kyoto for three years while a total of ten Kōfukuji appeals were lodged, marking the longest forceful protest in Japan's history.[79]

This incident is more than just a curious historical note; it is also an important indication that the *gōso* were much less effective than earlier, for the governmental bodies apparently felt less responsibility toward the elite religious institutions. A three-year-long protest in the twelfth or thirteenth centuries would have been inconceivable. The warrior leaders had little choice but to acknowledge the religious and military power of the established temples in the Kamakura age, but they were much less affected by their spiritual threats in the fourteenth century, as they promoted instead the new sects of Zen and Jōdo shinshū. It also appears that Kōyasan, whose position not far from the Yoshino headquarters of the Southern Court was well used by the clergy to entice favors from both sides, received tremendous favors from the bakufu, especially during the problematic Kannō years. For instance, on the nineteenth day of the sixth month of 1350, to woo the Kongōbuji clergy over, Yoshiakira prohibited invasions of Kōyasan estates and killings there by warriors, also hoping that he could prevent battles to be fought in those areas.[80] At the same time, the Southern Court was courting Kōyasan with more substantial bribes and donations, revealing a more active policy. For example, Kitabatake Chikafusa (1293–1354), the author of the famous *Jinnō shōtōki* (The Chronicle of the Direct Descent of

Gods and Sovereigns), written in defense of the Southern Court, donated a *jitō* office to Kōyasan's Rengajōin in the fourth month of 1352, ostensibly for prayers for his deceased father as well as his eldest son Akiie, who had died in battle for the Southern Court on the twenty-second day of the fifth month of 1338.[81] Since no temple siding with the Northern Court would have performed such prayers for Chikafusa, there was also an expectation of support for the Southern Court attached to that donation.

In general, Kōyasan was a more common recipient of favorable edicts from the Ashikaga Bakufu in land issues than were Enrya-kuji and Kōfukuji, and for good reasons. Kōyasan was one of the most crucial uncommitted forces in the war between the two courts on the Kii peninsula, and its consistent middle stance forced both sides to court the temple with confirmations and even donations of new land. The aforementioned case of 1348, when Kongōbuji ordered that monks were prohibited from joining the Northern Court but would nevertheless not be punished if they chose not to join the Southern Court in Yoshino, is an outstanding example of this balancing act. In addition, in that same year, Kōyasan turned to the Muromachi Bakufu when it faced problems in the Ōta estate, where a deputy *jitō* refused to forward the annual taxes to the proprietor. An agreement was eventually reached to split the taxes, which was confirmed by Tadayoshi in an edict of the twenty-seventh of the eighth month of 1348. The temple's request for Tadayoshi's confirmation of this *hanzei* indicates that Kōyasan was not completely confident that the local warrior-administrator would follow the contract, turning to the bakufu with hopes that it might be able to contain him. Indeed, although Kōyasan was also granted the *jitō* office for Ōta, which had been contested earlier, Takauji had to order the *shugo* and other commoners of Bingo Province to stop intruding onto the estate in the fourth month of the following year.[82]

The two-sided courting of Kōyasan continued also after the Kannō Disturbance and the turnovers of Kyoto. In the second month of 1354, the Southern Court confirmed the temple domain of Kōyasan as Go-Daigo had done earlier as well as the borders of Kongōbuji itself within the monastic complex.[83] Exactly a month later, Takauji responded to an appeal from the clergy of the Kongō sanmai'in, which the Ashikaga had remained close to since the late 1330s, appointing the monk Dōshun to administer the cloister's estate in Harima Province. In addition, Takauji sent one

of his vassals, Akamatsu Norisuke, to stop the intrusions performed on that estate by a local warrior. Another edict from
Takauji later that same year prohibited the intrusions and illegal
activities by various warriors and commoners on Kōyasan's Tera-
nishi estate of Settsu Province, further emphasizing the Muromachi Bakufu's support of the temple's established privileges.[84]
These various edicts indicate two crucial differences between the
two courts and their relationship with Kōyasan. First, the clergy
turned most frequently to the Ashikaga when dealing with intrusions by warriors. Not only did the Muromachi Bakufu have more
authority over the general warrior class, but warriors supporting
the Northern Court also had a better pretext to attack Kōyasan
estates because of its tie, albeit a weak one, with the southern
competitor. Conversely, Kongōbuji turned to the Southern Court
looking for confirmation of grants and traditional privileges, especially in competition with other temples. For example, both Kokawadera and Kōyasan appealed to the Southern Court in 1364 in a
renewed dispute over the borders between Mionoya and Nade
estates. Second, whereas the bakufu, based on its recognized authority over the warrior class, and the Northern Court focused on
confirming the rights of Kōyasan, the Southern Court was forced
to be more aggressive by granting new land in order to gain favor
with the temple. The Southern Court was, in other words, at a
clear disadvantage throughout the remaining years of the Nanbokuchō era, continuing to entice Kōyasan with new donations.
Late in 1359, for example, it donated the war tax of Ono village
in Kii Province for the reconstruction of the main gate, as it had
done the previous year.[85]

Overall, Kōyasan benefited immensely from the struggles between the two courts and from the fluctuating power of the Muromachi Bakufu. Not only did it obtain confirmations and expand
its landholdings and offices at the expense of less strategically
located proprietors, such as Iwashimizu Hachimangū, but through
innovative and bold policies, the temple's control of its land also
improved. Departing from the traditional *shōen* hierarchy where a
local strongman, most commonly a warrior with considerable freedom and ambitions of his own, served as administrator on behalf
of the proprietor, the temple now began to rule its estates more
directly. Kōyasan managed to extend its control into the Ategawa Estate, which previously had been dominated by the Yuasa,
who sided on occasion with the previous proprietor (Jakurakuji),

on occasion with Kōyasan, but always attempted to squeeze the farmers and extract additional resources for themselves. The fall of the Kamakura Bakufu and the war between the two courts prompted the decline of the Yuasa, as they joined the cause of the Southern Court after having supported Rokuhara before 1333. While Kōyasan thus received land confirmations from both sides, augmenting its authority vis-à-vis the Yuasa, other competing warrior families, such as the Kishi, received *jitō* appointments from the Ashikaga in Yuasa territories. By the end of the fourteenth century, the Yuasa band all but disappear from the records, extinguished by its unfortunate stance in this problematic era.[86] To survive in such a competitive atmosphere, Kōyasan began to implement a more direct control of its nearby estates in the late fourteenth century by performing detailed land surveys (preceding similar strategies used by the *sengoku daimyō*—regional warlords—in the sixteenth century), registering rice paddies and dry fields in a simplified manner without the multilayered exemptions and office fields that were still customary in Kōyasan's distant *shōen*. Such a direct proprietary control also favored naming cultivators with each piece of land, allowing more strict direct taxation and more security for the farmer on his land.[87] This type of "territorial lordship" also developed within the warrior class in the fourteenth century, revealing a preview of a more effectively centralized, yet localized, rulership that would dominate in the late fifteenth and sixteenth centuries.[88]

Land disputes in the mid–fourteenth century were quite complicated, as numerous studies have demonstrated. Yet even from this limited treatment of Enryakuji, Kōyasan, and Kōfukuji, three simultaneous processes can be seen to be at work. The first and most overarching trend is that of increasing warrior control of land at the local level. This territorial hegemony was the wave of the future, and it affected central proprietors heavily, as they gradually lost control of their *shōen*. Kōyasan stands apart from Enryakuji and Kōfukuji here, since it managed to establish a local warrior-like territorial rulership, benefiting from the chaos of the Nanbokuchō era. The era of the two courts provides a second factor that needs to be considered in fourteenth-century land conflicts. As demonstrated here, Kōyasan effectively used its position to enhance its position in Kii, while Enryakuji reaped minor benefits when the Southern Court made advances close to Kyoto. By contrast, Kōfukuji was torn, suffering devastating internal battles, inviting the support of local warriors on both sides. The main clergy was nearly helpless in its efforts to curtail the activities of the two disputing cloisters, attempting in vain to keep factional struggles separated from the administration and control of Kōfukuji. The bakufu's expanded authority over land, regardless of who was involved, is a third important consideration. Though it did not particularly favor the established religious centers, confirmation of the rights of Enryakuji, Kōfukuji, Kōyasan, and other central landowners was often necessary to maintain peace and stability amid severe social and economic changes. Acknowledgment of the rights of these temples was made, then, out of political need, as in the Kannō Disturbance, or out of a desire to limit local land intrusions and thus to control warriors. However, such acknowledgments of the proprietary rights of the old elites did not fundamentally compromise the bakufu's authority. To the contrary, its ability to adjudicate land issues across the board demonstrated that the Muromachi polity was built around the rule of the warrior.

Economic Privileges and Judicial Immunities

In addition to problems in securing income from their estates and their diminished religious importance in the Ashikaga polity, the *kenmitsu* temples in the capital region also faced challenges to other income-yielding practices that derived from their status as privileged elites. As can be seen most obviously in the case of Enryakuji, the ability of temples to control and protect guilds began to decline. Contrary to the changes in the religious hierarchy, however, these problems were not caused exclusively by the bakufu but by local persons who started to question the authority of the traditional elites. The term *"gekokujō,"* a contemporaneous concept for describing a range of sociopolitical changes, including in particular the advances made by the local warrior class over land, may thus also be applied to describe the period's economic challenges.

By using their judicial immunity, the *kenmon* temples served as patrons of trade and of merchant guilds *(za)*. These *za*, developed as groups of producers, came together under a proprietor for whom they provided products and services. The first *za* appear in documents as early as the eleventh century, but they became widespread when commerce and specialization developed outside the confines of the *shōen* during the Kamakura era. Many *za* under temple and shrine protection developed as occupational groups, supplying products for festivals and ceremonies, but other creative and commercial activities were gradually included from the twelfth century. Though both temples in Nara and Kyoto protected different *za* and supplied tax-free markets on their immune temple grounds, Enryakuji appears to have been the most prominent one, owing in particular to its influence in the capital, which remained the center of commerce and luxury consumption. In the 1280s the Enryakuji complex (including its branches) controlled some 80 percent of the sake brewers and moneylenders in Kyoto. Since the sake dealers and storehouse operators, who doubled as moneylenders, were among the most active merchants in the expanding trade of the thirteenth and fourteenth centuries, Enryakuji's profits were probably superior to those of all other temples in Japan at the time.[89]

The temple provided the guilds with protection, which included the lending out of manpower to put pressure on tardy debtors, and received taxes and dues in return. The members of a guild commonly resided on temple or shrine land, as in the case of Gion's cotton guild, which was located in the area of Sanjō and Shijō avenues close to the shrine. As shrine residents, the cotton guild members obtained the status of *jinnin*, thus justifying their special privileges. In general, Enryakuji retained its rights to tax and protect the guilds (especially from competition) in the fourteenth century, but changes within the commercial sector strained the old patron system. "New guilds" began to appear, challenging the monopolies enjoyed by the old *za*. In essence, whereas the older guilds developed in the service of the capital elites, the newer ones were geared to trade and business. Though they still paid their dues, their relationship with traditional patrons was more contractual. The movement from below that the new kinds of guilds represented initially provided the temple with more clients and thus more income. In the cotton trade, for example, the older guild, under the protection of the Gion shrine, lodged a complaint with the Northern Court in 1343 against merchants who were trading in the villages around Kyoto. The members of the guild disapproved of the new organization, whose members were allowed to trade by the Gion shrine for only a small annual fee. The court decided in favor of the original guild and prohibited the members of the newer guild from engaging in commerce.

However, the hierarchy of Gion, which did not mind the extra income, petitioned and ultimately convinced the court to reverse its verdict.[90]

Although the Gion shrine benefited from the addition of such new *za* in the 1340s, the growth of commerce made it more difficult for Enryakuji to maintain itself, in the end, as a successful patron. By contrast, the role of the bakufu became increasingly important as the authority of the old elites proved insufficient to control the conflicts between the old and the new guilds. This situation resulted in a diminished status for the former patrons and an enhanced authority for the bakufu in an area in which the preceding warrior government was not involved. The case of the Kitano sake malt guild provides an illustrative example not only of this development but also of its gradual progress to its conclusion in the fifteenth century.

The exclusive right to supply malt to the sake brewers of Kyoto was held by the sake malt guild under the protection of Kitano, another of Enryakuji's branch shrines. Starting in 1379, the bakufu acknowledged the guild's monopoly but also started to levy taxes of its own. Thus, when the sake brewers challenged the monopoly by getting cheaper malt elsewhere in 1419, the bakufu, not Enryakuji, responded by issuing edicts in support of the *za*, which was allowed to destroy the "illegal" malt chambers. That policy was continued for another two decades while the sake brewers, for their part, sought to weaken the monopoly. Finally, in 1444, the sake brewers openly refused to buy any malt from the *za*. The Kitano shrine tried to pressure the bakufu once again to support its monopoly, but both the bakufu and Enryakuji, Kitano's own patron, now found the monopoly increasingly unsustainable and disruptive to commerce. To the dismay and the anger of the members of the shrine, the bakufu reversed its earlier policies and supported the sake brewers. In the end, the bakufu had to subdue the shrine with force, after which the Kitano malt *za* was abolished and its surviving members forced out of the capital. A section within Enryakuji became the patron of the new *za*.[91]

The new social forces could accordingly no longer be controlled within the old patron-client system. Enryakuji itself collected taxes from the new guilds, though its control was less strict than it had been over their predecessors. Furthermore, while Enryakuji's authority as a patron of guilds declined, necessitating bakufu intervention to control conflicts among merchants and traders, the bakufu also imposed a tax of its own, increasing both its influence and its revenues. At the same time, Enryakuji lost more of its traditional rights as it was restricted in its adjudication of matters concerning its guilds. In 1370 the bakufu prohibited the Enryakuji clergy from harassing debtors in Kyoto on behalf of the guild of storehouse operators *(dōso za)*, whose members often doubled as moneylenders. That prohibition was repeated in an edict of 1386, when it was also added that disputes regarding late payments should be handled by the bakufu.[92] These edicts were designed to enhance the position of the bakufu in two ways. First, the bakufu needed to fulfill its policing duties and to maintain peace in the capital if it was to succeed as the country's legitimate government. Second, in seeking to realize this goal, the warrior regime was attempting to expand its authority in areas that had previously been under *kenmon* control. This attempt is further evident in the gradually increasing taxes on the sake producers and the storehouse operators. Temporary taxes on these establishments were not new. The imperial court had collected taxes from the sake brewers in 1315 to finance the reconstruction of some portable carts of Hiesha, and Takauji had also assessed taxes on the same establishments, though they were quite light. And, in 1370, a temporary tax was assessed on all *sakaya* and *dōso* for the retirement of Emperor En'yū. The bakufu, attempting to tap into this lucrative market, continued the practice, and this variety of irregular taxes was finally replaced by an annual tax by Yoshimitsu in 1393, retaining for the bakufu the exclusive right to appoint its own tax collectors. This measure marked not only an important stage in the development of Ashikaga jurisdiction, but also a serious limitation of the ability of Enryakuji to protect its guilds from and levy its own taxes on sake brewers and moneylenders.[93] The Ashikaga Bakufu was thus much less inclined than its predecessor to respect the judicial immunities of Enryakuji.

Whereas Enryakuji was the most influential patron of trade and commercial activities in Kyoto, Kōfukuji dominated Nara's three markets to an even higher degree. The first two markets developed just south and north of Nara in the mid–Kamakura period and came under the protection of the cloisters of Daijōin and Ichijōin, respectively. The main clergy of Kōfukuji added another market in the central part of the city, allowing for three regular markets in Nara by the early fifteenth century. The Hossō center provided protection for some eighty-five different *za*, dealing in fish, salt, cloth, paper, chopsticks, *eboshi* (court caps), tōfu, arrows, bells, rice, and even one that included prostitutes. As in the case of Enryakuji, each *za* belonged to a specific unit within Kōfukuji. For example, the most productive sake *za* was under the protection of Gangōji, which in turn was a branch temple of Kasuga's Wakanomiya. Some traders under Kōfukuji protection even lived in Kyoto, where some of the most sought after products, such as the famous Nara sake and tōfu, were sold. Interestingly, the Ashikaga Bakufu was far less aggressive against Kōfukuji's guilds than Enryakuji's despite its need for income. The Nara sake merchants, as Kasuga *jinnin* living in Kyoto, were exempted from taxes levied on other sake dealers in 1367, 1373, and 1457.[94] However, this leniency should not be misunderstood. The warrior government simply, and correctly, prioritized the Enryakuji sake brewers and sake producers, most of whom traded in the capital, since they generated the most income. In addition, though Nara was a considerable market, it was nowhere close to the size of Kyoto, also the bakufu headquarters, where it was also more pertinent for the bakufu to establish its judicial and economic superiority in the fourteenth century.

The authority of the bakufu expanded in several other traditional areas of *kenmon* control. For example, toll gates were an important source of income that the warrior regime now began to concern itself with. The seven highways entering the capital all had toll stations, which were controlled by traditional Kyoto aristocrats. In addition, other private barriers were occasionally erected and tolerated by the bakufu, if they were not an obstacle to the flow of goods.[95] As seen in the Nanzenji Gate incident, the bakufu also allowed toll gates to finance specific enterprises. However, by and large, the bakufu wished to restrict toll gates to allow the free flow of goods as well as to limit the income, and thereby a potential threat, of the major temples. On the tenth day of the seventh month of 1344, Retired Emperor Kōgon issued an edict, at the request of the bakufu, to prohibit new temple toll barriers, which naturally upset the clergies at all major temples, causing a particularly strong reaction from Kōfukuji. Instead of staging a protest, however, the Hossō monks resorted to the increasingly popular strategy of excommunicating a member of the Fujiwara family. The man in question was Shijō Takakage, an inconsequential Fujiwara who happened to be Kōgon's scribe, responsible for producing the actual edict. The members of the imperial court

were disturbed by the excommunication, but the bakufu was un-
moved and wanted to punish Kōfukuji by demolishing five of its
existing toll gates. In the meantime, the court attempted to persuade Kōfukuji to reinstate the scribe, who was eventually pardoned on the twenty-ninth day of the seventh month, without the
temple having obtained any exemptions from the prohibition of
new tolls.[96] The clergy was consequently already disappointed
when the imperial court turned down a Kōfukuji appeal to establish control of an existing toll gate in Settsu Province in the eleventh month of 1344. This time, the monks brought out the holy
sakaki branch, bringing it to the main temple building of Kōfukuji to prepare for a demonstration. Since the holy carts of Tōdaiji were also in the capital at the same time for an unrelated
complaint, the court was forced to scale down or cancel several
ceremonies and festivals for almost a year while the issues remained unresolved. Unfortunately, the sources give no indication
of a conclusion, and it appears that Kōfukuji's appeal was unsuccessful.[97] Still, Kōfukuji managed to retain its privileges for several
old toll gates despite the bakufu's reluctance to acknowledge any
territorial limitations to its jurisdiction in the capital region. For
instance, during a lengthy appeal against the intrusions on temple
land by one of the bakufu's warriors in the eighth month of 1366,
Ashikaga Yoshiakira tried to avoid punishing his own vassal by
allowing Kōfukuji to retain five existing toll gates. He additionally
canceled special pass permissions previously issued to warriors,
who were now forced to pay tolls, just like any other transporter
when passing these gates, allowing the Kōfukuji clergy to uphold
its traditional privileges and control of Yamato.[98]

Enryakuji, which appears to have controlled seven toll gates
close to Sakamoto on the shores of Lake Biwa, was affected in a
similar way, though it did not launch any full-scale protests against
the bakufu's limitations on new gates.[99] Since the bakufu respected
Enryakuji's rights to the old gates, there was little reason for the
temple to protest, but the warrior leaders also made it clear that
toll gates did not imply extraterritoriality. Thus, an edict issued in
1346 prohibited the erection of new toll barriers, and a similar
promulgation was made in 1363, when the bakufu specifically required that it grant permission to erect any new gates. Though it
granted exemptions on occasion, it became increasingly clear in
the 1360s that the bakufu intended to be the only source of legitimacy for toll gates. The very necessity of exemptions, or licenses

it issued to facilitate transport, from the bakufu, demonstrated that its own power was intended to supersede that of any of the *ken-mitsu* temples.[100] The right to collect toll dues was thus increasingly restricted by the bakufu's prohibitions and exemptions, which, to make matters worse for the established temples, most frequently benefited Zen temples.

On the whole, the Ashikaga Bakufu did not attempt to eradicate all judicial and economic privileges of the elite temples in Nara and Kyoto, but it made it clear that it retained the right to intervene and restrict these rights. Enryakuji and Kōfukuji felt the power and presence of the bakufu in different ways. Enryakuji on the one hand, as the most powerful patron of the most influential guilds in the profitable markets of Kyoto, became the target for severe restrictions of its judicial immunities as the bakufu began to assess new taxes on the sake brewers and combined money-lenders–storehouse operators. On the other hand, Kōfukuji's guilds, which were mostly located and operated in Nara, were not much of a concern to the bakufu. Instead, it was in the area of toll barriers that the Hossō center experienced the biggest challenges. With almost full control of Yamato Province, Kōfukuji reaped important income from transports coming through from the south to the capital, and the bakufu wanted not only to tap into this market but also to ensure a free flow of goods. In addition, since several of these barriers were located in an area that was contested between the forces of the Northern and Southern courts, the warrior government was interested in exerting some measure of control over who or what passed through these gates. In the end, the Ashikaga Bakufu did not extend its control into all corners of each sphere of judicial immunity for the *kenmon* temples, but it did its best to ensure that there was no doubt as to who held ultimate authority.

Ashikaga Yoshimitsu: The Final Blow to Cooperative Rulership

Judicial immunity was perhaps the most important privilege for the *kenmon* temples. Not only did it reflect a unique status awarded only to a privileged few who were the cornerstones of the imperial state, it was also the basis for other important benefits. *Kenmon* status led to tax-exempt estates, provided the ability to protect traders and artisans from taxes and competition, as well as brought

commoners streaming to the temple to make a career as administrators or simply as bullies under the religious umbrella. Among
the elite temples, none exerted more influence or enjoyed more
privileges and immunities than Enryakuji from the eleventh to
the fourteenth centuries. In part, it may have been the temple's
location close to the capital that gave it a slight edge over other
religious competitors, such as Kōfukuji and Tōdaiji. However,
there were also limitations to Enryakuji's power. It could not control the religious hierarchy or even its own sibling temple at times
because of the multitude of doctrines and temples that were involved in state ceremonies and were part of the cooperative system. The sharing of responsibilities thus remained the operative
concept among the various gates of power in the state as well
as within the religious establishment. Nevertheless, Enryakuji remained the most powerful of the temples and was virtually im-
pregnable to most rulers in Kyoto. Neither the court nor the
bakufu could restrict Enryakuji's immunities or control it directly
during the Kamakura period. Government officials had no jurisdiction on Mt. Hiei, and they would not even ascend the mountain without the clergy's permission. In fact, the Enryakuji compound was a sanctuary that was occasionally used by criminals to
escape punishment. Temples were expected to extradite such vil-
lains, but the records reveal that they refused in many cases. To
make matters worse for the secular powers, Enryakuji's military
strength could tip the balance in factional disputes in the capital,
and the secular powers repeatedly attempted to recruit its support. Failing to do so, the secular authorities attempted to prohibit the monks from carrying arms, but such edicts had little
effect, as evidenced by the continued activities of Enryakuji's
armed forces.[101]

Another common strategy to communicate with and control the
Enryakuji clergy was to use the head abbot, who was still appointed
by the imperial court. However, by the late Kamakura era, this
office had become little more than a lucrative source of income
for the sons of either nobles or the imperial family, who lacked
any substantial support within the temple complex in spite of
high expectations from their secular patrons.[102] Instead, the abbots
of the three largest cloisters—the Shōren'in, the Nashimoto
(Kajii), and the Myōhōin—emerged as the leaders through whom
the court and the bakufu attempted to communicate with the Enryakuji clergy. Similar developments occurred within Kōfukuji,

which was divided into three blocs with the two cloisters of Dai-jōin and Ichijōin heading the competition for titles and land, while the general clergy of the main temple (also known as *jimon*, "Temple Gate") was often caught in the middle. These divisions were mainly the result of the aristocratization of the elite temples, where sons of nobles attempted to dominate the religious complexes by establishing alternative centers of authority within the most powerful monasteries. However, this influx also brought about a greater distancing between the clergy and the temple leadership, and by the second half of the fourteenth century, changes in the temples' internal power structure had undermined the authority of these abbots substantially. New warrior leaders—part of the trend of *gekokujō*—who performed administrative and managerial duties at the cloisters, now began to challenge their masters. Within Kōfukuji, the aforementioned monk Seia was powerful enough to become a major figure in Yamato in the battles between the two courts and invading the property of the Kasuga Shrine in the 1340s. In addition, the Ochi family's occupation of the Ichijōin during the Kannō Disturbance and the main clergy's revolt against the cloisters further illustrate how lower-ranking monks and locals could aid in overturning a *kenmon* temple's hierarchy.

Similar developments within the Enryakuji complex resulted in the emergence of a new kind of commanders, who are sometimes even referred to as *daimyō*, from the 1360s. In fact, a marked change can be seen between the incidents of 1345 and 1368. In the earlier Tenryūji incident, the bakufu managed to contain the clergy by threatening to depose all three noble abbots and confiscate Enryakuji property if the portable shrines were brought into the capital. The same method was used in the Nanzenji Gate incident more than two decades later, but this time with no effect. The abbots were repeatedly asked to calm the monks and to stop them from entering Kyoto, but they failed, and two of them who had sided with the bakufu were even chased off Mt. Hiei in the fourth month of 1369. The Enryakuji clergy continued to demand that Nanzenji's gate be demolished through spiritual threats and demonstrations in the capital, but contemporary sources also indicate that there was a new level of preparedness for violence during the confrontations, indicating the role played by these monk-commanders. It is in this context that the bakufu responded on the fourth day of the seventh month of 1369 by creating a new post, called the Enryakuji magistrate *(sanmon bugyō),* designed to oversee the temple and specifically to ensure that the Hie *mikoshi* were removed from the capital.[103] But the new office did not accomplish what the bakufu leaders had in mind. The choice of Sasaki Takanaga, the *shugo* of Ōmi Province, was problematic from the start, since that family was an old enemy of Enryakuji. Disputes over rights to taxes and land had been a recurrent theme in their relationship since the 1190s, and Takanaga proved unable to exercise any real authority over Enryakuji. A new magistrate from the Kyōgoku family was appointed in the eighth month of 1370, but he as well seems to have achieved little success.[104] The magistrate appointments nonetheless reflected the bakufu's wish to assume direct control over the temple, thereby negating the older concept of cooperative rulership under the *kenmon.*

During the tenure and rule of the third shōgun, Ashikaga Yoshimitsu (shōgun 1368–1394), the problem of authority was resolved with the military figures within the temple, who first appear in the sources during the aftermath of the Nanzenji Incident. Although Enryakuji was victorious in the dispute itself, the problems continued as the bakufu, headed by Hosokawa Yoriyuki, procrastinated in assigning funds for the reconstruction of damaged carts. Among those who led the Enryakuji clergy to pressure the bakufu to comply with its own promise in the sixth month of 1377 were ten "mountain monks" (*"sansō,"* a term denoting lower-ranking monks), referred to as *"daimyō."* The identity of these monk-commanders is not well known, but there can be no doubt of their military prowess and relatively humble origins. Their appointment as Enryakuji constables *(sanmon shisetsu)* in 1379 proved to be a judicious match for both sides. Though the new commanders were powerful, they were also newcomers who lacked traditional status within the temple. The bakufu appointment gave them the official status and the additional authority to make them the undisputed powers on Mt. Hiei. Owing in particular to Yoshimitsu's ability to identify such well-placed allies within Enryakuji, the magistrates now came to serve the bakufu's purposes successfully in several areas. Their first assignment was to administer the reconstruction of the damaged carts, which was subsequently completed in 1380, only a year after their initial appointment. They subsequently acted as the bakufu's deputies, adjudicating internal conflicts, collecting and forwarding rents and taxes, and curtailing unruly monks. The *sanmon shisetsu* were, in short, *shugo*-like officials specific to Enryakuji. For that matter, they even had the right to levy the special taxes *(tanzen)* associated with *shugo* on Enryakuji estates.[105]

For Yoshimitsu's part, the magistrates were instrumental in expanding his authority both within Enryakuji and against competing warriors, such as the Rokkaku family, who held considerable power as *shugo* of Ōmi. Indeed, the timing of the creation of these offices indicates how important they were in the overall political scheme. The magistrates were appointed at the time of a palace coup (known as Kōryaku no seihen) in the fourth month of 1379, when Yoshimitsu ousted the increasingly unpopular Hosokawa Yoriyuki and took control of the bakufu himself. He was aided by Shiba Yoshimasa, who was reappointed *kanrei*, keeping that post until 1392. Under Yoshimasa's guidance and Yoshimitsu's rule, the Zen network, which had been put on hold after the disappointing setback during the Nanzenji Incident of 1368 to 1369, was reinvigorated, while monks who had formerly been deposed by Yoriyuki were reinstated.[106] It was with the intention of extending his rulership further and controlling the religious hierarchy more firmly, and thus establishing a much more centralized monarchical rulership, that Yoshimitsu established the *sanmon shisetsu* only a month after the coup against Yoriyuki, successfully subduing and controlling Enryakuji for the first time in centuries. The success of this policy is most evident in the astonishing absence of incidents involving Enryakuji monks for nearly the next half century.[107]

Yoshimitsu's measures appear less drastic vis-à-vis Kōfukuji, but he had similar ambitions there once he was in control in the capital. However, that was not the case in the tenth month of 1378, when Kōfukuji asked for help against a bothersome *kokumin*, Toichi Tōyasu, who had allied himself with the *shugo* of Settsu, Akamatsu Mitsunori, occupying and appropriating temple land in Yamato. Yoshimitsu responded by sending forces under the leadership of his trusted general Shiba Yoshimasa, in the first month the following year, to drive out Tōyasu. However, Tōyasu escaped and resorted to guerrilla warfare, while Yoshimasa was called back to Kyoto to help Yoshimitsu defeat Hosokawa Yoriyuki in the Kōryaku coup in the third month of 1379.[108] Though Yoshimitsu managed to establish himself as the undisputed leader of the bakufu in this coup, making Yoshimasa his right hand in the process, the Kōfukuji monks were not happy about his inability to resolve the situation with the Settsu *shugo* and the Toichi family. As a result, the clergy began to prepare a forceful protest in the seventh month of 1379, and on the fourteenth day of the eighth month they entered the capital with the holy *sakaki* branch. Instead of targeting the Fujiwara chieftain or the Chōkōdō, the sacred symbols were now taken to Yoshimitsu's Rokujō mansion: a clear indication that Japan had now entered the age of the warrior, since it was the first time the *shinmoku* was taken to a warrior's mansion. Yoshimitsu was not unaffected by the pressure, and he felt compelled to calm the monks in the ninth and tenth months, calling his advisers, and even the head abbot of Kōfukuji, to discuss the return of the *shinmoku* to Nara, but to no avail. In the eleventh month, the shōgun dispatched a considerable force of warriors from six different provinces to chastise the Toichi family. Discussions about the return of the holy branches in the twelfth month indicate that the campaign was only partially successful, and the problem was not entirely resolved until later the following year.[109]

The Kōfukuji clergy found new reasons to be unhappy with Yoshimitsu in 1380, when he pardoned the former abbot of the Ichijōin, Jitsugen, who was involved in the internal fighting in 1351 to 1353 and again in the destructive battles of 1371 to 1372. The clergy was deeply disappointed with the return of this alienated monk, but the protest was ignored, and the situation quickly became antagonistic within the temple as some rebellious temple servants supported Jitsugen. Finally, the clergy attacked Jitsugen's residence and burned it down in the third month of 1381. At this point, Kyōshin, who was involved in the earlier fighting and was also exiled in 1374, entered the conflict, attacking the Ichijōin. This time, the destructive confrontations spread throughout the monastery, and much of Kōfukuji was burned down during the ensuing battles, as was the Kasuga shrine, until Jitsugen escaped to Kyoto and peace was restored through the intervention of the bakufu in the sixth month of 1382.[110]

The problems at Kōfukuji turned out to be a blessing in disguise for Yoshimitsu, in reality offering an important opportunity to expand his own influence. The serious damage to the Kasuga complex necessitated an extensive reconstruction, and it was Yoshimitsu who stepped in to provide funding and oversee this project. Ignoring the precedents of the reconstruction following the Genpei War, when the Fujiwara chieftain managed the project,

Yoshimitsu now took charge personally, assessing taxes (*munebe-chisen*) all over the country to raise funds. Through these measures, he demonstrated not only that the Fujiwara family was no longer capable of providing for the shrine, but also that the shōgun's authority extended into the realms of one of the oldest and most privileged shrines in Japan. Yoshimitsu also increased his control of Yamato, which had remained under Kōfukuji-Kasuga rulership since the early Kamakura age, and even extracted a pledge of loyalty from the clergy and the *kokumin* of Kōfukuji.[111] In fact, Yoshimitsu was able to disregard earlier practices completely when he appointed the monk Jitsuga master of ceremonies at the Yuima'e without consulting the Fujiwara chieftain in 1395. The incumbent chieftain, Chancellor (*kanpaku*) Ichijō Tsunetsugu (1358–1418), noted with amazement in his diary: "In such matters, the head abbot should first contact the Fujiwara chieftain, after which the chieftain consults with Lord Muromachi [Yoshimitsu] regarding the [nominated] candidates. However, recently, the [temple's] letter of nominations was sent directly [to Yoshimitsu], and the chieftain merely obeyed [his command]. How can this be so?"[112] Furthermore, Yoshimitsu appointed another monk for a Buddhist ceremony at the imperial court in 1396, and the ambitious shōgun subsequently became increasingly involved in monk appointments within the Hossō center. According to a contemporary chronicle by the Kōfukuji head abbot Kōen, even minor offices such as overseers of maintenance, recording officers, and scribes were appointed based on the specific advice of Yoshimitsu. His subsequent involvement in religious matters in general is evidenced in confirmations of several appointments for offices at Kumano, Gion, Kitano, the Ichijōin, and Kōfukuji in 1398 alone—undeniable testimony of Yoshimitsu's unprecedented power as Japan's warrior leader. Another outstanding example of his unique influence can be found in 1404, when the newly resigned Daijōin abbot Kōjin went to Yoshimitsu's mansion to get his blessing before he went into seclusion. His successor also visited Yoshimitsu to confirm his new appointment, while neither of these transitions was ever brought to the attention of the imperial court, breaking all precedents.[113]

Thus, without any major innovations or any intrusions into Kōfukuji's traditional privileges, Yoshimitsu managed to gain control over the Hossō center. At Kōfukuji as at Enryakuji, he used internal upheavals and changes to his advantage to gain inside followers and control of what used to be highly independent temples. In fact, the success of this strategy was almost as complete with Kōfukuji as with the Tendai center. After 1382 there were only a few conflicts within Kōfukuji, and even fewer *gōso* in spite of a high frequency in the preceding decades. More important, Yoshimitsu also gained control of Yamato Province, and even though he allowed the temple to reassume its title as *shugo* in 1405, the appointment itself only verified his own prestige and control.[114]

As in the past, pilgrimages combined with participation in important ceremonies and appropriate grants were important means for confirming ties during Yoshimitsu's era. Yoshimitsu visited Kasuga in the eighth month of 1385, during its reconstruction, ordering that the completion of the shrine be enforced more speedily. By staying in charge of the reconstruction and by showing his personal support, Yoshimitsu was able to assume complete control of the *shugo* post of Yamato and increase the pressure on the Southern Court in Yoshino. He remained on close terms with the Kōfukuji-Kasuga complex, paying another visit in the ninth month of 1391, when he further proved his generosity by donating funds to the temple as well as to the two cloisters after having enjoyed both *dengaku* and *sarugaku* dance performances at Wakanomiya. Accompanied by several of his trusted retainers, Yoshimitsu made a similar visit early in 1394 and again in 1397. But the more auspicious ceremonies were held in the third month of 1399, when the reconstruction of Kōfukuji's halls were celebrated in a large initiation ceremony at the Kondō, which also had been repaired. The Fujiwara chieftain (Nijō Morotsugu) was with him, as were the abbots of the Ichijōin and the Daijōin, all now skillfully controlled by Yoshimitsu.[115]

Yoshimitsu's pilgrimage to Enryakuji and the Hie shrines in the ninth month of 1394 was also a grandiose one, with high-ranking members from both the imperial court and the warrior aristocracy attending, counting also the shōgun's mother Ki no Yoshiko, his wife Yasuko, and his adoptive son Yoshimochi among the participants. While offering further evidence of Yoshimitsu's pacification and control of Enryakuji, this pilgrimage also indicates an unheard of closeness between a shōgun and the Tendai center on Mt. Hiei. In addition, though Yoshimitsu took Buddhist vows (following his retirement as shōgun) according to Zen traditions in 1395, he also went to Enryakuji's Daikōdō, where he was initiated in the Tendai teachings the following year. As in the case of Kōfukuji, Yoshimitsu displayed his power by granting funding for reconstruction of ruined buildings, such as various temple halls close to the Grand Lecture Hall and the bell tower (which had been destroyed in 1332). The 1396 initiation ceremony that Yoshimitsu sponsored was characteristically the first one to take place without an imperial edict to that effect. There were a number of additional visits to Hie (1401) and Tendai branches (Tōnomine in 1403), as Yoshimitsu kept himself busy by honoring and controlling most religious institutions of status until his death in 1408.[116]

In terms of religious policies, Kōyasan was less of an urgent matter, largely because of its location away from the capital. Yet Yoshimitsu had plans much beyond the capital area, as evidenced by a successful extension of his direct authority over the Kantō and Kyushu in the 1390s. As his plans to eliminate the Southern Court became more concrete, Kōyasan came to play a more important role, and it is not surprising to find that he visited the complex in the ninth month of 1389, though the records are unclear as to his exact activities. Considering the timing, it appears more than likely, however, that he tried to lure the clergy away from its middle stance as he was contemplating strategies to merge the two courts.[117]

In the end, there can be no doubt as to Yoshimitsu's intentions and his unprecedented success in containing the most powerful of the established religious centers. Even as he used some proven strategies, he was attempting to break new ground, perhaps even aspiring to bring the *kenmitsu* sects under the same strict control as Zen. Finding allies within the monastic centers was probably the biggest obstacle, though he was nevertheless quite successful, owing to his recognition of the emerging warrior leaders within Enryakuji and his command over Kōfukuji's reconstruction. However, he also wished to control the *monzeki*, which had considerable wealth in land even if they were not always able to control the general clergy. Yoshimitsu therefore had six of his children take Buddhist vows, with Sonman and Yoshinori (who took the Buddhist name Gien, only to return later to the secular world, becoming the sixth Ashikaga shōgun) entering the Shōren'in (in 1389 and 1407 respectively), Yoshitsugu and Gijō going to the Sanzen'in (1407 and 1412), Yoshiaki to the Myōhōin (1406), and Hōzon to Ninnaji (1409). Five of his cleric sons thus settled at

Enryakuji cloisters, with two of them becoming Tendai *zasu* (Yoshi-nori and Gijō), indicating the attention it received from Japan's most powerful figure. Yoshimitsu was also the first bakufu leader to send direct orders to the Tendai *zasu* (a princely monk) in 1385. His retirement (1394) and tendencies to imitate earlier practices by retired emperors in other areas have prompted scholars to conclude that Yoshimitsu aimed to establish a Muromachi monarchy, and, as indicated by his unprecedented authority in the relgous sphere, he might have succeeded were it not for his death in 1408.[118]

Conclusion

The *kenmon* temples experienced drastic changes during the fourteenth century. Their status as proprietors and patrons was challenged first by local warriors and then by a growing number of merchants and entrepreneurs in a typical expression of the *gekokujō* trend. In addition to these slower-moving developments, there were also sudden political jolts caused by the establishment of the Ashikaga Bakufu in Kyoto. This new warrior regime envisioned a much less restricted authority than that of its predecessor, expanding its authority at the expense of the religious elites in three important areas. First, the bakufu's religious support was geared toward Zen from the start. Although this progress was successfully halted in the Nanzenji Incident of 1368, Yoshimitsu's rise to power and the reinstatement of Shiba Yoshimasa after the Kōryaku coup ensured that the early vision of a Zen temple network under bakufu control became reality. As a result, the public role of the *kenmitsu* temples as providers of doctrine and ceremonies was severely diminished. Moreover, the bakufu threatened to replace the whole multidoctrinal system with a religious hierarchy consisting of a single controllable doctrine. Enryakuji spearheaded the defense of the traditional sects and opposed this move but had little success.

Second, since the Ashikaga Bakufu lacked an extensive land base of its own and wished to establish its absolute authority as the single government, it limited the economic privileges of most temples and shrines. Enryakuji lost income as the bakufu allowed new guilds to emerge and because of the bakufu's own taxation of the most lucrative enterprises in Kyoto. Kōfukuji was more concerned with the limitations that the bakufu enforced on its toll barriers, which not only provided important income but also reinforced the temple's authority in Yamato Province. By the end of the fourteenth century, these matters essentially became a moot issue, as Yoshimitsu managed to take control of both the Hossō center and Yamato.

Third, during Yoshimitsu's tenure, Enryakuji's and Kōfukuji's judicial privileges, the most sacred of their rights, came to be severely restricted. Noting the declining authority of the traditional noble leaders of the elite temples, Yoshimitsu also recognized that lower-level clerics and warriors within the temple complexes were gaining power, and he began to use them to extend his own authority over the established sects. These policies resulted in an unprecedented expansion of bakufu authority through appointments of deputies within Enryakuji, which was now neutralized for half a century. The temple did not regain control over its own organization until the bakufu itself started to crumble in the mid–fifteenth century. Kōfukuji experienced a similar change, as its clergy and many of the local warriors (kokumin) pledged loyalty to Yoshimitsu when they realized that only his patronage could guarantee the reconstruction of Kasuga after its destruction in 1382. Yoshimitsu's involvement in monk appointments and his many visits to both Nara and Tendai centers in symbiosis with his more ground-breaking appointments of lower-ranking members within the monasteries reflect his successful pacification of the established sects in central Japan.

By contrast, Kōyasan continued on its own course throughout the fourteenth century. More than Enryakuji and Kōfukuji, it managed to adjust to the social changes and incorporate the emerging local powers into its own structure. In addition, it played its cards well during the battles between the two courts, thus managing to obtain confirmations of old and new land, as well as new donations to extend its local influence. Kōyasan's location was the basis for the different course it took, and it was allowed a certain degree of freedom since Shingon's headquarters was actually Tōji. It was thus possible for the monastic center on Mt. Kōya to transform itself into a powerful local landholder with growing forces and military strength into the fifteenth century.[119] By the end of the Sengoku Age (1467–1573), Kōyasan had become one of the most powerful temples in Japan, and it was the last one to succumb to the new warlords of the late sixteenth century, facing the much superior forces of Toyotomi Hideyoshi in 1588.

By employing Kuroda's *kenmon* terminology, these conclusions can be put in a slightly different light. First, even though the Shingon sect was an active participant in the *kenmitsu* system, Kōyasan displayed characteristics that indicates it was quite different from the elite temples in the capital district in the fourteenth century. Nonetheless, the Kōyasan clergy referred to its *kenmon* privileges as it used the fabricated legend of the temple's original domain to extend its local control close to Mt. Kōya. Yet at the same time, there was less concern with spiritual justification in the age of the warrior, and it was as a prominent landholder and ruler of a large number of supporters that Kōyasan was attractive to the disputing parties in the Nanbokuchō War. Second, Kuroda claimed that the *kenmon* system prevailed until the Ōnin War, but that conclusion cannot be accepted based on his own definition of *kenmon* cooperative rulership. The Ashikaga Bakufu not only favored but also controlled Zen. There was consequently no mutual dependence between the two. The traditional *kenmitsu* schools such as Enryakuji and Kōfukuji were simply excluded from the Ashikaga polity. It is not surprising that it was during this era that negative views and depictions of the established sects' secular power gained true momentum.

The most striking change can, however, be found in the limitation of old *kenmon* privileges such as immunity and self-rule, reflecting a tremendous expansion of the bakufu's and the warrior aristocracy's control of state matters. During its zenith, the bakufu indeed managed to control Enryakuji and Kōfukuji, but the Ashikaga hegemony did not last long enough to extinguish the power of the old elites. In the long run, the bakufu policies of the early Muromachi age resulted in an elimination of the fundamental conditions for *kenmon* cooperative rule, leaving the temple elites as separate and alienated powers. The old strategies of demonstrating were much less effective in the fourteenth century, as evidenced by Kōfukuji protests extending over several years and the increased use of excommunication of members of the Fujiwara clan. Furthermore, the negotiations between the religious and secular elites display a more violent component in the fourteenth century, when new terminology in contemporary diaries indicates a higher degree of violent confrontations and new monk-commanders are found within the monastic center of Enryakuji.

As a result, when the Muromachi Bakufu's power weakened in the middle of the fifteenth century, the old sects, especially Enryakuji and Kōyasan, resurfaced as independent and powerful military centers. The Ashikaga vision of religious institutions strictly in their own service therefore did not materialize until the late sixteenth century, when the new hegemons brought all major temples under their control.

8
Epilogue: Religious Power and the Power of Religion in Premodern Japan

The secular power of religious institutions from the late Heian to the late Muromachi eras earned the entire group of traditional Buddhist schools in central Japan a bad reputation among later observers and scholars. Tales compiled in the late thirteenth and fourteenth centuries offer images of ferocious monk-warriors and temple servants driven by their greed to stage violent protests in the capital. As noted in Chapter 6, these images, which are at variance with accounts in contemporary sources, were created during a period of extensive social change and of an increasing popularity among high and low of new Buddhist sects; both trends increased the opposition to the old established temples of Nara and Kyoto. The role of Buddhism and its institutions within the state was then dramatically redefined with the consolidation of the Tokugawa Bakufu early in the seventeenth century. While the political power of the largest monasteries was severely restricted, open criticism of the Buddhist establishment also became more manifest, as evidenced by the introduction of the term *"sōhei"* (monk-warriors) and the nationalistic *Dainihon shi,* which put much of the blame for the decline of the imperial state on Buddhist monks.[1] As a consequence, myths of rampaging monk-warriors and views of temples as a disruptive influence on legitimate government became reinforced. Furthermore, the separation of Buddhism and Shintō in 1868 led Japanese historians to accentuate their prejudice against temples; and the postwar constitution, which prohibits the state from engaging in religious activities, marked the culmination of more than half a millennium of prejudice against the secular power of Buddhism. In the West, where the division of politics and religion into separate entities is

346

several centuries old, historians willingly followed their Japanese colleagues in discrediting the Buddhist establishment.

Yet as some scholars have now managed to see through these many layers of prejudice, they have come to realize that the separation of religion and politics is a distinction that the premodern Japanese never knew. To the contrary, the secular influence of religious institutions can only be understood by relating them to the structures of government and the *mentalité* of the times. In short, rulership in the late Heian and Kamakura eras, roughly from the late eleventh to the late fourteenth centuries, was characterized by a division of responsibilities and a sharing of privileges among several elites. The basis for this rulership was the status that derived from their participation in the imperial government. The imperial hierarchy was the center of this state, but the noble elites were not the only gates to power *(kenmon)* and influence, as they relied on the warrior class to quell disturbances and maintain peace. The warrior leadership, for its part, was unwilling to overextend itself into the realms of religion and squabbles between the capital elites. The spiritual protection for this polity, which was united and symbolized by the emperor, was provided by the Buddhist-Shintō monastic centers. Since several sects took part in this sanctification throughout the Heian and Kamakura eras, it was not a specific doctrine but rather the ceremonies and ideological representations that supplied the ideological symbolism and reinforcement the noble elites needed to maintain and boost their power. The relationship between the Kamakura Bakufu and the imperial court was symbiotic, just as the prominence of these monastic centers was tied to the vigor of a system of codependency and shared rulership. As important providers of rituals and spiritual support for the state, Enryakuji, Kōfukuji, and Kōyasan earned the economic and judicial privileges of a *kenmon*. However, since competition and factionalism were also embedded in this system, the temples were forced to rely on their own ability to protect their private assets and to perform their religious functions. Even though this competition occasionally deteriorated into battles, it was never the clergies' intention to overturn the system itself, since it would have eliminated their own raison d'être. Seen in this light, the disruptions that were caused by the *gōso* must be interpreted as Enryakuji's and Kōfukuji's efforts to protect their status within this elite system, as evidenced by the fact that such protests became especially frequent and violent during the aggressive rulership of three former emperors.

Shirakawa's era marked the imperial family's joining the competition for private wealth and power, an important aspect of which were the retired emperor's new religious policies. By establishing a set of temples and religious ceremonies under his personal control, favoring in particular Shingon through extensive patronage of both Tōji and Kōyasan, Shirakawa created a spiritual counterweight to the dominance of monks from Tendai and Hossō. Besides obtaining more imperial control of important Buddhist functions, the new temples also brought financial benefits, since the princely abbots of those institutions became the holders of numerous private estates. In addition, Shirakawa appointed monks of his own choosing to mid-level affiliates of both Enryakuji and Kōfukuji, attempting to disqualify established branches as immune estates. In the process, however, the retired emperor inevitably challenged the religious establishment, leading to the first divine demonstrations staged by Buddhist centers. Both Enryakuji and Kōfukuji reacted strongly against Shirakawa's policies not only because of their traditional closeness to the imperial court, but also because the clergies felt their very existence and status threatened by being bypassed in state ceremonies. Significantly, such reactions and the responses to them reflect a governmental system where religious institutions already played an integral part. Though it is difficult to assess exactly when the sociopolitical structures took on the character of shared rulership, the connections with the weakening of the Fujiwara during Shirakawa's era are undeniable, as is the emergence of a new, more competitive polity consisting of elites from various sectors.

Because of the unruly times of the late twelfth century, the strategies of Go-Shirakawa were necessarily different from those of his predecessor. In short, the jockeying for control among the elites and the growing importance of military power both put their mark on the retired emperor's relations with the monastic centers in the capital region. In particular, Go-Shirakawa attempted to control Enryakuji early on, but, failing at that, he chose instead to promote Onjōji, aiming to weaken Enryakuji's domination of Tendai. Though fierce opposition from the monks on Mt. Hiei forced Go-Shirakawa to abandon this strategy, his attempts created problems that far transcended a simple sibling rivalry. As the Enryakuji clergy moved to establish a firmer grip on the leadership of Tendai, the monks of Kōfukuji correspondingly felt compelled to defend Onjōji. The tensions between Enryakuji and Kōfukuji eventually developed into one of the most serious religious incidents (1173) of the late Heian era. Whereas Enryakuji thus defended its privileged position within the imperial state by opposing the retired emperor's attempts to control Tendai, the Hossō center in Nara similarly maintained its prominence and interests, even as it acted against its main secular ally, the Fujiwara chieftain.

The *insei* of Go-Shirakawa also saw competition for land become intensified, leading to a greater need for military might to secure a steady flow of income. Both Enryakuji and Kōfukuji defended their landed interests by using a combination of followers in the provinces and spiritual pressure and allies in the capital. Conversely, the temples' wealth and power were quite appealing to ambitious courtiers and warriors. In fact, the capital area could not be governed at the time without at least the passive support of the established religious centers. The burning of Kōfukuji and Tōdaiji at the hands of Taira troops late in 1180 and the subsequent reconstruction efforts attest to their importance to the secular leaders. In addition, the retired emperor, the Taira, Kiso Yoshinaka, and Minamoto Yoshitsune all sought to control or to secure the support of Enryakuji during their brief stints in Kyoto. But it was the founder of the Kamakura Bakufu, Yoritomo, who was the most successful noncourtier to establish a relationship of trust with the Tendai center by his near total noninvolvement in religious issues and his support of the monasteries' traditional privileges. The Kamakura chieftain also took a personal interest and offered support in the reconstruction of the temples in Nara, earning him a reputation as a religious person quite contrary to Kiyomori. This success unquestionably owed much to the new warrior government's ability to restrain warrior challenges to temple estates. In other words, contrary to the traditional view, Enryakuji, Kōfukuji, and Kōyasan all welcomed the bakufu's establishment as an institutionalization of the warrior elites' role in the *kenmon* state. It halted the assault of the local warrior class on the estates and the privileges of the great monastic centers, in effect prolonging the life of that system for almost two centuries.

Following the defeat of the court in the Jōkyū War of 1221, the monastic centers were involved in relatively few incidents, mainly because there was no elite in Kyoto powerful enough to endanger their religious and political status. However, protests and violence reappeared during the *insei* of Go-Saga, who managed a partial revival of the imperial house. Interestingly, he used traditional methods in his efforts to control in particular Enryakuji, ignoring the failures of his predecessors. Throughout his rule, Go-Saga appointed imperial princes as head abbots of Tendai, though they had trouble keeping the confidence of the clergy because of their close relationship with the capital nobility. He later resorted to promoting Onjōji (an obvious imitation of Go-Shirakawa's policies), allowing the construction of an independent ordination platform and granting it the symbolically important abbotship of Shitennōji. However, this strategy proved equally inefficient and served only to exacerbate the mistrust and violence between the two Tendai centers.

The Fujiwara family saw its influence over Kōfukuji decline further during Go-Saga's era, as it was now wholly unable to contain the Hossō clergy through traditional means, forcing instead the retired emperor to step in. At the same time, the two main cloisters within Kōfukuji, often headed by the sons of members of the Fujiwara clan, began to dominate important offices within the Hossō sect, creating a widening breach between the general clergy and the noble abbots within the temple community. Such divisions would eventually result in a decline of Kōfukuji's coherence, though it remained the single most powerful religious institution south of the capital, based on its control of Yamato Province, in which it held the *shugo* post for most of the Kamakura era. Indeed, a vast majority of the monastic complexes were considerably less coherent units than has hitherto been assumed, as evidenced by the factions within Enryakuji during the Genpei War and the disputes between the two cloisters within Kōfukuji, which joined opposing sides in the Nanbokuchō era, quite apart from the general clergy.

Besides its location, Kōyasan had much in common with other *kenmon* temples, but it began to move in a different direction in the late thirteenth century. While the Kongōbuji clergy continued to claim the status of a religious elite and maintained distant estates like other religious *kenmon,* it also showed indications of a different kind of rulership by trying to extend its local control in a more direct manner. Estates close to Mt. Kōya were gradually incorporated into "the original temple domains" according to claims based on a mid-Heian document attributed to Kūkai's era.

By alternatively allying itself with local warriors and appealing to the bakufu to contain the ambitions of those same local powers when they got out of hand, Kōyasan attempted to establish itself as the local power par excellence, often supplanting the rights of more distant elites. Because of its popularity as a religious retreat and retirement haven both among courtiers and warrior aristocrats, these long-standing goals were eventually granted by the secular elites in Kyoto and Kamakura.

By shifting the perspective away from preconceived and modern expectations of the role of religion, this book has shown that the increase in divine demonstrations and the intensification of competition for religious offices during the Heian and Kamakura eras were the direct consequences of decisions made by the elites within the imperial court. The *kenmon* temples defended their status by staging *gōso* when the retired emperor became more aggressive in trying to control matters in the capital.[2] The conflicts examined here were, in other words, not caused by a secularized and degenerate clergy that was seeking to topple the imperial government, of which the monks and their supporters themselves were a part. Accordingly, the *gōso* were not considered illegal, but were simply the clergy's acknowledged vehicle to communicate, in a ritualized fashion, with allies, not with enemies. As such, they reflect not only political circumstances but also leading ideological constructs of the time.

The divine demonstrations may be seen as the embodiment of three important concepts of the eleventh through the fourteenth centuries. First, they illustrate the practical aspect of the *honji suijaku* idea, according to which the *kami* were the Japanese manifestations of the buddhas and the bodhisattvas. The native gods protected Buddhism and its physical representations in various ways, while the carrying of divine symbols to the capital provides convincing evidence of the important role played by the *kami*. Although the *shinmoku* (the holy *sakaki* branch) was the preferred symbol from Kasuga, portable shrines *(shin'yō* or *mikoshi)*, which were used by most other shrines, provided the most apparent symbolism, with mirrors representing the *kami* and a phoenix often placed on top. The efficiency of these protests, perhaps more than anything, attests to the power of these symbols and the *kami* themselves. Second, the *gōso* show that the *ōbō-buppō sōi* concept of mutual dependence of the imperial law and Buddhism provided the theoretical and religious base for the state's dominant ideology. The secular powers needed the support of Buddhism and thus were required to underwrite it financially and politically. The reconstruction of damaged palanquins at the court's expense and the punishments of warriors who incurred such damages effectively prove this point. Third, the *gōso* provide indisputable support for the idea of shared rulership. Protesting in the capital was the prerogative of the most prestigious religious elites (though other, less auspicious, means were available for temples just below the upper echelons), and their responsibilities as spiritual supporters for the leaders of the state gave them the right to both economic and judicial privileges. The *gōso* themselves thus represent the symbiosis of religious and political doctrines and the larger political history of the era. To put the matter in a different light, it is not possible to understand the role of religious institutions or the actions of the secular elites, warriors or nobles, vis-à-vis temples and shrines without an integrated treatment of religion and politics.

The end of the age of cooperative rulership among the various elites can be found in the mid– to late fourteenth century, but it is more difficult to pinpoint exactly when because of the many possible turning points. For example, the battles between the Ashikaga and Enryakuji forces, which even besieged the capital in the 1330s, appear to mark a breakdown of the cooperative spirit that characterized the relationship between the Kamakura Bakufu and the religious centers. Yet the shifting of loyalties during the early years of the Nanbokuchō age left the avenue open for a reconciliation, perhaps with a possibility that the established sects could maintain their position within the state in the mid–fourteenth century. But the Muromachi Bakufu, led by warriors who were less attached to the established sects, was built around different principles, in which there was no room for such sharing and independence, and its promotion of Zen was not compatible with a continuation of the old system. For example, the warrior aristocracy's lack of attachment to the old religious structures severely damaged the efficacy of protests, which tended to be more drawn out and violent in the fourteenth century. Enryakuji managed to halt this trend temporarily in the Nanzenji Incident of 1368, but it was clearly the *kenmitsu* sects' last stand against the transformation of the ruling structures. Yoshimitsu finally put an end to shared rulership as a working concept when he extended his control over both Enryakuji and Kōfukuji, by promoting mid-level monk-commanders and local warriors *(kokumin)* within the monasteries, to an unprecedented level.

The fourteenth century stands out as an important and often overlooked watershed in premodern Japan, as reflected in several other trends that are intimately related to the decline of the *kenmon*. First, it marked the end of rulership based on status— *kenmon* lordship—in favor of a more locally based territorial lordship, which was not only the trend among the warrior class but also for Kōyasan, as the temple successfully transformed itself into a regional power with direct control of its estates. In spite of a loss of public status within the state, Enryakuji went through similar adjustments, recovering its independence as the Ashikaga power declined in the fifteenth century. Like Kōyasan, Enryakuji's highest priority was then to maintain a firm hold over its local holdings, as it was now alienated from the workings of the state. By contrast, Kōfukuji found it harder to recover lost ground after Yoshimitsu. It lost its control of Yamato and was much less a factor than temples with strong local footholds, such as Kōyasan, Enryakuji, Negoroji, and Kokawadera, in the wars of the fifteenth and sixteenth centuries. Second, the means of negotiation between the various elites became increasingly obsolete with a new warrior aristocracy in power, effectively ending practices that had been in place since the late Heian period. As a result, the old elites were forced to resort to more violent strategies to defend their land and privileges, a trend that fit only too well into the warrior climate of the fourteenth century. Ironically, it was during this same period that the monasteries that were powerful enough to respond to these challenges became increasingly criticized for doing what everyone else in the warrior class was heralded for.

To return, finally, to Kuroda's *kenmon* synthesis, there can be no doubt that the concept of several elites sharing the responsibilities and privileges of government is fundamental in understanding late Heian and Kamakura Japan. Yet one must also acknowledge the limitations of this thesis and clarify the characteristics as well as the time frame of this type of governmental system. For example, Kuroda's contention that the *kenmon* consisted of three distinctive and equal blocs cannot be sustained. Although the warriors and the nobles both had their own governments and sociopolitical hierarchies, the religious establishment lacked that degree of unity and coherence. As emphasized in this study, several temples and shrines were employed by the secular elites in various state ceremonies, each holding governmental responsibilities and privileges as *kenmon* on their own. In fact, the secular powers promoted and maintained this power equilibrium in order to play one monastic center against another to shift the balance in their favor. Furthermore, even the secular blocs were characterized by internal tensions, though their leaders claimed to represent the interests of the whole class. Indeed, the most severe disturbances during the Heian and Kamakura eras (the Heiji and Hōgen incidents and the Genpei and Jōkyū wars) contained strong elements of intrabloc confrontations that inevitably involved allies in the different sectors. The outcome of these conflicts demonstrates that hegemons needed to encompass all spheres of rulership to govern Japan successfully. In other words, the period-defining ties of cooperation and interdependence can be found at the individual level, rather than in formal agreements between static blocs. For example, while Kiyomori failed to gain support from other *kenmon,* Yoritomo could restore peace, owing to his successful relations with individual courtiers and temples in the capital area. To cite one more case, though Go-Saga's rule marked the high point of bakufu-court cooperation, he was not as successful in securing the support of Enryakuji, causing occasional disruptions of peace. A successful rule demanded the control of one's own class as well as a working relationship with the most powerful elements of the other spheres. Shared rulership should not be seen in terms of blocs, but rather as consisting of individual gates of power from various sectors constituting what might be called the *kenmon* state.

Unfortunately, Kuroda also failed to see the temporal limitations of his synthesis. Though several of the elites survived the shakeup and social changes of the fourteenth century, they could only do so in a transformed form outside of the confines of the government and as independent lords, not unlike the emerging *daimyō.* As shown in Chapter 7, the *kenmitsu* sects lost many of their exclusive rights with the Muromachi Bakufu's promotion of Zen, and the privileges of the traditional elite temples were effectively eliminated during Yoshimitsu's rule. *Kenmon* rule, then, ranged from the inception of the *insei* to the late fourteenth century, which raises an interesting question of periodization. As this study suggests, the role of the elite religious institutions within the state remained the same not in spite of but thanks to the establishment of the Kamakura Bakufu. In fact, even at the peak of Kamakura power (during Go-Saga's *insei*), the bakufu limited its intervention to occasions when peace and stability were severely threatened. Contrary to contemporary observations, the age of cooperative rulership was not an age of decline of Buddhist influence on society, but rather the peak of such a configuration. As a consequence, the "*kenmon* era" designation seems closer to capturing the essence of an age of shared rulership than does the old division into sequential epochs of aristocratic and warrior dominance.

APPENDIX I
Conflicts Involving Enryakuji and Kōfukuji, 1061–1400

Five-year span	Protests	Internal	Fighting	Total
1061–1065				0
1066–1070	2		1	3
1071–1075		1	2	3
1076–1080	1			1
1081–1085			2	2
1086–1090	1			1
1091–1095	4	2	3	9
1096–1100	1	1		2
1101–1105	5	4	3	12
1106–1110	4		7	11
1111–1115	4	2	2	8
1116–1120	3	2	1	6
1121–1125	2	1	2	5
1126–1130	1		2	3
1131–1135	1	1	1	3
1136–1140	2	1	1	4
1141–1145		1	3	4
1146–1150	3	1	3	7
1151–1155		2	1	3
1156–1160	2	1	2	5
1161–1165	5	2	3	10
1166–1170	2	2		4
1171–1175	2	2	3	7
1176–1180	6	1	5	12
1181–1185		2	1	3
1186–1190	1	2	2	5
1191–1195	2		1	3
1196–1200		1		1
1201–1205	4	1		5

(continued)

Five-year span	Protests	Internal	Fighting	Total
1206–1210			2	2
1211–1215	4	2	5	·11
1216–1220	2			2
1221–1225		1	1	2
1226–1230	2	5	3	10
1231–1235	4	1	2	7
1236–1240	3		1	4
1241–1245	2	1		3
1246–1250	3	2	2	7
1251–1255		1	1	2
1256–1260	6		1	7
1261–1265	2	3	2	7
1266–1270	4	3	1	8
1271–1275	2	1		3
1276–1280	5		1	6
1281–1285	5		1	6
1286–1290	1			1
1291–1295	7	1	1	9
1296–1300	1		1	2
1301–1305	3		5	8
1306–1310	3			3
1311–1315	2		2	4
1316–1320	4		3	7
1321–1325	2	1		3
1326–1330	1	2		3
1331–1335	1	2	3	6
1336–1340	3	1	3	7
1341–1345	6		1	7
1346–1350	5		2	7
1351–1355	2	1	1	4
1356–1360	3	1		4
1361–1365	2			2
1366–1370	3	1	2	6
1371–1375	4	2		6
1376–1380	3		3	6
1381–1385		1		1
1386–1390			1	1
1391–1395				0
1396–1400		1		1

APPENDIX 2
Diagram of Enryakuji and Kōfukuji Conflicts, 1061–1400

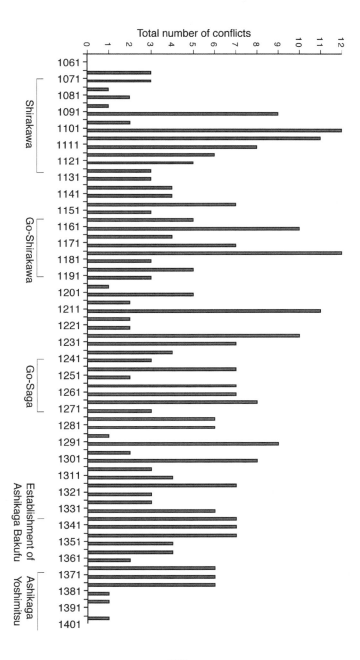

NOTES

Chapter 1   Introduction

1. Most notably, the works of pioneering scholars such as John Whitney Hall, Jeffrey P. Mass, H. Paul Varley, and Conrad Totman come to mind, but several excellent works from the next generation now also provide new and valuable insights. See, for example, recent monographs by Karl Friday, Bruce Batten, Eiko Ikegami, and others.

2. G. Cameron Hurst III was one of the first Western scholars to note the continuing vitality of the imperial court in the Kamakura era in his article "The Kōbu Polity: Court-Bakufu Relations in Kamakura Japan," in *Court and Bakufu in Japan: Essays in Kamakura History,* edited by Jeffrey P. Mass (Stanford: Stanford University Press, 1982), 3–28. However, the logical conclusion that the age of the warrior thus began later has not been expressed until quite recently.

3. The consensus regarding this interpretation seems overwhelming today among scholars. See *The Origins of Medieval Japan,* edited by Jeffrey P. Mass (Stanford: Stanford University Press, 1997), which is based on a conference featuring Western and Japanese scholars from a variety of fields held at Hertford College, Oxford, England, in August of 1994.

4. *"Kamogawa no mizu, sugoroku no sai, yama hosshi, sorezore chin ga kokoro ni shitagawanu mono."* *Genpei seisuiki,* volume 1 (Tokyo: Miyai shoten, 1994), 124; *Heike monogatari,* volume 1, in *Shinkō nihon koten shūsei,* edited by Mizuhara Hajime, (Tokyo: Shinkōsha, 1979), 93; Helen McCullough, *The Tale of the Heike* (Stanford: Stanford University Press, 1990), 50.

5. Missing character.

6. *Chūyūki,* in *Zōho shiryō taisei,* volumes 9–14 (Kyoto: Rinsen shoten, 1965), Tennin 1 (1108)/3/23; *Dainihon shiryō* (hereafter cited as *DNS*), edited by Shiryō hensan kakari (Tokyo: Tokyo daigaku zōhan, 1926–), series 3, volume 10 (3:10), p. 113.

7. George Sansom, *A History of Japan to 1334* (Stanford: Stanford University Press, 1958), 223. It should be noted, in Sansom's defense, that he relied on the interpretations of Japanese scholars and could hardly have been expected to view the influence of religious institutions in premodern Japan any differently.

8. For example, the secular power of the leading monastic centers and their

political role are completely neglected in volume three of the prestigious *Cambridge History of Japan* in deference to Zen and the populist Buddhist sects (Kozo Yamamura, ed., *The Cambridge History of Japan,* volume 3, *Medieval Japan* [Cambridge: Cambridge University Press, 1990]). Such an interpretation unquestionably misrepresents the political and ideological configurations of the premodern era. In fact, temples like Enryakuji, Onjōji, Tōdaiji, Tōji, Kōfukuji, and Kōyasan managed to maintain and, in several instances, even to improve their judicial and economic privileges, and their role as providers of religious rituals and spiritual protection continued throughout the period.

9. Neil McMullin, "Historical and Historiographical Issues in the Study of Pre-Modern Japanese Religions," *Japanese Journal of Religious Studies* 16:1 (1989), 26, 30.

10. Martin Collcutt, *Five Mountains: The Rinzai Zen Monastic Institution in Medieval Japan* (Cambridge: Harvard University Press, 1981); Neil McMullin, *Buddhism and the State in Sixteenth-Century Japan* (Princeton University Press: Princeton, 1984); Joan Piggott, "Tōdaiji and the Nara Imperium" (Ph.D. dissertation, Stanford University, 1987); Janet R. Goodwin, *Alms and Vagabonds: Buddhist Temples and Popular Patronage in Medieval Japan* (Honolulu: University of Hawai'i Press, 1994); Allan G. Grapard, *The Protocol of the Gods: A Study of the Kasuga Cult in Japanese History* (Berkeley: University of California Press, 1992).

11. Narratives of Enryakuji's protests are available in Katsuno Ryūshin's *Sōhei* (Tokyo: Shibundō, 1966), Hioki Shōichi's *Nihon sōhei kenkyū* (Tokyo: Heibonsha, 1934), Tsuji Zennosuke's "Sōhei no gen'yū" and "Akusō jinnin no katsudō" in his *Nihon bukkyō shi: jōsei hen* (Tokyo: Iwanami shoten, 1944), Hirata Toshiharu's *Sōhei to bushi* (Tokyo: Nihon kyōbunsha, 1965), and his "Nanto hokurei no akusō ni tsuite," in volume 3 of *Ronshū Nihon bukkyō shi: Heian jidai,* edited by Hiraoka Jōkai (Tokyo: Yūzankaku shuppan, 1986), 261–295. Though informative, these works do not relate religious conflicts to the shifts of power and factionalism among the secular elites. For a general history of Enryakuji, see Kageyama Haruki, *Hieizan* (Tokyo: Kadokawa shoten, 1975); idem, *Hieizanji: sono kōsei to sho mondai* (Tokyo: Kadokawa shoten, 1979); Murayama Shūichi, *Shinbutsu shugo shichō* (Kyoto: Heirakuji shoten, 1957); and idem, *Hieizan shi: tatakai to inori no seichi* (Tokyo: Tokyo bijutsu, 1994); idem, ed., *Hieizan to Tendai bukkyō no kenkyū* (Tokyo: Meishō shuppan, 1976).

12. For an extensive analysis of Oda Nobunaga's burning of Enryakuji and his crusade against the temples of central Japan, see McMullin, *Buddhism and the State in Sixteenth-Century Japan.*

13. *Kōtei zōho Tendai zasuki* (hereafter referred to as the *Tendai zasuki*), compiled by Shibuya Gaiji (Tokyo: Daiichi shobō, 1973). The *Tendai zasuki* referred to here was compiled from three different sources, ending with the appointment of the 247th *zasu* Kōei in 1927.

14. Grapard, *Protocol of the Gods,* 131.

15. See, for example, Nagashima Fukutarō, *Nara* (Tokyo: Yoshikawa kōbunkan, 1972), 130.

16. *Kōfukuji bettō shidai* is printed in *Dainihon bukkyō zensho: Kōfukuji sōsho* (Tokyo: Ushio shobō, 1931), volume 2, 1–59, and *Sōgō bunin* in volume 1, 61–288.

17. *Kōfukuji ryaku nendaiki,* in volume 29, part 2, of *Zoku gunsho ruijū* (Tokyo: Yoshikawa kōbunkan, 1965), 107–205. The *Kōfukuji ryaku nendaiki* was compiled

in 1725 by the monk Shōen, abbot of the noble cloister Daijōin within Kōfukuji, who appears to have recorded the section dating after 1576. The earlier parts come from various sources, dating from the thirteenth and fourteenth centuries.

18. Takamura Takashi, "Kōyasan ryō shōen kenkyū shi," in *Kōyasan ryō shōen no shihai to kōzō*, edited by Toyoda Takeshi (Tokyo: Gannandō shoten, 1977), 308; Inoue Mitsusada, "Kamakura bakufu seiritsu ki no bushi rangyō: Kii no kuni, Tanaka-no-shō Satō shi no ba'ai," *Nihon shi kenkyū* 110 (March 1970), 23.

19. Takamura, 307; Kuroda Toshio, "Buddhism and Society in the Medieval Estate System," translated by Suzanne Gay, *Japanese Journal of Religious Studies* 23: 3–4 (1996), 301–302.

20. Conflicts are defined as "overt, coercive actions of contending collectives." See Ted Robert Gurr, "Introduction," in *Handbook of Political Conflict*, edited by Ted Robert Gurr (New York: The Free Press, 1980), 1.

21. This summary of Kuroda's thesis is a slightly altered version of an account included in my "Enryakuji—an Old Power in a New Era," in *The Origins of Medieval Japan*, ed. Jeffrey Mass, 238–244.

22. See the memorial issue "The Legacy of Kuroda Toshio," *Japanese Journal of Religious Studies* 26:3–4 (fall 1996), edited by James C. Dobbins.

23. Kuroda Toshio, *Jisha seiryoku: mō hitotsu chūsei no shakai* (Tokyo: Iwanami shoten, 1980), 56. The entire quote is quite revealing of Kuroda's concern with other scholars' neglect of religious institutions: "If we refrain from meaningless moral judgments and try to reinterpret the complexities of the different powers, we will find that this [aggressive behavior of religious institutions] was a small-scale reflection of the social and political structures. Thus, though individual monk disturbances and riots have been examined, they must now be analyzed in conjunction with other political and military incidents."

24. Some notable exceptions should be mentioned here. Taira Masayuki, Kuroda's disciple and successor at Osaka University, has continued his mentor's legacy with a few adjustments (*Nihon chūsei no shakai to bukkyō* [Tokyo: Kōshobō, 1992]). In the West, Suzanne Gay has paid attention to Kuroda's work while studying the early development of the Muromachi Bakufu (see "Muromachi Bakufu Rule in Kyoto: Administrative and Judicial Aspects," in *The Bakufu in Japanese History*, edited by Jeffrey P. Mass and William B. Hauser [Stanford: Stanford University Press, 1985], 49–65; and "The Muromachi Bakufu in Medieval Kyoto" [Ph.D. dissertation, Yale University, 1982]).

25. I find it somewhat misleading that the recent tribute to Kuroda's scholarship in the *Japanese Journal of Religious Studies*—though laudable and an important contribution to Western Scholarship—is so dominated by translations of and debates concerning the *kenmitsu taisei*. As I see it, this belief system is only one part of a larger theory that cannot be correctly understood without taking into account also the prevailing ruling system, as Kuroda himself urged in his writings.

26. Kuroda presented the *kenmon* theory in the following works: *Jisha seiryoku: mō hitotsu chūsei no sekai; Nihon chūsei kokka to shūkyō* (Tokyo: Iwanami shoten, 1976); "Chūsei jisha seiryoku ron," in volume 6 of *Iwanami kōza, Nihon rekishi: chūsei 2*, edited by Asao Naohiro et al. (Tokyo: Iwanami shoten, 1975), 245–295; "Chūsei kokka to tennō," in volume 6 of *Iwanami kōza, Nihon rekishi: chūsei 2*, edited by Ienaga Saburō et al. (Tokyo: Iwanami shoten, 1963), 261–301.

27. Kuroda, *Nihon chūsei kokka to shūkyō*, 17–18, 31, 78; "Chūsei kokka to tennō," 265–279. The court-bakufu relationship has been described in English in G. Cameron Hurst III, "The Kōbu Polity: Court-Bakufu Relations in Kamakura Japan"; and Cornelius J. Kiley, "The Imperial Court as a Legal Authority in the Kamakura Age," in *Court and Bakufu in Japan*, ed. Jeffrey P. Mass, 29–44.

28. For an excellent treatment of Emperor Kammu and the move of the capital, see Ronald Toby, "Why Leave Nara?" *Monumenta Nipponica* 40:3 (1985), 331–347.

29. Kuroda, *Nihon chūsei kokka to shūkyō*, 20–21, 453; idem, "Chūsei kokka to tennō," 279–280.

30. Kuroda, *Nihon chūsei kokka to shūkyō*, 19; idem, "Chūsei kokka to tennō," 277–280.

31. Kuroda, *Nihon chūsei kokka to shūkyō*, 7–11, 367; idem, "Chūsei kokka to tennō," 269–270.

32. Kuroda, "Chūsei kokka to tennō," 268.

33. Ibid., 270, 275–276; Kuroda, *Nihon chūsei kokka to shūkyō*, 455–458.

34. Kuroda, *Nihon chūsei kokka to shūkyō*, 17–18, 21; idem, "Chūsei kokka to tennō," 275–279.

35. Our understanding of the Kamakura Bakufu has progressed greatly during the last two decades, thanks in particular to the work of Jeffrey Mass. See, for example, Mass, *Warrior Government in Early Medieval Japan: A Study of the Kamakura Bakufu, Shugo and Jitō* (New Haven: Yale University Press, 1974); Mass, "The Kamakura Bakufu," in *The Cambridge History of Japan,* volume 3; and Mass, ed., *Court and Bakufu in Japan: Essays in Kamakura History* (Stanford: Stanford University Press, 1982).

36. Kuroda, *Jisha seiryoku*, 255–256; idem, *Nihon chūsei kokka to shūkyō*, 454–455.

37. Kuroda, *Jisha seiryoku*, 257; Kuroda Toshio, "The Buddhist Law and the Imperial Law," translated by Jacqueline Stone, *Japanese Journal of Religious Studies* 23:3–4 (1996), 271–277.

38. Taira Masayuki, *Nihon chūsei no shakai to bukkyō*, 94–96.

39. Kuroda, *Nihon chūsei kokka to shūkyō*, 306, 456.

40. See also Taira Masayuki, "Kuroda Toshio and the *Kenmitsu taisei* Theory," *Japanese Journal of Religious Studies* 23:3–4, 441–442.

41. The term *"jike"* does appear in Kamakura sources, but it refers to individual temples, not the entire establishment, as in the case of the court nobles and the warrior aristocracy.

42. *Kōyasan monjo*, in *Dai nihon komonjo: iewake 1* (Tokyo: Tōkyō daigaku shiryō hensanjo, 1903–1907), volume 2, document 661, *Tōji chōja mikyōjō*, Kōan 6 (1283)/5/29 (pp. 79–80).

43. Suzuki Kunihiro, "Kōyasan ni okeru shōen seiteki kenryoku kōzō no tokushitsu, to sono henka," in *Kōyasan ryō shōen no shihai to kōzō*, edited by Toyoda Takeshi, 51–52.

44. *Kōyasan monjo* 7, document 1594, *Sarukawa no shō kumon sō Nōshin ukebumi*, Shōō 4 (1291)/9/19, (pp. 205–210); documents 1599 and 1600, *Sarukawa no shō kumon sō Nōshin ukebumi*, Kengen 1 (1302)/12/14 and 12/15, (pp. 217–223).

45. In this case, *"sōke"* appears to refer specifically to the patron *(honke),* the highest level in the *shōen* hierarchy. *Kōyasan monjo* 1, document 439, *Kongōbuji nenjo okibumi an*, Bun'ei 8 (1271)/7 (pp. 479–485); *Kamakura ibun*, compiled by

Takeuchi Rizō (Tokyo: Tōkyōdō shuppan, 1971–1992), volume 14, document 10856 (p. 290); Suzuki, Kunihiro, "Kōyasan," 66, 68–70.

46. Kuroda, *Nihon chūsei kokka to shūkyō*, 15–16, 31–32; James C. Dobbins, "Editor's Introduction: Kuroda Toshio and His Scholarship," *Japanese Journal of Religious Studies* 23:3–4 (1996), 220; Taira, "Kuroda Toshio and the *Kenmitsu taisei* Ideology," 432–433.

47. Kuroda, *Nihon chūsei kokka to shūkyō*, 306, 457, 460.

Chapter 2   Monastic Developments in the Heian Age

1. See, for example, Nagashima Fukutarō, *Nara*, 130, and idem, *Nara-ken no rekishi* (Tokyo: Yamakawa shuppansha, 1980), 63.

2. For an analysis of the important developments in the 660s and 670s, see Bruce Batten, "Foreign Threat and Domestic Reform," *Monumenta Nipponica* 41: 2 (1986), 199–219.

3. Matsushima Ken, *Kōfukuji*, in volume 3 of *Shinpen meihō Nihon no bijutsu* (Tokyo: Shōgakkan, 1990); Grapard, *Protocol of the Gods*, 48.

4. Grapard, *Protocol of the Gods*, 48–49; Nagashima Fukutarō, *Nara*, 50–52; Katsuno Ryūshin, *Hieizan to Kōyasan: Saichō to Kūkai wo chūshin toshite* (Tokyo: Shibundō, 1966), 32; *Kōfukuji ryaku nendaiki*, 105.

5. Grapard, *Protocol of the Gods*, 49–53; Nagashima Fukutarō, *Nara*, 86; *Kōfukuji ryaku nendaiki*, 106–108.

6. Nagashima, *Nara*, 87; *Kōfukuji ryaku nendaiki*, 122. The Yuima Sūtra describes the activities of Buddhist laypeople, indicating above all that people who have not taken the Buddhist vows can obtain considerable merit through their actions. The Yuima ceremony, which probably was promoted by Kamatari at Yamashinadera and then reintroduced by Fuhito at Kōfukuji in honor of his father, therefore became quite popular with the nobility in the Nara period (Nagashima, *Nara*, 34, 87).

7. Kamikawa Michio, "Chūsei jiin no kōzō to kokka," *Nihon shi kenkyū* 344 (1991), 32; *Bukkyō jiten* (Tokyo: Iwanami shoten, 1989), s.v. "*sōgō.*" Joan Piggott has provided an extensive chart of the *sōgō* organization from its inception to the late seventh century with meticulous translations. See Piggott, *The Emergence of Japanese Kingship* (Stanford: Stanford University Press, 1997), 94.

8. Paul Groner, *Saichō: The Establishment of the Japanese Tendai School* (Berkeley: University of California Press, 1984), 72–73; Grapard, *Protocol of the Gods*, 66; Nagashima Fukutarō, *Nara*, 80. Kōfukuji's expansion is evidenced in the transformation of Yakushiji, Hōryūji, and Kiyomizudera (in Kyoto) into Hossō temples. In addition, the abbotships of Saidaiji, Daianji, and Hokkeji—all Shingon temples —were eventually controlled by Kōfukuji (Nagashima, *Nara*, 80).

9. Groner, *Saichō*, 21–26; Hori Daiji, "Enryakuji no kaisō," in *Shinshū Ōtsu-shi shi*, volume 1: *Kodai* (hereafter *Ōtsu-shi shi*), compiled by Ōtsu shiyakusho (Nihon shashin insatsu kabushiki gaisha, 1978), 322; Kageyama, *Hieizan*, 45; Daigan Matsunaga and Alice Matsunaga, *Foundation of Japanese Buddhism* (Tokyo: Kenkyūsha, 1974), volume 1, 140.

10. Kageyama, *Hieizan*, 40–41; Hori, "Enryakuji no kaisō," 316–317; Groner, *Saichō*, 164.

11. Allan Grapard, "Linguistic Cubism: A Singularity of Pluralism in the Sannō Cult," *Japanese Journal of Religious Studies* 14:2–3 (1987), 213–214; Murayama,

Hieizan shi, 2; Kageyama Haruki, *Hieizan to Kōyasan* (Tokyo: Kyōikusha, 1980), 1–2, 12.

12. Grapard, *Protocol of the Gods,* 25–29. Grapard has convincingly demonstrated that since Buddhism lacked territorial grounding in Japan, the native cults became instrumental in communicating the new faith to potential believers. He aptly named this process a "reversed conversion" in which Buddhism adopted local cults, ideologies, creeds, and practices (Allan Grapard, "Institution, Ritual, and Ideology: The Twenty-two Shrine-Temple Multiplexes of Heian Japan," *History of Religions* 27:3 [1988], 252–254). There is ample historical evidence to support Grapard's view. For example, during the late Nara and early Heian periods, Buddhist monks built a specific kind of temple, called *jingūji* (temple for divine palaces), on shrine compounds. Furthermore, the Hachiman deity of Usa in Kyushu and the imperial temple of Tōdaiji in Nara developed a close relationship in the mid–eighth century (Ross Bender, "The Hachiman Cult and the Dōkyō Incident," *Monumenta Nipponica* 34:2 [1979], 134–136).

13. Groner, *Saichō,* 30; Hori, "Enryakuji no kaisō," 319–320; Kageyama, *Hieizan,* 48. Enryaku is the name of the era from 782 to 806. It was not unusual for temples in early Japan to be given names after the eras in which they were founded.

14. Groner, *Saichō,* 30; *Japanese-English Buddhist Dictionary* (Tokyo: Daitō shuppansha, 1991), s.v. *"ichijō."*

15. Groner, *Saichō,* 31–32; *Bukkyō jiten,* s.v. *"naigubu;"* Matsunaga and Matsunaga, 141. It is believed that Saichō made these vows *(ganmon)* shortly after he settled on Mt. Hiei (Groner, *Saichō,* 28–30).

16. Toby, "Why Leave Nara?" 342–345; Grapard, *Protocol of the Gods,* 50.

17. The Northern Fujiwara's advance during this period is a topic that deserves more attention. Although weak on critical assessment of its sources, the most informative treatment is probably Tsuruoka Shizuo, "Saichō to Fujiwara shi," in idem, *Kodai bukkyō shi no kenkyū* (Tokyo: Bungadō shoten, 1967).

18. Kageyama, *Hieizan to Kōyasan,* 35–38.

19. Katsuno, *Hieizan to Kōyasan,* 62–67; Kageyama, *Hieizan to Kōyasan,* 41–42.

20. Hakeda Yoshito, *Kukai: Major Works* (Columbia: Columbia University Press, 1972), 13–22; *Wakayama-ken shi: genshi, kodai,* compiled by Wakayama-ken shi hensan kakari inkai (Osaka: Dainihon insatsu kabushiki gaisha, 1994), 568–569; Katsuno, *Hieizan to Kōyasan,* 130–133. Legends indicate that Kūkai spent most of his time in the capital region as a wandering monk, perhaps even visiting Mt. Kōya, which is located at a walking distance of several days south of Nara.

21. Hakeda, 28; *Wakayama-ken shi: genshi, kodai,* 568; Katsuno, *Hieizan to Kōyasan,* 130–134.

22. The Mahāvairochana Sūtra is the most popular of the esoteric texts, presenting the Vairochana Buddha (the Ultimate Buddha) as the ultimate essence and claiming that enlightenment can be obtained by knowing the Three Mysteries of Body, Speech, and Mind (see *Japanese-English Buddhist Dictionary,* s.v. "Dainichi-kyō").

23. Hakeda, 29–33; *Wakayama-ken shi: genshi, kodai,* 571–572; Katsuno, *Hieizan to Kōyasan,* 138–143.

24. Groner, *Saichō,* 38–53; Matsunaga and Matsunaga, 141–142; Kageyama, *Hieizan,* 51–52; Robert Borgen, "The Japanese Mission to China, 801–806," *Monumenta Nipponica* 37:1 (1982), 6, 10–13, 17; Katsuno, *Hieizan to Kōyasan,* 68–70, 74–

75. In all, some 120 works in 345 facsimiles were copied and ultimately brought back to Japan.

25. The *kanjō* ritual was a ceremony in which water was sprinkled on the heads of the initiated (Groner, *Saichō*, 65–67).

26. The ordination system, which was initiated in 696, restricted the number of monks who could be ordained every year. During Saichō's time of increasing sectarianism (to which Saichō himself also contributed by trying to establish Tendai as an independent sect), the yearly ordinands became an issue of competition for supremacy among the different Nara schools. For an informative treatment of this system, see Hiraoka Jōkai, *Nihon jiin shi no kenkyū* (Tokyo: Yoshikawa kōbunkan, 1981, 457–462.

27. Groner, *Saichō*, 68–69; Sonoda Kōyū, "Heian bukkyō no seiritsu," in *Nihon bukkyō shi*, volume 1: *Kodai hen*, edited by Ienaga Saburō (Kyoto: Hōzōkan, 1967), 187; Hori, "Enryakuji no kaisō," 326–327; Kageyama, *Hieizan*, 58; Hiraoka, *Nihon jiin shi no kenkyū*, 457–459; Hakeda, 37; Katsuno, *Hieizan to Kōyasan*, 77–80.

28. Groner, *Saichō*, 71–72, 74.

29. Hakeda, 34–35, 38–40; Kuroda, *Jisha seiryoku*, 20; Katsuno, *Hieizan to Kōyasan*, 152–153; *Wakayama-ken shi: genshi, kodai*, 572–573.

30. Groner, *Saichō*, 87; *Wakayama-ken shi: genshi, kodai*, 572–573.

31. See, for example, Groner, *Saichō*, 77–87; Hakeda, 42–44; and Katsuno, *Hieizan to Kōyasan*, 163–167.

32. Groner, *Saichō*, 88–115; Joseph Kitagawa, *Religion in Japanese History* (New York: Columbia University Press, 1990), 60.

33. Nezu Masashi, *Tennō ke no rekishi*, volume 1 (Tokyo: San'ichi shobō, 1973), 175–177; *Kokushi daijiten* (Tokyo: Yoshikawa kōbunkan, 1979–), s.v. "Kusuko no hen." The dates of the incident are 810/9/10–12.

34. Groner, *Saichō*, 72–73; Toby, 345–346; *Kokushi daijiten*, s.v. "Kusuko no hen."

35. Groner, *Saichō*, 125; Hiraoka, 460–463; Katsuno, *Hieizan to Kōyasan*, 97–98. According to Tsuji Zennosuke, as many as twelve of the twenty-four monks went to the Hossō school (Tsuji Zennosuke, *Nihon bukkyō shi: jōsei hen* [Tokyo: Iwanami shoten, 1944], 270). Tsuruoka has suggested that it was Fujiwara no Fuyutsugu who encouraged Saichō to establish Tendai outside the control of the *sōgō* (Tsuruoka, 226).

36. Groner, *Saichō*, 118, 120, 123–126, 136; *Kōfukuji ryaku nendaiki*, 122–123; Hori, "Enryakuji no kaisō," 330.

37. There was one ordination platform at Tōdaiji in Nara, one at Kanzeonji in Echizen Province and one at Yakushiji in Shinano Province. *Bukkyō jiten*, s.v. "*kaidan.*"

38. Groner, *Saichō*, 129–158; Matsunaga and Matsunaga, 142, 148–149; Tsuji, *Nihon bukkyō shi: jōsei hen*, 285–290; Kageyama, *Hieizan*, 61–62; *Kōfukuji ryaku nendaiki*, 123.

39. This idea is expressed in two documents believed to be written by Saichō: *Sange gakushō shiki* and *Kenkai ron*. See Tsuji, *Nihon bukkyō shi: jōsei hen*, 323–324; Ishikawa Shiratsuru, *Tennōsei to chingō kokka no bukkyō* (Tokyo: Dentō to gendai sōsho, 1973), 57–58. Tsuruoka believes that the idea was ultimately suggested by the Fujiwara leaders (Tsuruoka, 212).

40. Groner, *Saichō*, 162–165; Kageyama, *Hieizan*, 63; Sonoda, 190; Kamikawa, 29. Other temples, though of much less significance than Enryakuji and Kōya-

san (which also obtained control of its own ordinations), also became immune to *sōgō* jurisdiction in the ninth century (Taira, 91).

41. *Wakayama-ken shi: genshi, kodai*, 573–574.

42. Hakeda, 48; *Wakayama-ken shi: genshi, kodai*, 574–575; Kageyama, *Hieizan to Kōyasan*, 18–19. Kūkai's request was granted in the seventh month of 816, though there is some doubt as to the authenticity of the donation document. First, it is a *daijō kanpu* (an imperial order), but such documents were not used at the time. Second, no borders of the area donated are listed except for a vague statement of "the four directions of the high mountain." Such vagueness is inconsistent with other documents granting land to temples in the early Heian age. It is therefore apparent that this document must be a forgery that is intentionally vague in defining the area, allowing the monks on Mt. Kōya to claim more land for the temple. This conclusion is further supported by a third point. The document mentions that the temple homestead borders Ishigaki kami-no-shō (again without any specific references to where the borders are), but this private estate was not created until 946. See *Wakayama-ken shi: genshi, kodai*, 574–576.

43. Kageyama, *Hieizan to Kōyasan*, 141–151; *Wakayama-ken shi: genshi, kodai*, 574; Katsuno, *Hieizan to Kōyasan*, 177–178.

44. Hakeda, 48–50; *Wakayama-ken shi: genshi, kodai*, 578–580; Katsuno, *Hieizan to Kōyasan*, 188–190; Kageyama, *Hieizan to Kōyasan*, 156, 168–169.

45. Hakeda, 52, 54–55; *Wakayama-ken shi: genshi, kodai*, 581. Tōji's main lecture hall was completed by 835 while Kūkai was still alive, but the five-storied pagoda that was begun in 826 was not finished until the early 880s (*Wakayama-ken shi: genshi, kodai*, 580).

46. Hakeda, 55. This request further supports the notion that Kūkai selected Mt. Kōya to keep his monks at some distance from the several other sects in Nara and Kyoto.

47. Hakeda, 56–57; *Wakayama-ken shi: genshi, kodai*, 581.

48. *Wakayama-ken shi: genshi, kodai*, 584–585. The Mishihō (Go-shichinichi no mishihō, or Mishuhō) was a ceremony held during the second week of the new year, with prayers for the emperor's health and for peace and stability in the imperial state.

49. Hakeda, 58–59; *Wakayama-ken shi: genshi, kodai*, 585; Miyasaka Yūshō, *Kōyasan shi* (Tokyo: Kōyasan bunka kenkyūkai, 1962), 14; Katsuno, *Hieizan to Kōyasan*, 209–210; *Shinkō Kōya shunjū hennen shūroku* (hereafter referred to as *Kōya shunjū*), compiled by Hinonishi Shinjō (Tokyo: Daimonsha, 1982), 18, 20.

50. The Dōkyō Incident has traditionally been seen as an attempt by the monk Dōkyō to usurp power from Empress Shōtoku. See, for example, Bender, "The Hachiman Cult and the Dōkyō Incident." However, Joan Piggott has convincingly demonstrated that Dōkyō was little more than a pawn in the factional struggles at the imperial court in the mid–eighth century and was victimized by his Fujiwara opponents at court, who also wrote their own history of the events surrounding the monk's rise to power. See Piggott, "Tōdaiji and the Nara Imperium," 72–79.

51. Shimosaka Mamoru, "Chūsei daijiin ni okeru 'jike' no kōzō," in *Kyōto-shi rekishi shiryōkan kiyō* 10, compiled by Kyōto-shi rekishi shiryōkan (Kyoto: Dōhō-sha, 1992), 159, 170; *Tendai zasuki*, 17.

52. The first lay administrators may have been appointed by 818, but there is

no extant appointment edict to substantiate this claim (Kikuchi Kyōko, "Zoku bettō no seiritsu," *Shirin* 51:1 [1968], 103–104).

53. Uejima Susumu, "Chūsei zenki no kokka to bukkyō," *Nihon shi kenkyū* 403 (1996), 37; Groner, *Saichō*, 162–163. It has been suggested that Saichō, inspired by a similar Chinese office, may himself have promoted the installation of a *zoku bettō* in order to retain the support of the government while also avoiding control by the *sōgō*. There may be some merit in this claim, since the responsibilities were first given to Fujiwara no Mimori and Ōtomo no Kunimichi, who had been among Saichō's most faithful supporters (Groner, *Saichō*, 269–271).

54. Groner, *Saichō*, 269–271; Kikuchi, 107–108; Itō Seirō, "Chūsei sō gōsei no kenkyū," *Rekishi* 53 (1979), 23; Okano Kōji, "Enryakuji zoku bettō to Tendai zasu," *Komazawa shigaku* 33 (1985), 94; idem, "Kōfukuji zoku bettō to Kangakuin," *Bukkyō shigaku kenkyū* 34:2 (1991), 67–69; *Wakayama-ken no rekishi*, 588, 638, 724; Joan Piggott, "Hierarchy and Economics in Early Medieval Tōdaiji," in *Court and Bakufu in Japan*, ed. Jeffrey Mass, 50.

55. The first set of practical and administrative rules were written by three of Saichō's disciples in 824/5. These rules were approved by the *zoku bettō* in the seventh month of that year (Okano, "Enryakuji zoku bettō to Tendai zasu," 94–95).

56. Gishin returned to Enryakuji in 813 after an eight-year retreat in his native Sagami.

57. Groner, *Saichō*, 162, 286; Neil McMullin, "The Sanmon-Jimon Schism in the Tendai School of Buddhism: A Preliminary Analysis," *Journal of the International Association of Buddhist Studies* 7:1 (1984), 84; Hori Daiji, "Enryakuji no kaisō," 334; Sonoda, 190; Matsunaga and Matsunaga, 162. In retrospect, Gishin has been seen as the first *zasu* (head abbot) of Enryakuji. However, in the edict of Tenchō 1 (824)/6/22, as cited in the *Tendai zasuki*, the term "*zasu*" itself is not mentioned. The term used is "*isshū no sōshu*," meaning "head of the monks of the whole [Tendai] sect." See *Tendai zasuki*, 6.

58. Groner, *Saichō*, 290; Matsunaga and Matsunaga, 164–165; Tsuji, *Nihon bukkyō shi: jōsei hen*, 825–826. The edict appoints Enchō *denpōshi* (Transmitter of the Law), but there are also contemporary notes referring to him as *zasu* (*Tendai zasuki*, 8).

59. Kōjō's recognition as leader of Tendai came first on 854/4/3, when he was appointed head administrator *(bettō)*. It is probably no coincidence that this appointment took place on the same day that Ennin was appointed head abbot (*Tendai zasuki*, 9–10).

60. Groner, *Saichō*, 281–282, 292–298; McMullin, "Sanmon-Jimon Schism," 85; Tsuji, *Nihon bukkyō shi: jōsei hen*, 826; Murayama, *Hieizan shi*, 80.

61. Matsunaga and Matsunaga, 163; Edwin O. Reischauer, *Ennin's Diary: The Record of a Pilgrimage to China in Search of the Law* (New York: Ronald Press Company, 1955), 32, 35–36, 46, 174; Hori Daiji, "Yokawa to Onjōji," in *Ōtsu-shi shi*, 343–345, 346; Tsuji, *Nihon bukkyō shi: jōsei hen*, 342–343; Sonoda, 221; *Tendai zasuki*, 10.

62. Hori Daiji, "Yokawa to Onjōji," 349; Okano, "Enryakuji zoku bettō to Tendai zasu," 98–102; Groner, *Saichō*, 283–284, 298; *Tendai zasuki*, 9–10, 16–17; Taira, *Nihon chūsei no shakai to bukkyō*, 94.

63. Sonoda, 223–225; *Tendai zasuki*, 22; Groner, *Saichō*, 283; Hori Daiji, "Yokawa to Onjōji," 354; Tsuji, *Nihon bukkyō shi: jōsei hen*, 353–354.

64. Hori Daiji, "Yokawa to Onjōji," 346–347.

65. Hiraoka Jōkai, *Nihon jiin shi,* volume 2, 107–108.

66. The edict, a *daijō kanchō* dated Jōgan 8 (866)/5/14, is noted in *Shiga-ken shi,* volume 2: *Jōdai-chūsei,* compiled by Shiga-ken (Tokyo: Sanshūsha, 1927), 191, note 102. Although this work does not specify the source for this edict, it is likely that the author relied on a quotation in *Onjōji denki,* in volume 127 of *Dainihon bukkyō zensho* (Tokyo: Busshō kankōkai, 1916), 58. Other scholars do not appear to pay much attention to this edict. See Tsuji, *Nihon bukkyō shi: jōsei hen,* 352–353; *Ōtsu-shi shi,* 150, 155. It is also of some interest that the Ōtomo family in that same year was ousted from the capital by Fujiwara Yoshifusa in the Ōtenmon incident. The relationship between this incident and Onjōji's conversion into a Tendai *betsuin* needs to be further scrutinized.

67. *Daishi yuigon,* Kanpyō 3 (891)/10/17, in *Tendai zasuki,* 25–27; Sonoda, 225. Some scholars believe that this document is a forgery by the Saichō-Ennin branch, but no concrete evidence is provided to support this view (*Kyōto no rekishi 1: Heian no shinkyō,* compiled by Kyōto-shi [Tokyo: Gakugei shorin, 1973], 352). The claim may still have some validity, since the document is suspiciously favorable to the Saichō-Ennin branch.

68. *Tendai zasuki,* 28–42. McMullin counts nine out of ten Gishin-Enchin abbots directly after Enchin, but he does not show how he arrived at that figure ("Sanmon-Jimon Schism," 88). Murayama counts seven out of eight from that branch, but he also acknowledges that two of them are listed as Saichō-Ennin followers in other sources (*Hieizan shi,* 111). In fact, the division may not have been as clear-cut as many scholars believe. Gikai, the fourteenth *zasu,* was a disciple of masters from both branches. See Figure 1.

69. Hirabayashi Moritoku, *Ryōgen* (Tokyo: Yoshikawa kōbunkan, 1976), 33–34, 158; McMullin, "Sanmon-Jimon Schism," 88–89, 102; idem, "The *Lotus Sutra* and Politics in the Mid-Heian Period," in *The Lotus Sutra in Japanese Culture,* edited by George Tanabe Jr. and Willa Jane Tanabe (Honolulu: University of Hawai'i Press, 1989), 119, 123–125.

70. Hirabayashi, 83; McMullin, "The *Lotus Sutra* and Politics," 129–133; Murayama, *Hieizan shi,* 125–127. Ryōgen's most successful appearance was at the Ōwa religious debate, which took place on 963/8/21–26, three years before Ryōgen's appointment as *zasu.*

71. Hirabayashi, 47–49, 58; Neil McMullin, "The Enryaku-ji and the Gion Shrine-Temple Complex in the Mid-Heian Period," *Japanese Journal of Religious Studies* 14:2–3 (1987), 169–171; Toyoda Takeshi, *Nihon shūkyō seido shi no kenkyū* (Tokyo: Kōseikaku, 1938), 78; Kageyama, *Hieizan,* 142.

72. Wada Teruo, "Chūsei Kōyasan kyōdan no soshiki ni tsuite," in *Kōyasan ryō shōen no shihai to kōzō,* edited by Toyoda Takeshi, 25–26.

73. *Wakayama-ken no rekishi,* 588, 638, 725; Miyasaka, 13–15; *Kōya shunjū,* 20–21.

74. *Wakayama-ken no rekishi,* 723–728; *Kōya shunjū,* 28–30; Miyasaka, 14. It should be noted that the Great Pagoda on Mt. Kōya was probably not completed by 861, and the "repairs" were consequently intended to finish the construction.

75. *Wakayama-ken no rekishi,* 728–729; Miyasaka, 14–15; *Kōya shunjū,* 32. These thirty scrolls, known as *sanjū jō sakushi,* are today a National Treasure in Japan, kept at Ninnaji in northern Kyoto.

76. *Wakayama-ken no rekishi,* 728–730; *Kōya shunjū,* 34, 36; Wada, 26.

77. Kuroda, *Jisha seiryoku,* 35; *Wakayama-ken no rekishi,* 731–733; *Kōya shunjū,* 36–39; Miyasaka, 20.

78. *Wakayama-ken no rekishi*, 30, 733–736; Miyasaka, 14–15, 20–21; Kuroda, *Jisha seiryoku*, 35; Wada, 27–28; Katsuno, *Hieizan to Kōyasan*, 215; *Kōya shunjū*, 40–42.

79. Kuroda, *Jisha seiryoku*, 35; *Wakayama-ken no rekishi*, 734, 737; Miyasaka, 16, 21; Wada, 26; *Kōya shunjū*, 44.

80. Taira Masayuki, "Kamakura bukkyō no sho mondai," in *Ronshū Nihon jiin shi*, volume 4: *Kamakura*, part 1, edited by Hiraoka Jōkai, 106–107; *Wakayama-ken no rekishi*, 737–738; Miyasaka, 21–22; Katsuno, *Hieizan to Kōyasan*, 216.

81. Okano Kōji, "Kōfukuji zoku bettō to Kangakuin," 67. Samuel Morse has also pointed out that Hossō temples continued to be constructed in the capital region in the ninth and tenth centuries, thus refuting the outdated view that only the newer Tendai and Shingon temples received extensive patronage in the early Heian age ("Competing Agendas: Image Making and Religious Authority in Ninth-Century Japan" [unpublished paper, presented at the conference "From Precepts to Practice: New Perspectives on Japanese Buddhist Culture," Yale University, October 17, 1998]).

82. *Kōfukuji bettō shidai*, 1.

83. Grapard, *Protocol of the Gods*, 120; Nagashima, *Nara*, 83, 90–91; Nagashima, *Nara-ken no rekishi*, 58; *Kōfukuji bettō shidai*, 2–3.

84. *Kōfukuji bettō shidai*, 3–7; *Kaitei shinpan konsaisu Nihon jinmei jiten* (Tokyo: Sanshōdō, 1996), s.v. "Shūen."

85. Okano, "Kōfukuji zoku bettō to Kangakuin," 81.

86. Nagashima, *Nara*, 85–86, 105–107, 115–117; Grapard, *Protocol*, 57–61, 76–77.

87. Nagashima, *Nara*, 119–120; Suzuki Motokazu, "Kōfukuji gakuryō, roppō ni tsuite," *Nihon rekishi* 88–89 (1955), 57; Muraoka Motomasa, "Chūsei Kasuga sha no jinnin soshiki," *Ritsumeikan bungaku* 521 (1991), 550–551.

88. Groner, *Saichō*, 271; Shimosaka, "Chūsei daijiin," 155; Murayama, *Hieizan shi*, 71; Inaba Nobumichi, *Chūsei jiin no kenryoku kōzō* (Tokyo: Iwanami shoten, 1997), 191, 200–201. The first *sangō* at Enryakuji were appointed on 824/6/24 (*Tendai zasuki*, 6).

89. Shimosaka, "Chūsei daijiin," 149, 171, note 12; Inaba, 190–191, 202.

90. Toyoda Takeshi, *Nihon shūkyō seido shi no kenkyū*, 81, 92, 97–98; Hori Daiji, "Sōhei no seikatsu," in *Ōtsu-shi shi*, volume 1, 479–480; Hirata, *Sōhei to bushi*, 108–111; Hioki, 55.

91. McMullin, "Sanmon-Jimon Schism," 86–87; Hirabayashi, 119; Kageyama, *Hieizan*, 69, 74, 133.

92. Inaba, 223–224; Nagashima, *Nara*, 133–134; Suzuki Motokazu, 53–54; Hioki, 155.

93. Nagashima, *Nara*, 119, 134; Arai Takashige, *Chūsei akutō no kenkyū* (Tokyo: Yoshikawa kōbunkan, 1990), 90.

94. Wada, 5–7; Miyasaka, 47–49; Kageyama, *Hieizan to Kōyasan*, 223–226. For an extensive study in English of important aspects of such *hijiri*, see Janet R. Goodwin, *Alms and Vagabonds: Buddhist Temples and Popular Patronage in Medieval Japan*.

95. Miyasaka, 48.

96. Kageyama, *Hieizan*, 68, 126–127; Murayama Shūichi, "Heian bukkyō no tenkai: sono ichi," in *Nihon bukkyō shi*, volume 1: *Kodai hen*, edited by Ienaga Saburō (Kyoto: Hōzōkan, 1968), 245; Taira, 468–469. Kageyama suggests that the original area of Hieizanji was not more than four kilometers by four kilometers (*Hieizan*, 68).

97. Taira, *Nihon chūsei no shakai to bukkyō*, 468–469.

98. Kuroda Toshio, "Shōen sei shakai to bukkyō," in *Nihon bukkyō shi*, volume 2: *Chūsei hen*, edited by Akamatsu Toshihide (Kyoto: Hōzōkan, 1967), 393; Murayama, *Hieizan shi*, 238.

99. Miyasaka, 22–23; *Wakayama-ken shi: genshi, kodai*, 31, 673–676, 740; Wada, 3; Katsuno, *Hieizan to Kōyasan*, 216–219.

100. Wada, 29; *Kōya shunjū*, 92; Kageyama, *Hieizan to Kōyasan*, 171; Kuroda, *Jisha seiryoku*, 42.

101. *Wakayama-ken shi: genshi, kodai*, 31–32, 668–670, 741–744; Miyasaka, 23; Hiraoka, *Nihon jiin shi: chūsei*, 108; Toyoda Takeshi, "Kōyasan jiryō no hensen," in Toyoda, ed., *Kōyasan ryō shōen no shihai to kōzō*, 464; Katsuno, *Hieizan to Kōyasan*, 220.

102. Grapard, *Protocol*, 128, 267, note 40, citing Atsuta Kō, "Jisha shōen no arawashi," *Rekishi kōron* 5, 98–105.

103. Hiraoka, *Nihon jiin shi: chūsei*, 108–109; Nagashima, *Nara*, 119; Kamikawa, 31. For an extensive treatment of the association between the main deities of Kasuga and the buddhas of Kōfukuji, see Grapard, *Protocol*, 82–97.

104. Nagashima, *Nara*, 108–109, 121–123; Grapard, *Protocol*, 93–97.

105. Nagashima, *Nara*, 124–127, 152–153; idem, *Nara-ken*, 62; Hiraoka, *Nihon jiin shi no kenkyū: chūsei*, 107–108.

106. Although Kōyasan was also affiliated with shrines and *kami* in the vicinity of Mt. Kōya, they do not appear to have played a crucial role in securing support from the capital elites. While Kasuga and Hiesha were both ranked among the most important shrines for the state, none of Kōyasan's shrines (such as Amanosha) was.

107. Tsuji, *Nihon bukkyō shi: jōsei hen*, 354, 448–449, 452–453; Sonoda 225; Grapard, "Linguistic Cubism," 212–216; Murayama, *Hieizan shi*, 2. The imperial deity alluded to earlier was transformed into Ōhie and the local agricultural deity into Kobie (see Takatori Masao, "Shinbutsu shūgo," in *Ōtsu-shi shi*, volume 1: *Kodai*, 380).

108. Grapard, "Linguistic Cubism," 214–215; Takatori, 379–385.

109. Kuroda Toshio, *Jisha seiryoku*, 52; Toyoda, *Nihon shūkyō seido shi no kenkyū*, 44–47; McMullin, "The Enryaku-ji and the Gion," 168–169; Kuroda, *Jisha seiryoku*, 52.

110. The Tado shrine-temple in Ise, for example, became a Tendai *betsuin* in 839, but this tie was terminated only two years later. Following that break, Tado became a Shingon *betsuin* in 849. The Gion shrine complex became a Tendai *betsuin* in the 970s but was later transformed into a *massha* (McMullin, "The Enryaku-ji and the Gion," 165, 168–169).

111. Toyoda, *Nihon shūkyō seido shi no kenkyū*, 38–39.

112. Toyoda, *Nihon shūkyō seido shi no kenkyū*, 40; McMullin, *Buddhism and the State*, 21. The figure is probably exaggerated, but at the very least it shows that Enryakuji's network of branches was quite extensive at the time.

113. Kuroda Toshio, *Jisha seiryoku*, 31–32. The title of this Tokugawa work is *Kansai hikki* (ibid.). Hirata claims that the term was first used in the *Dainihon shi* (*Heian ridai no kenkyū* [Tokyo: San'ichi shobō, 1943], 145), which is also a Tokugawa work.

114. Kuroda Toshio, *Jisha seiryoku*, 31–32; Hori Daiji, "Sōhei no katsudō," 474–476.

115. Hirata, *Sōhei to bushi*, 157–158.

116. Hioki, 109; Tsuji, *Nihon bukkyō shi: jōsei hen*, 771; Kageyama, 107.

117. Kuroda, *Jisha seiryoku*, 34.

118. McMullin, "Sanmon-Jimon Schism," 91, 93–95.

119. *Shiga-ken shi*, 202; McMullin, "Sanmon-Jimon Schism," 96–97; Murayama, *Hieizan shi*, 135–136; Hioki, 85; *Tendai zasuki*, 46. For an informative account of Hosshōji and its establishment, see Hiraoka, *Nihon jiin shi no kenkyū*, 581–586.

120. Jinzen was the first Tendai head abbot born of the highest-ranking nobles in the capital (Murayama, *Hieizan shi*, 144).

121. *Tendai zasuki*, 46–48; Tsuji, *Nihon bukkyō shi: jōsei hen*, 830.

122. Tsuji, *Nihon bukkyō shi: jōsei hen*, 830–831; Kageyama, *Hieizan*, 122; McMullin, "Sanmon-Jimon Schism," 98–99.

123. Previous scholars seem to have exaggerated the extent of the separation in 993. Indeed, in 1035, Myōson of Onjōji had a residence on Mt. Hiei (*Sakeiki*, volume 6 of *Zōho shiryō taisei* [Kyoto: Rinsen shoten, 1965], Chōgen 8 [1035]/4/4).

124. Onjōji was clearly not a branch temple at this juncture, but it is possible that it was designated a detached cloister of Enryakuji in 866 (see note 66).

125. Tsuji, *Nihon bukkyō shi: jōsei hen*, 833–835; *Tendai zasuki*, 54–56; *Shiga-ken shi: jōdai, chūsei*, 281–283; Murayama, *Hieizan shi*, 147.

126. Hori Daiji, "Sōhei no katsudō," 480–485.

127. Kageyama, *Hieizan*, 123.

128. Miyasaka, 24–25; *Kōya shunjū*, 94–95.

129. Miyasaka, 24–27; *Wakayama-ken no rekishi*, 744; Miyasaka, 33; *Kōya shunjū*, 96–99; Kuroda, *Jisha seiryoku*, 87; Toyoda, 465; *Konsaisu Nihon jinmei jiten*, s.v. "Kakuban."

130. McMullin, "The Enryaku-ji and the Gion Shrine Temple Complex," 171; idem, "The *Lotus Sutra* and Politics," 128.

131. The story is summarized in English by McMullin in "The Enryaku-ji and the Gion Shrine Temple Complex," 161–163.

132. Ibid., 161–163, 167, 169. Hirabayashi dates the takeover of Gion to 974/5/7, when Kan'eiji of the Gion complex became a Tendai *betsuin* (Hirabayashi, 130).

133. *Tendai zasuki*, 46–52, 92–95.

134. *Kōfukuji bettō shidai*, 13–14; Hiraoka, *Ronshū Nihon bukkyō shi: Heian jidai*, 248, 251; Nagashima, *Nara*, 97–98.

135. Murayama, *Hieizan shi*, 156–158; Hirata, *Sōhei to bushi*, 105–107.

136. Paul Groner has perceptively noted this trend in his "Annen, Tankei, Henjō, and Monastic Discipline in the Tendai School: The Background of the *Futsū jubosatsukai kōshaku*," *Japanese Journal of Religious Studies* 14:2–3 (1987), 129.

137. Paul L. Swanson, "Editor's Introduction," *Japanese Journal of Religious Studies* 14:2–3 (1987), 74.

138. This view is held by Hirata Toshiharu, as quoted in Adachi Naoya, "Hōshinnō no seijiteki igi," in *Shōen sei shakai to mibun kōzō*, edited by Takeuchi Rizō (Tokyo: Azekura shobō, 1980), 174, and by Nagashima (*Nara*, 97). See also McMullin, *Buddhism and the State* (20–21), which cites Tamamura Taijō, "Heian chō matsu jiin no shakai shiteki kōsatsu," *Shigaku zasshi* 42 (1932), 58–59.

139. Murayama, "Heian bukkyō no tenkai," 245.

140. Adachi, 180, 192; Taira, 96–97, 471.

141. Adachi, 175–176. For further discussion of the *hōshinnō*, see Chapter 3.

142. *Kōya shunjū*, 92–93; Katsuno, *Hieizan to Kōyasan*, 221.

143. The case was also the same with Tōdaiji (Piggott, "Hierarchy and Economics in Early Medieval Tōdaiji," 60).

144. Kuroda, *Jisha seiryoku*, 133.

145. Kageyama, *Hieizan*, 163–164.

146. Murayama, *Hieizan shi*, 246; Kageyama, *Hieizan*, 165. The son of the forceful Fujiwara no Tadamichi, Jien entered that cloister in 1165 and was appointed Tendai *zasu* in 1192. He was dismissed four years later at the same time that his older brother Kujō Kanezane lost favor in the capital. Jien's appointment as head abbot three additional times (in 1201, 1212, and 1213) indicates how important political considerations were in *zasu* appointments. It is also indicative of the uncertain conditions that influenced Jien to write his famous work. See Delmer Brown and Ichirō Ishida, *The Future and the Past: A Translation and Study of the Gukanshō, an Interpretative History of Japan Written in 1219* (Berkeley: University of California Press, 1979), 236–237, 408; Itō Toshikazu, "Shōren'in monzeki no keisei to bō mandokoro," *Komonjo kenkyū* 35 (1990), 11–12.

147. Adachi, 182; Hisano Nagayoshi, "Sanmon-jimon no sōkoku," in *Ōtsu-shi shi*, volume 2: *Chūsei*, 93–95; Kageyama, 163–167; Itō Toshikazu, 18, 24; Kuroda Toshio, "Chūsei jisha seiryoku ron," 263; Murayama, "Heian bukkyō no tenkai," 247.

148. *Kōfukuji bettō shidai*, 13–14; Hiraoka, *Ronshū Nihon bukkyō shi: Heian jidai*, 248, 251; Nagashima, *Nara*, 97–98.

149. Kuroda, *Jisha seiryoku*, 129; Nagashima, *Nara*, 96–98; idem, *Nara-ken*, 72; Hiraoka, *Ronshū Nihon bukkyō shi: Heian jidai*, 270; Grapard, *Protocol*, 107–109.

150. Adachi, 190; Hisano, 119.

151. Adachi, 188; Itō Toshikazu, 12–14.

152. Grapard, *Protocol*, 131; Nagashima, *Nara*, 154–156.

Chapter 3   Capital Politics and Religious Disturbances in the Shirakawa Era (1072–1129)

1. My account of the political development during this period is based on Cameron Hurst's *Insei: Abdicated Sovereigns in the Politics of Late Heian Japan, 1086–1185* (New York: Columbia University Press, 1976), and "The Development of the *Insei*: A Problem in Japanese History and Historiography," in *Medieval Japan: Essays in Institutional History*, edited by John W. Hall and Jeffrey P. Mass (Stanford: Stanford University Press, 1974), unless otherwise indicated. These accounts still stand out as the best studies in English of the political developments in the late Heian period.

2. There were no specific rules stating which of the male heirs should be designated crown prince, even though the son of the highest-ranking consort as well as the firstborn son were prime candidates. These customs invited ambitious siblings to compete for the throne, allowing for factionalism to become a key feature of the imperial court throughout much of the premodern era.

3. William McCullough's "Japanese Marriage Institutions in the Heian Period," *Harvard Journal of Asiatic Studies* 27 (1967), 103–167, remains the standard account on this topic.

4. Hurst, *Insei*, 103–106. See also the imperial genealogy in Figure 5.

5. Ibid., 110. The full name of the *kirokujo* was *kiroku shōen kenkeisho,* meaning Office for Investigation of Estate Documents.

6. Hurst, *Insei,* 117.

7. Suga Shinjō, "Hokkyō san'e no seiritsu," *Shigaku kenkyū* 206 (1994), 1–6; Yamashita, *Insei* (Tokyo: Kindai bungeisha, 1995), 34.

8. Motoki Yasuo, *Insei ki seiji shi kenkyū* (Kyoto: Shibunkaku shuppan, 1996), 100.

9. Hurst, *Insei,* 144–145.

10. Gomi Fumihiko, *Insei ki shakai no kenkyū* (Tokyo: Yamakawa shuppansha, 1984), 43; Sakaki Michio, *Insei jidai shi ronshū* (Tokyo: Zoku gunsho ruijū kansei-kai, 1993), 376. Tadazane broke with Shirakawa in 1122, when he refused to give one of his daughters as a consort to Emperor Toba, Shirakawa's grandson.

11. Motoki, *Insei ki seiji shi kenkyū,* 104; Yamashita Takashi, *Insei* (Tokyo: Kindai bungeisha, 1995), 41; Yasuda Motohisa, *Nihon rekishi,* volume 7: *Insei to heishi* (Tokyo: Shogakkan, 1974), 51; Hurst, *Insei,* 148; Hashimoto Yoshihiko, "Kizoku seiken no seiji kōzō," in *Iwanami kōza, Nihon rekishi* volume 4: *Kodai* (Tokyo: Iwanami shoten, 1976), 14–15.

12. Hurst, *Insei,* 128, 146; idem, "The Development of *Insei,*" 71.

13. Gomi, *Insei ki shakai no kenkyū,* 140, 164–165.

14. Ibid., 139, 141, 164–165. The provincial proprietors were yet another expression of the privatization process of government that had been under way since the eleventh century. Tadazane was, for example, the proprietor of Owari and Tango in 1113, but the governorships were held by Minamoto no Morotoshi (ibid., 138–141).

15. Among Japanese scholars, Satō Hiroo has expressed this view most lucidly. See, for example, his *Nihon chūsei kokka to bukkyō* (Tokyo: Yoshikawa kōbunkan, 1987), 139.

16. *Tendai zasuki,* 68–70; Nezu Masashi, *Tennō ke no rekishi* (Tokyo: San'ichi shobō, 1973), volume 1, 258–259. For an analysis of these privileges, see David Moerman, "The Ideology of Landscape and the Theater of State: Insei Pilgrimage to Kumano (1090–1220)," *Japanese Journal of Religious Studies* 24:3–4 (1997), 347–374.

17. Tsuji, *Nihon bukkyō shi: jōsei hen,* 727; Hiraoka, *Nihon jiin shi no kenkyū,* 388; Inoue Mitsusada, *Nihon jōdōkyō no seiritsu no kenkyū* (Tokyo: Yamakawa shuppan-sha, 1956), 268.

18. Motoki Yasuo, "Insei ki Kōfukuji kō," *Otemae joshi daigaku ronshū* 21 (1987), 182–183; Uejima, 36, 48. Tendai monks occasionally led the Yuima'e and the other Sandai'e in the ninth and early tenth centuries, but this custom ended with Keiun, who led the Yuima'e in 990 (*San'e jōikki,* in *Dainihon bukkyō zensho: Kōfukuji sōsho,* part 1 [Tokyo: Bussho kan kōkai, 1931], 300).

19. Suga, 2–6; *Tendai zasuki,* 60–61; Uejima, 48–49.

20. Suga, 11–13; Motoki Yasuo, "Insei ki seiji shi no kōzō to tenkai," *Nihon shi kenkyū* 283 (1986), 59–60. Though their pronunciation is identical, Shirakawa's Hosshōji (Temple for the Victory of the Law) is different from the Hosshōji (Temple of the Nature of the Law) that was constructed by Fujiwara no Tadahira in 925.

21. Suga, 8–9; Nezu, 258; Hurst, *Insei,* 263–265; Hiraoka, *Nihon jiin shi no kenkyū,* 607–610; Hayashiya Tatsusaburō, *Koten bunka no sōzō* (Tokyo: Tōkyō daigaku

shuppankai, 1964), 164–166, 168, 170; Nishiguchi Junko, "Shirakawa goganji shōron," in *Ronshū Nihon bukkyō shi,* volume 3: *Heian jidai,* edited by Hiraoka Jōkai (Tokyo: Takayama kaku shuppan, 1986), 240–241; *Tendai zasuki,* 55–56; Hiraoka, *Nihon jiin shi no kenkyū,* 607–611; Motoki, *Insei ki seiji shi kenkyū,* 101.

22. *Suisaki,* volume 8 of *Zōho shiryō taisei* (Kyoto, Rinsen shoten, 1965), Shōryaku 1 (1077)/12/18; *Tendai zasuki,* 67 (Eihō 3 [1083]/10/1); Hayashiya, 169; Taira, *Nihon chūsei no shakai to bukkyō,* 124–125; Suga, 16; Nishiguchi, 242. By Go-Shirakawa's era, these imperial temples were often referred to as Rikushōji (or Rokushōji), "the Six Temples of Victory," after the pronunciation of the Chinese character for "victory" (*shō*). The temples included Hosshōji (built by Shirakawa), Sonshōji (built during Horikawa's reign but generally attributed to Shirakawa), Saishōji (Toba), Enshōji (Taikenmon'in), Jōshōji (Sutoku), and Enshōji (Konoe).

23. Hiraoka, *Nihon jiin shi no kenkyū,* 626–631; Taira, *Nihon chūsei no shakai to bukkyō,* 471; Hayashiya, 167; Nishiguchi, 247–251.

24. Nishiguchi, "Shirakawa goganji shōron," 242, 251; Hioki, *Sōhei,* 105; Suga, 9.

25. Three *hōshinnō* were appointed during Shirakawa's era, three by Toba, and six during the *insei* of Go-Shirakawa. In addition to extending the imperial family's control over certain temples and religious ceremonies, the princely abbots also became an alternative to giving surnames to superfluous princes, which was becoming increasingly expensive (Hirata, *Sōhei to bushi,* 81, 89–90).

26. *Honchō seiki,* volume 9 of *Shintei zōho kokushi taikei* (Tokyo: Yoshikawa kōbunkan, 1935), Kōwa 1 (1099)/1/3 (p. 297); Adachi, 175–176; Hirata, *Sōhei to bushi,* 87; Hiraoka, *Nihon jiin shi no kenkyū,* 634–635.

27. Sakaki, 244; Murayama, *Hieizan shi,* 157–158.

28. Adachi, 178–179; Taira, *Nihon chūsei no shakai to bukkyō,* 471; Sakaki, 214.

29. Motoki Yasuo correctly notes that there were no Kōfukuji demonstrations in the capital over monk appointments before Shirakawa, indicating that the subsequent increase in violence and frequency of temple protests were caused by Shirakawa's attempt to gain control of the religious hierarchy at the expense of the Fujiwara ("Insei ki Kōfukuji kō," 180–184). Unfortunately, he does not explain why Enryakuji also became involved in more protests or why there were marked increases in demonstrations during the rulership of other ambitious retired emperors as well.

30. *Suisaki,* Eihō 1 (1081)/6/9. Hirata sees in this incident the first evidence in court diaries of "evil monks" (*akusō*), i.e., armed monks ("Nanto hokurei no akusō ni tsuite," 267–269).

31. The *honjo hō*—the law of *shōen* proprietors—was loosely based on customs and precedent, allowing for aggressive proprietors and estate managers to impose arbitrary taxes at any time. Such urges were, however, counterbalanced by the farmers themselves, who could leave their fields in protest against unreasonable taxation. In the end, it was in the proprietor's own interest to achieve a workable tax rate lest the farmers abscond, leaving him with no revenues at all.

32. *Suisaki,* Eihō 1/8/18; *Fusō ryakki,* volume 12 of *Shintei zōho kokushi taikei* (Tokyo: Yoshikawa kōbunkan, 1965), Eihō 1/4/15 (p. 322).

33. The edict was an imperial directive (*senji*), but Minamoto no Toshifusa, the Minister of the Left, indicates in his diary that the decision was made by the high-ranking members of the imperial court without much participation by Emperor Shirakawa (*Suisaiki,* Eihō 1/8/18).

34. *Suisaki,* Eihō 1/8/1, 18; *Hyakurenshō,* volume 11 of *Shintei zōho kokushi taikei*

(Tokyo: Yoshikawa kōbunkan, 1965), Eihō 1/6/9, 17; *Fusō ryakki,* Eihō 1/6 (p. 322); *Tendai zasuki,* 64–65.

35. *Suisaki,* Eihō 1/8/20; *Fusō ryakki,* Eihō 1/8/20. Claiming ignorance of incidents or of the whereabouts of criminals was a common strategy among temples to protect the members of their communities. In theory, the judicial immunity of temples and shrines was not unconditional, since criminals could expect to be extradited. However, in practice, the court and its warriors could do little if the religious centers did not cooperate. For all intents and purposes, Enryakuji thus enjoyed complete immunity for its members.

36. *Suisaki,* Eihō 1/9/14, 16, 17, 20, 10/4; *Hyakurenshō,* Eihō 1/9/14, 15; *Fusō ryakki,* Eihō 1/9 (pp. 323–324); *Tendai zasuki,* 65; *Tamefusa kyōki,* Eihō 1/10/1, *Shishū* (Komazawa daigakuin shigakkai kodai shi bukai) 10 (1979), 102; Hirata, "Nanto hokurei no sōhei ni tsuite," 268–269.

37. *Chūyūki,* volumes 9–14 of *Zōho shiryō taisei* (Kyoto: Rinsen shoten, 1965), Hōan 1 (1120)/4/28, 29, 5/4; *Hyakurenshō,* Hōan 1/4/29.

38. Claiming a lack of original documents while soliciting the support of Enryakuji, local monks and warriors, including a former governor of Izu (Minamoto no Kunifusa) and his son, Mitsukuni—both opportunistic warriors of local stature —challenged Tōji's control of Tado on several occasions from 1075 to 1107 (see *Heian ibun,* edited by Takeuchi Rizō [Tokyo: Tōkyō shuppan, 1963–1974], volume 3, document 1115, Shōhō 2 [1075]/5/12; document 1128, Shōhō 3 [1076]/3/ 23; document 1131, Shōhō 3/5/25; volume 4, document 1646, Chōji 2 [1105]/ 7/14; *Tōji monjo,* in *DNS* 3:8, 280–281; *Heian ibun* 4, documents 1663, Kajō 1 [1106]/8/14; and 1681, Kajō 2 [1107]/12/28; *DNS* 3:9, 737–738; *Heian ibun* 5, documents 1881–1882, Eikyū 5 [1117]/12/23; *Sonpi bunmyō* [Tokyo: Yoshikawa kōbunkan, 1962], volume 3, 141).

39. Tsuji, *Nihon bukkyō shi: jōsei hen,* 852.

40. *Sochiki,* volume 5 of *Zōho shiryō taisei* (Kyoto: Rinsen shoten, 1965), Shōryaku 5 (1081)/3/9; *Suisaki,* same date; *Kōfukuji ryaku nendaiki,* Eihō 1/3 (p. 141); *Hyakurenshō,* Eihō 1/3/6; Hioki, 93.

41. *Sochiki,* Shōryaku 5/3/9, 13, 15, 16, 25, 26, 12/4; *Suisaki,* Shōryaku 5/3/ 9, 12/5; *Kōfukuji ryaku nendaiki,* Eihō 1/3 (p. 141).

42. *Denryaku,* in volume 4 of *Dainihon kokiroku,* parts 1–4 (Tokyo: Iwanami shoten, 1956), Tennin 1 (1108)/9/12, 13, 14, 15; *Chūyūki,* Tennin 1/9/11, 14: *DNS* 3:10, 302, 304; *Kōfukuji ryaku nendaiki,* Tennin 1/9/12 (p. 143); *Hyakurenshō,* same date.

43. *Chūyūki,* Tennin 1/9/11, 16; *Denryaku,* Tennin 1/9/14, 17; *DNS* 3:10, 304–305.

44. *Chūyūki,* Tennin 1/9/2, 18, 19; *Kōfukuji bettō shidai,* 11; *Denryaku,* Tennin 1/9/20; *DNS* 3:10, 303, 305–307.

45. *Chūyūki,* Tennin 1/9/24, 26, 29; *Denryaku,* Tennin 1/9/24, 29; *DNS* 3:10, 307.

46. *Chūyūki,* Tennin 1/9/29; *DNS* 3:10, 307–308.

47. *Chūyūki,* Tennin 1/10/4, 5, 6; *Eishōki,* Ten'ei 1 (1110)/6/21; *DNS* 3:10, 308, 922–926.

48. *Denryaku,* Ten'ei 1/8/16; *DNS* 3:11, 9.

49. The travel time to Kōyasan for an imperial pilgrimage is noted in the *Kōya shunjū,* Kanji 2 (1088)/2/26 (pp. 78–79).

50. *Wakayama-ken shi: genshi, kodai,* 677–678; Miyasaka, 21–23; *Wakayama-ken*

shi: kodai shiryō, volume 1, compiled by Wakayama-ken shi hensan kakari inkai (Osaka: Dainihon insatsu kabushiki gaisha, 1981), "Heian jidai 1," document 224, *Daijō kanpu,* Kankō 1 (1004)/9/25 (pp. 474–476).

51. *Wakayama-ken shi: genshi, kodai,* 678; Egashira Tsuneharu, *Kōyasan ryō shōen no kenkyū* (Tokyo: Nihon keizai shi kenkyū sho, 1938), 31–37; *Wakayama-ken shi: kodai shiryō* 1, "Heian jidai 2," document 407, *Kanshōfu no shō jūninra gesu,* Tenji 2 (1125)/7/13 (pp. 897–899); document 436 (pp. 920–921), *Kanshōfu no shō jūninra ureijō,* Daiji 4 (1129)/1/29; *Kōyasan monjo* 7, documents 1628, 1629 (pp. 266–273).

52. Hioki, 109–110.

53. *Go-Nijō Moromichi ki,* in volume 5 of *Dainihon kokiroku* (Tokyo: Iwanami shoten, 1956), Kanji 6 (1092)/9/18; *Chūyūki,* 9/18, 29; *DNS* 3:2, 665, 667, 669.

54. *Go-Nijō Moromichi ki,* Kanji 6/9/22, 23, 28; *Chūyūki,* Kanji 6/9/20, 28; *Tendai zasuki,* 70; *DNS* 3:2, 667–670.

55. *Fusō ryakki,* Kanji 7 (1093)/6/27, *Kugyō bunin:* both in *DNS* 3:2, 959, 962; *Chūyūki,* Kahō 1 (1094)/3/5; *DNS* 3:3, 259.

56. *Chūyūki,* Kahō 2 (1095)/10/23, 24, 25, 11/1; *DNS* 3:3, 930–932; *Tendai zasuki,* 71; Tsuji, *Nihon bukkyō shi: jōsei hen,* 793; Hirata, "Nanto hokurei no akusō ni tsuite," 275.

57. *Chūyūki,* Kahō 2/10/23; *DNS* 3:3, 931; *Heike monogatari,* in *DNS* 3:3, 933, 938; *Genpei seisuiki,* in *DNS* 3:3, 944. See also Helen McCullough, *The Tale of the Heike,* 50.

58. *Genpei seisuiki* (Tokyo: Miyai shoten, 1994), volume 1, 125–126; *DNS* 3:3, 944–945; McCullough, *Tale of the Heike,* 51–52. The curse is described in some detail in Chapter 6.

59. *Ichidai yōki,* volume 1 of *Kaitei sekishū shūran* (Tokyo: Kondō kappansho, 1900), Hōan 4 (1123)/7/18, 23 (p. 216); *Tendai zasuki,* 80.

60. *Go-Nijō Moromichi ki,* Kanji 7 (1093)/8/6; *Fusō ryakki,* Kanji 7/8/22; *DNS* 3:2, 986, 988.

61. *Go-Nijō Moromichi ki,* Kanji 7/8/25, 26, 27, 28; *Hyakurenshō,* Kanji 7/8; *Fusō ryakki,* Kanji 7/8/26, 27; *DNS* 3:2, 987, 990–991; *Kōfukuji ryaku nendaiki,* Kanji 7/8/28 (p. 142). The *Hyakurenshō* states that the monks carried with them the holy *sakaki* tree at this juncture (Kanji 7/8/26; *DNS* 3:2, 987), though it is not mentioned in any of the other sources.

62. *Fusō ryakki,* Kanji 7/8/27; *DNS* 3:2, 987. Tameie was reappointed on Kahō 1 (1094)/6/5.

63. Hurst, *Insei,* 126; Yamashita, 45, quoting from Ōe no Masafusa's diary, *Gōki.*

64. *Chūyūki,* Hōan 1 (1120)/8/16, 21, 22, 23; *Kōfukuji ryaku nendaiki,* Hōan 1/8/22 (p. 145); *Hyakurenshō,* Hōan 1/8/23 (p. 52). The governor was a certain Fujiwara no Masataka, a minor member of the Fujiwara clan.

65. *Chūyūki,* Kōwa 4 (1102)/7/10, 8/1, 2, 6, 7, 8; *Denryaku,* Kōwa 4/7/29; *Kōfukuji ryaku nendaiki,* Kōwa 4 (pp. 142–143); *DNS* 3:6, 457–459; Motoki, "Insei ki Kōfukuji kō," 184; idem, *Insei ki seiji shi kenkyū,* 251–252.

66. Motoki, *Insei ki seiji shi kenkyū,* 252–253; Nishiguchi, "Shirakawa goganji shōron," 248, 251, 257, note 30; *Kōfukuji bettō shidai,* 11.

67. *Chūyūki,* Kōwa 4/8/6, 8; *Denryaku,* Kōwa 4/8/6, 7, 8; *DNS* 3:6, 517–518; Motoki, "Insei ki Kōfukuji kō," 184. Jōshin held the rank of *jōza* (a senior lecturer who oversaw the education of younger monks).

68. *Chūyūki*, Kōwa 4/8/8, 12; *DNS* 3:6, 518–519.

69. *Chūyūki*, Kōwa 4/8/15, 18, 21, 23, 26; *Denryaku*, 8/18, 21, 29; *DNS* 3:6, 519, 543–544.

70. *Chūyūki*, Kōwa 4/9/4, 5, 28, 29, 10/9, 17; *Denryaku*, 9/28, 10/9; *DNS* 3:6, 556–558, 584–586, 601–605.

71. *Chūyūki*, Kōwa 5 (1103)/3/25, 29, 4/1, 5/10, 12, 16; *Honchō seiki*, Kōwa 2/3/26, 4/1; *Hyakurenshō*, Kōwa 5/3/26; *Ichidai yōki*, same date; *Denryaku*, Kōwa 5/5/9, 12, 16, 7/6–7; *DNS* 3:6, 941–943; *DNS* 3:7, 4–6; *Kōfukuji ryaku nendaiki*, 142–143.

72. This lecture meeting was one of the imperially sponsored "Lecture Meetings of the Northern Capital" (Hokkyō no san'e), and it was thus considered an important appointment that reflected the status of the monk as well as of the temple.

73. *Chūyūki*, Chōji 2/1/1–2; *Eishōki*, Chōji 2/1/1–2; *DNS* 3:7, 899–900.

74. *Chūyūki*, Tennin 1/3/20, 23; *DNS* 3:10, 112–113.

75. *Chūyūki*, Tennin 1/3/23; *DNS* 3:10, 114.

76. *Chūyūki*, Tennin 1/3/30, 4/1; *DNS* 3:10, 123–124.

77. *Chūyūki*, Tennin 1/4/2; *DNS* 3:10, 124. This promise was, however, broken by Shirakawa in 1112, when Enryakuji complained over renewed favoritism of Tōji monks (*Denryaku*, Ten'ei 3/3/13, 21; *Chūyūki*, same date; *DNS* 3:13, 9–10).

78. *Chūyūki*, Tennin 1/4/2; *DNS* 3:10, 124.

79. *Hyakurenshō*, *Chūyūki*, Kanji 5 (1091)/2/17, Kōwa 5 (1103)/11/25; *Honchō seiki*, Kōwa 5/11/25; *Kōya shunjū*, 85; *DNS* 3:2, 129–133; *DNS* 3:7, 276–282; Tsuji, *Nihon bukkyō shi*, 733.

80. Tsuji, *Nihon bukkyō shi*, 745; Nishiguchi, 252, 258.

81. Iwashimizu Hachimangū was founded by the monk Gyōkyō in the ninth century. He enshrined the Hachiman deity from the Usa shrine in Kyushu, and the complex became one of the top-ranking shrines in the Heian age, commanding considerable landed wealth. Although the founder was a Shingon monk and there were connections with other temples, Iwashimizu remained unattached throughout the premodern era.

82. *Dazaifu chō*, Chōji 2 (1105)/1, in *DNS* 3:7, 992–993.

83. *Chūyūki*, Kahō 1 (1094)/int. 3/8. Unfortunately, no other contemporary sources note this incident, but it may be related to the resignation of Ryōshin in the eighth month of 1093. Ryōshin served as the Tendai leader for twelve years but was forced to resign after an attack on his residence by his own clergy, which drove him away from Mt. Hiei (*Tendai zasuki* 67–70). Perhaps the Daisenji monks opposed this act or perhaps they simply disapproved of the new head abbot Ninkaku. The records do not provide any further information on this issue, but the Daisenji appeal in the capital was apparently considered important enough to be represented in one of very few pictorial representations of monk demonstrations in the late fourteenth century. For a more extensive analysis of this illustration, see Chapter 6 and Figure 20.

84. *Chūyūki*, Chōji 2/6/2; *Hyakurenshō*, same date; *DNS* 3:8, 149; Murayama, *Hieizan shi*, 167.

85. *Tendai zasuki*, 72–73; *Chūyūki*, Chōji 2 (1105)/10/30; *DNS* 3:8, 272; Murayama, *Hieizan shi*, 167. It is conceivable that Shirakawa made the appointment knowing that Keichō, for reasons that cannot be determined from historical sources, would not protest.

86. *Chūyūki*, Chōji 1 (1104)/10/7, 29.

87. *Chūyūki*, Chōji 1/10/14; *Sanjū gobun shū*, in *DNS* 3:7, Chōji 2 (1105)/1 (pp. 992–993); *Chūyūki*, Chōji 2/10/30; *DNS* 3:8, 272–273; Murayama, *Hieizan shi*, 167.

88. *Chūyūki*, Chōji 2/5/4, 8, 6/14, 8/30; *Denryaku*, Chōji 2/6/14, 8/30; *DNS* 3:8, 128–129, 154, 226–227.

89. *Chūyūki*, Chōji 2/10/10, 12, 16, 25, 28, 30; *Denryaku*, Chōji 2/10/22, 23, 24; *DNS* 3:8, 255–256, 259, 270–272.

90. *Chūyūki*, Chōji 2 (1105)/11/1, 4, 12/21, 26, 29; *DNS* 3:8, 260, 274–776, 331, 352–353.

91. Sakaki, 51, 216; Gomi, *Insei ki shakai no kenkyū*, 378–379. The Kawada estate is mentioned in *Taikenmon'in chō kudashibumi*, Chōshō 3 (1134)/int. 12/15, published in *Heian ibun* 5, document 2310 (p. 1956). Kawada-no-shō and Lady Mino also appear in a document (a lawsuit) of 1184, which has been translated by Jeffrey Mass (*The Kamakura Bakufu: A Study in Documents* [Stanford: Stanford University Press, 1976], document 7, pp. 32–34).

92. See *Chūyūki*, Chōji 2/10/30; *DNS* 3:8, 272–273.

93. *Kanetaka ki*, Eikyū 1 (1113)/int. 3/20, 21, cited in *Eikyū gannenki*, in *DNS* 3:14, 139–140.

94. *Denryaku, Chōshūki, Eikyū gannenki*, Eikyū 1/int. 3/20, 21, 22, all in *DNS* 3:14, 137–140.

95. *Denryaku*, Eikyū 1 (1113)/int. 3/29, 4/1; *Chūyūki*, Eikyū 1/4/1; *Tendai zasuki*, 77–78; *DNS* 3:14, 145–147.

96. *Chūyūki*, Eikyū 1/4/1, 6; *Chōshūki*, Eikyū 1/4/9; *DNS* 3:14, 145–146, 152–153.

97. *Denryaku, Chūyūki*, Eikyū 1/4/13–18; *DNS* 3:14, 160–163.

98. Gomi makes the interesting observation that Shirakawa broke the normal chain of command in dispatching these government warriors. The retired emperor indeed bypassed the chief of staff of the imperial police even though the forces were headed by captains of that police force (Gomi, *Insei ki shakai no kenkyū*, 23; *Chūyūki*, Eikyū 1/4/30; *DNS* 3:14, 180). This point further attests to Shirakawa's direct control of the court, including its warriors, in the post-Kōwa era.

99. *Chūyūki*, Eikyū 1/4/30, 5/4; *Kōfukuji ryaku nendaiki*, Eikyū 1/4/29; *Hyakurenshō*, same date (p. 49); Nagashima, *Nara*, 132; *DNS* 3:14, 179–180, 182–183. This episode as well as the general development of the whole incident are briefly described in Wayne Farris' *Heavenly Warriors: The Evolution of Japan's Military, 500–1300* (Cambridge, Mass.: Harvard University Press, 1992), 261–263. Unfortunately, Farris has neglected to place what he calls "religious riots" in context, merely claiming that they were "part of a general trend towards domestic violence in late Heian Japan, and . . . a by-product of economic decline" (p. 261). It is unclear to me what "economic decline" Farris is referring to, since the period is characterized by commercial expansion and rising agricultural productivity. Moreover, Farris seems to assume that all religious protests were designed to be violent and that they had little connection with decisions made at the imperial court. As shown in this chapter, not only were the two closely connected, it was factionalism at the imperial court and attempts to shift the balance among the established sects that caused the most violent religious incidents.

100. *Chūyūki*, Eikyū 1/4/30; *DNS* 3:14, 180. Munetada refers to the famous uprising of 939 in which Taira Masakado attempted to create an imperium of his own in the east after a disappointing career in Kyoto.

101. *Chūyūki*, Eikyū 1/4/30; *Tendai zasuki, Kōfukuji ryaku nendaiki*, in *DNS* 3:14, 179–180, 185.

102. *Chūyūki*, Eikyū 2 (1114)/5/29, 10/26; Motoki, "Insei ki Kōfukuji kō," 185; Kamikawa, 41–43.

103. *Denryaku*, Eikyū 4 (1116)/10/11; *San'e jōikki*, 22–23; Motoki, "Insei ki Kōfukuji kō," 185–186; Kamikawa, 41–43.

104. *Denryaku*, Ten'ei 1 (1110)/8/3, 9/5; Motoki, "Insei ki Kōfukuji kō," 187; idem, *Insei ki seiji shi kenkyū*, 255. Fujiwara no Akiyoshi (the grandson of Tamefusa) harassed Kōfukuji servants in Sanuki Province, where Akiyoshi served as governor, in a dispute over land (*Kasuga kannushi Kanetaka ki*, Eikyū 4 [1116]/5; *Denryaku*, Eikyū 4/7/13–14, 23–24, 26–28, 8/3, 13, 15).

105. *Denryaku*, Kōwa 4 (1102)/5/7, *Chūyūki*, 5/9; *DNS* 3:6, 352–354.

106. For a comprehensive description of the construction of Hōjōji and the ensuing competition for its abbotship between Enryakuji and Onjōji, see Hiraoka, *Nihon jiin shi no kenkyū*, 586–600.

107. *Chūyūki*, Kōwa 4/int. 5/22, 6/27; *DNS* 3:6, 396, 418; *Denryaku, Chūyūki*, Kōwa 4/7/3; *DNS* 3:6, 433–434.

108. The pledge is not extant, but according to contemporary diaries, it contained ten clauses all of which stated the monks' promise to stop their evil deeds (*Denryaku, Chūyūki, Eishōki, Chōshūki*, Ten'ei 2 [1111]/12/25; *DNS* 3:12, 106–108).

109. *Chūyūki*, Kajō 1 (1106)/2/23, 25, 29, 3/16; *Denryaku*, Kajō 1/2/23, 29; *DNS* 3:7, 530–531.

110. *Chūyūki*, Kajō 1/3/29.

111. *Genpei seisuiki*, volume 1, 123–124; McCullough, *Tale of the Heike*, 50.

Chapter 4 Temples as Allies or Divine Enemies during the Tumultuous Years of Go-Shirakawa (1155–1192)

1. Hurst, *Insei*, 156–157, 166.

2. The discord was ostensibly caused by Tadazane, who, contrary to an earlier agreement, refused to give his daughter Taishi as consort to Emperor Toba. However, there seems to have been more to this estrangement, since Taishi in fact became Toba's consort and was made empress in 1134, after Shirakawa's death (Hurst, *Insei*, 155, 160).

3. Motoki, "Insei ki Kōfukuji kō," 190–191; idem, *Insei ki seiji shi kenkyū*, 260–261. Shinjitsu is one of the most fascinating monks to head armed forces in Japan's history. He was of Minamoto descent and was active at Kōfukuji for over three decades before the Hōgen Disturbance of 1156. See, for example, Hirata, "Nanto hokurei no akusō ni tsuite," 282–286.

4. Hurst, *Insei*, 168–169; Motoki, "Insei ki seiji shi no kōzō to tenkai," 65; *Hyakurenshō*, Ninpyō 1 (1151)/1/10 (p. 69); *Kugyō bunin*, part 1, *Shintei zōho kokushi taihei*, volume 13 (Tokyo: Yoshikawa kōbunkan, 1937), 429. Toba may have elevated Yorinaga not only to challenge Tadamichi, but also in order to weaken the Fujiwara regency in general, by making the brothers almost equal in ranking (Motoki, "Insei ki seiji shi no kōzō to tenkai," 65).

5. Hurst, *Insei*, 160–162, 166, 168–169, 175; Motoki, *Insei ki seiji shi kenkyū*, 282.

6. Motoki, *Insei ki seiji shi kenkyū*, 129–132. Shinzei was the son of Fujiwara no Sanekane but had been adopted by Takashina Tsunetoshi, a member of the provincial governor class (*zuryō*). It is possible that Shinzei's comparatively low status was the very reason for his success; low-ranking retainers had a tendency to be

more loyal to their masters. Go-Shirakawa promoted Taira no Kiyomori, whose lineage also belonged to the large middle stratum of courtiers, in a similar fashion.

7. Hurst, *Insei*, 187–190; Motoki, *Insei ki seiji shi kenkyū*, 135–149; Mass, *Warrior Government in Early Medieval Japan*, 18.

8. Mass, *Warrior Government*, 20–21.

9. Ibid., 26–27; Mass, "The Kamakura Bakufu," 53.

10. Mass, *Warrior Government*, 72–73.

11. Mass, *Warrior Government*, 125, 127; idem, "The Kamakura Bakufu," 47, 57; Hurst, "The Kōbu Polity: Court-Bakufu Relations in Kamakura Japan," 8–9.

12. See, for example, Sansom, *A History of Japan to 1334*, 331.

13. See *Gyokuyō*, 3 volumes (Tokyo: Meicho kankōkai, 1993), Angen 2 (1176)/ 4/27; *Kitsuki*, volumes 29–30 of *Zōho shiryō taisei* (Kyoto: Rinsen shoten, 1965), same date; *Tendai zasuki*, 105; Nagahara Keiji, ed., *Tennō kenryoku no kōzō to tenkai: sono ichi* (Tokyo: Shimizu shoten, 1992), 147–161; David Moerman, "The Ideology of Landscape and the Theater of State," 349. Go-Shirakawa was also ordained at Tōdaiji on 1176/4/20 (*Tendai zasuki*, 105).

14. Janet Goodwin, "The Buddhist Monarch: Go-Shirakawa and the Rebuilding of Tōdai-ji," *Japanese Journal of Religious Studies* 17:2–3, 219–242.

15. The imperial edict *(senji)* itself is not extant, but the document is cited in *Heihanki*, in volume 19 of *Zōho shiryō taisei* (Kyoto: Rinsen shoten, sixth edition, 1992), Hōgen 1 (1156)/int. 9/18. A nearly identical edict, containing five articles, was issued by the imperial government on 1157/3/17 (*Heian ibun*, volume 6, *Daijō kanpu an*, document 2876). See also Gomi, *Insei ki shakai no kenkyū*, 26–29, 287; Hirata, *Sōhei to bushi*, 192–194; Tanaka Fumihide, *Heishi seiken no kenkyū* (Kyoto: Shibunkaku shuppan, 1994), 166–169. The juxtaposition of shrine service people with evil monks appears illogical, but the terms themselves do not imply that they were criminals. Rather, the term *"akusō,"* which frequently appears in contemporary sources, reflects the court's view of monks who were exceedingly occupied with secular issues, including warfare. The *jinnin* were secular followers who frequently joined the clergy in demonstrations and other activities that could benefit them. It is also interesting to note that the edict mentions specific institutions for each group; the unruly *jinnin* were mainly from Ise, Iwashimizu Hachimangū, Kamo, Kasuga, Sumiyoshi, Hie, and Gion, whereas the "evil monks" belonged to Kōfukuji, Enryakuji, Onjōji, Kumano, and Yamato's Kinpusen (*Heihanki*, Hōgen 1/int. 9/18).

16. See appendixes 1 and 2, and Hioki, "Nihon sōhei shi nenpyō," 8–9, in the appendix of *Nihon sōhei kenkyū*. Several violent conflicts involving religious complexes during the 1145–1150 era were caused by neighboring land claims between Enryakuji and Onjōji, and between Kōfukuji and Kinpusen. In the capital itself, only two incidents stand out during this era. The first one occurred in the sixth month of 1146, when followers of Taira no Tadamori became involved in a brawl with service people of the Gion shrine during one of its festivals. Tadamori sent his son, Kiyomori, whose warriors attacked the Gion people with their bows and arrows. As a result, it was reported that thousands of monks protested in the capital, demanding that the Taira leaders be exiled. Fujiwara no Tadazane and his son Yorinaga supported the appeal, but Toba protected his Taira retainers, who thereby escaped punishment (Hioki, 111–112). The second confrontation was caused by an Enryakuji demonstration at Retired Emperor Toba's residence

in the fourth month of 1147, in which the monks wanted a temple (Hakusanji) in Echizen Province confirmed as an Enryakuji branch. Toba obliged the monks on 5/4, but there were several confrontations between Enryakuji supporters and Taira warriors following the demonstration. See, for example, *Taiki*, in volume 23 of *Zōho shiryō taisei* (Kyoto: Rinsen shoten, 1965), entries for Kyūan 3 (1147)/ 4, 6, 7, 8, 10; *Honchō seiki*, Kyūan 3/7, 8, 10.

17. *Tendai zasuki*, 92. Tendai *zasu* began to reside in the capital during Shira-kawa's era, though they also maintained, or constructed, their own cloisters on Mt. Hiei. By Go-Shirakawa's time it became increasingly common to reside solely in Kyoto, and the court elites probably favored this custom, since it gave them an opportunity to influence the abbots of important cloisters and temples. See Inoue, *Nihon jōdōkyō seiritsu shi no kenkyū*, 283–284, 296–297.

18. Adachi, 195; Inoue, 93. Masamichi was a retainer as well as the brother-in-law of Fujiwara no Ienari (Gomi, *Insei ki shakai no kenkyū*, 425–456, 439). Ienari, in turn, was a close retainer of Go-Shirakawa and also the father of Narichika, who became one of Go-Shirakawa's most important confidants.

19. *Heihanki*, Hōgen 3 (1158)/6/16–19.

20. *Hyakurenshō*, Nin'an 2 (1167)/2/3. The character for "bright," which makes up the first part of Myōun's name, may also be pronounced *"mei"* (thus "Meiun"), a pronunciation used by the editors of *Heike monogatari* (*Shinkō Nihon koten shūsei: Heike monogatari*, volume 1, 111–123) and by Helen McCullough in her translation of that war tale. However, the *Heike monogatari* is part of a particu-lar literary tradition where stylistic changes were common throughout the trans-mission of the work, and it has little relation to Tendai matters. Thus, based on contemporary Buddhist names and terms, as in the Buddhist deity Fudō Myōō (The King of Immovable Light), I have preferred Myōun. See also *Kaitei shinpan konsaisu Nihon jinmei jiten*, s.v. "Myōun." Myōun became a very important leader within Tendai. Go-Shirakawa, for example, attempted to tie him to the imperial family by placing his son, the princely monk Ninjō, as a disciple of Myōun (*Gyokuyō;* and *Sankaiki*, in *Shiryō taisei*, volumes 19–21 [Tokyo: Naigai shoseki kabu-shiki gaisha, 1936], Angen 1 [1175]/8/16), who also led the retired emperor's esoteric initiation ceremony in 1176.

21. Adachi, 192–193.

22. *Jimon kōsōki*, in volume 28, part 1 of *Zoku gunsho ruijū* (Tokyo: Zoku gun-sho ruijū kanseikai, 1978), 76; *Onjōji denki*, volume 127 of *Dainihon bukkyō zensho* (Tokyo: Bussho kankōkai, 1916), Kaō 1 (1169)/6/17 (p. 87). See also Tanaka Fumihide, "Go-Shirakawa insei ki no seiji kenryoku to kenmon jiin," *Nihon shi kenkyū* 256 (1983), 8, 14.

23. Though ceremonial differences seem to have been more important than doctrinal ones in the premodern era, institutional and political concerns played the most dominant role in factionalism among the religious elites. There were, for example, ceremonial differences among the different cloisters at Enryakuji, but few, if any, conflicts concerned such issues.

24. Tanaka, "Go-Shirakawa insei ki no seiji kenryoku to kenmon jiin," 8, citing from the *Gukanshō*. The Byōdōin was built in 1052 by Fujiwara no Yorimichi on a location close to the Fujiwara residence in Uji. It was designated a *betsuin* (de-tached temple) of Onjōji, and the reputable monk Myōson (971–1063), who also had attempted to become Tendai *zasu*, was named the founder.

25. *Sankaiki*, Eiryaku 2 (1161)/4/7–9.

26. *Tendai zasuki*, 95; *Hyakurenshō*, Ōhō 2 (1162)/int. 2/1 (p. 76); *Kōfukuji betō shidai*, 19.

27. *Tendai zasuki*, 95, 98; *Hyakurenshō*, Ōhō 2/int. 2/1, Chōkan 1 (1163)/3/29 (pp. 76–77).

28. *Tendai zasuki*, 98; *Hyakurenshō*, Chōkan 1/5/22, 29 (p. 77). Kakuchū's appointment to head Hosshōji just several days earlier seems related to Go-Shirakawa's concession.

29. *Hyakurenshō*, Chōkan 1/5/22, 29 (p. 77); *Kōfukuji betō shidai*, 19; Hioki, 135.

30. *Tendai zasuki*, 98; *Hyakurenshō*, Chōkan 1/6/9, 23, 7/22, Chōkan 2/4/26 (pp. 77–78); *Kōfukuji betō shidai*, 19. This visit also reinforces the impression that Go-Shirakawa changed his policies toward Enryakuji following the problems with Saiun's replacement.

31. The *Tendai zasuki* (p. 99) indicates that the destroyed buildings were on Mt. Hiei, but it seems improbable that the Kōfukuji monks would have been able to ascend the mountain and cause such damage without help from a considerable force of armed followers. More important, there is no mention of such rampaging in any of the contemporary sources. The *Tendai zasuki* may be referring to cloisters on the western foot of the mountain and to Tendai branches in the Kyoto area or it may simply be offering an excuse for the clergy's subsequent attack on Kiyomizudera.

32. *Tendai zasuki*, 99; *Hyakurenshō*, Eiman 1 (1165)/8/9, 10/26, 28 (p. 79); *Akihiro ōki*, in volume 5 of *Shiga-ken shi*, compiled by Shiga-ken (Tokyo: Sanshūsha, 1928), 69–70; *Akihiro ōki* (Kunaichō shorikubu, Tokyo, unpublished), Eiman 1/8/12, 13, 30.

33. *Hyakurenshō*, Chōkan 1 (1163)/7/25, (pp. 77–78); *Kōfukuji betō shidai*, 19; *Kōfukuji ryaku nendaiki*, 150.

34. *Kōfukuji betō shidai*, 18–19.

35. *Sankaiki*, Nin'an 2 (1167)/4/19, 23, 5/7, 15; *Gyokuyō*, Nin'an 2/4/18, 19; *Heihanki*, Nin'an 2/5/15; *Kōfukuji betō shidai*, 19; *Kōfukuji ryaku nendaiki*, 151. There is some uncertainty regarding where Eshin actually ended his days. The *Kōfukuji betō shidai* quotes one source that indicates that he died in Izu on 1170/9/25, but another claims that it was in Ōmi on 1171/9/25 (*Kōfukuji betō shidai*, 19).

36. *Gyokuyō*, Jōan 3 (1173)/5/20; *Tōnomine ryakki*, in volume 2 of *Jishi sōsho*, in *Dainihon bukkyō zensho* (Tokyo: Bussho kankōkai, 1913), Jōan 3/6/8.

37. *Tōnomine ryakki*, Jōan 2 (1172)/9/6, int. 12/24.

38. *Gyokuyō*, Jōan 3 (1173)/6/21, 25, 27, 30; *Tōnomine ryakki*, Jōan 3/6/20; *Hyakurenshō*, Jōan 3/6/25, 26, 29.

39. *Gyokuyō*, Jōan 3/7/1, 7, 12–15, 21. The quote can be found in the entry for 7/21.

40. *Gyokuyō*, Jōan 3/8/9, 19, 27, 28, 9/3.

41. *Gyokuyō*, Jōan 3/9, 11/11, 12, 12/3; *Hyakurenshō*, Jōan 3/11/3, 4, 6, 7, 9, 11; *Kōfukuji betō shidai*, 21–22; *Kōfukuji ryaku nendaiki*, 152; Hioki, 96–97; *Heian ibun*, volume 7, document 3652, *Kansenji*, Jōan 4 (1174)/1/18; Arai, 67. The records are silent about the punishments except for a brief entry in *Kōfukuji ryaku nendaiki* (p. 152), which notes that the monk Kakkō was exiled to Harima.

42. *Wakayama-ken shi: genshi, kodai*, 686; *Wakayama-ken shi: kodai shiryō*, 2 "Heian

jidai 5," document 114, *Tōji montora sōjōan,* Ōho 2 (1162)/11 (pp. 372–374); document 115, *Tōji montora mōshijō an,* same date (pp. 374–375); *Kōyasan monjo* 8, document 1798 (pp. 144–147).

43. *Wakayama-ken shi: genshi, kodai,* 687; *Wakayama-ken shi: kodai shiryō* 2, "Heian jidai 5," document 50, *Go-Shirakawa in-no-chō kudashibumi,* Heiji 1 (1159)/5/28 (p. 325); document 55, *Bifukumon'in ryōji,* Heiji 1/7/17 (p. 329); document 60, *Bifukumon'in ryōji,* Heiji 1/11/3; document 114, *Tōji montora sōjō an,* Ōho 2 (1162)/11 (pp. 372–374); *Kōyasan monjo* 1, documents 326 (p. 338), 327 (p. 339), 343 (pp. 352–355); *Heian ibun* 5, documents 3000 (pp. 2460–2462), 3015 (p. 2464); *Heian ibun* 6, document 2979 (pp. 2449–2451); *Kōya shunjō,* Heiji 1 (1159)/5/28, 7/8, 17 (pp. 106–107); Inoue, "Kamakura seiritsu ki no bushi rangyō," 24–26. Bifukumon'in died the following year and was, despite prohibitions against women on Mt. Kōya, buried within the temple compound (*Wakayama-ken shi: genshi, kodai,* 687).

44. *Wakayama-ken shi: genshi, kodai,* 680–690; *Wakayama-ken shi: kodai shiryō* 2, "Heian jidai 5," document 114 *Tōji montora sōjō an,* Ōho 2 (1162)/11 (pp. 372–374); and document 136, *Gon dainagon Taira Kiyomori ke mandokoro kudashibumi,* Chōkan 2 (1164)/6 (pp. 399–400); *Kōya shunjū,* Eiryaku 1 (1160)/10/22 (p. 108); *Heihanki,* Nin'an 2 (1167)/1/27; Inoue, "Kamakura seiritsu ki no bushi rangyō," 29. Tamenaga is listed as one of Kiyomori's twenty-five *keishi* in the 1/27 entry of the *Heihanki.*

45. *Wakayama-ken shi: genshi, kodai,* 690; *Wakayama-ken shi: kodai shiryō* 2, "Heian jidai 5," document 127, *Sakyō gon daifu Taira Nobunori shojō,* Chōkan 1 (1163)/7/25 (p. 397); *Heian ibun* 7, documents 3109, 3110, 3111, 3113, 3114 (pp. 2508–2511), 3264 (p. 2598); *Kōya shunjū,* Ōho 2 (1162)/4/15, 28, 5/24, Chōkan 1 (1163)/6/3, 25, 8/8 (pp. 108–109).

46. *Gyokuyō,* Shōan 1 (1171)/9/23; *Kugyō bunin,* part 1, 473–476.

47. For a detailed description of these incidents in Japanese, see Tanaka Fumihide, *Heishi seiken no kenkyū,* 182–203, though the analysis is quite conventional, positing Enryakuji's protest as a challenge against the imperial state (p. 193).

48. *Heihanki,* Kaō 1 (1169)/12/17; *Gyokuyō,* 12/23. According to later sources, Masatomo had encountered the Hirano *jinnin* at an inn when they were on their way to sell flour for their rents. For some reason, he put ink into the flour, destroying the product completely (Tanaka, "Go-Shirakawa in seiki no seiji kenryoku to kenmon jiin," 16; *Genpei seisuiki,* volume 2, 15–16).

49. Kaō 1/12/23, in *Gyokuyō, Heihanki,* and *Gumaiki* (Kyoto: Yōmei bunkō, unpublished); *Tendai zasuki,* 103. Fujiwara no Narichika was a career commander with ambitions in the imperial court. As a twenty-two year-old, he sided with Fujiwara no Nobuyori in the Heiji Disturbance of 1159–1160 against both Go-Shirakawa and Taira no Kiyomori. Narichika was spared execution because of his marriage to Kiyomori's daughter, but he was stripped of his offices. He was reinstated in 1161 but was immediately involved in another incident centering on the newly born Prince Tadahito (Go-Shirakawa's seventh son, later Emperor Takakura, who ruled from 1168 to 1180), resulting in his exile. Narichika was pardoned the following year, and, resuming his career as a hired sword, received Owari Province in 1166.

50. Kaō 1/12/23, 24, in *Gyokuyō, Heihanki, Gumaiki.*

51. Tanaka, "Go-Shirakawa in seiki no seiji kenryoku to kenmon jiin," 18–19.

52. Kiyomori was apparently also reluctant to attack Enryakuji followers in 1165 during the conflict between Enryakuji and Kōfukuji, despite requests to that effect from the retired emperor (Hioki, 143–144). The *Genpei seisuiki* cites Kiyomori as stating that "the descent of monks from Mt. Hiei to the capital is not a matter of the Taira clan" (*Genpei seisuiki,* volume 1, 59).

53. *Gyokuyō,* Kaō 1/12/24, 30; *Heihanki,* Kaō 1/12/24, 27, 29; *Gumaiki,* Kaō 1/12/24; *Hyakurenshō,* Kaō 1/12/28; *Kugyō bunin* 1, Nin'an 4 (p. 469).

54. *Gyokuyō,* Kaō 2 (1170)/2/2, 8; *Hyakurenshō,* Kaō 2/1/13, 22, 23, 27. Tokitada and Nobunori were recalled in exchange for Narichika (*Hyakurenshō,* Kaō 2/2/6). For the reinstatement of Narichika, see *Kugyō bunin* 1, Kaō 2.

55. The *Genpei seisuiki,* which is heavily biased against both Kiyomori and Enryakuji, even suggests that Kiyomori planned a revolt against Go-Shirakawa in 1169 and therefore encouraged the monks of Enryakuji to protest against Narichika (*Genpei seisuiki,* volume 1, 91–92).

56. *Akihiro ōki* (unpublished), Jishō 1 (1177)/4/13; *Gyokuyō,* Jishō 1/3/21; *Tendai zasuki,* 105; McCullough, *The Tale of the Heike,* 48–50. Hakusanji was given to the Tendai *zasu* Kakushū by Retired Emperor Toba in 1147 (*Taiki,* Kyūan 3/3/7).

57. Jishō 1/4/13 in *Akihiro ōki* (unpublished), *Gumaiki,* and *Nakasuke ōki* (Tokyo: Kunaichō shorikubu, unpublished); *Tendai zasuki,* 105.

58. *Gumaiki,* Jishō 1/4/14, 15, 16; *Gyokuyō,* Jishō 1/4/14, 17; *Akihiro ōki* (unpublished), Jishō 1/4/14; *Tendai zasuki,* 106.

59. *Gyokuyō, Gumaiki, Hyakurenshō,* Jishō 1/4/20; *Tendai zasuki,* 106.

60. *Nakasuke ōki* (unpublished), *Akihiro ōki* (unpublished), Jishō 1/5/4; *Gumaiki,* Jishō 1/5/9, 11; *Gyokuyō,* Jishō 1/5/10, 11; *Tendai zasuki,* 106. The new head abbot was Kakukai (the seventh son of Toba), whose ability to lead the Enryakuji monks was severely limited, since he spent most of his time as a monk in the capital. In fact, he did not ascend Mt. Hiei for a whole month after his appointment (*Gyokuyō,* Jishō 1/5/10; *Nakasuke ōki,* Jishō 1/6/14). The punishment of Myōun can only be described as remarkable, especially considering that Go-Shirakawa had received the Tendai precepts in 1176 and had placed his son as a disciple with the monk.

61. *Nakasuke ōki* (unpublished), Jishō 1/5/21; *Gumaiki,* Jishō 1/5/13, 14, 16; *Akihiro ōki* (unpublished), Jishō 1/5/21; *Gyokuyō,* Jishō 1/5/20.

62. *Nakasuke ōki* (unpublished), *Akihiro ōki* (unpublished), Jishō 1/5/23; *Gumaiki,* Jishō 1/5/23, 24; *Tendai zasuki,* 106; *Gyokuyō,* Jishō 1/5/11, 29; Inoue, 275–276.

63. Uwayokote Masataka, "Genpei sōran," in *Ōtsu-shi shi,* volume 2: *Chūsei,* 39.

64. Moromitsu—a minor member of the Fujiwara—was promoted by Shinzei, who was killed early in the Heiji Incident of 1159–1160. He followed his mentor's example, taking Buddhist vows and the name Saikō, while continuing to be involved in capital politics as a retainer of Go-Shirakawa.

65. Jishō 1/6/9, in *Akihiro ōki, Nakasuke ōki, Hyakurenshō, Genpei seisuiki.* The Shishigatani Incident is well known through a number of sources, *Gyokuyō* being one of the most reliable and comprehensive. Though the *Heike monogatari* is a later source, its account does not differ substantially from contemporary sources. It is especially recommendable in its English translation by Helen Craig McCullough (*Tale of the Heike,* 63–66). See also Gomi Fumihiko, *Kamakura to kyō,*

volume 5 of *Taikei Nihon no rekishi* (Tokyo: Shogakkan, 1988), 52–53. Kiyomori had Narichika killed in Bizen on Jishō 1 (1177)/7/9 *(Akihiro ōki, Gyokuyō, Hyakurenshō, Genpei seisuiki).*

66. McCullough, *Tale of the Heike,* 57; *Gyokuyō,* Jishō 1/6/1; Tsuji, *Nihon bukkyō shi: jōsei hen,* 907; Gomi, *Kamakura to kyō,* 48; Inoue, 272.

67. *Gyokuyō,* Jishō 1/6/1. One should not rule out the possibility that the treatment of Myōun could have been used as a justification for Kiyomori's execution of Saikō. However, given Kiyomori's long-standing support of Myōun and the monk's designation as his Buddhist master, it is more probable that he considered the punishment of Myōun as a threat almost equal in gravity to the plot against himself.

68. *Gyokuyō,* Jishō 1/6/1.

69. Mass, "The Kamakura Bakufu," 51.

70. Nagashima, *Nara,* 136–137; *Nara-ken no rekishi,* 72, Hirata, *Sōhei to bushi,* 206–207.

71. *Gyokuyō,* Shōan 2 (1172)/12/21, 24; *Hyakurenshō,* Shōan 2/12/21, 27.

72. For a proponent of this view, see Hioki, 159.

73. *Nakasuke ōki* (unpublished), Angen 3 (1177)/6/5, 12/19; Uwayokote, "Genpei sōran," 39; Gomi, *Kamakura to kyō,* 48. Though Kiyomori did not take complete control of the capital until his coup in the eleventh month of 1179, his ability to restore Myōun's estates indicates that he had assumed new powers already following the Shishigatani Affair.

74. *Gyokuyō,* Jishō 2 (1178)/1/20, 2/5, 7; *Sankaiki,* Jishō 2/1/20, 2/10, 5/16, 20; *Hyakurenshō,* Jishō 2/2/1; Hioki, 144.

75. Tsuji states that the conflict began after some scholar-monks invaded a *shōen* that belonged to the worker-monks *(Nihon bukkyō shi: jōsei hen,* 912). Inoue provides some additional information, explaining that the conflict originated in 1177, when a scholar-monk, named Eishun, of the Tōtō section attacked worker-monks in Etchū Province. This incident caused the *dōshū* to build fortifications on Mt. Hiei, leading to a gradual decline in the relationship between the two groups (Inoue, 273–274, 281, citing from the later *Genpei seisuiki).*

76. *Genpei seisuiki,* volume 2, 75–76, Jishō 2 (1178)/8/6, 9/20; *Akihiro ōki* (unpublished), *Hyakurenshō,* Jishō 2/10/4; *Gyokuyō,* Jishō 2/10/4, 11/5.

77. *Gyokuyō,* Jishō 3 (1179)/6/5, 10, 7/25, 9/11, 10/3, 11/2; *Sankaiki,* Jishō 3/10/3, 25, 11/2; *Hyakurenshō,* Jishō 3/10/3, 11/2, 5, 7. Inoue suggests that the three estates that were attacked provided shelter for former thieves, mountain marauders, and pirates who supported the *dōshū* (p. 274). Again, Inoue relies entirely on the later *Genpei seisuiki.*

78. Tanaka, *Heishi seiken no kenkyū,* 209, 225, 228; Motoki, *Insei ki seiji shi kenkyū,* 309, 329; *Sankaiki,* Jishō 3/11/27; *Gyokuyō,* Jishō 3/12/3.

79. *Gyokuyō,* Jishō 3/11/16; *Sankaiki,* Jishō 3/11/17; *Tendai zasuki,* 108; *Hyakurenshō,* Jishō 3/11/16, 22; *Kōfukuji ryaku nendaiki,* 152–153; Murayama, *Hieizan shi,* 178; Tsuji, *Nihon bukkyō shi: jōsei hen,* 913; Hiraoka, *Nihon jiin shi no kenkyū,* volume 2: *Chūsei, kinsei,* 2–3.

80. *Gyokuyō,* Jishō 4 (1180)/3/17, 5/17, 18; Jishō 4 (1180)/5/17, 18, in *Meigetsuki (Shiryō sanshū* [Tokyo: Zoku gunsho ruijū, 1967], volume 6), *Sankaiki,* and *Hyakurenshō;* McCullough, *Tale of the Heike,* 145–146.

81. McCullough, *Tale of the Heike,* 146–147.

82. *Gyokuyō*, 5/25; *Sankaiki*, 5/17. One Enryakuji monk—a certain Ekōbō Chinkei—actually joined Onjōji with three hundred of his own men after failing to convince the Enryakuji clergy to side with Prince Mochihito (Hirata Toshiharu, "Nanto hokurei no akusō ni tsuite," 289).

83. *Sankaiki*, Jishō 4 (1180)/5/27; *Hyakurenshō*, same date.

84. Kenreimon'in is Taira no Tokuko, the daughter of Kiyomori and the mother of Antoku, who had become emperor on 1180/2/26.

85. *Gyokuyō*, Jishō 4/5/26.

86. Ibid., Jishō 4/5/26, 27.

87. Ibid., Jishō 4/5/27.

88. See, for example, McCullough, *Tale of the Heike*, 163–164.

89. Hioki, 145; McCullough, *Tale of the Heike*, 131–132. Takakura did visit the Hie shrines on his return from Itsukushima late in the third month (McCullough, *Tale of the Heike*, 133).

90. Hioki, 149. For a more detailed description of the Fukuhara episode and the resistance of temples, see also Hirata, *Sōhei to bushi*, 205–227.

91. *Gyokuyō*, Jishō 4/7/1, 10/20, 28, 11/27, 12/3; *Tendai zasuki*, 108–109; *Sankaiki*, Jishō 4/11/6; Motoki, *Insei ki seiji shi kenkyū*, 335.

92. *Gyokuyō*, Jishō 4/12/9–14.

93. *Gyokuyō*, Jishō 4/12/15, 16, 22, 24. It appears that Enryakuji, from which Kiyomori still received some support through Myōun, played a crucial role in Kiyomori's decision to return to Kyoto. See *Kitsuki*, Jishō 4/11/15; Hioki, 149; Hirata, *Sōhei to bushi*, 222–223; and *Genpei seisuiki*, volume 4, 164–167.

94. *Gyokuyō*, Jishō 4/12/25, 29; *Hyakurenshō*, Jishō 4/12/28.

95. *Gyokuyō*, Jishō 4/12/29.

96. *Gyokuyō*, Jishō 5 (1181)/1/5, 7, 8, int. 2/20; *Hyakurenshō*, Jishō 5/1/4, 8; Nagashima, *Nara*, 139.

97. *Gyokuyō*, Jishō 5/1/6, 22, 29, 30, int. 2/20, 6/15; *Kitsuki, Ichidai yōki*, Jishō 5/6/20; Nagashima, *Nara*, 139–140.

98. *Gyokuyō*, Jishō 5/1/5, 3/11, 6/14.

99. *Tendai zasuki*, 109. Rokushōji (or Rikushōji) translates as "The Six Victorious Temples" and included the aforementioned Hosshōji (built by Shirakawa), Sonshōji (Horikawa), Saishōji (Toba), Enshōji (Taikenmon'in), Jōshōji (Sutoku), and Enshōji (Konoe).

100. *Gyokuyō*, Jūei 1 (1182)/4/15, 16; *Hyakurenshō*, Jūei 1/4/15.

101. *Gyokuyō*, Jūei 2 (1183)/7/24, 25; Uwayokote, "Genpei sōran," 45; McCullough, *Tale of the Heike*, 237–239.

102. *Kitsuki*, Jūei 2/7/12; *Hyakurenshō*, Jūei 2/7/8; McCullough, *Tale of the Heike*, 239–240.

103. *Gyokuyō*, Jūei 2/7/22, 23, 25, 26; *Tendai zasuki*, 109–110; Uwayokote, "Genpei sōran," 46.

104. *Wakayama-ken shi: genshi, kodai*, 691–692; *Wakayama-ken shi: kodai shiryō* 2, document 62, excerpt from the *Gukanshō* (pp. 335–337); document 65, excerpt from the *Heiji monogatari* (pp. 339–340); documents 403–404, excerpts from the *Heike monogatari* (pp. 541–542). Muneshige thereafter became one of Kiyomori's main retainers, and he participated in the Taira leader's siege of Mt. Hiei in the tenth month of 1179, during the dispute between scholar-monks and worker-monks (*Heike monogatari*, volume 1, 202–204; also quoted in *Kii no kuni Ategawa*

no shō shiryō, volume 1, compiled by Nakamura Ken (Tokyo: Yoshikawa kōbunkan, 1976, hereafter referred to as *Ategawa* 1), document 27 [pp. 58–59]).

105. *Wakayama-ken shi: genshi, kodai,* 706–707; *Wakayama-ken shi: kodai shiryō* 2, "Heian jidai 5," document 496, *Aragawa no shō hyakuseira gonjō jō an,* Jishō 5 (1181)/4/24 (p. 587); *Heian ibun* 8, document 3946, *Takakura jōō chō kudashibumi,* Jishō 4 (1180)/12 (pp. 3010–3011); Inoue, "Kamakura bakufu seiritsu ki no bushi rangyō," 30–31.

106. *Wakayama-ken shi: genshi, kodai,* 707–708; *Wakayama-ken shi: kodai shiryō* 2, "Heian jidai 5," document 558, excerpt from the *Azuma kagami,* Jūei 3 (1184)/2/21 (p. 617).

107. *Gyokuyō,* Jūei 2 (1183)/int. 10/19, 26.

108. *Gyokuyō,* Jūei 2/11/22; Uwayokote, "Genpei sōran," 48; Mass, "The Kamakura Bakufu," 54; idem, *Warrior Government,* 72–73; McCullough, *Tale of the Heike,* 276–278; *Tendai zasuki,* 110.

109. *Gyokuyō,* Jūei 2/12/8, 9, Genryaku 1 (1184)/1/22; *Tendai zasuki,* 110–111; McCullough, *Tale of the Heike,* 284–293.

110. Nagashima, *Nara,* 140; idem, *Nara-ken no rekishi,* 74.

111. *Gyokuyō,* Jūei 2 (1183)/10/4; *Kōya shunjū,* 120; Tsuji, *Nihon bukkyō shi: chūsei* 1 (Tokyo: Iwanami shobō, 1947), 8–9.

112. *Kōya shunjū,* 119–120; *Kōyasan monjo* 1, document 416, *Minamoto no Yoritomo kudashibumi,* Genryaku 1 (1184)/7/2; *Ategawa* 1, document 32, *Kongōbuji shuto ureijō,* Jūei 3 (1184)/3 (p. 62); document 36, *Minamoto no Yoshitsune shojō,* Genryaku 1 (1184)/5/2 (p. 66); document 37, *Minamoto no Yoritomo kudashibumi,* Genryaku 1 (1184)/7/2 (p. 66–67); document 38, excerpt from the *Azuma kagami,* Genryaku 1/7/2 (p. 67); *Wakayama-ken shi: kodai shiryō* 2, documents 583–584 (pp. 638–639); Nakamura Ken, "Jitō hihō no katakana gonjōjō: Kii no kuni Ategawa no shō," in *Shōen no sekai* (Tokyo: Tōkyō daigaku shuppankai, 1985), edited by Inagaki Yasuhiko, 212–213; Nakamura Ken, *Shōen shihai kōzō no kenkyū* (Tokyo: Yoshikawa kōbunkan, 1978), 4; Egashira, 103. The Kōyasan clergy was quite active in seeking confirmations from Yoritomo in 1184. For instance, it also received exemptions from war taxes on Nanaka Estate in Kii on 1184/5/24 (Mass, *The Kamakura Bakufu: A Study in Documents,* document 2 (pp. 26–27).

113. Tsuji, *Nihon bukkyō shi: chūsei* 1, 19. Some of these dates may be incorrect, since Tsuji is relying on the *Azuma kagami,* a later source that has been proven to be questionable in several accounts of the early years of the bakufu. For a comprehensive analysis of this early development of the Kamakura Bakufu, see Mass, *Warrior Government,* 124–127.

114. Nakamura, "Jitō hihō katakana gonjōjō," 213–215; *Gyokuyō,* Bunji 1 (1185)/int. 7/ 9, 10, 16; *Ategawa* 1, documents 50–52 (pp. 78–79), documents 58–60 (pp. 87–89); *Wakayama-ken shi: kodai shiryō* 2, "Kamakura jidai," documents 51–53 (pp. 705–706).

115. *DNS* 4:1, Bunji 2 (1186)/5/20 (p. 381); *Kōya shunjū,* 121; *Wakayama-ken shi: kodai shiryō* 2, "Kamakura jidai," document 60, *Kōyasan jūsōra gesu,* Bunji 2 (1186)/5 (pp. 716–722); Inoue, "Kamakura bakufu seiritsu ki no bushi rangyō," 37–41.

116. Mass, *Warrior Government in Early Medieval Japan,* 131–132, 155; *Kamakura ibun* 1, document 42, *Hōjō Tokimasa kudashibumi,* Bunji 2 (1186)/1/29 (p. 17); document 131, (p. 87); *Kamakura ibun* 2, document 867 (p. 198); *Kōyasan*

monjo 1, document 3, *Go-Shirakawa in in-no-chō kudashibumi*, Bunji 2/5 (pp. 4–7); documents 4–5, *Daijō kanpu*, (pp. 8–12); document 52, *Kongō buji konpon daitō gusō gesu an*, Kenkyū 1 (1190)/11 (pp. 48–51); *Wakayama-ken shi: kodai shiryō* 2, "Kamakura jidai," documents 54–56 (pp. 707–711); Jeffrey Mass, *The Development of Kamakura Rule, 1180–1250*, (Stanford: Stanford University Press, 1979), 212 (document 59); Egashira, 40, 234–235; *Azuma kagami*, 6 volumes, compiled by Nagahara Keiji and Kishi Shōzō (Tokyo: Shin jinbutsu jūraisha, 1976–1979), Bunji 2/7/24; *Kōya shunjū*, 121.

117. Nagashima, *Nara*, 145. Although Kōfukuji's Kondō was completed in 1194, four years before Tōdaiji's main temple hall, the size of the Tōdaiji building heavily overshadowed that of Kōfukuji's main hall. In addition, most other Hossō temple halls and Buddhist images lagged behind the Tōdaiji reconstruction by a wide margin (*Kōfukuji ryaku nendaiki*, 154–155; Matsushima, "Nenpyō," in volume 3 of *Shinpen meihō Nihon no bijutsu: Kōfukuji*).

118. *Gyokuyō*, Bunji 4 (1188)/5/22; *DNS* 4:2, Bunji 4/5/22 (pp. 375–377), Bunji 5 (1189)/7 (pp. 715–716); *DNS* 4:3, Kenkyū 1 (1190)/5/2 (pp. 143–145).

119. *Gyokuyō*, Kenkyū 2 (1191)/4/2, 3, 6; *Hyakurenshō*, Kenkyū 2/4/26; Uwayo-kote Masataka, "Shugo Sasaki shi," in *Shinshū Ōtsu-shi shi*, volume 2: *Chūsei*, compiled by Ōtsu shiyakusho Ōtsu: Nihon insatsu kabushiki gaisha, 1978), 59; Mura-yama, *Hieizan shi*, 239; Kuroda Toshio, "Enryakuji shuto to Sasaki shi," in *Shōen sei to buke shakai*, edited by Takeuchi Rizō hakushi kanreki kinnenkai (Tokyo: Yoshi-kawa kōbunkan, 1969), 75; Takahashi Masaaki, "Heian matsu, Kamakura jidai no Sasaki shi," in *Yōkaichi-shi shi*, volume 2: *Chūsei* (Yōkaichi-shi: Yōkaichi-shi yakusho, 1983), 43.

120. *Gyokuyō*, Kenkyū 2/4/5, 6, 26, 29; *Azuma kagami*, Kenkyū 2/5/3; *Hyaku-renshō*, Kenkyū 2/4/26, 27, 28, 30, 5/1; Uwayokote, "Shugo Sasaki shi," 60–61; Kuroda Toshio, "Enryakuji shuto to Sasaki shi," 76; Takahashi, 43–44.

121. Kuroda Toshio, "Enryakuji shuto to Sasaki shi," 76–77; Uwayokote, "Shugo Sasaki shi," 62–63; idem, *Kamakura jidai seiji shi kenkyū* (Tokyo: Yoshikawa kōbunkan, 1991), 178. The *Tendai zasuki* states that Sadashige was killed because of "the murder of the shrine servants and because of his evil acts in Echigo Province" (p. 118).

122. Hirata, *Sōhei to bushi*, 233–234.

123. Kuroda, "Enryakuji shuto to Sasaki shi," 76–77; *Azuma kagami*, Kenkyū 4 (1193)/4/26, 29, 10/28, 12/20; Takahashi Masaaki, 44.

124. The Sasaki family was involved in several fascinating incidents with both the bakufu and Enryakuji. For example, during the Jōkyū War of 1221, some members sided with the court against the bakufu, perhaps motivated, in part, by Yoritomo's "treachery" thirty years earlier (Mass, *The Development of Kamakura Rule, 1180–1250*, 22; idem, *Lordship and Inheritance in Early Medieval Japan: A Study of the Kamakura Sōryō System* [Stanford: Stanford University Press, 1989], 55). An inci-dent that occurred in 1235 between the Sasaki and Enryakuji has been summa-rized in Hitomi Tonomura, *Community and Commerce in Late Medieval Japan: The Corporate Villages of Tokuchin-ho* (Stanford: Stanford University Press, 1992), 29–30, 217.

125. Uwayokote, *Kamakura jidai seiji shi kenkyū*, 170.

126. *Gyokuyō*, Bunji 2 (1186)/9/19, 20, 21, 22, 28; *DNS* 4:1, Bunji 2/9/22, (pp. 609–613).

127. *Gyokuyō*, Bunji 2 (1186)/9/28; Hirata, *Sōhei to bushi*, 230.

128. Uwayokote, "Shugo Sasaki shi," 59; *Azuma kagami*, in *DNS* 4:2, Bunji 4 (1188)/10/17; Hirata, *Sōhei to bushi*, 231. One of the monks (Shunshō) accompanied Yoshitsune to the northern provinces. The other monk (Zenkōbō) was punished because he was caught with a letter from Yoshitsune stating that he intended to return to Kyoto (Uwayokote, *Kamakura jidai seiji shi kenkyū*, 177).

129. Tsuji, *Nihon bukkyōshi: chūsei* 1, 28; Hirata, *Sōhei to bushi*, 229. As mentioned in the previous note, Zenkōbō was later arrested for supporting Yoritomo's brother.

130. *Gyokuyō*, Kenkyū 1 (1190)/3/2–7; *DNS* 4:3, 65–68; *Tendai zasuki*, 115; *Hyakurenshō*, Kenkyū 1/3/4, 7; Tsuji, *Nihon bukkyō shi: chūsei* 1, 5–7; Uwayokote, "Shugo Sasaki shi," 51.

131. Tsuji, *Nihon bukkyō shi: chūsei* 1, 28–30; Hirata *Sōhei to bushi*, 233–234.

132. See Kuroda, *Chūsei no kokka to shūkyō*, 17–18, 53–55.

Chapter 5   Religious Conflicts and Shared Rulership in the Late Thirteenth Century

1. During Go-Saga's *insei* (1246–1272) alone, there were more forceful appeals (*gōso*) involving Enryakuji than during the first six decades of the Kamakura period. In addition, counting *gōso*, internal disputes, battles with other elites, and mobilizations (*hōki*), there were twenty-seven incidents during Go-Saga's tenure, averaging just about one per year. By contrast, no other emperor or retired emperor experienced as many Enryakuji disturbances. Go-Horikawa's reign (1221–1232) saw nine incidents, but six of those did not affect the capital, since they were internal affairs within the temple complex. There were also four *gōso* during Kameyama's *insei* (1274–1287), but they were all related to incidents and developments from Go-Saga's time. See appendixes 1 and 2.

2. There were a total of twelve forceful protests during Go-Saga's era, as opposed to sixteen during the preceding six decades. See, for example, Katsuno, *Sōhei*, 171–179; and Hioki, "Nihon sōhei shi nenpyō," 14–19, in *Nihon sōhei kenkyū*.

3. Mass, *The Development of Kamakura Rule, 1180–1250*, 11; idem, "The Kamakura Bakufu," 67–68.

4. Mass, "The Kamakura Bakufu," 67–68; Carl Steenstrup, *Hōjō Shigetoki (1198–1261) and His Role in the History of Political and Ethical Ideas in Japan* (London and Malmö: Curzon Press, 1979), 14–15; Ishii Susumu, *Kamakura bakufu*, volume 7 of *Nihon no rekishi* (Tokyo: Chūō kōronsha, 1967), 274–276, 289–296.

5. Mass, *The Development of Kamakura Rule*, 16–18.

6. Ibid., 12, 36–39; Hurst, "The Kōbu Polity," 16.

7. Hurst, "The Kōbu Polity," 17; Mass, *The Development of Kamakura Rule*, 37.

8. Andrew Goble, "The Hōjō and Consultative Government," in Mass, ed., *Court and Bakufu in Japan: Essays in Kamakura History*, 175–176, 179; H. Paul Varley, "The Hōjō Family and Succession to Power," in ibid., 161; Hurst, "The Kōbu Polity," 17–18.

9. Hurst, "The Kōbu Polity," 18–19; Mori Shigeaki, *Kamakura jidai no chōbaku kankei* (Kyoto: Shibunkaku shuppan, 1991), 15–18; Ishii, *Kamakura bakufu*, 233–235.

10. Mori, *Kamakura jidai*, 18–23; Hurst, "The Kōbu Polity," 19.

11. Hurst, "The Kōbu Polity," 18; Nezu Masashi, *Tennō ke no rekishi,* volume 2, 14–17; Mass, *The Development of Kamakura Rule,* 113.

12. Hurst, "The Kōbu Polity," 19; Mori, *Kamakura jidai,* 23.

13. Steenstrup, 17–18; Mori, *Kamakura jidai,* 24.

14. Mori, *Kamakura jidai,* 24–25, 27.

15. Hurst, "The Kōbu Polity," 20–21; Mori, *Kamakura jidai,* 26–29, 40; Nezu, *Tennō ke no rekishi,* volume 2, 17.

16. Hurst, "The Kōbu Polity," 22; Goble, "The Hōjō and Consultative Government," 188; Ishii Susumu, "The Decline of the Kamakura Bakufu," in *The Cambridge History of Japan,* volume 3: *Medieval Japan,* 133, 161–162; Hurst, "The Kōbu Polity," 21; Nezu, 14.

17. During a serious incident involving Kōfukuji in 1246 (discussed later in this chapter), it was Retired Emperor Go-Saga who controlled the decision-making process, overshadowing not only the bakufu but also the Fujiwara chieftain (*Yōkōki,* volume 8 of *Shiryō sanshū* [Tokyo: Zoku gunsho ruijū kanseikai, 1971], Kangen 4 [1246]/4). In addition, he also single-handedly confirmed several landholdings for Tōdaiji during the 1250s (Mass, *The Development of Kamakura Rule,* 206–207).

18. Mass, *The Development of Kamakura Rule,* 41.

19. Mass, "The Kamakura Bakufu," 88; Miyama Susumu, "Munetaka shinnō," in *Kamakura shōgun shikken retsuden,* edited by Yasuda Motohisa (Tokyo: Akida shoten, 1974), 210; Ishii, "Decline of the Kamakura Bakufu," 161–163; Hurst, "The Kōbu Polity," 23–24; Andrew Edmund Goble, *Kenmu: Go-Daigo's Revolution* (Cambridge: Harvard University Press, 1996), 4–7; Nezu, 23–24.

20. *Tendai zasuki,* 205, 207–208.

21. Ibid., 209–210. The ritual was the Shijōkōhō (The Ritual of the Blazing Light), described in detail in the *Mon'yōki* (volumes 11–12 of *Taishō shinshū daizōkyō: zuzō* [Tokyo: Daizō shuppan, 1933–1934]). See also *DNS* 5:14, entry for Ninji 3 (1242)/1/24 (pp. 93–103). Several other ceremonies that were performed for the imperial court can be found in *DNS* 5:14, Ninji 3/4/8, 7/3; *DNS* 5:15, Ninji 3/9/21, 10/15; *DNS* 5:16, Kangen 1 (1243)/4/18, 7/6, int. 7/27, 9/27; *DNS* 5:17, Kangen 1/10/17, 12/15, Kangen 2 (1244)/2/26, 5/1, 6/29; *DNS* 5:18, Kangen 2/10/10, Kangen 3 (1245)/3/7; *DNS* 5:19, Kangen 3/7/26, 10/1, 11/3, 11/22, 12/22; *DNS* 5:20, Kangen 4 (1246)/3/20; *DNS* 5:21, Kangen 4/12/5, Kangen 5 (1247)/1/28.

22. *Tendai zasuki,* 213–217; Mori, *Kamakura jidai,* 152, 154.

23. *Tendai zasuki,* 213.

24. Ibid., 217, 221; *Yōkōki, Hyakurenshō, Mon'yōki,* in *DNS* 5:21, Hōji 1 (1247)/3/25 (pp. 415–430).

25. *DNS* 5:19, 393–395; *Yōkōki,* Kangen 4 (1246)/8/17, 18, 21, 23, 24, 28, 29, 9/12, 17, 28, 10/5, 10.

26. *Yōkōki,* Hōji 2 (1248)/12/28, int. 12/1.

27. Ibid., Hōji 1 (1247)/4/29, 5/8, 11, 16, 24, 6/1, 2; *DNS* 5:22, 22–24.

28. *Yōkōki,* Hōji 2/8/7, 16–18, 9/6, 11/28, 30; *DNS* 5:26, 351–352, 392; *DNS* 5:27, 235.

29. Dōkaku performed a ritual for the safe child delivery of a consort of Go-Saga on Hōji 1/9/5 (*DNS* 5:22, 323–347) and led other services at the retired emperor's palace on Hōji 2/3/22 (*DNS* 5:26, 110–111) and Hōji 2/10/21 (*DNS* 5:27, 51–74).

30. *Tendai zasuki,* 222–223; *Hyakurenshō,* Hōji 2/3/4 (p. 225).

31. *Tendai zasuki,* 173.

32. *Hyakurenshō,* Kangen 4 (1246)/1/8, 9, 11, 15, 17, 18 (p. 211), Hōji 1/2/9, 16 (p. 218), Hōji 2/9/8 (p. 226), Kenchō 2 (1250)/3/11, 4/5 (p. 229), Kenchō 3 (1251)/1/13 (p. 230).

33. The pilgrimages took place on Shōka 1 (1257)/3/21 (*Kōya shunjū,* p. 165) and Shōka 2 (1258)/3/26 (*Masu kagami,* in volume 21, part 2 of *Shintei zōho kokushi taikei* [Tokyo: Yoshikawa kōbunkan, 1940], 78; *Hyakurenshō,* p. 250).

34. *Kōya shunjū,* 99; Miyasaka, 24–27, 33; *Wakayama-ken no rekishi,* 744; Kuroda, *Jisha seiryoku,* 87; Toyoda, "Kōyasan jiryō no hensen," 465; Wada, 29.

35. *Kōya shunjū,* 112.

36. *DNS* 5:14, Ninji 3 (1242)/7/13 (pp. 450–455); *Hyakurenshō,* Ninji 3/7/13 (p. 194); *Kōya shunjū,* 154; *DNS* 5:15, Kangen 1 (1243)/1/25, 7/13, 11/18 (pp. 151–154); Toyoda, "Kōyasan jiryō no hensen," 468.

37. *Yōkōki, Kōyasan monjo,* in *DNS* 5:20, Kangen 4 (1246)/4/15 (p. 177); *Negoro yōsho, Buke mikyōjō an,* in *DNS* 5:22, Hōji 1 (1247)/5/13 (pp. 25–26): Miyasaka, 39; Wada, 34–35.

38. Go-Saga visited Gion on 1251/2/13 and 1254/2/23, and Hiesha on 1252/9/1 (*Tendai zasuki,* 227–229).

39. *Yōkōki,* Hōji 2 (1248)/11/21, 26, 12/2; *DNS* 5:27, 231–233; *Kachō yōryaku, Mon'yōki,* both in *DNS* 5:27, 410–415. Apparently, Go-Saga consulted the records of the influential *zasu* Jien (1155–1225), whose will stipulated that the estates should be managed by the head abbot in office.

40. *Tendai zasuki,* 224–225; *Hyakurenshō,* Kenchō 1 (1249)/9/6.

41. During Sonkaku's tenure, Go-Saga made pilgrimages to shrines affiliated with Enryakuji on Kenchō 2 (1250)/2/10, Kenchō 3 (1251)/2/13, and Kenchō 4 (1252)/9/1 (all to Hiesha), and to Gionsha on Kenchō 6 (1254)/2/23 (*Tendai zasuki,* 226–229). Go-Saga made no more visits to the Enryakuji complex until 1264, just after a lengthy conflict that involved Enryakuji and Onjōji, treated later in this chapter.

42. Nezu, 19.

43. *Tsunetoshi kyōki* (Kunaichō shorikubu, Tokyo, unpublished), Shōka 1 (1257)/3/27, int. 3/1, 7, 7/16; *Tendai zasuki,* 230. The postponement could also have been a means to punish Enryakuji, since Kitano—dedicated to the spirit of the late-ninth-century courtier Sugawara no Michizane—was one of its branch shrines. At any rate, it reveals that the issue was still unsettled some three months after the edicts from the imperial court and the Kantō.

44. *Azuma kagami* (Tokyo: Shin jinbutsu jūraisha, 1976–1979), Shōka 1/10/13.

45. *Tendai zasuki,* 231–233; *Azuma kagami,* Shōka 2 (1258)/4/21, 5/6; *Hyakurenshō,* Shōka 2/4/17, 19, 5/1, 18 (pp. 250–251). The *Hyakurenshō* notes that only two carts were carried to Kyoto during the protest.

46. *Tendai zasuki,* 234–238; *Zokushi gushō,* in *Shintei zōho kokushi taikei* (Tokyo: Yoshikawa kōbunkan), volume 13, Bun'ō 1 (1260)/1/4–6 (pp. 7–8); *Azuma kagami,* Shōgen 2 (1260)/1/10; *Myōkaiki, Kachō yōryaku,* in *Shiga-ken shi,* volume 5, 79–80.

47. *Zokushi gushō,* Bun'ō 1/1/8, 11, 14, 17, 19, 2/1, 3/11, 13, 4/12; *Azuma kagami,* Shōgen 2/1/26, 29, 2/3, 3/1 (see also *Azuma kagami,* in *Shintei zōho kokushi taikei* [Tokyo: Yoshikawa kōbunkan, 1936], volume 33, 726–727); *Tendai zasuki,* 238–243.

48. *Tendai zasuki,* 246–249.

49. Murayama Shūichi, *Hieizan shi: tatakai to inori no seichi*, 84; *Jimon kōsōki*, in *Zoku gunsho ruijū*, 83–84; *Tennōji bettō shidai*, in *Zoku gunsho ruijū* (Tokyo: Keizai zasshisha, 1904), volume 4, 433–434; *Shitennōji rekidai bettō shumu jijo*, in *Zoku gunsho ruijū*, volume 4, 688–689. Unfortunately, these sources show some discrepancies, making it difficult to know the exact order of abbots. For example, monks of Onjōji claimed that thirteen consecutive abbots had been appointed from their temple beginning with Saisan in 1057, but other sources do not substantiate this claim. There was at least one monk from Ninnaji breaking this streak (*Jimon kōsō denki*, 84–90). Nevertheless, all sources do confirm Onjōji's near monopoly of the post in the last century of the Heian period.

50. *Tennōji bettō shidai*, 437; McCullough, *Tale of the Heike*, 164; Uwayokote, "Genpei sōran," 40.

51. *Tennōji bettō shidai*, 437; *Jimon kōsō denki*, citing the appeal from the Onjōji clergy, *Tennōji bettō shiki sossho sōjō*, Yōwa 2 (1182)/1/17 (pp. 79–80), and Go-Shirakawa's edict *Go-Shirakawa in onchōsen* of Bunji 5 (1189)/4/14 (pp. 81–82).

52. *Jimon kōsō denki*, citing the Enryakuji clergy's statement *Enryakuji sanzen shu-tora shinsei*, Kenkyū 7 (1196)/10/28 (pp. 85–88); *Sanchōki*, Kenkyū 7 (1196)/10/28; *DNS* 4:5, 266–270; *Tennōji bettō shidai*, 437–438; *Shitennōji bettō shumu jijo*, 689–690.

53. *Tendai zasuki*, 207, 223; *Kachō yōryaku*, 68; *Hyakurenshō*, *Ichidai yōki*, in *DNS* 5:12, Ennō 1 (1239)/9/20 (pp. 538–540); *DNS* 5:14, Ninji 3 (1242)/3/10 (p. 216).

54. *Saimyōji monjo* (unpublished, Tokyo daigaku shiryō hensanjo Tokyo), Kenchō 1 (1249)/8/14; *Ichidai yōki*, Kenchō 1/8/14, 9/6 (p. 344); *Hyakurenshō*, same dates (p. 228); *Tendai zasuki*, 223–225.

55. *Geki nikki*, volume 1 of *Zoku shiseki shūran* (Tokyo: Kondō shuppansha, 1930), Bun'ei 1 (1264)/1/15, 3/23; *Tendai zasuki*, 249–250; *Ichidai yōki*, Bun'ei 1/3/23 (p. 363). The *Geki nikki* states that a total of nine buildings were destroyed.

56. An *inzen* quoted in the *Tendai zasuki* states that "there has never been another temple besides this [Enryakuji] designated the original temple [*dōjō*] of the emperor" and that "the altars of the seven Hie shrines protect [the capital] from the direction of the gate of demons" (Bun'ei 1/3/27, p. 252). See also Chapter 6 for more on these doctrines.

57. *Ichidai yōki*, Bun'ei 1/3/25, 27; *Zokushi gushō*, Bun'ei 1/3/24, 25, 27; *Geki nikki*, Bun'ei 1/3/25; *Tendai zasuki*, 250–252. Sanefuji was exiled to Awaji on the sixth day of the fourth month (*Geki nikki*, Bun'ei 1/4/6; *Kamakura ibun* 12, document 9071, *Daijō kanpu*, Bun'ei 1/4/6 [p. 324]; *Tendai zasuki*, 253; *Kugyō bunin*, part 2, *Shintei zōho kokushi taihei*, volume 14 (Tokyo: Yoshikawa kōbunkan, 1937), p. 198).

58. *Tendai zasuki*, 253–254; *Zoku shi gushō*, Bun'ei 1/3/29; *Geki nikki*, Bun'ei 1/3/29, 4/18; *Ichidai yōki*, Bun'ei 1/3/29, 4/16, 18. The attacking monks were later apprehended and handed over to the Rokuhara headquarters (*Geki nikki*, *Zokushi gushō*, Bun'ei 1/4/18).

59. *Geki nikki*, *Zoku shi gushō*, Bun'ei 1/5/2–6; *Tendai zasuki*, 254.

60. *Geki nikki*, Bun'ei 1/5/10, 15, 24, 27, 6/1, 6; *Tendai zasuki*, 255–256.

61. *Tendai zasuki*, 255 (Bun'ei 1/10/26); *Geki nikki*, Bun'ei 1/12/14.

62. *Geki nikki*, Bun'ei 2 (1265)/2/15; *Tendai zasuki*, 256–257. The prohibition of secular followers for monks is a strong indication that the religious forces

and the violence associated with protests involved a substantial number of noncleric. Similar edicts condemning the use of arms by clerics were issued by the bakufu against Kōyasan in the late 1220s and against Enryakuji in 1230 (Hioki, 157).

63. *Tendai zasuki*, 258. See also *Kamakura ibun* 13, document 9335.

64. *Geki nikki*, Bun'ei 2/3/18, 19.

65. *Tendai zasuki*, 258–259, 262; Tsuji, *Nihon bukkyō shi: chūsei* 1, 54; *Geki nikki*, Bun'ei 4 (1267)/1/2. Saijo was Tendai head abbot from 1286 to 1288 (*Tendai zasuki*, 294–295).

66. *Kanchūki*, volumes 26–27 of *Shiryō taisei* (Tokyo: Naigai shoseki kabushiki gaisha, 1931–1944), Kōan 5 (1282)/10/16.

67. *Masu kagami*, in *Ōkagami, Masu kagami* (Tokyo: Kadokawa shoten, 1976), Kōan 6 (1283)/1/6 (p. 132); *Sanemi kyōki, Dainihon kokiroku*, volumes 20–21 (Tokyo: Iwanami shoten, 1991–1994), *Kanchūki*, Kōan 6/1/6.

68. Though the bakufu's criticism of the warriors was harsh, it immediately pardoned all of them because of the threat of a Mongol invasion from the continent. Japan had already been attacked twice—in 1274 and 1281—by Kublai Khan's armadas, and the threat of yet another invasion was still felt in both Kyoto and Kamakura in 1283.

69. *Kinhira kōki*, in *Shiryō sanshū* (Tokyo: Zoku gunsho ruijū kanseikai, 1968), Kōan 6/7/2, 10, 22. See also *Kankenki* (another name for *Kinhira kōki*), in *Shiga-ken shi*, volume 5, 82.

70. *Sanemi kyōki* (unpublished), Shōō 4 (1291)/3/8, 15, 16, 17; *Tennōji bettō shidai*, 437; *Tendai zasuki*, 294.

71. Mori, *Kamakura jidai*, 152, 154; *Tendai zasuki*, 217, 221.

72. Mori, *Kamakura jidai*, 152; *Ichidai yōki; Tendai zasuki*, 268–269.

73. *Tendai zasuki*, 285–295; *Kinhira kōki*, Kōan 6 (1283)/7/2; Mori, *Kamakura jidai*, 152–153.

74. *Yōkōki*, Kangen 4 (1246)/4, int. 4, 5/3, 13.

75. *Hyakurenshō*, Hōji 1 (1247)/5/18, 22, 23; *Kōfukuji bettō shidai*, 33.

76. *Tsunetoshi kyōki*, Shōgen 1 (1259)/3/17; Mori, *Kamakura jidai*, 143, 145.

77. See, for example, *Chūsei hōsei shiryō shū*, volume 1: *Kamakura bakufu hō*, edited by Satō Shin'ichi and Ikeuchi Yoshisuke (Tokyo: Iwanami shoten, 1969), Ennō 2 (1240)/6/21 (pp. 124–125), Kōchō 2 (1262)/5/23 (pp. 217–218), Kōan 7 (1284)/5/20 (p. 250).

78. *Azuma kagami*, in *Shintei zōho kokushi taikei*, Katei 1 (1235)/5/23, 7/24 (pp. 152–153, 162); *Hyakurenshō*, Katei 1/6/3 (p. 178); Tsuji, *Nihon bukkyō shi: chūsei* 1, 83–84; Katsuno, *Sōhei*, 30.

79. The imperial court's claim appears to be incorrect. Iwashimizu Hachimangū's holy carts were indeed carried around by the clergy on 1104/2/11 in response to the deposition of assistant abbot Kōshin (*Chūyūki, Tamefusa kyōki*, Chōji 1/2/16). It is, however, unclear whether the carts actually reached the imperial palace during this incident.

80. *Azuma kagami*, in *Shintei zōho kokushi taikei*, Katei 1/7/24 (p. 163); *Hyakurenshō*, Katei 1/int. 6/19–21, 23, 27, 28 (p. 178); Tsuji Zennosuke, *Nihon bukkyō shi: chūsei* 1, 84–85; Katsuno, *Sōhei*, 31.

81. *Azuma kagami*, in *Shintei zōho kokushi taikei*, Katei 1/7/24 (p. 163); Tsuji, *Nihon bukkyō shi: chūsei* 1, 84–85. According to Hioki, the decision to depose Shūsei

marked the first time that the bakufu issued a verdict against a monk ("Nihon sōhei shi nenpyō," 16, in Hioki, *Nihon sōhei kenkyū*).

82. *Azuma kagami,* in *Shintei zōho kokushi taikei,* Katei 1/12/29 (p. 168); *Hyakurenshō,* Katei 1/12/21, 25 (p. 180); Tsuji, *Nihon bukkyō shi: chūsei* 1, 85; Katsuno, *Sōhei,* 31.

83. Tsuji, *Nihon bukkyō shi: chūsei* 1, 85–86; *Hyakurenshō,* Katei 2 (1236)/1/1, 5.

84. *Azuma kagami,* in *Shintei zōho kokushi taikei,* Katei 2/2/28, 3/21 (pp. 173–174,), 7/24 (p. 177), 8/20 (p. 183), 10/2, 5, 6 (p. 184); *Hyakurenshō,* Katei 2/2/19, 21, 7/28 (p. 181); Tsuji, *Nihon bukkyō shi: chūsei* 1, 86–87; Katsuno, *Sōhei,* 32.

85. *Azuma kagami,* in *Shintei zōho kokushi taikei,* Katei 2/11/13, 14 (p. 184); *Hyakurenshō,* Katei 2/10/6, 10, 16, 11/2; Tsuji, *Nihon bukkyō shi: chūsei* 1, 87; Hioki, *Nihon sōhei kenkyū,* 156.

86. *Kanchūki,* Kōan 5 (1282)/2; *San'e jōikki,* Kōan 4 (1281) and Kōan 5 (pp. 364–365); Tsuji, *Nihon bukkyō shi: chūsei* 1, 88–89.

87. *Tsunetoshi kyōki,* Shōka 1 (1257)/4/23, 6/11; *Kasuga monjo,* Shōka 2 (1258)/12/25.

88. *Bun'ei gannen Nakatomi Sukemasa ki,* Bun'ei 1 (1264)/5/5, 6/6, 9/2, in *Kasugasha kiroku,* part 13, printed in volume 47 of *Zōho zoku shiryō taisei* (Kyoto: Rinsen shoten, 1983), 377–381, 413–414. War taxes *(hyōrōmai)* were first levied by Taira no Kiyomori as well as by Yoritomo during and after the Genpei War. After that, such taxes were assessed on an as-needed basis, during particular campaigns or conflicts, as proclaimed by the bakufu. The irregular taxes assessed on the Kōfukuji estates in 1264 included both war levies and special dues for transportation (*Bun'ei gannen Nakatomi Sukemasa ki,* Bun'ei 1/6/10, 8/1, 2 [pp. 379, 390, 391]).

89. *Bun'ei gannen Nakatomi sukemasa ki,* Bun'ei 1 (1264)/8/19, 9/2 (pp. 407, 414); *Kōfukuji ryaku nendaiki,* Katei 1 (1235), Shōka 2 (1258)/7/2, 8/2 (pp. 160, 162).

90. *Bun'ei gannen Nakatomi Sukemasa ki,* Bun'ei 1/6, 1/7/2, 3, 26, 8/6, 12, 21 (pp. 376–406); *Kōfukuji ryaku nendaiki,* Bun'ei 1/7/2, 8/2 (p. 163); *Geki nikki,* Bun'ei 1/7/2, 27, 8/2, 3.

91. *Bun'ei gannen Nakatomi Sukemasa ki,* Bun'ei 1/8/11–14, 19–23, 26 (pp. 403–411). The *Geki nikki* states that Nagatoki died on the twenty-first (Bun'ei 1/8/21).

92. *Bun'ei gannen Nakatomi Sukemasa ki,* Bun'ei 1/9/1–3, (pp. 413–415), Bun'ei 2 (1265)/6/28 (pp. 433–434), 7/22 (p. 439); *Kōfukuji bettō shidai,* 34; *Geki nikki,* Bun'ei 1/9/22.

93. *Bun'ei gannen Nakatomi Sukemasa ki,* Bun'ei 2/8/1 (p. 441); *Entairyaku,* Bun'ei 3 (1266)/4/4; *Geki nikki,* Bun'ei 3/7/8; *Kōfukuji ryaku nendaiki,* Bun'ei 5 (1268)/8/26 (p. 62); *Ichidai yōki,* Bun'ei 5/8/26.

94. The term *"gekokujō"* appears in the late Heian period (Hioki, *Nihon sōhei,* 155), but it becomes more commonplace in the late thirteenth and fourteenth centuries, when the authority of the central elites was seriously and widely challenged.

95. Hioki, *Nihon sōhei,* 155–156.

96. *DNS* 5:18, Kangen 2 (1244)/8/9; *Hyakurenshō,* same date; *Yōkōki,* Hōji 2 (1248)/12/28; *Okanoya kanpaku ki,* part 2 of *Yōmei sōsho kiroku monjo hen* (Kyoto: Shibunkaku shuppan, 1984), Hōji 2/12/28, int. 12/1.

97. *Yōkōki,* Kangen 4 (1246)/8/7; *DNS* 5:19, 393.

98. Katsuno, *Sōhei*, 51–52; *Kanchūki*, Kōan 7 (1284)/8/28, 9/7 (quoting the entire imperial edict), 8, 15, 16, 10/10. The excommunicated scribe, Kanenaka, is the author of *Kanchūki*, though he unfortunately refrains from making any extensive comments about his predicament.

99. *Kanchūki*, Shōō 2 (1289)/2/26; *Shōō ninen Nakatomi Sukeharu ki*, Shōō 2/2/25, in *Kasugasha kiroku*, part 28, in volume 49 of *Zōho zoku shiryō taisei*, p. 241; Hioki, *Nihon sōhei*, 135.

100. *Kōfukuji ryaku nendaiki*, 168; *Fushimi in goki*, Shōō 5 (1292)/1/14, in volume 3 of *Zōho shiryō taisei* (Kyoto, Rinsen shoten, 1965), p. 305; Hioki, 136; *San'e jōikki*, 372.

101. Toyoda, "Kōyasan jiryō no hensen," 468–471.

102. *Kōyasan monjo* 2, document 634, *Kantō mikyōjō*, Jōō 2 (1223)/6/28 (pp. 54–55); Hioki, "Nihon sōhei shi nenpyō," 14, in idem, *Nihon sōhei kenkyū*.

103. Kokawadera was situated in the northwest corner of Kii (present-day Wakayama) and was an important local competitor to Kōyasan.

104. *Kōyasan monjo* 4, document 113, *Kongōbuji shuto chinjō an*, Ninji 2 (1240) (pp. 247–250); document 114, *Kongōbuji shuto chinjō an*, Ninji 2/7 (pp. 250–254); document 115, *Kongōbuji shuto chinjō an*, Ninji 2/7 (pp. 254–258); Takahashi Osamu, "Shōen kōryō wo meguru ryōshū to minshū," in *Wakayama-ken shi: chūsei*, compiled by Wakayama-ken shi hensan kakari inkai (Osaka: Dainihon insatsu kabushiki kaisha, 1994), 99.

105. Takahashi Osamu, 101–102; *DNS* 5:16, Kangen 1 (1243)/7/16. The bakufu's disengagement can only be described as surprising, since the bakufu's jurisdiction was not restricted geographically. Though it should not be taken to reflect a general principle, it demonstrates the warrior government's limited knowledge of conditions in Kii and its reluctance to overextend its authority in a conflict between two temples, even if a *jitō* was also involved.

106. Takahashi Osamu, 101–105; *Kōya shunjū*, Kenchō 2 (1250)/12/2 (p. 158); *Kōyasan monjo* 1, document 396, *Kansenji*, Kenchō 2/12/2 (pp. 427–435).

107. Takahashi Osamu, 104–105; Ōishi Naomasa, "Nade no shō Mionoya mura yōsui sōron no shinryō," in *Kōyasan ryō shōen no shihai to kōzō*, ed. Toyoda Takeshi, 209–210; *Kōya shunjū*, Kenchō 3 (1251)/2/16 (p. 158); *Kōyasan monjo* 4, document 120, *Fujiwara no Toshinao narabi ni sōkan chūbunjō*, Kenchō 5 (1253)/7/18, (pp. 264–265), 121, *Mionoya mura jitō Shinagawa Kiyohisa sōjō*, Shōka 1 (1257)/8, (p. 266).

108. Takahashi Osamu, 105–106; Ōishi, 210–213; *Kōyasan monjo* 1, document 402, *Rokuhara meshibumi mikyōjō*, Kōchō 3 (1263)/8/18, (pp. 438–439); *Kōyasan monjo* 4, document 121 (pp. 266–267).

109. *Kōyasan monjo* 7, document 1665, *Kantō gechijō an*, Jōō 1 (1222)/9/13 (pp. 529–530).

110. *DNS* 5:22, Hōji 1 (1247)/6 (pp. 191–194); *Kōyasan monjo* 2, document 264, *Kōyasan jūsō gejō*, Hōji 1/6 (pp. 409–414).

111. *Kōyasan monjo* 1, document 1, *Go-Shirakawa in in-no-chō kudashibumi*, Kaō 1 (1169)/11/23 (pp. 1–3); document 3, *Go-Shirakawa in in-no-chō kudashibumi*, Bunji 2 (1186)/5 (pp. 4–7); document 10, *Minamoto no Yoritomo shojō*, Bunji 2/7/24 (p. 17); see also documents 4–5, 8–9, 11; Egashira, 232–234, 263–265; Mass, *The Kamakura Bakufu: A Study in Documents*, 90, 125, 165–166, 192, 212, 258.

112. *Kōyasan monjo* 1, document 54, *Kantō mikyōjō*, Katei 1 (1235)/10/25 (pp. 54–56); document 88, *Kantō gechijō*, Katei 1/10/25 (pp. 81–82); Egashira, 277.

113. *Kōya shunjū*, Kōchō 3 (1263)/8/4 (p. 168), Bun'ei 9 (1272)/1/20, 5/20 (p. 172); *Kōyasan monjo* 1, document 92, *Kantō gechijō*, Bun'ei 9/1/20, (p. 86); Egashira 278–281.

114. Egashira, 281–284; *Kōya shunjū*, 173; *Kōyasan monjo* 1, document 93, *Rokuhara segyōjō*, Kōan 9 (1286)/int. 12/28 (pp. 86–87); document 94, *Kantō gechijō*, Shōan 4 (1302)/6/23 (pp. 87–90); *Kōyasan monjo* 8, document 1937; *Ōta no shō Ōtakata jitōra chinjō*, Bun'ei 11 (1274)/7 (pp. 574–577), document 1938, *Ōta no shō Ōtakata hongō teramachi shōkan hyakuseira gonjōjō*, Shōan 2 (1300)/1 (pp. 577–583).

115. See, for example, Takamura Takashi, "Kōyasan ryō shōen kenkyū shi," and Endō Iwao, "Izumi no kuni Kogi-no-shō bashaku chōto jōri sei no seikaku," 272–274, both in Toyoda, *Kōyasan ryō shōen no shihai to kōzō*.

116. *Kōyasan monjo* 7, document 1534, *Aragawa hyakuseira sojō an*, Kenchō 7 (1255)/11 (pp. 118–120); Tashiro Osamu, "Kōyasan kenryoku to nōmin no dōkō: chūsei goki no Aragawa no shō," in Toyoda, *Kōyasan ryō shōen no shihai to kōzō*, 221.

117. Takahashi Osamu, 108–109; Tashiro, 221.

118. Takahashi Osamu, 109–110; Tashiro, 221–222; *Kōyasan monjo* 7, document 1543, *Kōyasan shuto chinjō an*, Shōō 4 (1291)/11 (pp. 127–130). See also documents 1544 and 1545, and *Kōyasan monjo* 1, document 360, *Aragawa Gen'ya Yoshinori kishōmon*, Shōō 3 (1290)/8/8 (pp. 373–374).

119. Takahashi Osamu, 110–113; *Kōyasan monjo* 7, document 1543, *Kōyasan shuto chinjō an*, Shōō 4 (1291)/11 (pp. 127–130). See also documents 1544 and 1545; document 1565, *Sō Hōshin sojō narabi ni gūsho an*, Shōō 4/9 (pp. 152–155); document 1567, *Kōyasan shuto sojō an*, Shōō 4/9 (pp. 157–159); document 1568, *Rokuhara segyō mikyōjō an*, Shōō 4/10/5 (pp. 159–160); documents 1569–1580; *Kōyasan monjo* 8; document 1745, *Aragawa Nade ryōshō akutō kyōmyō chūmon*, Shōō 4/9 (pp. 47–50).

120. *Ategawa* 1, document 124, *Kongōbuji shuto ureijō an*, Kenchō 8 (1256)/6 (pp. 140–143); document 127, *Ategawa no shō shōkan chūshinjō*, Shōka 1 (1257)/8/17 (pp. 145–146); *Tsunetoshi kyōki*, Shōka 1/6/18.

121. *Kōya shunjū*, Shōgen 1 (1259)/10; *Kōyasan monjo* 5, document 1158, *Ategawa kami no shō jitō Yuasa Mitsunobu sojō an*, Shōgen 1 (1259)/10 (pp. 723–726); *Ategawa* 1, document 141 (pp. 160–161). For other examples of the Yuasa legal skills, see *Kōyasan monjo* 5, documents 1156, *Yuasa nyūdō Chigan mōshijō an*, Bun'ei 6 (1269)/3 (pp. 716–718), and 1157, *Yuasa nyūdō Chigan mōshijō an*, Bun'ei 6/6 (pp. 718–720), regarding an appeal to have a Kyoto residence secured to Yuasa Chigan. These documents are also reprinted in *Ategawa* 1, documents 186, 187.

122. *Ategawa* 1, document 168, *Ategawa no shō zasshō chinjō an*, Bun'ei 3 (1266)/4/23 (pp. 186–188); *Geki nikki*, Bun'ei 3 (1266)/4/15; *Kōyasan monjo* 6, document 1415, *Rokuhara meshibumi mikyōjō an*, Bun'ei 4 (1267)/5/30 (pp. 476–477); document 1416, *Rokuhara meshibumi mikyōjō an*, Bun'ei 4/12/6 (p. 477).

123. *Kōyasan monjo* 1, document 182, *Ategawa no shō kami no mura zasshō Jūren gonjō an*, Kenji 1 (1275)/9 (pp. 203–205); *Kōyasan monjo* 5, document 1125, *Ategawa no shō zasshō mōshijō an*, Kenji 2 (1276)/6/5 (pp. 671–672); document 1130, *Ategawa no shō hyakuseira kanete gonjō*, Kenji 1/5 (pp. 679–680); document 1132, *Ategawa no shō jitō Yuasa Munechika chinjō an*, Kenji 2 (1276)/6 (pp. 682–685); document 1152, *Ategawa no shō jitō Yuasa Munechika chinjō an*, Kenji 2/7 (pp. 710–

713); documents 1154–1155; *Kōyasan monjo* 6, document 1423, *Ategawa no shō Kami no mura hyakuseira gonjōjō* (pp. 486–490); Egashira, 138–141, 168–169; *Ategawa* 2, documents 207, 211, 213, 216–218, 219 (the famous Kana letter of 1275/10/28); Nakamura Ken, "Jitō hihō to katakana gonjōjō," in *Shōen no sekai,* edited by Inagaki Yasuhito (Tokyo: Tōkyō daigaku shuppankai, 1985), 223, 227–228; Takahashi Osamu, 120–125, 156–170; Inoue, "Kamakura bakufu seiritsu ki no bushi rangyō," 22–24.

124. *Ategawa* 1, document 244, *Kōyasan shuto keijō ukebumi,* Kōan 1 (1278)/8 (pp. 52–53); *Ategawa* 2, document 276, *Gouda in inzen,* Kengen 2 (1303)/6/9 (p. 79); document 277, *Ategawa no shō kami no mura azukari dokoro ukebumi,* Kengen 2/6 (pp. 79–80); document 278, *Kameyama in inzen,* Kagen 1 (1303)/8/13 (pp. 80–81); *Kōyasan monjo* 5, document 1139, *Kōyasan shuto gejō an,* Kagen 2 (1305)/3/5 (pp. 692–694); see also documents 1142–1144, 1150; *Kōyasan monjo* 2, document 681, *Gouda in inzen,* Kengen 2/6/9 (p. 98); document 682, *Kōyasan shuto keijō ukebumi,* Kōan 1 (1278)/8 (pp. 99–100). See also *Kōya shunjū,* Shōō 1 (1288)/12/9 (p. 182), Einin 4 (1296)/8/22 (p. 185), Kengen 1 (1302)/8/20 (p. 188), and Kengen 2/3/7, 10 (p. 189); Toyoda Takeshi, "Kōyasan jiryō no hensen," 474; Inoue, "Kamakura bakufu seiritsu ki no bushi rangyō," 34–36.

Chapter 6   Protesting and Fighting in the Name of the *Kami* and the Buddhas

1. Hioki calculates that more than two hundred divine demonstrations were staged from the late tenth to the sixteenth centuries (Hioki, 120). Enryakuji staged around one hundred divine protests, while some seventy *gōso* can be attributed to Kōfukuji (Nagashima, *Nara,* 135). For a brief but informative account of demonstrations staged by Tōdaiji, see Katsuno, *Sōhei,* 57–64.

2. *Entairyaku,* Kōei 3 (1344)/11/18, in *DNS* 6:8, 509; and *Gukanki,* Jōji 1 (1362)/7/3, in *DNS* 6:24. The most paradigmatic example of the anachronistic usage can be found in the important source collection *Dainihon shiryō,* where headings to several entries in the Heian and Kamakura series frequently contain the term *"gōso"* although it is not to be found in the sources themselves. See, for example, *DNS* 3:2, 898, entry for Chōji 2 (1105), first month.

3. Nagashima, *Nara,* 145; Katsuno, *Sōhei,* 17–18, 26. The *sakaki* seems to have no equivalent in English, though it is known as *Cleyera ochnacea* to botanists.

4. Katsuno, *Sōhei,* 21–22; Nagashima, *Nara,* 120–121; Hirata, *Sōhei to bushi,* 123–124, 132–136; Hioki, 109.

5. *Gonki,* in volumes 4–5 of *Zōho shiryō taisei* (Kyoto: Rinsen shoten, 1965), Kankō 3 (1006)/7/13, 15; *Hyakurenshō,* Kankō 3/7/13 (13); Katsuno, *Sōhei,* 22–23.

6. Tsuji, *Nihon bukkyō shi: jōsei hen,* 833–835; *Tendai zasuki,* 54–56.

7. Nagashima, *Nara,* 119; *Kokushi daijiten,* s.v. *"gōso"* (pp. 420–421); Hioki, 112; Katsuno, *Sōhei,* 24–25, citing from *Kasuga kannushi Sukemasa ki.* See also document 1264, in *Heian ibun* 4, Kanji 2 (1088)/8/10 (pp. 1249–1250).

8. Hioki, 112–113.

9. *Go-Nijō Moromichi ki, Chūyūki,* Kanji 6 (1092)/9/18, 28; *DNS* 3:2, 665, 667, 669; Hirata, *Sōhei to bushi,* 142; *Fusō ryakki,* Kanji 7 (1093)/8/22, 26, 27 (p. 334); Katsuno, *Sōhei,* 24–25.

10. *Chūyūki,* Kahō 2 (1095)/10/23, 24; *DNS* 3:3, 931–932.

11. *Denryaku, Eishunki, Chūyūki,* Chōji 2 (1105)/1/1, 2; *DNS* 3:7, 899–901.

The *Tendai zasuki* notes that this was the first time that the Gion palanquins were carried around during a protest (p. 73).

12. *Chūyūki*, Chōji 2/6/2, 14, 23; *DNS* 3:8, 149, 154–155. Jien notes in his *Gukanshō* that this incident marks the first time palanquins from Mt. Hiei itself (Hiesha) entered the capital, but writing over a century after these events, Jien was obviously misinformed here (*Gukanshō*, in *DNS* 3:8, 276).

13. *Denryaku*, Tennin 1 (1108)/3/20, 23; *Chūyūki*, Tennin 1/3/20–23; *DNS* 3:10, 111–114; Nagashima, *Nara*, 131.

14. *Denryaku*, Eikyū 1 (1113)/int. 3/29, 4/1; *Chūyūki*, Eikyū 1/4/1; *DNS* 3:14, 145–146.

15. Motoki Yasuo, "Insei ki Kōfukuji kō," 175–193.

16. *Chūyūki*, Kōwa 5 (1103)/3/25, 29, 4/1; *Honchō seiki*, Kōwa 5/3/26, 4/1; *Hyakurenshō*, Kōwa 5/3/26; *Ichidai yōki*, Kōwa 5/3/26; *DNS* 3:6, 941–943.

17. *Chūyūki*, Eikyū 1/4/30, *DNS* 3:14, 180; Katsuno, *Sōhei*, 18.

18. *Ichidai yōki*, Hōan 4 (1123)/7/18, 23 (p. 216); *Hyakurenshō*, same dates (pp. 52–33).

19. *Teiō hennenki*, volume 12 of *Shintei zōho kokushi taikei* (Tokyo: Yoshikawa kōbunkan, 1965), 332.

20. *Heihanki*, Kaō 1 (1169)/12/23.

21. *Tendai zasuki*, 99; *Hyakurenshō*, Eiman 1 (1165)/8/9 (p. 79); *Akihiro ōki*, in *Shiga kenshi*, 69–70; *Gyokuyō*, Jōan 3 (1173)/9, 11/11, 12, 12/3; Hioki, 96–97, Nagashima, *Nara*, 135.

22. Hioki, 113.

23. Wayne Farris, for example, calls the demonstrations of 1092 (involving no more than thirty service people of Hiesha) and 1095 attacks on the capital and further claims that the religious protests were "unique to the late eleventh and twelfth centuries" (Farris, 261). Religious protests were common from the twelfth to the fifteenth centuries, and there was nothing unique about the ones in the late Heian period except that they mark the beginning of a ritualized form of protest.

24. *Chūyūki*, Chōji 2 (1105)/5/4, 8, 6/2, 14, 8/30, 10/10, 12, 16, 30; *Denryaku*, Chōji 2/6/14, 8/30; *Hyakurenshō*, Chōji 2/6/2; *DNS* 3:8, 128–129, 149, 154, 226–227, 255–256, 270–272.

25. *Chūyūki*, Hōan 1 (1120)/8/16, 21, 22. The governor was a certain Fujiwara no Masataka, a minor member of the Fujiwara clan.

26. *Heihanki*, Kaō 1 (1169)/12/17, 23, 24; *Gyokuyō, Gumaiki*, Kaō 1/12/23, 24.

27. *Ichidai yōki*, Bun'ei 1 (1264)/3/23, 25, 27 (p. 363); *Zokushi gushō*, Bun'ei 1/3/25, 27; *Geki nikki*, Bun'ei 1/3/23, 25, 28; *Tendai zasuki*, 250–252.

28. *Heihanki, Gumaiki*, Kaō 1 (1169)/12/24; *Gyokuyō*, Kaō 1/12/24, Kaō 2 (1170)/2/2, 8; *Hyakurenshō*, Kaō 2/1/13, 22, 23, 27.

29. *Hyakurenshō*, Katei 1 (1235)/12/21, 25, Katei 2 (1236)/1/1, 5; Tsuji, *Nihon bukkyō shi: chūsei* 1, 85–86; Katsuno, *Sōhei*, 31.

30. The shrines and their Buddhist deities were Ōmiya or Ōhie (Shaka nyō-rai), Ninomiya or Kobie (Yakushi nyōrai), Seishinshi (Amida nyōrai), Hachiōji (Senshu Kannon), Marōdo (Jūichimen Kannon), Jūzenshi (Jizō bosatsu), and Sannomiya (Fuken bosatsu).

31. Hirata, *Sōhei to bushi*, 139. Another example can be found on a folding

screen panel from the middle of the Edo period (*Hie sannō gongen: kami to hotoke no bijutsu,* compiled by Shiga kenritsu biwako bunka kan [Ōtsu shi: Dainihon insatsu, 1991], 16, 80–81, 111).

32. *Hie sannō gongen: kami to hotoke no bijutsu,* 79.

33. Nagashima, *Nara,* 135; Katsuno, *Sōhei,* 18.

34. Toyoda, *Nihon shūkyō seido shi no kenkyū,* 81, 92, 97–98.

35. *Tengu sōshi,* in *Tengu sōshi, Zegaibō e,* volume 27 of *Shinshū Nihon emakimono zenshū* (Tokyo: Kadokawa shoten, 1978), color plate 2; *Tsuchigumo sōshi, Tengū sōshi, Ōeyama ekotoba,* volume 26 of *Zoku Nihon no emaki* (Tokyo: Chūō kōronsha, 1993), 20–21.

36. *Tengu sōshi,* in *Zoku Nihon no emaki,* volume 26, p. 39.

37. Most scholars agree that these scrolls, known as *Hōnen shōnin eden,* were completed in 1307, probably by Shunjō, a ninth-generation direct disciple of Hōnen. The accompanying text was contributed by prominent courtiers and emperors within the next decade. See *Hōnen shōnin eden,* in *Zoku Nihon no emaki* (Tokyo: Chūō kōronsha, 1990), volume 1, 1; volume 3, 118, 120; *Emakimono sōran* (Tokyo: Kadokawa shoten, 1995), 273. Hōnen (1133–1212), who initially studied at Enryakuji, claimed that salvation could only be achieved with the help of Amida Buddha. Thus rejecting all esoteric practices of Tendai and Shingon, he proposed that a continuous repetition of Amida's name—a practice known as *nenbutsu*—would be enough to allow one to be reborn in the Pure Land.

38. *Hōnen shōnin eden,* in *Zoku Nihon emaki taisei* (Tokyo: Chūō kōronsha, 1981), volume 2, 114–115; also in *Zoku Nihon no emaki,* volume 2, 114–115; *Chion'in to Hōnen shōnin eden,* compiled by Kyōto kokuritsu hakubutsukan (Kyoto: Ōtsuka kōgeisha, 1982), 132–133.

39. *Hōnen shōnin eden,* in *Zoku Nihon emaki taisei,* volume 2, 120–121; *Chion'in to Hōnen shōnin eden,* 134. See also Harper Coates and Ishizuka Ryugaku, trans., *Hōnen the Buddhist Saint: His Life and Teachings* (Kyoto and Tokyo: Sanshusha, 1925), 550–554.

40. *Hōnen shōnin eden,* in *Zoku Nihon no emaki,* volume 2, 120–122, 205; *Chion'in to Hōnen shōnin eden,* 134–135. Kōfukuji's appeal can be found in *Kōfukuji sōjō,* in *Dainihon bukkyō zensho: Kōfukuji sōsho,* part 2 (Tokyo: Bussho kankōkai, 1931), 103–109, and in part in Coates and Ishizuka, 557–558.

41. For a long time, scholars believed that the *Genpei seisuiki,* which consists of forty-eight scrolls, was compiled between 1247 and 1249, but, because of its literary style, there now seems to be a general consensus that the work was actually written in the Nanbokuchō era (1336–1392). Though believed to based on the *Heike monogatari,* the *Genpei seisuiki* tells the tale of the Heike and the Genpei War in a slightly different manner. In particular, the detailed accounts of Enryakuji are intriguing, but they also reveal a critical view of the temple that is not uncommon in the war tales produced in the Kamakura era. See *Shiseki kaidai jiten: kodai, chūsei* (Tokyo: Tōkyōdō shuppan, 1995), s.v. "Genpei seisuiki"; *Nihon reki-shi daijiten* (Tokyo: Kawade shobō shinsha, 1973), s.v. "Genpei seisuiki."

42. See Kuroda, *Jisha seiryoku,* 62–63; Hirata, *Sōhei to bushi,* 111; Hioki, 70, and Hori Daiji, "Sōhei no seikatsu," 479–480.

43. "Hall-entering-staff."

44. *Genpei seisuiki,* volume 1, 135–136.

45. Miya Jirō, "Emaki ni yoru engi to sōden," in *Ronshū Nihon bukkyō shi,* volume 4: *Kamakura jidai,* edited by Hiraoka Jōkai (Tokyo: Yūzankaku shuppan, 1988), 311–324; Kuroda, *Jisha seiryoku,* 168.

46. Arai, 99–104.

47. *Go-Nijō Moromichi ki,* Kanji 7/8/25, 26; *DNS* 3:2, 990.

48. For an enlightening account of the combat strategies and the sneak attacks of the warrior class according to various war chronicles, see Paul Varley, *Warriors of Japan, as Portrayed in the War Tales* (Honolulu: University of Hawai'i Press, 1994).

49. *Chūyūki,* Tennin 1/3/30, 4/1; *DNS* 3:10, 123–124.

50. Though from the middle of the Edo period, a folding screen kept at Enryakuji offers an interesting view of this process, showing the protesters descending to the capital on the trail (*Hie sannō gongen,* 79). The Kirara-zaka trail, now sunken some twenty feet into the mountainside at certain places after more than a thousand years, is still a popular climb in visiting Enryakuji. The trail begins close to the imperial villa of Shūgakuin and reaches a plateau on Mt. Hiei (which unfortunately is the site of an artificial ski slope today). From there, the trail continues to Saitō and Tōtō in an easy thirty-minute walk.

51. *Chūyūki, Denryaku,* Chōji 2/6/14, 10/28, 30; *DNS* 3:8, 154, 272. In a similar incident, Taira no Kiyomori and his father Tadamori incurred the wrath of the Gion shrine in the sixth month of 1147. Apparently, retainers of the two Taira became involved in a brawl with service people, and they even fired arrows at the palanquins. As a consequence, protests were lodged, and father and son found themselves temporarily suspended (*Honchō seiki,* Kyūan 3 (1147)/6/15, 24; *Taiki,* Kyūan 3/8/13).

52. *Tendai zasuki,* 73; *DNS* 3:7, 899–901.

53. *Heihanki,* Kaō 1 (1169)/12/23.

54. *Go-Nijō Moromichi ki, Chūyūki,* Kanji 6 (1092)/9/18; *DNS* 3:2, 665, 667.

55. *Zoku shi gushō, Geki nikki, Ichidai yōki,* Bun'ei 1 (1264)/3/25; *Tendai zasuki,* 250–252.

56. Nagashima, *Nara,* 135; idem, *Nara-ken no rekishi,* 69; Katsuno, *Sōhei,* 18.

57. *DNS* 3:2, 987–991.

58. Tsuji, *Nihon bukkyō shi: chūsei* 1, 88–89; Katsuno, *Sōhei,* 18.

59. Thomas Keirstead, *The Geography of Power in Medieval Japan* (Princeton: Princeton University Press, 1992), 75, 81.

60. *Kōfukuji bettō shidai,* 11.

61. *Tendai zasuki,* 207–208, 224–225, 234–235; *Hyakurenshō,* Kenchō 1 (1249)/9/6.

62. *Hyakurenshō,* Kyūan 3 (1112)/8/9; *Taiki,* Kyūan 3 (1147)/8/13, 10/17; *Honchō seiki,* Kyūan 3/8/11, 13, 10/8; *Tendai zasuki,* 79, 90; Hioki, 116; Murayama Shūichi, *Hieizan shi: tatakai to inori no seichi,* 155.

63. *Hyakurenshō,* Chōkan 2/7/35, (pp. 77–78); *Kōfukuji bettō shidai,* Chōkan 2/8/25, (p. 19); *Bun'ei gannen Nakatomi Sukemasa ki,* Bun'ei 1 (1264)/5/5, 6/6, 9/2, in part 13 of *Kasugasha kiroku,* 377–381, 413–414.

64. *Chūyūki,* Gen'ei 1 (1118)/5/22; *DNS* 3:20, 17.

65. See, for example, *Gyokuyō, Gumaiki, Hyakurenshō,* Jishō 2 (1177)/4/20;

Gyokuyō, Kenkyū 2 (1191)/4/26, 29; *Azuma kagami*, Kenkyū 2/5/3; Uwayo-kote, "Shugo Sasaki shi," 60–61; Kuroda Toshio, "Enryakuji shuto to Sasaki shi," 76.

66. *Taiki*, Kyūan 6 (1150)/8/10, 16, 17, 21; *Hyakurenshō*, Kyūan 6/8/5–15 (pp. 68–69); Katsuno, *Sōhei*, 28–29; *Heihanki*, Kaō 1 (1169)/12/24. For other examples, see *Azuma kagami*, in *Shintei zōho kokushi taikei*, Shōka 2 (1258)/5/17, and *Ichidai yōki*, Bun'ei 6 (1270)/1/10.

67. See, for example, Kuroda, *Jisha seiryoku*, 62–63; and Wayne Farris, 261.

68. See, in particular, Thomas Keirstead, *The Geography of Power in Medieval Japan*, chapter 4, "The Theater of Protest," for a pioneering effort in this area.

69. Neil McMullin, "On Placating the Gods and Pacifying the Populace: The Case of the Gion *Goryō* Cult," *History of Religions* 27:3 (1988), 272. The 1364–1366 Kōfukuji protest, when the Kasuga *shinmoku* was left in the capital for almost two years and various strange events and diseases were blamed on the anger of the gods, provides a particularly telling example. See Chapter 7 for a detailed treatment of this incident.

70. McCullough, *Tale of the Heike*, 51–52.

71. The war tale states that eight demonstrators were killed, while contemporary sources indicate no fatal injuries at all.

72. *Chūyūki*, Chōji 2 (1105)/10/30; *DNS* 3:8, 259.

73. *Gyokuyō*, *Gumaiki*, *Hyakurenshō*, Jishō 2 (1177)/4/13, 20.

74. *Azuma kagami*, *Hyakurenshō*, *Tendai zasuki*, in *DNS* 5:10, 184–186, 200–202, Katei 1 (1235)/7/23, 29.

75. Tsuji, *Nihon bukkyō shi: chūsei* 1, 88–89.

76. *DNS* 6:27, Jōji 5 (1366)/6 (pp. 327–328); *Yoshida nichiji ki*, *Kasuga kannushi Sukekata ki*, *Taiheiki*, in *DNS* 6:27, Jōji 5 (1366)/8/8, 8/12, (pp. 343–356, 361–390). According to the head priest of Kasuga, it is believed that the monks intentionally brought a withering branch with them at the beginning of a protest. This branch was then magically revived (replaced) after Kōfukuji had received a favorable verdict (visit to and interview at Kasuga Taisha, June 17, 1997).

77. *Zokushi gushō*, Bun'ō 1 (1260)/1/21, 3/11, 13, 4/12; *Tendai zasuki*, 243; *Azuma kagami* (in *Shintei zōho kokushi taikei*), 727; *Ichidai yōki*, *Geki nikki*, Bun'ei 1 (1264)/3/23.

78. *Zokushi gushō*, Bun'ei 6 (1269)/7/14 (p. 61); *Tendai zasuki*, 280, Bun'ei 12 (1275)/3/14.

79. *Tendai zasuki*, 255 (Bun'ei 1/10/26). The court also sent messengers to Hiesha, Gionsha, and Kitano in the fifth month of that year to thank the gods for help in bringing the sacred palanquins back to their shrines after a protest at the palace (*Geki nikki*, Bun'ei 1/5/15).

80. *Sochiki*, Shōryaku 5 (1081)/3/25, 26, 12/4; *Fusō ryakki*, Shōryaku 5/3/28; *Suisaki*, Shōryaku 5/12/5.

81. *Denryaku*, *Chūyūki*, Eikyū 1/4/13–18; *DNS* 3:14, 160–163; Hioki, 126, 129.

82. This notion conforms with Keirstead's analysis of peasant protests (Keirstead, 75). See also *Chūyūki*, Eikyū 1 (1113)/4/1; *DNS* 3:14, 145–146.

83. *Genpei seisuiki*, volume 4, 169.

84. Hirata, *Sōhei to bushi*, 154. The *Ōkagami*, written in the late Heian period, notes that "even when there is no righteousness in the grievance of Yamashi-

nadera [Kōfukuji], there is not much one can do against the *Yamashina dōri*" (ibid., 154).

85. *Gyokuyō,* Jōan 3 (1173)/7/21, and Kenkyū 2 (1191)/4/26; *Kamakura ibun* 2, document 1009, *Kōfukuji chōjō,* Kenkyū 9 (1198)/11/1 (pp. 320–323); Arai, 90; Hirata, *Sōhei to bushi,* 153–155.

86. See Kuroda Toshio, *Jisha seiryoku,* 69.

87. Hirata, *Sōhei to bushi,* 124.

88. Ibid., 125–126; *Heian ibun,* volume 3, document 702, *Mino no kuni Senbu shōshi jūninra gesu,* Tengi 1 (1053)/7 (pp. 834–835); Kuroda, *Jisha seiryoku,* 48. For quotes by Kujō Kanezane and Go-Toba, see Hirata, *Sōhei to bushi,* 126.

89. For treatments in English of the *mappō* concept, see Ishida Ichirō, "Structure and Formation of *Gukanshō* Thought," in *The Future and the Past: A Translation and Study of the Gukanshō, an Interpretative History of Japan Written in 1219,* edited by Delmer M. Brown and Ichirō Ishida, 420–450; and Michele Marra, "The Conquest of *Mappō:* Jien and Kitabatake Chikafusa," *Japanese Journal of Religious Studies* 12:4 (1985), 319–341.

90. *Daisenji engi,* 103–104. The original picture scroll, believed to have been created in the early Muromachi period (probably in 1398), was destroyed in a fire on 1925/4/22. The version that remains available today is compiled from *shahon* (copies of the original) from Tokyo University and Tōkyō kokuritsu hakubutsukan.

91. *Hie sannō gongen,* 16, 79–81. The first screen is kept at Enryakuji, whereas the second one belongs to Shiga kenritsu biwako bunkakan.

92. Conversation with Mr. Ueno Ryōshin, curator at Shiga kenritsu bunkakan, June 19, 1997.

93. McCullough, *Tale of the Heike,* 52–54.

94. Missing character.

95. *Chūyūki,* Tennin 1 (1108)/3/23; *DNS* 3:10, 113.

96. Hirata, *Sōhei to bushi,* 157–158. A similar observation was also made by Kuroda Toshio, who noted that the protests were not direct confrontations with other blocs, but rather pressure on the court (Kuroda, *Chūsei kokka to tennō,* 278).

97. *Chūyūki,* Eikyū 1 (1113)/4/30; *DNS* 3:14, 179–180.

98. *Sankaiki,* Nin'an 2 (1167)/4/19, 23; *Kōfukuji bettō shidai,* 19.

99. See, for example, *Chūyūki,* Chōji 2 (1105)/10/29; *DNS* 3:8, 271.

100. *Hyakurenshō,* Kyūan 6 (1150)/8/5 (p. 68).

101. This method is still in use among several temples in Japan. In 1986, when the government threatened to impose a new tax on temples, several major tourist attractions such as Kinkakuji and Ginkakuji closed their gates to the public in Kyoto. In another more selective protest in 1993, Kiyomizudera prohibited visitors from a certain hotel to enter its premises because the hotel's plans for a new annex would ruin the scenic view from the temple.

102. *Meigetsuki,* Kenpō 1 (1213)/8/3–8; *DNS* 4:12, 650–664; Hirata, *Sōhei to bushi,* 130; *Hyakurenshō, Azuma kagami, Enryakuji gokoku engi,* in *DNS* 5:10, 184–188, Katei 1 (1235)/7/23; *Tendai zasuki,* 198–199.

103. Hirata, *Sōhei to bushi,* 129; *Hyakurenshō,* Chōkan 1 (1163)/6/9, 23, 7/22 (pp. 77–78).

104. *DNS* 5:14, 216; *Tsunetoshi kyōki* (unpublished), Shōka 1 (1257)/int. 3/1, 7;

Tendai zasuki, 230–231; *Azuma kagami* (in *Shintei zōho kokushi taikei*), Bun'ō 1 (1260)/2/3; *Ichidai yōki,* Bun'ō 1/3/17.

105. Hirata, *Sōhei to bushi,* 129.

106. Hioki, 238.

107. *Azuma kagami,* Katei 1 (1235)/7/24 (p. 163); *Hyakurenshō,* Katei 1/int. 6/19–21, 23, 27, 28 (p. 178); Tsuji, *Nihon bukkyō shi: chūsei* 1, 84–85; Katsuno, *Sōhei,* 31. As noted in Chapter 5 (note 79), Iwashimizu's *shin'yō* were actually brought out in 1104 in support of the assistant abbot Kōshin, but it is not clear how far they were taken (*Chūyūki, Tamefusa kyōki,* Chōji 1/2/16). There is conclusive evidence, though, that a *gōso* was staged in Kyoto by the shrine in 1279, although the holy carts were left at Tōji (indicating an affiliation between these two centers) instead of at the imperial palace (Katsuno, *Sōhei,* 128–129). The lack of precedence thus had its limitations.

108. Katsuno, *Sōhei,* 51, citing Ōya Tokujō, *Nihon bukkyō shi no kenkyū* (Tokyo: Kokusho kankōkai, 1928); Hioki, 136.

109. *Kōfukuji sōgō dai hosshira sōjō,* in *Kōfukuji sōsho,* volumes 123–124 of *Dainihon bukkyō zensho* (Tokyo: Bussho kankōkai 1917), part 2, 101; Hirata, *Sōhei to bushi,* 151; Katsuno, *Sōhei,* 48, 50.

110. Katsuno, *Sōhei,* 51; Hirata, *Sōhei to bushi,* 152; Hioki, 135.

111. *Entairyaku, Kugyō bunin,* Kōei 3 (1344)/3/4, 7/10, in *DNS* 6:8, 154–155, 319; Hirata, *Sōhei to bushi,* 136; Katsuno, *Sōhei,* 54.

112. Hirata notes that Enryakuji attacked and burned Onjōji in 1121, 1140, 1162, 1214, 1264, and 1317 (*Sōhei to bushi,* 167). Parts of the temple were also destroyed in 1280 (*Zokushi gūsho,* Kōan 3/6/29).

113. *Chūyūki, Denryaku,* Chōji 2 (1105)/10/29, 30; *DNS* 3:8, 270–271.

114. *Chūyūki,* Eikyū 1 (1113)/4/30; *DNS* 3:14, 179–180; *Gyokuyō,* Jōan 3 (1173)/9, 11/11, 12, 12/3; Hioki, 96–97.

115. *Chūyūki,* Eikyū 1/4/30; *DNS* 3:14, 179–180.

116. See McCullough, *Tale of the Heike,* 153–154, *Chūyūki,* Chōji 1 (1104)/10/7; Hirata, "Nanto hokurei sōhei ni tsuite," 283–284; Motoki, "Insei ki Kōfukuji kō," 189–190; Hirata, *Sōhei to bushi,* 176; *Heian ibun* 6, document 2937, *Kōfukuji shūsōra mōshijō,* Hōgen 3 (1158)/7 (pp. 2419–2422); *Kōfukuji bettō shidai,* 16–19.

Chapter 7   Religious Elites and the Ashikaga Bakufu: Collapsing the Gates of Power

1. See *The Origins of Medieval Japan,* edited by Jeffrey Mass. This chapter draws from my own contribution, titled "Enryakuji—an Old Power in a New Era."

2. Though Zen consists of several different schools, I use the term here in a more limited way to refer to the monks and institutions of the Ashikaga-favored Rinzai sect.

3. Kuroda, *Nihon chūsei no kokka to shūkyō,* 533, 539–543; idem, "Chūsei kokka to tennō," 291–294; idem, *Jisha seiryoku,* 203–205.

4. Kuroda, *Nihon chūsei no kokka to shūkyō,* 535–538; idem, *Jisha seiryoku,* 207–208.

5. Taira, *Nihon chūsei no shakai to bukkyō,* 335, 339–342; Hisano, 77–79; *Shiga-ken shi* 2, 423; Ōsumi Kazuo, "Buddhism in the Kamakura Period," in volume 3 of *The Cambridge History of Japan: Medieval Japan,* edited by Kozo Yamamura (Cambridge: Cambridge University Press, 1990), 564.

6. Ōsumi, 566; Martin Collcutt, *Five Mountains,* 50–52.

7. Kuroda, *Nihon chūsei no kokka to shūkyō,* 537–541; idem, "Chūsei kokka to tennō," 291, 296–300; Suzanne Gay, "The Muromachi Bakufu in Medieval Kyoto," (Ph.D. dissertation, Yale University, 1982), 195.

8. Nagahara Keiji, "Nihon kokka shi no ichi mondai," *Shisō* 475:1 (1964), 48.

9. Goble, *Kenmu: Go-Daigo's Revolution,* 48–52.

10. *Tendai zasuki,* 329–335; Collcutt, *Five Mountains,* 95. Goble claims that Go-Daigo established a "hegemony over the religious world" (*Kenmu: Go-Daigo's Revolution,* 75–76), but his repeated courting of and lack of support from the leading temples during the 1330s indicate that his control was temporary at best, hinging on donations and other momentary favors.

11. Inaba, 277, 290. The Fujiwara had alienated themselves from the temple, often neglecting to provide for Kōfukuji's financial base. Instead, much energy was spent on trying to dominate the temple through the two powerful cloisters of Daijōin (courted by the Kujō, Ichijō, and Nijō branches) and Ichijōin (the Konoe branch), inducing the clergy to become more amenable to other patrons and allies while seeking more independence from the aristocratic families (Nagashima, *Nara-ken no rekishi,* 90).

12. Goble, *Kenmu: Go-Daigo's Revolution,* 99–102; *Tendai zasuki,* 330–331, 333, 339; Hioki, 180–181; Helen Craig McCullough, trans., *The Taiheiki: A Chronicle of Medieval Japan* (Rutland, Vt., and Tokyo: Charles E. Tuttle, 1985), 28–30.

13. Hioki, 180–182, 186; McCullough, *Taiheiki,* 30.

14. Goble, *Kenmu: Go-Daigo's Revolution,* 121; Hioki, 182–183; *Tendai zasuki,* 332–333; McCullough, *Taiheiki,* 31, 58–62.

15. Goble, *Kenmu: Go-Daigo's Revolution,* 121–122; Hioki, 183; *Tendai zasuki,* 333–334; McCullough, *Taiheiki,* 31, 63–64.

16. Goble, *Kenmu: Go-Daigo's Revolution,* 122–124; McCullough, *Taiheiki,* 79–82.

17. Hioki, 184–185; Goble, *Kenmu: Go-Daigo's Revolution,* 124–125; McCullough, *Taiheiki,* 101, 105–106; *Tendai zasuki,* 335; Tsuji, *Nihon bukkyō shi: chūsei* 3, 67.

18. Goble, *Kenmu: Go-Daigo's Revolution,* 127–128; Hioki, 186; *Wakayama-ken shi: chūsei,* 286; McCullough, *Taiheiki,* 176–177, 192–200.

19. Goble, *Kenmu: Go-Daigo's Revolution,* 129–130; *Wakayama-ken shi: chūsei,* 287–289; McCullough, *Taiheiki,* 217–222.

20. Goble, *Kenmu: Go-Daigo's Revolution,* 132–135; Mc Cullough, *Taiheiki,* 205–221, 237–240, 250–259, 320–321.

21. Mc Cullough, *Taiheiki,* 340, 344; Goble, *Kenmu: Go-Daigo's Revolution,* 185; *Tendai zasuki,* 339; Kuroda, *Chūsei kokka to tennō,* 535–538.

22. In 1308, after having received an esoteric initiation, Go-Uda granted the posthumous title of Grand Master *(daishi)* to Yakushin (827–906), the founder of the lineage that performed the ceremony. Since this title had only been granted to Saichō, Kūkai, Ennin, and Enchin, the Enryakuji monks sensed that this was an attempt to make Tōji the main provider of ceremonies for the imperial court. After a rejected appeal, the monks even burned down parts of Hiesha in protest, and the issue was temporarily resolved when Go-Uda was forced to step down as retired emperor that same year. The conflict continued until 1312, when the bakufu was forced to oblige the Tendai monks. See *Tendai zasuki,* 312–317; Tsuji, *Nihon bukkyōshi: chūsei* 1, 60–73.

23. Goble, *Kenmu: Go-Daigo's Revolution,* 188–189.

24. Tsuji, *Nihon bukkyō shi: chūsei* 3, 66–68; Atsuta Tadashi, "Chūsei goki no shōen to sonraku," in *Wakayama-ken shi: chūsei*, 425–428; *Kōyasan monjo* 1, document 456, *Go-Daigo tennō rinji*, Genkō 1 (1331)/9/23 (pp. 522–523); document 30, *Go-Daigo tennō rinji*, Genkō 3 (1333)/10/8 (p. 32); *Kōyasan shunjū*, 204–205; Toyoda, "Kōyasan jiryō no hensen," in idem, *Kōyasan ryō shōen no shihai to kōzō*, 476.

25. Goble, *Kenmu: Go-Daigo's Revolution*, 190–192.

26. Ibid., 192–197.

27. Hioki, 186; *Tendai zasuki*, 340; McCullough, *Taiheiki*, 344; Goble, *Kenmu: Go-Daigo's Revolution*, 247–253.

28. Hioki, 187–188; *Tendai zasuki*, 341; Goble, *Kenmu: Go-Daigo's Revolution*, 252–256; Nagashima, *Nara-ken no rekishi*, 90; Atsuta, "Chūsei goki no shōen to sonraku," 428.

29. Hioki, 188; *Tendai zasuki*, 342; Goble, *Kenmu: Go-Daigo's Revolution*, 258–259.

30. Hioki, 189–190; *Tendai zasuki*, 342–343; Goble, *Kenmu: Go-Daigo's Revolution*, 259.

31. Hioki, 190; *Tendai zasuki*, En'en 1 (1336)/7/16 (p. 343).

32. Hioki, 190–191; Goble, *Kenmu: Go-Daigo's Revolution*, 261; *Wakayama-ken shi: chūsei*, 295.

33. *Wakayama-ken shi: chūsei*, 296; Atsuta Tadashi, "Shugo ryō kokusei no tenkai," in *Wakayama-ken shi: chūsei*, 390–391.

34. Tsuji, *Nihon bukkyō shi: chūsei* 3, 69; Hioki, 191–192. Kōfukuji's Ichijōin cloister, which was headed by the younger brother of Konoe Tadatsune, a supporter of Go-Daigo, did in fact express its support for the Southern Court in 1336, but it did not provide any substantial assistance (Nagashima, *Nara-ken no rekishi*, 92–93).

35. For example, on the one hand, Ashikaga Takauji responded to a Kōyasan appeal on Kenmu 4 (1337)/2/13 by ordering one of his vassals to ensure that intrusions of an estate in Harima would be stopped and that the land would remain under the control of the temple's Kongō sanmai'in cloister (*Kongō sanmai'in monjo*, in *DNS* 6:4, 79–81). On the other hand, the Southern Court confirmed Miyoshi Sukemasa's donation of land to Kōyasan in the twelfth month of 1337 (*Kōyasan monjo*, in *DNS* 6:4, Engen 2/12/24, 483–484).

36. Hioki, 179, 192–193; Nagashima, *Nara-ken no rekishi*, 93.

37. *Nibu monjo*, in *DNS* 6:5, Ryakuō 1 (1338)/8/2, (p. 2); *Kōyasan monjo*, in *DNS* 6:5, Ryakuō 2 (1339)/2/25 (pp. 433–434), Ryakuō 2/11/26, (pp. 814–815); Tsuji, *Nihon bukkyō shi: chūsei* 3, 71.

38. Atsuta, "Chūsei goki no shōen to sonraku," 428–435.

39. *Kokin saiyō shō, Entairyaku*, both in *DNS* 6:6, Ryakuō 3 (1340)/10/23 (pp. 376–377); *Kasuga jinja monjo*, in *DNS* 6:6, Ryakuō 3/11/3 (pp. 385–387); *Chūin ippon ki*, Ryakuō 3/12/17–19, in *DNS* 6:6, 424–428; Hioki, 193–195, 207; Nagashima, *Nara-ken no rekishi*, 93.

40. See *DNS* 6:6, Ryakuō 3/11/8 (pp. 387–388); Ryakuō 3/12/19 (pp. 424–428); Ryakuō 4 (1341)/1/1 (pp. 543–552), Ryakuō 4/1/7 (pp. 572–593), 1/8 (pp. 593–594), 1/11 (p. 596), 1/16 (pp. 605–615), 2/7 (pp. 650–652), 2/9 (pp. 653–654). Among the sources noted are *Gyokuei kishō, Chūin ippon ki, Kasuga jinja monjo, Kokin saiyō shō, Moromori ki*, and *Zoku shi gushō*.

41. Hioki, 194–195, 207.

42. *Kōyasan monjo*, in *DNS* 6:11, Jōwa 4 (1348)/3 (pp. 439–440), Jōwa 4/8 (p. 804); *Kōya shunjū*, Jōwa 4/3/10 (p. 211); Toyoda, "Kōyasan jiryō no hensen," 476; Hioki, 195–196.

43. Collcutt, *Five Mountains*, 57–61.

44. A brawl between Tōji and Enryakuji monks in 1367 represents the only instance of a conflict between Enryakuji and other *kenmitsu* temples during the whole of the period from the establishment of the Ashikaga Bakufu to the end of the fourteenth century (*Moromori ki*, in *Shiryō sanshū*, 11 volumes [Tokyo: Zoku gunsho ruijū kanseikai, 1968], Jōji 6 (1367)/8/18, 19, 20; *DNS* 6:22, 247–272). As for Kōfukuji, it was involved in a fight with Tōdaiji in the ninth month of 1349, when about five monks were killed on each side (Jōwa 5 [1349]/9/6, in *DNS* 6:12, 913–914). It is clear from these rare cases of conflicts between the *kenmitsu* temples that a severe shift within the Buddhist establishment had occurred, indicating that the early Ashikaga period does indeed mark the end of an era.

45. Collcutt, *Five Mountains*, 103–105; Hioki, 216–218; Tsuji, *Nihon bukkyō shi: chūsei* 3, 118.

46. The entire set of appeals and complaints has been recorded in various sources and can be found in *DNS* 6:9, 121–143, 190–212, and in Hioki, 219–233.

47. *Sanzen'in monjo*, Kōei 3/12; *Sanmon uttaemōsu*, Kōei 4/6/29; *Kōei yonnen sanmon uttaemōsu*, Kōei 4/7/3, in *DNS* 6:9, 121–124.

48. *Kōei yonnen sanmon uttaemōsu*, Kōei 4/7/3, 7/4, 7/20, in *DNS* 6:9, 122–125, 128, 130–132; Hioki, 220–223, 225–226. I am grateful to Carl Bielefeldt for sharing crucial information regarding Kagenji and Kenninji. The former was never built, as Enryakuji pressure dissuaded Emperor Go-Uda from carrying out his plans to construct this Zen temple in the Higashiyama area. Kenninji was constructed for Eisai—one of the Zen founders in Japan—in 1202, but Enryakuji managed to have it confirmed as a Tendai branch. Enryakuji thus claimed that Zen temples could only exist as branches of Enryakuji, referring to these precedents (Ogisu Jundō, *Nihon chūsei zenshū shi* [Tokyo: Mokujisha, 1965], 217–218). It should also be noted, however, that Kenninji eventually became an exclusive Zen temple in 1268, before becoming officially recognized as such by the Ashikaga in 1334.

49. *Kōei yonnen sanmon uttaemōsu*, *Entairyaku*, in *DNS* 6:9, Kōei 4/7/4, 8, 18, 20, 23 (pp. 124–126, 129–133); Hioki, 224, 227–230; *Tendai zasuki*, 354–355; Tsuji, *Nihon bukkyō shi: chūsei* 3, 121–128; *Kōfukuji ryaku nendaiki*, 181.

50. *Entairyaku*, *Moromori ki*, Kōei 4/7/23, *Sanmon uttaemōsu*, Kōei 4/8/3, 8, *Moromori ki*, Kōei 4/8/15, *Taiheiki*, volume 24, all in *DNS* 6:9, 191–211; Hioki, 230–233; *Saisai yōki*, in volume 1 of *Zoku shiseki shūran* (Kyoto: Rinsen shoten, 1984), 11–12; *Kōfukuji ryaku nendaiki*, Kagen 3 (1305)/4/6 (pp. 174–175); Tsuji, *Nihon bukkyō shi: chūsei* 3, 145.

51. *Entairyaku*, in *Shiryō sekishū: kokiroku hen* (Tokyo: Zoku gunsho ruijū kanseikai, 1970–1986), Kōei 4/8/8; *DNS* 6:9, 198–199; Hioki, 232–235; *Moromori ki*, Kōei 4/8/29, 8/30; Collcutt, 105–106; Tsuji, *Nihon bukkyō shi: chūsei* 3, 148–150.

52. *Moromori ki*, Jōji 6/6/18, 26, 7/2; *DNS* 6:27, 127–128; *Gukanki*, volumes 1–4 of *Zoku shiryō taisei* (Kyoto: Rinsen shoten, 1967), Jōji 6 (1367)/8/8; Hioki, 236; Tsuji, *Nihon bukkyō shi: chūsei* 3, 295.

53. "The Enryakuji monks are merely the monkeys of the seven [Hie] shrines. They look like humans but they are not" (*Zoku shōbōron* in *DNS* 6:29, 477). See

also Tsuji, *Nihon bukkyō shi: chūsei* 3, 296–298. Jōzan is making a pun here, refer-ring to the numerous monkeys that inhabited the area around the Hie shrines on the eastern slopes of Mt. Hiei.

54. *Nanzenji taiji soshō,* Ōan 1/int. 6, in *DNS* 6:29, 483–486; Satō Hiroo, 209; Tsuji, *Nihon bukkyō shi: chūsei* 3, 37, 299–303.

55. The bakufu uses the rhetoric of the victor here, equating loyalty to the state with the interests of the Ashikaga clan even before the establishment of the Muromachi Bakufu.

56. *Sanmon gōsoki,* Ōan 1/7/10, in *DNS* 6:29, 489–492; Tsuji, *Nihon bukkyō shi: chūsei* 3, 306–307; Hioki, 238–239.

57. *Nanzenji taiji soshō,* Ōan 1/8/4, in *DNS* 6:30, 21; Tsuji, *Nihon bukkyō shi: chūsei* 3, 308–328.

58. Hioki, 200. Another example, also involving the Sasaki family, occurred in 1357–1358 (Hioki, 202; *Sugaura monjo,* in *DNS* 6:21, 427–432, 522–524; *Gukanki,* Enbun 3 [1358]/2/3; *DNS* 6:21, 737).

59. *Gukanki,* Ōan 1/7/5; *DNS* 6:29, 494–495.

60. *Moromori ki,* Ōan 7/6/20; *Hie shin'yō gojuraku kenmon ryakki, Gukanki, San-mon gōsoki,* in *DNS* 6:30, Ōan 1/8/28 (pp. 38–42); *Tendai zasuki,* 380–382; Tsuji, *Nihon bukkyō shi: chūsei* 3, 330–332; Hioki, 240–242.

61. *Gogumaiki* and *Gion shaki,* in *DNS* 6:30, Ōan 2 (1369)/4/20; 415–419; *Gukanki,* Ōan 2/4/2, 4, 8, 20, 7/19, 28; *Gogumaiki,* Ōan 2/7/4, 20, 27; *DNS* 6:31, 29–31; Hioki, 242–243; *Tendai zasuki,* 382–384; Collcutt, 119–122; Tsuji, *Nihon bukkyō shi: chūsei* 3, 332–333.

62. *Kaei sandaiki,* Ōan 5 (1372)/7/11, in *DNS* 6:36, 23–24; *Gukanki,* Ōan 6 (1373)/6/19, 29, 8/10, Ōan 7 (1374)/6/20, Ōan 8 (1375)/7/27, Eiwa 5 (1379)/ 2/9, /6/8, 14; *Gogumaiki,* Ōan 6/8/10, in *DNS* 6:38, 60–61; *Gukanki, Gogumaiki, Moromori ki, Kaei sandaiki,* Ōan 7/6/20, in *DNS* 6:41, 22–27; *Kaei sandaiki* (in *Shinkō gunsho ruijū: zatsubu* [Tokyo: Naigai shoseki kabushiki gaisha, 1938]), Eiwa 5/6/8; *Hie shin'yō gojuraku kenmon ryakki* (in *Shinkō gunsho ruijū, jingibu* 1 [Tokyo: Naigai shoseki kabushiki gaisha, 1938], p. 472), Kōryaku 2 (1380)/6/30; Hioki, 244; *Tendai zasuki,* 387, 389; *Chūsei hōsei shi shiryō shū,* volume 2: *Muromachi bakufu hō,* document 127, Kōryaku 1 (1379)/7/25 (pp. 54–55); Tsuji, *Nihon bukkyō shi: chūsei* 3, 334–335; Mori Shigeaki, *Nanbokuchō ki kōbu kankei shi no kenkyū* (Tokyo: Bunken shuppan, 1984), 263. Hosokawa Yoriyuki (1329–1392) left Kyoto for Sanuki Province after he was ousted by shōgun Yoshimitsu in 1379, but he resur-faced in 1390, when he was appointed *shugo* of Bingo. His son, Yorimoto, became *kanrei* the next year, allowing Yoriyuki to resume an important position within the bakufu.

63. *Moromori ki,* Jōji 6 (1367)/8/18, 19, 20; *DNS* 6:22, 247–272; Hioki, 202–204; *Kōfukuji ryaku nendaiki,* Jōji 6/8/19 (p. 183); *Taiheiki,* volume 40, in *DNS* 6:28, Jōji 6/8/18 (pp. 286–287).

64. See, for example, *Chūsei hōsei shi* 2, document 1, Kenmu 4 (1337)/10/7; document 6, Ryakuō 3 (1340)/4/15; document 55, Kannō 2 (1351)/6/13; document 56, Kannō 3 (1352)/7/24; document 57, Kannō 3/8/21; documents 79–83, Enbun 2 (1357)/9/10; documents 84–85, Jōji 6 (1368)/6/27; documents 96–97, Ōan 1 (1368)/6/17.

65. "Nanbokuchō nairan," in *Wakayama-ken shi: chūsei,* 306.

66. Satō Shin'ichi, "Kyōto sōdatsusen," in volume 9 of *Chūō kōronsha Nihon reki-*

shi: Nanbokuchō no dōran (Tokyo: Chūō kōronsha, 1967), 270–272; "Nanbokuchō nairan," in *Wakayama-ken shi: chūsei,* 307.

67. *Ashikaga shogun daidai gechijō,* in *DNS* 6:14, Kannō 2/1/8 (p. 386); *Entairyaku,* Kannō 2/1/9; *Kachōyō ryaku,* Bunna 1 (1352)/3/18, 4/2, in *DNS* 6:16, 370, 412–413; *Kyōto teikoku daigaku shozō monjo,* Enbun 5 (1360)/3/18, in *DNS* 6:23, 82; *Gogumaiki,* Jōji 2 (1363)/4/13, in *DNS* 6:25, 56–57.

68. *Gokyojōtō shitsuji hikitsuke,* in *DNS* 6:13, Kannō 1 (1350)/8/5 (pp. 782–783), Kannō 1/8/23 (p. 824), Kannō 1/8/26 (pp. 829–830), Kannō 1/8/27 (p. 831), Kannō 2 (1351)/4/17 (p. 964); *Gokyojōtō shitsuji hikitsuke,* in *DNS* 6:14, Kannō 1/ 11/23 (p. 52); *Tōkondō saisai yōki, Taiheiki,* in *DNS* 6:14, Kannō 2/1/22 (pp. 673– 675).

69. *Tōkondō saisai yōki, Entairyaku, Kōfukuji sangō bunin,* in *DNS* 6:15, Kannō 2 (1351)/5/18 (pp. 15–21); *Entairyaku, Kanetsuna kōki, Tōkondō saisai yōki,* in *DNS* 6:15, Kannō 2/7/6 (pp. 108–116); Hioki, 207–208; Nagashima, *Nara-ken no rekishi,* 90–91; *Saisai yōki,* Kannō 2/7 (p. 28).

70. Nagashima, *Nara-ken no rekishi,* 93–95; *Saisai yōki nukigaki,* in *Dainihon bukkyō zensho: Kōfukuji sōsho,* part 2 (Tokyo: Bussho kankōkai, 1931), 182–183; *Saisai yōki,* Kannō 2/8/6, 9, 10 (pp. 28–29).

71. *Gokyojōtō shitsuji hikitsuke,* in *DNS* 6:16, Shōhei 7 (1352)/6/21 (pp. 591– 592); ibid., in *DNS* 6:17, Bunna 1 (1352)/9/4 (pp. 7–8), 9/26 (pp. 49–50), 12/8 (pp. 288–289); Nagashima, *Nara-ken no rekishi,* 95; Hioki, 208.

72. *Gokyojōtō shitsuji hikitsuke,* in *DNS* 6:18, Bunna 2 (1353)/5/16 (p. 77), Bunna 3 (1354)/2/3 (p. 714), 2/11 (pp. 718–720), 3/21 (p. 746); ibid., in *DNS* 6:19, Bunna 3 (1354)/5/8 (pp. 49–50), 8/8 (p. 128), 9/24 (p. 160), int. 10/5 (p. 198); ibid., in *DNS* 6:20, Bunna 4 (1355)/10/3 (pp. 28–29), 10/9 (p. 34); *Gukanki,* Enbun 1 (1356)/7/11, 13, 23, Enbun 2 (1357)/2/11; *Entairyaku,* Enbun 1/7/13, Enbun 2/2/13, 3/4; *DNS* 6:20, Enbun 1/7/13 (pp. 651–653); *DNS* 6:20, 223; *DNS* 6:21, 204–206; *Saisai yōki nukigaki,* 188–189; *Saisai yōki,* Bunna 5 (1356)/7/12.

73. *Shinboku juryakki, Daijōin nikki mokuroku,* in *DNS* 6:26, Jōji 3 (1364)/12/19, (pp. 408, 410); Satō Shin'ichi, *Ashikaga Yoshimitsu: Chūsei ōken e no chōsen* (Tokyo: Heibonsha, 1994), 105.

74. *Daijōin nikki mokuroku, Shinboku juryakki,* and other sources, listed in *DNS* 6:26, Jōji 3 (1364)/12/20 (pp. 408–424); Katsuno, *Sōhei,* 43–44.

75. *Zokushi gushō,* Jōji 4 (1365)/11/1, Jōji 5 (1366)/6; *DNS* 6:27, 67, 327–328, 362.

76. *Yoshida nichijiki, Kasuga kannushi ki, Taiheiki, Shinboku godōza tabitabi dairan ruijū, Tōkondō saisai yōki, Gogumaiki, Moromori ki,* and other sources in *DNS* 6:27, Jōji 5/8/8 (pp. 343–356), 8/12 (pp. 361–390), 9/3 (p. 428); Satō Shin'ichi, *Ashikaga Yoshimitsu,* 106.

77. *Saisai yōki nukigaki,* Ōan 4 (1371)/9, 12 (pp. 199–200); *Kōfukuji ryaku nendaiki,* 183–184; *Gukanki,* Ōan 6 (1373)/1/21, in *DNS* 6:36, 358; Hioki, 209.

78. *Gukanki, Gogumaiki,* in *DNS* 6:38, Ōan 6/11/12, 13, (pp. 282–284); *Saisai yōki nukigaki,* Ōan 5 (1372)/10/7 (p. 201); *Saisai yōki,* 290–291; *Kaei sandaiki, Kasuga shinboku gojuraku kenmon ryakki,* in *DNS* 6:40, Ōan 7 (1374)/5/26 (pp. 574–575).

79. *Kaei sandaiki, Daijōin nikki mokuroku, Monzeki den,* in *DNS* 6:41, Ōan 7 (1374)/6/12 (pp. 16–17); *Gukanki, Moromori ki, Kaei sandaiki, Kasuga shinboku*

gojuraku kenmon ryakki, Gogumaiki, in *DNS* 6:41, Ōan 7/11/3 (pp. 236–241); *Gukanki, Gogumaiki, Moromori ki, Kokin saiyō shō, Daijōin nikki mokuroku, Kōfukuji ryaku nendaiki,* in *DNS* 6:41, Ōan 7/12/17 (pp. 333–340); Hioki, 209; *Kōfukuji ryaku nendaiki,* 184.

80. *Kōyasan monjo* 1, document 510, *Ashikaga Yoshiakira kinsei,* Kannō 1 (1350)/ 6/19 (pp. 560–561); *DNS* 6:13, 702–704; *Kōya shunjū,* Kannō 1/4/25, 6/25, 10/27 (p. 212).

81. *Kōyasan monjo* 1, document 293, *Kitabatake Chikafusa rengajōin kangaku ryōsho kishinjō,* Shōhei 7 (1352)/4/1 (p. 314); in *DNS* 6:16, 409–410.

82. *Kōyasan monjo* 1, document 146, *Ōta no shō zasshō jitōdai wayōjō,* Jōwa 4 (1348)/8/27 (pp. 168–170); document 1962, in ibid., volume 8 (pp. 625–627); *DNS* 6:11, 804–809; *Kōyasan monjo* 1, document 35, *Go-Murakami tennō rinji,* Shōhei 6 (1351)/10/27 (p. 35); *Kōyasan monjo,* in *DNS* 6:14, Kannō 2 (1351)/4/ 25 (p. 973).

83. *Kōyasan monjo* 1, document 190, *Go-Murakami tennō rinji,* Shōhei 9 (1354)/ 2/21 (pp. 210–211), document 544, *Tōji chōja mikyōjō,* same date (p. 585); *DNS* 6:18, 728.

84. *Kōyasan monjo,* in *DNS* 6:18, Bunna 3 (1354)/3/21 (pp. 746–748); *DNS* 6:19, Bunna 3/9/17 (pp. 155–156).

85. *Kōyasan kyūki, Sanpōin kyūki,* in *DNS* 6:22, Shōhei 14 (1359)/10/22 (pp. 721–722); "Nanbokuchō nairan," in *Wakayama-ken shi: chūsei,* 312.

86. Atsuta, "Shugo ryō kokusei no tenkai," in *Wakayama-ken shi: chūsei,* 353–354.

87. Atsuta, "Chūsei goki no shōen to sonraku," 434–440; Kuroda, *Nihon chūsei kokka to shūkyō,* 204. A number of land survey and tax evaluations remain in particular from the Ōei years (1394–1428). See for example documents 999–1018 in *Kōyasan monjo* 5. Kuroda maintained that this adjustment saved the *kenmon* temples from declining together with the *shōen* (*Nihon chūsei kokka to shūkyō,* 204). However, based on my analysis, it appears more appropriate to conclude that Kōyasan survived the changing conditions of the fourteenth and fifteenth centuries not as a *kenmon*—whose status and authority were insufficient to secure proprietorship at this time—but as a new kind of local power. Disengaged form Tōji and capital politics, the Kōyasan complex relied exclusively on local rulership and control of land instead of participation in ceremonies and religious status, suggesting that a cooperative rulership *(kenmon taisei)* was no longer functional.

88. See Thomas Conlan, "Largesse and the Limits of Loyalty in the Fourteenth Century," in *The Origins of Medieval Japan: Courtiers, Clerics, Warriors and Peasants in the Fourteenth Century,* edited by Jeffrey Mass, 42.

89. Toyoda Takeshi and Sugiyama Hiroshi, "The Growth of Commerce and Trade," in *Japan in the Muromachi Age,* edited by John W. Hall and Toyoda Takeshi (Berkeley: University of California Press, 1977), 131–132; Toyoda Takeshi, *Za no kenkyū* (Tokyo: Yoshikawa kōbunkan, 1982), 104–105.

90. Toyoda, *Za no kenkyū,* 113–114; Gay, "The Muromachi Bakufu in Medieval Kyoto," 85; Wakita Haruo with Susan B. Hanley, "Dimensions of Development: Cities in Fifteenth and Sixteenth Century Japan," in *Japan before Tokugawa: Political Consolidation and Economic Growth,* edited by John W. Hall, Nagahara Keiji, and Kozo Yamamura (Princeton: Princeton University Press, 1981), 319; Kozo Yamamura, "The Development of Za in Medieval Japan," *Business History Review* 47:4 (winter 1973), 447–451; Toyoda Takeshi and Sugiyama Hiroshi, "The Growth of

Commerce and Trade," 137; *Gion shitsugyō nikki,* Kōei 2 (1343)/7, in *DNS* 6:7, 757–759.

91. Gay, "The Muromachi Bakufu in Medieval Kyoto," 117–119; *Kitano tenmangū shiryō: komonjo,* edited by Kitano tenmangū shiryō kankōkai (Kyoto: Kitano tenmangū, 1978), documents 7 and 8, Ōei 26 (1419)/9/12, 9/14; Yamamura, "The Development of *Za,*" 449–454.

92. *Chūsei hōsei shiryō shū,* volume 2: *Muromachi bakufu hō,* document 105, Ōan 3 (1370)/12/16; document 145, Shitoku 3 (1386)/8/25.

93. Toyoda, "Za to dōso," in volume 6 of *Iwanami kōza Nihon rekishi: chūsei,* part 2 (Tokyo: Iwanami shoten, 1967), 177, 180; Toyoda, "The Growth of Commerce and Trade," 132; Gay, "The Muromachi Bakufu in Medieval Kyoto," 117; Kozo Yamamura, "The Growth of Commerce in Medieval Japan," in volume 3 of the *Cambridge History of Japan,* edited by Kozo Yamamura (Cambridge: Cambridge University Press, 1990), 389–391; *Kitano tenmangū shiryō: komonjo,* documents 3, Kōryaku 1 (1379)/9/20, and 4, Kakei 1 (1387)/9/16; Toyoda, *Za no kenkyū,* 130–133.

94. Toyoda Takeshi, "Za to dōso," 162–166; idem, "The Growth of Commerce and Trade," 134, 137; Nagashima, *Nara,* 178–180, 185–188; Toyoda Takeshi, *Za no kenkyū,* 71, 112, 116–118, 275–276; Ono Kōji, *Nihon chūsei shōgyō shi no kenkyū* (Tokyo: Hōsei daigaku shuppan, 1989), 55–57.

95. Gay, "The Muromachi Bakufu in Medieval Kyoto," 92–93.

96. *Entairyaku,* Kōei 3 (1344)/7/11, 12, 22, 24, 25, 28, 29, in *DNS* 6:8, 317, 319–322; Hioki, 136.

97. *Entairyaku,* Kōei 3/11/18, in *DNS* 6:8, 509; Jōwa 1 (1345)/1/1, in *DNS* 6:8, 679–680.

98. *Kasuga jinja monjo,* in *DNS* 6:27, Jōwa 5 (1366)/8/3 (p. 342).

99. There is no exact information on Enryakuji's toll gates during the fourteenth century. However, seven toll stations (Honzeki, Dōmuseki, Kōdōseki, Yokawaseki, Chūdōseki, Taniseki, and Saitōseki) are mentioned in a document of 1448/9 (Shimosaka Mamoru, "Sanmon shisetsu seido no seiritsu to tenkai," *Shirin* 58:1 [1975], 106, 110, 112; *Nanzenji monjo,* cited in Imatani Akira, *Sengoku ki no Muromachi bakufu* [Tokyo: Kadokawa shoten, 1975], 92–93).

100. *Moromori ki,* Jōji 2 (1363)/int. 1/26; *Chūsei hōsei shiryō shū,* volume 2: *Muromachi bakufu hō,* document 17 (p. 17); *Rinsenji kasanegaki anmon,* Jōji 5 (1366)/8/11, in *DNS* 6:27, 360–361; ibid., Jōji 6 (1366)/8/21, in *DNS* 6:28, 305–306; Toyoda, "Za to dōso," 133; Shimosaka, "Sanmon shisetsu seido," 106.

101. In 1268 Hōjō Tokimune issued an edict threatening to punish the monks, who were fighting among themselves, if they did not make peace. See Hisano, "Sanmon-jimon no sōkoku," 91–95. Edicts proclaiming the restriction of arms were also issued on 1188/2/22, in 1189/2, and on 1212/3/22 and 1265/8/21.

102. All thirty-four head abbots appointed from 1336 to 1400 were aristocrats or imperial princes who were brought up in Kyoto (*Tendai zasuki,* 339–404).

103. Shimosaka, "Sanmon shisetsu seido," 82, 89–92 (citing *Hie shin'yō gojuraku kenmon ryakki*); *Entairyaku,* entry for Jōwa 1 (1345)/8/8; *DNS* 6:9, Jōwa 1/8/14 (199); *Gukanki,* Ōan 2 (1369)/4/7, 7/4; *Gogumaiki,* Ōan 2/4/7. The term *"daimyō"* was usually reserved for warriors of magnate status.

104. *Kaei sandaiki,* Ōan 3 (1370)/8/6, in *DNS* 6:32, 223.

105. Shimosaka, "Sanmon shisetsu seido," 85–95, 113; Shimosaka, "Nanboku-chō jidai no Rokkaku shi," in *Yōkaichi-shi shi,* volume 2: *Chūsei,* edited by Naka-mura Ken (Yōkaichi-shi: Yōkaichi shiyakusho, 1983), 165.

106. Shimosaka, "Sanmon shisetsu seido," 91–92; idem, "Nanbokuchō jidai no Rokkaku shi," 166–167; Usui Nobuyoshi, *Ashikaga Yoshimitsu* (Tokyo: Yoshi-kawa kōbunkan, 1974), 56; Imatani Akira, *Muromachi no ōken: Ashikaga Yoshimitsu no ōken sandatsu keikai* (Tokyo: Chūō kōronsha, 1990), 67–68. Imatani Akira be-lieves that Yoshimitsu's involvement in the coup was limited. However, as Shimo-saka points out, the sources reveal that Yoshimitsu was in close contact with the new magistrates in the fifth month of 1379 (Shimosaka, "Sanmon shisetsu seido," 91). There should be no real doubt as to his personal involvement in the new policies. For an extensive treatment of the Gozan Zen network and its expansion under Yoshimitsu, see Collcutt, 119–123.

107. I have only found two *gōso*—in 1415 and 1428—and one appeal (1427) by Enryakuji for the whole of the period from 1378 to 1433. Clearly, this lack of disturbances indicates that the temple had been effectively contained for the first time. The Eikyō incident of 1433 marked the beginning of the end of the bakufu's successful intervention. An uprising by the temple constables was easily suppressed by Ashikaga Yoshinori, but it also resulted in a substantial loss of in-fluence by the bakufu within the temple. The principal source for this incident is the *Mansai jugō nikki* (Kyoto: Kyoto daigaku, 1920; also published in *Zoku gunsho ruijū, bui,* edited by Zoku gunsho ruijū kanseikai, 1974–1975). See also Shimo-saka, "Sanmon shisetsu seido."

108. *Kaei sandaiki,* Kōryaku 1 (1379)/1/6; Nagashima, *Nara-ken no rekishi,* 97; *Kōfukuji ryaku nendaiki,* 184; *Saisai yōki,* 298–300; Hioki, 210.

109. *Gukanki,* Kōryaku 1/7/16, 8/16, 9/17, 10/20, 11/22, 12/23; *Gogumaiki,* Kōryaku 1/8/16; *Kōfukuji ryaku nendaiki,* 184–185; *Saisai yōki,* 301; Hioki, 210

110. *Saisai yōki nukigaki,* Kōryaku 2 (1380)/12/12, Kōryaku 3 (1381)/3/3, 5/ 1 (p. 208), Eitoku 2 (1382)/6/13 (p. 209), *Gukanki,* Eitoku 1/3/4, 5/7, 8, 8/28; *Gogumaiki,* Eitoku 1/5/1; Hioki, 210–211.

111. Nagashima, *Nara-ken no rekishi,* 96–97.

112. Imatani, *Muromachi no ōken,* 68, citing from Tsunetsugu's diary *Kōryaku.*

113. Imatani, *Muromachi no ōken,* 68–70, 72–73; Akira Imatani and Kōzo Yama-mura, "Not for a Lack of Will or Wile: Yoshimitsu's Failure to Supplant the Impe-rial Lineage" (an article summarizing Imatani's views from *Muromachi no ōken),* *Journal of Japanese Studies* 18:1 (1992), 55, 57.

114. Nagashima, *Nara-ken no rekishi,* 96–97.

115. Nagashima, *Nara-ken no rekishi,* 96–97; Usui, 62, 88, 104–105, 150–151; Imatani, *Muromachi no ōken,* 131–132.

116. *Tendai zasuki,* 394, 403; Usui, 88–89, 102–103; Imatani, *Muromachi no ōken,* 126–128; Imatani and Yamamura, 56–57. Yoshimitsu followed the procedures of Go-Shirakawa's pilgrimage to Enryakuji in 1176 and Go-Saga's in 1269 to the letter, with identical titles granted to the abbots of the cloisters (Usui, 103).

117. *Kōya shunjū,* 221; Atsuta, "Shugo ryō kokusei no tenkai," 317–318, 338; Usui, 60–61, 151; Lorraine F. Harrington, "Regional Outposts of Muro-machi Rule: The Kantō and Kyushu," in *The Bakufu in Japanese History,* edited by Jeffrey P. Mass and William B. Hauser (Stanford: Stanford University Press, 1985), 89–90.

118. Imatani, *Muromachi no ōken,* 73–74; *Tendai zasuki,* 393, 405, 409, 428; Mori, *Nanbokuchō ki kōbu kankei shi no kenkyū,* 502; Imatani and Yamamura, 45–78.

119. See also Satō Hiroo, 203–204.

Chapter 8 Epilogue: Religious Power and the Power of Religion in Premodern Japan

1. The earliest use of the term *"sōhei"* in Japan has been traced to 1715, in a work titled the *Kansai hikki.* Kuroda believes that the expression was introduced from Korea (*Jisha seiryoku,* 31–32). The *Daiaihon shi* is a 397-volume work that was begun in the Mito domain in 1693. It was completed in 1906.

2. Such views have been expressed in Japanese by Uejima ("Chūsei zenki no kokka to bukkyō," 54) and Motoki Yasuo ("Insei ki Kōfukuji kō," 186–188).

Glossary of Terms
and Names

bettō 別当

Head administrator in a variety of organs, ranging from headquarters of a noble household, the imperial police, to certain temples. The term was most commonly used for smaller temples and branches, but also denoted the head abbot for Kōfukuji.

Chōkōdō 長講堂

A Buddhist hall that was originally built within Go-Shirakawa's Rokujō mansion in the southeastern part of Kyoto. It became quite wealthy in the Kamakura period, as it received numerous estates, becoming one of the main assets for the Jimyōin (Senior) Line of the imperial family. The Chō-kōdō was the main target for Kōfukuji protests in Kyoto in the fourteenth century.

Daidenpōin 大伝法院

The headquarters for the Shingi Shingon sect, located at Negoroji. The Daidenpōin was originally established as a cloister on Mt. Kōya by Kakuban in 1130, but when Toba granted it special status and stated that the head of the cloister should also be the abbot of Kongōbuji (Kōyasan), new frictions emerged. Kakuban was driven off Mt. Kōya, and the tensions continued for over a century until 1288, when the monk Raiyu moved the cloister to its present location at Negoroji, marking the establishment of the new Shingon sect.

daijō daijin 太政大臣

Grand Minister of the imperial state. The highest-ranking title in the imperial court hierarchy.

dōshū 堂衆

Worker-monks. The rank and file of most large temple communities. Their main responsibilities included menial tasks such as maintenance, preparation for rituals, and other daily practical matters.

Enjitsu 円実

(1212–?) The son of Kujō Michiie, Enjitsu was appointed head abbot of the Fujiwara clan temple in 1235 at age twenty-three but resigned later that year.

He was reappointed in 1258 and headed Kōfukuji until 1264, when his lack of support of a protest lodged by the clergy led to violent confrontations and his deposition. He attempted a comeback with the help of armed supporters in 1266 but was beaten and managed to retire in the vicinity of Nara only with the help of his noble peers in Kyoto.

Fujiwara no Narichika　藤原成親

(1137–1177) Narichika was a career commander with ambitions within the imperial court. As a twenty-two-year-old, he sided with Fujiwara no Nobuyori in the Heiji Disturbance of 1159–1160 against both Go-Shirakawa and Taira no Kiyomori. Narichika escaped execution because of his marriage to Kiyomori's daughter, but he was stripped of his offices. He was reinstated in 1161 but was immediately involved in another incident centering on the newly born Prince Tadahito (Go-Shirakawa's seventh son, later Emperor Takakura, who ruled 1168–1180), resulting in his exile. Narichika was pardoned the following year and, resuming his career as a hired sword, received Owari as a proprietary province in 1166. He was Enryakuji's main opponent in a dispute over land in Owari in 1169 and sided against the temple and Taira no Kiyomori in 1176–1177.

gekokujō　下剋上

"The lower overthrowing those above." A historical term that describes the social and political upheavals that started in the late Kamakura period, before becoming a nationwide trend and problem in the fourteenth century. Signs of this trend can be found within the major religious institutions as early as the late Heian period, when lower-ranking monks began to oppose their increasingly distant noble abbots.

gesu　下司

A local land steward (estate manager) under the jurisdiction of the proprietor. See Mass, *The Kamakura Bakufu: A Study in Documents.*

Goshuin engi　御手印縁起

Kūkai's "Hand-Imprinted Legend," according to which Kōyasan claimed that a substantial area close to the mountain was granted to the founder. The legend was created in the mid–Heian period, as the Kongōbuji clergy attempted to expand the temple's influence in Kii Province. Though clearly a fabrication, the claim was eventually acknowledged in the early fourteenth century, as local rulership began to spread and the imperial family sought the support of powerful Buddhist institutions such as Kōyasan.

gōso　嗷訴（強訴）

A forceful protest, which featured monks and shrine people demonstrating in the capital with divine symbols associated with their shrines.

Hōjōji　法成寺

Completed in 1020 under the patronage of Fujiwara no Michinaga, this Buddhist temple became an important stronghold in Kyoto for the Fujiwara in the Kamakura era. Following the destruction of the Kangakuin in a great fire in Kyoto in 1177, Hōjōji became the new Fujiwara administrative headquarters in the capital, until it, too, was destroyed in 1317.

hōshinnō　法親王

Imperial Prince of the Law. Sons of emperors who took Buddhist vows and lived as prestigious monks in specially constructed cloisters (*monzeki*), often in the capital area. *Hōshinnō* headed important temples with considerable landed wealth in the Kamakura era, providing the imperial family with direct influence within the religious establishment.

Hossō　法相

The most influential of the six Nara sects, Hossō had Kōfukuji as its head-quarters. The sect sought to distinguish the real nature of things from their worldly appearance through intensive studies of several sacred texts. It ori-ginated in India but reached Japan from China for the first time in 653. Because of its focus on reading and intellectual activities, the Hossō sect became especially popular among the ultimate elites, as it also served to dis-tinguish the well educated and cultured from members of the lower nobility.

Iwashimizu Hachimangū　岩清水八幡宮

A shrine-temple complex located south of Kyoto, founded by the monk Gyōkyō in 860 as a worship hall for the war god Hachiman. The complex soon became a sacred protector for the imperial state, assuming a place among the highest-ranking shrines in Japan. It was a prominent presence in Yamashiro Province and received consistent patronage and visits from the Kyoto nobility. Contrary to many other prestigious shrines, Iwashimizu lacked a strong affiliation with any of the *kenmon* temples.

Jigen　慈源

(1218–?) The son of Kujō Michiie and the brother of shōgun Kujō Yoritsune, Jigen became head abbot of Tendai in 1238 at the age of twenty. Jigen re-mained in Kyoto, involving himself in both religious and political matters. His failure to control the clergy induced him to resign in 1239, but he was reappointed on 1241/1/17, remaining Tendai head until 1247, when he resigned again in protest of the ousting of his brother in Kamakura.

jin-no-tō　陣頭

The location for the meetings of the highest court council (the *kugyō*). The meetings (*jin-no-sadame*) took place at the headquarters of the inner palace guard (*konoefu;* see Hurst, *Insei*, 29), located just inside the Yomei Gate of the Greater Palace area. It was to this location that the Enryakuji protesters directed their demonstrations.

jitō　地頭

A land steward under the jurisdiction of the warrior government. The office was used by Minamoto no Yoritomo, the founder of the Kamakura Bakufu, to control a large portion of the warrior class, although many *jitō* were difficult to contain even for the warrior leaders. See in particular the works of Jeffrey Mass for extensive treatments of this important office.

Kajii monzeki　梶井門跡

See Sanzen'in

Kakushin　覚信

(1065–1121) Kakushin was the son of Fujiwara no Morozane (clan chieftain from 1075 to 1094) and the first member of the chieftain's line to become head abbot of Kōfukuji (1100). He was, however, opposed by Shirakawa, who temporarily relieved him of his duties in 1102. Kakushin was reinstated the following year and remained *bettō* until his death in 1121.

Kangakuin　勧学院

The Fujiwara chieftain's administrative headquarters in Kyoto. Most of the *sekkanke*'s orders were issued from the Kangaku'in, and the Kōfukuji clergy consequently directed their forceful protests to this location.

kanpaku　関白

Most commonly translated as "chancellor," the *kanpaku* was a regent for an adult emperor, invented by Fujiwara no Mototsune in 880.

kantō mōshitsugi　関東申次

The Kamakura Bakufu's liaison with the imperial court in Kyoto.

kenmitsu　顕密

Exoteric and esoteric. "*Kenmitsu*" was the combined term for the six Nara schools and the two Heian sects (Tendai and Shingon). Tendai and Shingon were particularly popular in the late Heian and Kamakura periods, since they combined exoteric (*ken*) scriptures with esoteric (*mitsu*), orally transmitted rituals in their teachings. Kuroda Toshio claimed that the *kenmitsu* teachings were the ideological paradigm from the early Heian to the mid–Muromachi era.

kenmon　権門

"Gates of power" or "influential families." A historical term referring primarily to the noble elites in the late Heian to Muromachi eras, though Kuroda Toshio used it to denote any of the religious, military, or noble elites who coruled Japan.

kokujin　国人

"Men of the provinces." Local warriors who developed a considerable degree of control of land and men at the provincial level from the fourteenth century.

Kongōbuji　金剛峰寺

The proper name for the Shingon monastic center on Mt. Kōya, also known as Kōyasan.

kugyō　公卿

The Imperial Court Council, consisting of nobles of the third rank and above. The *kugyō* assembly was undoubtedly the most important organ within the imperial court, as even the most powerful members of the Fujiwara were expected to discuss important decisions at this venue.

Kujō Michiie　九条道家

(1193–1251) The grandson of Kujō Kanezane (1149–1207), Michiie was raised to restore the glory of the Kujō lineage within the dominating regent's branch of the Fujiwara. He became Minister of the Left (*sadaijin*) in 1218 and regent for Emperor Chūkyō in 1221. Although Michiie maintained a middle stance in the Jōkyū War of 1221, he was forced to resign as regent. However, he was able to resume the regency in 1228, two years after his fourth son, Kujō Yoritsune, had become shōgun in Kamakura, much with the help of his distant relative Saionji Kintsune. Michiie remained highly active in court politics, attempting to dominate both Kyoto and Kamakura, until Yoritsune's failed uprising against shogunal regent Hōjō Tokiyori in 1246.

Kujō Yoritsune　九条頼経

(1218–1256) The fourth son of Kujō Michiie, Yoritsune was sent to Kamakura at the age of one, following the assassination of the third shōgun, Sanetomo, in an effort to create a bond between the warrior government and the imperial court. Yoritsune became the fourth shōgun of the Kamakura Bakufu in 1226, though real control of the Kantō government rested with his Hōjō regents. He was forced to resign in 1244 in favor of his young son, Yoritsugu, but returned to Kamakura the next year in an attempt to build his own following and overthrow the Hōjō. Yoritsune was defeated by the young Hōjō Tokiyori in 1246, after which he was sent back to Kyoto.

mikoshi　御輿

See *shin'yō*

Minamoto no Tameyoshi　源為義

(1096–1156) The head of the Seiwa Genji, who made his career as a respected military noble in the capital area. He served as Imperial Police Captain and was an important retainer of the *sekkanke*. He sided with the losing side in the Hōgen Disturbance (1156), after which he was decapitated.

monzeki　門跡

Noble cloister. Originally a term for sects or groups of disciples, but from the late Heian period it was used to refer to the special residential and temple areas of noble abbots, often located in the outskirts of Kyoto, where they could enjoy the benefits of aristocratic lifestyles. The *monzeki* were constructed in the popular *shinden* style of the Heian nobility with a U-shaped structure facing into a garden with a pond, instead of the more austere settings of the traditional Buddhist monasteries. The term also came to denote the noble abbot himself.

Myōun　明雲

(?–1183) A Minamoto descendant who became one of the most prominent Tendai head abbots in the premodern era. Well liked by the Enryakuji clergy, he was appointed Tendai *zasu* in 1166 but deposed by Go-Shirakawa in 1177. Owing to his close ties with Taira no Kiyomori, Myōun was reinstated in 1179. He remained a supporter of the Taira during the Genpei War but made peace with Go-Shirakawa, which cost him his life in 1183, when he stayed at the retired emperor's palace in Kyoto as Kiso Yoshinaka attacked the capital.

Nashimoto monzeki　梨本門跡

See Sanzen'in

Onjōji　園城寺

Also known as Miidera, Onjōji was established southeast of Mt. Hiei facing Lake Biwa in the early 670s by Emperor Tenji. After being destroyed in the Jinshin War of 671–672, the Ōtomo family rebuilt the temple between 680 and 686, renaming it Onjōji soon afterwards. The fourth Tendai head abbot, Enchin, received this temple as a donation in 862, and it was probably made into a Tendai detached cloister (*betsuin*) some four years later. The Onjōji compound, located away from the main temple building on Mt. Hiei, became the center for Enchin's religious lineage, challenging for the sect's leadership from 993, when Onjōji was organizationally separated from the rest of the Tendai clergy.

risshi 律師

Preceptor. The third and lowest-ranking office in the *sōgō*.

Ryōgen 良源

(912–985) One of the best-known Tendai head abbots, Ryōgen entered Enryakuji in 923 and settled at the Yokawa section. His close relationship with Fujiwara no Morosuke (908–960) made it possible for Ryōgen to revive Yokawa and Enryakuji after a long period of decline. He became *zasu* at the mere age of fifty-four in 966 and managed to stabilize and consolidate the monastery's internal structures, in part by excluding competitors from Onjōji.

Saionji Kintsune 西園寺公経

(1171–1244) A member of one of the minor Fujiwara branches, Kintsune started out as a mid-level courtier before reaching the top echelons in 1198. Since he opposed Go-Toba's failed uprising against the Kamakura Bakufu of 1221 (the Jōkyū War), Kintsune quickly rose through the ranks. He was promoted to Grand Minister (*daijō daijin*), served as the court liaison (*Kantō mōshitsugi*) with the bakufu, and saw his son-in-law, Kujō Yoritsune, become the fourth shōgun of the Kamakura Bakufu.

Sandai'e 三大会

The three annual lecture-rituals, performed for the imperial court and the welfare of the state. They were the Yuima'e held at Kōfukuji, the Saishō'e at Yakushiji (both located in Nara), and the Gosai'e at the imperial palace, largely controlled by the Fujiwara chieftain. Participation in and performance of these ceremonies were also crucial for determining promotion of monks to the Office of Monastic Affairs (the *sōgō*), which determined the ranking of clerics in the religious hierarchy. The Sandai'e were also referred to as "*sanne*" and "*nankyō/nanto san'e*" (the Three Meetings of the Southern Capital).

Sanzen'in 三千院

One of the three most important noble cloisters (*monzeki*) at Enryakuji. Also known as the Kajii or the Nashimoto monzeki, it was founded in the 1050s. Originally located in the Tōtō section, monks of the Sanzen'in were often involved in disputes over estates and the Tendai head abbot post with the Shōren'in clergy in the thirteenth and fourteenth centuries.

sekkanke 摂関家

The Regent's Line of the Fujiwara clan, which evolved from the Northern Fujiwara (the *hokke*) branch. The *sekkanke* monopolized the offices of regent (*sesshō*) and chancellor (*kanpaku*), through which the head also served as the chieftain of the Fujiwara clan. The *sekkanke* was gradually divided, however, from the thirteenth century, resulting in a decline of support from and loyalty within the clan.

sesshō 摂政

Regent for a minor or sometimes female emperor. Prince Shōtoku (574–622) is generally considered to have functioned as regent for his aunt, Empress Suiko. The first nonimperial member to serve as *sesshō* was Fujiwara no Yoshifusa in 858, after which the Fujiwara monopolized the post for centuries.

Shingon 真言

The True Word sect, founded by Kūkai (774–835) early in the ninth century, with one center at Tōji in Kyoto and one at Kongōbuji on Mt. Kōya. Secret words, hand gestures, and cosmic maps (Mandalas) were crucial aspects to obtain enlightenment, as taught in the most popular esoteric text, the Mahāvairochana Sūtra (*Dainichi-kyō* in Japanese).

shinmoku (*shinboku*) 神木

The Holy Tree, referring to a branch (or branches) of the sacred *sakaki* tree (*Cleyera ochnacea*) that was carried to the capital in protest by certain shrines, including Kumano and Kasuga. The branch was put on a platform and equipped with sacred mirrors before it was taken out for a *gōso*. It is believed that protesters often carried a branch with withering leaves to the capital to indicate the deteriorating state of the shrine and the anger of the gods, replacing it with a fresh one when they had been obliged.

shin'yō 御輿

Divine palanquins that were taken out from shrines for protests (*gōso*) as well as for festivals. The carts are believed to contain the *kami* residing in the shrine and must thus be treated with much caution. There is usually a sacred object, such as a mirror, inside, while other mirrors are also hung outside to reflect the power of the *kami*. An alternative reading is "*mikoshi*," which is the contemporary term for these carts.

Shōren'in 青蓮院

The most important of Enryakuji's five *monzeki* (noble cloisters). It was established as the residence of the forty-eighth head abbot, Gyōgen (1093–1152), in the Tōtō section in the 1130s but was moved to the Sanjō-Shirakawa intersection in the eastern part of Kyoto by the mid–twelfth century. The best-known abbot of the Shōren'in was unquestionably Jien (1155–1225), who wrote the well-known *Gukanshō*, an interpretative history of Japan.

shugo 守護

A provincial military governor first appointed by the Kamakura Bakufu to oversee and control local warriors under bakufu jurisdiction. Though limited in power in the thirteenth century, these regional warriors became increasingly influential in the Muromachi Age.

sōgō 僧綱

The Office of Monastic Affairs. The *sōgō* was a government organ established in 624 for the purpose of supervising all Buddhist sects, monks, and nuns. Its responsibilities included ordinations, registration of monks, and reviewing the rules for each sect. The court staffed the *sōgō* with high-ranking monks of its own choice, even though nominations were made by a monk's teacher or his temple, based on his services within the temple and merits accumulated through the performance of prestigious Buddhist rituals for the imperial court. The composition of the *sōgō* tended to reflect the political balance among the different sects, but it was in particular dominated by Hossō monks in the early Heian age.

sōjō 僧正

Grand Master. The highest-ranking office in the *sōgō*.

sōzu 僧都

Monk supervisor or director. The second-ranking office in the *sōgō*.

Tendai 天台

A Buddhist sect of the Mahāyāna school that preached that all human beings had the potential for enlightenment. It is based primarily on the Lotus Sūtra, which suggests that all beings have the ability to reach enlightenment after this life. Tendai was known in Japan before Saichō (766/7–822), but he has been credited with establishing it as a separate sect early in the ninth century with Enryakuji on Mt. Hiei as its headquarters. It incorporated esoteric rites, Zen, and the traditional rules for monks, becoming the most syncretic of all the Buddhist sects in Japan.

Tōnomine 多武峰

A temple-shrine complex, located some twenty miles south of Nara (close to present-day Sakurai City). The Tōnomine peak became the location for the mausoleum of Fujiwara no Kamatari, the Fujiwara patriarch, probably in the Nara period. However, a monk named Son'ei, who was trained at Enryakuji's Mudōji cloister, retired to Tōnomine, where he began to attract many students with his Tendai teachings in the early years of the eleventh century. Son'ei was succeeded at Mudōji by a certain Kenmei, who was close to the most dominating courtier at the time, Fujiwara no Michinaga. Since Tōnomine lacked affiliation with a central temple, Son'ei asked Michinaga to make it a branch of Enryakuji. Despite protests from Kōfukuji, Michinaga allowed Son'ei's temple, now known as Myōrakuji, to become affiliated with Enryakuji, making the shrine-temple complex a Tendai foothold in Yamato. Disputes were subsequently common between Tōnomine and Kōfukuji in the late Heian and Kamakura eras.

Yuima'e 維摩会

A ceremony performed annually for the court and the imperial state at Kōfukuji. It was based on the Yuima Sūtra, which describes the activities of Buddhist laypeople, indicating that people who had not taken the Buddhist vows could perform meritorious deeds. The Yuima ceremony, which is said to have originated at Yamashinadera under the patronage of Fujiwara no Kamatari (614–669) and then reintroduced by Fuhito at Kōfukuji in honor of his father, therefore became quite popular with the nobility in the Nara and Heian eras.

zasu 座主

A term indicating leadership of certain religious sects, most notably Tendai. It was also used to denote the abbotship for the monastic complex (Kongōbuji) on Mt. Kōya.

zoku bettō　俗別当

    Lay administrators for one of the elite temples. The first *zoku bettō* were appointed for Enryakuji in 823, in an attempt to establish some measure of insight into the Tendai center's affairs, since the temple was the first one to be granted an ordination platform of its own. The office quickly became popular among other temples as well, as Kōfukuji, Tōdaiji, Kongōbuji, and Kōji all were connected with lay administrators in the first half of the ninth century. Though the office became superfluous in the late Heian period, *zoku bettō* were sporadically appointed even in the Kamakura period.

REFERENCES

Annotated Bibliography of Primary Sources

Sources included only in the *Dainihon shiryō* series are not cited under individual entries.

Akihiro ōki. Unpublished. Kunaichō shorikubu, Tokyo.

———. In *Shiga-ken shi,* volume 5, compiled by Shiga-ken. Tokyo: Sanshūsha, 1928.

———. *Zoku shiryō taisei,* volume 21. Kyoto: Rinsen shoten, 1967.

    A little-used diary written by Prince Akihiro, a sixth-generation descendant of Emperor Kazan who was adopted by a mid-ranking Minamoto. Akihiro served at the Jingikan (Department of Divine Affairs), and his diary, which unfortunately is scattered and incomplete, contains entries for the years 1161–1178.

Ategawa. See *Kii no kuni Ategawa no shō shiryō*

Azuma kagami. Shintei zōho kokushi taikei, volumes 32–33. Tokyo: Yoshikawa kōbunkan, 1936.

———. Compiled by Nagahara Keiji and Kishi Shōzō. 6 volumes. Tokyo: Shinjinbutsu jūraisha, 1976–1979. Cited as *Azuma kagami.*

    The official chronicle of the Kamakura Bakufu for the years 1180–1266. Though many details are offered for the early years of the bakufu, this source has the typical weaknesses of an official history, as it attempts to legitimize the Hōjō family's control of the shogunate. It is probably most reliable for its historical contents for the later years.

Chūsei hōsei shiryō shū. Ed. Satō Shin'ichi and Ikeuchi Yoshisuke. Tokyo: Iwanami shoten, 1987.

    A compilation of warrior law codes and other legal edicts issued during the Kamakura and Muromachi eras.

Chūyūki. Zōho shiryō taisei, volumes 9–14. Kyoto: Rinsen shoten, 1965.

    Fujiwara no Munetada's (1062–1141) diary begins in 1087 and ends in 1139. Munetada was a mid-ranking Fujiwara who reached the top level within the imperial hierarchy, but it is in particular his years as head administrator for the chieftain that gives his diary a unique insight. By far one of the most important sources for the early *insei* era, giving an insider's view not only of the issues facing the clan as a whole but also of the procedures that mid- to high-level courtiers occupied themselves with.

Dainihon shiryō. Series 1–6. Ed. Shiryō hensan kakari. Tokyo: Tokyo daigaku zōhan, 1926–. Cited as *DNS.*

The most ambitious collection of sources of premodern Japanese history. Now almost three-quarters of a century in the making, the series publishes historical documents in chronological order. There are several series in this collection, and most are yet to be completed. Though the *Dainihon shiryō* lacks an index, it is the most helpful source collection for a chronological approach. The scholar must proceed with caution, though, as some of the early volumes have many errors and misprints.

Daisenji engi. Unpublished document at Tōkyō daigaku shiryō hensanjo.

A chronicle of Daisenji, written mostly in the form of a hagiography. Unfortunately, the original document, believed to date from the early Muromachi period (probably from 1398), was destroyed in a fire on 1925/4/22. The version that remains available today is compiled from *shahon* (copies of the original) from Tokyo University and Tōkyō kokuritsu hakubutsukan. It contains several pictorial representations of the activities of the monks at Daisenji, which was a powerful monastic center outside the capital region.

Denryaku. Dainihon kokiroku, volume 4, parts 1–4. Tokyo: Iwanami shoten, 1956.

The diary of Fujiwara no Tadazane (1078–1162), who served as clan chieftain from 1099 and as regent on several occasions. The diary that remains covers the years from 1098 to 1118. It is a valuable source for the struggles of the chieftain during Shirakawa's years, but many entries are disappointingly brief even regarding important events.

DNS. See *Dainihon shiryō*

Entairyaku. 7 volumes. In *Shiryō sekishū: kokiroku hen.* Tokyo: Zoku gunsho ruijū kanseikai, 1970–1986.

An extensive diary written by Tōin Kinkata (1291–1360), covering almost five decades from 1311 to his death. A valuable source for various aspects of the first half of the fourteenth century, offering great insights into political circumstances. The diary also contains frequent references to precedents and entries dating to the thirteenth century.

Fushimi in goki (Fushimi tennō shinki). Zōho shiryō taisei, volume 3. Kyoto: Rinsen shoten, 1965.

The diary of Emperor Fushimi (1265–1317), covering the years 1287–1311. Only nine of the original scrolls written by the emperor himself remain today. Nevertheless, it is a valuable source for the late Kamakura period, since Fushimi, as the son of Go-Fukakusa of the Jimyōin line, was involved in the split of the imperial line.

Fusō ryakki. Shintei zōho kokushi taikei, volume 12. Tokyo: Yoshikawa kōbunkan, 1965.

A Buddhist chronicle compiled from various other histories, monk appointment records, and legends by the Tendai monk Kōen, who is believed to have lived in the late twelfth to early thirteenth centuries. The chronicle covers the period from the legendary Emperor Jimmu to Horikawa (1094). It contains mostly brief entries with some useful information from sources that are now lost.

Geki nikki. Zoku shiseki shūran, volume 1. Tokyo: Kondō shuppansha, 1930.

An unusual source in which many documents issued by the *daijōkan* (the Council of State) were recorded in chronological order by various scribes *(geki),* who were responsible for recording precedents and edicts issued. The collection is far from complete, covering a broad span from 790 to 1186, and little is known about its author(s) and origins, but there are some valuable entries in this collection for the Heian era.

Genpei seisuiki. 4 volumes. Tokyo: Miyai shoten, 1994.
A war tale that chronicles the conflicts in the capital region during the last years of the Heian age. Many scholars believed that the *Genpei seisuiki,* which consists of forty-eight scrolls, was compiled between 1247 and 1249, but, because of its literary style, there is now a general consensus that the work was written in the Nanbokuchō era (1336–1392). Though believed to be based on the *Heike monogatari,* the *Genpei seisuiki* tells the tale of the Heike and the Genpei War in a slightly different manner. In particular, the detailed accounts of Enryakuji are intriguing, but they also reveal a critical view of the temple that is not uncommon in the war tales produced in the Kamakura era.

Go-Nijō Moromichi ki. In *Dainihon kokiroku,* volume 5, parts 1–3. Tokyo: Iwanami shoten,1956.
The diary of Fujiwara no Moromichi (1062–1099), written from 1083 to 1099. Although Moromichi died young, he rose quickly as the son of Regent Morozane, becoming himself regent and Fujiwara chieftain in 1094. A valuable diary for the early years of Shirakawa's retirement.

Gonki. Zōho shiryō taisei, volumes 4–5. Kyoto: Rinsen shoten, 1965.
The *Gonki* was written by Fujiwara no Yukinari (972–1027) between 991 and 1011. Yukinari served as a middle-ranking official at the Heian court, and his diary provides insight into the peak of the Fujiwara regency. Some sections are missing, but the coverage is in all fairly even.

Gukanki. Zoku shiryō taisei, volumes 1–4. Kyoto: Rinsen shoten, 1967.
The diary of Konoe Michitsugu, who served as regent for the Northern Court, covering the years from 1356 to 1383. Though four years are missing and many entries are disappointingly brief, it is a valuable source for capital politics during the age of the two courts.

Gumaiki. Unpublished. Yōmei bunko, Kyoto.
Sanjō Sanefusa's diary covers the years from 1166 to 1195, although several segments are missing today. Sanefusa was a mid- to high-ranking courtier about whom not much is known, though he did reach the rank of Minister of the Left and Minister of the Right before retiring in 1196. Another valuable source for the eventful decades at the end of the twelfth century, the *Gumaiki* has unfortunately not been printed in one comprehensive series, since the remaining copies of the diary are kept at different locations.

Gyokuyō. 3 volumes. Tokyo: Kokusho kankōkai sōsho, 1906. Reprinted in 1993 (Tokyo: Meicho kankōkan).
The diary of Fujiwara (Kujō) no Kanezane (1149–1207), chieftain and regent in the early Kamakura era. By far the most important and comprehensive contemporary source for the years leading up to and following the Genpei War. The diary begins on 1164/10/17, when Kanezane was appointed to the second rank of the court hierarchy at the age of fifteen, and ends in 1203.

Heian ibun. Ed. Takeuchi Rizō. 13 volumes. Tokyo: Tōkyō shuppan, 1963–1974.
One of the most valuable source collections for the study of Heian Japan. It contains all known documents issued during this age, arranged in chronological order with a convenient index available. The scrupulous editing of Professor Takeuchi makes this collection highly useful and reliable.

Heihanki (Hyōhanki). Zōho shiryō taisei, volumes 18–22. Kyoto: Rinsen shoten, 1965.
Taira no Nobunori's (1112–1187) diary, covering the period from 1132 to 1171.
Though not as detailed as the *Gyokuyō*, perhaps lacking the kind of insight that Kanezane had since Nobunori was a mid-ranking courtier serving the *sekkanke*, it is an
extremely valuable source for the Hōgen and Heiji incidents. Nobunori was also
made scapegoat in 1169 during the Narichika Incident but was recalled in 1171,
owing to Kiyomori's intervention.

Heike monogatari. 3 volumes. In *Shinkō Nihon koten shūsei,* ed. Mizuhara Hajime.
Tokyo: Shinkōsha, 1979.
A war tale that chronicles the rise and fall of the Taira in the twelfth century.
Extant versions of the chronicle date to the Tokugawa age, but the work was probably produced first in the thirteenth century. Though some descriptions are undoubtedly exaggerated, many entries can be verified in other, more contemporary
sources.

Hie shin'yō gojuraku kenmon ryakki. In *Shinkō gunsho ruijū: jingibu,* volume 1. Tokyo:
Naigai shoseki kabushiki gaisha, 1938.
A record focusing on the *gōso* staged with the holy carts from the Hie shrines dur-
ing slightly more than a decade in the fourteenth century. Compiled by a monk of
Enryakuji's Mudōji section, it covers protests from 1368 to 1380.

Honchō seiki. Shintei zōho kokushi taikei, volume 9. Tokyo: Yoshikawa kōbunkan,
1935.
A chronicle of Japan from Emperor Uda to Horikawa, written during the 1150s by
Fujiwara no Michinori (1106?–1159). Several sections are missing today, but the
chronicle contains some reliable information from events during the *insei* era.

Hōnen shōnin eden. Zoku Nihon emaki taisei, volumes 1–3. Tokyo: Chūō kōronsha,
1981.
————. *Zoku Nihon no emaki,* volumes 1–3. Tokyo: Chūō kōronsha, 1990.
The *Hōnen shōnin eden* is a tribute to the Buddhist saint Hōnen (1133–1212), glorify-
ing his life while vilifying many of his opponents. It was completed in 1307, probably
by Shunjō, a ninth-generation direct disciple of Hōnen. The accompanying text was
contributed by prominent courtiers and emperors within the next decade.

Hyakurenshō. Shintei zōho kokushi taikei, volume 11. Tokyo: Yoshikawa kōbunkan,
1965.
A chronicle beginning in the year 968 of Emperor Reizei's reign, ending in 1259 of
Emperor Go-Fukakusa's era. The author of this work is unknown, but it was compiled from various sources sometime in the late thirteenth century. Its focus is overwhelmingly on conditions in the capital region.

Ichidai yōki. In *Kaitei sanshū shūran,* volume 1. Tokyo: Kondō kappansho, 1900.
An imperial chronicle that begins with the legendary emperors and ends with Emperor Hanazono, written late in the thirteenth century by an unknown author. The
chronicle offers valuable information not only on emperors but also regarding other
important officials and consorts within the imperial court.

Jimon kōsōki. In *Zoku gunsho ruijū,* volume 28, part 1. Tokyo: Zoku gunsho ruijū
kanseikai, 1978.
An appointment record of high-ranking Onjōji monks, probably written around
1289. The author is not known, and four of the original ten volumes are lost. A good
source for the platform disputes with Enryakuji and for Onjōji's relations with various patrons of the Minamoto, Taira, and Fujiwara. Like the *Tendai zasuki,* the *Jimon
kōsōki* is especially valuable for its full, and fairly reliable, quotes of lost edicts.

Kachō yōryaku. Dainihon bukkyō zensho, volumes 128–130. Tokyo: Bussho kankōkai, 1931.
> A massive chronicle of Tendai's Shōren'in *monzeki.* The twenty-ninth abbot of the Shōren'in, princely monk Sonshin, ordered it written, and it was probably completed in 1803, at which time the cloister was located in Kyoto. It focuses mainly on rituals and other procedures relating to the Shōren'in.

Kaei sandaiki. In *Shinkō gunsho ruijū: zatsubu.* Tokyo: Naigai shoseki kabushiki gaisha, 1938.
> A record of warrior matters (thus also known as *Buke nikki* or *Muromachi ki*) in the Muromachi period, covering the period from 1367 to 1396.

Kamakura ibun. Compiled by Takeuchi Rizō. 42 volumes. Tokyo: Tōkyōdō shuppan, 1971–1992.
> The standard document collection for the Kamakura era, which today contains edicts and documents arranged in chronological order. It is an invaluable source for the era, especially for litigation and land issues. The collection is now complete with useful indexes thanks to the meticulous work of Takeuchi Rizō.

Kanchūki. Shiryō taisei, volumes 26–27. Tokyo: Naigai shoseki kabushiki gaisha, 1931–1944. *Zōho shiryō taisei,* volumes 34–36. Kyoto: Rinsen shoten, 1965.
> (Fujiwara) Kadenokōji Kanenaka's diary, kept from 1274 to 1300, though several years in addition to shorter sections are missing. As a member of a minor Fujiwara branch, Kanenaka served in the mid-level ranks of the Kyoto bureaucracy. His diary is particularly rich in information on matters of litigation within the imperial court as well as on religious issues in the frightful times and aftermath of the Mongol invasions.

Kankenki. See *Kinhira kōki*

Kasugasha kiroku. Zōho zoku shiryō taisei, volume 47–49. Kyoto: Rinsen shoten, 1983.
> A chronicle written by the shrine heads of Kasuga. The entire collection chronicles events related to the shrine from the 1180s to 1290, as recorded by various shrine heads, totaling about thirty, of the Nakatomi clan. It is especially valuable for its entries regarding Kōfukuji *gōso* that emanated from Kasuga. *Bun'ei gannen Nakatomi Sukemasa ki* (part 13) and *Shōō ninen Nakatomi Sukeharu ki* (part 28) are specifically cited in this study.

Kii no kuni Ategawa no shō shiryō. Compiled by Nakamura Ken. 2 volumes. Tokyo: Yoshikawa kōbunkan, 1976. Cited as *Ategawa.*
> A collection of documents and other sources pertaining exclusively to Ategawa-no-shō. Well annotated and useful for research of local conditions as well as of the workings of *shōen* matters in general. The documents relating to the Yuasa *jitō* and the protests lodged by local peasants are especially fascinating.

Kinhira kōki. 5 volumes. In *Shiryō sanshū.* Tokyo: Zoku gunsho ruijū kanseikai, 1968.
> A courtier diary written by Saionji Kinhira (1264–1315), which covers a thirty-two-year-long period from 1283 to 1315, much of which still remains. It is also included in the Saionji family's source collection known as the *Kankenki.* The *Kinhira kōki* is very useful for its coverage of the imperial court and its relationship with the bakufu in the late Kamakura era.

Kitano tenmangū shiryō: komonjo. Ed. Kitano tenmangū shiryō kankōkai. Kyoto: Kitano tenmangū, 1978.
> A source collection of documents relating to the Kitano shrine. A useful publication for issues pertaining to the shrine, its landholdings, and commercial activities in the capital during the Kamakura and Muromachi eras.

Kitsuki. Zōho shiryō taisei, volumes 29–30. Kyoto: Rinsen shoten, 1965.
The diary of Yoshida Tsunefusa (1143–1200), a mid- to high-ranking courtier, who served as the first *Kantō denso,* conveying messages between Kyoto and Kamakura. It covers the years from 1166 to 1193 and is an important source concerning the early court-bakufu relationship.

Kōfukuji bettō shidai. In *Dainihon bukkyō zensho: Kōfukuji sōsho,* part 2, 1–59. Tokyo: Bussho kankōkai, 1917.
A temple record of the head abbots of Kōfukuji, starting in the mid–Nara age and ending with the tenure of Kōson in 1570. Though not as detailed as the *Tendai zasuki,* this appointment record on occasion offers some insight into the most important developments at Kōfukuji.

Kōfukuji ryaku nendaiki. In *Zoku gunsho ruijō,* volume 29, part 2, 107–205. Tokyo: Yoshikawa kōbunkan, 1965.
The *Kōfukuji ryaku nendaiki* was compiled into its current form in 1725 by the monk Shōen, abbot of the noble cloister Daijōin within Kōfukuji, who appears to have recorded the section dating after 1576. The earlier parts are extrapolated from various sources, dating to the thirteenth and fourteenth centuries.

Kōfukuji sōjō. In *Dainihon bukkyō zensho: Kōfukuji sōsho,* part 2, 103–112. Tokyo: Bussho kankōkai, 1917.
A copy of the appeals forwarded to the imperial court to have Hōnen exiled in 1205. Though it is difficult to know how close these versions are to the original appeals, scholars appear to agree about their general authenticity.

Kōfukuji sōsho. Dainihon bukkyō zensho, volumes 123–124. Tokyo: Bussho kankōkai, 1915, 1917.
A collection of sources and documents that contains appointment records, founding myths, a limited number of appeals, and several chronicles pertaining to Kōfukuji. Since few original documents from the Hossō center remain, valuable information can be extrapolated from these two volumes, though each source must be subjected to a thorough scrutiny of authenticity and reliability.

Kōtei zōho Tendai zasuki. Compiled by Shibuya Gaiji. Tokyo: Daiichi shobō, 1973. Cited as *Tendai zasuki.*
The *Tendai zasuki* is a monk appointment record that covers the Tendai sect's head abbots from Saichō, ending with the appointment of the 247th *zasu* Kōei in 1927. It was compiled from three different sources and contains ample information not only about the head abbots and their ancestry and religious teachers, but also about important events and ceremonies that took place during their tenures. Several important documents otherwise lost, some of which are reprinted in the reputable source collections *Heian ibun* and *Kamakura ibun,* are included in the chronicle.

Kōya shunjū. See *Shinkō Kōya shunjū hennen shūroku*

Kōyasan monjo. 8 volumes. In *Dainihon komonjo: iewake* 1. Tokyo: Tokyo daigaku shiryō hensanjo, 1903–1907.
A much-used collection of documents from the archives of Mt. Kōya. The records cover a wide variety of topics from religious ceremonies to the management of and verdicts regarding various estates. Though a valuable publication, it is sometimes inconvenient, as the documents have been published as they were archived, and no comprehensive index is yet available.

Kugyō bunin. Shintei zōho kokushi taikei, volumes 13–14. Tokyo: Yoshikawa kōbunkan, 1937.

A useful appointment record for the imperial court in Kyoto, the *Kugyō bunin* contains notes not only for promotions but also for demotions and exiles.

Mansai jugō nikki. Kyoto: Kyoto daigaku, 1920. Also published in *Zoku gunsho ruijū, bui.* Tokyo: Zoku gunsho ruijū kanseikai, 1974–1975.
A diary written by the Shingon monk Mansai (1378–1435), who served as abbot of Daigoji and as one of the leaders of Tōji, while being a close supporter of Ashikaga Yoshinori. The diary is an extensive and important source, covering the years from 1411 to 1435 in forty-eight volumes.

Masu kagami. Shintei zōho kokushi taikei, volume 21, part 2. Tokyo: Yoshikawa kōbukan, 1940.

Masu kagami. In *Ōkagami, Masu kagami.* Tokyo: Kadokawa shoten, 1976.
A historical chronicle in seventeen volumes, beginning with the birth of Go-Toba in 1180 and ending with the return of Emperor Go-Daigo to Kyoto in 1333. Written in the simplified *kana* syllabary, perhaps for a more general population, by an unknown author in the late fourteenth century, it offers insights into noble society in Kyoto.

Meigetsuki. Shiryō sanshū, volume 6. Tokyo: Zoku gunsho ruijū, 1967.
The diary of Fujiwara no Sadaie (1162–1241), a member of the Northern Fujiwara *(hokke)* branch who was an accomplished scholar and poet, though he never reached the top of the court hierarchy. Sadaie wrote consistently in his diary from the age of eighteen to his death, covering some six decades of the early Kamakura era. One of the most valuable sources for the early Kamakura age.

Mon'yōki. Taishō shinshū daizōkyō: zuzo, volumes 11 and 12. Tokyo: Daizō shuppan, 1933–1934.
A detailed Tendai work that chronicles various monk appointments, ceremonies, and procedures of the Shōren'in in 130 parts. It was authored by the princely monk Son'en, about whom unfortunately very little is known. The original chronicle covers Tendai from the late twelfth to the early fifteenth century, when it was probably authored. More sections were added in the Tokugawa era by other princely monks. Since the work lacks a chronological structure and an index, it is somewhat inconvenient to use.

Moromori ki. 11 volumes. In *Shiryō sanshū.* Tokyo: Zoku gunsho ruijū kanseikai, 1968.
A diary written by Nakahara Moromori (years unknown), who served as a scribe, as did many others of his family line, for the imperial court in Kyoto. This is an extensive work, written between 1339 and 1374, dealing mostly with court procedures, but it also reflects the sentiments and struggles during the era of the two courts.

Nakasuke ōki. Unpublished. Kunaichō shorikubu, Tokyo.
———. In *Zoku shiryō taisei.* Kyoto: Rinsen shoten, 1965.
The diary of Prince Nakasuke, who served in the Jingikan. It contains entries from eight different years during the period from 1177 to 1213. Though parts of the diary have been printed in various source publications, a comprehensive work has yet to appear. Remaining handwritten copies are spread out in a number of source collections.

Okanoya kanpaku ki. Yōmei sōsho kiroku monjo hen, part 2. Kyoto: Shibunkaku shuppan, 1984.
The diary of Konoe Kanetsune (1210–1259), who was the fourth head of the Konoe line of the Fujiwara clan. He served as regent for Shijō (1237–1242), Go-Saga (1242/

1–3), and Go-Fukakusa (1247–1252), deeply involved in the competition for the headship of the Fujiwara with Kujō Michiie. It is believed that Kanetsune kept a diary for most of his life, perhaps from 1222 to 1257 (when he took Buddhist vows), but the last five years as well as many parts in between are missing.

Onjōji denki. Dainihon bukkyō zensho, volume 127. Tokyo: Bussho kankōkai, 1916.
A temple record in ten volumes that covers the history and legends of Onjōji. Though brief in several cases, it contains some useful information regarding Onjōji's conflicts with Enryakuji.

Saimyōji monjo. Unpublished. Tōkyō daigaku shiryō hensanjo, Tokyo.
A document collection belonging to Saimyōji, a Tendai branch located at the western foot of Mt. Hiei.

Saisai yōki. In *Zoku shiseki shūran,* volume 1, 231–310. Kyoto: Rinsen shoten, 1984.

Saisai yōki nukigaki. In *Dainihon bukkyō zensho: Kōfukuji sōsho,* part 2, 177–215. Tokyo: Bussho kankōkai, 1917.
A Kōfukuji chronicle (also known as *Tōkondō saisai yōki*) in seven volumes that documents especially events pertaining to the cloisters within the temple complex from 1333 to 1391. It was written by Jitsugon, an abbot of one of Kōfukuji's smaller cloisters. The early entries are especially interesting and appear to be reliable even though the chronicle is not contemporaneous.

Sakeiki. Zōho shiryō taisei, volume 6. Kyoto: Rinsen shoten, 1965.
A diary written by Minamoto no Tsuneyori (985–1035), who served as a mid-ranking bureaucrat at the imperial court. Covering the years 1016–1036, the diary is one of the earliest written by a Minamoto, offering insight into the workings of the imperial court and the Fujiwara clan's organization.

San'e jōikki. In *Dainihon bukkyō zensho: Kōfukuji sōsho,* part 1, 289–432. Tokyo: Bussho kankōkai, 1917.
An appointment record of monks performing the three main lecture-rituals in Nara and the imperial palace from the mid-tenth to the mid-sixteenth centuries. Contains brief but interesting notes about the appointed lecturers.

Sanemi kyōki. Unpublished. Tōkyō daigaku shiryō hensanjo, Tokyo.
———. *Dainihon kokiroku,* volumes 20–21. Tokyo: Iwanami shoten, 1991–1994.
The diary of Sanjō Tsuneyori (985–1039), who served in the imperial court bureaucracy as well as in the provincial administration during the important years of Fujiwara no Michinaga and Yorimichi. The diary covers the years 1009–1039 and contains useful information regarding the workings of the Heian governmental structures.

Sankaiki. Shiryō taisei, volumes 19–21. Tokyo: Naigai shoseki kabushiki gaisha, 1936.
The diary of Nakayama Tadachika (1132–1195), the son of Fujiwara no Munetada (see *Chūyūki*), who reached mid- to high-ranking courtier offices, serving in particular consorts at the imperial court. Tadachika's diary spans the years from 1151 to 1194, though much of it has been lost. In fact, there is not one single complete year remaining today. Tadachika, an accomplished writer and poet, does, however, offer an interesting inside view of the imperial court.

Shinkō Kōya shunjū hennen shūroku. Compiled by Hinonishi Shinjō. Tokyo: Daimonsha, 1982. Cited as *Kōya shunjū.*
"The Springs and Falls of Mt. Kōya." A temple chronicle that notes important events pertaining to Kōyasan, including imperial pilgrimages and disputes over estates. It begins in 816 with Kūkai and ends in 1718, when it was completed by the monk Kaiei, who became abbot at Kongōbuji around that time.

Shitennōji rekidai bettō shumu jijo. In *Zoku gunsho ruijū,* volume 4. Tokyo: Hideya, 1904.

An appointment record of various offices within Shitennōji. It is not very extensive, but it offers some insight regarding the appointments to the important abbotship of Shitennōji.

Sochiki. Shiryō taisei, volume 5. Tokyo: Naigai shoseki kabushiki gaisha, 1936.
————. *Zōho shiryō taisei,* volume 5. Kyoto: Rinsen shoten, 1965.

The diary of Minamoto no Tsunenobu (1016–1097), who was a successful courtier of the upper-middle nobility. He reached the rank of *dainagon* (Senior Counselor) before his appointment in 1094 to the Heian court's office in Kyushu, where he later died. A large part of the diary has been lost, leaving only entries for some four years during Shirakawa's era.

Sōgō bunin. In *Dainihon bukkyō zensho: Kōfukuji sōsho,* part 1, 61–288. Tokyo: Bussho kankōkai, 1915.

The appointment record for the Office of Monastic Affairs *(sōgō).* Many versions remain, but the one from Kōfukuji is the most extensive, beginning with appointments in 623 and ending in 1142, when the office had lost most of its leverage. It rarely contains any information beyond the appointment and the monk's name and religious lineage.

Sonpi bunmyō. 5 volumes. Tokyo: Yoshikawa kōbunkan, 1962.

A genealogy of several of the main noble families that can be helpful in tracing important family and clan connections.

Suisaki. Zōho shiryō taisei, volume 8. Kyoto: Rinsen shoten, 1965.

Minamoto no Toshifusa's (1035–1121) diary. One of the more extensive diaries for Shirakawa's early years, covering the years from 1062 to 1108, though there are several missing entries. Toshifusa reached the rank of *sadaijin* (Minister of the Left) before he retired from politics just before his death in 1121.

The Taiheiki: A Chronicle of Medieval Japan. Trans. Helen Craig McCullough. Rutland, Vt., and Tokyo: Charles E. Tuttle, 1985.

A war chronicle in forty volumes covering Go-Daigo's reign from 1318 through the Kemmu Restoration to the 1360s. The author appears to have been a monk, perhaps of Tendai or Zen lineage, who was sympathetic to the Southern Court. The majority of the chronicle was completed around 1371, but other sections appear to have been added on later. Though sometimes tedious in its descriptions of battles, there is some valuable information regarding the various factions and the involvement of religious institutions.

Taiki. Zōho shiryō taisei, volumes 23–25. Kyoto: Rinsen shoten, 1965.

The diary of Fujiwara no Yorinaga (1120–1156), the son of Tadazane, who staged the failed coup in 1156 against Go-Shirakawa after having been promoted hastily by his father in opposition to his older brother, Tadamichi. Yorinaga was a highly respected scholar as well as an accomplished writer despite his youth. Most of the diary has been lost, but sporadic entries remain for the years 1136–1155.

The Tale of the Heike. Trans. Helen McCullough. Stanford: Stanford University Press, 1990.

See note under *Heike monogatari.*

Tamefusa kyōki. Shishū (Komazawa daigakuin shigakkai kodai shi bukai), 10 (1979), 67–130.

The diary of Fujiwara no Tamefusa (1049–1115), a mid-level Fujiwara who served as a retainer of Go-Sanjō and Shirakawa. Though the diary originally covered the years from 1072 to 1104, many sections have been lost. The entries for the year 1081 are among the most extensive.

Teiō hennenki. Shintei zōho kokushi taikei, volume 12. Tokyo: Yoshikawa kōbunkan, 1965.

A compiled history in twenty-seven volumes, covering various events from the early Heian age to Emperor Go-Fushimi (1298–1301). The date and authorship of this work are unknown, and the entries are usually brief, but it can be useful for a general chronology of certain events.

Tendai zasuki. See *Kōtei zōho Tendai zasuki*

Tengu sōshi. In *Tengu sōshi, Zegaibō e. Shinshū Nihon emakimono zenshū,* volume 27. Tokyo: Kadokawa shoten, 1978.

———. In *Tsuchigumo sōshi, Tengū sōshi, Ōeyama ekotoba. Zoku Nihon no emaki,* volume 26. Tokyo: Chūō kōronsha, 1993.

Composed in the late Kamakura period (perhaps in 1296), this picture scroll shows the many misdeeds caused by small demons *(tengu)* that were believed to inhabit the mountains. Many of the scenes are set at Enryakuji, Onjōji, Kōfukuji, Kōyasan, and Tōdaiji, which are heavily discredited in this work. The images must thus be analyzed with great caution, though they do reveal the growing opposition the established sects faced in the late Kamakura era.

Tennōji bettō shidai. In *Zoku gunsho ruijū,* volume 4, 688–691. Tokyo: Hideya, 1904.

An appointment record for the abbotship of Shitennōji covering the years 837–1463. The document is very spartan, noting only the names of the abbots and their years of appointment.

Tōkondō saisai yōki. See *Saisai yōki*

Tōnomine ryakki. In *Dainihon bukkyō zensho: Jishi sōsho,* volume 2. Tokyo: Bussho kankōkai, 1913.

A chronicle of the Tōnomine complex, written in 1197 by a monk named Jōin. The chronicle is divided into several sections, including Buddhist procedures and specific information regarding buildings and construction. The early parts of the chronicle are especially useful for Tōnomine's initial developments and the Kōfukuji attacks on the complex.

Tsunetoshi kyōki. Unpublished. Kunaichō shorikubu, Tokyo.

The diary of Yoshida Tsunetoshi (1214–1276), who served as a mid- to high-ranking courtier (reaching the second highest rank) at the imperial court in Kyoto. The diary originally covered over four decades, from 1237 to 1276, in over 150 volumes, though extensive parts have been lost. It is particularly useful for the day-to-day operations at the court in the mid-Kamakura era.

Wakayama-ken shi: kodai shiryō. Compiled by Wakayama-ken shi hensan kakari inkai. 2 volumes. Osaka: Dainihon insatsu kabushiki gaisha, 1981.

A collection of documents and other historical sources pertaining to Wakayama Prefecture. The entries are conveniently compiled and can be useful for studies beyond the region itself. Many chapters from the accompanying history volume *(Wakayama-ken shi)* refer explicitly to documents in the source collection.

Yōkōki. Shiryō sanshū, volume 8. Tokyo: Zoku gunsho ruijū kanseikai, 1971.

The diary of Hamuro Sadatsugu (1208–1272), who served as a mid-level courtier for both Go-Saga and the *sekkanke* Fujiwara. Contains detailed information about court rituals and procedures, spanning from the early 1230s to the early 1250s, though many parts have disappeared.

Zokushi gushō. Shintei zōho kokushi taikei, volume 13. Tokyo: Yoshikawa kōbunkan, 1929.
> A history of Japan from Emperor Kameyama (1259–1274) to Go-Hanazono (1429–1464), written in the late Tokugawa period. It centers on the developments in Kyoto and events in court circles.

Bibliography of Secondary Sources

Adachi Naoya. "Hōshinnō no seijiteki igi." In *Shōen sei shakai to mibun kōzō,* ed. Takeuchi Rizō, 173–201. Tokyo: Azekura shobō, 1980.

Adolphson, Mikael. "Enryakuji—an Old Power in a New Era." In *The Origins of Japan's Medieval World,* ed. Jeffrey Mass, 237–260. Stanford: Stanford University Press, 1997.

Arai Takashige. *Chūsei akutō no kenkyū.* Tokyo: Yoshikawa kōbunkan, 1990.

Atsuta Tadashi. "Shugo ryō kokusei no tenkai." In *Wakayama-ken shi: chūsei,* compiled by Wakayama-ken shi hensan kakari inkai, 328–424. Osaka: Dainihon insatsu kabushiki kaisha, 1994.

———. "Chūsei goki no shōen to sonraku." In *Wakayama-ken shi: chūsei,* 425–487.

Batten, Bruce. "Foreign Threat and Domestic Reform." *Monumenta Nipponica* 41:2 (1986), 199–219.

Bender, Ross. "The Hachiman Cult and the Dōkyō Incident." *Monumenta Nipponica* 34:2 (1979), 125–153.

Borgen, Robert. "The Japanese Mission to China, 801–806." *Monumenta Nipponica* 37:1 (1982), 1–28.

———. *Sugawara no Michizane and the Early Heian Court.* Cambridge, Mass.: Harvard University Press, 1986.

Brown, Delmer, and Ichirō Ishida. *The Future and the Past: A Translation and Study of the Gukanshō, an Interpretative History of Japan Written in 1219.* Berkeley: University of California Press, 1979.

Bukkyō jiten. Tokyo: Iwanami shoten, 1989.

Chion'in to Hōnen shōnin eden. Compiled by Kyōto kokuritsu hakubutsukan. Kyoto: Ōtsuka kōgeisha, 1982.

Coates, Harper, and Ishizuka Ryugaku, trans. *Hōnen the Buddhist Saint: His Life and Teachings.* Kyoto and Tokyo: Sanshusha, 1925.

Collcutt, Martin. *Five Mountains: The Rinzai Zen Monastic Institution in Medieval Japan.* Cambridge: Harvard University Press, 1981.

Conlan, Thomas. "Largesse and the Limits of Loyalty in the Fourteenth Century." In *The Origins of Japan's Medieval World: Courtiers, Clerics, Warriors and Peasants in the Fourteenth Century,* ed. Jeffrey Mass, 39–64. Stanford: Stanford University Press, 1997.

Dobbins, James C. "Editor's Introduction: Kuroda Toshio and His Scholarship." *Japanese Journal of Religious Studies* 26:3–4 (1996), 217–232.

———, ed. "The Legacy of Kuroda Toshio." Commemorative issue of *Japanese Journal of Religious Studies* 26:3–4 (fall 1996).

Egashira Tsuneharu. *Kōyasan ryō shōen no kenkyū.* Tokyo: Nihon keizai shi kenkyū sho, 1938.

Emakimono sōran. Tokyo: Kadokawa shoten, 1995.

Endō Iwao. "Izumi no kuni Kogi no shō bashaku chō to jōri sei no seikaku." In *Kōyasan ryō shōen no shihai to kōzō,* ed. Toyoda Takeshi, 267–303. Tokyo: Gannandō shoten, 1977.

Farris, Wayne. *Heavenly Warriors: The Evolution of Japan's Military, 500–1300.* Cambridge, Mass.: Harvard University Press, 1992.

Gay, Suzanne. "The Muromachi Bakufu in Medieval Kyoto." Ph.D. dissertation, Yale University, 1982.

———. "Muromachi Bakufu Rule in Kyoto: Administrative and Judicial Aspects." In *The Bakufu in Japanese History,* ed. Jeffrey P. Mass and William B. Hauser, 49–65. Stanford: Stanford University Press, 1985.

Goble, Andrew. "The Hōjō and Consultative Government" In *Court and Bakufu in Japan: Essays in Kamakura History,* ed. Jeffrey Mass, 169–190. Stanford: Stanford University Press, 1982.

———. "Go-Daigo and the Kemmu Restoration." Ph.D. dissertation, Stanford University, 1987.

———. *Kenmu: Go-Daigo's Revolution.* Cambridge: Harvard University Press, 1996.

Gomi Fumihiko. *Insei ki shakai no kenkyū.* Tokyo: Yamakawa shuppansha, 1984.

———. *Kamakura to kyō.* Taikei Nihon no rekishi, volume 5. Tokyo: Shogakkan, 1988.

Goodwin, Janet R. "The Buddhist Monarch: Go-Shirakawa and the Rebuilding of Tōdai-ji." *Japanese Journal of Religious Studies* 17:2–3, 219–242.

———. *Alms and Vagabonds: Buddhist Temples and Popular Patronage in Medieval Japan.* Honolulu: University of Hawai'i Press, 1994.

Grapard, Allan. "Linguistic Cubism: A Singularity of Pluralism in the Sannō Cult." *Japanese Journal of Religious Studies* 14:2–3 (1987), 211–233.

———. "Institution, Ritual, and Ideology: The Twenty-two Shrine-Temple Multiplexes of Heian Japan." *History of Religions* 27:3 (1988), 246–269.

———. *The Protocol of the Gods: A Study of the Kasuga Cult in Japanese History.* Berkeley: University of California Press, 1992.

Groner, Paul. *Saichō: The Establishment of the Japanese Tendai School.* Berkeley: University of California Press, 1984.

———. "Annen, Tankei, Henjō and Monastic Discipline in the Tendai School: The Background of the *Futsū jubosatsukai kōshaku.*" *Japanese Journal of Religious Studies* 14:2–3 (1987), 129–160.

Gurr, Ted Robert . "Introduction." In *Handbook of Political Conflict,* ed. Ted Robert Gurr, 1–16. New York: The Free Press, 1980.

Hakeda Yoshito. *Kukai: Major Works.* Columbia: Columbia University Press, 1972.

Harrington, Lorraine F. "Regional Outposts of Muromachi Rule: The Kantō and Kyushu." In *The Bakufu in Japanese History,* ed. Jeffrey P. Mass and William B. Hauser, 66–98. Stanford: Stanford University Press, 1985.

Hashimoto Yoshihiko. "Kizoku seiken no seiji kōzō." In *Iwanami kōza, Nihon rekishi,* volume 4: *Kodai,* 1–42. Tokyo: Iwanami shoten, 1976.

Hayashiya Tatsusaburō. *Koten bunka no sōzō.* Tokyo: Tōkyō daigaku shuppankai, 1964.

Hie sannō gongen: kami to hotoke no bijutsu. Compiled by Shiga kenritsu biwako bunka kan. Ōtsu-shi: Dainihon insatsu, 1991.

Hioki Shōichi. *Nihon sōhei kenkyū.* Tokyo: Heibonsha, 1934.

Hirabayashi Moritoku. *Ryōgen.* Tokyo: Yoshikawa kōbunkan, 1976.

Hiraoka Jōkai. *Nihon jiin shi no kenkyū.* Tokyo: Yoshikawa kōbunkan, 1981.

———, ed. *Ronshū Nihon bukkyō shi,* volume 3: *Heian jidai,* and volume 4: *Kamakura jidai.* Tokyo: Yūzankaku shuppan, 1986–1988.

Hirata Toshiharu. *Heian jidai no kenkyū.* Tokyo: San'ichi shobō, 1943.

―――. *Sōhei to bushi.* Tokyo: Nihon kyōbunsha, 1965.

―――. "Nanto hokurei no akusō ni tsuite." In *Ronshū Nihon bukkyō shi,* volume 3: *Heian jidai,* ed. Hiraoka Jōkai, 261–295. Tokyo: Yūzankaku shuppan, 1986.

Hisano Nagayoshi. "Sanmon-jimon no sōkoku." In *Shinshū Ōtsu-shi shi,* volume 2: *Chūsei,* compiled by Ōtsu shiyakusho, 71–98. Ōtsu: Nihon shashin insatsu kabushiki gaisha, 1978.

Hori Daiji. "Enryakuji no kaisō." In *Shinshū Ōtsu-shi shi,* volume 1: *Kodai,* compiled by Ōtsu shiyakusho, 313–342. Ōtsu: Nihon shashin insatsu kabushiki gaisha, 1978.

―――. "Yokawa to Onjōji." In *Shinshū Ōtsu-shi shi,* volume 1: *Kodai,* compiled by Ōtsu shiyakusho, 343–372. Ōtsu: Nihon shashin insatsu kabushiki gaisha, 1978.

―――. "Sōhei no seikatsu." In *Shinshū Ōtsu-shi shi,* volume 1: *Kodai,* compiled by Ōtsu shiyakusho, 465–492. Ōtsu: Nihon shashin insatsu kabushiki gaisha, 1978.

Hori Kyotsu. "The Mongol Invasions and the Kamakura Bakufu." Ph.D. dissertation, Columbia University, 1967.

Hurst, G. Cameron III. "The Development of the *Insei:* A Problem in Japanese History and Historiography." In *Medieval Japan: Essays in Institutional History,* ed. John W. Hall and Jeffrey P. Mass, 60–90. Stanford: Stanford University Press, 1974.

―――. *Insei: Abdicated Sovereigns in the Politics of Late Heian Japan, 1086–1185.* New York: Columbia University Press, 1976.

―――. "The Kōbu Polity: Court-Bakufu Relations in Kamakura Japan." In *Court and Bakufu in Japan,* ed. Jeffrey P. Mass, 3–28. Stanford: Stanford University Press, 1982.

Ienaga Saburō, ed. *Nihon bukkyō shi,* volume 1: *Kodai hen.* Kyoto: Hōzōkan, 1968.

Imatani Akira. *Sengoku ki no Muromachi bakufu.* Tokyo: Kadokawa shoten, 1975.

―――. *Muromachi no ōken: Ashikaga Yoshimitsu no ōken sandatsu keikaku.* Tokyo: Chūō kōronsha, 1990.

Imatani, Akira, and Kōzo Yamamura. "Not for a Lack of Will or Wile: Yoshimitsu's Failure to Supplant the Imperial Lineage." *Journal of Japanese Studies,* 18:1 (1992), 45–78.

Inaba Nobumichi. *Chūsei jiin no kenryoku kōzō.* Tokyo: Iwanami shoten, 1997.

Inagaki Yasuhiko, ed. *Shōen no sekai.* Tokyo: Tōkyō Daigaku shuppan kai, 1985.

Inoue Mitsusada. *Nihon jōdōkyō seiritsu shi no kenkyū.* Tokyo: Yamakawa shuppansha, 1956.

―――. "Kamakura bakufu seiritsu ki no bushi rangyō: Kii no kuni, Tanaka-no-shō Satō shi no ba'ai." *Nihon shi kenkyū* 110 (March 1970), 23–41.

Ishida Ichirō. "Structure and Formation of *Gukanshō* Thought." In *The Future and the Past: A Translation and Study of the Gukanshō, an Interpretative History of Japan Written in 1219,* ed. Delmer M. Brown and Ichirō Ishida, 420–450. Berkeley: University of California Press, 1979.

Ishii Susumu. *Kamakura bakufu.* Nihon no rekishi, volume 7. Tokyo: Chūō kōronsha, 1967.

―――. "The Decline of the Kamakura Bakufu." In *The Cambridge History of Japan,* volume 3: *Medieval Japan,* ed. Kozo Yamamura, 128–174. Cambridge: Cambridge University Press, 1990.

Ishikawa Shiratsuru. *Tennō-sei to chingō kokka no bukkyō.* Tokyo: Dentō to gendai sōsho, 1973.

Itō Seirō. "Chūsei sōgō sei no kenkyū." *Rekishi* 53 (1979), 20–35.

Itō Toshikazu. "Shōren'in monzeki no keisei to bō mandokoro." *Komonjo kenkyū* 35 (1990), 11–29.

Japanese-English Buddhist Dictionary. Tokyo: Daitō shuppansha, 1991.

Kageyama Haruki. *Hieizan.* Tokyo: Kadokawa shoten, 1975.

——. *Hieizanji: sono kōsei to sho mondai.* Tokyo: Kadokawa shoten, 1979.

——. *Hieizan to Kōyasan.* Tokyo: Kyōikusha, 1980.

Kaitei shinpan konsaisu Nihon jinmei jiten. Tokyo: Sanseidō, 1996.

Kamikawa Michio. "Chūsei jiin no kōzō to kokka." *Nihon shi kenkyū* 344 (1991), 26–56.

Katsuno Ryūshin. *Sōhei.* Tokyo: Shibundō, 1966.

——. *Hieizan to Kōyasan: Saichō to Kūkai wo chūshin toshite.* Tokyo: Shibundō, 1977.

Keirstead, Thomas. *The Geography of Power in Medieval Japan.* Princeton: Princeton University Press, 1992.

Kikuchi Kyōko. "Zoku bettō no seiritsu." *Shirin* 51:1 (1968), 103–133.

Kiley, Cornelius J. "The Imperial Court as a Legal Authority in the Kamakura Age." In *Court and Bakufu in Japan,* ed. Jeffrey P. Mass, 29–44. Stanford: Stanford University Press, 1982.

Kitagawa, Joseph. *Religion in Japanese History.* New York: Columbia University Press, 1990.

Kokushi daijiten. Tokyo: Yoshikawa kōbunkan, 1979–.

Konsaisu Nihon jinmei jiten. See *Kaitei shinpan konsaisu Nihon jinmei jiten*

Kuroda Toshio. "Chūsei kokka to tennō." In *Iwanami kōza, Nihon rekishi,* volume 6: *Chūsei* 2, ed. Ienaga Saburō et al., 261–301. Tokyo: Iwanami shoten, 1963.

——. "Shōen sei shakai to bukkyō." In *Nihon bukkyō shi,* volume 2: *Chūsei hen,* ed. Akamatsu Toshihide, 376–412. Kyoto: Hōzōkan, 1967.

——. "Enryakuji shuto to Sasaki shi." In *Shōen sei to buke shakai,* ed. Takeuchi Rizō hakushi kanreki kinnenkai, 69–97. Tokyo: Yoshikawa kōbunkan, 1969.

——. "Chūsei jisha seiryoku ron." In *Iwanami kōza, Nihon rekishi,* volume 6: *Chūsei* 2, ed. Asao Naohiro et al., 245–295. Tokyo: Iwanami shoten, 1975.

——. *Nihon chūsei no kokka to shūkyō.* Tokyo: Iwanami shoten, 1976.

——. *Jisha seiryoku: mō hitotsu chūsei no shakai.* Tokyo: Iwanami shoten, 1980.

——. "Shintō in the History of Japanese Religions." *Journal of Japanese Studies* 7 (1981), 1–21.

——. "The Buddhist Law and the Imperial Law." Trans. Jacqueline Stone. *Japanese Journal of Religious Studies* 23:3–4 (1996), 271–286.

——. "Buddhism and Society in the Medieval Estate System." Trans. Suzanne Gay. *Japanese Journal of Religious Studies* 23:3–4 (1996), 287–320.

Kyōto no rekishi. Volume 1: *Heian no shinkyō,* compiled by Kyōto-shi. Tokyo: Gakugei shorin, 1973.

Marra, Michele. "The Conquest of *Mappō:* Jien and Kitabatake Chikafusa." *Japanese Journal of Religious Studies* 12:4 (1985), 319–341.

Mass, Jeffrey. *Warrior Government in Early Medieval Japan: A Study of the Kamakura Bakufu, Shugo and Jitō.* New Haven: Yale University Press, 1974.

————. *The Kamakura Bakufu: A Study in Documents.* Stanford: Stanford University Press, 1976.

————. *The Development of Kamakura Rule, 1180–1250: A History with Documents.* Stanford: Stanford University Press, 1979.

————. *Lordship and Inheritance in Early Medieval Japan: A Study of the Kamakura Sōryō System.* Stanford: Stanford University Press, 1989.

————. "The Kamakura Bakufu." In *The Cambridge History of Japan,* volume 3: *Medieval Japan,* ed. Yamamura Kozo, 46–88. Cambridge: Cambridge University Press, 1990.

————, ed. *Court and Bakufu in Japan: Essays in Kamakura History.* Stanford: Stanford University Press, 1982.

————, ed. *The Origins of Medieval Japan: Courtiers, Clerics, Warriors, and Peasants in the Fourteenth Century.* Stanford: Stanford University Press, 1997.

Matsunaga, Daigan, and Alice Matsunaga. *Foundation of Japanese Buddhism,* volume 1. Tokyo: Kenkyūsha, 1974.

Matsushima Ken. *Shinpen meihō Nihon no bijutsu.* Volume 3: *Kōfukuji.* Tokyo: Shōgakkan, 1990.

McCullough, Helen Craig, trans. *The Taiheiki: A Chronicle of Medieval Japan.* Rutland, Vt., and Tokyo: Charles E. Tuttle, 1985.

————. *The Tale of the Heike.* Stanford: Stanford University Press, 1990.

McCullough, William. "Japanese Marriage Institutions in the Heian Period." *Harvard Journal of Asiatic Studies* 27 (1967), 103–167.

McMullin, Neil. *Buddhism and the State in Sixteenth-Century Japan.* Princeton: Princeton University Press, 1984.

————. "The Sanmon-Jimon Schism in the Tendai School of Buddhism: A Preliminary Analysis." *Journal of the International Association of Buddhist Studies* 7:1 (1984), 83–105.

————. "The Enryaku-ji and the Gion-Shrine Temple Complex in the Mid-Heian Period." *Japanese Journal of Religious Studies* 14:2–3 (1987), 161–184.

————. "On Placating the Gods and Pacifying the Populace: The Case of the Gion *Goryō* Cult." *History of Religions* 27:3 (1988), 270–293.

————. "Historical and Historiographical Issues in the Study of Pre-Modern Japanese Religions." *Japanese Journal of Religious Studies* 16:1 (1989), 3–40.

————. "The *Lotus Sutra* and Politics in the Mid-Heian Period." In *The Lotus Sutra in Japanese Culture,* ed. George Tanabe Jr. and Willa Jane Tanabe, 119–141. Honolulu: University of Hawai'i Press, 1989.

Miya Jirō. "Emaki ni yoru engi to sōden." In *Ronshū Nihon bukkyō shi,* volume 4: *Kamakura jidai,* ed. Hiraoka Jōkai, 295–328. Tokyo: Yūzankaku shuppan, 1988.

Miyama Susumu. "Munetaka shinnō." In *Kamakura shōgun shikken retsuden,* ed. Yasuda Motohisa, 227–240. Tokyo: Akida shoten, 1974.

Miyasaka Yūshō. *Kōyasan shi.* Tokyo: Kōyasan bunka kenkyūkai, 1962.

Moerman, David. "The Ideology of Landscape and the Theater of State: Insei Pilgrimage to Kumano (1090–1220)." *Japanese Journal of Religious Studies* 24: 3–4 (1997), 347–374.

Mori Shigeaki. *Nanbokuchō ki kōbu kankei shi no kenkyū.* Tokyo: Bunken shuppan, 1984.

————. *Kamakura jidai no chōbaku kankei.* Kyoto: Shibunkaku shuppan, 1991.

Morse, Samuel. "Competing Agendas: Image Making and Religious Authority in Ninth-Century Japan." Unpublished paper, Yale University, 1998.

Motoki Yasuo. "Insei ki seiji shi no kōzō to tenkai." *Nihon shi kenkyū* 283 (1986), 58–75.

———. "Insei ki Kōfukuji kō." *Otemae joshi daigaku ronshū* 21 (1987), 175–195.

———. *Insei ki seiji shi kenkyū*. Kyoto: Shibunkaku shuppan, 1996.

Muraoka Motomasa. "Chūsei Kasugasha no jinnin soshiki." *Ritsumeikan bungaku* 521 (1991), 550–576.

Murayama Shūichi. *Shinbutsu shugo shichō*. Kyoto: Heirakuji shoten, 1957.

———. "Heian bukkyō no tenkai: sono ichi." In *Nihon bukkyō shi*, volume 1: *Kodai hen*, ed. Ienaga Saburō, 241–298. Kyoto: Hōzōkan, 1968.

———. *Hieizan shi: tatakai to inori no seichi*. Tokyo: Tōkyō bijutsu, 1994.

———, ed. *Hieizan to Tendai bukkyō no kenkyū*. Tokyo: Meishō shuppan, 1976.

Nagahara Keiji. "Nihon kokka shi no ichi mondai." *Shisō* 475:1 (1964), 42–51.

———. *Tennō kenryoku no kōzō to tenkai: sono ichi*. Tokyo: Shimizu shoten, 1992.

Nagashima Fukutarō. *Nara*. Tokyo: Yoshikawa kōbunkan, 1972.

———. *Nara-ken no rekishi*. Tokyo: Yamakawa shuppansha, 1980.

Nakamura Ken. *Shōen shihai kōzō no kenkyū*. Tokyo: Yoshikawa kōbunkan, 1978.

———. "Jitō hihō to katakana gonjōjō: Kii no kuni Ategawa no shō." In *Shōen no sekai*, ed. Inagaki Yasuhiko, 203–237. Tokyo: Tōkyō daigaku shuppankai, 1985.

Nezu Masashi. *Tennō ke no rekishi*. 2 volumes. Tokyo: San'ichi shobō, 1973.

Nihon rekishi daijiten. Tokyo: Kawade shobō shinsha, 1973.

Nishiguchi Junko. "Shirakawa goganji shōron." In *Ronshū Nihon bukkyō shi*, volume 3: *Heian jidai*, ed. Hiraoka Jōkai, 239–260. Tokyo: Takayama kaku shuppan, 1986.

Ogisu Jundō. *Nihon chūsei zenshū shi*. Tokyo: Mokujisha, 1965.

Ōishi Naomasa. "Nade no shō Mionoya mura yōsui sōron no shinryō." In *Kōyasan ryō shōen no shihai to kōzō*, ed. Toyoda Takeshi, 205–214. Tokyo: Gannandō shoten, 1977.

Okano Kōji. "Enryakuji zoku bettō to Tendai zasu." *Komazawa shigaku* 33 (1985), 93–114.

———. "Kōfukuji zoku bettō to Kangakuin." *Bukkyō shigaku kenkyū* 34:2 (1991), 67–95.

Ono Kōji. *Nihon chūsei shōgyō shi no kenkyū*. Tokyo: Hōsei daigaku shuppan, 1989.

Ōsumi Kazuo. "Buddhism in the Kamakura Period." In *The Cambridge History of Japan*, volume 3: *Medieval Japan*, ed. Kozo Yamamura, 544–582. Cambridge: Cambridge University Press, 1990.

Ōtsu-shi shi. See *Shinshū Ōtsu-shi shi*

Piggott, Joan. "Hierarchy and Economics in Early Medieval Tōdaiji." In *Court and Bakufu in Japan*, ed. Jeffrey P. Mass, 45–91. New Haven: Yale University Press, 1982.

———. "Tōdaiji and the Nara Imperium." Ph.D. dissertation, Stanford University, 1987.

———. *The Emergence of Japanese Kingship*. Stanford: Stanford University Press, 1997.

Reischauer, Edwin O. *Ennin's Diary: The Record of a Pilgrimage to China in Search of the Law*. New York: Ronald Press Company, 1955.

Sakaki Michio. *Insei jidai shi ronshū.* Tokyo: Zoku gunsho ruijū kanseikai, 1993.

Sansom, George. *A History of Japan to 1334.* Stanford: Stanford University Press, 1958.

Satō Hiroo. *Nihon chūsei no kokka to bukkyō.* Tokyo: Yoshikawa kōbunkan, 1987.

Satō Shin'ichi. "Kyōto sōdatsusen." In *Chūō kōronsha Nihon rekishi,* volume 9: *Nanbokuchō no dōran.* Tokyo: Chūō kōronsha, 1967.

———. *Ashikaga Yoshimitsu: Chūsei ōken e no chōsen.* Tokyo: Heibonsha, 1994.

Shiga-ken shi. Compiled by Shiga-ken. 5 volumes. Tokyo: Sanshūsha, 1927.

Shimosaka Mamoru. "Sanmon shisetsu seido no seiritsu to tenkai." *Shirin* 58:1 (1975), 67–114.

———. "Nanbokuchō jidai no Rokkaku shi." In *Yōkaichi-shi shi,* volume 2: *Chūsei,* ed. Nakamura Ken, 122–175. Yōkaichi-shi: Yōkaichi shiyakusho, 1983.

———. "Chūsei daijiin ni okeru 'jike' no kōzō." In *Kyōto-shi rekishi shiryōkan kiyō,* volume 10, compiled by Kyoto-shi rekishi shiryōkan, 147–174. Kyoto: Dōhōsha, 1992.

Shinshū Ōtsu-shi shi. Volume 1, *Kodai,* and volume 2, *Chūsei.* Compiled by Ōtsu shiyakusho. Ōtsu: Nihon shashin insatsu kabushiki gaisha, 1978. Cited as *Ōtsu-shi shi.*

Shiseki kaidai jiten: kodai, chūsei. Tokyo: Tōkyōdō shuppan, 1995.

Sonoda Kōyū. "Heian bukkyō no seiritsu." In *Nihon bukkyō shi kenkyū,* volume 1: *Kodai hen,* ed. Ienaga Saburō, 175–240. Kyoto: Hōzōkan, 1967.

Steenstrup, Carl. *Hōjō Shigetoki (1198–1261) and His Role in the History of Political and Ethical Ideas in Japan.* London and Malmö: Curzon Press, 1979.

Suga Shinjō. "Hokkyō san'e no seiritsu." *Shigaku kenkyū* 206 (1994), 1–20.

Suzuki Kunihiro. "Kōyasan ni okeru shōen seiteki kenryoku kōzō to tokushitsu, to sono henka." In *Kōyasan ryō shōen no shihai to kōzō,* ed. Toyoda Takeshi, 37–109. Tokyo: Gannandō shoten, 1977.

Suzuki Motokazu. "Kōfukuji gakuryō, roppō ni tsuite." *Nihon rekishi* 88–89 (1955), 53–60.

Swanson, Paul L. "Editor's Introduction." *Japanese Journal of Religious Studies* 14: 2–3 (1987), 71–78.

Taira Masayuki. "Kamakura bukkyō no sho mondai." In *Ronshū Nihon jiin shi,* volume 4: *Kamakura,* part 1, ed. Hiraoka Jōkai, 83–124. Tokyo: Yoshikawa kōbunkan, 1981.

———. *Nihon chūsei no shakai to bukkyō.* Tokyo: Kōshobō, 1992.

———. "Kuroda Toshio and the *Kenmitsu taisei* Theory." Trans. Thomas Kirchner. *Japanese Journal of Religious Studies* 23:3–4 (1996), 427–448.

Takahashi Masaaki. "Heian matsu, Kamakura jidai no Sasaki shi." In *Yōkaichi-shi shi,* volume 2: *Chūsei,* 12–120. Yōkaichi-shi: Yōkaichi-shi yakusho, 1983.

Takahashi Osamu. "Shōen kōryō wo meguru ryōshū to minshū." In *Wakayama-ken shi: chūsei,* compiled by Wakayama-ken shi hensan kakari inkai, 37–173. Osaka: Dainihon insatsu kabushiki gaisha, 1994.

Takamura Takashi. "Kōyasan ryō shōen kenkyū shi." In *Kōyasan ryō shōen no shihai to kōzō,* ed. Toyoda Takeshi, 305–358. Tokyo: Gannandō shoten, 1977.

Takatori Masao. "Shinbutsu shūgo." In *Shinshū Ōtsu-shi shi,* volume 1: *Kodai,* compiled by Ōtsu shiyakusho, 373–398. Ōtsu: Nihon shashin insatsu kabushiki gaisha, 1978.

Tanaka Fumihide. "Go-Shirakawa insei ki no seiji kenryoku to kenmon jiin." *Nihon shi kenkyū,* 256 (1983), 1–42.

———. *Heishi seiken no kenkyū.* Kyoto: Shibunkaku shuppan, 1994.

Tashiro Osamu. "Kōyasan kenryoku to nōmin no dōkō: chūsei goki no Aragawa-no-shō." In *Kōyasan ryō shōen no shihai to kōzō,* ed. Toyoda, 215–266. Tokyo: Gannandō shoten, 1977.

Toby, Ronald. "Why Leave Nara?" *Monumenta Nipponica* 40:3 (1985), 331–347.

Tonomura, Hitomi. *Community and Commerce in Late Medieval Japan: The Corporate Villages of Tokuchin-ho.* Stanford: Stanford University Press, 1992.

Toyoda Takeshi. *Nihon shūkyō seido shi no kenkyū.* Tokyo: Kōseikaku, 1938.

———. "Za to dōso." In *Iwanami kōza Nihon rekishi,* volume 6: *Chūsei,* part 2. Tokyo: Iwanami shoten, 1967.

———. "Kōyasan jiryō no hensen." In Toyoda, ed., *Kōyasan ryō shōen no shihai to kōzō,* 461–482.

———. *Za no kenkyū.* Tokyo: Yoshikawa kōbunkan, 1982.

———, ed. *Kōyasan ryō shōen no shihai to kōzō.* Tokyo: Gannandō shoten, 1977.

Toyoda Takeshi and Sugiyama Hiroshi. "The Growth of Commerce and Trade." In *Japan in the Muromachi Age,* ed. John W. Hall and Toyoda Takeshi, 129–144. Berkeley and Los Angeles: University of California Press, 1977.

Tsuji Zennosuke. *Nihon bukkyō shi: jōsei hen.* Tokyo: Iwanami shoten, 1944.

———. *Nihon bukkyō shi: chūsei 1.* Tokyo: Iwanami shobō, 1947.

Tsuruoka Shizuo. *Kodai bukkyō shi no kenkyū.* Tokyo: Bungadō shoten, 1967.

Tyler, Susan. "*Honji Suijaku* Faith." *Japanese Journal of Religious Studies* 16:2–3 (1989), 227–250.

Uejima Susumu. "Chūsei zenki no kokka to bukkyō." *Nihon shi kenkyū* 403 (1996), 31–64.

Usui Nobuyoshi. *Ashikaga Yoshimitsu.* Tokyo: Yoshikawa kōbunkan, 1974.

Uwayokote Masataka. "Genpei sōran." In *Shinshū Ōtsu-shi shi,* volume 2: *Chūsei,* compiled by Ōtsu shiyakusho, 26–49. Ōtsu: Nihon insatsu kabushiki gaisha, 1978.

———. "Shugo Sasaki shi." In *Shinshū Ōtsu-shi shi,* volume 2: *Chūsei,* compiled by Ōtsu shiyakusho, 50–70. Ōtsu: Nihon insatsu kabushiki gaisha, 1978.

———. *Kamakura jidai seiji shi kenkyū.* Tokyo: Yoshikawa kōbunkan, 1991.

Varley, H. Paul. "The Hōjō Family and Succession to Power." In *Court and Bakufu in Japan: Essays in Kamakura History,* ed. Jeffrey Mass, 143–167. Stanford: Stanford University Press, 1982.

———. *Warriors of Japan, as Portrayed in the War Tales.* Honolulu: University of Hawai'i Press, 1994.

Wada Teruo. "Chūsei Kōyasan kyōdan no soshiki ni tsuite." In *Kōyasan ryō shōen no shihai to kōzō,* ed. Toyoda Takeshi, 1–35. Tokyo: Gannandō shoten, 1979.

Wakayama-ken shi: chūsei. Compiled by Wakayama-ken shi hensan kakari inkai. Osaka: Dainihon insatsu kabushiki gaisha, 1994.

Wakayama-ken shi: genshi, kodai. Compiled by Wakayama-ken shi hensan kakari inkai. Osaka: Dainihon insatsu kabushiki gaisha, 1994.

Wakita Haruo with Susan B. Hanley. "Dimensions of Development: Cities in Fifteenth and Sixteenth Century Japan." In *Japan before Tokugawa: Political Consolidation and Economic Growth,* ed. John W. Hall, Nagahara Keiji, and Kozo Yamamura, 295–326. Princeton: Princeton University Press, 1981.

Yamamura, Kozo. "The Development of Za in Medieval Japan." *Business History Review* 47:4 (winter 1973), 438–465.

———. "The Growth of Commerce in Medieval Japan." In *Cambridge History of Japan,* volume 3: *Medieval Japan,* ed. Kozo Yamamura, 344–395. Cambridge: Cambridge University Press, 1990.

———, ed. *The Cambridge History of Japan,* volume 3: *Medieval Japan.* Cambridge: Cambridge University Press, 1990.

Yamashita Takashi. *Insei.* Tokyo: Kindai bungeisha, 1995.

Yasuda Motohisa, ed. *Kamakura shōgun shikken retsuden.* Tokyo: Akida shoten, 1979.

———. *Nihon rekishi,* volume 7: *Insei to heishi.* Tokyo: Shogakkan, 1974.

INDEX

ABOUT THE AUTHOR

Raised next to a medieval castle in Kalmar, Sweden, MIKAEL ADOLPH-SON was educated as a historian at the University of Lund, at Stanford, and at Kyoto University. He is currently assistant professor at the Department of East Asian Languages and Civilizations at Harvard University.

Carleton College Library
One North College Street
Northfield, MN 55057-4097

WITHDRAWN